Using Google Apps

by

Meghen Ehrich
Instructional Technology Specialist
Prince George's County Public Schools
Prince George's County, Maryland

Monica Kinney
Instructional Technology Specialist
Prince George's County Public Schools
Prince George's County, Maryland

Publisher
The Goodheart-Willcox Company, Inc.
Tinley Park, Illinois
www.g-w.com

Manufactured in the United States of America.

Library of Congress Catalog Card Number 2013009207

ISBN 978-1-61960-297-7

1 2 3 4 5 6 7 8 9 – 14 – 18 17 16 15 14 13

Library of Congress Cataloging-in-Publication Data
Ehrich, Meghen.
Using Google Apps / by Meghen Ehrich, Monica Kinney.
pages cm
Includes index.
ISBN 978-1-61960-297-7
1. Google Apps—Juvenile literature. 2. Application software—Juvenile literature. I. Kinney, Monica. II. Title.
TK5105.8885.G643E47 2013
025.04252—dc23
2013009207

Cover photos: LilKar/Shutterstock.com, Oleksiy Mark/Shutterstock.com

Introduction

Using Google Apps gives students and instructors an opportunity to incorporate an alternative software application solution into daily computer use. By studying this text, students can learn the skills needed to be productive and efficient in their use of Google apps.

This text provides structured instruction for the basic concepts and skills associated with various Google apps. Each chapter builds on the previous chapter to offer sound instruction and user comprehension. Self-assessment opportunities are provided throughout to measure understanding and comprehension of what has been presented.

Focus is placed on those tools used for communication, such as Google Mail, Google Chat, Google Sites, and Google Groups. Coverage is also included for collaboration (Google Drive), media (Picasa and Google News), and location (Google Maps). Through practical exercises, students are introduced to real-world applications of these tools.

Creating a Google Account

Many of the lessons in this textbook require a Google account. Signing up for a Google account is free and easy.

1. Using your Internet browser, navigate to www.google.com.
2. Click the **Sign In** button in the upper-right corner of the web page.
3. On the new page that is displayed, click the **Sign Up** button. The Create a new Google Account page is displayed, as shown in **Figure A.**
4. Enter the requested information. The user name will be the name others see for you and your Gmail address, so choose it wisely.
5. Enter the verification code and click the **Next Step** button.
6. If you left some of the required information blank, then those fields will be highlighted and the sign-up process is not complete. If everything was filled in and the verification code entered correctly, a new page is displayed.
7. On the profile page that is displayed, click the **Next step** button. A Welcome page is displayed and the current e-mail address you provided will be sent an e-mail.
8. Click the **Get Started** button on the Welcome page to sign in. When you do so, the Google home page is displayed, and your user name is displayed in the upper-right corner to show that you are signed in, as shown in **Figure B.**

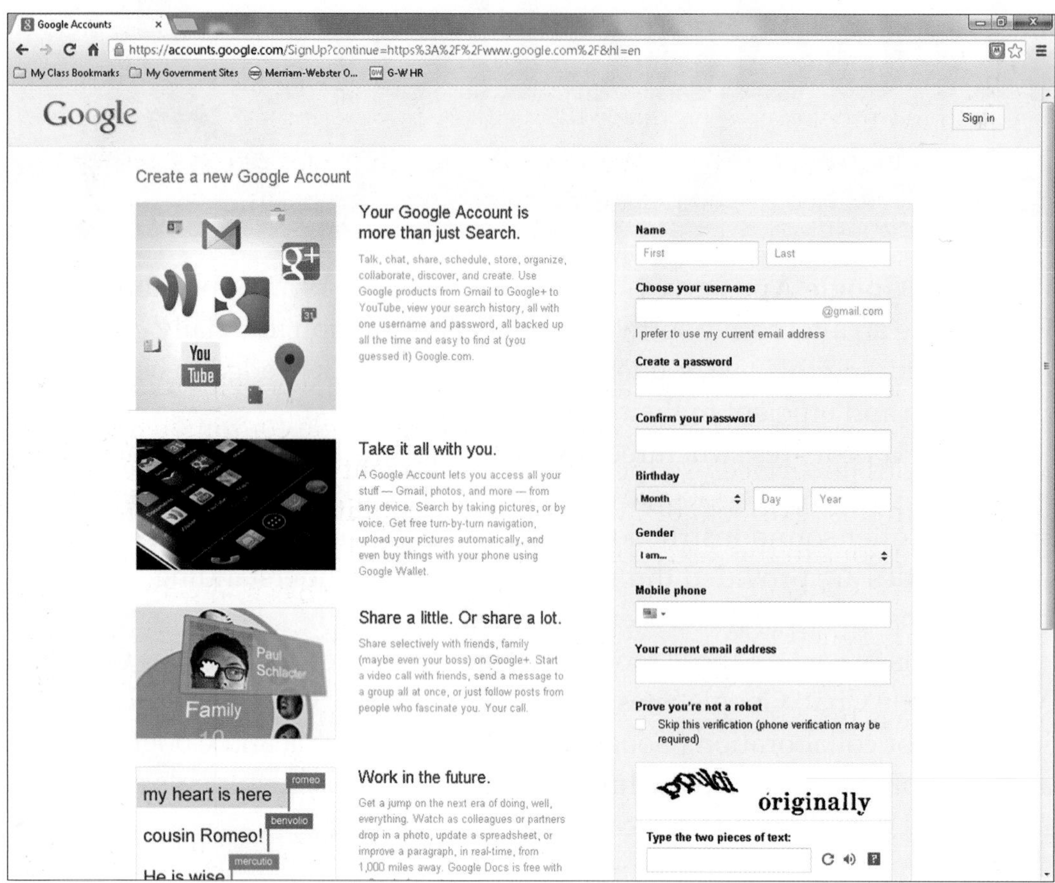

Figure A *Goodheart-Willcox Publisher*

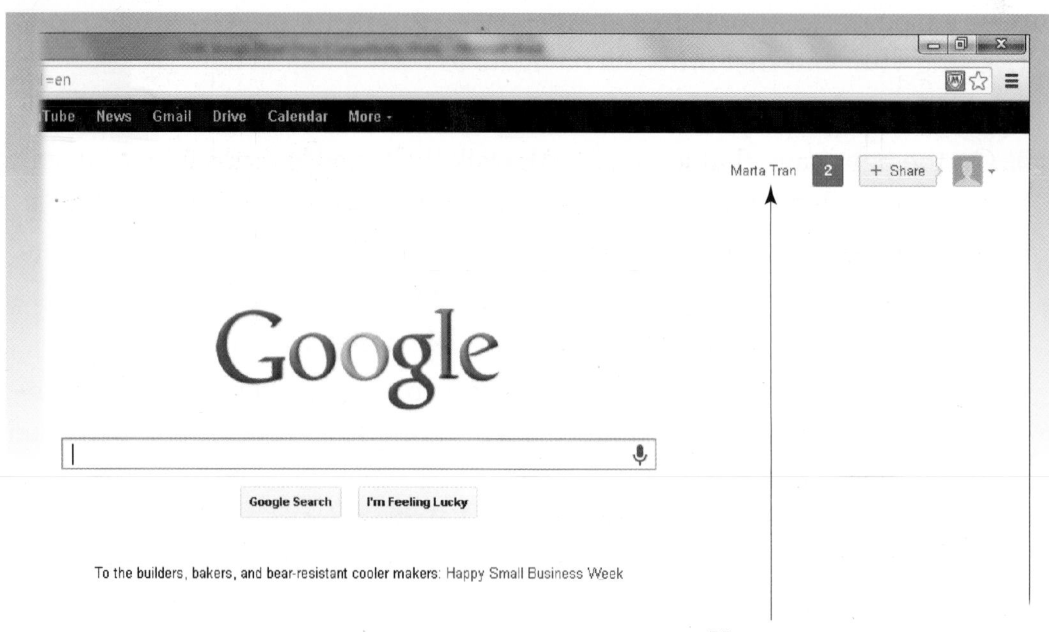

Figure B *Goodheart-Willcox Publisher*

9. To sign out from Google, click your user name, and then click the **Sign Out** button in the flyout menu that is displayed.
10. To sign in to Google, navigate to the Google home page, click the **Sign In** button in the upper-right corner of the page, and enter your user name (you do not need to include @gmail.com) and password.

Updates and Equipment

The descriptions and instructions in this textbook were vigorously tested and correct at the time of publication. However, Google continuously improves and upgrades its services, so the current functionality may differ from what is presented in this textbook. Be aware of this possibility when using this textbook.

Some lessons in this textbook require additional hardware. In order to fully complete these lessons, a microphone, speakers, or web cam need to be installed and properly functioning. Review the lessons in each chapter prior to beginning the lessons to determine what, if any, additional hardware is required. Ensure each device is functioning before starting a lesson that requires it.

About the Authors

Meghen Ehrich is a Google Certified Trainer and Instructional Technology Specialist for a large, urban school district in the Washington, DC, metropolitan area. As part of the Google Apps implementation team for her district, she has been creating and delivering professional development and training resources for Google Apps since 2008.

Monica Kinney is an Instructional Technology Specialist for a large, urban school district in the Washington, DC, metropolitan area. She has been delivering professional development training on Google Apps to teachers and administrators since her school district implemented Google Apps in 2008. She is pursuing Google Certified Trainer qualification.

Reviewers

The authors and publisher would like to thank the following individuals for providing assistance and guidance in developing this textbook.

Georgiann Andersen
Business and Computer Instructor
Tri-Center High School
Neola, Iowa

M. Lynne Archer
Teacher, Career and Technical Education Department
Cactus Shadows High School
Cave Creek, Arizona

Tom Bartz
Technology Teacher and Technology Coordinator
James A. Garfield Local Schools
Garrettsville, Ohio

William E. Bishop, Jr.
Director
Haleyville Center of Technology
Haleyville, Alabama

Mark Bowman
Instructor, Computer Repair and Networking
South Branch Career and Technical Center
Petersburg, West Virginia

Kristi A. DeBruyne
Instructional Technology Coordinator, Business and IT Department
Medford Area Senior High School
Medford, Wisconsin

Carolyn Barnette Diaz
Teacher and CATE Department Head
Irmo High School
Columbia, South Carolina

DeAnna Donahue, MAT
Career and Technical Education Teacher
Ereckson Middle School
Allen, Texas

Don Dunlap
Business and Entrepreneurship Instructor
Patrick Henry High School
Stockbridge, Georgia

Dixie Durkee
Computer Instructor
Anna Local School
Anna, Ohio

David Glavach
Business Education Teacher
Yale Public Schools
Yale, Michigan

Donna M. Guillot
Business and Computer Science Department
Killingly High School
Dayville, Connecticut

Sherie M. Moran, M.A.
Business, Economics, and Social Studies Teacher
Idaho Digital Learning Academy
Meridian, Idaho

Dr. Johann Ngo
CTE Business Teacher
Alchesay High School
Whiteriver, Arizona

Linda Phillips
Business and Information Technology Teacher
Elko County School District
West Wendover, Nevada

Jon Rogers
Work Based Learning Teacher
North Pole High School
North Pole, Alaska

Paulette Roundtree
Multimedia Instructor
Corsicana High School
Corsicana, Texas

Melissa Scott
Education Programs Professional
Nevada Department of Education
Las Vegas, Nevada

Sherry B. Stone, NBCT
Teacher
Irmo High School
Columbia, South Carolina

Arthur Turnbull
Technology Manager
Mai-Tech Interactive & Graphics
Chicago, Illinois

Renee Waters
Teacher and Department Chair
Whitewater High School
Fayetteville, Georgia

Paula Williams
Instructor
Arkansas Northeastern College
Blytheville, Arkansas

Monica Winchester
Business Teacher
Yale Public School
Yale, Michigan

Brief Contents

Expanded Table of Contents

Handbooks

Content Connected

Formative Assessment

Pretest and Posttest

The chapter pretest is a self-assessment guide to what you already know and what you need to focus on while completing the chapter. The chapter posttest is a guide to how successfully you have learned the material in the chapter.

Skill Review

The skill review at the end of each chapter provides an opportunity to measure your knowledge of the content presented in the chapter.

Lesson Application

The lesson application section at the end of each chapter provides an opportunity to apply the skills you learned in the chapter to real-world tasks. Skills learned in previous chapters are also applied in these exercises.

Summative Assessment

Unit Review

The unit reviews present a scenario and activities to be completed. The skills needed to complete the activities are drawn from all chapters within the unit.

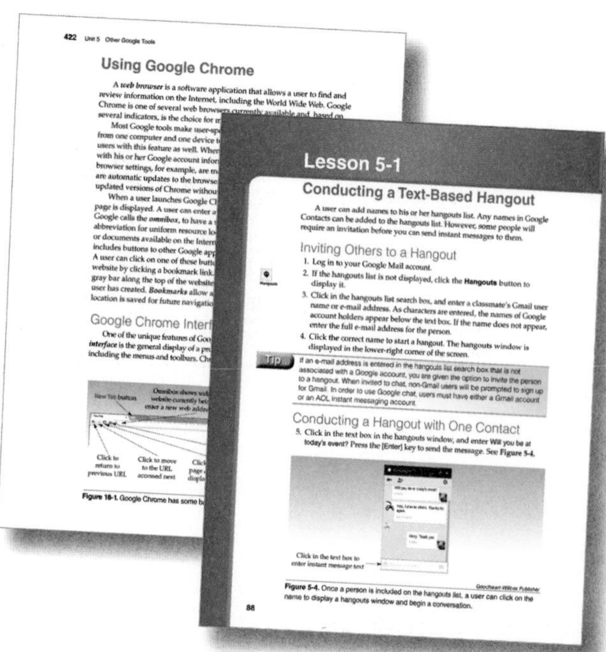

Features Spotlighted

Reading Material

Each chapter begins with reading material related to the skills being presented. The reading material discusses and explains features and uses of the software.

Chapter Lessons

The chapter lessons are hands-on applications of the skills presented in the chapter. Each lesson is a tutorial to be completed step by step.

Technology Applied

Technology is an important part of your world. So, it should be part of your everyday learning. In this textbook, you will find the following.

- Each lesson applies web-based technology.
- A pretest and posttest are provided for each textbook chapter for self-assessment, which are accessed by scanning the QR code to visit the mobile site or you can visit the companion website to take the test.
- Data files needed for lessons are provided on the companion website.

G-W Learning Companion Website

The G-W Learning companion website for **Using Google Apps** is a study reference that contains matching vocabulary games, e-flash cards, and interactive quizzes. Also included are data files for lessons. www.g-wlearning.com/informationtechnology/

G-W Learning Mobile Site

The G-W Learning mobile site* is a study reference to use when you are on the go. The mobile site is easy to read, easy to use, and fine-tuned for quick access.

For **Using Google Apps**, the G-W Learning mobile site contains chapter pretests and posttests and e-flash card vocabulary practices. If you do not have a smartphone, these same features can be accessed using an Internet browser to visit the G-W Learning companion website.

G-W Learning mobile website:
www.m.g-wlearning.com

Scan now!

Goodheart-Willcox QR Codes

This Goodheart-Willcox product contains QR codes*, or quick response codes. These codes can be scanned with a smartphone bar code reader to access information or online features. For more information on using QR codes and a recommended QR reader, visit the G-W Learning companion website at www.g-wlearning.com.

Scan now!

*An Internet connection is required to access the QR code destinations. Data-transfer rates may apply. Check with your Internet service provider for information on your data-transfer rates.

Unit 1

Google Mail

Google Mail, or Gmail, is one of the most popular browser-based e-mail services. The ability to retrieve and send e-mail using a browser allows people access to it on any computer, tablet, or smartphone connected to the Internet. Like many e-mail services, Google Mail provides tools for users to organize their mail, store contact information, and create and manage tasks. Using Google tools to organize an inbox can ease the process of finding messages that require the user to take action. Gmail Contacts allows the user to store information about family, friends, coworkers, and business associates within his or her e-mail interface, where it will likely be needed. Gmail users can also create a to-do list, known as a task list, based on information in their Gmail messages.

Chapters

Chapter 1

Sending and Receiving Messages

Objectives

After completing this chapter, you will be able to:

- **Compose** a formatted e-mail message.
- **Reply** to e-mail messages.
- **Send** an e-mail with an attached file.
- **Search** for e-mails meeting certain criteria.
- **Select** a picture to represent you on your Google account.
- **Use** an e-mail signature.
- **Select** a theme for your Google account.

alexmillos/Shutterstock.com

Check Your Google Apps IQ

Before you begin this chapter, see what you already know about Google Apps by taking the chapter pretest.

www.m.g-wlearning.com
www.g-wlearning.com/informationtechnology/

Navigating Gmail

E-mail, short for electronic mail, is a system for sending messages from one device to another over an electronic network. E-mail services provide users with an e-mail client by which e-mail can be sent and received. Some e-mail clients are software programs installed on a computer. Other e-mail clients are browser-based, which means the e-mail software is accessed through the Internet via a website.

Once a user logs in to his or her Gmail account, the Mail page is displayed. The list of received e-mail messages, known as the ***inbox,*** occupies most of the browser window. Each entry in the list of received messages includes the name of the person or business that sent the message. The subject line of the message is displayed to the right of the sender's name. The last piece of information included is the date the message was received. When the sender's name, subject, and date information for a message are displayed in bold text, it indicates that the message has not been opened or read.

Many people are used to storing e-mail messages in folders. Gmail uses labels rather than folders to store e-mail messages. ***Labels*** are used to organize e-mails in the same way folders are used to organize files on a computer. The advantage of labels over folders is that messages can be assigned to more than one label at a time. The labels list appears to the left of the e-mail list. There are default labels that are part of the Gmail system. The default or system labels include **Inbox**, **Starred**, **Important**, **Sent Mail**, **Drafts**, and **All Mail**, as seen in **Figure 1-1.** Some of these system labels appear in the label list only after the user completes certain actions. For example, the **Trash** label may be displayed only after the first time a message has been deleted. Gmail users can also create new labels, as discussed in Chapter 2.

Composing and Sending E-mail Messages

To reach someone using e-mail, a Gmail user must compose a new message. To ***compose*** a message is to create and write it. The first step is to address the message by entering one or more e-mail addresses in the **To** text box. Next, add a subject to the message by entering the text in the **Subject** text box. The ***subject*** of an e-mail should give the recipient an idea of what the message is about in 130 characters or less. It is similar to the headline of a news article. The ***message*** itself is the information being communicated. It is entered in the large text box below the **Subject** text box. Once the message text is complete, the user sends the e-mail.

The ***sender*** is the person who sends the e-mail. The ***recipient*** is the person to whom the e-mail is sent.

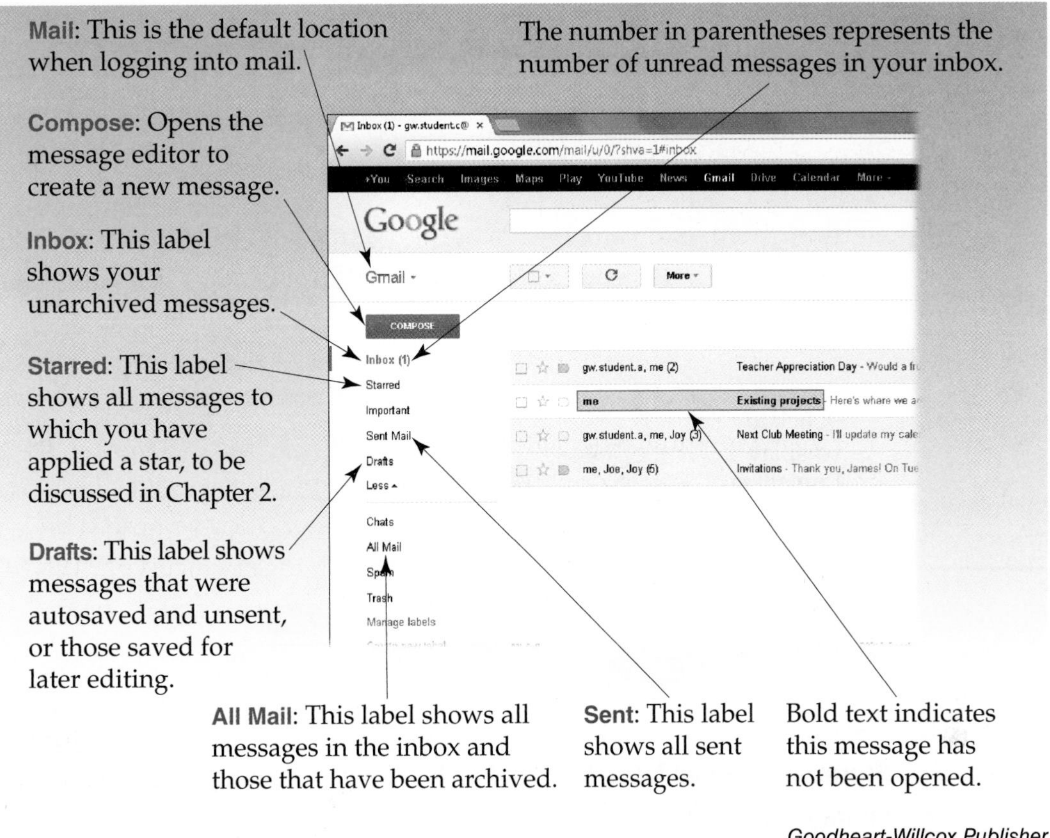

Goodheart-Willcox Publisher

Figure 1-1. Gmail system labels, which are used rather than folders to store e-mail messages, are displayed to the left of the e-mail list.

Addressing and Formatting Messages

Google provides tools to give users additional options in addressing and formatting e-mail. When users write a new e-mail, they can include recipients who are not the user's primary audience. These recipients can be carbon copied on an e-mail to keep them informed about the topic. ***Cc*** stands for carbon copy. The names and address of those that have been carbon copied are visible to all other recipients. ***Bcc*** stands for blind carbon copy. Names and addresses entered in the **Bcc** text box are not visible to other recipients. Including recipients as a bcc rather than a cc is typically done to protect the identity of the recipients.

Below the message text box users can access formatting options, as seen in **Figure 1-2.** These buttons are similar to those found on the formatting toolbar of a word processor. The Gmail tools include those that change the look of the text such as bold, italic, underline, font type, font size, and text color. Other tools allow users to format entire lines or paragraphs of text, such as the tools for creating automatically numbered or bulleted lists. When using these tools, however, keep in mind that Gmail formatting may not be supported by the recipient's e-mail software. In those cases, the formatting added to an e-mail in Gmail could be stripped out of the message.

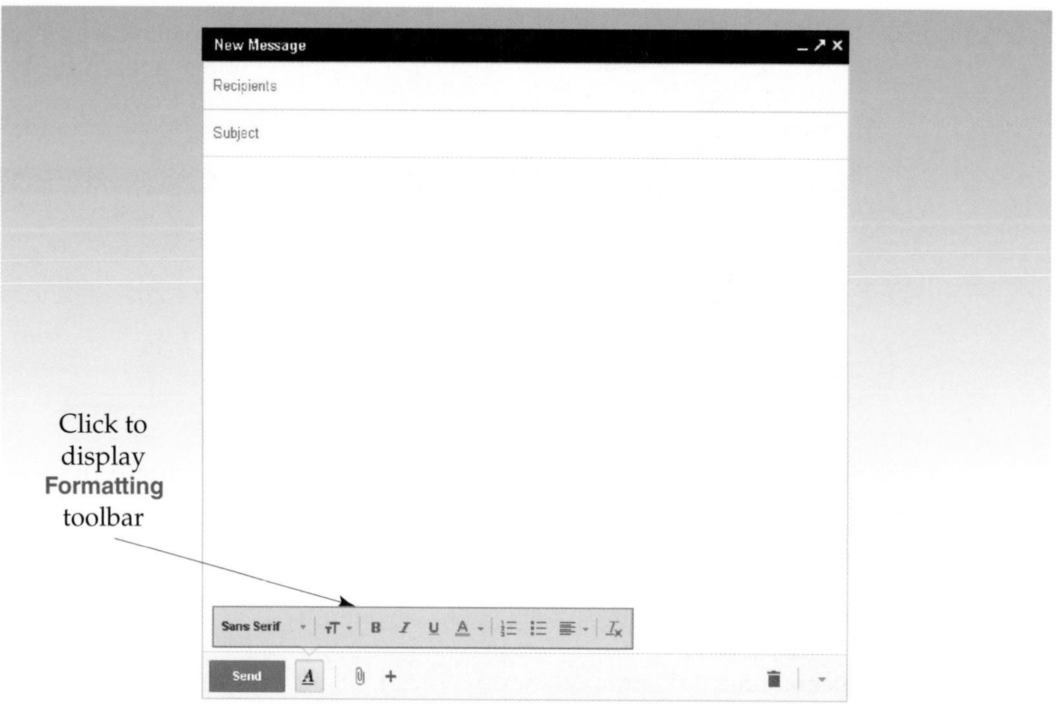

Goodheart-Willcox Publisher

Figure 1-2. Gmail formatting tools allow users to change the look of a single word or entire paragraphs.

Responding to Messages

At the bottom of every message received are options for the Gmail user to reply to or forward the message. ***Reply*** opens a window allowing the responder to enter a message and send it to the person who sent the message without entering his or her e-mail address. When the original e-mail includes more than one recipient, a **Reply to all** link is displayed. ***Reply to all*** sends the response to the sender and anyone else who received the original e-mail. ***Forward*** sends the e-mail to a new recipient. When forwarding a message, the Gmail user needs to enter the e-mail address of the new recipient.

Attaching Files to Messages

Whether responding to a received message or creating a new message, Gmail users can send files via e-mail. ***Attachments*** are the files sent via e-mail. People send documents, presentations, and picture files, for example, via e-mail. There are some rules regarding attachments. Google allows users to attach most file types to messages, except executable (EXE) files. Executable files make a computer perform tasks, and as a result they can be used to spread computer viruses.

Gmail users can attach multiple files to a message. However, the total size of the attachments must be less than 25 megabytes (MB). As long as the file type and size requirements are met, users can send attachments along with their e-mail messages.

Searching for Messages

The inbox can quickly fill up with messages. Finding the e-mail to which you need to respond may require a search. There are several ways to search for messages in Gmail. The search box at the top of the Gmail window can be used to perform a quick search. This quick search allows users to enter a sender's name, an e-mail address, or a word to be found in a subject line or in the message text. Users can also conduct an advanced search using the search wizard.

Messages Versus Conversations

Most e-mail services list incoming messages individually, regardless if the e-mail is new or a response. Gmail works differently. All e-mail messages are grouped together into conversations. A ***conversation*** is a collection of messages with the same subject line. If you begin with a new e-mail, every response to that message is grouped into a single entry in the inbox. So, what may appear to be a single e-mail could in fact be a conversation containing several e-mails.

Conversations can help organize the inbox because all responses to an e-mail are on one line in the inbox rather than searching for pieces of the conversation. Another benefit of conversations is that actions taken on a conversation affect all of its contents. As a result, you can move or delete all of the messages in a conversation with a single action.

Gmail displays who has responded to a conversation and the number of messages within the conversation, as seen in **Figure 1-3.** The senders are also visible. A number is displayed in parentheses to the right of the sender name.

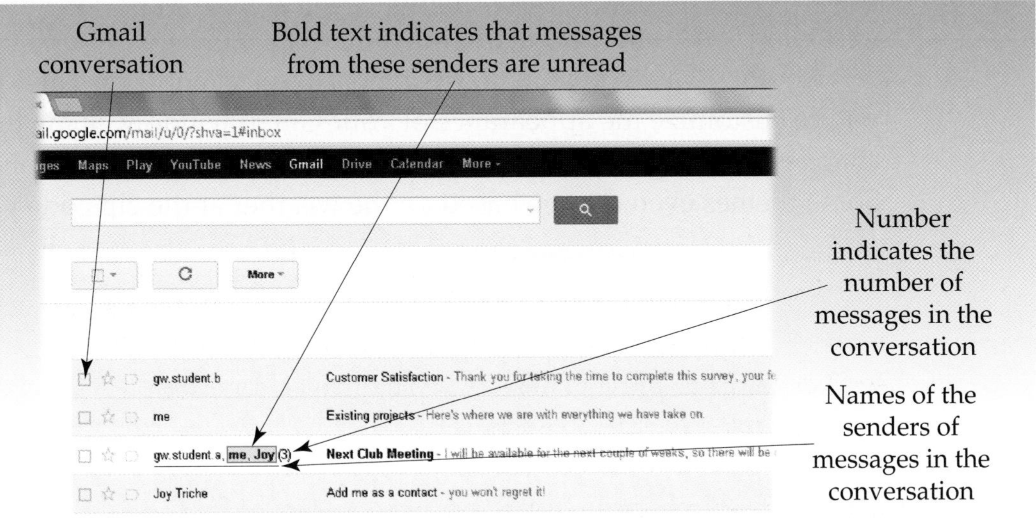

Goodheart-Willcox Publisher

Figure 1-3. Google groups all e-mail messages with the same subject line into a single entry in the inbox, which is then called a conversation.

This number refers to the number of messages in a conversation. The names in bold indicate the senders of unread messages. The user can respond to any e-mail in the conversation, although often the most recent e-mail is the one to which a response is sent.

Personalizing Gmail

Users can customize the Gmail window in the **Settings** menu. This can include choosing a profile photo, setting up a signature, and selecting a theme. Customizing Gmail in these ways allows users to have it reflect their personality.

Users can select a photo that will represent them for other Gmail users. Some people choose to use a photo of themselves. Others choose to use a photo of an object of something that represents them. Once chosen, the user can decide if the photo will be seen by everyone or just people with whom the user has agreed to chat. Chatting is discussed in Chapter 5. If the user chooses to have the photo visible by everyone, the photo will appear when other users place their cursor over the user's name in their inboxes, contacts, chat lists, or when someone looks at the user's public Google profile.

The sender of an e-mail message usually enters his or her name as part of the closing of the message. With some messages, information in addition to a name is appropriate. In these cases, it can be helpful to create a signature. A ***signature*** is text that is automatically included in all outgoing messages. A signature usually includes your name and contact information. If the user is sending e-mail for work, the signature often includes his or her work title, business contact information, and business website address. Rather than entering this information every time, a signature allows the user to set it up once and have it included in every message.

Another way to personalize Gmail is to select a theme. ***Themes*** allow you to customize the appearance of your Gmail window. Some themes change the background of the Gmail page to an image or to a solid color. Some themes even change based on the weather at the zip code you enter.

Lesson 1-1

Composing a New Message

Using Gmail to compose e-mail allows you to format the text. When a message is formatted appropriately, it helps the recipient understand the message.

1. Log in to your Google Mail account.
2. Click the **Compose Mail** button. A form is displayed for composing the e-mail, as shown in **Figure 1-4.**

COMPOSE

3. Click in the **To** text box and enter the e-mail address of a classmate.
4. Click **Cc** next to the **To** text box. The **Cc** text box appears. Enter your e-mail address in the **Cc** text box.
5. Click in the **Subject** text box and enter Make Planning Events Easy.
6. Click in the main text editor area, and enter the following as the body of the message.

> Good morning,
>
> M&M Event Planning is Maryland's leading company for premier events and is located in downtown Baltimore. We specialize in large events for over 200 people, but we are happy to plan smaller events as well. The company has been recognized in newspapers and magazines for hosting elegant, yet affordable, events. Some of our events have included:

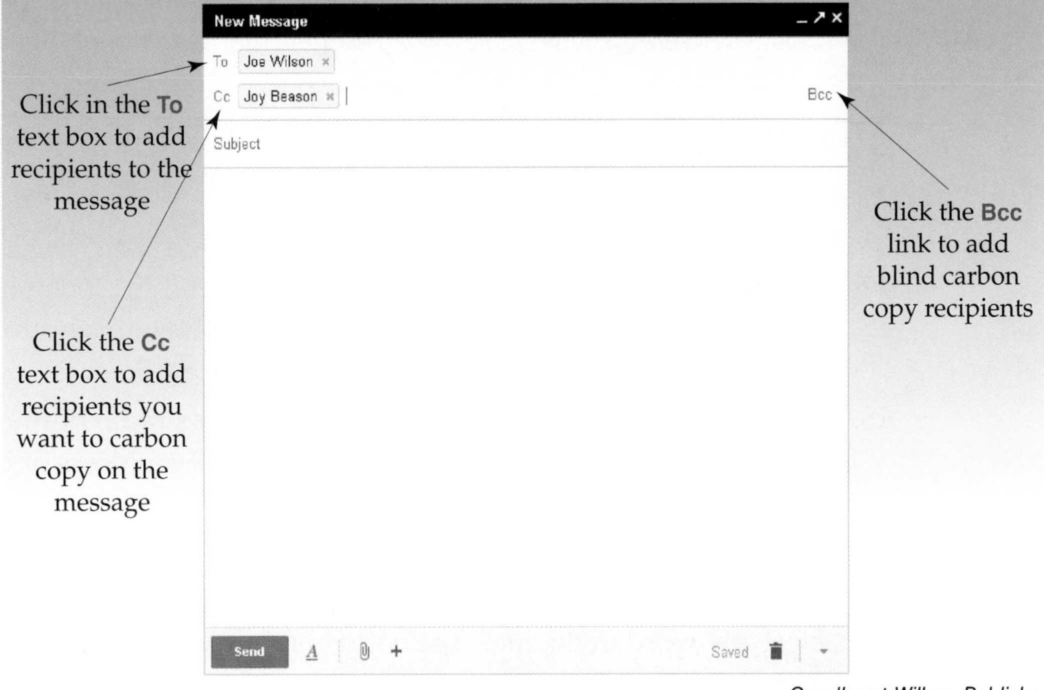

Goodheart-Willcox Publisher

Figure 1-4. The form for composing e-mail includes options for addressing the message, adding a subject to the message, and entering the main content of the message.

7. Scroll over the text M&M Event Planning to select it.

Formatting Options

8. Click the **Formatting Options** button at the bottom of the text editor to display the **Formatting** toolbar.

Tip: To hide the **Formatting** toolbar, click the **Formatting Options** button a second time.

Bold

9. Click the **Bold** button on the toolbar to make the selected text bold.

Text Color

10. Click the **Text Color** button to display a color palette. Click a purple color swatch to make the selected text purple.
11. Click at the end of the last line of text to place the cursor there, then press the [Enter] key to start a new line.

Bulleted List

12. Click the **Bulleted List** button to place a bullet at the beginning of the line.
13. Enter the following text. The bullets will be automatically added each time a new line is started by pressing the [Enter] key.

- weddings;
- parties;
- company meetings; and
- conferences.

Bulleted List

14. Press the [Enter] key to start a new line, and then click the **Bulleted List** button to end creating the bulleted list.
15. Enter the remaining text:

For more information about M&M Event Planning, call our office or visit our website: www.m&mplanning.com. We are open Tuesday through Sunday. We would love to host your next event.

Sincerely,

your name

16. Scroll over the text www.m&mplanning.com to select it.

Link

17. Click the **Link** button. If needed, click the + to show this button. The **Edit Link** dialog box is displayed, as shown in **Figure 1-5.**
18. In the **Edit Link** dialog box, click the **Web address** radio button. Then, click in the text box to the right of it and enter the address of the website (www.m&mplanning.com).
19. Click the **OK** button to close the dialog box and assign the hyperlink. Notice the text is replaced by a hyperlink in the message body.
20. Select any word in the message body and introduce a spelling error.

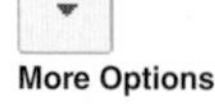

More Options

21. Click the **More Options** button at the lower-right corner of the text editor, and click **Check spelling** from the drop-down menu. All suspected spelling errors in the message are highlighted in yellow.

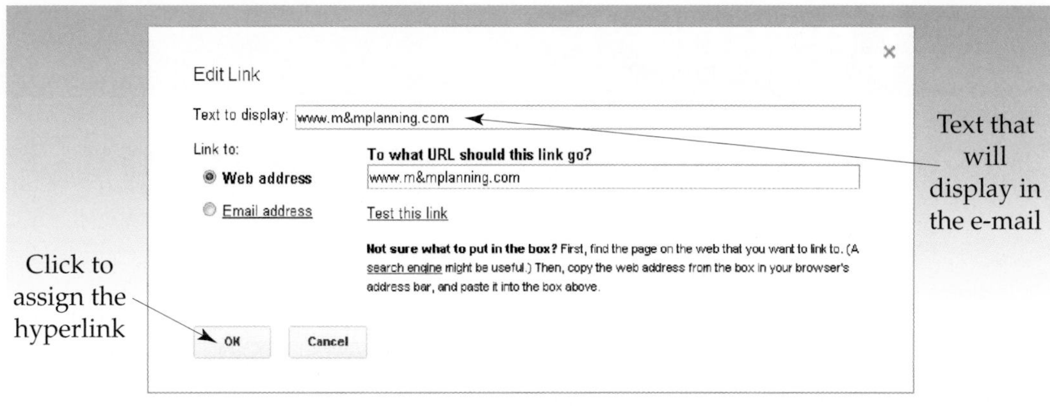

Goodheart-Willcox Publisher

Figure 1-5. Along with editing the text to display for the link, the **Edit Link** dialog box provides users with the opportunity to test a hyperlink before including it in an e-mail.

22. Click a highlighted word. A list of suggestions appears, as shown in **Figure 1-6.** Click the correct spelling in the list or click **Ignore**.
23. Click the **X** on the spelling toolbar to end the spell check.
24. Click the **Send** button to send the e-mail.

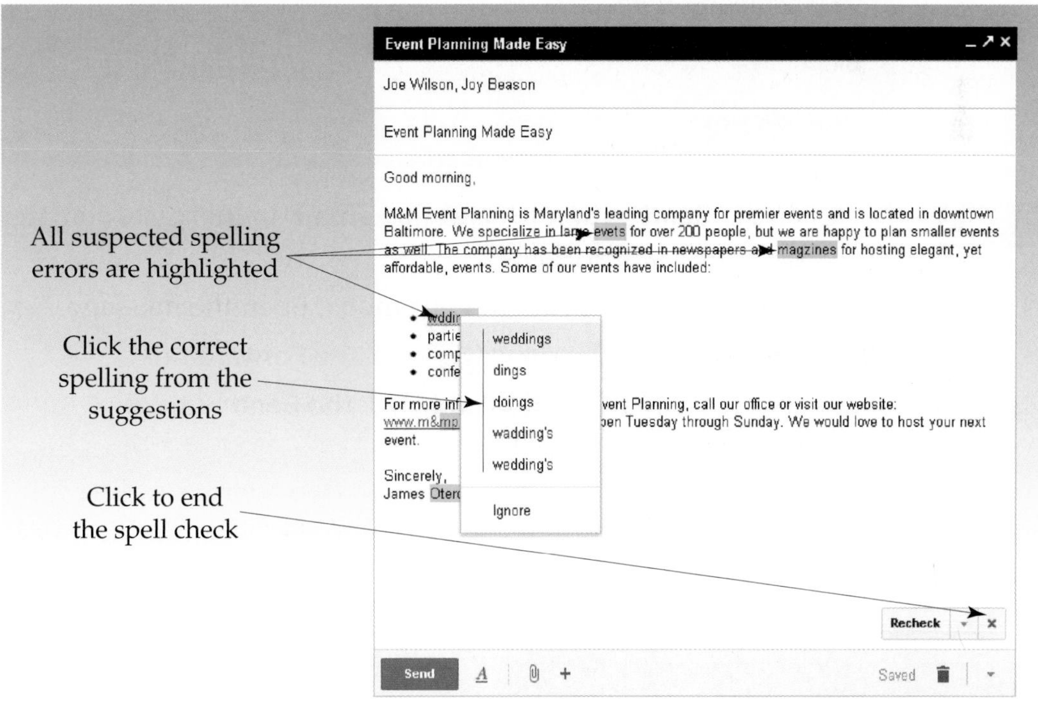

Goodheart-Willcox Publisher

Figure 1-6. The spell-check feature in Gmail provides suggestions for suspected spelling errors once you click a highlighted word.

Lesson 1-2

Replying To and Forwarding Messages

When users reply to messages, they can respond to just the sender or everyone else on the message. If the message needs to be sent to an entirely new recipient, the message can be forwarded.

1. Log in to your Google Mail account.
2. In the inbox, find the message with the subject Make Planning Events Easy.
3. Click the message subject to open the message.
4. At the bottom of the message, click the **Reply** link.
5. Enter the following text.

> Good afternoon,
>
> My organization is very interested in seeing if your company can plan our next company retreat. Your e-mail stated your company has been recognized in newspapers and magazines. Can you please send me the articles that feature your company or direct me to where I can find them online?
>
> Sincerely,
>
> Tran Nguyen

Send

6. Click the **Send** button to send the e-mail. In this case, you are replying to your own e-mail address.
7. When the reply appears in your inbox, open the message.
8. At the bottom of the message, click the **Forward** link.
9. Enter your e-mail address and click the **Send** button.

Attaching Files to E-mail

Gmail users can e-mail documents to others by attaching them to a message. Users need to adhere to file type and size parameters when using the attachments feature.

1. Navigate to the student companion website (www.g-wlearning.com/informationtechnology/), and download the MM News Article data file to your working folder.
2. Log in to your Google Mail account.
3. Locate the conversation with the subject Make Planning Events Easy. This contains the e-mail you forwarded to yourself in Lesson 1-2. Click the conversation to view it.
4. Click the **Reply** link to add a new e-mail to the conversation.

Attach files

5. Click the **Attach files** button at the bottom of the text editor. A standard Windows open dialog box is displayed, as shown in **Figure 1-7.**
6. Browse to the file downloaded in step 1 and select it.

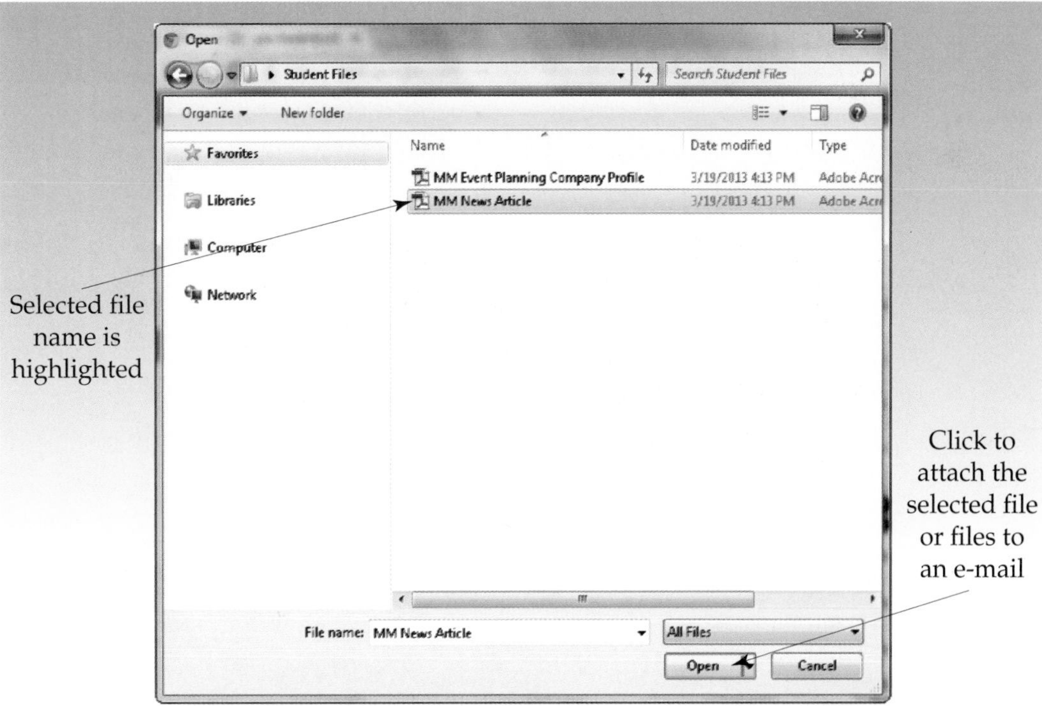

Goodheart-Willcox Publisher

Figure 1-7. A standard Windows open dialog box is displayed for Gmail users to browse for and select a file to attach to a message.

Multiple files can be attached by holding the [Ctrl] key and selecting each file. Adobe Flash must be installed to use this feature.

7. Click the **Open** button to attach the file to the e-mail. There may be a brief pause as Google uploads the file.

8. Click the **Send** button to send the e-mail with the attached file.

Lesson 1-4

Searching for Messages

Google provides tools to help users find messages they need. A quick search can be conducted from the default Gmail window. Users can also complete a more focused search using the advanced search feature.

Performing a Basic Search

1. Log in to your Google Mail account.
2. In the search text box at the top of the Mail page, enter Tran Nguyen, as shown in **Figure 1-8.**

3. Click the **Search Mail** button. All messages that have Tran Nguyen in the subject line or the body are listed in the Mail page. If there are more than twenty messages, the messages appear on multiple pages. Click the arrows to view the other pages.
4. Click the **Inbox** label to clear the search and view all of the messages in your inbox.

Performing an Advanced Search

5. Click the drop-down arrow to the right of the search text box. The **Search** dialog box shown in **Figure 1-9** is shown.
6. In the **Has the words** text box, enter M&M Event Planning.

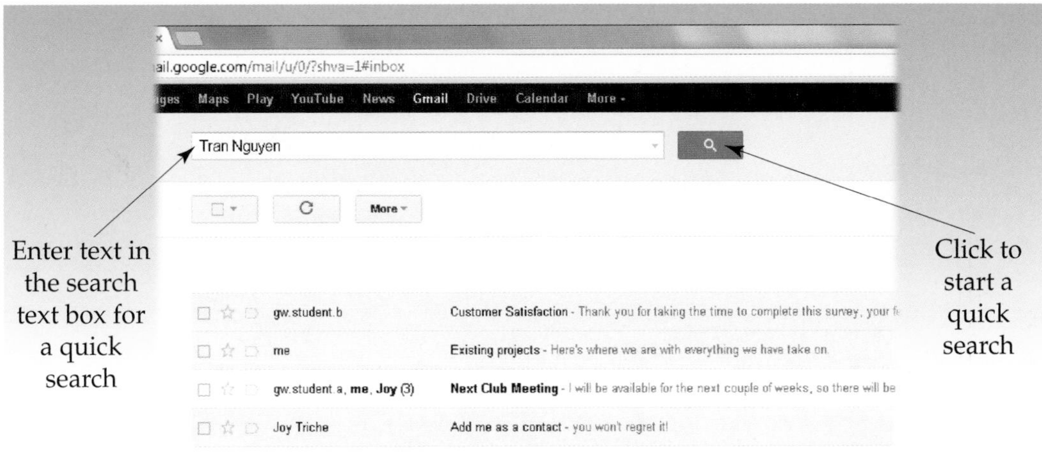

Goodheart-Willcox Publisher

Figure 1-8. The basic or quick search can be more convenient for users than the advanced search, but the search criteria are limited.

Search
All Mail
From
To
Subject
Has the words
M&M Event Planning
Doesn't have
Has attachment
Date within 1 day of
Examples: Friday, today, Mar 26, 3/26/04
Create filter with this search »

Click to start an advanced search

Goodheart-Willcox Publisher

Figure 1-9. There are many criteria by which a user can search for a message using the advanced search feature.

7. Click the **All Mail** button at the top of the dialog box to display a drop-down menu.
8. Click **Mail & Spam & Trash** in the drop-down menu. This will search all possible locations for messages that match the search criteria.

9. Click the **Search Mail** button in the dialog box. The search results are displayed in the Mail page.

Lesson 1-5

Using the My Picture Settings

Users can select a picture to represent them to other Gmail users. The picture should be appropriate for the way you use Gmail. For users that send Gmail for their business, they could use their company logo as their picture.

1. Navigate to the student companion website (www.g-wlearning.com/informationtechnology/), and download the M-M Logo data file to your working folder.
2. Log in to your Google Mail account.

Settings

3. Click the **Settings** button in the upper-right corner of the Mail page to display a drop-down menu.
4. Click **Settings** in the drop-down menu. The Settings page is displayed.
5. Click the **General** tab, if it is not already displayed.
6. Scroll down to the **My picture:** section of the page.
7. Click the **Select a picture** link. A dialog box is displayed in which you can specify a picture for the account, as shown in **Figure 1-10.**
8. Click **My Computer** on the left side of the dialog box to tell Google the file is located on your hard drive. You can also select a picture from your Picasa album or a web address.
9. Click the **Choose File** button to display a standard Windows open dialog box.
10. Browse to the file downloaded in step 1 and select it.
11. Click the **Open** button to upload the image. The image is displayed for cropping, as shown in **Figure 1-11.**

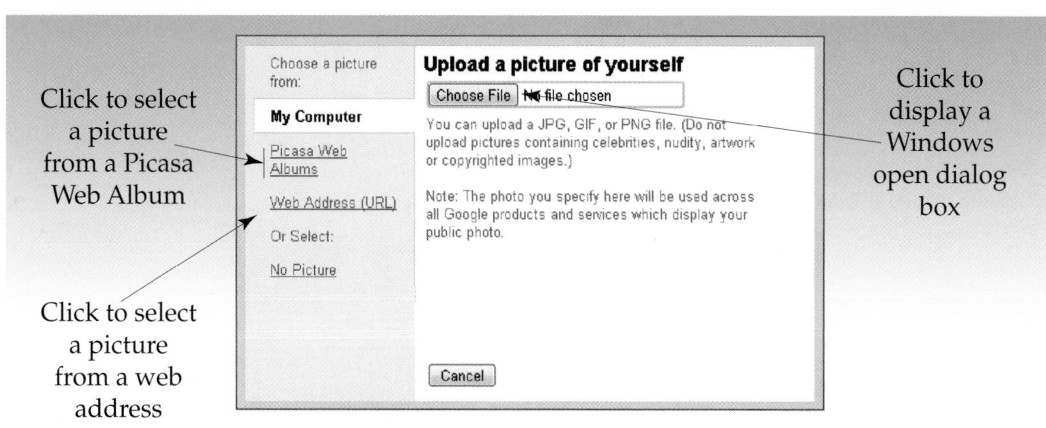

Goodheart-Willcox Publisher

Figure 1-10. A user can select an appropriate picture to display when someone looks at his or her Google profile.

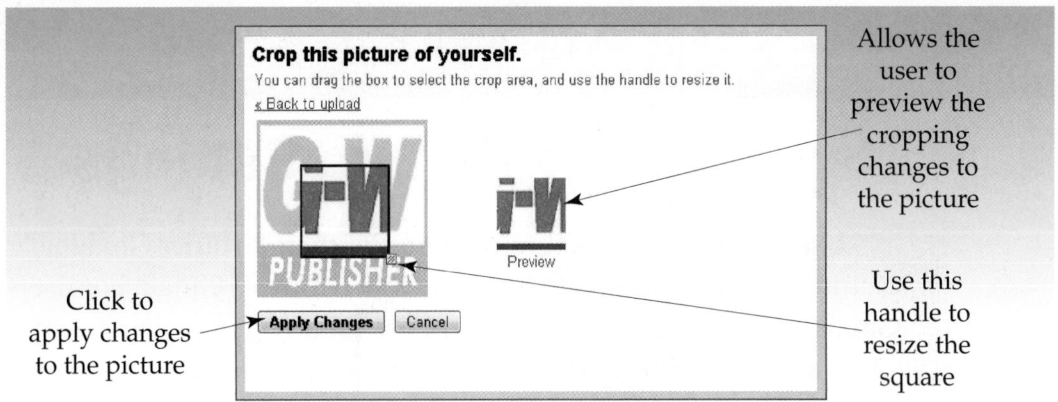

Goodheart-Willcox Publisher

Figure 1-11. Pictures can be cropped from within Gmail, but must retain the square shape.

12. Move the square box over the image to specify the portion to be used. The box can be resized using the handle at its bottom-right corner, but it will remain square.
13. Click the **Apply Changes** button to crop the image and set it as the profile image.
14. Scroll to the bottom of the Settings page and click the **Save Changes** button. If the button is grayed out, Google has automatically saved the changes.

Lesson 1-6

Setting Up a Signature

Creating a signature customizes Gmail and can save users time. Also, signature can be changed or updated easily.

1. Log in to your Google Mail account.

Settings

2. Click the **Settings** button in the upper-right corner of the Mail page to display a drop-down menu.
3. Click **Settings** in the drop-down menu. The Settings page is displayed.
4. Click the **General** tab, if it is not already displayed.
5. Scroll down to the **Signature:** section of the page.
6. Click inside the large text box. Notice that the radio button above the text box is automatically turned on.
7. Enter the following. Use the formatting options on the toolbar above the text box to match the formatting shown.

Your Name

Marketing Team

M&M Event Planning

800-555-1234

8. Scroll to the bottom of the Settings page and click the **Save Changes** button. If the button is grayed out, Google has automatically saved the changes.

Lesson 1-7

Using Themes

The way the Gmail window looks can reflect your personality. The themes feature allows users to radically or subtly change the look of the Gmail window.

1. Log in to your Google Mail account.
2. Click the **Settings** button in the upper-right corner of the Mail page to display a drop-down menu.

   Settings

3. Click **Themes** in the drop-down menu. The Settings page is displayed with the **Themes** tab current. See **Figure 1-12.**
4. Scroll down, locate the Tree theme, and click it. A dialog box appears asking for your city. This particular theme changes based on the location you enter.
5. Enter your city in the dialog box.
6. Click the **Save** button to display the selected theme.

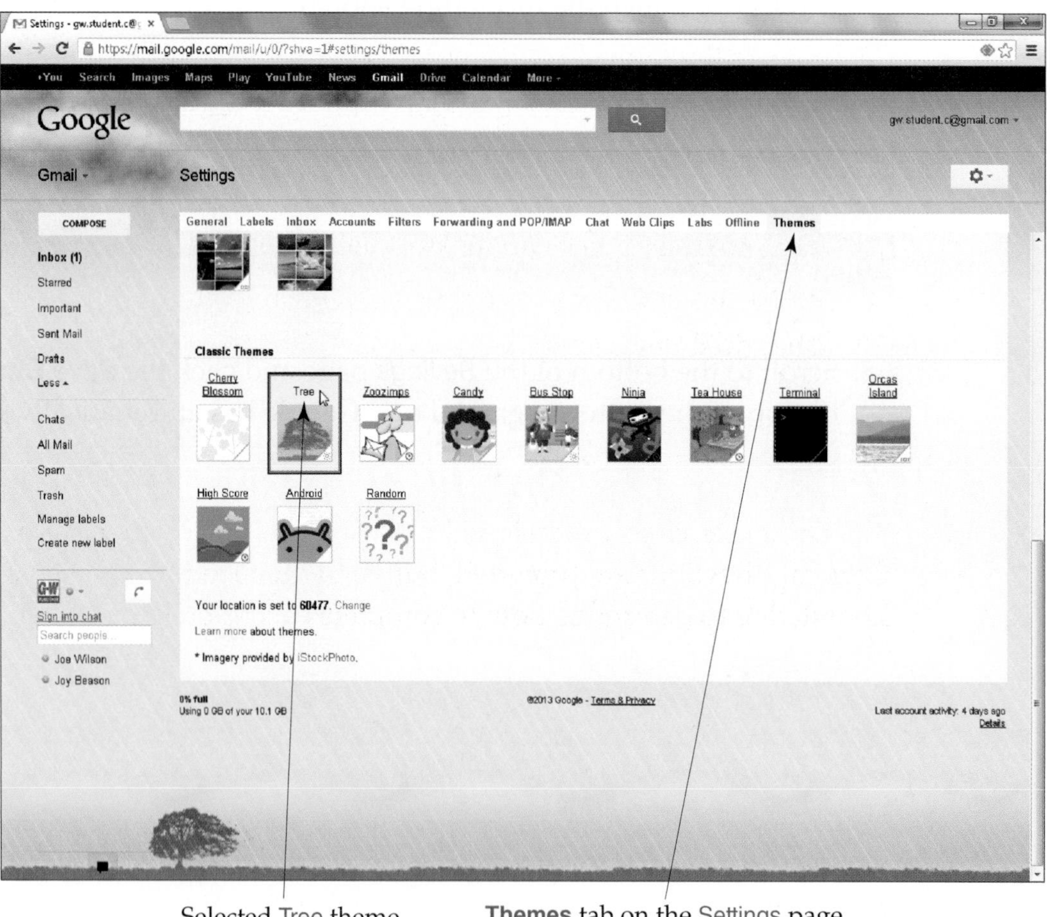

Goodheart-Willcox Publisher

Figure 1-12. Users can change the look of their Gmail window by choosing a new theme from the **Theme** tab on the Settings page.

Check Your Google Apps IQ

Now that you have finished this chapter, see what you know about Google Apps by taking the chapter posttest.
www.m.g-wlearning.com
www.g-wlearning.com/informationtechnology/

Skill Review

Answer the following questions on a separate sheet of paper.

1. Where does the list of incoming mail appear in Gmail?
2. What is the recipient?
3. Describe the difference between cc and bcc.
4. Which option will send a response to everyone who received the original message?
5. What is the maximum size for an e-mail attachment?
6. In Gmail, messages are grouped into ______ based on the subject line.
7. If a number appears in parentheses after the sender name, what does this indicate?
8. What are the three locations from where a profile picture can be selected?
9. Briefly describe the purpose of a Gmail signature.
10. What do themes allow?

Lesson Application

These exercises are designed to apply the skills learned in this chapter. General directions are provided, but you will need to draw on your knowledge to determine how to complete each exercise.

Exercise 1-1
Compose a New Message with an Attachment

Before beginning this activity, navigate to the student companion website (www.g-wlearning.com/informationtechnology/), and download the MM Company Brochure data file to your working folder. Take the steps needed to compose a new e-mail and attach this file to it. Use the following text as the body of the message.

Good morning Ms. Strong,

Our marketing team forwarded your information to us. We would love to work with your company to plan your retreat. We have attached our company brochure that provides an overview of our services.

Sincerely,

your name

Send the e-mail to the Gmail address of one of your classmates. One of your classmates should send an e-mail to you.

Exercise 1-2 Searching for E-mails with an Attachment

Take the steps needed to perform an advanced search of your e-mail. Look for e-mails that have an attachment and include the word review in the subject or body of the message. The search should return the e-mail created in Exercise 1-1. Open that conversation, reply to it, and cc another classmate.

Exercise 1-3 Creating a Signature

Create an e-mail signature for your Gmail account. Include your name, your job title, and your company or town. Format the signature so your name is bold and in a color other than black. Format the other elements of the signature so they are personalized to your tastes.

Exercise 1-4 Changing Your Profile

Select a photo to use as a profile picture. You may use freeware images or clipart, or you may use a digital camera to take a photograph of yourself. Use image-editing software as needed to make the image square. Then, take the steps needed to set the photograph as the profile picture for your Google account.

Chapter 2

Organizing the Inbox

Objectives

After completing this chapter, you will be able to:

- **Explain** how to delete, archive, and restore messages.
- **Create** labels to group messages.
- **Use** stars to call attention to important messages.
- **Create** filters that automatically organize messages.

alexmillos/Shutterstock.com

Check Your Google Apps IQ

Before you begin this chapter, see what you already know about Google Apps by taking the chapter pretest.

www.m.g-wlearning.com
www.g-wlearning.com/informationtechnology/

Organizational Tools

The average person receives around 100 e-mail messages each day. With this volume of e-mail coming in, it helps to have an organized inbox. Google provides several tools to aid users in keeping their e-mail organized. Gmail organizational tools include deleting and archiving messages. Stars and importance markers are other organizational tools. Stars can be used to differentiate messages that require follow up, for example. The creation of custom labels provides users with a method of grouping similar messages. The filters feature automates the application of organizational tools based on user-defined criteria.

Deleting and Archiving Gmail Messages

Often the two first steps in organizing messages are removing items that will not be needed at all and storing items that will not be needed on a regular basis. In the Gmail inbox, these two actions are referred to as deleting and archiving. ***Deleting*** a message will remove it from the **Inbox** label and move it to the **Trash** label, as shown in **Figure 2-1**. Deleted messages remain in the **Trash** label for 30 days before they are permanently deleted. ***Archiving*** allows Gmail users to move messages

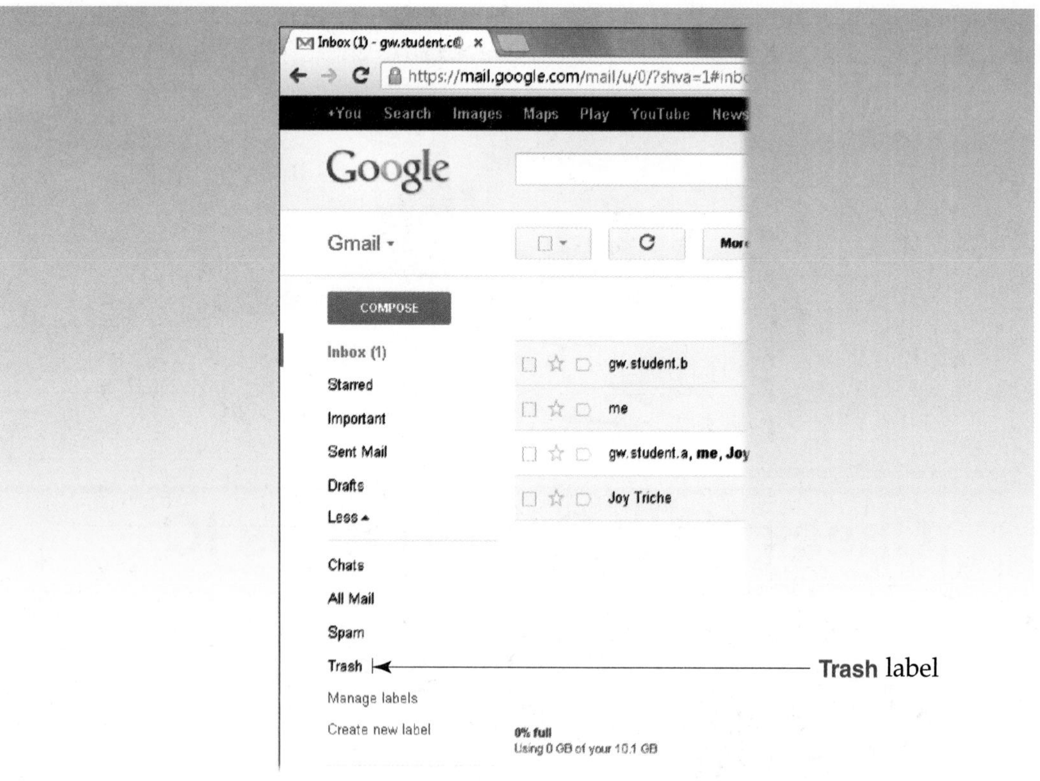

Goodheart-Willcox Publisher

Figure 2-1. Deleted messages are available for 30 days in the **Trash** label.

from the **Inbox** label without permanently deleting them. Archived mail is displayed within the **All Mail** label. Unlike deleted messages, archived messages will appear in search results of Gmail. Archived messages also will be displayed in the **Inbox** label if a new message in the conversation is received.

Using Stars, Importance Markers, and Labels

For the messages that remain in the **Inbox** label, Gmail users can use stars, importance markers, and customized labels to organize them. By using these organizational tools, users can highlight messages according to importance or action within the **Inbox** label or distinguish them being part of a particular group of messages.

Stars are symbols that provide a quick way to make a visual distinction between messages. Some e-mail messages require the user to respond right away, while other messages do not require any response. Applying stars to differentiate the type of action needed on a message can help organize the inbox. The default symbol is a yellow star, but other colored stars and symbols are available, as shown in **Figure 2-2**. Because symbols can be quickly changed or removed at any time, Gmail users could also use a combination of colored stars and symbols as a way to track the progress in resolving messages. For example, a yellow star could indicate a message that requires action. The star could be changed to a green check mark when the action is complete. Only the Gmail user will see the symbol or understand its significance. Another advantage of using this tool is that starred messages show up in the default **Starred** label.

Star	Name
★	Yellow-Star
★	Orange-Star
★	Red-Star
★	Purple-Star
★	Blue-Star
★	Green-Star

Star	Name
!	Red-Bang
»	Orange-Guillement
!	Yellow-Bang
✔	Green-Check
i	Blue-Info
?	Purple-Question

Goodheart-Willcox Publisher

Figure 2-2. There are 12 stars (symbols) that can be used to visually categorize messages.

The ***importance marker*** is similar to the stars feature in that it visually tags messages. Unlike the stars feature, it is intended to always point out e-mails the user deems important. Google analyzes what messages the user has tagged to try to predict what messages should have the importance marker assigned in the future. As a result, you may notice that messages will have an importance marker without having assigned it yourself. If a message has been inappropriately tagged with the importance marker, you can remove the marker. Doing so helps Google learn what to mark in the future. All e-mails with the importance marker are displayed in the **Important** label.

In addition to the **Important** and **Starred** labels, Gmail has several system labels, such as: **Inbox**, **Sent Mail**, **Drafts**, and **All Mail**. Gmail users can add to these system labels and create customized labels to further organize their inboxes. For example, if you are planning a party, you could create a label called **Party Planning**. Any messages received about that event could be moved to the **Party Planning** label.

Gmail users can take labels a step further by using sublabels. With ***sublabels,*** also referred to as *nested labels,* users create a new label within a custom label to further organize messages. For example, within the **Party Planning** label, you could create the sublabel **Catering** under which all food-related messages for the party would be stored.

Using Filters

Gmail users can create filters to support their efforts at organizing their inboxes. ***Filters*** automatically screen all e-mails based on criteria the user has defined. Users can create filters that analyze e-mails based on:

- the e-mail address the message is from;
- the e-mail address the message was sent to;
- text within the subject line of the e-mail;
- text included in the body of the message;
- text excluded from the body of the message; and
- whether or not the message has an attachment.

Based on those criteria, the filter can be set up to complete several actions. Some of the actions include starring the message, applying a label to the message, forwarding the message, deleting the message, archiving the message, or marking the message as important. One or more of these actions can be assigned to a filter. Creating filters that support the way you use the Gmail organizational tools can be helpful in finding messages quickly and easily.

Gmail has a default spam filter. ***Spam*** is unwanted and unsolicited e-mail. E-mails that meet the criteria outlined in the spam filter are automatically sent to the **Spam** label. Sometimes an e-mail the user actually wants is sent to the **Spam** label, so it is a good idea to check that label from time to time.

Lesson 2-1

Deleting and Archiving Messages

Two ways of removing messages from the **Inbox** label are deleting and archiving. When a message is deleted, it is moved to the **Trash** label. Archiving a message moves it from the **Inbox** label to the **All Mail** label.

Deleting a Message

1. Send yourself an e-mail with the subject line Family Reunion.
2. Once the message appears in the inbox, check the check box to the left of the Family Reunion message.
3. Click the **Delete** button. The message is moved to the **Trash** label.
4. To see the contents of the **Trash** label, click **More** in the list of labels, then click the **Trash** label, as shown in **Figure 2-3**.

Delete

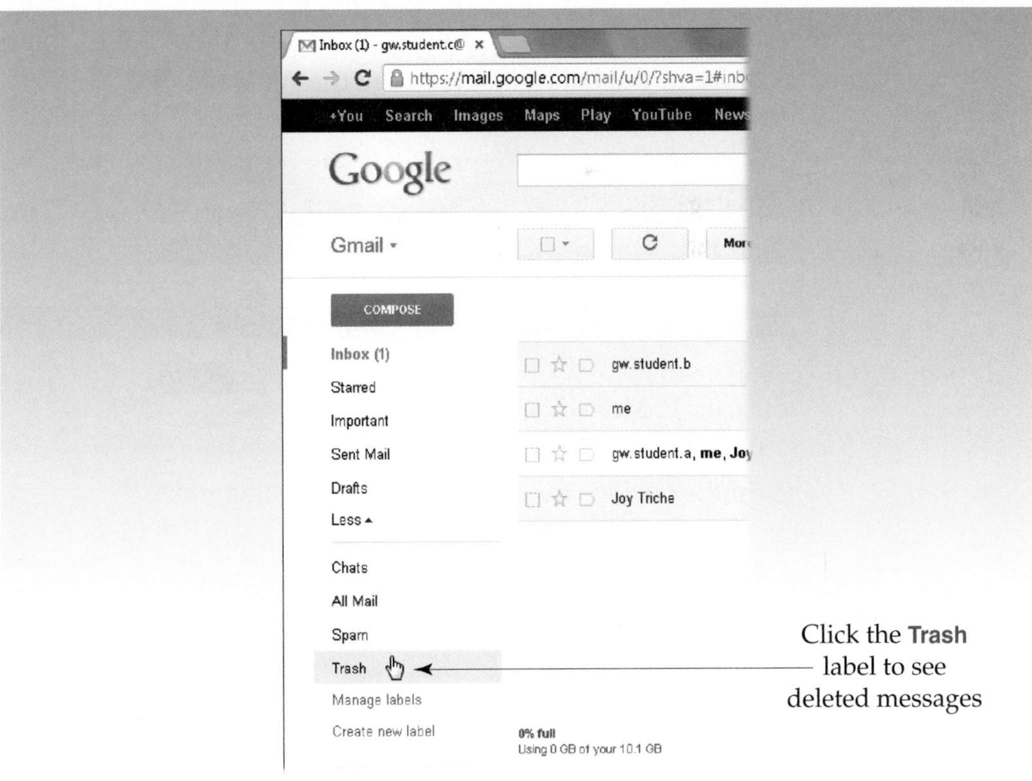

Goodheart-Willcox Publisher

Figure 2-3. The **Trash** label contains deleted messages.

Recovering a Deleted Message

5. Display the contents of the **Trash** label, if not already displayed. You may need to click **More** or move the cursor over the list of labels to see the **Trash** label.
6. Check the check box to the left of the deleted message to be recovered. In this case, the Family Reunion message is to be recovered, so check the check box to the left of that message.

Move to

7. Click the **Move to** button to display a drop-down menu, as shown in **Figure 2-4**.
8. Click **Inbox** in the drop-down menu.
9. The message is moved to the **Inbox** label, and a message stating that is displayed at the top of the page.

Archiving a Message

10. Display the contents of the **Inbox** label.
11. Check the check box to the left of the Family Reunion message.

Archive

12. Click the **Archive** button.
13. The message is moved to the **All Mail** label, as shown in **Figure 2-5**, and a message stating that is displayed at the top of the page. You may need to click **More** in the list of labels to see the **All Mail** label.

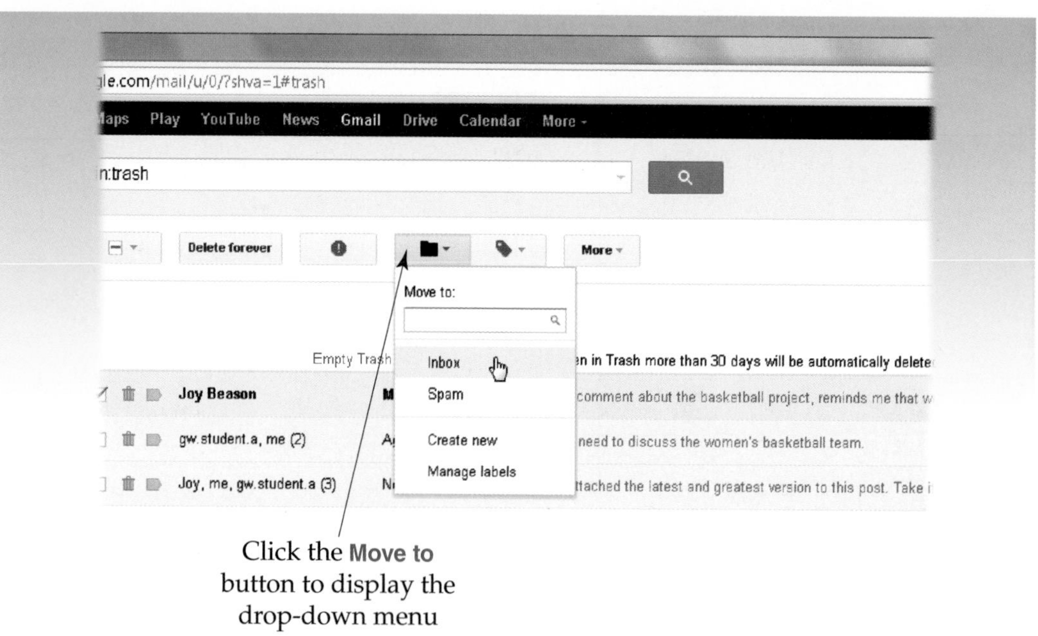

Goodheart-Willcox Publisher

Figure 2-4. The **Move to** button is used to move a message from one label to another.

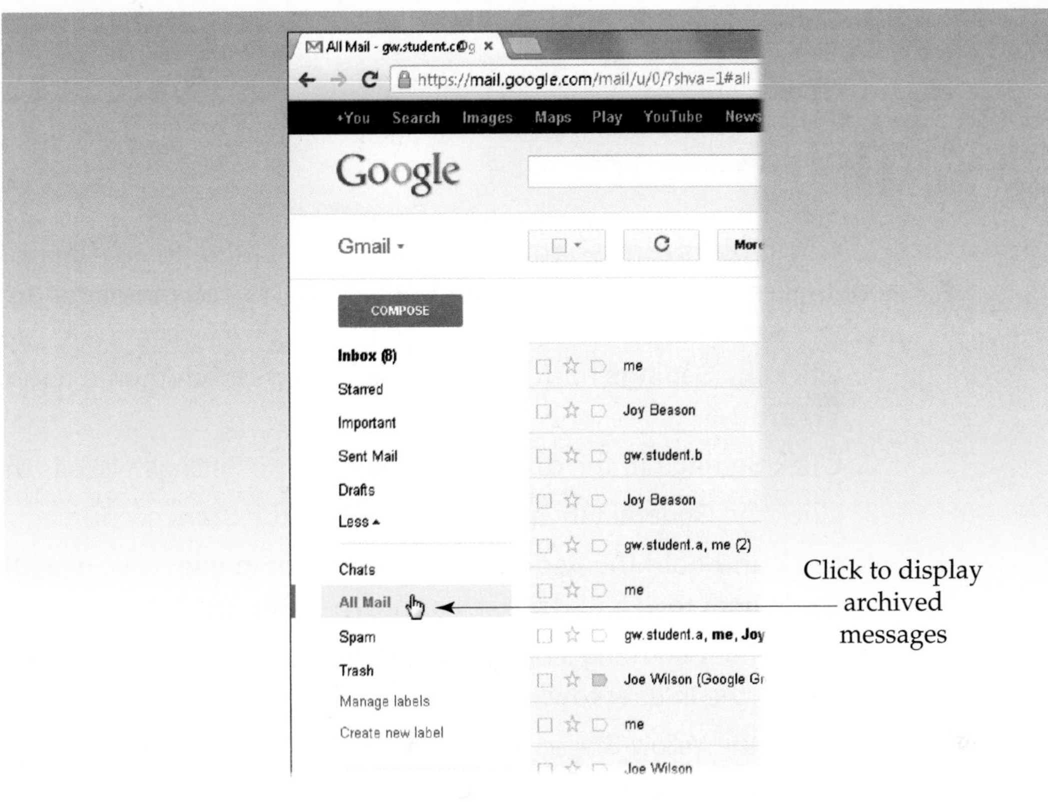

Goodheart-Willcox Publisher

Figure 2-5. Archived messages appear in the **All Mail** label.

Unarchiving a Message

14. Display the contents of the **All Mail** label, if not already displayed.
15. Check the check box to the left of the Family Reunion message.
16. Click the **Move to Inbox** button. The Family Reunion message is moved to the **Inbox** label, and a message stating that is displayed at the top of the screen.

Move to Inbox

Lesson 2-2

Using Stars

Gmail users can assign a star or another symbol to an e-mail. Using this tool makes certain messages stand out. Also, starred messages are displayed in the **Starred** label.

1. Click the **Settings** button to display a drop-down menu, as shown in **Figure 2-6**.
2. Click **Settings** in the drop-down menu. The Settings page is displayed.

Settings

3. Click the **General** tab and scroll down to the **Stars** section.
4. Click and hold the Red-Star icon in the **Not in use:** row, drag the icon to the **In use:** row, and drop it, as shown in **Figure 2-7**.
5. Move the Red-Bang icon and the Purple-Question icon from the **Not in use:** row to the **In use:** row.
6. Move the Yellow-Star icon from the **In use:** row to the **Not in use:** row.
7. Move the Red-Star icon to the far left of the **In use:** row. This will make it the first symbol that appears when clicked. The order in which the symbols appear in the **In use:** row determines the order in which they will be displayed when clicked.

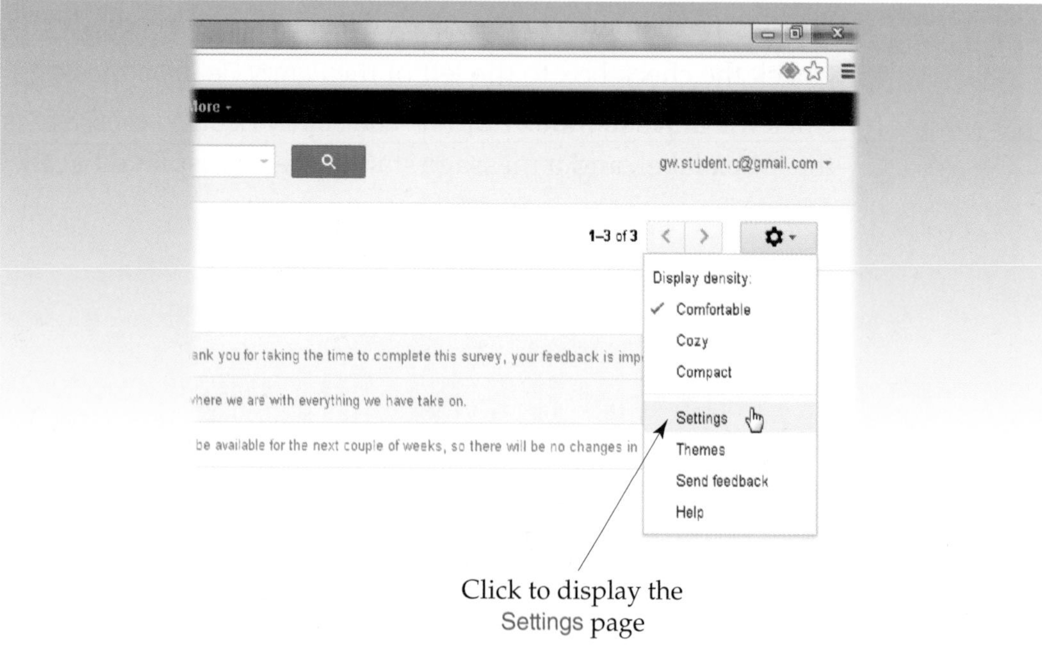

Figure 2-6. To select which stars are available, click the **Settings** button to display the Settings page.

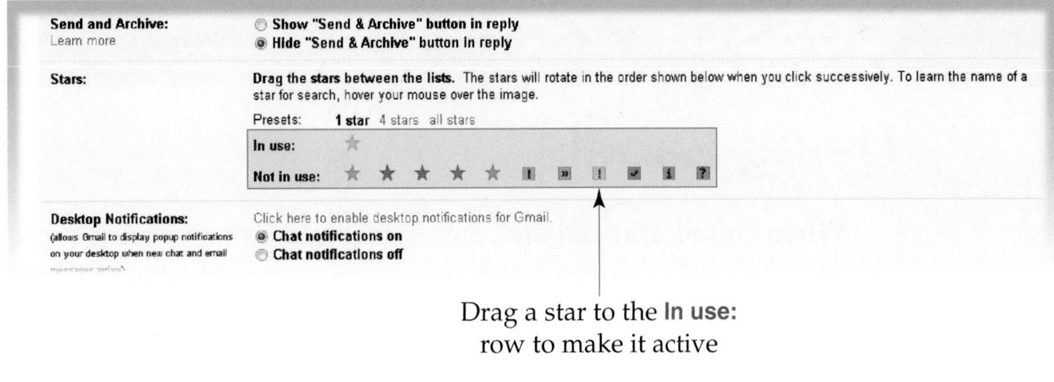

Goodheart-Willcox Publisher

Figure 2-7. Making a star available to use as a symbol on a message.

8. Scroll to the bottom of the page and click the **Save Changes** button.
9. Display the contents of the **Inbox** label, if not already displayed.
10. Click the empty star to the left of the Family Reunion message. The star should turn red, as shown in **Figure 2-8**.
11. Click the red star. The next symbol that was set in the **In use:** list is displayed. If the clear star is displayed, too much time passed between displaying the red star and clicking it again. To display the symbols in sequence, do not pause between clicking each symbol.

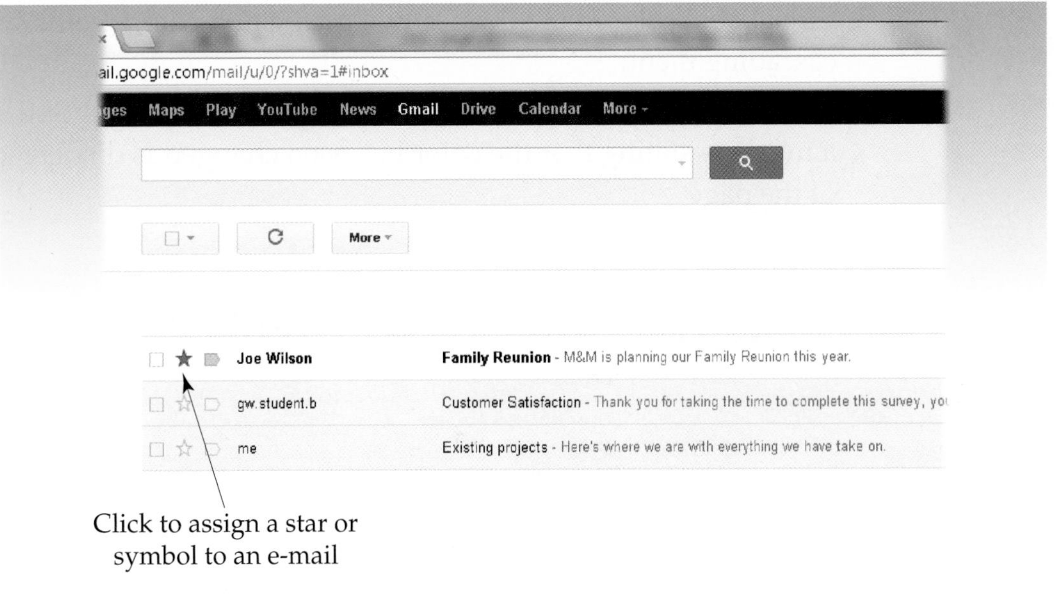

Goodheart-Willcox Publisher

Figure 2-8. The message has been flagged with a red star.

Lesson 2-3

Using Labels

When Gmail users create custom labels, they can group similar messages together. Within a custom label, users can create sublabels to further group related messages.

Creating a Label

1. Click **More** in the list of labels or move the cursor over the list of labels to see the expanded list.
2. Click the **Create new label** link. The **New Label** dialog box shown in **Figure 2-9** is displayed.
3. In the **Please enter a new label name:** text box, enter Reunions.
4. Click the **Create** button to create the label.
5. The **Reunions** label appears in the list of labels on the left.

Assigning a Color to a Label

6. Move the cursor over the **Reunions** label so it is highlighted.
7. Click the button to the right of the label name to display a drop-down menu, as shown in **Figure 2-10**.
8. Click **Label color** in the drop-down menu, and click a color swatch in the cascading menu.
9. The selected color appears as a small square to the right of the label, and a message stating that the color has been changed is displayed at the top of the page.

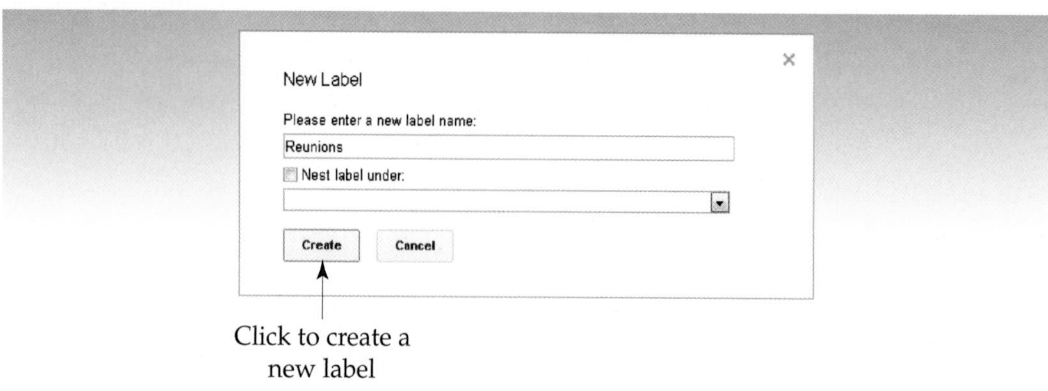

Goodheart-Willcox Publisher

Figure 2-9. Creating a new label.

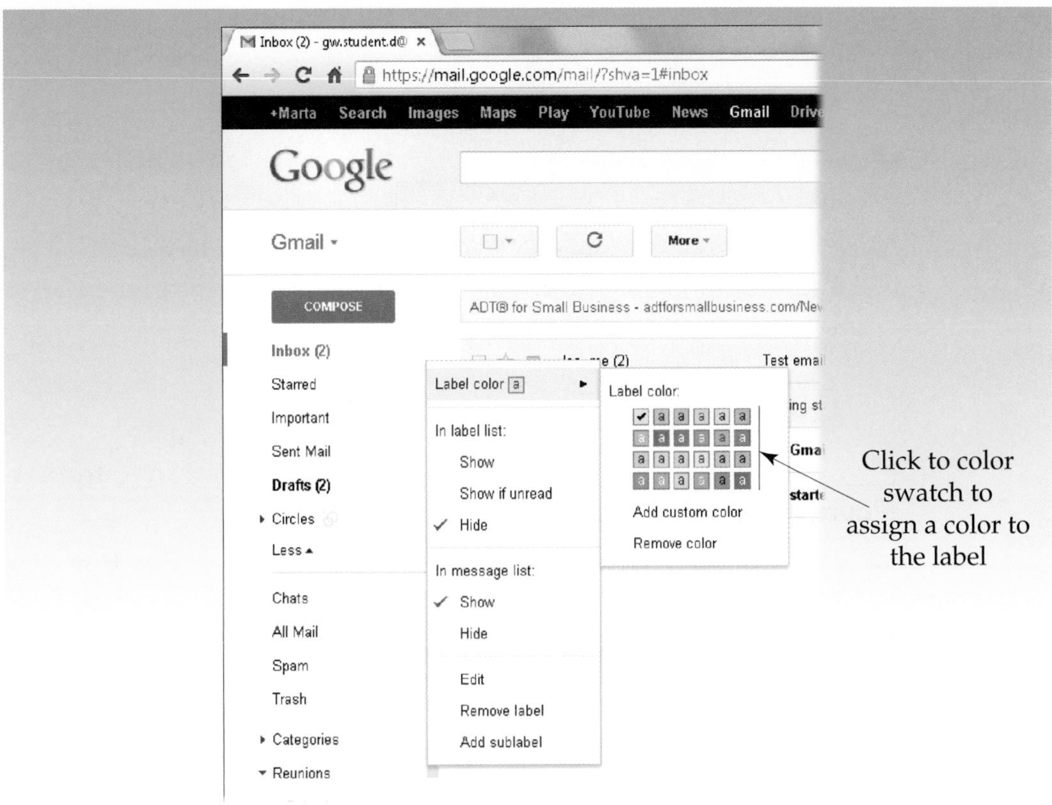

Goodheart-Willcox Publisher

Figure 2-10. Assigning a color to a label.

Assigning a Label

10. Display the contents of the **Inbox** label, if not already displayed.
11. Check the check box to the left of the Family Reunion message.

Labels

12. Click the **Labels** button to display a drop-down menu.
13. In the drop-down menu, check the check box next to **Reunions**, as shown in **Figure 2-11**.
14. Click **Apply** in the drop-down menu. The **Reunions** label appears on the message in the inbox.
15. Click the **Reunions** label in the list of labels. The Family Reunion message is displayed in the contents. Any other message assigned this label also appears in the **Reunions** label contents.

Tip To label a message *and* archive it in one step, use the **Move to** button instead of the **Label** button.

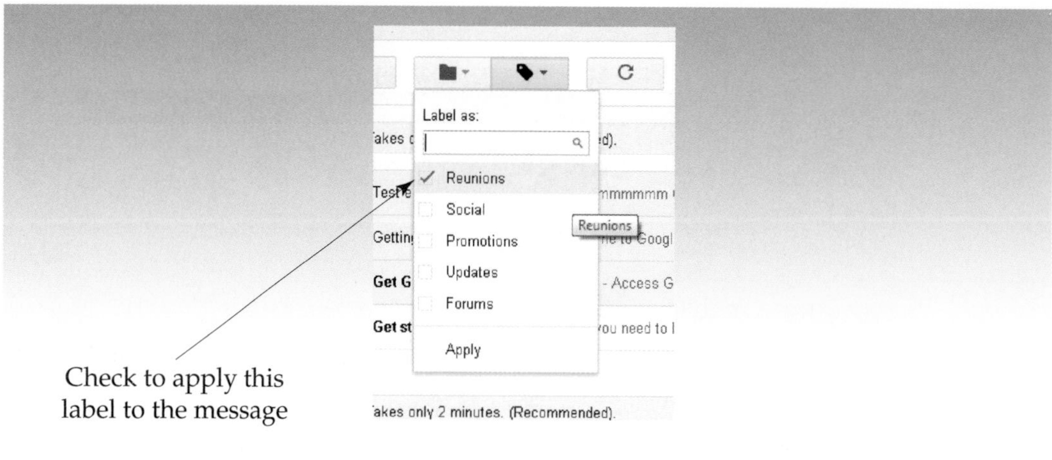

Goodheart-Willcox Publisher

Figure 2-11. Assigning a label to a message.

Creating Sublabels

16. Move the cursor over the **Reunions** label so it is highlighted.
17. Click the button to the right of the label name to display a drop-down menu.
18. Click **Add sublabel** in the drop-down menu. The **New Label** dialog box is displayed, as shown in **Figure 2-12**. Note that the **Nest label under:** check box is checked and **Reunions** is selected in the drop-down list.
19. Enter School in the **Please enter a new label name:** text box.
20. Click the **Create** button.
21. A small triangle is displayed to the left of the **Reunions** label in the list of labels. Click the triangle to expand the list of sublabels under the **Reunions** label.

To turn an existing label into a sublabel, click the button to the right of the label and click **Edit** in the drop-down menu. In the **Edit Label** dialog box, check the **Nest label under** check box and select where to nest the label in the drop-down list.

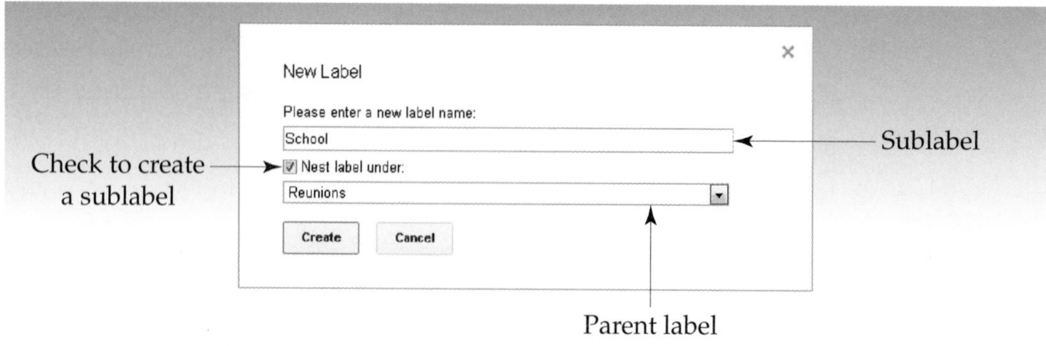

Goodheart-Willcox Publisher

Figure 2-12. Creating a sublabel nested below a parent label.

Manage Labels

22. Move the cursor over the **Reunions** label so it is highlighted.
23. Click the button to the right of the label name to display a drop-down menu.
24. In the **In label list:** section of the drop-down menu, click **Hide**, as shown in **Figure 2-13**. This places the label in the expanded area of the label list, which is displayed by clicking **More**.
25. Expand the list of labels, and move the cursor over the **Reunions** label so it is highlighted.
26. Click the button to the right of the label name to display a drop-down menu.
27. In the **In label list:** section of the drop-down menu, click **Show**. This makes the label visible even when the list of labels is not expanded.

Tip To delete a label, click the button to the right of the label and select **Remove label** in the drop-down menu. This does not delete any messages within that label.

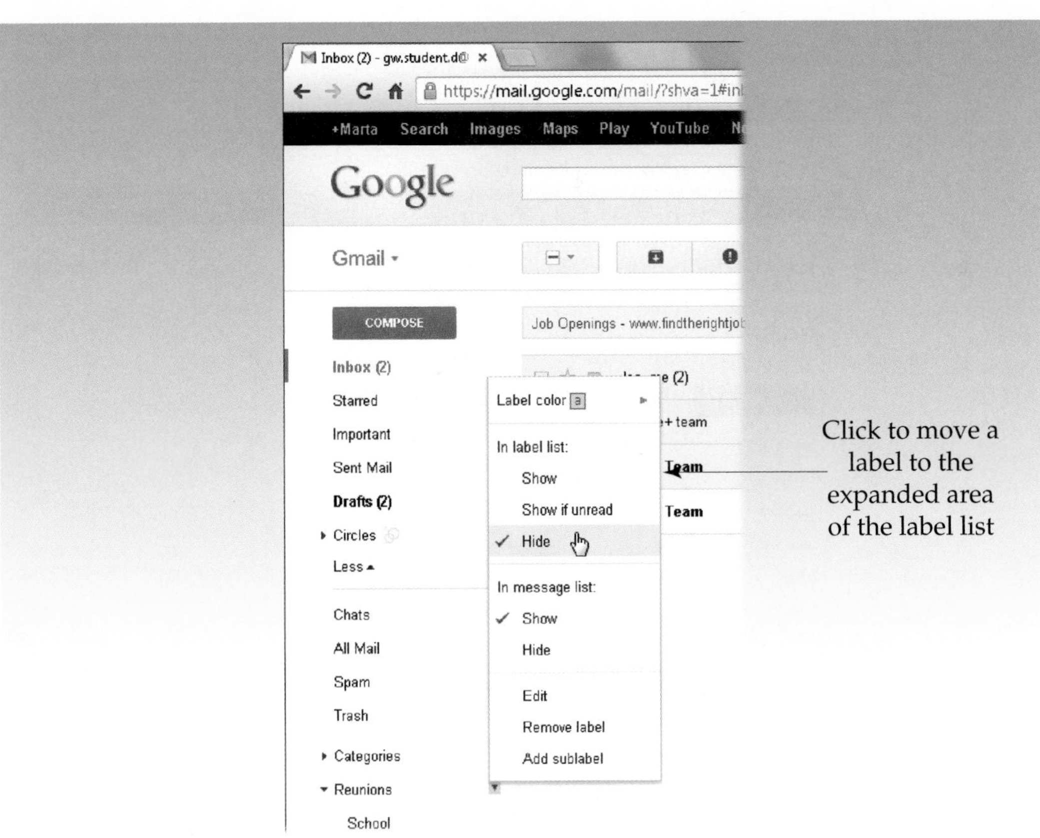

Goodheart-Willcox Publisher

Figure 2-13. Setting a label so it appears in the expanded area of the label list.

Lesson 2-4

Creating and Using Filters

There are two basic steps in creating a filter: establish the search criteria, and then set the actions to be taken on messages that meet those criteria. A filter can be created with criteria entered in one or more of the fields.

Setting Up a Filter

1. Move the cursor over the search box at the top of the Gmail page, and click the drop-down button on the right side of the search box. A filter form is displayed, as shown in **Figure 2-14**.
2. In the **Has the words** text box, enter Reunion as the search criterion.
3. Click **Create filter with this search** at the bottom of the filter form. A second page to the filter form is displayed, as shown in **Figure 2-15**.
4. Click the **Choose label...** button and select **Reunions** in the drop-down list. You can select as many or as few actions as needed.

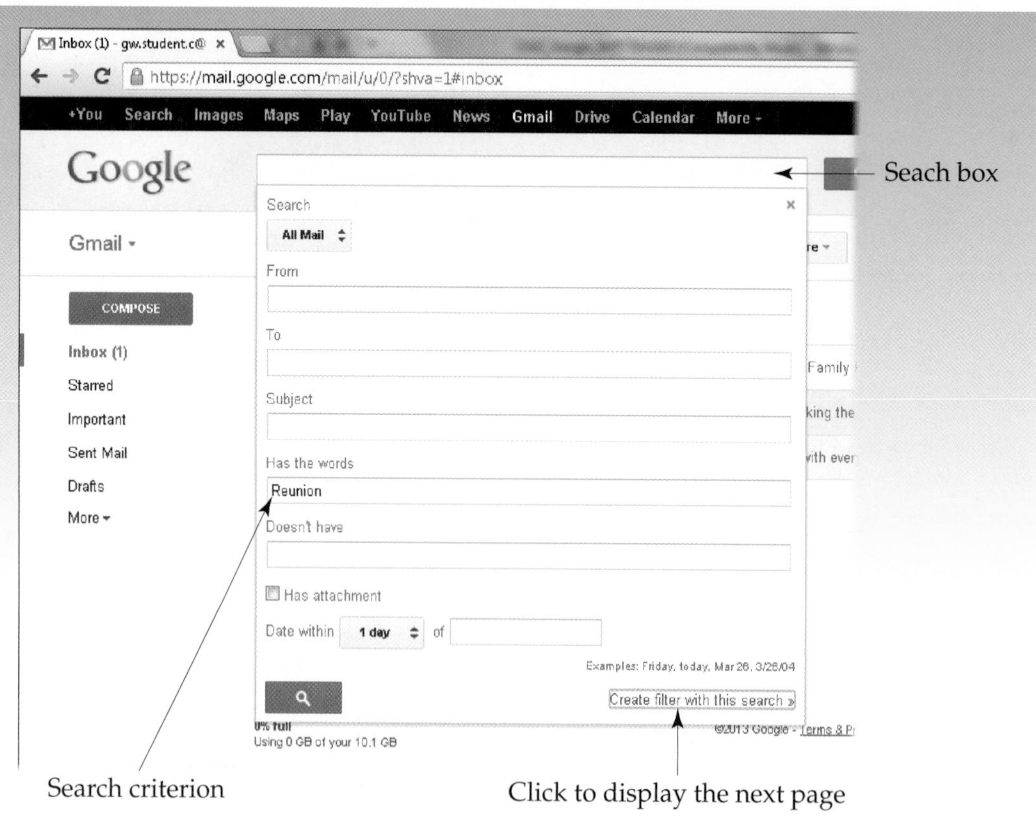

Goodheart-Willcox Publisher

Figure 2-14. The first page of the form used to create a filter.

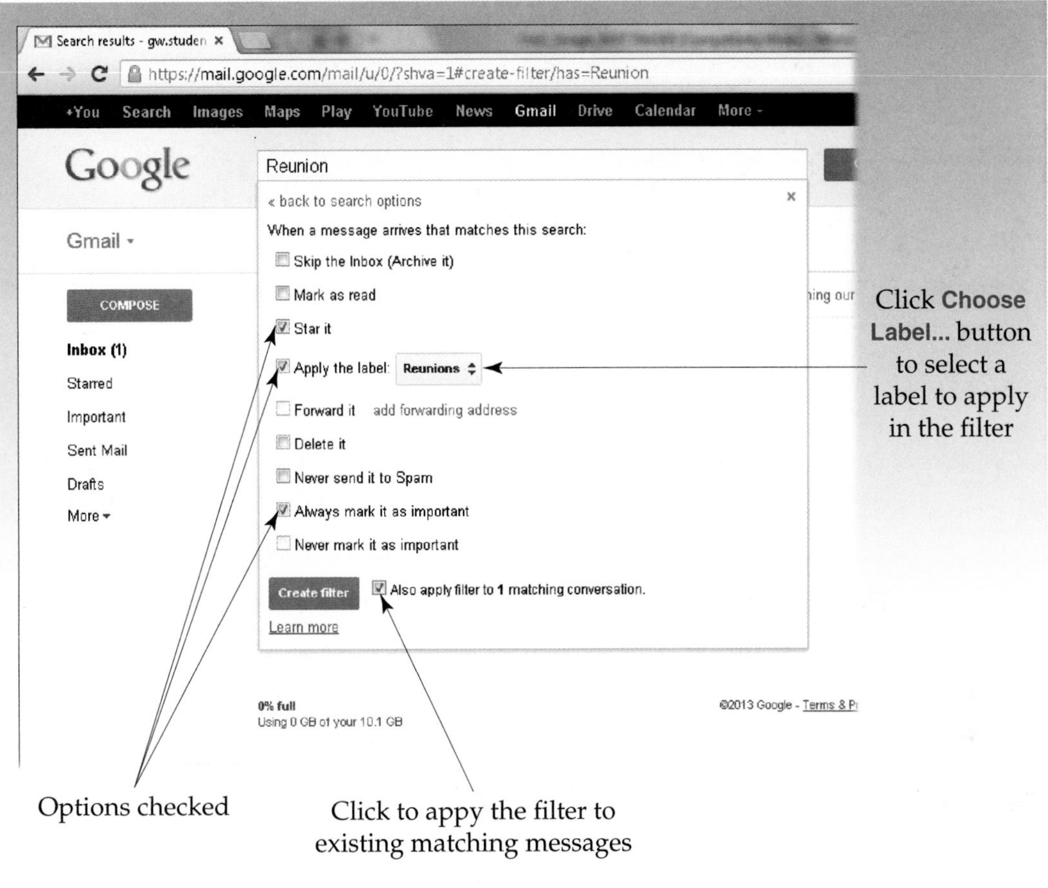

Goodheart-Willcox Publisher

Figure 2-15. The second page of the form used to create a filter.

5. To apply the filter to messages that have already been delivered, check the **Also apply filter to matching conversations** check box. If this check box is not checked, the filter will only apply to new messages.

6. Click the **Create filter** button to apply the filter. A message appears at the top of the page to indicate the filter was created.

A filter can also be created from within a message by clicking the **More** button and **Filter messages like this** in the drop-down menu. The filter form will be displayed with the sender's e-mail inserted in the search criteria.

Editing Filters

7. Click the **Settings** button, and then click **Settings** in the drop-down menu to display the Settings page.
8. On the Settings page, click the **Filters** tab, as shown in **Figure 2-16**.

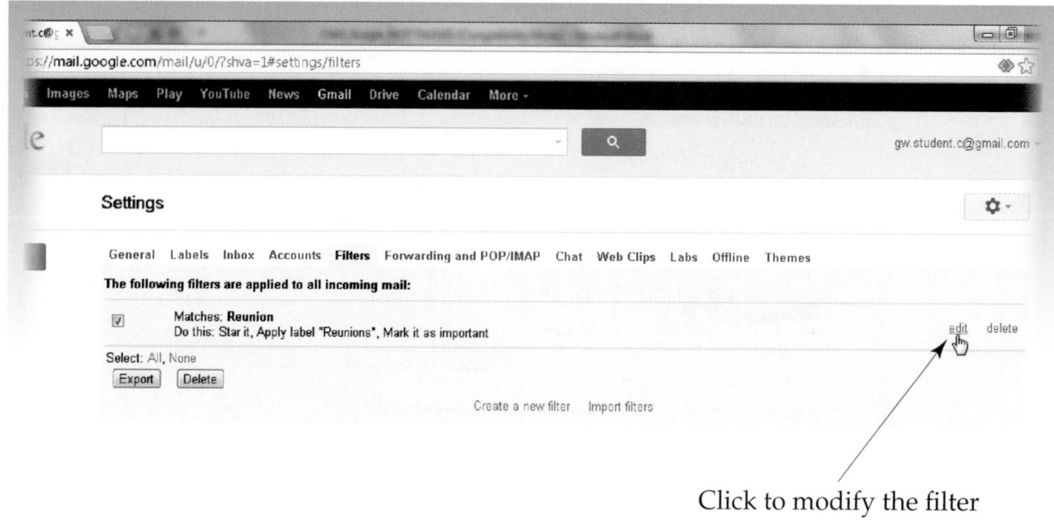

Goodheart-Willcox Publisher

Figure 2-16. A filter is selected for editing on the Settings page.

9. Click the **edit** link for the filter to modify.

Update filter

10. Change the filter form as needed, then click the **Update filter** button.
11. To permanently remove a filter, click the **delete** link. This only deletes the filter, not the individual messages matching the filter criteria.

Check Your Google Apps IQ

Now that you have finished this chapter, see what you know about Google Apps by taking the chapter posttest.
www.m.g-wlearning.com
www.g-wlearning.com/informationtechnology/

Skill Review

Answer the following questions on a separate sheet of paper.

1. What are the two basic ways in which to clean up the Gmail inbox?
2. A deleted message will remain in the **Trash** label for ______ days.
3. Which appears in a search result, archived messages, deleted messages, or both?
4. How can a deleted message be recovered?
5. What is the purpose of assigning a star to a message?
6. What determines the order in which stars are displayed when the symbol for a message is clicked?
7. A(n) ______ is a nested label below a parent label.
8. Briefly describe how to assign a color to a label.
9. ______ can be used to locate messages matching certain criteria.
10. Briefly describe how to edit a filter.

Lesson Application

These exercises are designed to apply the skills learned in this and previous chapters. General directions are provided, but you will need to draw on your knowledge to determine how to complete each exercise.

Exercise 2-1
Using Stars

Remove all of the currently available stars and symbols. Select three stars and three other symbols to make available for your use. Send yourself an e-mail with the subject line Save the Date Notices. Once the message appears in the inbox, assign one of the symbols to it.

Exercise 2-2
Creating Labels and Sublabels

Create a label called **Google Class Files**. Assign the color of your choice to the label. Set the label so it appears in the expanded area of the label list. Create a label called **Business**. Assign the color of your choice to the label. Create two sublabels named **Customers** and **Sales**.

Reorganize the **Reunion** label created in the chapter so it is a sublabel under **Google Class Files**. Edit the **Google Class Files** label so it always appears without expanding the list of labels.

Exercise 2-3
Creating a Filter

Create a filter that searches for the subject line Making Planning Events Easy created in Chapter 1. From within the filter, create a new label named **Sales**. Set the filter to include in this new label any e-mails found matching the criterion.

Exercise 2-4
Deleting and Archiving Messages

Archive the e-mail with the subject line Family Reunion. Then move it back to the **Inbox** label. Delete this same message, and then recover it.

Chapter 3

Contacts

Objectives

After completing this chapter, you will be able to:

- **Create** an individual contact.
- **Manage** contact groups.
- **Import** contact information from a file.
- **Export** contact information to a file.

alexmillos/Shutterstock.com

Check Your Google Apps IQ

Before you begin this chapter, see what you already know about Google Apps by taking the chapter pretest.

www.m.g-wlearning.com
www.g-wlearning.com/informationtechnology/

Using Gmail Contacts

In Gmail Contacts, Gmail users store information about people and businesses with whom they communicate. ***Contact information*** may include e-mail addresses, phone numbers, and street addresses, which can be convenient to have in a central location. Like other Gmail features, contact information is not tied to a specific computer. It can be accessed as long as a user can get online. Using Gmail Contacts can make addressing e-mail messages faster and easier.

Google uses the information in Gmail Contacts in its auto-complete feature. ***Auto-complete*** suggests e-mail addresses as characters are entered in the **To** line of an e-mail. For example, if you enter D in the **To** line of an e-mail, contacts beginning with the letter d will be displayed. Also, when the **To** label itself is clicked in a new e-mail message, the names and e-mail addresses that are displayed in a dialog box are pulled from Gmail Contacts.

Gmail Contacts are set up to house more information than just names and e-mail addresses. Phone numbers, birth date, job title, company name, a photo, and the nickname for a contact are examples of the other information that can be stored about a person in Gmail.

Gmail Contact Groups

Contact groups are used to organize contacts. Google puts contacts into three default groups—My Contacts, Most Contacted, and Other Contacts, as shown in **Figure 3-1.** The My Contacts group includes contact information that has been created in Gmail, imported from another Gmail account or

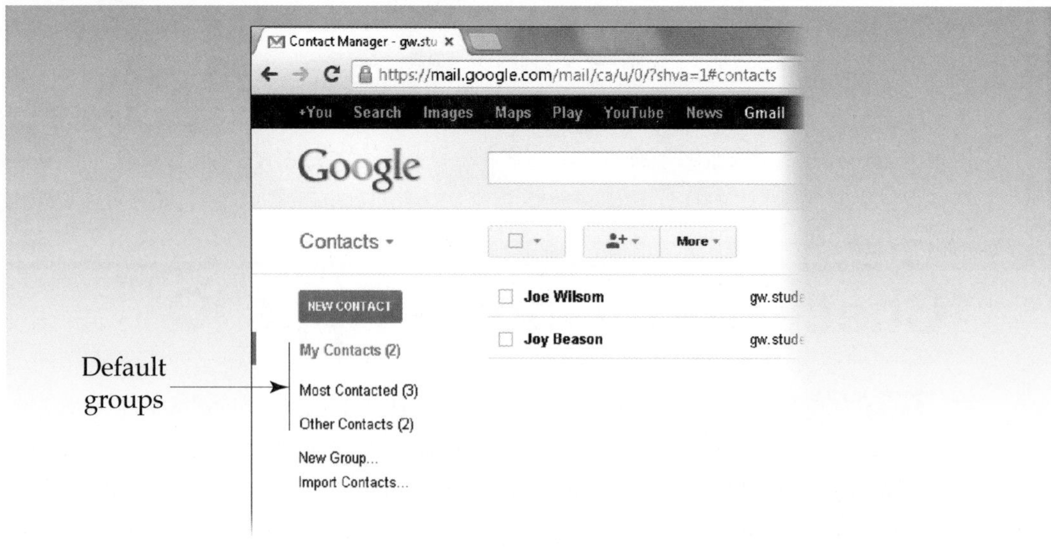

Figure 3-1. There are three default contact groups.

another program, or moved from the Other Contacts group. The Most Contacted group includes the 20 contacts used most frequently. The Other Contacts group includes contact information that has been created or used, but has not been assigned to any other category. Every contact group has a number in parentheses that is displayed next to its label name. This is the number of contacts within the group.

Contacts can be associated with more than one group. When viewing contacts, all of the groups associated with that contact will be displayed. Contacts that are assigned to a group will be displayed in the **My Contacts** label along with any custom group.

In addition to the default groups, Gmail users can create new contact groups. Like the custom label feature in Mail discussed in Chapter 2, users can organize their contacts by grouping similar contacts under a custom group. The new contact group is displayed under the list of default groups. Existing and new contacts can be assigned to these new custom groups.

Organizing contacts into custom groups can make sending e-mails to a group of people easier. When addressing an e-mail, a Gmail user can choose a contact group as the recipient of the e-mail, rather than an individual. For example, you could create a group with the e-mail addresses of every member of your book club. When sending an e-mail to the book club, you could address the e-mail to the contact group rather than entering the e-mail address of each member.

Importing and Exporting Contacts

Contact information is sometimes stored in software other than Gmail. Having contact information centrally located outside of Google can be helpful. Contact entries can be imported from other software programs and apps. ***Importing*** is the process of loading information from a file. Google supports importing comma-separated values (CSV) files and vCard files. vCard is a standard file type for electronic business cards. Several software programs and apps, such as Outlook, Outlook Express, Yahoo! Mail, Hotmail, Eudora, and Apple Address Book, support these file types. Once imported, contact entries can be edited and grouped like those created within Gmail.

Conversely, contact information in Gmail can be shared with others, added to another Gmail account, or exported for use with another software program or app. ***Exporting*** is the process of extracting information and saving it to a file. Exporting contacts also makes them available when an Internet connection is not available. Gmail users can choose to export a single contact, a group of contacts created by the user, a default contact group, or all contacts. Contacts are exported as a CSV or a vCard file. Once exported, the file can be imported into other software following the steps specific to that software program or app.

Lesson 3-1

Individual Contacts

Gmail Contacts can be an efficient place to store contact information. Gmail users can create new contacts in the Contacts section of Gmail or from the Mail section. Contacts can be edited with updated or new information or deleted when a contact is no longer needed.

Creating a Contact

1. Log in to your Google Mail account.
2. Click **Mail** at the upper-left corner of the Mail page to display a drop-down menu, as shown in **Figure 3-2.**

Tip The **Mail** button may display **Gmail** or **Mail**, depending on the version of Google Mail you are using.

3. Click **Contacts** in the drop-down menu to display the Contacts page.

4. Click the **New Contact** button. A form is displayed to add a contact.
5. In the **Add Name** text box, enter your name. Refer to **Figure 3-3.** If **Add Name** is not automatically highlighted, click on it to activate the text box.

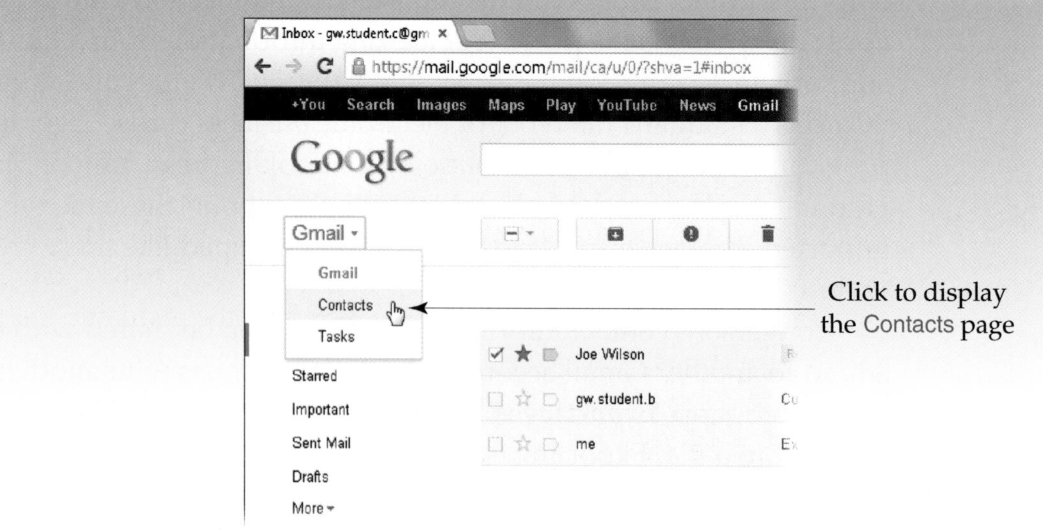

Goodheart-Willcox Publisher

Figure 3-2. Displaying the Contacts page.

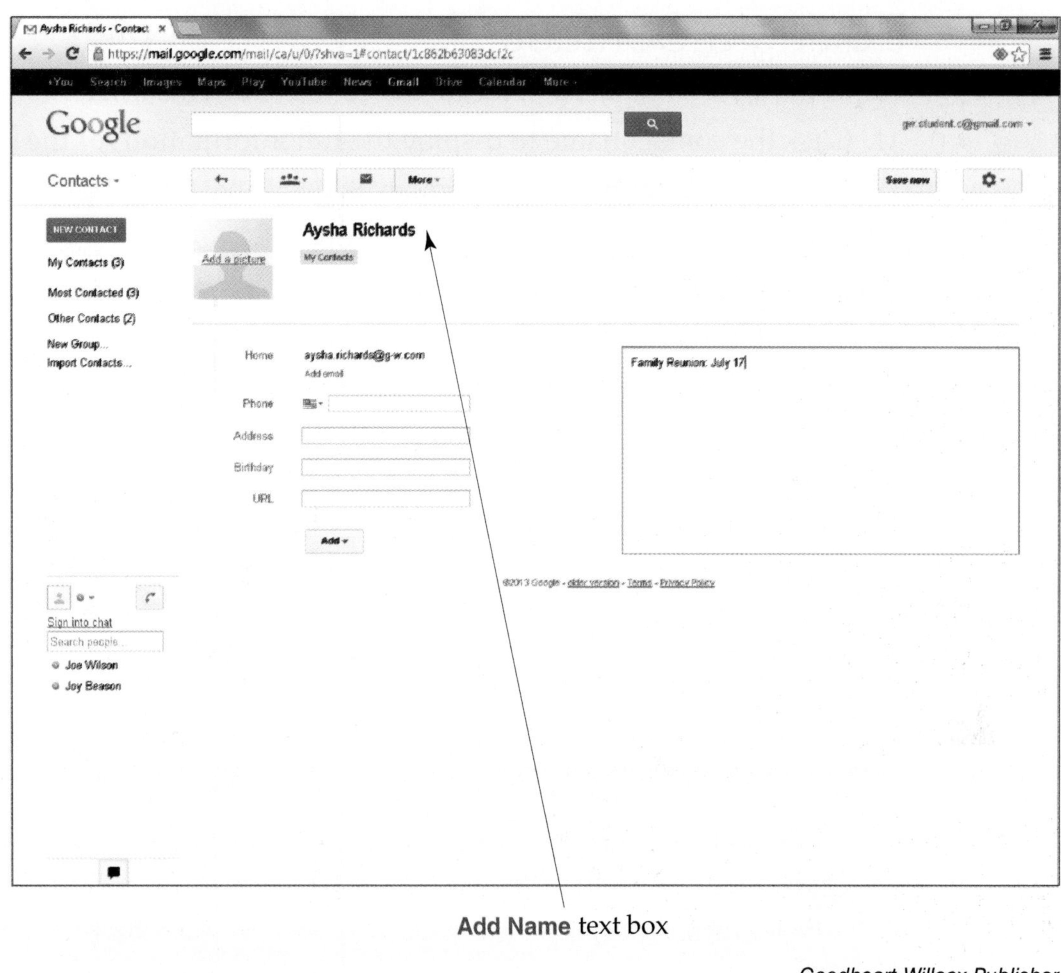

Goodheart-Willcox Publisher

Figure 3-3. Creating a new contact.

6. Click in the **Email** text box and enter your e-mail address. Note: when you click in the text box, the label changes to **Home**. Clicking the drop-down arrow to the right of **Home** displays a menu that allows you to select which e-mail to add. There can be separate e-mails for home, business, and "custom."
7. Click inside the **Add a note** text box and enter Family Reunion: July 17. This text box can be used to add any details that need to be included in the contact information that are not covered by the available fields.

Save now

8. Click the **Save now** button. If this button is grayed out and labeled **Saved**, it is because Google has automatically saved changes made to fields. The **Save now** button is only enabled when there are unsaved changes.

Tip Click the **Add** button to select additional fields to include in the contact information.

9. Click the **My Contacts** label to display all contacts.

Editing a Contact

10. In the **My Contacts** label, locate the contact added earlier.
11. Click the contact name to display the full information for the contact.
12. Click in the **Phone** text box and key 800-555-1234.
13. Update any other information as needed.
14. Click the **Save Now** button, if it is enabled.
15. Click the **My Contacts** label to display all contacts.

Tip You can use the search box at the top of the page to quickly find a contact.

Deleting a Contact

16. In the **My Contacts** label, locate the contact added earlier.
17. Check the check box to the left of the contact.
18. Click the **More** button to display a drop-down menu.
19. Click **Delete Contact** in the drop-down menu, as shown in **Figure 3-4.**

More ▾

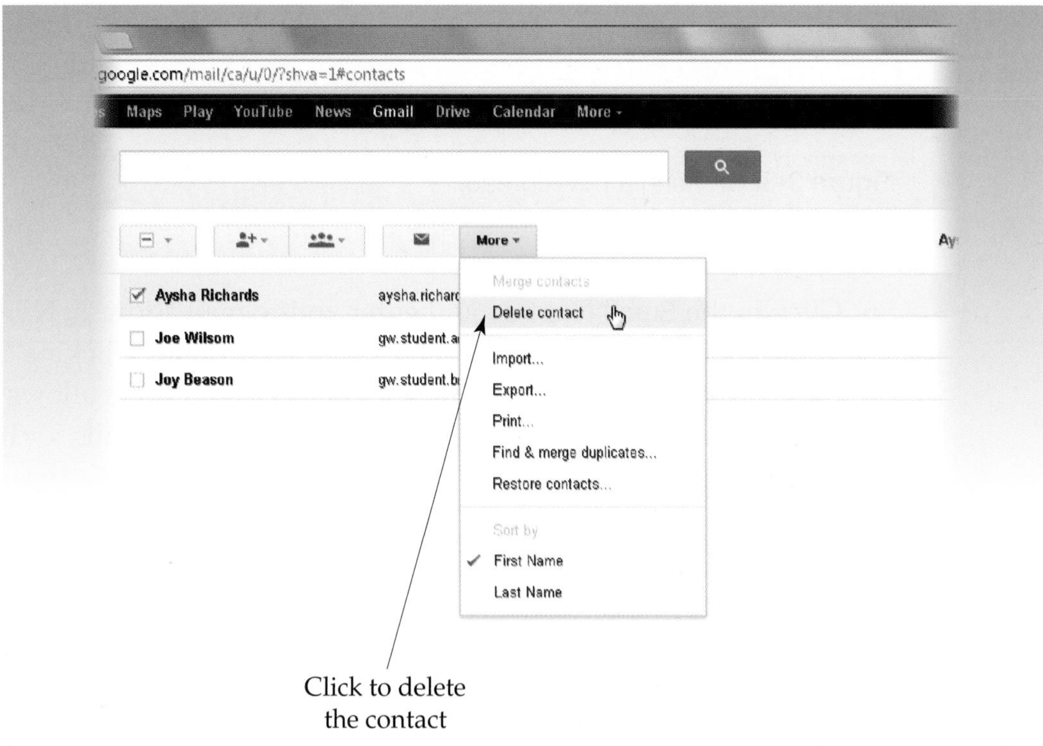

Goodheart-Willcox Publisher

Figure 3-4. Deleting a contact.

Lesson 3-2

Contact Groups

Contact groups can help Gmail users easily find information about people they need to contact. Contact groups can also provide an easy method of sending e-mail to several recipients at one time.

Creating a Contact Group

1. Log in to your Google Mail account.
2. Click **Mail** at the upper-left corner of the Mail page, and click **Contacts** in the drop-down menu to display the Contacts page.
3. Click the **New Group...** label. The **New group** dialog box is displayed, as shown in **Figure 3-5.**
4. In the **Please enter a new group name** text box, enter Reunion Customers.
5. Click the **OK** button to close the dialog box and create the group. The new group appears between the **My Contacts** and **Most Contacted** labels.

Adding Contacts to a Contact Group

6. Click the **My Contacts** label to display all contacts.
7. Check the check box to the left of the contacts to add to a group.
8. Click the **Groups** button to display a drop-down menu, as shown in **Figure 3-6.**

Groups

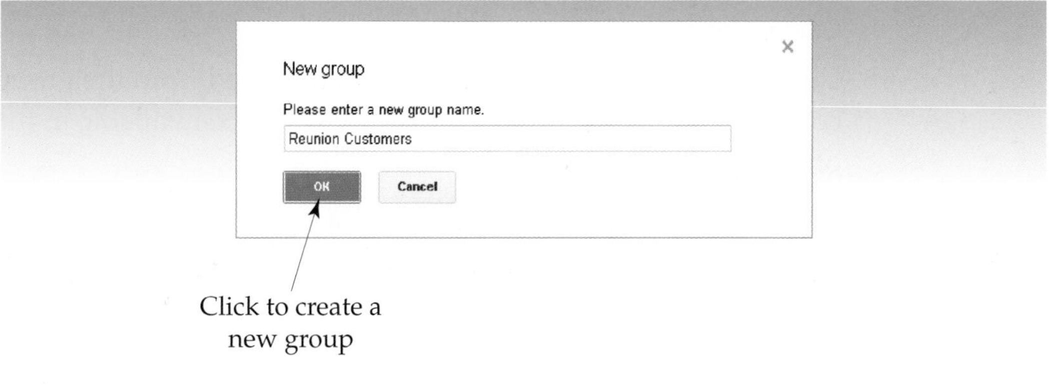

Goodheart-Willcox Publisher

Figure 3-5. Creating a new contact group.

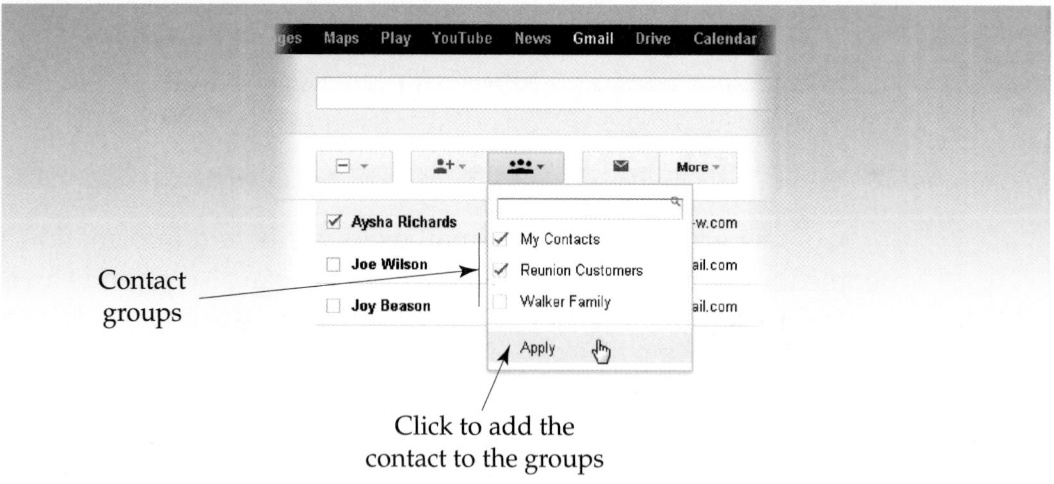

Goodheart-Willcox Publisher

Figure 3-6. Setting the contact groups to which a contact is assigned.

9. Check the check box to the left of the group name Reunion Customers.
10. Click the **Apply** button in the drop-down menu. The contact is added to the group(s) checked in the drop-down menu.

Tip If a contact name does not appear in the contents of the **My Contacts** label, use the search tool or look in the contents of the **Other Contacts** label.

Removing a Contact from a Contact Group

11. Click the **Reunion Customers** label to display the contacts in the group.
12. Check the check box to the left of the contact to remove.
13. Click the **Groups** button.

Groups

14. In the drop-down menu, uncheck the check box to the left of the Reunion Customers group.
15. Click the **Apply** button. The contact is removed from the group. If the contact is not in any other group, it will still be available in the contents of the **Other Contacts** label.

Tip To delete a group, click the group name, click the **More** button, and choose **Delete group**.

Sending an E-mail to a Contact Group

16. Click **Contacts** at the upper-left corner of the Contacts page, and click **Mail** in the drop-down menu to display the Mail page.
17. Click the **Compose Mail** button.
18. Click in the **To:** text box.
19. Begin keying the name of the contact group Reunion Customers. As the name is entered, Google compares the characters to contact names and groups and makes suggestions in a drop-down list, as shown in **Figure 3-7.**
20. When **Reunion Customers** appears as a suggestion in the drop-down list, click on it. The e-mail addresses of the group members appear in the **To:** field.
21. Compose the e-mail and click the **Send** button.

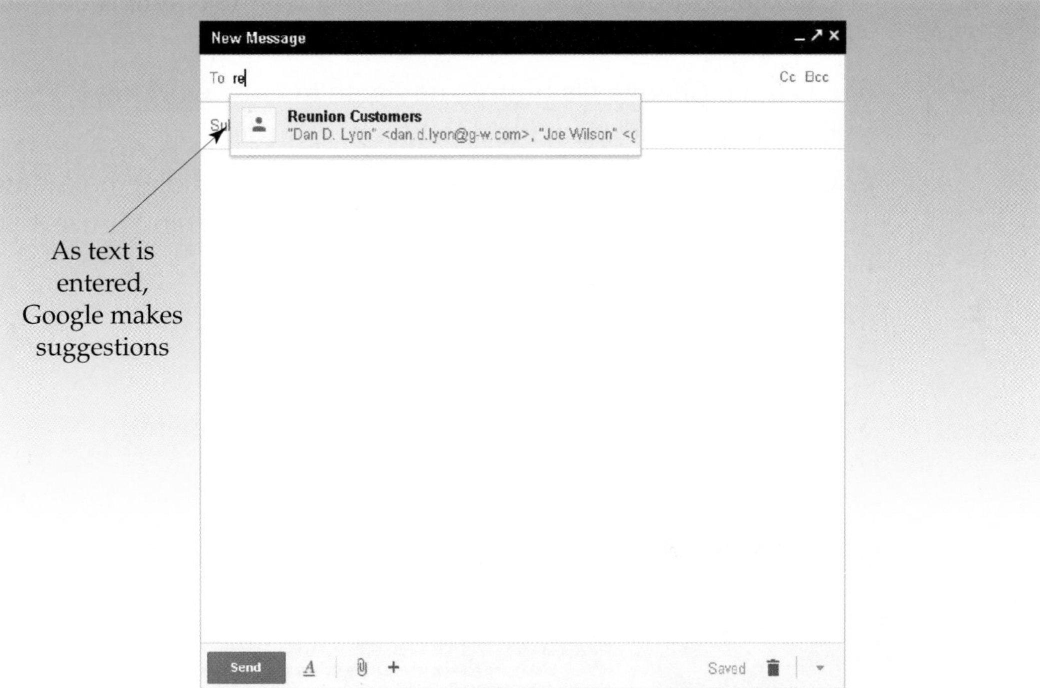

Goodheart-Willcox Publisher

Figure 3-7. Google suggests contact names and groups as characters are entered.

Lesson 3-3

Importing Contact Information

Having contact information in more than one software program can make addressing Gmail messages challenging. However, contacts can be imported into Gmail Contacts from other software programs.

Importing a Contact Group

1. Navigate to the student companion website (www.g-wlearning.com/informationtechnology/), and download the Walker Family data file to your working folder.
2. Log in to your Google Mail account.
3. Click **Mail** at the upper-left corner of the Mail page, and click **Contacts** in the drop-down menu to display the Contacts page.
4. Click **Import Contacts...** in the list of labels. The **Import contacts** dialog box is displayed, as shown in **Figure 3-8.**
5. Click the **Choose file** button, navigate to your working folder, and open the Walker Family data file downloaded earlier.
6. Click the **Import** button in the **Import contacts** dialog box. A new contact group named **Imported** *date* is created, as shown in **Figure 3-9.**

Renaming a Contact Group

7. Click the **Imported** *date* group.

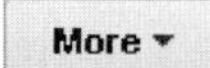

8. Click the **More** button to display a drop-down menu.

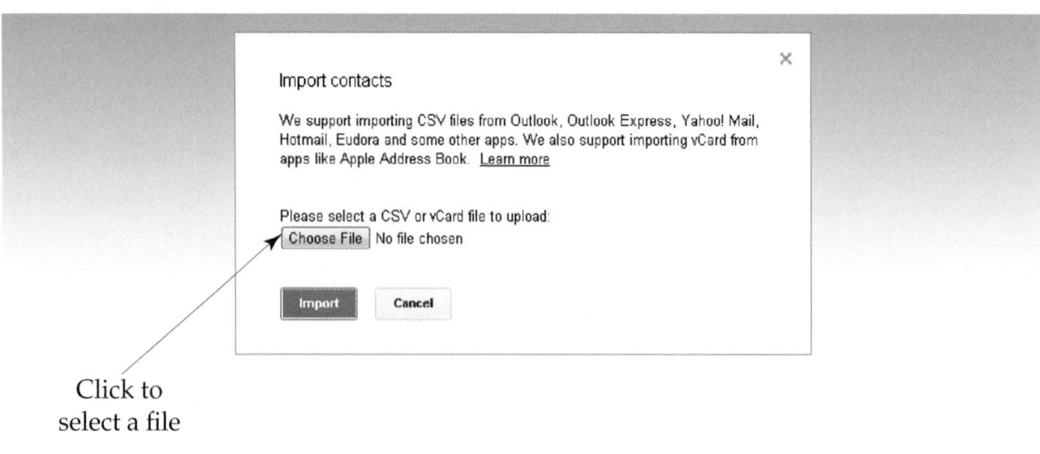

Goodheart-Willcox Publisher

Figure 3-8. Importing contacts.

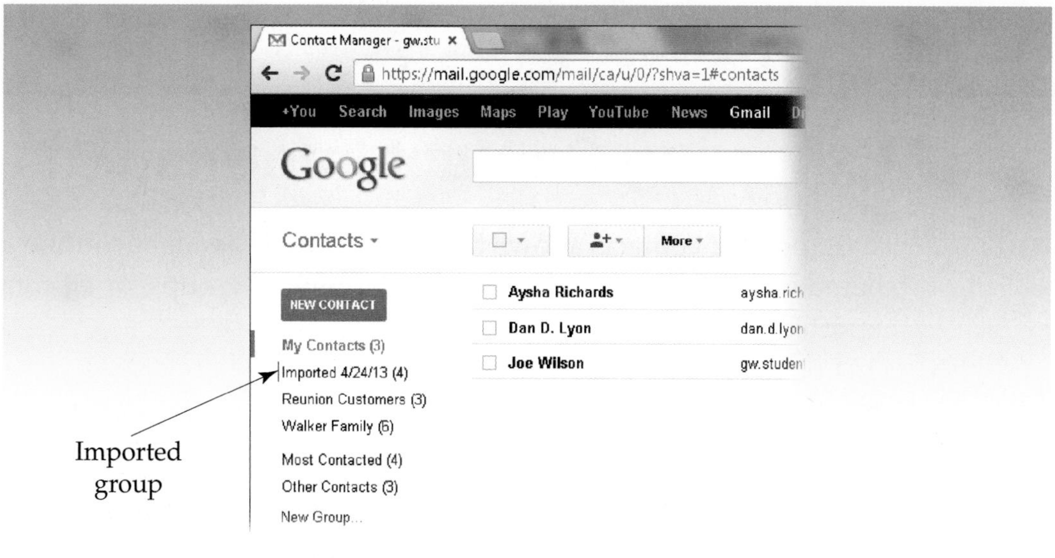

Goodheart-Willcox Publisher

Figure 3-9. When contacts are imported, a contact group named **Imported** *date* is created for those contacts.

9. Click **Rename group** in the drop-down menu, as shown in **Figure 3-10.**
10. In the **Rename group** dialog box that is displayed, enter the new name for the group, in this case Walker Family.
11. Click the **OK** button to close the **Rename group** dialog box and rename the group.

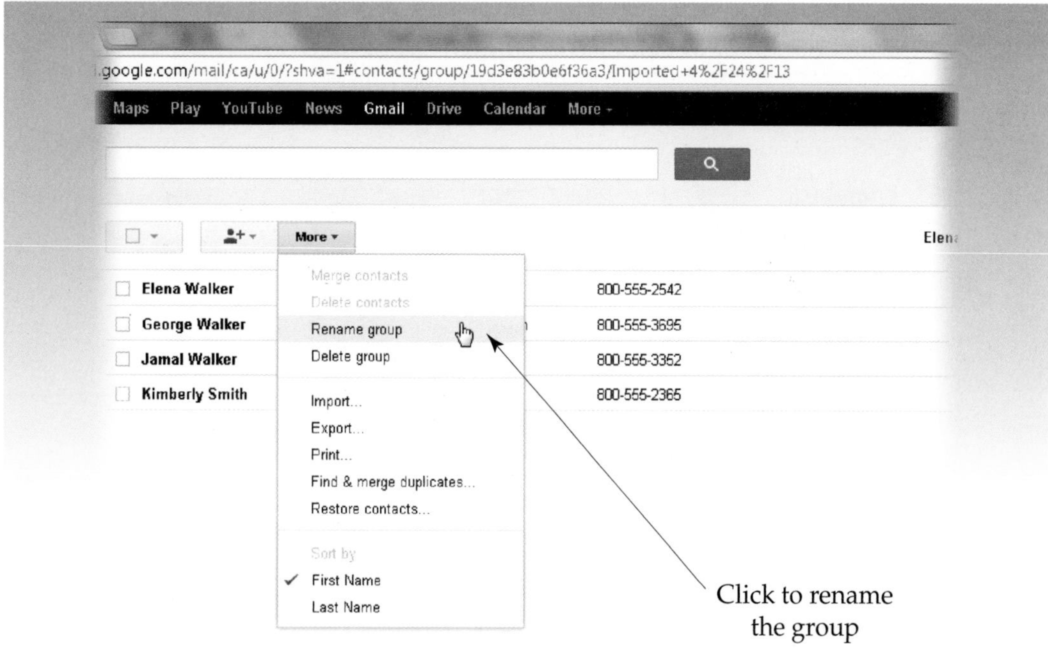

Goodheart-Willcox Publisher

Figure 3-10. Renaming a contact group.

Lesson 3-4

Exporting Contact Information

Exporting contacts allows the contacts to be available offline and to be shared with others. Individual contacts, contact groups, or all contacts can be exported.

1. Log in to your Google Mail account.
2. Click **Mail** at the upper-left corner of the Mail page, and click **Contacts** in the drop-down menu to display the Contacts page.
3. Click the **More** button, and select **Export...** from the drop-down menu. The **Export Contacts** dialog box is displayed, as shown in **Figure 3-11.**
4. In the **The group** drop-down list, select **Reunion Customers**. This is the contact group that will be exported.
5. Click the **Export** button. The file is saved on your local hard drive in your My Documents\Downloads folder. A button also appears at the bottom of the document window for the downloaded document.
6. Click the arrow on the button for the downloaded document to display a drop-down menu.
7. Click **Show in folder** in the drop-down menu. This displays the folder in which the file was downloaded.
8. Close the folder window.

More ▾

Tip To print Contacts, click the **More** button and select **Print...**. Then users can print select contacts, specific groups, or all contacts.

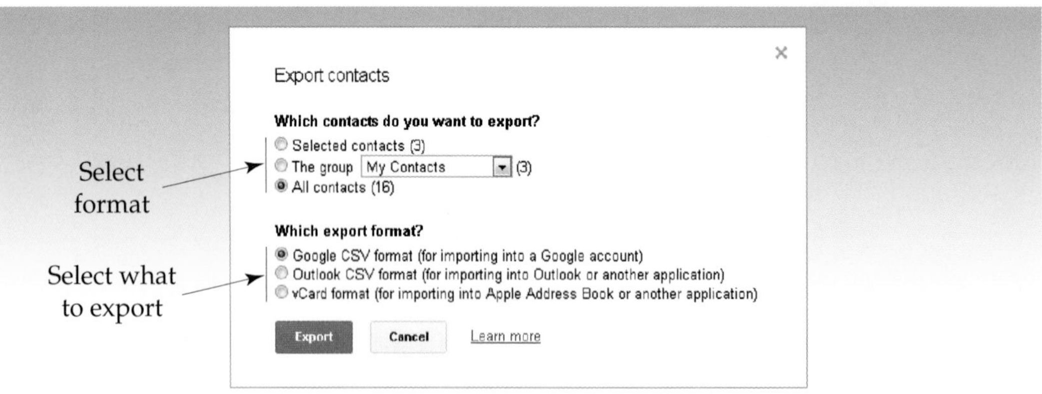

Goodheart-Willcox Publisher

Figure 3-11. Exporting contacts.

Check Your Google Apps IQ

Now that you have finished this chapter, see what you know about Google Apps by taking the chapter posttest.
www.m.g-wlearning.com
www.g-wlearning.com/informationtechnology/

Skill Review

Answer the following questions on a separate sheet of paper.

1. What are the three default contact groups?
2. When the Mail page is displayed, how do you display the Contacts page?
3. Up to ______ most recently used contacts are displayed in the **Most Contacted** group.
4. What does the number enclosed in parentheses at the end of a contact group name indicate?
5. What would be an easy way to create a personal mailing list for sending an e-mail to a group of people?
6. What are the two types of files that can be imported as a contact group?
7. The ______ text box in the contact form is used for any additional information about the contact not covered by the available fields.
8. To add contacts from a file, click ______ in the label list on the Contacts page.
9. How is the name of a contact group changed?
10. In order to share contacts with someone else, the contacts must first be ______ to a file.

Lesson Application

These exercises are designed to apply the skills learned in this and previous chapters. General directions are provided, but you will need to draw on your knowledge to determine how to complete each exercise.

Exercise 3-1
Creating a Contact

Work with two classmates. Create an individual contact for each of them, and provide information for them to create an individual profile of yourself. Do not provide any personal information you are not comfortable sharing with the class. Use of fake personal information is acceptable. Include name, e-mail addresses, and phone numbers. If a digital camera is available, take a photograph of each person and save it to your working folder. If a camera is not available, use an image from Microsoft Office clipart. Then, use what you know about how to add data to the contact information to include the photograph.

Exercise 3-2
Creating a Contact Group

Create a contact group called Classmates. Add yourself and the two classmates from Exercise 3-1 to the group. Use the search function to locate another person to add to the group. This could be your instructor or another classmate. If there are no additional contacts, add a new contact and place it in the Classmates contact group.

Exercise 3-3
Importing and Exporting Contacts

Navigate to the student companion website (www.g-wlearning.com/informationtechnology/), and download the M&M Company Employees data file to your working folder. Take the steps needed to import this file into your Google account as contacts in a group named Employees.

Export the contact group named Classmates that was created in Exercise 3-2. Save this file as a CSV file named Classmates Contacts in your working folder. E-mail this file to another classmate, and have another classmate e-mail his or her contacts file to you. Import the new file as contacts in a group named New Classmates.

Delete all contact groups created in this chapter. Delete all contacts added in this chapter.

Chapter 4

Tasks

Objectives

After completing this chapter, you will be able to:

- **Explain** how to create tasks manually and using e-mails.
- **Describe** the use of Gmail organizational tools to manage tasks.
- **Discuss** creating multiple task lists and moving tasks between lists.

alexmillos/Shutterstock.com

Check Your Google Apps IQ

Before you begin this chapter, see what you already know about Google Apps by taking the chapter pretest.

www.m.g-wlearning.com
www.g-wlearning.com/informationtechnology/

Using Gmail Tasks

With so much communication occurring via e-mail, e-mail messages can result in many tasks for Gmail users. A ***task*** is any action that must be completed, usually by a specified date or time. For example, users could receive requests via e-mail to complete an assignment for work or a portion of a group project for school, or to find information about a new store coming to the neighborhood. The Gmail Tasks feature allows users to compile tasks generated from Gmail messages into a task list. A ***task list*** is simply a collection of individual actions to remind the user what needs to be done. Users can also manually add tasks to a task list. Due dates and notes can be assigned to tasks to provide users with complete information about their tasks.

A single task could include several components. In those cases, subtasks can be created. A ***subtask*** is one of the actions required to complete a larger, or parent, task. For example, a parent task may be to paint the living room. Subtasks for this may include buying paint, masking the molding, spackling holes, washing the walls, painting the ceiling, painting the walls, and cleaning up.

Task List

Unlike other features, the Gmail task list is normally displayed in a window at the bottom of the Gmail window, as seen in **Figure 4-1.** When the task list is visible, the rest of the Gmail window does not change in content. A user can display e-mail or contacts while the task list is open. The task list can also be displayed in a separate window, or popped out, from the Gmail window, as shown in **Figure 4-2.** The separate window allows the task list to be visible so the user stays aware of tasks that need to be completed, but moved around the screen as needed. A user can view easily his or her to-do list when receiving other task requests.

Organizational Tools

People often use to-do lists to organize the tasks they are responsible to complete, so keeping that list organized can be important. Google provides organizational tools for Gmail Tasks. Users can rearrange tasks into an order that is most helpful for them. For example, tasks can be arranged based on their due dates or based on their level of importance to the users. Users drag and drop tasks to rearrange them in the task list. Users can automatically sort tasks by their due date by selecting **Sort by due date** by clicking the **Actions** button in the **Tasks** window. Also, tasks

Goodheart-Willcox Publisher

Figure 4-1. The **Tasks** window is usually displayed at the bottom of the Gmail window.

can be marked complete or deleted. Deleting a task immediately removes it from the task list. To mark a task complete does not automatically remove it from the default view of the task list. This action changes the appearance of the task so lines called *strikethrough* appear through the task. To remove completed tasks, the user can select **Clear Completed Tasks** in the drop-down menu displayed by clicking the **Actions** button in the **Tasks** window.

Gmail users can create multiple task lists to further organize their tasks. For example, you may create one list for each class, or one for homework and one for work. Additional lists can be created within the menu displayed by clicking the **Switch List** button in the **Tasks** window. Tasks can be moved between lists. Only one task list is displayed at a time, but users can easily switch back and forth between lists.

The **Tasks** window can be moved around once it has been popped out

Goodheart-Willcox Publisher

Figure 4-2. The **Tasks** window can be popped out in a separate window that can be minimized to reduce clutter on the screen.

Lesson 4-1

Creating Tasks

Creating tasks in Gmail can be helpful when users receive task requests via e-mail. Gmail Tasks allows users to manually create tasks and create tasks from e-mail messages in a single location.

Manually Creating Tasks

1. Log in to your Google Mail account.
2. Click **Mail** at the upper-left corner of the Mail page to display a drop-down menu, as shown in **Figure 4-3.**
3. Click **Tasks** in the drop-down menu to display the **Tasks** window. The window is displayed in the bottom-right corner of the screen, as shown in **Figure 4-4.**
4. Click inside the **Tasks** window and enter the task:

Send quotes for Brown Anniversary Party

5. Press the [Enter] key to start a new task.
6. Press the [Tab] key to create a subtask. The subtask is indented to the right.
7. Enter Catering for the subtask.

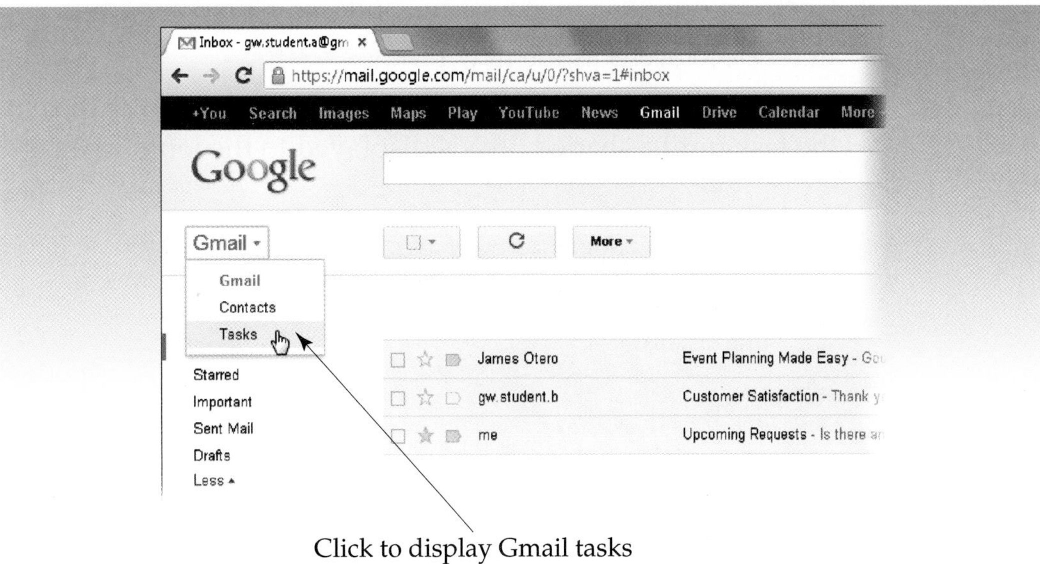

Goodheart-Willcox Publisher

Figure 4-3. Once a user clicks **Tasks** in the drop-down menu, the **Tasks** window appears at the bottom of the Gmail window.

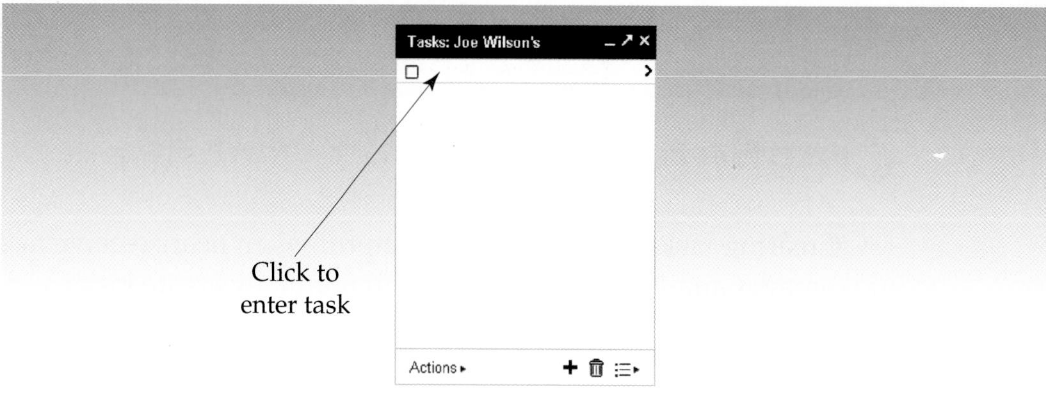

Goodheart-Willcox Publisher

Figure 4-4. To create a subtask, press the [Tab] key or click the **Actions** button and select **Indent Task** from the drop-down menu.

8. Hover the cursor over the task, and then click the chevron (>) symbol on the right end of the task. A details page for the task is displayed in the **Tasks** window, as shown in **Figure 4-5.**

Calendar

9. Click the **Calendar** button to display a minicalendar.
10. Click a date in the minicalendar to set a due date. For this lesson, click a date that is one week away.
11. Click inside the **Notes** text box. The default text Notes is replaced by a standard text editor cursor.
12. Enter Beverages, Appetizers, Buffet, Desserts.
13. Click the **<Back to list** link at the top of the **Tasks** window to return to the first page of the task list. The details and due date appear below the Catering task.

Add Task

14. Click the **Add Task** button at the bottom of **Task** window
15. Enter Decorations as the new task.
16. Notice the task was added at the top of the list. Hover the cursor over the task until a shaded area is displayed to the left of the task.

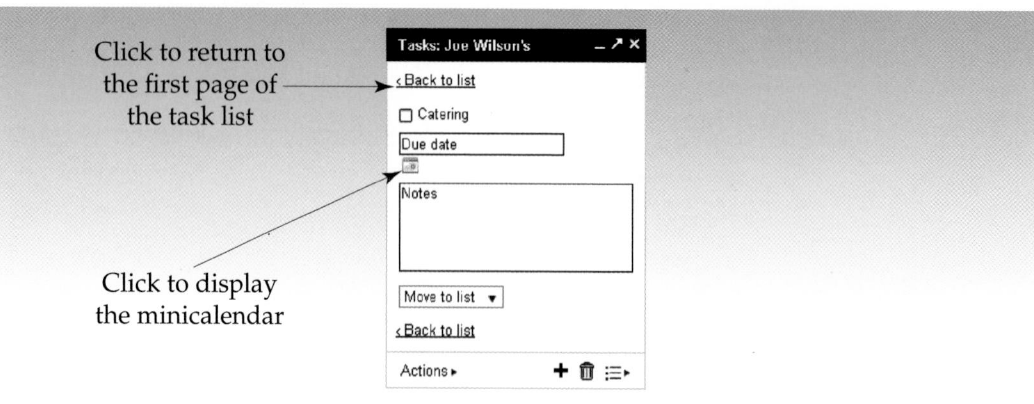

Goodheart-Willcox Publisher

Figure 4-5. The due date and notes for a task are added in the task details page.

17. Click and hold on the shaded area, drag the task below Catering, and drop to reorder the tasks. Notice that the task is automatically indented as a subtask.
18. Add details to the Decorations task. Enter notes of your choice, but select a completion date earlier than that of the Catering task.
19. Close the **Tasks** window by clicking the **X** in the upper-right corner of the window.

Creating a Task from an E-mail

20. Send yourself a message with Invitations as the subject.
21. Open the message.

22. Click the **More** button, and click **Add to Tasks** from the drop-down menu, as shown in **Figure 4-6.**
23. The **Tasks** window is opened and a new task is added to the top of the list. The name of the task is the same as the subject line of the e-mail.
24. Leave the **Tasks** window open and click the **Inbox** label to display the contents of the inbox.
25. Click the **Related email** hyperlink in the **Tasks** window. The contents of the message are displayed in the Gmail window.

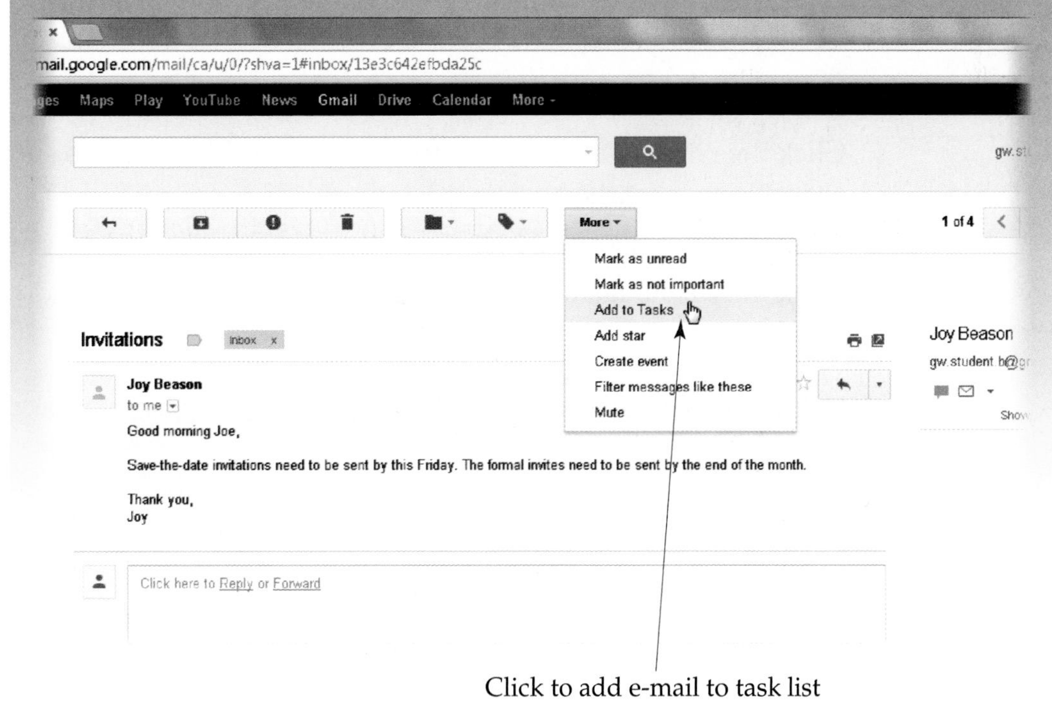

Goodheart-Willcox Publisher

Figure 4-6. When an e-mail is added to the task list, a user can display the e-mail by clicking the **Related email** link in the task.

Lesson 4-2

Managing Tasks

Gmail organizational tools can help users manage their tasks and task lists. It can be efficient to view only tasks that have not been completed.

Marking a Task as Completed

1. Click **Mail** at the upper-left corner of the Mail page, and click **Tasks** in the drop-down menu to display the **Tasks** window.
2. Check the check box to the left of the Catering task. The task text is struck through to indicate the task is completed.
3. Similarly, mark the Decorations task as completed.

Viewing Completed Tasks

Actions ▾

4. Click the **Actions** button at the bottom of the **Tasks** window to display a drop-down menu.
5. Click **View Completed Tasks** in the drop-down menu. Only the completed tasks are displayed, sorted by completion date, as shown in **Figure 4-7.** Today's date appears at the top of the list.
6. Click the **< Back to list** link to return to the main task list.

Deleting a Task

7. Click the check marks next to the Catering and Decorations tasks so they are no longer marked as completed.
8. Click the Decorations task name so the task is active (highlighted).

9. Click the **Delete task** button at the bottom of the **Tasks** window. The task is deleted.

Figure 4-7. Viewing completed tasks in the **Tasks:** window.

Lesson 4-3

Creating Additional Task Lists

For some users, managing tasks works best when the tasks are divided into several lists. The user determines how tasks are divided. As a result, additional task lists can be separated by subject area or task type, for example.

Creating a Task List

1. Click **Mail** at the upper-left corner of the Mail page, and click **Tasks** in the drop-down menu to display the **Tasks** window.

Switch List

2. Click the **Switch List** button at the bottom-right corner of the **Tasks** window to display a drop-down menu.
3. Click **New List** in the drop-down menu, as shown in **Figure 4-8.** A dialog box appears asking for a name for the new list.
4. Enter Reunions in the dialog box, and then click the **OK** button to create the list. The new list is displayed in the **Tasks** window.

Moving Items Between Task Lists

Switch List

5. Click the **Switch List** button. The names of the available task lists are displayed at the bottom of the drop-down menu. The current task list is shown with a check mark on its name.
6. Click the name of the default task list in the drop-down menu to display that list in the **Tasks** window. The name of the default task list is your user name.

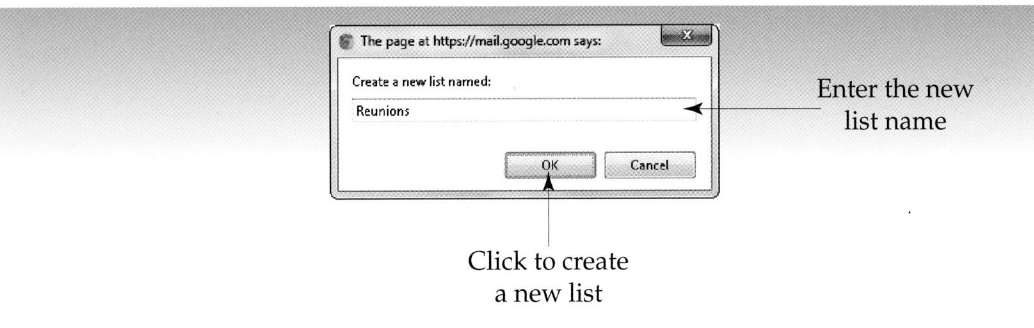

Goodheart-Willcox Publisher

Figure 4-8. The default list has a standard name, but the user determines the names of additional lists.

7. Click the chevron (>) symbol for the Invitations task created from an e-mail to display the details page.
8. Click the **Move to list** button on the details page for the task to display a drop-down menu, as shown in **Figure 4-9.**
9. Select **Reunions** in the drop-down menu to move the task to that task list.
10. Click the **Switch List** button, and click **Reunions** in the drop-down menu. Notice that the task has been moved to the list.

The only way to share your task list with someone else is to e-mail or print it. Both options are available in the drop-down menu displayed by clicking the **Actions** button.

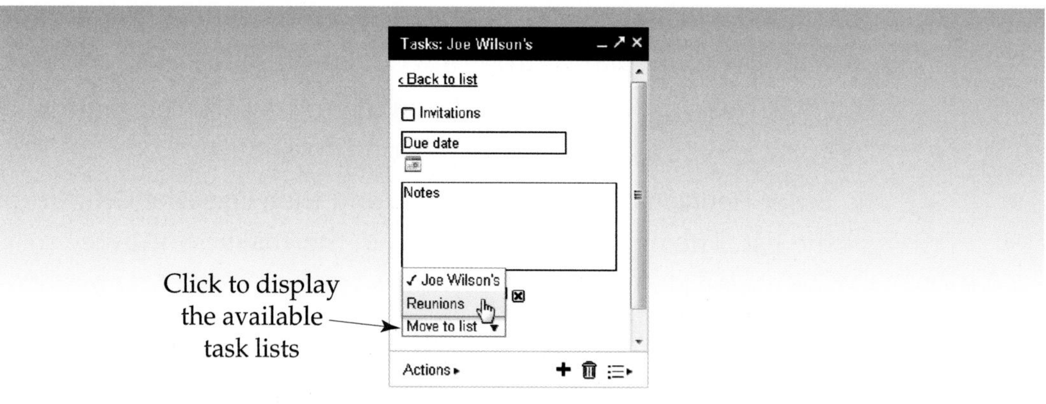

Goodheart-Willcox Publisher

Figure 4-9. Tasks can be moved on any task list available.

Check Your Google Apps IQ

Now that you have finished this chapter, see what you know about Google Apps by taking the chapter posttest.
www.m.g-wlearning.com
www.g-wlearning.com/informationtechnology/

Skill Review

Answer the following questions on a separate sheet of paper.

1. Briefly describe how to display the **Tasks** window.
2. What are the two basic ways to add tasks to a task list?
3. List two pages that can be displayed when the **Tasks** window is open.
4. Briefly describe how users can rearrange tasks in the **Tasks** window.
5. How does a user display the details page for a task?
6. ______ a task will immediately remove it from the task list.
7. Briefly describe how to create a subtask.
8. To add a due date to a task, a user must access the ______.
9. Which button is used to create a new list?
10. On the details page for a task, which button is used to switch the task to another list?

Lesson Application

These exercises are designed to apply the skills learned in this and previous chapters. General directions are provided, but you will need to draw on your knowledge to determine how to complete each exercise.

Exercise 4-1
Creating a Task and Subtasks

Create a task called Singh Sweet Sixteen. Then send yourself an e-mail with Decorations as the subject line. Once the e-mail is displayed in the inbox, add it as a subtask of the Singh Sweet Sixteen task. Create another subtask called Entertainment.

Exercise 4-2
Adding Task Details

Create a new task called Moy Wedding. Add a due date to the task that is two months away. In the notes field, add location, City Ballroom. Add a due date to the Singh Sweet Sixteen task that is one week away.

Exercise 4-3
Completing a Task

Mark the task Moy Wedding and the subtask Decorations of the Singh Sweet Sixteen task as complete. Change the **Tasks** window so only the completed tasks are displayed.

Exercise 4-4
Creating New Lists

Create a new task list called Parties. Move the Singh Sweet Sixteen task and all of its subtasks to the new list. Create a new task list called Weddings. Move the Moy Wedding task and all of its subtasks to the new list.

Unit 1 Review

Scenario

The M&M Event Planning company has been asked to plan a graduation party for the Perkins family. The party will have over 75 guests. Use the information learned in this unit to complete the activities. As much as possible, these activities should be completed without referring to the chapters for information.

Activities

1. Draft a short e-mail to the Perkins family asking them about the event. Ask questions regarding a theme, music, food, and any other details needed to plan the party. Send this e-mail to yourself, and then forward it to one classmate and your instructor.
2. Draft an e-mail about possible invitation ideas for the graduation party. Assign a yellow exclamation point star to the e-mail, and send it to the **Tasks** label. Add Guest list and Venue Information subtasks to the list. Assign a due date and a note to each subtask. E-mail the task list to your instructor.
3. In the task list, create a label titled Perkins Graduation Party with sublabels titled Venue, Decorations, and Food. Give each label a different color. Move an e-mail to the Graduation Party label. Set up a filter to star all e-mail that has the words Perkins party.
4. Create a contact group for the people involved in the planning process for the event. Include yourself, your instructor, and at least two classmates. Name the group Perkins Planning Team. Send an e-mail to the group suggesting a possible theme for the graduation party.

5. Navigate to the student companion website (www.g-wlearning.com/informationtechnology/), and download the Perkins Guests data file from the Chapter 4 area to your working folder. This is a CVS file. Import the file into contacts and name the group Perkins Guest List. Add yourself as an additional contact to the Perkins Guest List.

Google Hangouts, Calendar, and Groups

Google provides tools that allow users to interact with others outside of e-mail correspondence. Users can interact with others in real time using instant messages. Instant messaging can be text- or video-based using Google Hangouts. Google Calendar helps users keep track of events on their schedules. It can also be a collaborative tool. Google Calendar allows users to share event information or share entire calendars with others. Google Groups are online forums developed to facilitate interaction between people. There are Google Groups on many varied topics, such as health, home, and schools. Users can choose to join a Google Groups or create groups.

Chapters

Chapter 5

Google Hangouts

Objectives

After completing this chapter, you will be able to:

- **Invite** another user to a hangout.
- **Conduct** a video hangout.

alexmillos/Shutterstock.com

Check Your Google Apps IQ

Before you begin this chapter, see what you already know about Google Apps by taking the chapter pretest.

www.m.g-wlearning.com
www.g-wlearning.com/informationtechnology/

Instant Messaging

When people send e-mail messages, sometimes they receive immediate responses or it can take several days before replies appear. When users need an instant response or want to share a quick thought, they might use an instant messenger (IM) service rather than e-mail. An ***instant messenger service*** is an application or a feature of an application that offers quick transmission of messages in real time. Text messages sent using a mobile phone are the equivalent of instant messages sent using an IM service. Instant messenger services, also known as *online chat services,* can provide users with the ability to connect with others through audio and video as well. There are two types of instant messaging available for Google users: text- and video-based messaging. Hangouts is Google's instant messenger service.

Using Google Hangouts

When a user logs into Gmail, the hangouts list is displayed. The ***hangouts list*** is a list of contacts with whom the Gmail user can send instant messages. The user's name and profile photo appear at the top of the hangouts list. As long as he or she is signed in, a green line will be displayed under his or her name. Likewise, under each name in the hangouts list a green line appears if the user is signed in. If the user has added Gmail profile image, it will appear to the left of his or her name in the list.

The hangouts list is displayed in the lower-left corner of the Gmail window under the label list, as seen in **Figure 5-1.** When a user hovers the cursor over a name in the hangouts list, a profile card is displayed. The profile card includes the name of the contact along with a profile photo, if selected.

In order to exchange instant messages with someone, his or her name must be in the hangouts list. By default, Google adds to the list anyone with a Gmail account that the user e-mails frequently. Also, a user can add people to the hangouts list. To add someone, you enter his or her e-mail in the **New Hangout** text box.

Text-Based Hangouts

A user can begin an instant message session through a profile card by clicking the **Hangout with this contact** button or by clicking a name in the hangouts list. Either way, a hangouts window is displayed. The hangouts window is visible in the lower-right corner of the Gmail window like the task list. Also, e-mail or contacts can be displayed while the hangouts window is visible, as seen in **Figure 5-2**. The hangouts window can also be popped out from the Gmail window.

Goodheart-Willcox Publisher

Figure 5-1. With Google Hangout, the hangouts list is displayed in the lower-left corner of the Gmail window under the label list. The profile card is displayed when a user hovers over a name in the chat list.

To send instant text messages, the user enters text in the text box, and then presses [Enter] to send a message. Emoticons can be used to express a feeling during a hangout. An ***emoticon*** is an icon or combination of characters that represents the user's feeling or emotion. Users can choose from five categories of emoticons. Each category includes many options.

Images and video can also be shared in a hangout. Images can be uploaded from your computer, selected from your Google Photos albums, or taken from a web camera. You can also search for and share a video from YouTube.

Users can have an instant message session with multiple people. You can have more than one hangouts window open at a time to have several one-on-one hangouts simultaneously. There is also the option of having a group hangout. A ***group hangout*** is an instant message session where multiple people are added to the same instant messaging session.

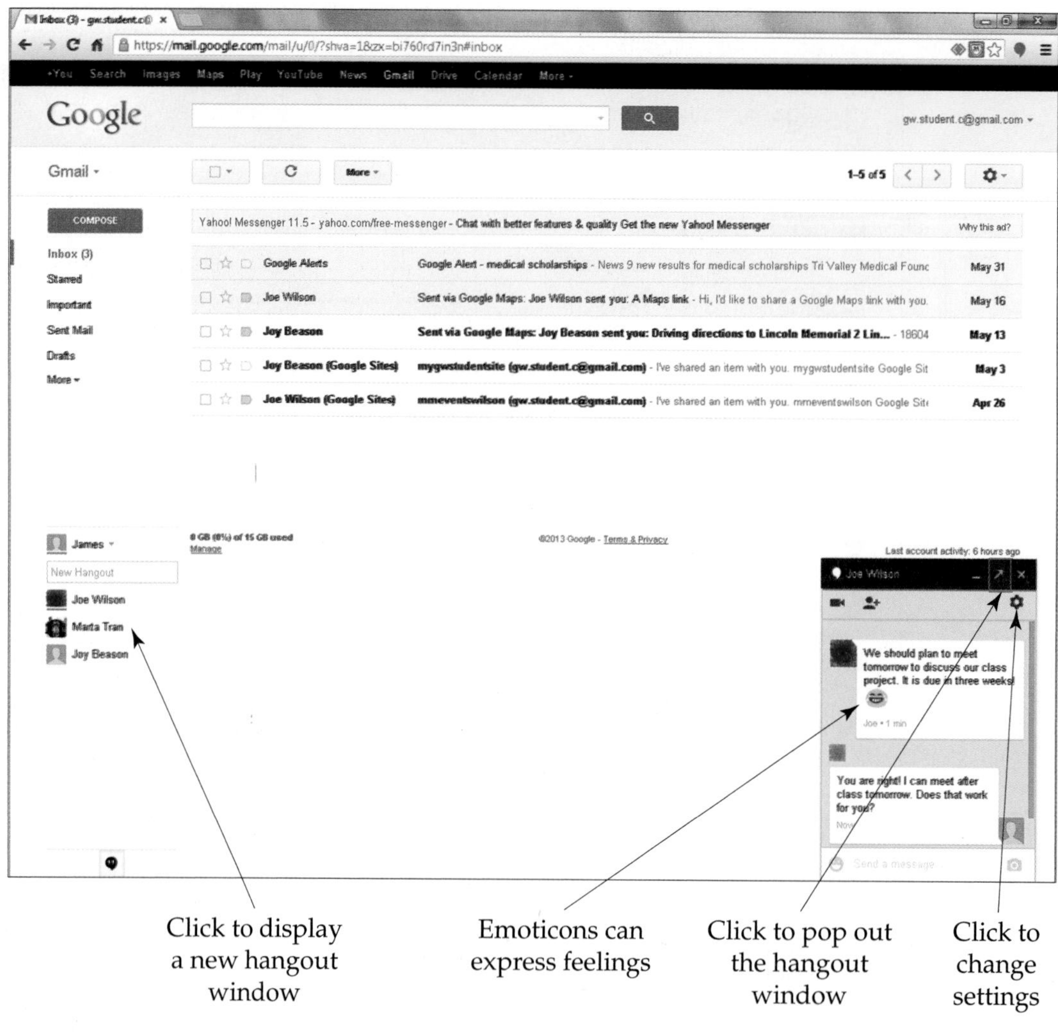

Goodheart-Willcox Publisher

Figure 5-2. The **Mail** window or the **Contacts** window remains visible when the hangouts window is displayed.

Group hangouts can be good for a brief discussion of a topic. Any participant of the group can invite others to join a hangout. There is no maximum number of people that can participate in a group hangout. See **Figure 5-3** for some guidelines to follow having a one-on-one instant message session or one with a group.

Transcripts of hangouts are automatically saved and can be viewed under the **Chat** label. In the hangouts settings, notifications for future messages from that person can be turned off or on. The next time that person sends you a message, his or her name will appear at the top of the hangouts list in bold. Archiving a hangout closes the discussion. The next time you start a hangout with this person, it will start as a new conversation. Deleting a hangout removes the history from the **Chat** label as well as from the hangouts list.

Guideline	Why It Is Important
Wait for a response before continuing to instant message.	This creates a linear conversation, avoiding overlapping comments and confusion.
Avoid typing in all capital letters.	Typing in all capital letters is considered shouting.
Consider the time of day you are initiating a hangout.	Initiating an instant message very early or late at night can be disruptive to another person.
Use proper grammar when sending instant messages.	Texting language is not universal and using it can lead to miscommunication.

Goodheart-Willcox Publisher

Figure 5-3. Following general guidelines when chatting with people can improve the clarity of the conversation.

Google Video Hangouts

Text-based instant message conversations can get too complex for the medium. Hearing the other person's voice and seeing his or her facial expressions can be important to the communication. In these cases, it can be useful to conduct a video-based instant message. People can see and hear each other in real time while communicating.

A video hangout requires preparation not needed for text-based instant messages. Headphones or speakers, a microphone, and a web camera are needed for a video hangout. Also, the hangouts plug-in must be installed before the video hangout will function.

When users are members of Google Plus, more features for Hangouts become available. For Google Plus members, users can add up to nine participants to a video hangout, for a total of ten people. Users and participants that are Google Plus members can also watch YouTube videos, share what is displayed on their computer monitors, and access and edit files on their Google Drive during a video hangout.

Lesson 5-1

Conducting a Text-Based Hangout

A user can add names to his or her hangouts list. Any names in Google Contacts can be added to the hangouts list. However, some people will require an invitation before you can send instant messages to them.

Inviting Others to a Hangout

1. Log in to your Google Mail account.

2. If the hangouts list is not displayed, click the **Hangouts** button to display it.
3. Click in the hangouts list search box, and enter a classmate's Gmail user name or e-mail address. As characters are entered, the names of Google account holders appear below the text box. If the name does not appear, enter the full e-mail address for the person.
4. Click the correct name to start a hangout. The hangouts window is displayed in the lower-right corner of the screen.

Tip If an e-mail address is entered in the hangouts list search box that is not associated with a Google account, you are given the option to invite the person to a hangout. When invited to chat, non-Gmail users will be prompted to sign up for Gmail. In order to use Google chat, users must have either a Gmail account or an AOL instant messaging account.

Conducting a Hangout with One Contact

5. Click in the text box in the hangouts window, and enter Will you be at today's event? Press the [Enter] key to send the message. See **Figure 5-4.**

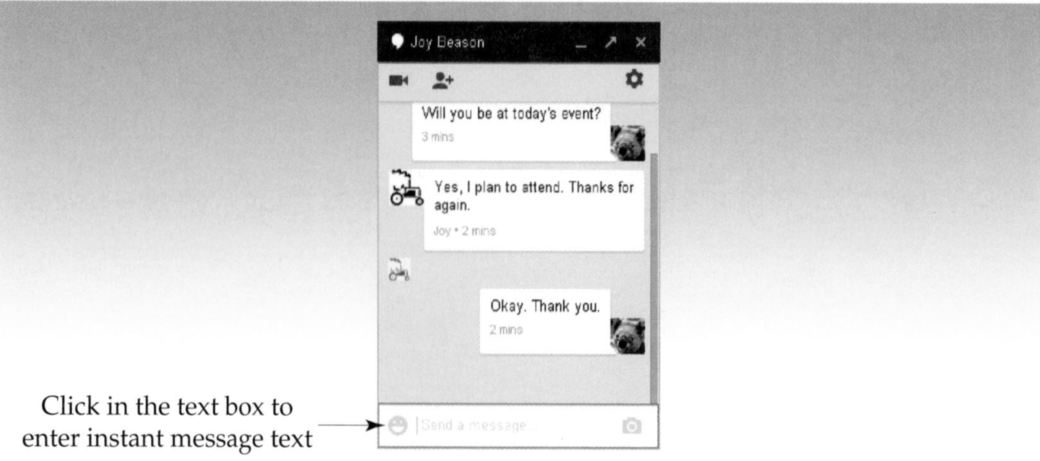

Goodheart-Willcox Publisher

Figure 5-4. Once a person is included on the hangouts list, a user can click on the name to display a hangouts window and begin a conversation.

6. Wait for the other person to respond.
7. When a response is received, enter Okay. Thank you. in the text box and press the [Enter] key to send the reply.
8. Click the close button in the upper-right corner of the hangouts window to end the session and close the window.

Conducting a Group Hangout

9. Click a classmate's name in the hangouts list. The hangouts window is opened.

Create a group hangout

10. Click the **Create a group hangout** button in the hangouts window, as shown in **Figure 5-5.**
11. In the text box that appears at the top of the hangouts window, enter the name of another classmate.
12. When the correct name is displayed, click the name.

Add people

13. Click the **Add people** button. A new hangouts window is displayed, and the number of people in the hangout in addition to yourself is displayed next to the "add people" button.
14. Click in the text box at the bottom of the hangouts window, and enter I have to change the time of today's meeting to 2:00 p.m.; does that work for everyone?
15. Press the [Enter] key to send the message to the group.
16. Wait for the responses of the other people in the group hangout.
17. When the last response is received, enter Thank you. and press the [Enter] key.
18. Close the window to leave the conversation.

If you leave a group hangout, the other participants can continue to chat. In order to rejoin the same hangout, simply click it in the hangouts list.

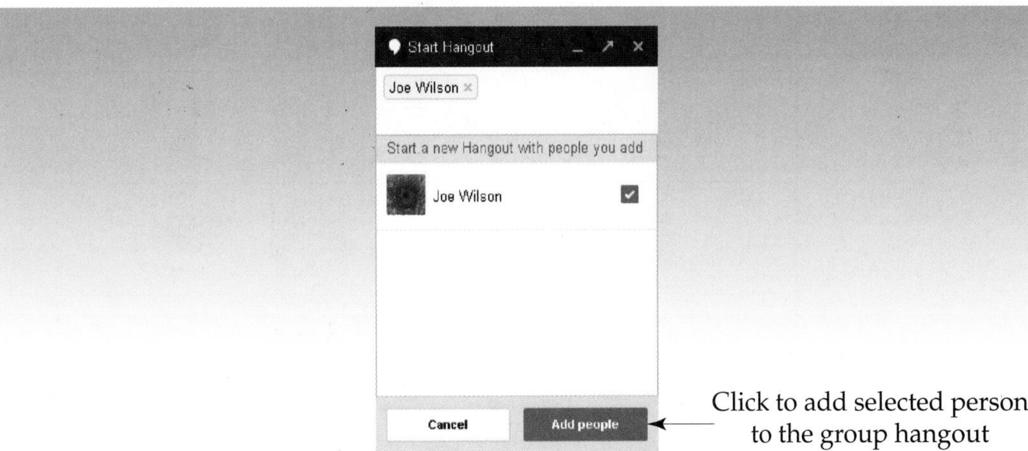

Goodheart-Willcox Publisher

Figure 5-5. Any participant, not just the person who started the hangout, can invite others to a group hangout.

Using Emoticons during a Hangout

19. Click a classmate's name in the hangouts list. A hangouts window is opened.
20. In the text box, enter Hello, but do not press the [Enter] key.
21. Click the smiley face icon to the left of the text box, as shown in **Figure 5-6.** A pop-up menu appears containing emoticons in five sets. See **Figure 5-7.**
22. Select an emoticon from one of the sets.
23. Press the [Enter] key to send the message with the emoticon.
24. Close the hangouts window.

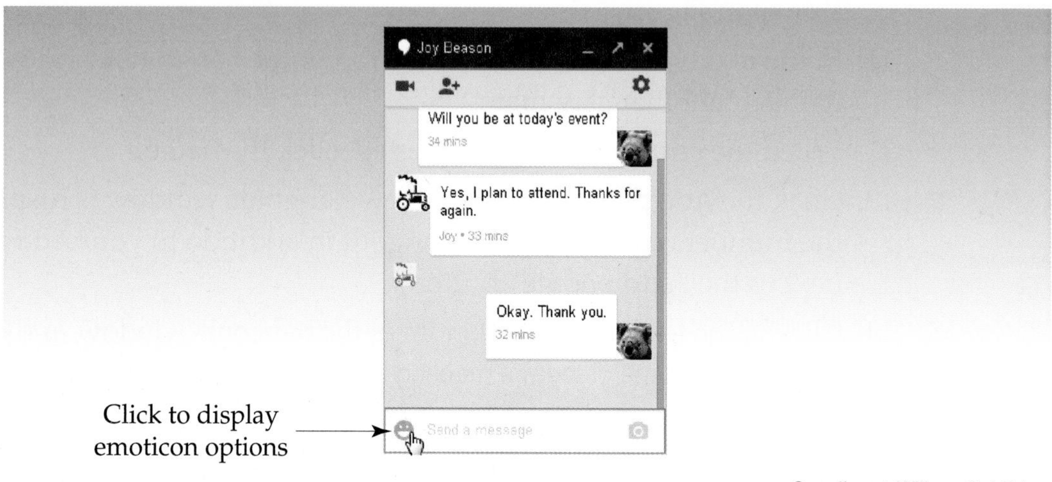

Goodheart-Willcox Publisher

Figure 5-6. Emoticons can help users quickly convey an emotion.

Category	Such as...
	Recently used emoticons from any category

Goodheart-Willcox Publisher

Figure 5-7. There are many emoticons available to use in a hangout.

Lesson 5-2

Conducting a Video Hangout

In some cases, audio and video are needed to make an online chat more productive. A web camera, a microphone, and headphones or speakers are needed for this lesson.

Installing the Hangouts Plug-in

1. Log in to your Google Mail account.
2. Click a classmate's name in the hangouts list. A hangouts window is opened.

Video call

3. Click the **Video call** button in the hangouts window. A new window is displayed in which the video hangout will take place.
4. Click the **Install Plugin** button in the window. Click the **Close** button in the message that appears indicating the installation is complete. If the hangouts plug-in is already installed, this message will not appear and you can skip to the next section entitled Conducting a Video Hangout Chat.
5. Close the window for the video hangout.

Tip You can click the **Join** button in the window for the video hangout to directly enter the hangout after the plug-in is installed.

Conducting a Video Hangout

6. Click a classmate's name in the hangouts list. A hangouts window is opened.

Video call

7. Click the **Video call** button in the hangouts window. A new window is displayed in which the video hangout will take place, as shown in **Figure 5-8**, and an invitation is sent to your classmate.
8. The person to whom the invitation was sent will be presented with **Answer** and **Decline** buttons. If he or she clicks the **Answer** button, you will be able to conduct a two-way conversation that includes video. If he or she clicks the **Ignore** button, a message is displayed indicating the person is unavailable.
9. Conduct a conversation with your classmate about an upcoming school event.

Exit

10. To conclude the video chat, either party can click the **Exit** button or the standard close button.
11. Close the hangouts window.

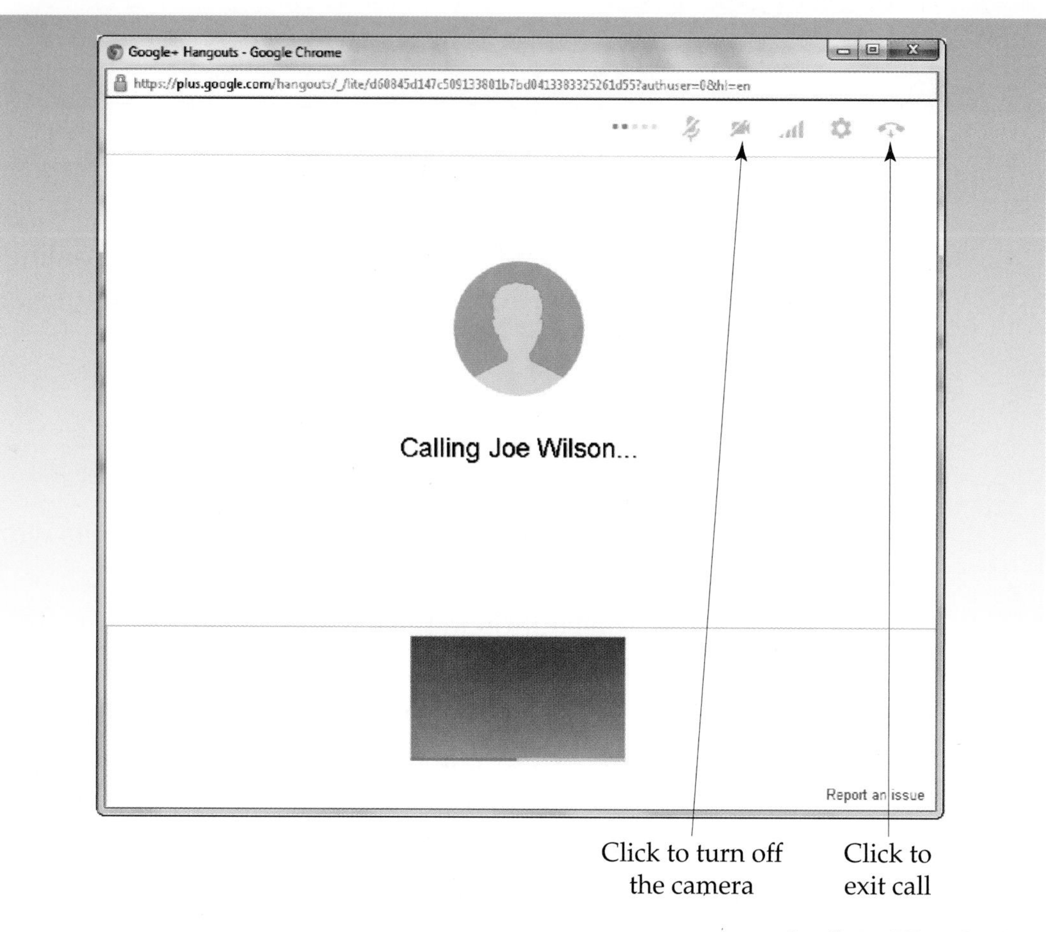

Goodheart-Willcox Publisher

Figure 5-8. A video hangout can be started from within a hangouts window.

Check Your Google Apps IQ

Now that you have finished this chapter, see what you know about Google Apps by taking the chapter posttest.
www.m.g-wlearning.com
www.g-wlearning.com/informationtechnology/

Skill Review

Answer the following questions on a separate sheet of paper.

1. What is an instant messenger service?
2. What is the Google app that allows for text- or video-based instant messaging?
3. A(n) ______ line beneath the person's profile picture means the person is logged into Google Hangouts.
   A. green
   B. red
   C. gray
   D. orange
4. Describe the two ways you can start a hangout.
5. Briefly describe the purpose of emoticons.
6. A(n) ______ is an instant message session where multiple people are added to the same session.
   A. one-on-one hangout
   B. video hangout
   C. contact group
   D. group hangout
7. What is the maximum number of people that can be in a group text-based hangout?
8. In a text-based hangout, why is it a good idea to wait for a response before continuing to instant message?
9. The additional equipment needed for a video hangout is ______, ______, and ______.
10. For Google Plus members, up to ______ people can join a video hangout.

Lesson Application

These exercises are designed to apply the skills learned in this and previous chapters. General directions are provided, but you will need to draw on your knowledge to determine how to complete each exercise.

Exercise 5-1
Conducting an Individual Hangout

Work with one classmate. If he or she is not in your hangouts list, take the steps needed to add him or her to the hangouts list. Conduct a text-based hangout about an upcoming school event. Use proper grammar, not texting language. However, you may use emoticons to express your feelings. The hangout should have several entries from both parties.

Exercise 5-2
Conducting a Group Hangout

Work with two classmates. Have one member of the group create a group hangout with the other two. Conduct a text-based hangout with the group discussing a few ways hangouts can be a beneficial way to communicate with others. Each member must participate in the conversation using proper grammar. Use emoticons during the hangout as appropriate.

Exercise 5-3
Conducting a Video Hangout

A microphone, speakers or a headset, and a web camera are required for this exercise. Work with one classmate. Decide who will initiate the video hangout, and then conduct a brief conversation comparing and contrasting the advantages of video and text hangout. Send an e-mail to your instructor summarizing your conversation. Send a carbon copy of the e-mail to your partner.

Chapter 6

Google Calendar

Objectives

After completing this chapter, you will be able to:

- **Create** events on a Google calendar.
- **Explain** how to change the calendar view and print the calendar.
- **Edit** an event.
- **Invite** guests to an event.
- **Create** additional calendars.
- **Discuss** the reasons for sharing calendars.
- **Describe** modifying calendar settings.

alexmillos/Shutterstock.com

Check Your Google Apps IQ

Before you begin this chapter, see what you already know about Google Apps by taking the chapter pretest.

www.m.g-wlearning.com
www.g-wlearning.com/informationtechnology/

Using Google Calendar

Google Calendar allows Gmail users to keep track of their schedules on a calendar that they can access from most web-enabled devices. With Google Calendar, users can document one-time appointments, repeating meetings, and annual occasions. These activities can then be viewed in a variety of ways on the Calendar page. Users can also invite people to events and share their entire calendar with others using Google Calendar.

To access Google Calendar, Gmail users click on the **Calendar** link along the top of the Gmail window. The Calendar page is displayed on a separate tab or in a separate window. The calendar occupies most of the browser window. As seen in **Figure 6-1**, to the left of the calendar there are three calendar labels: **Mini calendar**, **My calendars**, and **Other calendars**. By default

Goodheart-Willcox Publisher

Figure 6-1. The default view of the calendar displays an entire month in the center of the window with a minicalendar and labels along the left.

the **Mini calendar** label is expanded. When expanded, the label changes to display the name of the current month and year with a minicalendar of the current month. Users can click on the chevron symbols (< and >) to the right of the month name to display previous and subsequent months.

Every Gmail user is provided with a default calendar. Additional calendars can also be created. The default calendar, any user-created calendars, and the user's task list are found in the **My calendars** label. The **Other calendars** label includes public calendars and calendars other users have shared.

Creating Calendar Events

Doctor appointments, study group meetings, and friends' birthdays are examples of information that can be added to the Google Calendar. Google refers to each of these as an event. ***Events*** are occurrences that are added to the Google Calendar.

Many details can be added to events in Google Calendar. The start and end time can be specified. An event can also be set to last all day. All-day events can span multiple days. The location of the event can be added. A user can enter a casual name for a location, such as school library, or a complete street address. A description of the event can be added as well. Reminders can be helpful to include when creating an event. A reminder is a notification to be received by the user in a pop up window or can be received in an e-mail about an event before the event is scheduled to take place. Reminders can be set to display at a certain time before the scheduled start time of an event.

Often users will have events that occur at regular intervals, such as a class or club meeting. To save time, users can create the event once and then set it as a repeating or recurring event. A recurring event is an event that repeats at regular intervals. Events can be set to repeat daily, weekly, monthly, or once per year with other options in between.

There are several ways to create events in Google Calendar: the **Create** button, clicking directly on the calendar, clicking a date in an e-mail message, or the Quick Add feature. After creating an event, a user can change one or all of the details.

Clicking the **Create** button to display a form with fields will create an event. Also, clicking on a day in the calendar displays a dialog box with a text box to create an event.

The Quick Add feature allows users to create an event by entering a phrase in the **Quick Add** text box. The text must include an event title, such as study group meeting or dinner with Arthur. **Figure 6-2** provides tips that can help you use the Quick Add feature more effectively.

If you enter	Google Quick Add feature will
A time with no date for an event	Create an event on the earliest future date
An event without a start time or end time	Create an all day event
An event without an end time	Create a one-hour event
A date range (i.e., 1/12-15) for an event	Create an event that spans multiple days
Someone's e-mail address	Add he or she as a guest of the event

Goodheart-Willcox Publisher

Figure 6-2. The Quick Add feature allows users to create events for Google Calendar by simply entering a phrase.

Viewing the Calendar and Searching for Events

Every Google Calendar can be displayed in several different ways. Users can choose to view a day, four days, a week, or a month in the calendar section of the browser window. On the Settings page the four-day view can be changed to another time span. With these views only the time span selected and the events scheduled during it are visible. All of the days within the time span are displayed even if events are not scheduled on them. Google Calendar can also be displayed in agenda view. An ***agenda*** is a list of things to be done. The Agenda view in Google Calendar displays events in list format. Only the days on which events are scheduled are displayed.

A user can print the calendar in any view. To print, click the **More** button and then **Print**. A **Calendar Print Preview** window is displayed. In this window, the user can choose to change the time span that will print. The font size and page orientation can be changed in this window as well. The user can also choose whether to print all events to which he or she has been invited, but has declined to attend. Finally, if the user has access to a color printer, he or she can choose to print the calendar in color or in black and white.

Similar to the Mail or Contacts pages, the Calendar page includes the quick search box at the top of the window. Users can search for past and future events based on event title or location. This quick search allows users to enter text to search for specific events. Users can also conduct an advanced search using the search wizard, as seen in **Figure 6-3**.

Sharing Events and Calendars

A Gmail user can expand the reach of his or her Google Calendar by sharing events and calendars. A user can invite guests to events, create additional calendars, and share calendars. Inviting guests to an event allows

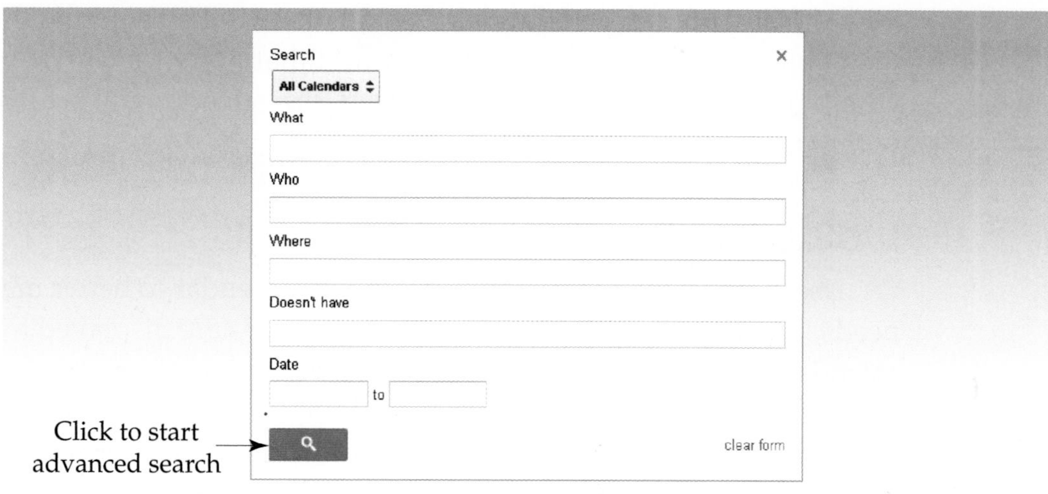

Goodheart-Willcox Publisher

Figure 6-3. In addition to a quick search, users can conduct an advanced search for an event using the search wizard.

a user to share event details with people and to track their responses to the invitation. Guests can be added as required or as optional attendees. When a guest accepts an invitation, the event is automatically added to his or her Google Calendar.

A Gmail user automatically has a default calendar in the **My calendar** label. It can be helpful to create additional calendars for specific activities such as sports schedules or special projects. Each calendar can be displayed one at a time or multiple calendars can be displayed at once.

When a user sets up a new calendar, a calendar name, description, and location are specified. A time zone can also be set for a calendar. A user can select a color for the calendar. All events associated with that calendar will be displayed in the selected color. This can be helpful when viewing multiple calendars.

Calendars can be shared with the public or specific people. To set a calendar or document as shared is to provide others with access to it. Sharing a calendar with the public makes it accessible to anyone. Many businesses and organizations make public calendars to inform a large audience about their events. Sharing a calendar with specific users allows them to view it from their calendar page. In setting up the shared calendar, you determine if other users can add events or just view events. The permission settings determine what level of access other users will have to events in a shared calendar.

A user can also add calendars to his or her Calendar page under the **Other calendars** label. There are several ways to add calendars. Google provides users with basic calendars, such as holiday calendars, that can be added. Users can import calendars from other software programs. To import them, files must be iCal or CSV format. The iCal file format is calendar application file for Macs. Public calendars can be added as well by entering the URL for the public calendar. A user can also request that friends share their calendars with him or her. If the request is accepted, the calendar will be displayed within the **Other calendars** label.

Customizing the Calendar

Users can change the settings in Google Calendar to better meet their needs. Users can specify how the dates and times are displayed in the calendar. The day that is set as the first day of the week can be changed to Monday, Sunday, or Saturday. There are also options to alter how events are displayed on the calendar. For example, users can determine if certain types of events are dimmed on the calendar. Dimmed events are displayed in colored text that is lighter than the majority of the text to downplay their presence.

Lesson 6-1

Adding Events to a Calendar

The Google Calendar can help users manage their schedules. Adding events to the calendar can be the first step in the process.

Accessing Your Calendar

1. Log in to your Google Mail account.
2. Click the **Calendar** link on the bar at the top of the Mail page, as shown in **Figure 6-4.** Depending on which browser is being used, you may need to click the **More** link to display a drop-down menu, and then click **Calendar** in the menu.
3. Depending on which browser is being used and its settings, the calendar is displayed in a new tab or a new browser window.

Tip The first time Google Calendar is displayed, you may be asked to set some defaults.

Creating an Event

CREATE

4. Click the **Create** button in the upper-left corner of the Calendar page. A new page is displayed with a form for entering information about the event, as shown in **Figure 6-5.**

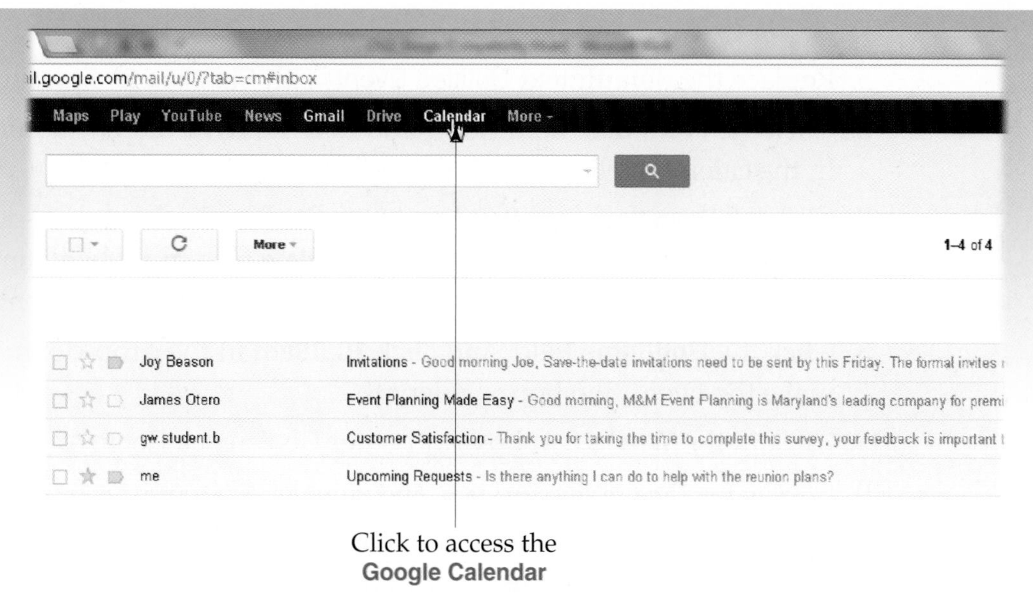

Goodheart-Willcox Publisher

Figure 6-4. When a user clicks the **Calendar** link, the Google Calendar is displayed in a new browser window or tab.

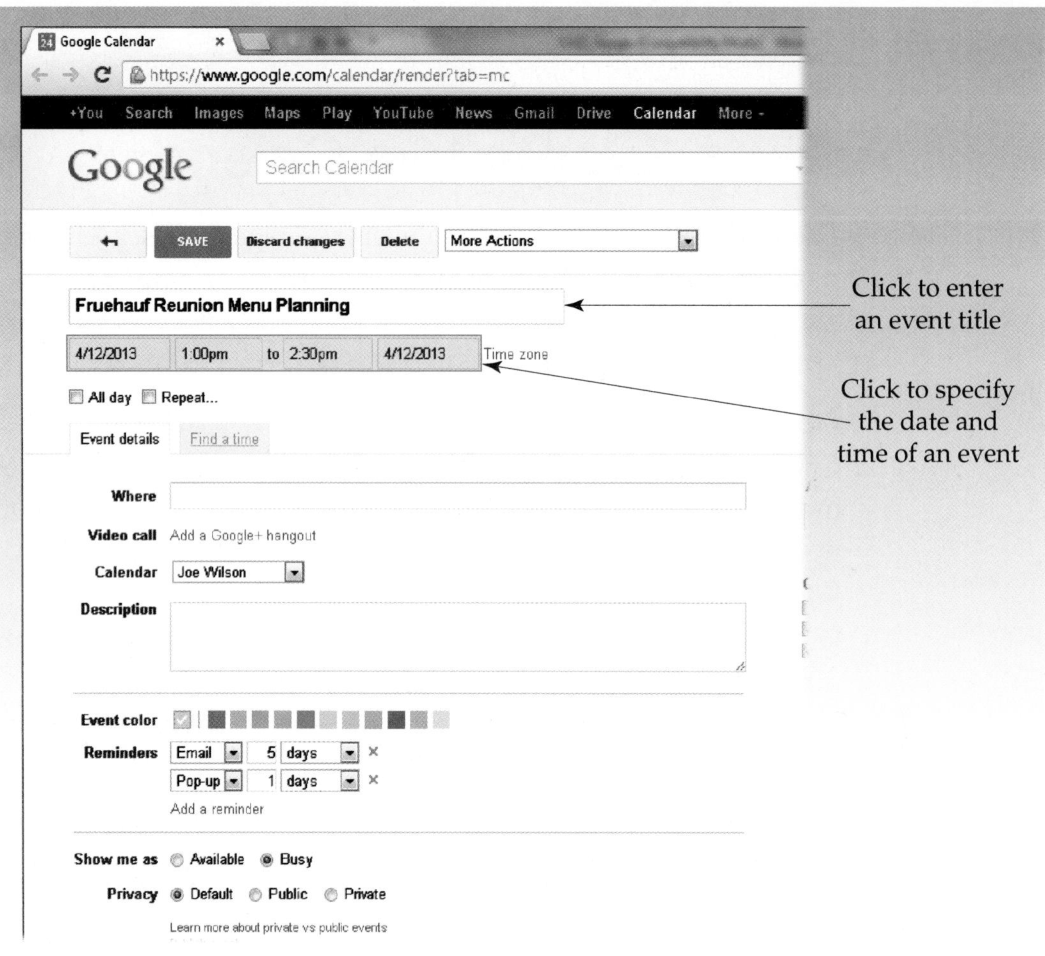

Goodheart-Willcox Publisher

Figure 6-5. Many details can be added to events such as start and end time, location, and description.

5. Replace the default text Untitled Event with Planning for Fruehauf Reunion.
6. Click the **From date** field (left-hand date field) to display a minicalendar. In the calendar, click a Friday that is two weeks away.
7. Click the **From time** field (left-hand time field) to display a drop-down list, and click **8:00am** in the list. The **Until time** field (right-hand time field) automatically changes to **9:00am** because events are one hour long by default.
8. Click the **Until time** field, and click **10:00am** in the drop-down list to make the event two hours in length.
9. Click in the **Where** text box, and enter Conference Room A.
10. Click in the **Description** text box, and enter Initial planning for the Fruehauf reunion.
11. Click one of the **Event color** swatches to assign a color to the event. The event is displayed in this color in the calendar.

Tip Use the same color for events of the same type. For example, you can always use red for deadlines and blue for staff meetings.

12. In the **Reminders** area of the page, click the **Add a reminder** link, click the **Reminder type** drop-down list, and select **Email**. This specifies the reminder will be an e-mail to you.
13. Click in the **Reminder time** text box and enter 5. This specifies how many units of time before the event the reminder will be given. The unit of time is set in the **Reminder time** drop-down list.
14. Click the **Reminder time** drop-down list and click **days** in the list. The reminder is now set to send an e-mail five days before the event.
15. Click the **Add a reminder** link to add a third second. Set the second reminder to be a pop-up that is displayed one day before the event.

SAVE

16. Click the **Save** button at the top of the page to save the event and return to the Calendar page.

Creating an Event Directly in the Calendar

Month

17. On the Calendar page, click the **Month** button to display a full month.
18. Locate the Planning for Fruehauf Reunion event.
19. Click the number of the date in the calendar to display the day view of that date, as shown in **Figure 6-6.**

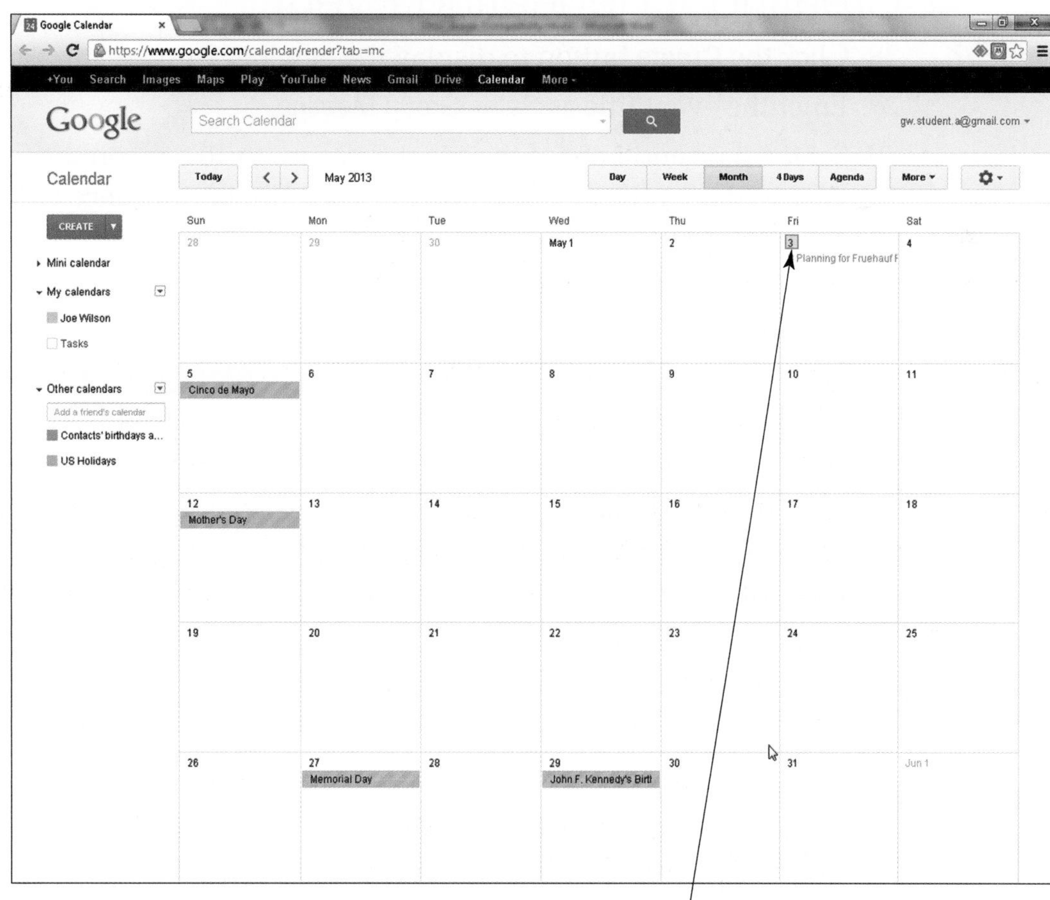

Goodheart-Willcox Publisher

Figure 6-6. A user can click the **Day** button to display the day view of the selected date.

20. Click the calendar at 1:00 p.m., hold, drag down to 2:30 p.m., and release the mouse button. A dialog box is displayed, as shown in **Figure 6-7.**
21. Click in the **What:** text box in the dialog box, and enter Fruehauf Reunion Menu Planning.
22. Click the **Create Event** button in the dialog box to add the event.

Creating an Event Using Quick Add

CREATE

23. Select the arrow to the right of the **Create** button to display the **Quick Add** dialog box, as shown in **Figure 6-8.**
24. In the text box in the **Quick Add** dialog box, enter Fruehauf Reunion Food Tasting 5 p.m. along with text that indicates a date one week after the related planning meeting.
25. Click the **Add** button or press the [Enter] key. The event is added to the calendar on the date and at the time entered in the text box. The event is one hour by default.

Creating a Repeating Event

CREATE

28. Click the **Create** button to display the new page for creating an event.
29. Enter the event title as Sales Group Meeting.
30. Set the date and time of the event to 8 a.m. to 10 a.m. on the first Wednesday of the next month. This is the first occurrence of the repeating event.

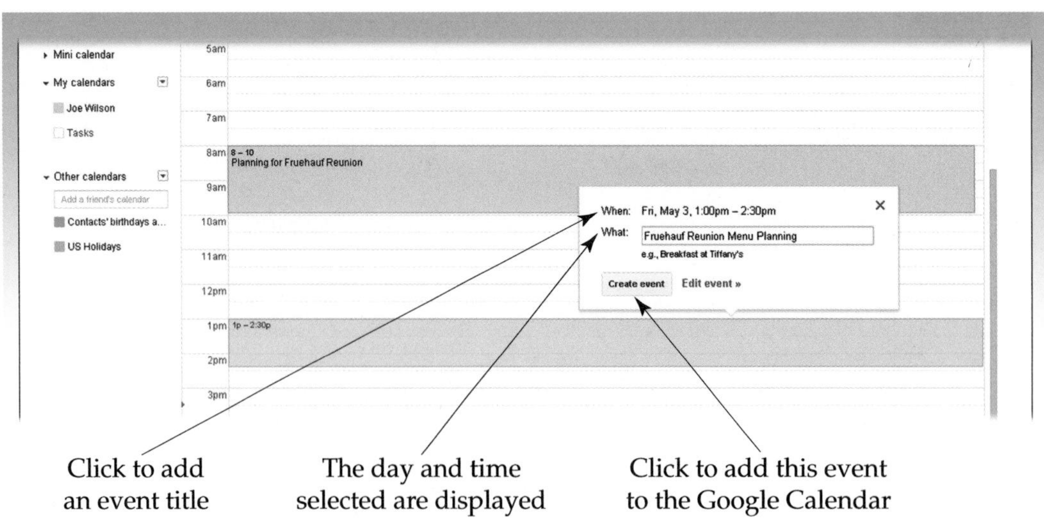

Goodheart-Willcox Publisher

Figure 6-7. To add more details to an event created directly in the calendar, click the **Edit event** link.

Goodheart-Willcox Publisher

Figure 6-8. If a user enters an event using the Quick Add feature without a start time or end time, an all-day event is automatically created. To edit details of a quick add event, click the event title in the calendar view.

31. Check the **Repeat...** check box. The **Repeat** dialog box is displayed, as shown in **Figure 6-9.**
32. In the **Repeats:** drop-down list, click **Monthly**. This sets the event to occur every month.
33. In the **Repeat every:** drop-down list, click **1**. This sets the event to occur once a month.
34. In the **Repeat by:** area, click the **day of the week** radio button. This sets the event to occur on the first Wednesday of each month, because the first Wednesday of the month was set as the first event. If the **day of the month** radio button is selected, the event will occur on the same date (day number) each month.
35. The **Starts on:** text box displays the date of the first event. This is a read-only text box.

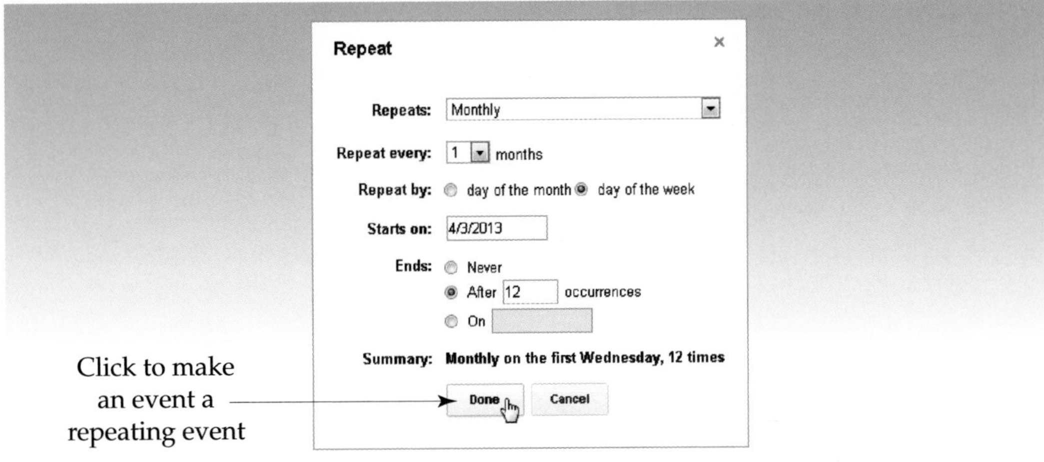

Goodheart-Willcox Publisher

Figure 6-9. An event can be set to repeat daily, weekly, monthly, or annually. An event can also be set to repeat every weekday; every Tuesday and Thursday; or every Monday, Wednesday, and Friday.

36. In the **Ends:** area, click the **After** radio button and enter 12 corresponding in the text box. This sets the event to occur 12 times, or in this case for one year (12 months).
37. The **Summary:** area at the bottom of the dialog box indicates the current settings for the event. In this case, it should read Monthly on the first Wednesday, 12 times.

Done

38. Click the **Done** button to close the **Repeat** dialog box. The page for specifying the details of the event is redisplayed.
39. Click in the **Where** text box, and enter Conference Room A.
40. Set the first reminder to send an e-mail 20 minutes before the event.

SAVE

41. Click the **Save** button to add the repeating event to the calendar.

Lesson 6-2

Changing the Calendar View and Printing the Calendar

The calendar can be displayed in a list format or showing various time spans, such as a single day or the entire month. The calendar view selected can determine the way in which the calendar will print.

Changing the Calendar View

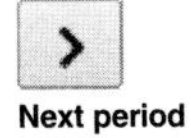

1. Log in to your Google Mail account.
2. Click the **Calendar** link to display the Calendar page.
3. Click the **Week** button, if needed, to display one week.
4. If the current week is not displayed, click the **Today** button to display the week containing the current day.
5. Click the **Next period** button to advance the calendar one week, as shown in **Figure 6-10.**

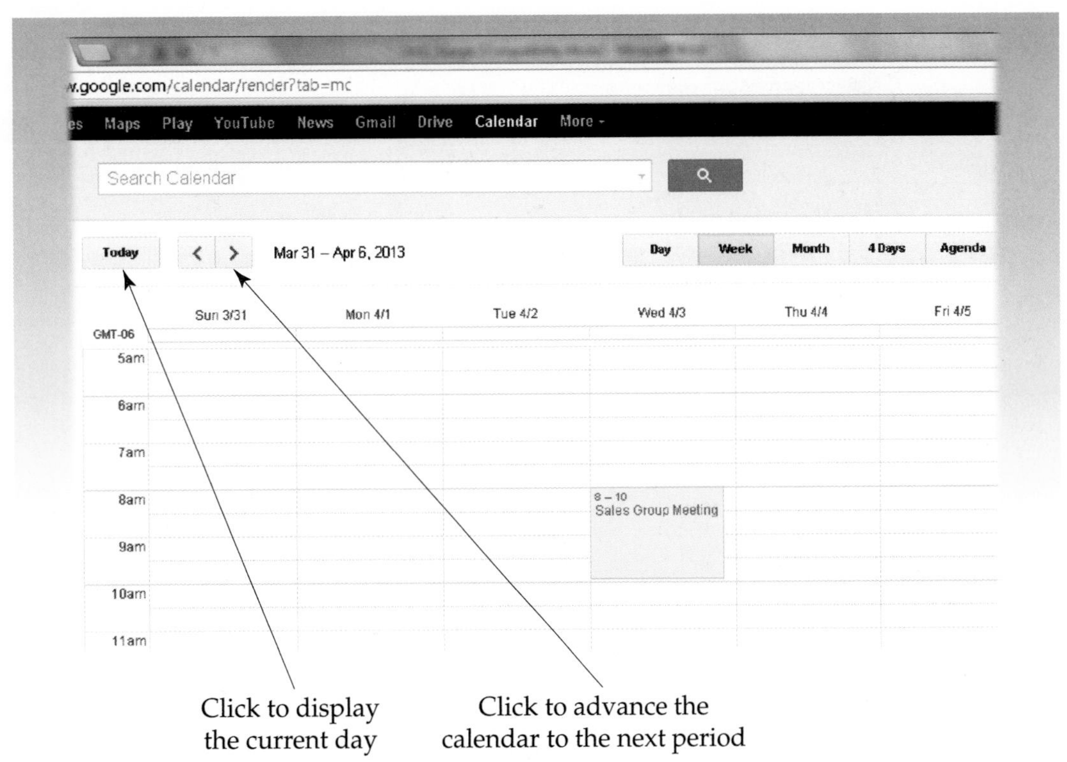

Goodheart-Willcox Publisher

Figure 6-10. To have the calendar displayed in other views, click the corresponding time span button or the **Agenda** button in the top right section of the window.

6. Advance the calendar until you see the planning events created in Lesson 6-1.
7. Click the **Agenda** button. A view of upcoming events is displayed, as shown in **Figure 6-11.**

Printing the Agenda

8. Click the **More** button, and click **Print** in the drop-down menu. The print preview is displayed in a new window, as shown in **Figure 6-12.**

Tip The current view displayed for the calendar determines what is printed. If the agenda is displayed, it is printed; if the calendar is displayed, it is printed.

9. Click the **Print Range:** drop-down list, and click in the left-hand date field. In the calendar, click a date that is three weeks away. This specifies the date range that will be printed.
10. Click the **Font size:** drop-down list, and click **Big**. This specifies the font size for the printed text.
11. Click the **Orientation:** drop-down list, and select how the information will be printed on the page.

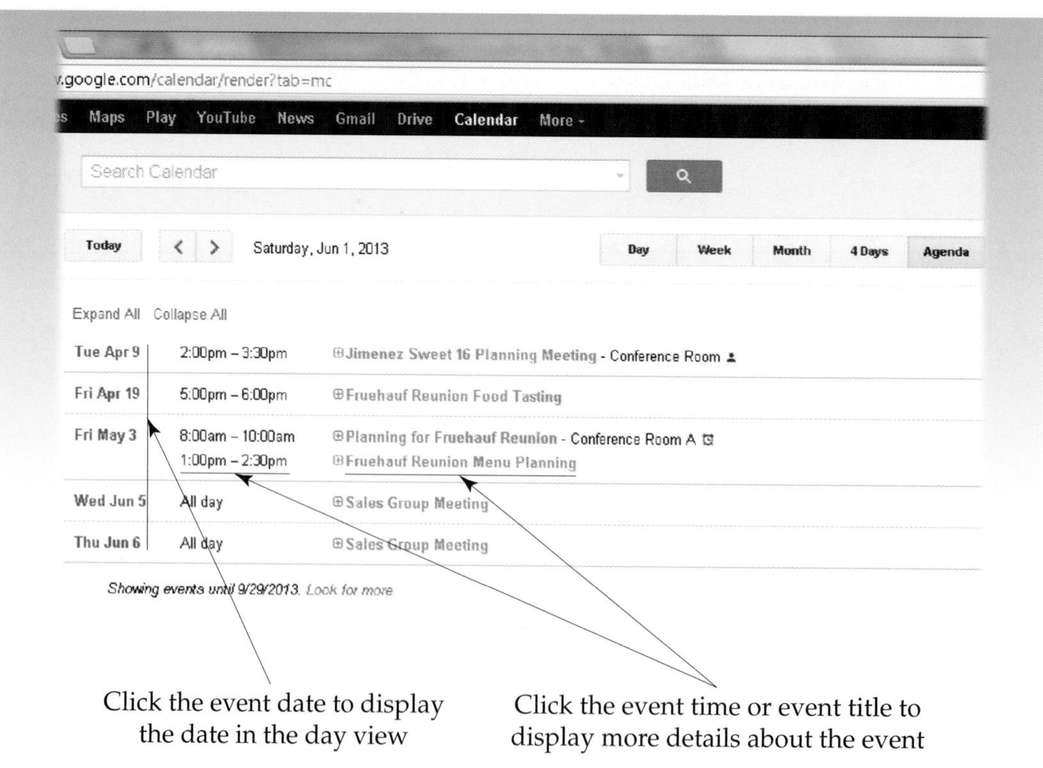

Goodheart-Willcox Publisher

Figure 6-11. In the agenda view of the calendar, only days with events scheduled are displayed.

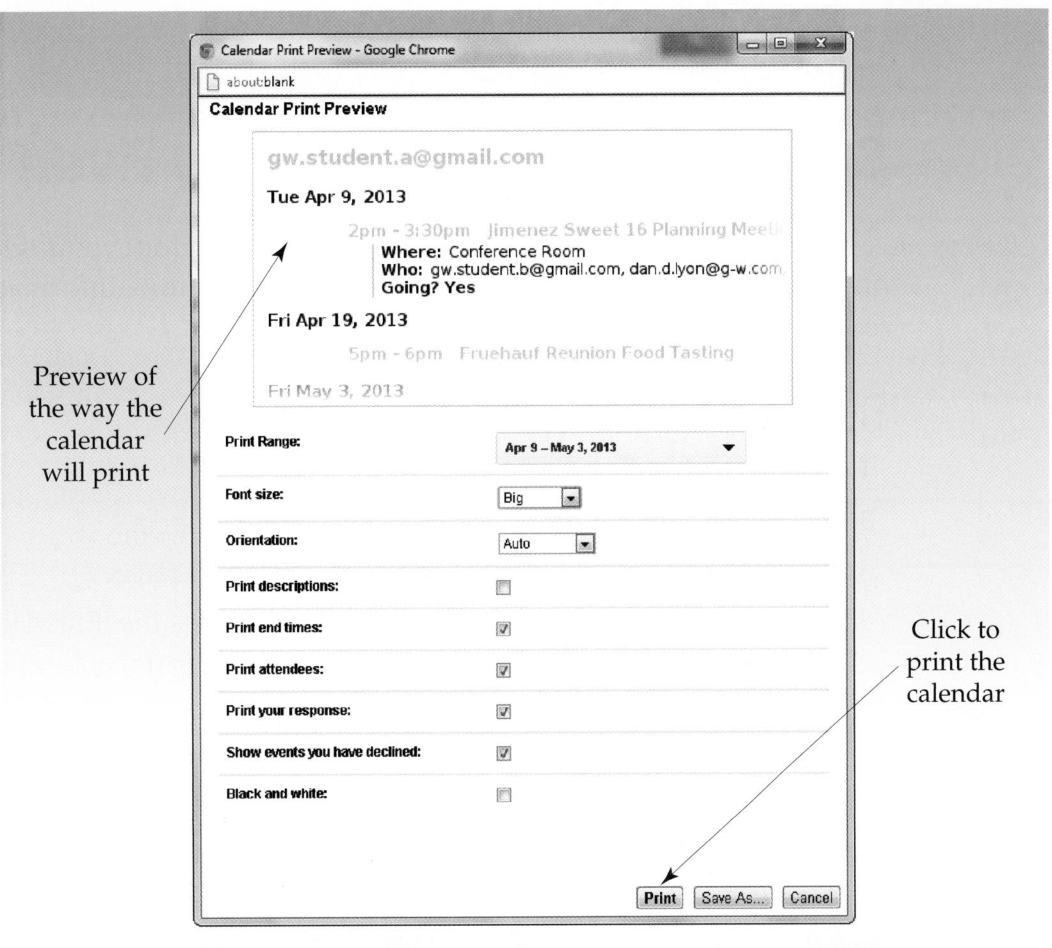

Goodheart-Willcox Publisher

Figure 6-12 In the Calendar print preview window, a user can make some changes to the way the calendar will print, such as the date range and the size of the font.

12. Check the check boxes next to the information to be printed.
13. Click the **Print** button to display the **Print** dialog box.
14. Make any changes needed to the printer settings, then click the **Print** button to print the calendar as specified.
15. Click the **Cancel** button in the print preview to close the preview.

Lesson 6-3

Searching for and Editing Events

Google provides users with the ability to search for events. Once users find an event, they can modify it to ensure only accurate information is recorded in the calendar.

Searching for an Event

1. Log in to your Google Mail account.
2. Click the **Calendar** link to display the Calendar page.
3. Click in the search box at the top of the Calendar page.
4. Enter the search term Fruehauf Reunion, and press the [Enter] key. The search results are displayed in an agenda format, as shown in **Figure 6-13.**
5. Click the event time, the event title, or the plus sign (+) to expand the details for a specific event.

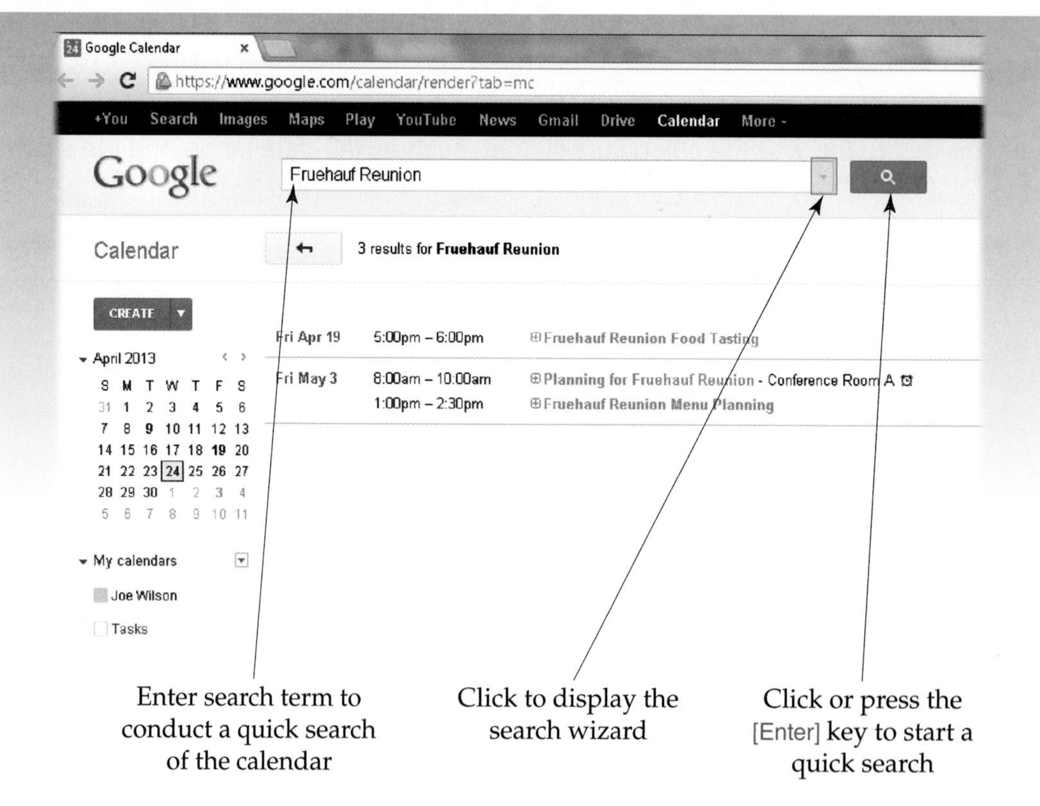

Goodheart-Willcox Publisher

Figure 6-13. Having the ability to search for an event can be helpful, especially for those events set for future dates.

Editing an Event

6. If in the agenda view, click the **Back to Calendar** button to display the Calendar page.

Tip Editing an event can be initiated from the agenda view or any of the calendar views.

7. Locate the event called Fruehauf Reunion Food Tasting.
8. Display the day view for that event's date.
9. Hover the cursor over the bottom line of the colored box for the event in the calendar. The cursor changes to a standard Windows resize cursor.
10. Click, hold, drag the cursor down to 11:30 p.m., and release the mouse button. This edits the duration of the event. Note that as you drag the end time of the event is changed.
11. Click anywhere on the colored block of the event except the event name. A pop-up window is displayed, as shown in **Figure 6-14.**
12. Click the name of the event in the pop-up window. The name of the event appears in a text box.
13. Move the cursor to the end of the event name and add (clean up the ballroom).
14. Click the color swatch to the left of the event name, and select a different color for the event.
15. Click the **Edit event** link in the pop-up window. The details page for the event is displayed.

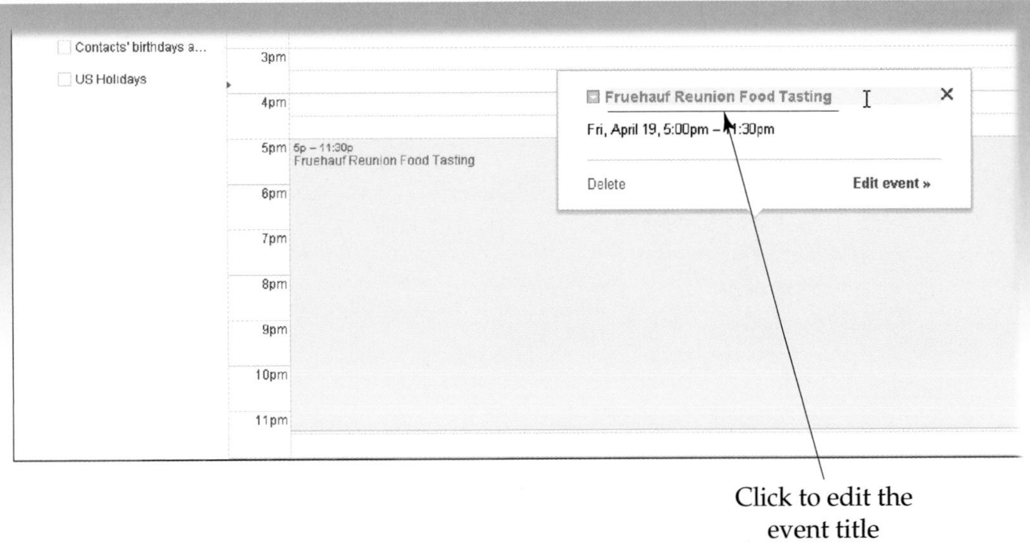

Goodheart-Willcox Publisher

Figure 6-14. Click the **Edit event** link to make changes to the details of the event.

The details page for the event can be displayed by clicking the event name in the colored block in the calendar.

16. On the details page, enter Ballroom in the **Where** text box and Remove decorations and serving supplies. in the **Description** text box.

SAVE

Back to Calendar

17. Click the **Save** button to save the changes and return to the calendar. If there have been no changes, you can click the **Back to Calendar** button.

Lesson 6-4

Inviting Guests

Guests can be invited either while creating a new event or when editing an existing one. Sending invitations this way can help save time when setting up events such as staff meetings and working on team projects.

Creating a New Event

CREATE

1. Log in to your Google Mail account.
2. Click the **Calendar** link to display the Calendar page.
3. Click the **Create** button to add a new event.
4. Enter Jimenez Sweet 16 Planning Meeting as the event name.
5. Select Tuesday of next week as the date of the event.
6. Set 2:00 p.m. as the start time for the event and 3:30 p.m. as the end time for the event.
7. Enter Conference Room as the location of the event.

Inviting Guests

8. Click in the **Add guests** text box.
9. Enter the e-mail address of a classmate, as shown in **Figure 6-15.** If the classmate is a contact, his or her name will appear in the autocomplete as characters are entered.

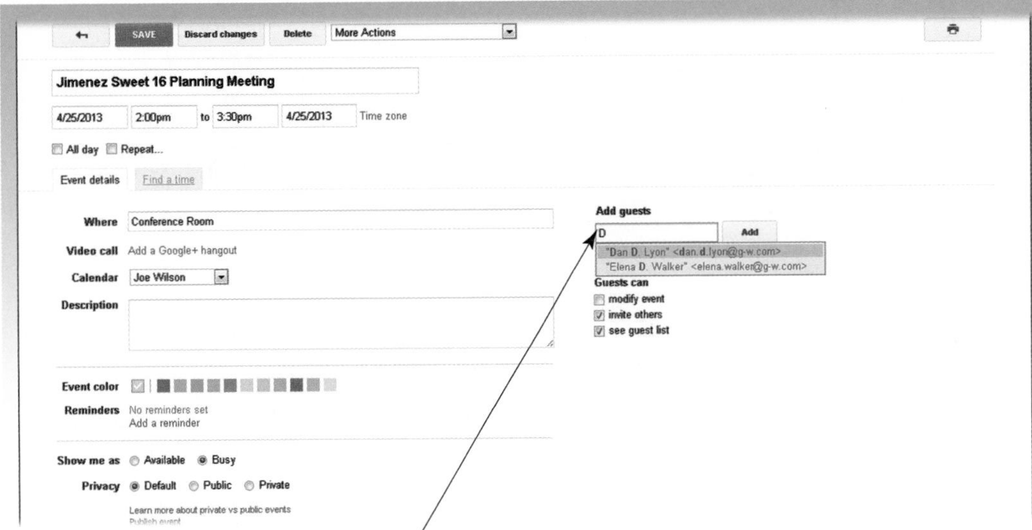

Goodheart-Willcox Publisher

Figure 6-15. No more than 500 guests can be added to Google Calendar events, and they do not need a Gmail account to receive an invitation.

Calendar invitations can be sent to people who do not have a Google account. They can reply to the invitation, but there will not be a connection between the event in your Google Calendar and their calendars.

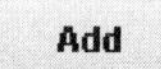

10. When the correct name is highlighted, press the [Tab] key to add that person as a guest. His or her name is added to the list in the **Guests** area, as shown in **Figure 6-16.** If the person is not a contact, enter the full e-mail address and click the **Add** button.
11. Invite a total of at least four classmates to the event.

Tip

Guests lists are limited to 500 guests per event. For events with guest lists that exceed 500 people, create additional events.

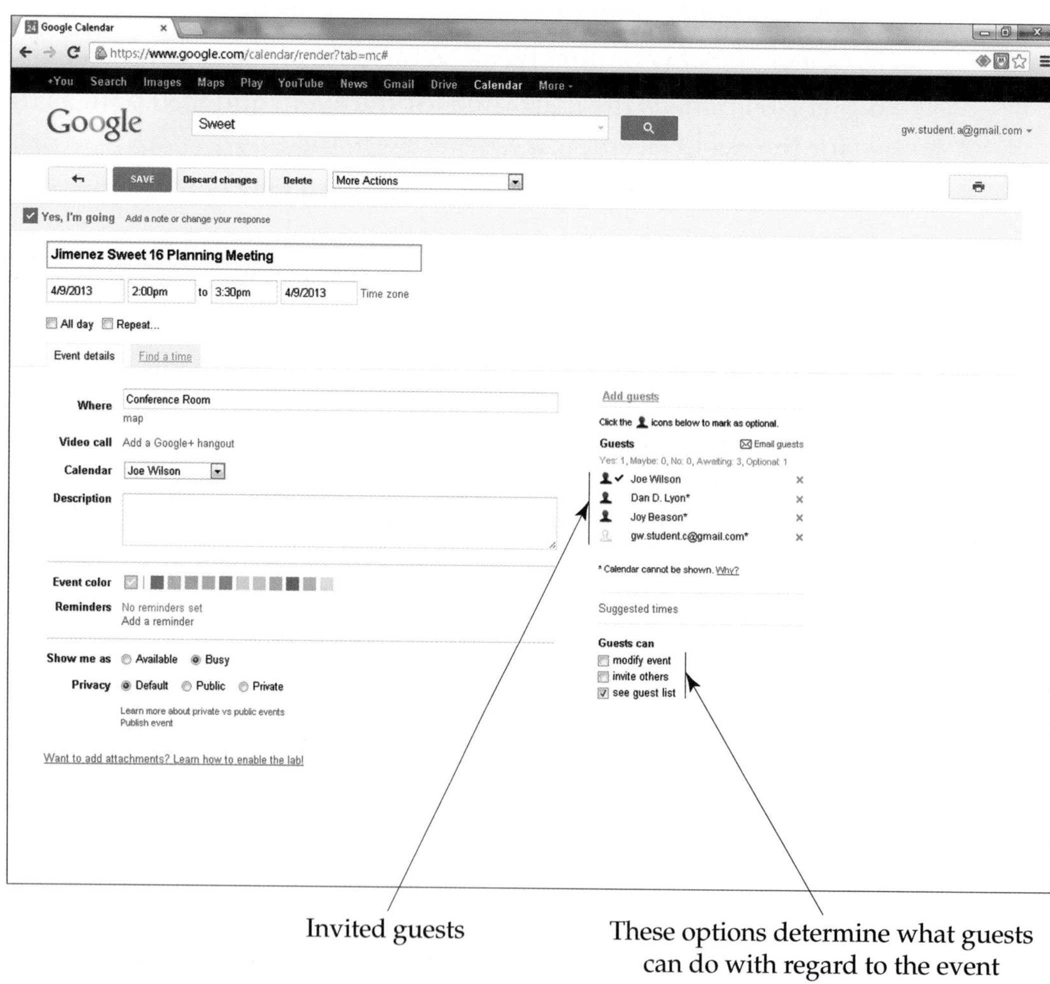

Figure 6-16. The name of each guest that receives an invitation is displayed on the guest list in the event detail window.

12. Click the silhouette icon to the left of one of the guest names to make that person an optional attendee. The icon changes from filled-in to an outline.
13. Make sure the **modify event** check box is unchecked. This prevents any of the guests from changing any of the event details.
14. Uncheck the **invite others** check box. This prevents any of the guests from adding more guests to the event. Only you will be able to invite more guests.
15. Make sure the **see guest list** check box is checked. This allows all guests in the event to see who else is invited and how each person has responded.
16. Click the **X** to the right of one attendee name. This removes the person from the guest list.

SAVE

17. Click the **Save** button. A dialog box appears asking if you want to send invitations to the guests.
18. Click the **Send** button in the dialog box so the guests receive an e-mail alerting them to the event.
19. When you receive an invitation from a classmate, respond to it accepting the event by clicking the **Yes** link in the e-mail.

Checking Invitation Responses

20. Locate the event on your calendar.
21. Edit the event so the details page is displayed.
22. Look at the **Guests** list on the details page. Directly to the left of the guest's name will be an icon or a blank that indicates how the person has replied. **Figure 6-17** illustrates the status icons.

Icon	Meaning
✓	Guest will attend.
⊘	Guest will not attend.
	Guest has not yet replied.
?	Guest may attend.

Goodheart-Willcox Publisher

Figure 6-17. The icon to the left of each guest's name indicates his or her response to the invitation.

Lesson 6-5

Creating Additional Calendars

A user can create additional calendars to organize different parts of his or her life. Each calendar created by the user will display in the **My calendars** label.

Creating a Calendar

1. Log in to your Google Mail account.
2. Click the **Calendar** link to display the Calendar page.
3. Click the triangle to the left of **My calendars** to display a list of all calendars. If the list is already displayed, clicking the triangle hides the list.
4. Click the drop-down arrow to the right of **My calendars** to display a menu.
5. Click **Create new calendar** in the drop-down menu. The Create New Calendar page is displayed, as shown in **Figure 6-18.**

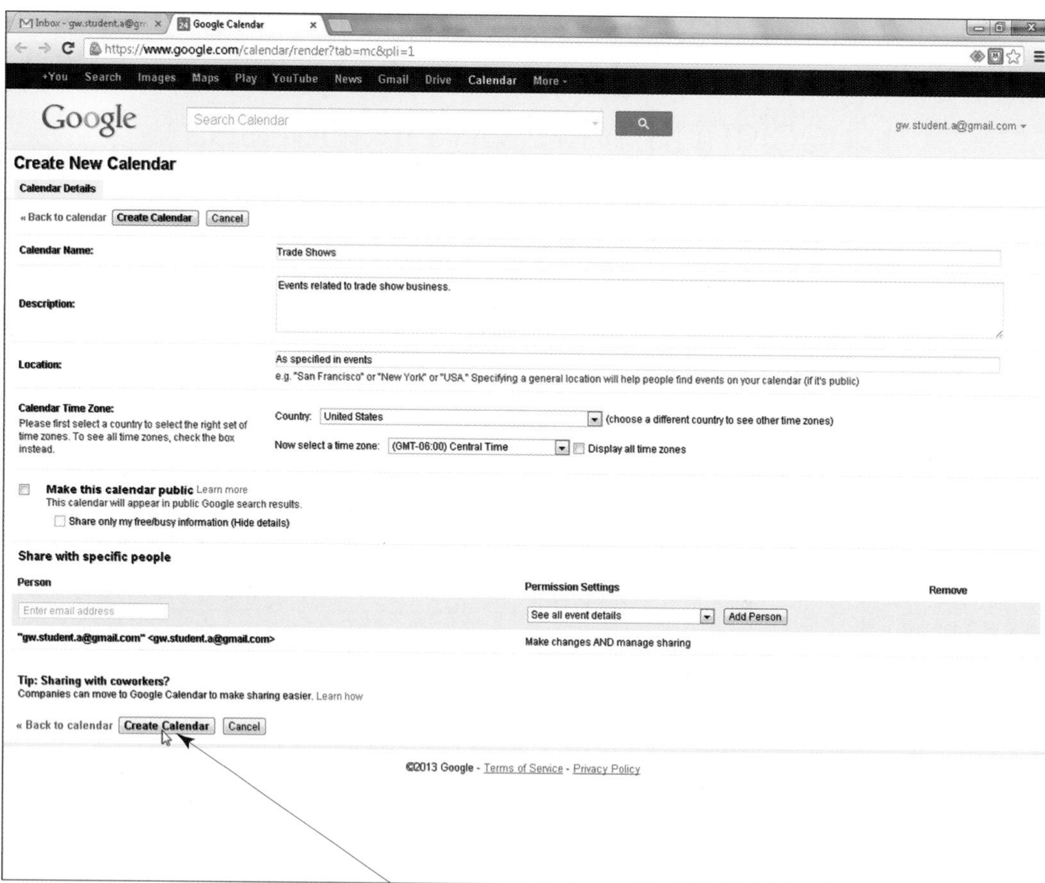

Goodheart-Willcox Publisher

Figure 6-18. On the Create New Calendar page, a user can create a calendar in addition to the default calendar to isolate events for specific activities.

6. Click in the **Calendar Name:** text box, and enter Trade Shows.
7. Click in the **Description:** text box, and enter Events related to trade show business.
8. Click in the **Location:** text box, and enter As specified in events.
9. In the **Calendar Time Zone:** area, set the United States as the country and select the time zone for your location.

Create Calendar

10. Click the **Create Calendar** button. The Calendar page is displayed. The new calendar appears in the list of calendars under **My calendars**.

Adjusting the Appearance of the Calendar

11. Hover over the name of a calendar in the list below **My calendars**. A drop-down arrow appears to the right of the calendar name.
12. Click the drop-down arrow to display a menu, as shown in **Figure 6-19.**
13. Click a color swatch in the menu to change the color of the calendar. Each calendar should have a different color to make it easier to distinguish them.
14. Hover over the calendar name, and click the drop-down arrow.
15. Click **Display only this calendar** in the drop-down menu. Only the events in this calendar are displayed in the Calendar page. The color swatch for the other calendars changes to an empty square to indicate their events are not being shown.
16. Click the name or color swatch for a calendar in the list below **My calendars**. The display of the events in the calendar is toggled on or off. If displayed when clicked, they are hidden. If hidden when clicked, they are displayed.

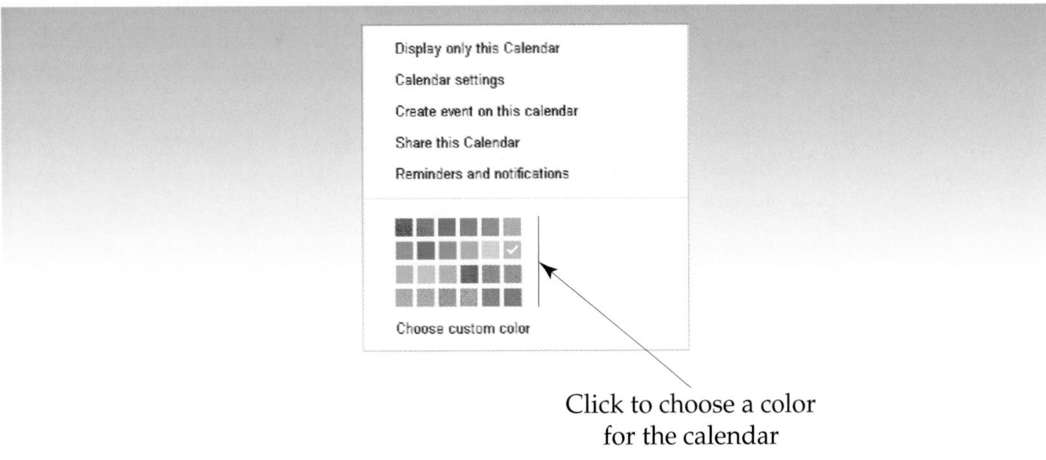

Goodheart-Willcox Publisher

Figure 6-19. The color a user chooses for a new calendar dictates the default color for all events added to that calendar.

Creating an Event on a Specific Calendar

CREATE

17. Click the **Create** button to add a new event.
18. Enter Reunion Planners USA as the event name.
19. Select a start date that is sometime in the next month.
20. Select an end date that is three days after the start date.
21. Check the **All day** check box. This specifies the entire day as the duration for the event. In this case, it is the entire day each of three consecutive days. Notice that the **From time** and **Until time** fields are hidden when the **All day** check box is checked.
22. In the **Where** text box, enter Tulsa, OK as the location.
23. Click the **Calendar** drop-down menu, and click **Trade Shows** in the menu, as shown in **Figure 6-20.** This is the calendar to which the event will be added.

Make sure to select the correct calendar on which the event will appear. Otherwise, the event will be added to the wrong calendar.

SAVE

24. Click the **Save** button to create the event and add it to the Trade Shows calendar.

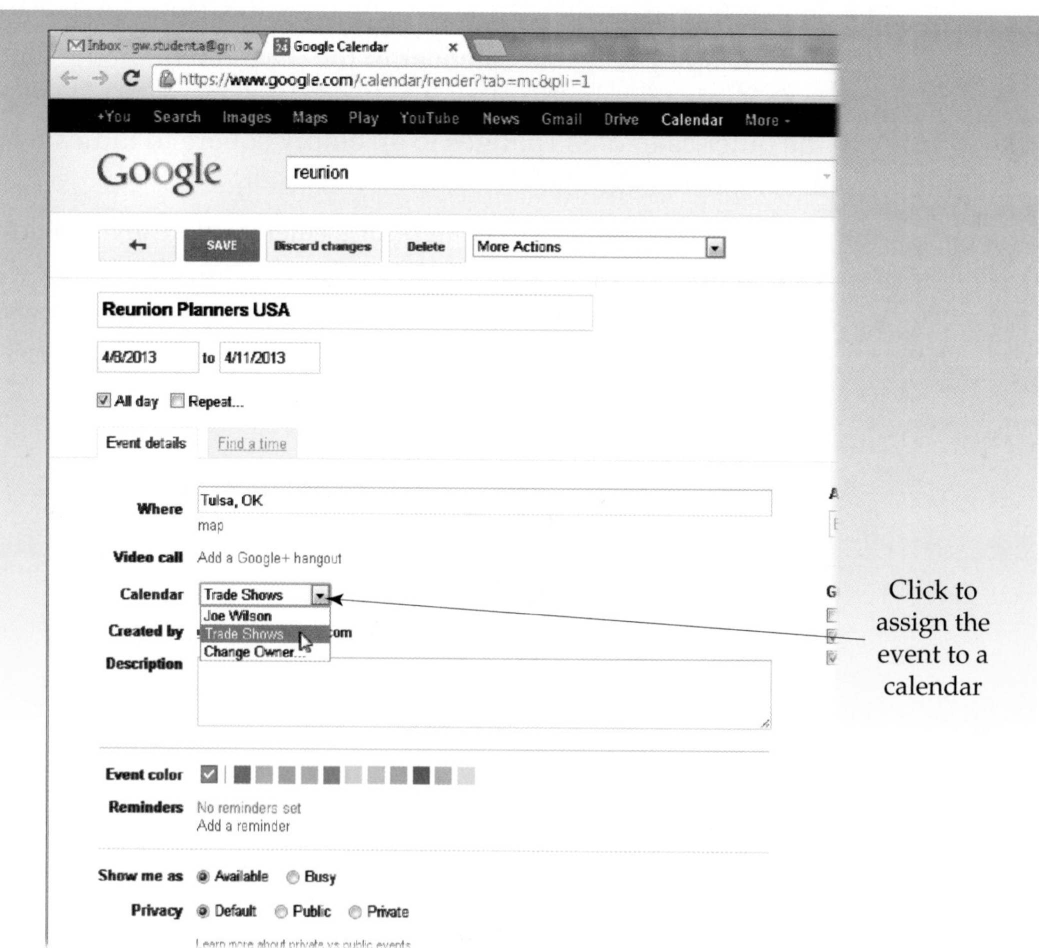

Goodheart-Willcox Publisher

Figure 6-20. A user can select on which calendar the event will be displayed.

Lesson 6-6

Sharing Calendars

Users can share calendars they have created with other users. They can also add publicly shared calendars to their Google Calendar.

Sharing a Calendar with a Large Group

1. Log in to your Google Mail account.
2. Click the **Calendar** link to display the Calendar page.
3. If needed, click the triangle to the left of **My calendars** to display a list of all calendars.
4. Click the drop-down arrow to the right of the Trade Show calendar.
5. Click **Share this Calendar** in the drop-down menu, as shown in **Figure 6-21.** The details page for the Trade Show calendar is displayed with the **Share this Calendar** tab active, as shown in **Figure 6-22.**
6. Check the **Make this calendar public** check box. This makes the calendar appear in public Google searches.

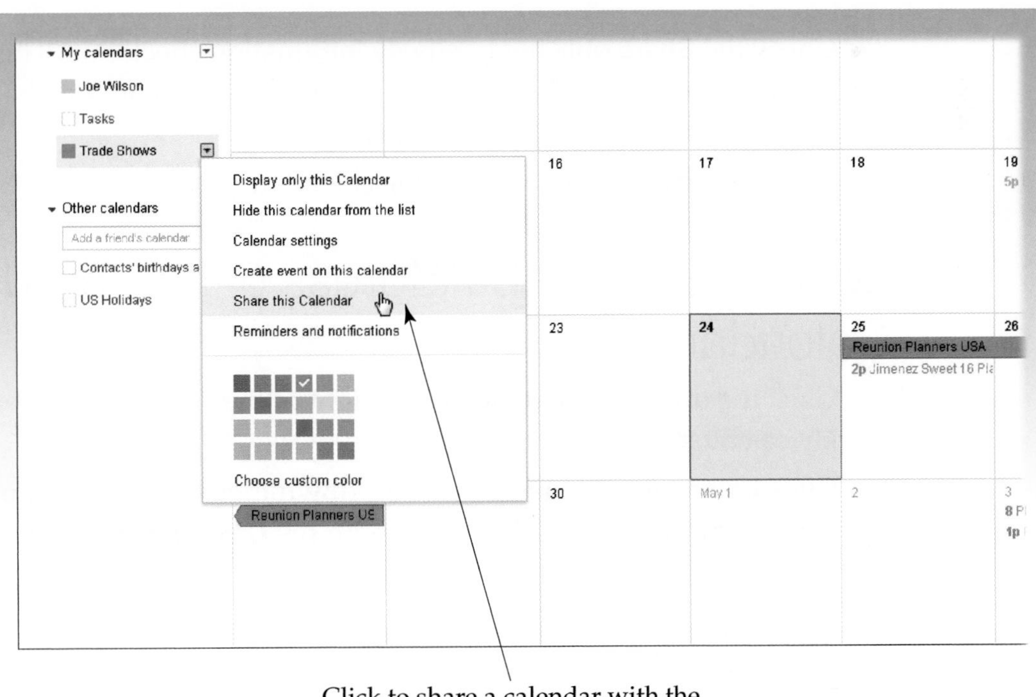

Goodheart-Willcox Publisher

Figure 6-21. Users can change the display of additional calendars from this menu.

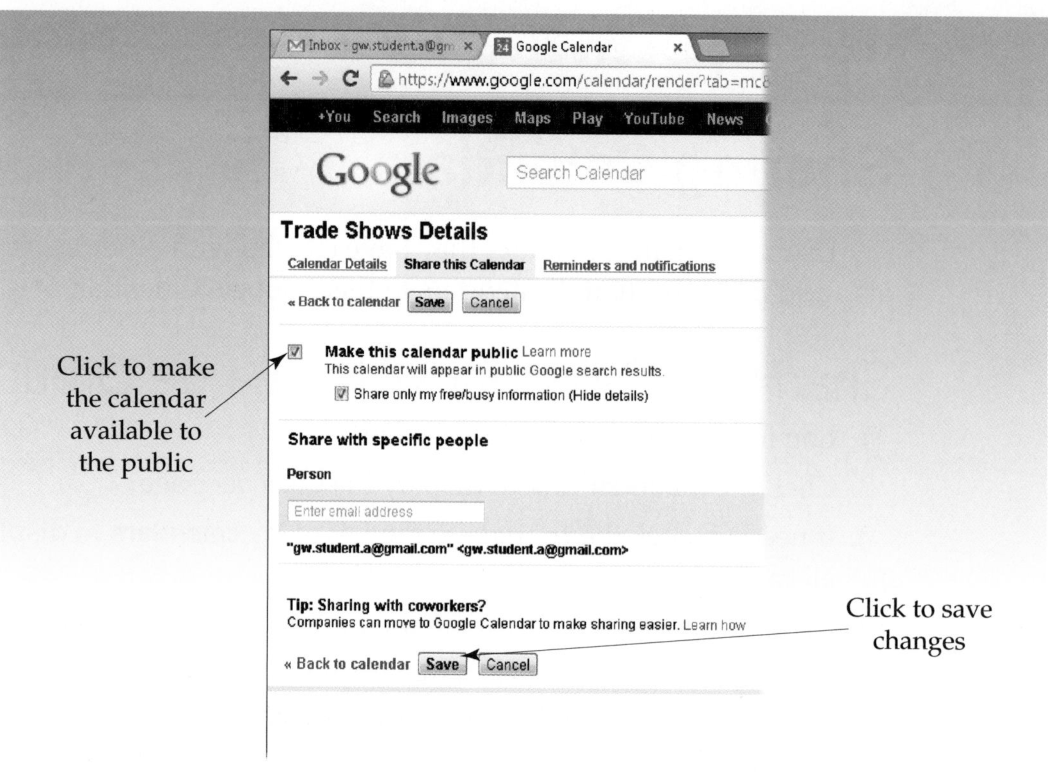

Goodheart-Willcox Publisher

Figure 6-22. Organizations often make public calendars to inform a large audience about their events.

7. Check the **Share only my free/busy information** check box. This prevents the details of events from appearing in public Google searches. Only your status will appear in searches.
8. Click the **Save** button to share the calendar.

Locating the Web Address of a Shared Calendar

9. Click the drop-down arrow to the right of the Trade Show calendar in the **My calendars** list.
10. Click **Calendar settings** in the drop-down menu. The details page for the Trade Show calendar is displayed with the **Calendar Details** tab active.
11. In the **Calendar Address:** area of the page, click on the **HTML** button. A dialog box is displayed with a hyperlink to the web address of the calendar, as shown in **Figure 6-23.**

Tip The web address for the calendar can also be obtained in XML or iCal format. Click the appropriate button.

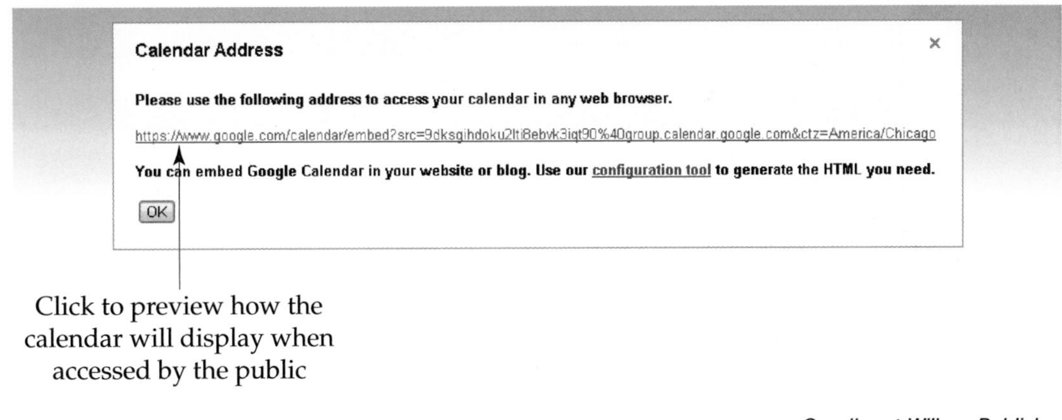

Goodheart-Willcox Publisher

Figure 6-23. The hyperlink in the **Calendar Address** dialog box is the web address of the public calendar.

12. Click the hyperlink to display the calendar in your default Internet browser. The address can be copied from the browser's address field and then included in the coding for a web page.
13. Close the browser window, and then close the dialog box.
14. Click the **Back to calendar** link to return to the Calendar page.

Sharing a Calendar with a Specific Person

15. Click the drop-down arrow to the right of the Trade Show calendar in the **My calendars** list.
16. Click **Share this Calendar** in the drop-down list.
17. On the details page, click in the **Person** text box.

Add Person

18. Enter the e-mail address of a classmate. When the correct person is displayed in the autocomplete field, press the [Tab] key. Or, enter the complete e-mail address and click the **Add Person** button.
19. Click the drop-down arrow to the right of the person's e-mail address.

Tip To stop sharing a calendar with a specific person, click the trash can icon to the right of his or her e-mail address.

20. Select the permission level in the drop-down list, as shown in **Figure 6-24.**

SAVE

21. Click the **Save** button to share the calendar with this specific person and return to the Calendar page.

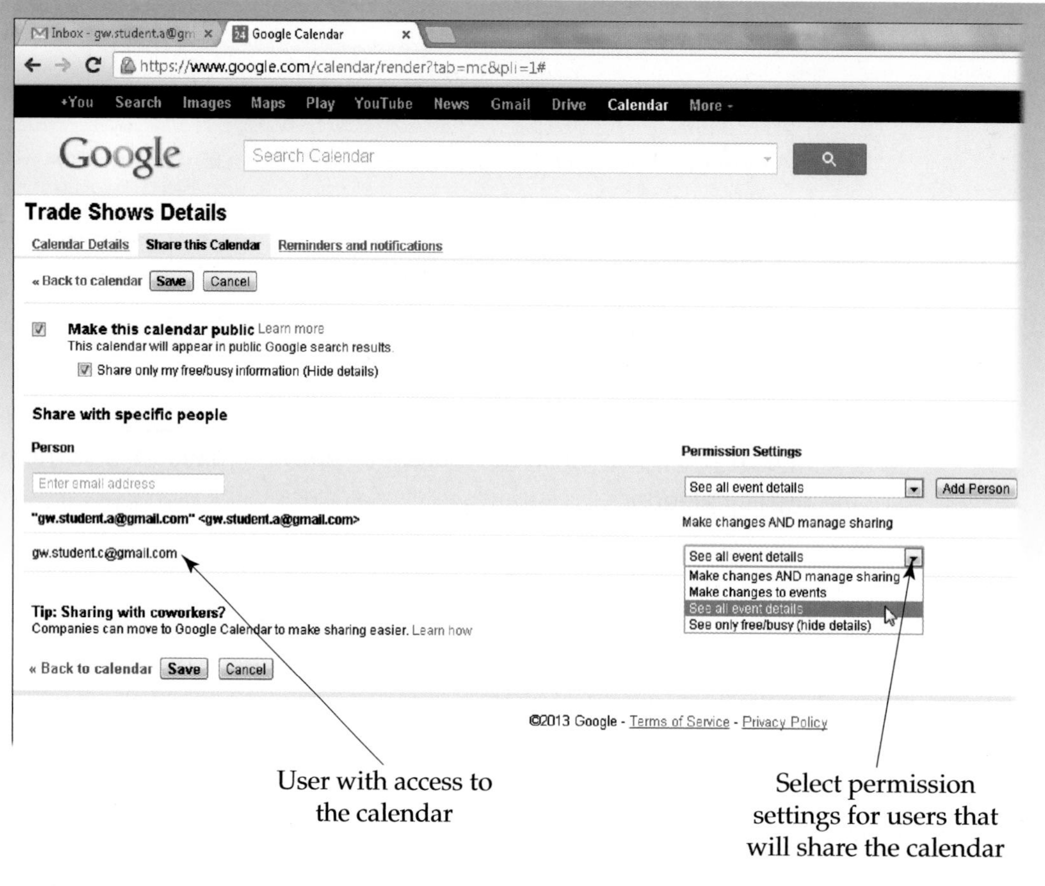

Goodheart-Willcox Publisher

Figure 6-24. A user can assign a different permission setting for each person that will have access to the shared calendar.

Lesson 6-7

Changing Calendar Settings

The calendar settings allow a user to customize the appearance and navigation of his or her calendar. A user can also hide/show calendars from the list of calendars.

1. Log in to your Google Mail account.
2. Click the **Calendar** link to display the Calendar page.
3. Click the **Settings** button, and click **Settings** in the drop-down menu. The details page for the calendar is displayed with the **General** tab active, as shown in **Figure 6-25.**

Settings

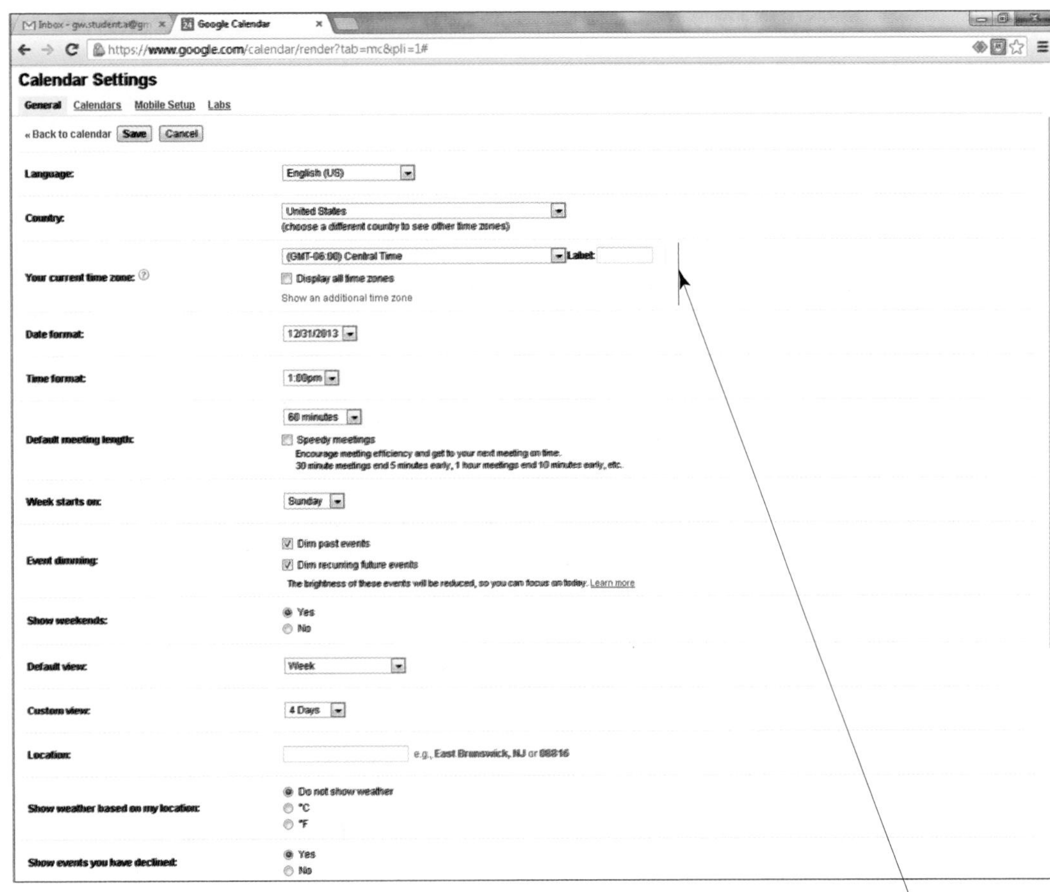

Goodheart-Willcox Publisher

Figure 6-25. Users can change the way the calendar date, time, and weeks are displayed in order to better meet their needs.

4. Click the drop-down list in the **Default meeting length:** area, and click **30 minutes** in the list. This changes the default duration of all new events to 30 minutes.
5. Click the drop-down list in the **Default view:** area, and click **Month** in the list. This sets the default calendar view to be a full month.
6. Click the drop-down list in the **Custom view:** area, and click **6 Days** in the list. This changes the custom view to six days, and a **6 Days** button will appear on the Calendar page.
7. In the **Show events you have declined:** area, click the **No** radio button. This prevents events from showing that you have declined.

SAVE

8. Click the **Save** button to return to the Calendar page.

Check Your Google Apps IQ

Now that you have finished this chapter, see what you know about Google Apps by taking the chapter posttest.
www.m.g-wlearning.com
www.g-wlearning.com/informationtechnology/

Skill Review

Answer the following questions on a separate sheet of paper.

1. What is the basic purpose of Google Calendar?
2. A(n) ______ is an occurrence that is added to the Google Calendar.
3. What is a reminder?
4. Which calendar view displays events in list format?
5. Describe how to adjust the date or time of an event by clicking and dragging.
6. What is the limit to the number of guests an event can have?
   A. 10
   B. 50
   C. 100
   D. 500
7. Who can view a publically shared calendar?
8. Describe why the color of a calendar would be changed.
9. What file types can be imported as a calendar?
10. Which days can be selected as the first day of the week for a calendar?

Lesson Application

These exercises are designed to apply the skills learned in this and previous chapters. General directions are provided, but you will need to draw on your knowledge to determine how to complete each exercise.

Exercise 6-1
Creating Events

Create three new events. One event should be titled Jazz Festival Planning, one event should repeat every Tuesday and Thursday for 6 weeks, and one event should be a week-long event. All should begin within the next 30 days. Set a reminder for each event.

Exercise 6-2
Searching for and Editing Events

Search for the event titled Jazz Festival Planning. Edit it by changing the date to tomorrow and inviting at least four classmates. Check your e-mail for an invite to the event from a classmate, and respond to it. Open the Jazz Festival Planning event in Calendar to check your guests' responses.

Exercise 6-3
Creating a Calendar

Create a new calendar called M & M Events. Assign a color of your choice to the calendar. Add two events to the calendar; one should be an all-day event, and one should be a recurring event. Both should begin within the next 30 days. Locate the Jazz Festival Planning event, and edit it so it is on the M & M Events calendar.

Exercise 6-4
Sharing a Calendar

Share the M & M Events calendar with three classmates and your instructor. Assign different permission settings for each person. Take the steps needed to e-mail the calendar to your instructor.

Exercise 6-5
Managing a Calendar

In the task list, create two new tasks, each with a due date within the next 30 days. Ensure that all calendars and the task list are displayed in the **My Calendars** label and **Other Calendars** label. Print the calendar in the monthly view, and then print in the agenda view. Turn in the printouts to your instructor.

Chapter 7

Google Groups

Objectives

After completing this chapter, you will be able to:

- **Join** an existing group.
- **Participate** in a group.
- **Modify** user membership settings.
- **Create** a new group.

alexmillos/Shutterstock.com

Check Your Google Apps IQ

Before you begin this chapter, see what you already know about Google Apps by taking the chapter pretest.

www.m.g-wlearning.com
www.g-wlearning.com/informationtechnology/

Using Google Groups

Google Groups provide a way for people to connect with others via an online discussion board or an e-mail list. A group is typically created around a common interest that members discuss or about which members share information. Group members create topics related to the common interest shared by the group. A ***topic*** is a statement with a prompt or question that serves as the starting point of a new discussion within a group. Members then respond to topics. Both topics and responses are often referred to as *posts*.

There are three types of Google Groups: web forum, e-mail list, and Q&A forum. The web forum type of group allows users to interact with the group through the Topics page, as seen in **Figure 7-1**. The Topics page for

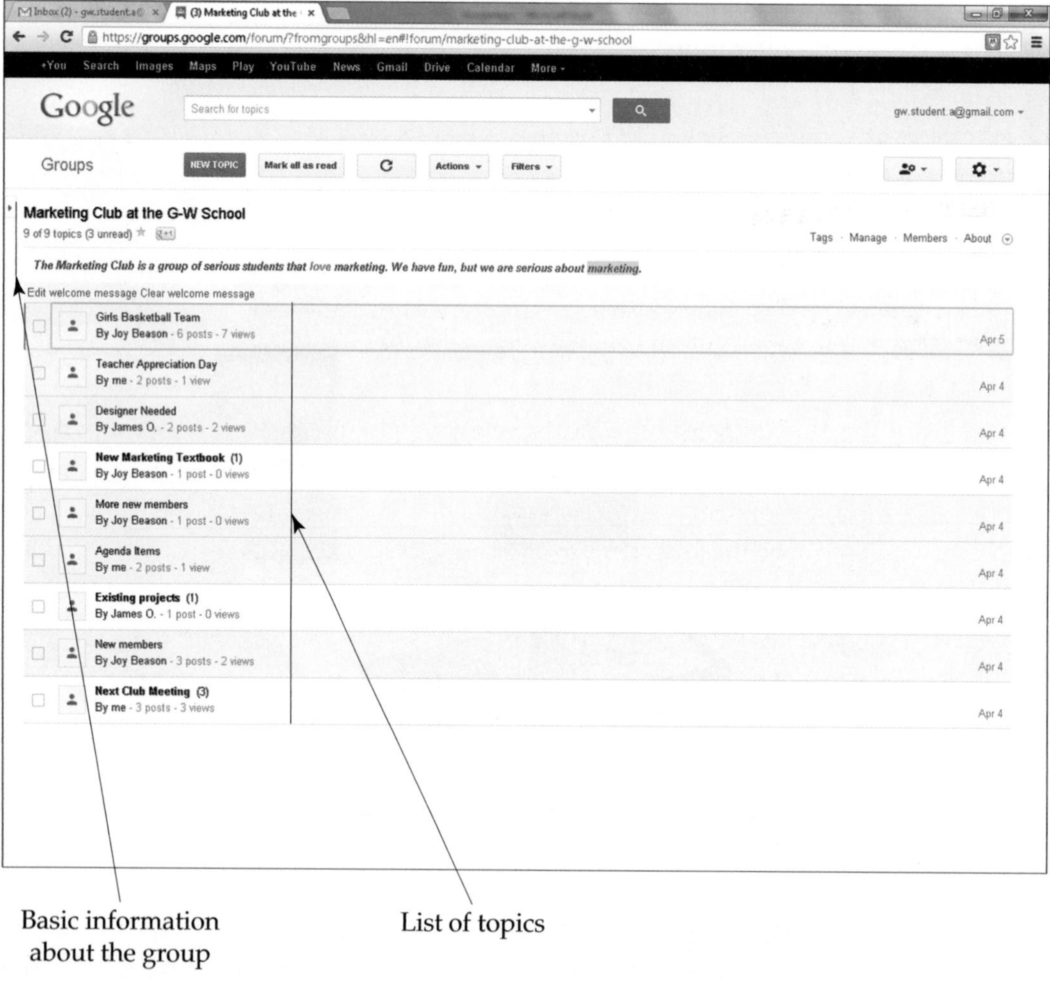

Goodheart-Willcox Publisher

Figure 7-1. The Topics page includes basic group information at the top with the list of posts organized by topic.

a group displays group information at the top with the list of topics and related posts. With an e-mail list type of group, users primarily communicate with the group via e-mail. Q&A forums allow members to post questions via the web and answers are posted via the web or e-mail. Members can identify which answers are the best and mark questions in which they are also interested.

Exploring Groups

Google has categories of groups that can be browsed. These broad categories can be further divided into more focused interests. For example, the health category is divided into several subcategories including disabilities, fitness, and child health. Each subject category is further divided by location or region. Groups based in the United States can also be associated with a specific state. Groups are further organized by the language in which the group members communicate.

Users can explore available groups. Google provides a page with a list of the broad subject categories. Users can click a category link that interests them to display the related subcategories. They can continue clicking through the categories to find groups that interest them. Users can also use the search function to find groups. Like the quick search text box on the Mail page, users can use the quick search feature at the top of the Groups page to enter text to search for groups. Group names, topics, and posts that meet the criteria will be displayed in the search results.

With either method of exploring groups, a list of groups is displayed. Listed groups often include a one- or two-sentence description of the group. Users can explore some groups further by looking at the threaded discussions shared in the group. A ***threaded discussion*** is the topic and its responses in an online group. Some groups require that users join before being able to view group discussions.

Joining, Organizing, and Participating in Groups

Once users find groups that interest them, there are different ways to join a group. The way users join a group depends on the group settings. With some groups anyone can join. In these cases, users click the **Join group** button on that specific group's page. Users are then automatically a member of that group. For other groups, users must send a request to join the group. People can choose to apply for membership to the group or contact the owner of the group to request to join. Users may also receive an invitation to join a group. The invitation will appear in the inbox as an e-mail. To join the group, users can accept the invitation within the e-mail.

Google provides tools to organize groups. A user can organize groups using the labels in the navigation panel. The default labels are **My groups**, **Home**, **Starred**, **Announcements**, **Recently viewed**, **Recent searches**, **Recently posted to**, and **Favorites**. Groups and topics are organized within the labels, as shown in **Figure 7-2**. Most labels are automatically populated based on the behavior of the user. However, the contents of the **Favorites** label and the **Starred** label are chosen by the user. A user can mark a group as a favorite and it will be displayed in the **Favorites** label. A user can create custom labels within the **Favorites** label to further organize his or her groups. The **Starred** label is for topics rather than groups. Within a group discussion, a user can mark a topic with a star. These topics will then be displayed within the **Starred** label on the Groups page.

To participate in a web or Q&A forum group, a user can create topics and post responses. The group's settings will determine whether or not members can create new topics. Creating a topic is similar to starting an e-mail message. Users create a subject line, and then can format the body text, insert images or links, and attach files to topics. Users can post a response to the topic or to posts related to the topic. In responding, users have the same formatting, inserting, and attaching tools as the user that created the topic. When a topic has not had any activity for 60 days, the option to post a reply is removed and the message is archived.

With an e-mail list group, most communication is relayed to the group members using e-mail. New topics are sent via e-mail. Group members can respond to topics by replying to the e-mail. Users can access the Topics page to see the e-mail correspondence. This is one of the characteristics of an e-mail list group that makes it different from a contact group. Contact groups are discussed in Chapter 3.

Labels	Label Contents
My groups	All groups to which the user has joined.
Starred	All topics that have been starred by the user. Users cannot star groups, only topics.
Announcements	Notices from Google to users regarding groups.
Recently viewed	Groups the user has viewed.
Recent searches	Searches conducted by the user in Groups.
Recently posted to	Groups to which the user has posted.
Favorites	Groups marked as favorites by the user.

Goodheart-Willcox Publisher

Figure 7-2. Groups and topics are organized within the default labels. Custom labels in the **Favorites** and **Starred** labels can further organize groups and topics.

Editing Membership Settings

A user can designate membership settings for each group. The membership settings allow a user to set how his or her information is seen by group members. A user can choose how his or her name will be displayed for each group. For example, for a small group of classmates, a user could choose to display just his or her first name. For a group of business contacts, the user could choose to display his or her full name.

How often a user receives e-mail updates about the group can also be decided in membership settings. There are four options. A user can receive a daily e-mail summary of group updates. He or she can choose to have up to 25 updates grouped together into a single e-mail. Receiving an update for every new topic or response post is another option. E-mailed updates can be turned off completely, as well. These settings allow a user to manage the amount of information he or she will receive for each group.

Creating Groups

A Google user can create a group to communicate with a school club or to exchange ideas on a topic of interest. For example, a user could create a group to organize the online resources for other students in the class. Before creating a Google group, it can be helpful to decide if the group will be a private or public group. A ***private group*** has its membership confined to a specific group of people. A ***public group*** does not have restrictions on its membership. Any Gmail user that finds the group can join a public group.

Setting up a Group

There are three basic roles in Google Groups. The user that creates the group is the ***group owner.*** The group owner determines if the group is private or public. An owner can delete the group, add members to the group, and define who can participate and how. The level of participation in a group is determined by the way the owner assigns the group member roles. Along with the owner, groups are comprised of managers, members, and the public. ***Group managers*** can create topics, post responses, and manage members and messages. ***Group members*** can create topics and post responses to the group. Public access can either have the ability to post responses to the group or only view threaded discussions. Even if the group is public, the group owner can add members to the group by inviting people or by adding them directly.

When a user chooses to create a group in Google Groups, basic information must be provided, as seen in **Figure 7-3**. He or she will need to enter the group name. Just like e-mail addresses, Google requires a group name to be unique. The group name is automatically used to create a group e-mail address, although the e-mail address can be changed.

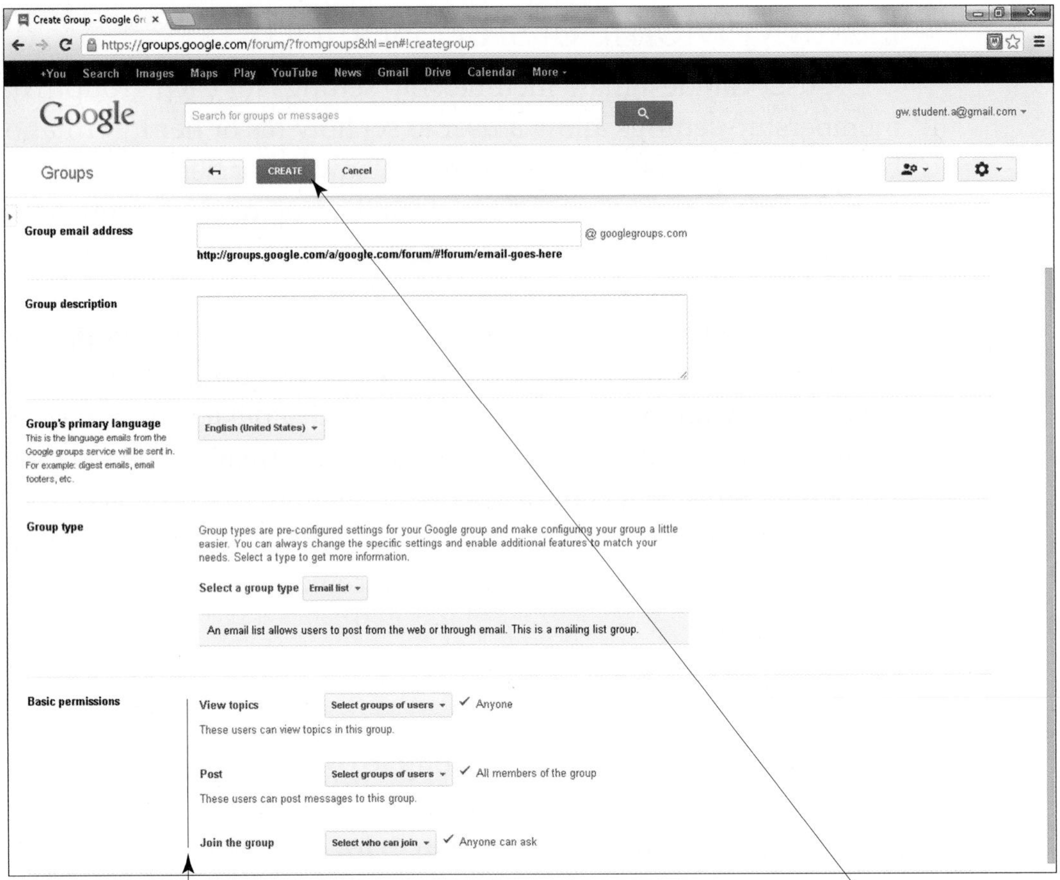

Selections in **Basic permissions** determine if the group is private or public

Click to create a new group

Goodheart-Willcox Publisher

Figure 7-3. Basic information is required when a user first creates a group in Google Groups.

The group type—web forum, e-mail list, or Q&A forum—must be selected as well. Then the group owner determines the basic permissions. These permissions determine if the group is private or public.

Managing Permissions

The basic permissions include three categories: who can view topics, who can post, and who can join the group. With regard to who can view topics, a user has four options. The owner can allow managers of the group, all members of the group, anyone, or only owners to view the group topics. The default is to allow anyone to view the topics. In determining who can post, a user has the same four options. The default here is to exclude anyone. The final basic permission to be determined is who can join the group. The group owner has three options in this category: anyone, only invited users, and anyone can ask. The third option is the default setting. To create a private group, do not select **Anyone** in any of the basic permissions categories. A group owner could select **Anyone can ask** in the **Who can join** category because the owners of the group would be required to approve any request to join.

Managing Group Membership

In addition to receiving requests to join a group, a group owner can invite or add members and change the roles of group members. The user can send invitations to people to invite them to join the group. The recipients do not need a Gmail account to join a Google Group. The e-mail invitation includes a message from the group owner and a link to click to accept the invitation. If a group owner has e-mail addresses of people that he or she knows want to be part of the group, these people can be added as members. Adding a member directly does not give them the opportunity to decline the membership. As a sresult, this feature should be used with care. The group owner can also change the roles of group members or transfer ownership to another user.

Lesson 7-1

Finding, Joining, and Organizing Groups

There are Google groups for many different interests. Users often find more than one group that matches their interests. Once joining a group, Google's organizational tools can provide users with easy access to them.

Finding a Group

1. Log in to your Google Mail account.
2. Click the **Groups** link on the bar at the top of the Mail page. Depending on which browser is being used, you may need to click the **More** link to display a drop-down menu, click **Even More** in the menu, and click the **Groups** link in the **Social** area of the new page that is displayed. See **Figure 7-4.**

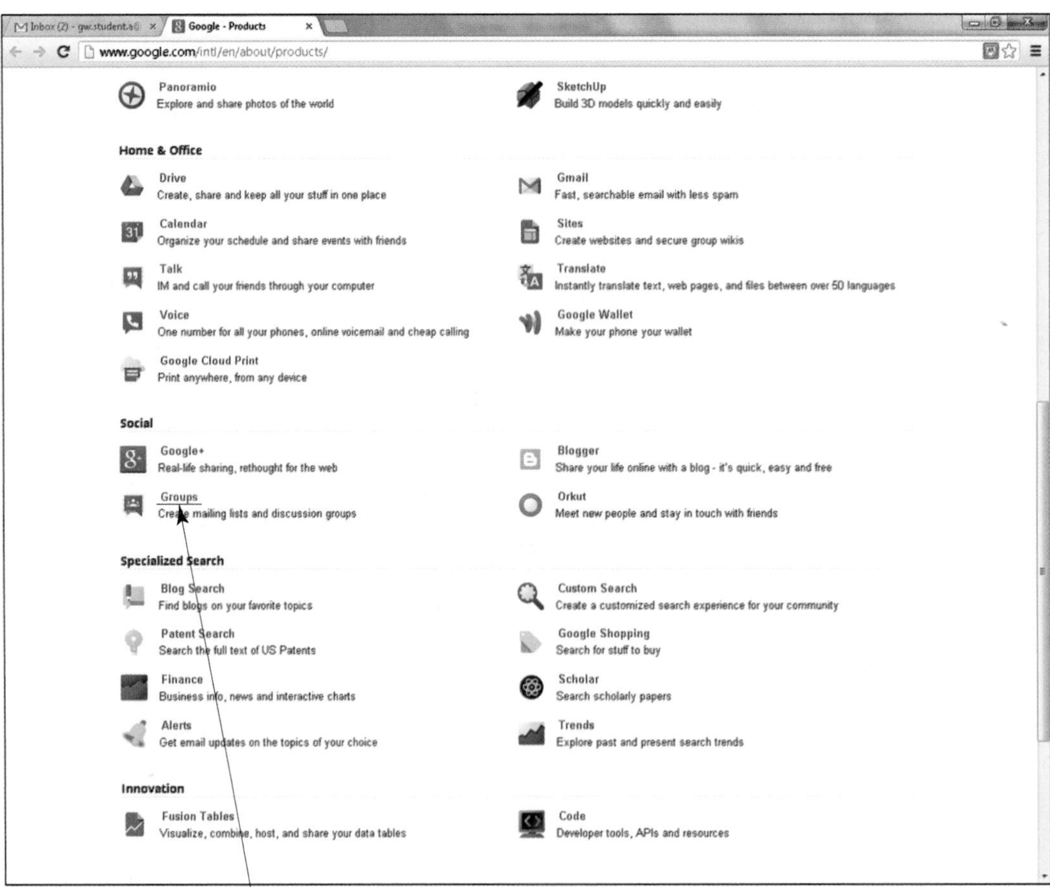

Goodheart-Willcox Publisher

Figure 7-4. To access the Google Groups page users may need to click the **More** link on the bar at the top of the Mail page.

3. On the Groups page that is displayed, click the **Browse all** link. A new page is display containing links to different categories of links.

Search

4. Click in the search box at the top of the page, enter high school biology or other search term provided by your instructor, and click the **Search** button. Google Groups matching the search criteria are displayed at the top of the page, while topics matching the search criteria are listed at the bottom of the page.
5. Below the listing of groups is the **See all** *xx* link as shown in **Figure 7-5.** The number indicates how many topics in the groups match the criteria. Click this link to display all groups containing topics matching the search criteria.

Goodheart-Willcox Publisher

Figure 7-5. The results of the quick search are divided into two sections: groups that meet the criteria at the top and topics that meet the criteria at the bottom.

Joining a Group

6. Click the name of the group to join.

7. Click the **Join group** button. A dialog box appears that contains membership information, as shown in **Figure 7-6.** The information shown here can be changed at any later time.

Tip Depending on the settings of the group, the button to click to join the group could display **Join to post to this group** or something else.

8. Click the **edit** link in the **My display name:** area, and enter your first name and last initial in the text box that is displayed.

Tip If you choose to link to your profile, other group members will be able to view your name, photo, and any other personal information you have added to your profile.

9. Click the drop-down list in the middle of the dialog box, and click **Send me an email for every new message** in the drop-down list.
10. Click the **Join this group** button to join the group.

Organizing Groups

11. Click **Groups** in the upper-left corner of the screen to display the main Groups page.
12. On the Groups page, click the triangle below the page name to display the navigation panel, as shown in **Figure 7-7.**

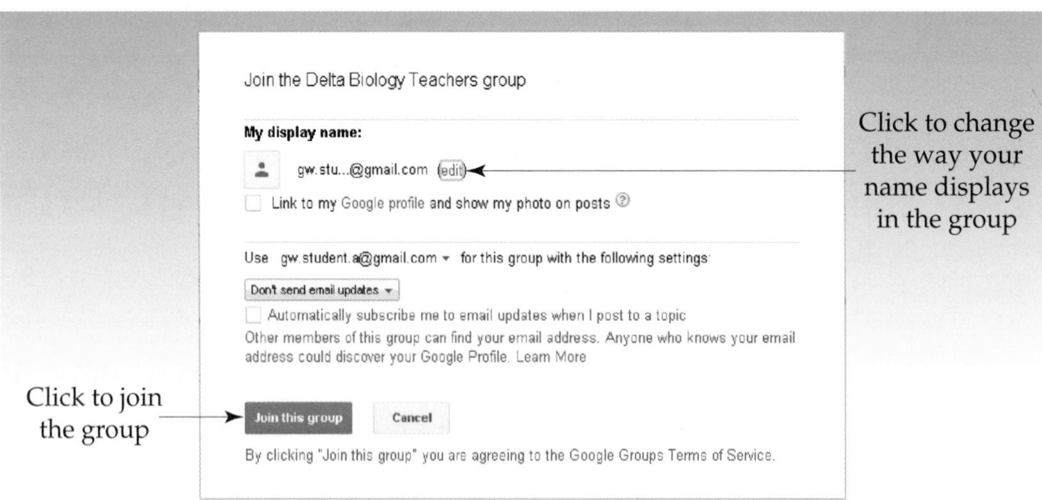

Goodheart-Willcox Publisher

Figure 7-6. The settings a user selects for this group can be different for other groups he or she joins.

Goodheart-Willcox Publisher

Figure 7-7. The labels in the navigation panel allow a user to organize his or her groups.

Tip On the **Groups** page, click the **My Groups** link to display the list of your groups.

13. Click **My groups** in the navigation panel to display a list of your groups.
14. Identify a group to add to the **Favorites** label, and click the star to the left of the group name. A message is displayed indicating the group is now in the **Favorites** label.

Tip Only *groups* appear in the **Favorites** label. Any *topics* that are starred appear under the **Starred** label. Starring a topic is useful when you need to easily access specific posts, such as this week's class discussions.

15. Hover the cursor over the **Favorites** label in the navigation panel to display a drop-down arrow. Click the arrow to display a drop-down menu.

16. Click **New Folder...** in the drop-down menu. A dialog box is displayed in which a folder name can be entered, as shown in **Figure 7-8.**
17. Click in the text box, enter School, and click the **OK** button to create the new folder (label) under the **Favorites** label.
18. Hover the cursor over a group name in the **Favorites** label to display a drop-down arrow. Click the arrow to display a drop-down menu.
19. Click the name of a folder to which to move the group, **School** in this case. The group is moved to the folder.

Tip A group can also be dragged and dropped into a folder in the navigation panel.

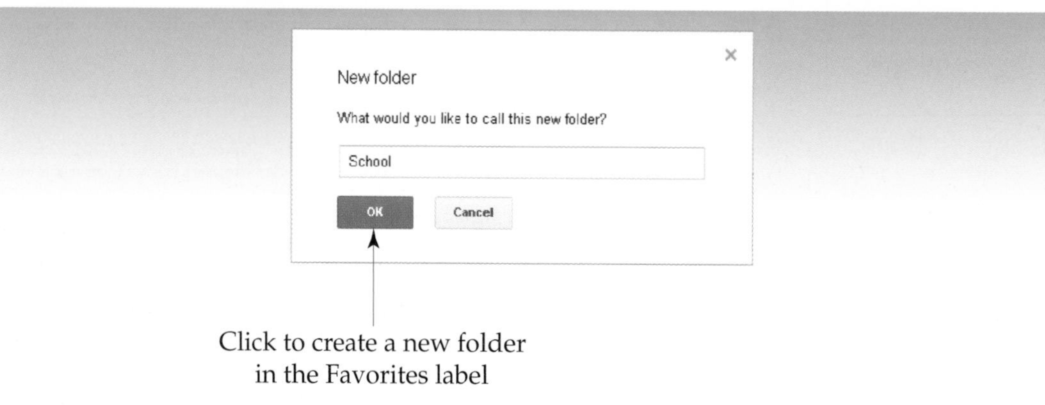

Goodheart-Willcox Publisher

Figure 7-8. Custom labels or folders can be created in the **Favorites** label to organize groups.

Lesson 7-2

Reading, Replying To, and Creating Topics

Participating in threaded discussions in a Google group is similar to writing and responding to e-mail messages. There are many of the same formatting tools available to apply to posts.

Participating on the Web

1. Log in to your Google Mail account.
2. Display the Groups page, and display the navigation panel if it is not already displayed.
3. Click the **My groups** label.
4. Click the name of the group for which you want to read or post messages. The Topics page for that group is displayed. Topics with unread messages appear in bold text and have a white background. Those with no unread messages have a gray background, as shown in **Figure 7-9.**

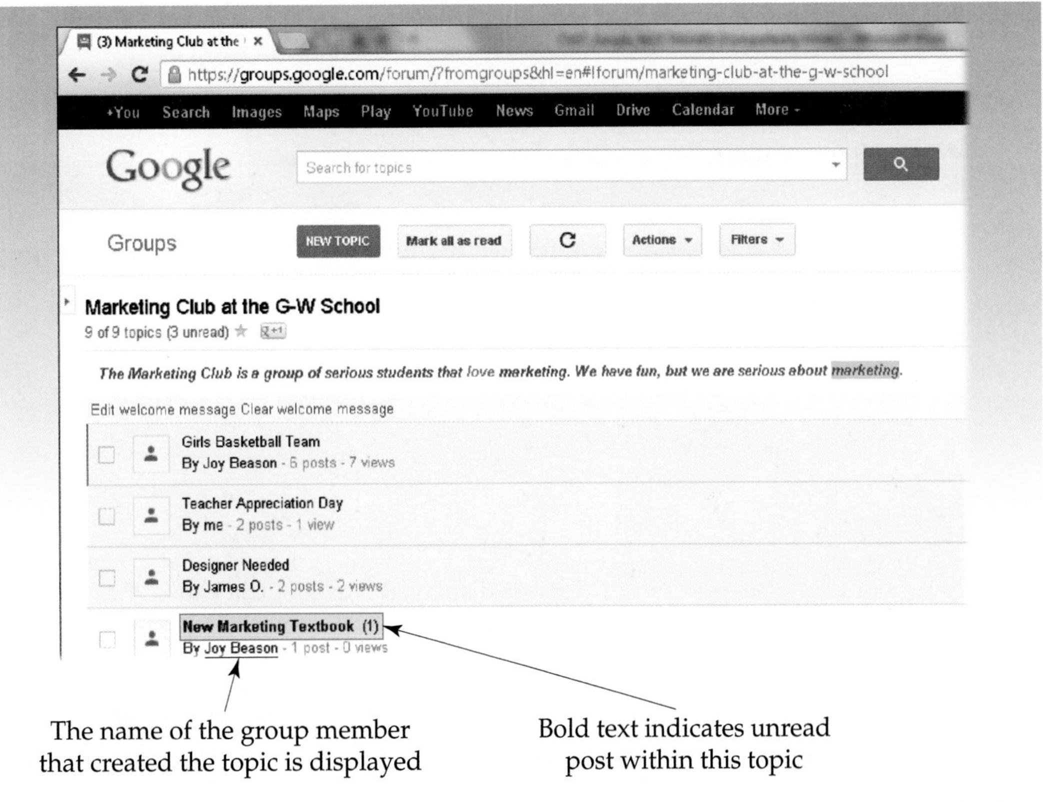

Goodheart-Willcox Publisher

Figure 7-9. Topics with unread posts appear in bold text. The number that will be displayed to the right of the topic reflects the number of unread posts.

6. Click the name of a topic to see the posts in it. The original post is displayed at the top, as shown in **Figure 7-10.**

Post Reply

7. Click the **Reply** link below the post or click the **Post Reply** button in the upper-right corner of the post. A text box is displayed with standard text-formatting tools. If the post is a reply to previous posts, quotes of all previous messages appear in the text box. The options for a reply are shown in **Figure 7-11.**
8. Enter the reply to the message in the text box.
9. Use the formatting tools to change the appearance of the response as needed.

Post

10. Click the **Post** button to complete the reply.

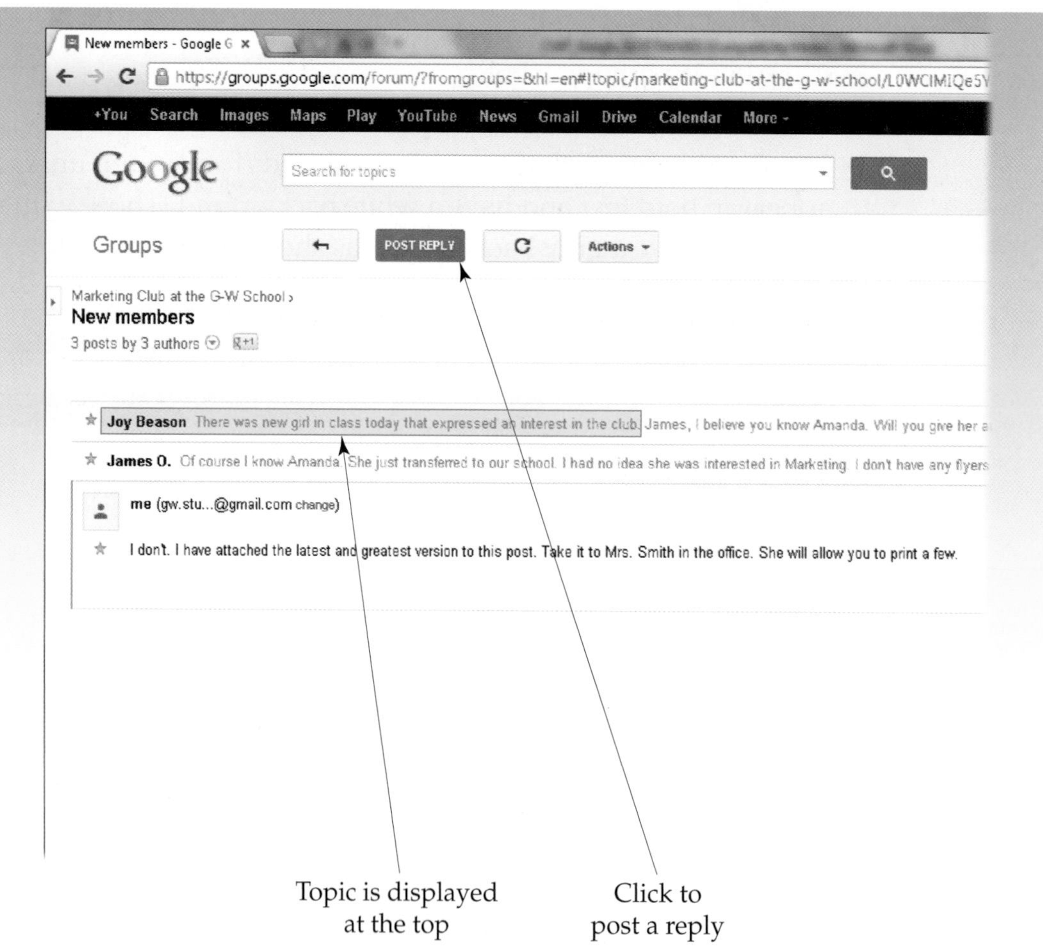

Goodheart-Willcox Publisher

Figure 7-10. The posts in response to a topic are listed beneath the topic in the order in which they were posted. The last post in the list is the most recent.

Message Options	Action
Attach a File	Allows a file 25 MB or smaller to be included in the post.
Add a Reference	Allows a web page to be included in the post. A thumbnail of the page appears in the post, and clicking the thumbnail displays the page in a new tab or window.
Edit the Subject	Allows the title of the reply to be different from the topic. The post appears in this topic, but arrives as a separate conversation in e-mail.
Quote Original	Inserts the message to which you are replying into the reply message.
Add Cc	Enter the e-mail addresses of anyone who should receive an email copy of the reply.

Goodheart-Willcox Publisher

Figure 7-11. A user can attach a file, format text, and add a reference to a post.

Participating by E-mail

11. Click the **Gmail** link at the top of the page to display the Mail page. New discussions from any groups you are subscribed to with e-mail alerts are shown in the inbox.
12. Click the discussion for a group to display the messages.
13. Read the discussion, and click the **Reply** link at the bottom of the discussion. A text box is displayed in which a reply can be entered.
14. Enter a reply to the message in the text box.

Send

15. Click the **Send** button to post the reply to the group. A new e-mail from the group also appears in the inbox.

Managing Posts

16. Display the Groups page, and display the navigation panel if it is not already displayed.
17. Click **My groups** to display the groups to which you are subscribed.
18. Click a group to display the topics it contains.
19. Click a topic name to display the posts it contains.
20. Click the star next to a post. The post now appears under the **Starred** label in the navigation panel.
21. Click on a post that you submitted. A thin blue bar appears on the left of the post to indicate it is selected.

22. Click the drop-down arrow next to the **Post Reply** button in the message to display a drop-down menu, as shown in **Figure 7-12.**
23. Click **Delete Post** in the drop-down menu. The message is removed, and a notification bar is displayed in its place to let members know a message has been removed.

Creating a New Topic

24. Display the Groups page, and display the navigation panel if it is not already displayed.
25. Click **My groups** to display the groups to which you are a member.
26. Click the name of a group to which you want to add a new topic. The topics in the group are displayed.

NEW TOPIC

27. Click the **New Topic** button. A new page is displayed on which a new topic can be created, as shown in **Figure 7-13.**

Depending on a group's settings, a new topic can also be created directly from e-mail by sending an e-mail to the group's e-mail address.

28. Click in the **Subject** text box, and enter the title of the topic.
29. Click in the main text box, and enter the message.
30. Use the formatting tools to adjust the appearance of the message text as needed.

Post

31. Click the **Post** button.

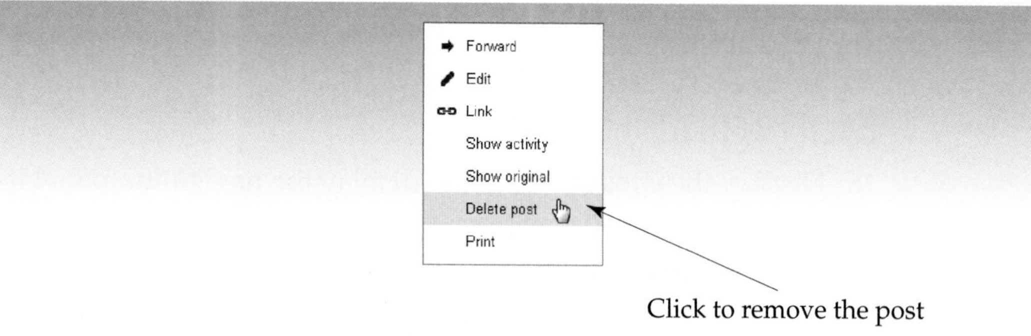

Goodheart-Willcox Publisher

Figure 7-12. When a user deletes a post, a gray bar with the text This message has been deleted will be displayed within the detail page for the topic.

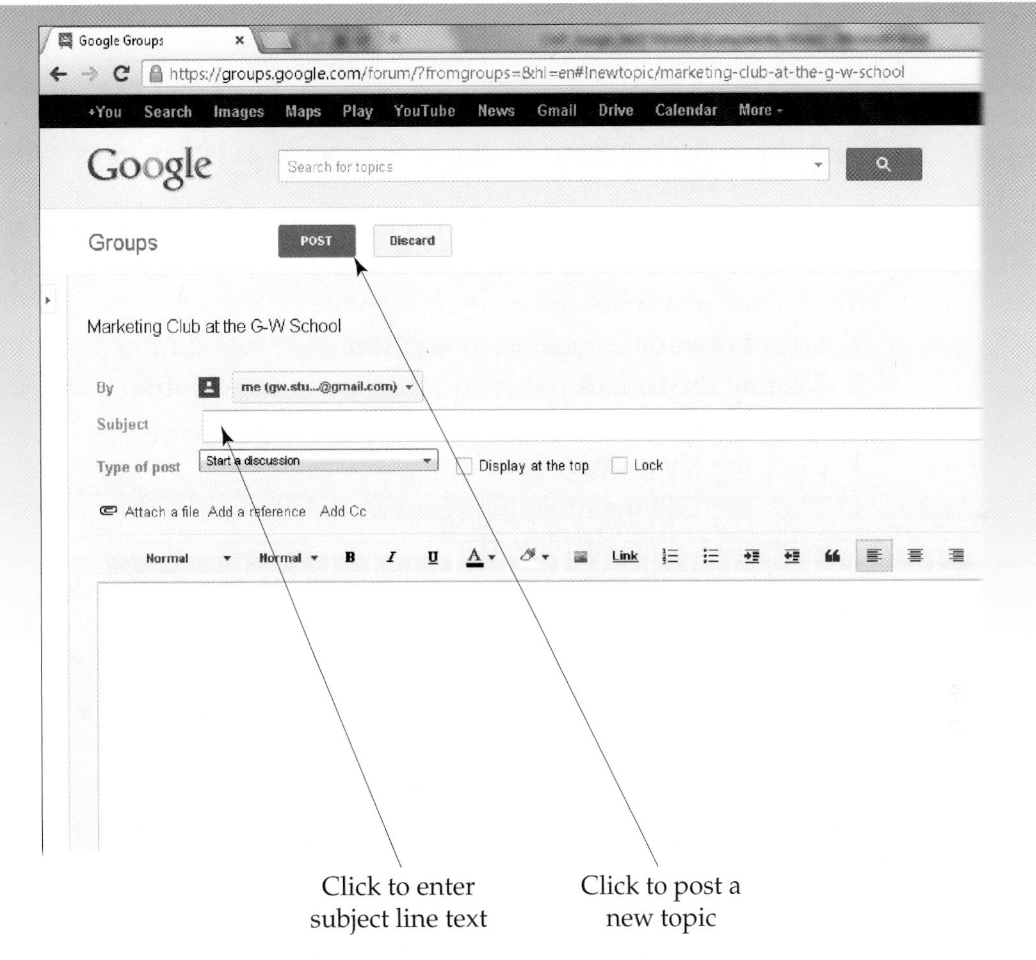

Goodheart-Willcox Publisher

Figure 7-13. Topics are created to initiate a new threaded discussion within the group.

Lesson 7-3

Editing Membership Settings

In addition to setting the way a user's name will appear in the group, a user can control how many updates he or she will receive regarding the group. Group updates are sent via e-mail.

1. Log in to your Google Mail account.
2. Display the Groups page, and display the navigation panel if it is not already displayed.
3. Click the **My groups** label.

Edit memberships

4. Click the **Edit memberships** button. A list of all of the groups you are subscribed to is displayed.
5. Click on the drop-down menu to the right of a group name, as shown in **Figure 7-14.** Change the e-mail subscription settings according to one of the options described in **Figure 7-15.**
6. Click the **Back to My Groups** link or click the **My groups** label to return to the list of groups to which you are subscribed.
7. Click the name of a group to which you want to unsubscribe.

My settings

8. Click the **My settings** button to display a drop-down list.
9. Click **Leave Group** in the drop-down menu. A dialog box appears asking you to confirm leaving the group.
10. Click the **Leave Group** button to unsubscribe from the group.

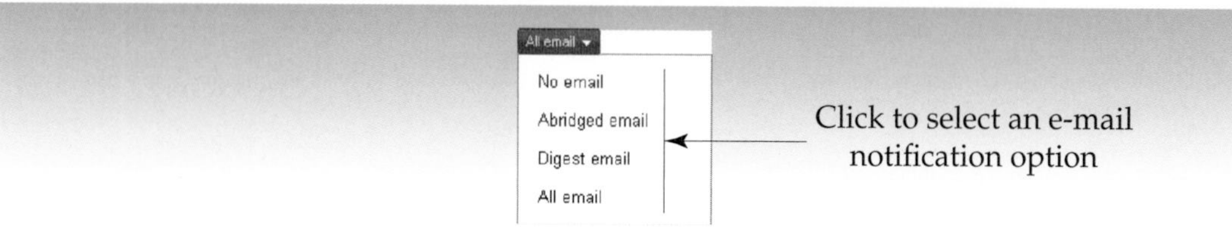

Goodheart-Willcox Publisher

Figure 7-14. In membership settings a user can choose how frequently he or she is notified with group updates.

Setting	Meaning
No Email	No e-mail notifications of new posts are sent.
Abridged Email	A daily summary of posts is sent by e-mail.
Digest Email	Updates are combined and sent by e-mail, up to 25 messages per e-mail.
All Email	An e-mail is sent for each new message.

Goodheart-Willcox Publisher

Figure 7-15. Being a member of an active group can result in receiving many e-mail messages. Membership settings can be decided based on how active a group is and how often the member needs updates.

Lesson 7-4

Creating a Group

While there are many Google groups, often a user will find the need to create a new group. A user can create a private group to address a topic with a specific group of people. Public groups can also be created to exchange ideas or information on a topic with a potentially large group of people.

Creating a Group

1. Log in to your Google Mail account.
2. Access Google Groups

CREATE GROUP

3. Click the **Create Group** button. A new page is displayed for creating the group, as shown in **Figure 7-16.**

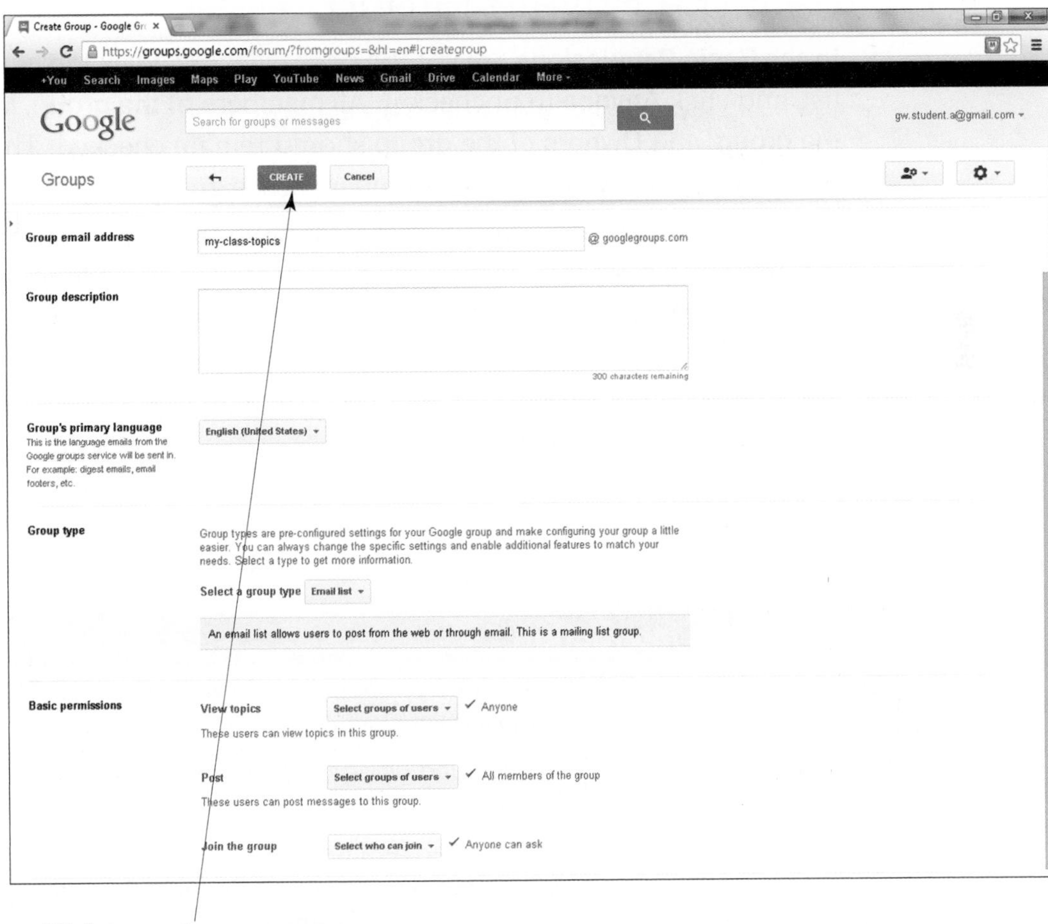

Goodheart-Willcox Publisher

Figure 7-16. Proper planning before creating a group should include deciding if the group will be a private group or a public group.

4. Click in the **Group Name** text box and enter the name of the group. This is how others will identify the group in search results.
5. By default the e-mail address for the group is the group name with hyphens in place of spaces. To change the e-mail address, click in the **Group email address** text box, and edit the default address as needed. For example, you may want to remove any unnecessary dashes. The e-mail address will always end with @googlegroups.com.
6. Click in the **Group description** text box, and enter a brief overview of the group. This should provide some basic information about the group in 300 characters or less.
7. Click the **Group's primary language** drop-down list and choose the language in which e-mails from the group will be sent.
8. In the **Group type** area of the page, click the **Select a group type** drop-down list. The three options are outlined in **Figure 7-17.** For this lesson, click **Web forum** in the drop-down list.

Creating a Private Group

9. In the **Basic Permissions** area of the page, click the **View topics** drop-down list, and click **Anyone** to uncheck it. **All members of the group**, **Managers of the group**, and **Owners of the group** should remain checked. This specifies that posts can only be read by members of the group.
10. Click the **Post** drop-down list, and click **Anyone** to uncheck it. **Owners of the group**, **All members of the group**, and **Managers of the group** should remain checked. This specifies that only members of the group can post messages.
11. Click the **Join the group** drop-down list, and click **Anyone can ask** to check it. This specifies that anybody can request to be a member of the group, but the request must be approved by the owner or the manager of the group. The settings in steps 8–10 create a private group.

Group type	Interaction
Email list	Posts can be added either using the web or e-mail. The group is bascially a mailing list.
Web forum	Posts must be added using the web. Users can receive e-mail updates of posts.
Q & A forum	Questions are posted and responses are added as answers. Answers can be rated by users. Posts must be added using the web, but users can receive e-mail updates.

Goodheart-Willcox Publisher

Figure 7-17. All group types allow members to discuss or share information about a common interest.

12. Click the **Create** button to create the group.
13. Click **Groups** in the upper-left corner of the page to return to the Groups page.

Adding a Welcome Message

14. On the Groups page, click the triangle below the name to display the navigation panel.
15. Click **My groups** in the navigation panel to display a list of your groups.
16. Click the name of the group you created in the Create a Private Group section. A new page is displayed on which details for the group can be changed.
17. Click the **Add welcome message** link for the group. A large text box is displayed with formatting tools.
18. Click in the text box, and enter Welcome to *your group's name*! Here we can discuss our project.

19. Click the **Insert Image** button on the formatting toolbar for the text box. The **Select a File** dialog box is displayed, as shown in **Figure 7-18.**

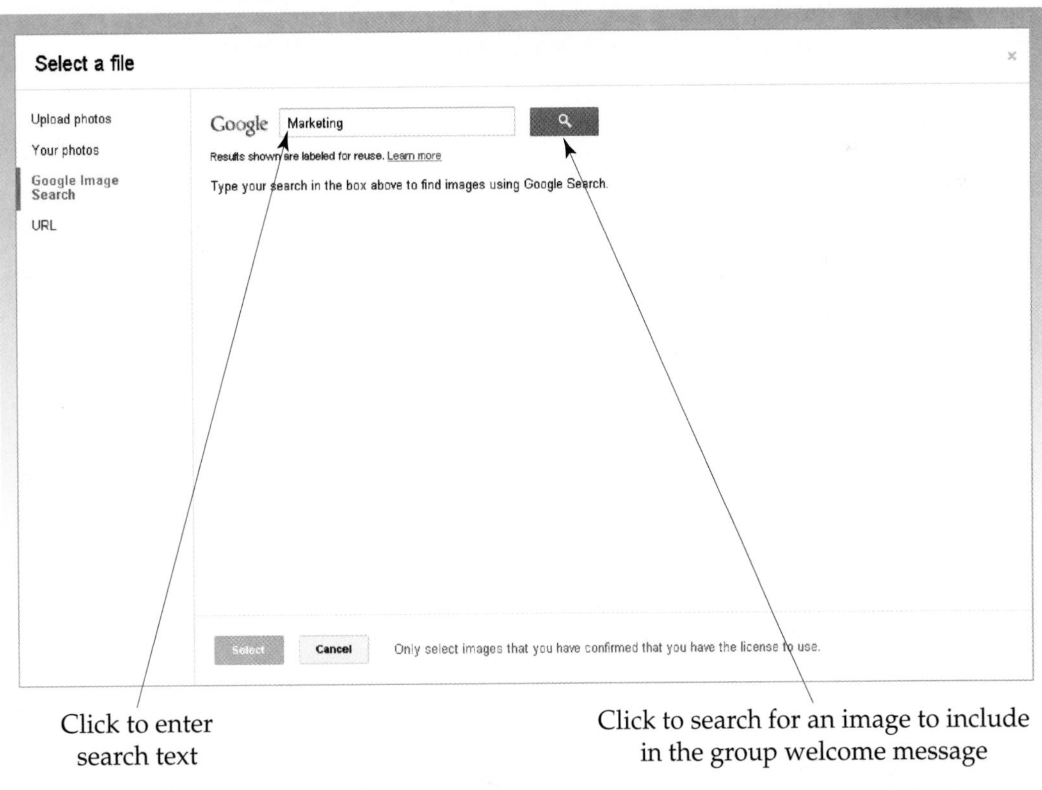

Goodheart-Willcox Publisher

Figure 7-18. A user can search for an image file to include in his or her group welcome message in one of four places: uploaded photos, the user's photos, Google Images, and on the web.

20. Click the **Google Image Search** link.

21. Click in the search text box, enter a word related to the group topic, and click the **Search** button to locate images.
22. Click on an appropriate image, then click the **Select** button to insert the image into the welcome message.
23. Click the **Save** button below the text box to save the welcome message.
24. Click **Groups** in the upper-left corner of the page to return to the Groups page.

Managing Group Settings

25. Click **My groups** in the navigation panel to display a list of your groups.
26. Click the name of the group to manage.
27. Click the **Manage** link in the upper-right corner. A list of group members and their roles is displayed, as shown in **Figure 7-19.**

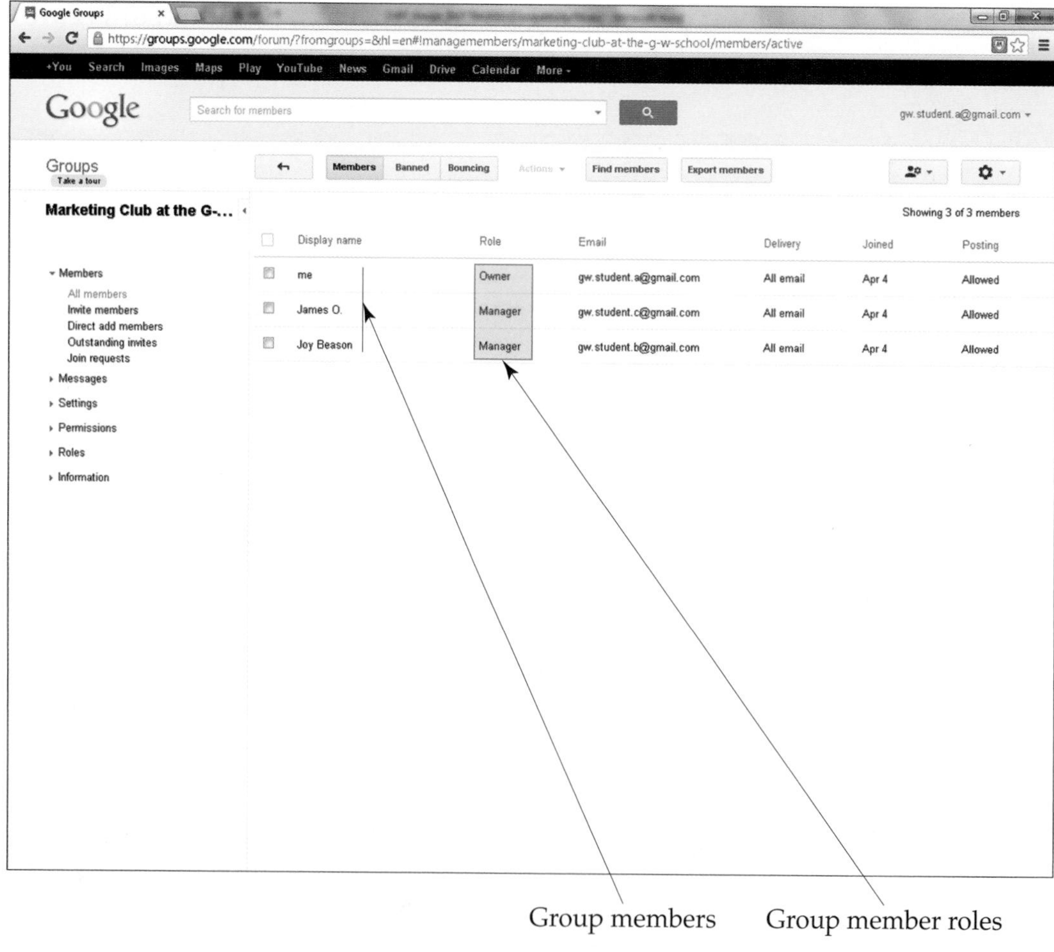

Goodheart-Willcox Publisher

Figure 7-19. A group owner can change the roles of group members from the Manage page.

If nobody has yet joined the group, only the owner of the group is displayed. Also notice the navigation panel on the left displays options for managing the group, which are described in **Figure 7-20.**

Inviting Members

28. Click **Members** in the navigation panel to expand that list.
29. Click **Invite member** in the navigation panel. A page is displayed on which to enter the e-mail address of a person to invite to the group.

If any invitations have already been sent, click the **Invite more** button at the top of the new page.

30. Click in the **Enter email addresses of people to invite** text box, and enter the e-mail address of at least two classmates.
31. Click in the **Write an invitation message** text box, and enter Please join our class discussion group.

Send invites

32. Click the **Send invites** button to e-mail the invitations.
33. If a verification screen appears, enter the requested information and click the **Continue** button.

Adding Members

34. Click **Members** in the navigation panel if needed to expand that list.
35. Click **Direct Add Members** in the navigation panel. A page is displayed on which to enter the e-mail address of a specific person to add to the group.

Option	Description
Members	Manage who is a member of the group by inviting people to join, directly adding new members, or approving requests for membership.
Messages	Approve or reject moderated messages.
Settings	Set e-mail options, which categories are moderated, limits on the number of new members, allow tagging of messages, and require messages to have a category.
Permissions	Set group-wide permissions related to content and types of messages, who can perform specific actions on messages, and what type of member information is visible to other members.
Roles	Modify what specific owners, managers, and members can do.
Information	Edit the general information about the group, subscribe the group to other groups, set archive options, and disable or delete the group.

Goodheart-Willcox Publisher

Figure 7-20. There are several management options for users occupying the owner or manager role in a Google group.

36. Click in the **Enter email addresses to add as members** text box, and enter the e-mail address of a classmate.
37. Note that the welcome message defaults to the one previously used. To change the message, click in the **Write a welcome message** text box, and enter a new message.
38. In the **Email subscription options** area, click the radio button corresponding to how the new member will receive messages. The new members can change this later by modifying his or her personal settings.
39. Click the **Add** button to add the new member.

Modifying Roles

40. Click **Members** in the navigation panel if needed to expand that list.
41. Click **All members** in the navigation panel. A list of approved members is displayed. In this case, these should be your classmates.
42. Check the check box to the left of the name of one of your classmates.
43. Click the **Actions** button to display a drop-down menu, as shown in **Figure 7-21.**
44. Click **Add to role** in the drop-down menu, and then click **Manager** in the cascading menu. This sets the member as a manager of the group, and he or she can perform all managerial tasks.

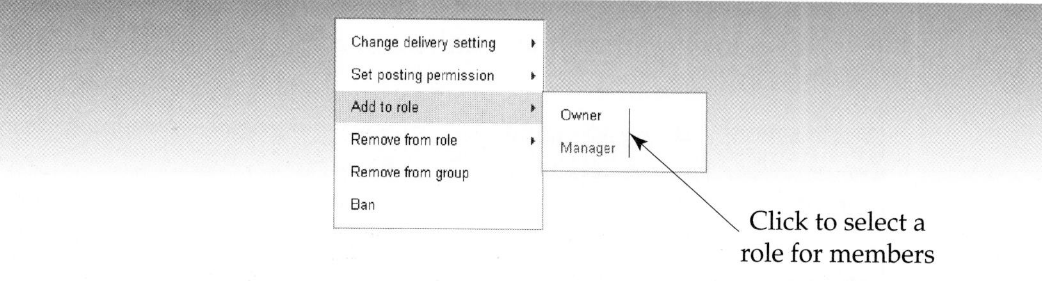

Goodheart-Willcox Publisher

Figure 7-21. Owners and managers can modify the roles of group members.

Check Your Google Apps IQ

Now that you have finished this chapter, see what you know about Google Apps by taking the chapter posttest.
www.m.g-wlearning.com
www.g-wlearning.com/informationtechnology/

Skills Review

Answer the following questions on a separate sheet of paper.

1. What is a topic in a group?
2. ______ is a group type in which users post from e-mail primarily, but also on the web.
3. Define threaded discussion.
4. What is the purpose of the **Favorites** label for groups?
5. What determines if and how you can join a group?
6. Briefly describe the difference between a public and a private group.
7. What is the user who created a group called?
8. List the three main roles in a group.
9. A group contains a list of ______.
10. Topics are comprised of multiple ______.

Lesson Application

These exercises are designed to apply the skills learned in this and previous chapters. General directions are provided, but you will need to draw on your knowledge to determine how to complete each exercise.

Exercise 7-1
Creating a Group

Create a group with a name of your choice or as specified by your instructor. Make the group private. Invite your instructor and at least four classmates to the group. Post a topic in the group to initiate a discussion on what the group should be about. Participate in the discussion, and then choose an image for the group and add it.

Exercise 7-2
Managing a Group

Join at least three other groups created by classmates in Exercise 7-1. Participate in the discussions started on those pages. Add two of the groups to your **Favorites** label. Star at least six topics within your classmates' groups and your own group. Send an e-mail to your instructor indicating which groups you joined, which groups you added to your **Favorites** label, and which topics you added to your **Starred** label.

Unit 2 Review

Scenario

You have been asked to plan the senior prom for Wilkins High School. You need to get input from colleagues as you plan this event. Use the information learned in this unit to complete the activities. As much as possible, these activities should be completed without referring to the chapters for information.

Activities

1. Invite two classmates to a group chat to discuss the music for the upcoming prom. Change your chat status to a busy custom message that reflects you are working on the senior prom. After concluding the chat, e-mail the chat history to your instructor.
2. Invite one classmate to a voice or video chat to discuss possible committees needed to plan the prom. Agree on which person will record the ideas, and that person should e-mail the list to the other person. After the chat, set your classmate's name to always be visible on your chat list.
3. Create a planning meeting on the calendar that repeats every Thursday afternoon in March. Include the time, location, a description, and an e-mail reminder. Choose and assign an event color for the meeting. Invite two classmates to the meeting, making one of them optional.
4. Create a calendar titled Wilkins School Events to be used by the students in the school. Make the calendar public so everyone can view it, and assign a color to the calendar. Add an event on this calendar that shows the date the prom money is due. Share the link to the calendar with your instructor.
5. Locate the Google group specified by your instructor. Create a topic with Possible Prom Themes—*YourName* as the subject. Enter an appropriate message, such as Suggest a possible theme and explain why you think the students will like the theme. Wait for classmates to post messages, and reply to two classmates' posts.

Unit 3

Google Drive Apps

Google Drive Apps include several online apps that can be created, edited, and stored online in Google Drive. As a result, files can be accessible via any computer, web browser, or web-enabled device, such as a mobile phone or tablet computer. These apps include a word processing tool, a spreadsheet tool, a presentation tool, a form creation tool, and a drawing tool. Files created using these tools can be shared with other users. Once shared, users can collaborate on the development of documents. Google Drive Apps allows users to view the same file simultaneously and make changes to it in real time. In addition to sharing, users can publish files to make them available to anyone via a unique web address. Then, when changes are made to published work, they are automatically updated; there is no need to republish.

Chapters

Chapter 8

Google Drive List

Objectives

After completing this chapter, you will be able to:

- **Create** a folder in Google Drive.
- **Share** a Google Drive folder.
- **Upload** files to Google Drive.
- **Search** for items in Google Drive.

alexmillos/Shutterstock.com

Check Your Google Apps IQ

Before you begin this chapter, see what you already know about Google Apps by taking the chapter pretest.

www.m.g-wlearning.com
www.g-wlearning.com/informationtechnology/

Using Google Drive

Google Drive is a cloud-based service used to store files. A ***cloud*** is a web-based location where a user can store files and create folders that can be accessed from anywhere with an Internet connection. Google Drive stores Google Docs, Google Sheets, Google Slides, Google Forms, and Google Drawings files as well as non-Google files the user uploads. Non-Google files that can be uploaded to Google Drive include, but are not limited to, the following.

- Microsoft Word files
- Microsoft PowerPoint files
- Microsoft Excel files
- PDF documents
- video files
- image files
- audio files

Files stored on Google Drive can be accessed through a web browser, an app on a mobile device, or through an application on a computer. A Gmail user can access Google Drive from a web browser, and they can log into Drive directly. The Google Drive app is available for many mobile devices. A Google Drive application can be downloaded and installed on a computer. The user can drag and drop files into the application to copy them to his or her Google Drive. The files are then synchronized across devices and available in the user's **My Drive**.

Navigating Google Drive

To access Google Drive, a user clicks on the **Drive** link along the top of the Gmail window. The Drive page is displayed on a separate tab or in a separate window, depending on the browser settings. The Drive page allows users to easily navigate to stored files and folders. The label list on the left side of the window includes default labels that store files, as shown in **Figure 8-1.**

The files and folders stored in Google Drive are displayed in the main area of the Drive page. The label selected in the label list determines what is displayed in the main area. Files are displayed in one of two ways: list view or grid view. The list view provides users with a listing of each file and folder with information about each. Each entry begins with an icon that indicates the file type or if the entry is a folder followed by the name of the file, the owner of the file, and the date the file was last changed. The grid view provides users with a visual representation of each file. In some cases, a preview of the file is provided in the grid view.

Label	Contents
My Drive	Files and folders created or uploaded by the user.
Shared with Me	Files and folders that have been specifically shared with the user, as well as shared items manually added to **My Drive**; does not include files shared publicly.
Starred	Files and folders starred as important.
Recent	All files created, uploaded, or shared that have been opened recently; folders are not included in this label.
Activity	All files that have been edited recently by the user or, for shared documents, collaborators.
All items	All files in the Google Drive.
Trash	Items that have been moved to the trash.

Goodheart-Willcox Publisher

Figure 8-1. The label list includes several default labels to provide users with easy access to categories of files.

Users can open, share, organize, remove, and preview files from Google Drive. To select a file or folder, users must check the check box to the left of the entry. Once a file or folder is selected, buttons are displayed along the top of the Drive page. To take action on the selected file or folder, users can make the appropriate selection from the buttons or the drop-down list that is displayed when the **More** button is clicked.

Creating and Sharing Folders

In addition to using the default labels, a user can organize his or her files by creating folders in Google Drive. ***Folders*** are virtual containers that can hold files or subfolders. ***Subfolders*** are folders created within a parent folder. Most labels are automatically populated based on the behavior of the user. Folders can be created, named, and the contents determined by the user. For example, a user can create a folder for each of his or her classes and store the assignments for each class in the appropriate folder.

Unlike files, folders are displayed in the label list under the **My Drive** label, as seen in **Figure 8-2.** Unlike labels, folders are visible in the main part of the Drive window among the files in the list or grid view. Many of the actions a user can take on a file can be applied to a folder.

A user can also create folders to share a group of documents with other Gmail users. Created folders can be set up to be shared. A ***shared folder*** is a folder that has been set up so other users can access it and its contents. When a user chooses to share a folder, he or she determines the visibility and the level of access of the folder. When a user shares a folder in Google Drive, all of the files added to the folder carry the same visibility and access settings

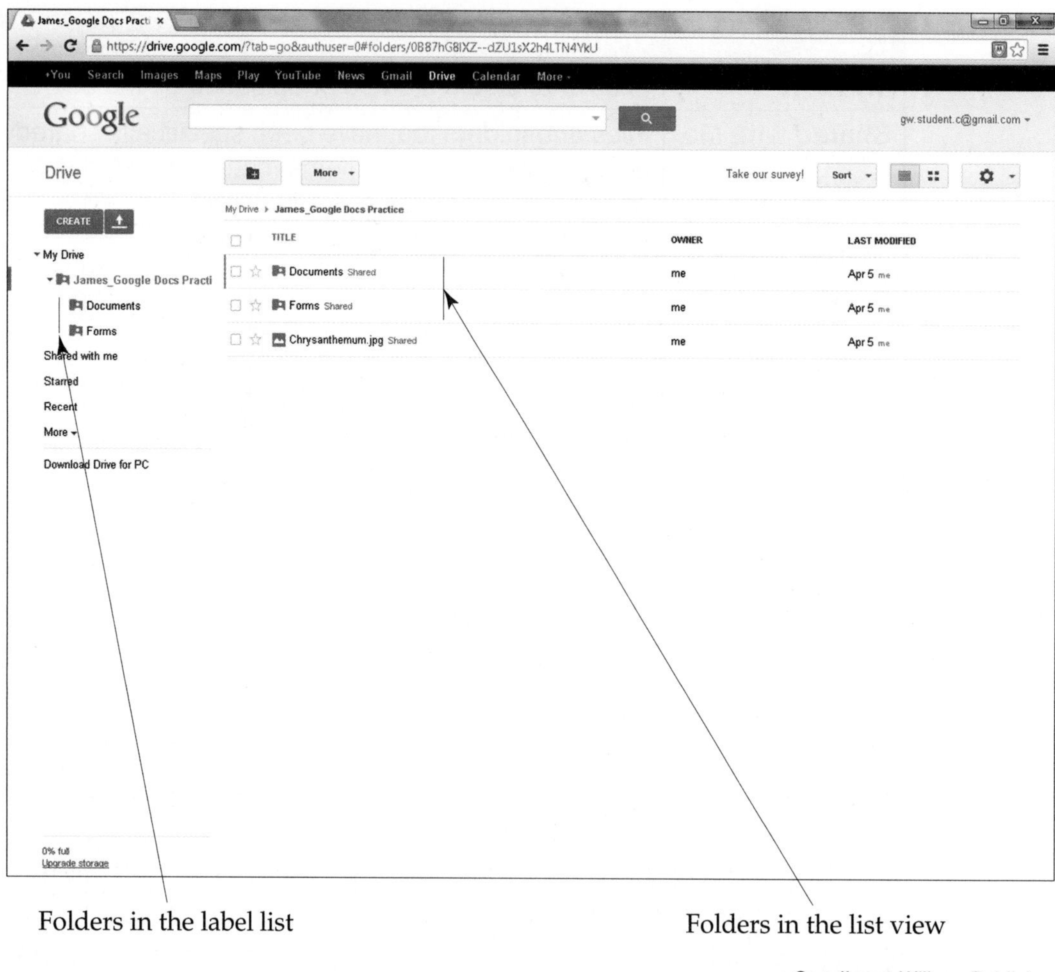

Goodheart-Willcox Publisher

Figure 8-2. Folders can be displayed in the Google Drive list or the label list. Files can be dragged and dropped into folders.

as the folder itself. When a user shares a folder, the folder icon includes the silhouette of a person. When a folder has been shared with a user, it is displayed in the **Shared with Me** label.

With regard to visibility, options may include: public, anyone with the link, and private. When a user selects **Public**, all of the documents in that folder can appear in anybody's Google search results. This is best for documents that should be easily found or widely accessible. To access folders and files set to **Anyone with the link** visibility, users must have the direct link. These documents will not appear in Google search results. This setting is best for documents which should not be open to everyone, but need to be open to a large group. The **Private** setting is the default and allows the folder or file owner to share the document with specific people. This setting is best for personal documents or for collaborating with a few other people.

A user can choose between four types of access when sharing a folder or files. By default, the creator of the document or the user that uploads the document is the owner. The document ***owner*** is the user that can delete a document for all collaborators. An owner can transfer ownership to another user. There may be only one owner for each document. When a user selects the **Can edit** access level, he or she allows another user to add or edit the content of the file. This edit level also allows people to use the comment feature within the file. Those with the edit access level can also share the folder or files with other users. With the **Can comment** access level, people can only comment on the file. People can view, but not modify or comment on the file, when they are assigned the **Can view** access level.

Searching for Files and Folders

As users create more documents, they will need a way to easily find files and folders. Google Drive provides a quick search box and an advanced search option. The quick search box can be used to easily locate a file or folder by entering a name or phrase for the item. For a more advanced search, search filters can help narrow the results and quickly find the item. A ***search filter*** contains criteria defined by the user that limits search results to only those matching the specifications. Filters can be set for the file type, the level of visibility assigned to a document, or the ownership. Users can also combine filters for a narrower search. Using search operators is another way to find files. See **Figure 8-3** for common Google Drive search operators.

Search Operator	How It Works
"" (quotation marks)	Use around a phrase to identify documents that contain that exact phrase.
or	Use between two words when a document may contain one of the two words.
before: *YYYY-MM-DD* after: *YYYY-MM-DD*	Use these operators to identify documents that were edited before or after a certain time. Only one of these operators, either the before or the after operator, can be used when searching.
to: *e-mail address* from: *e-mail address*	Use this to search for documents shared with or from someone. An e-mail address must be added after the colon.

Goodheart-Willcox Publisher

Figure 8-3. Using search operators can help people focus their search based on their knowledge of the file or folder for which they seek.

Lesson 8-1

Creating a Folder

Folders can help a user organize his or her files stored in Google Drive. Also, subfolders can be created as needed. Created and uploaded files can be moved into folders and subfolders.

Creating a Folder

1. Log in to your Google Mail account.
2. Click the **Drive** link in the menu bar at the top of the page. A new browser window or tab is opened with the Drive page displayed.

CREATE

3. Click the **Create** button to display a drop-down menu, as shown in **Figure 8-4.**
4. Click **Folder** in the drop-down menu. A dialog box is displayed in which a folder name is entered.

Tip A new folder can also be created within the current folder using the **New Folder in** *folder name* button at the top of the **Drive** page.

5. Click in the text box in the dialog box, and enter *Your Name*_Google Docs Practice.
6. Click the **Create** button to add the folder to your Google Drive. The folder appears under the **My Drive** label.

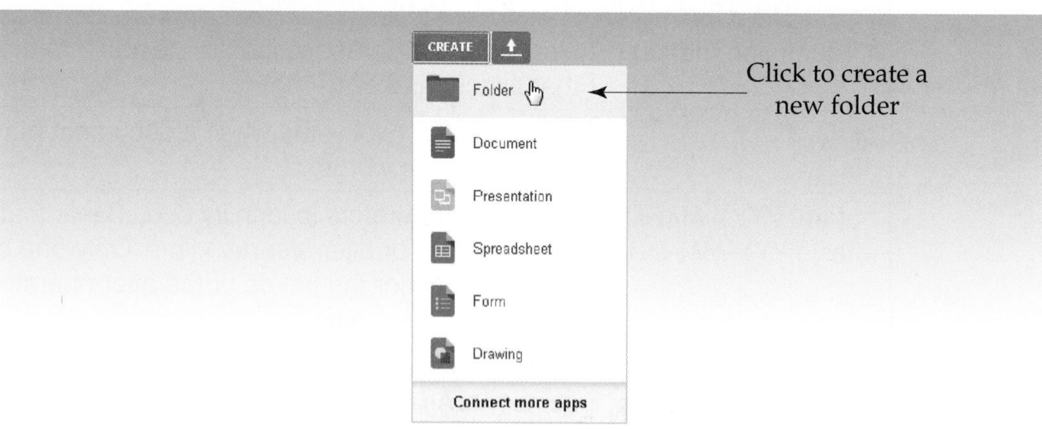

Goodheart-Willcox Publisher

Figure 8-4. New folders can be created using the **Create** button or the **New Folder in** *folder name* button.

Creating a Subfolder

7. Click the arrow to the left of the **My Drive** label if needed to expand the list of your folders.
8. Click the name of the folder to which the subfolder will be added, in this case *Your Name_***Google Docs Practice**.

New Folder In

9. Click the **New Folder In** button at the top of the page.
10. In the **New Folder** dialog box, enter Documents in the text box and click the **Create** button.
11. Add a second subfolder to *Your Name_***Google Docs Practice** named Forms.

Lesson 8-2

Sharing a Folder

Sharing a folder allows users to easily share all of the files within the folder without having to share each file individually. The permissions assigned to a folder are automatically transferred to any file or subfolder in the folder.

Sharing a Folder

1. Log in to your Google Mail account.
2. Click the **Drive** link in the menu bar at the top of the page to display the Drive page.
3. Check the check box next to the folder to share, in this case the *Your Name*_**Google Docs Practice** folder. Additional buttons appear at the top of the page.
4. Click the **Share** button. The **Sharing Settings** dialog box is displayed in which settings for sharing the folder are made, as shown in **Figure 8-5.**

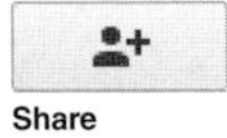

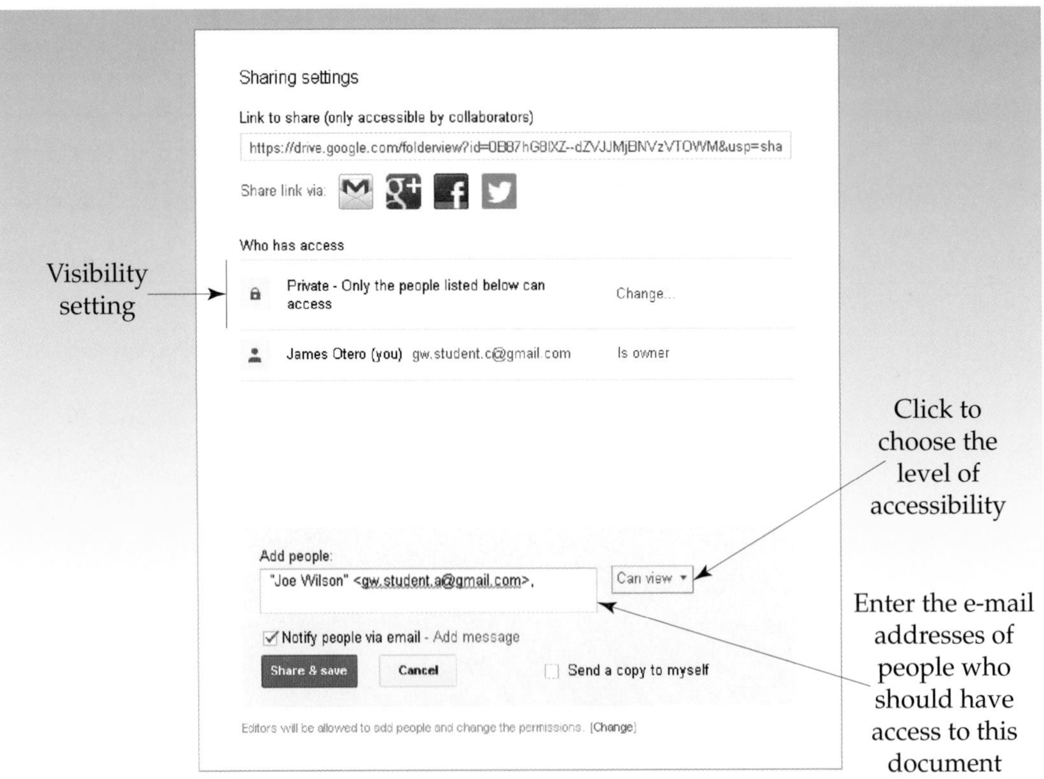

Goodheart-Willcox Publisher

Figure 8-5. By default, files within a shared folder inherit the visibility and access settings are determined by the folder's properties.

Setting Sharing Permissions

5. Click in the **Add people:** text box at the bottom of the dialog box. The lower area of the dialog box expands with additional options, as shown in **Figure 8-5.**
6. Enter the e-mail address of a classmate as assigned by your instructor in the text box.
7. Click the drop-down list next to the text box, and click **Can view** in the list. This specifies that the person can see the folder, but cannot edit or delete content.
8. Click the **Add message** link below the text box. An additional text box is displayed in which a message can be entered.
9. Click in the new text box, and enter This is *Your Name*'s folder for the Google Docs unit.
10. Check the **Send a copy to myself** check box at the bottom of the dialog box.
11. Click the **Share & Save** button to share the folder with the person. The name of the person is now listed in the **Sharing Settings** dialog box.
12. Click in the **Add people:** text box again, and enter your instructor's e-mail address.
13. Set the permission to **Can edit** to allow your instructor to edit and delete content in the folder.
14. Click the **Add message** link and include the same message used earlier.
15. Click the **Share & Save** button.
16. Click the **Done** button to close the dialog box. On the Drive page, the folder now has Shared to the right of the name.

Lesson 8-3

Uploading Files

A Gmail user can upload and store files not created using Google Apps. When a user accesses such files, they can choose to open them in the Google Drive as a view only file.

1. Log in to your Google Mail account.
2. Click the **Drive** link in the menu bar at the top of the page to display the Drive page.
3. Click the name of the folder to which to add a file, in this case *Your Name*_Google Docs Practice.

4. Click the **Upload** button to display a drop-down menu.
5. Click **Files...** in the drop-down menu. A standard file-open dialog box is displayed.
6. Navigate to a file on your local or network drive, as specified by your instructor; select an image file, such as a JPEG; and click the **Open** button. A dialog box appears asking if you want to upload the file.
7. Click the **Upload and Share** button to upload the file. A window appears showing the progress of the upload and then that it is complete. See **Figure 8-6.** The file is now in the folder.
8. Click the name of the Documents subfolder. The contents of the folder are displayed. In this case, the folder is empty.

9. Click the **Upload** button, and click **Files...** in the drop-down menu.
10. Navigate to a different image file on your local or network drive, as specified by your instructor, and upload the file.
11. When the upload is complete, close the status window.
12. If the folder tree is not displayed in the list of labels, click the triangle next to the **My Drive** label. You should see the Google Docs Practice folder and the Documents subfolder in a tree format similar to what is displayed in the default file manager. You may need to expand the tree again to see the subfolder.
13. Click the Google Docs Practice folder to make it active and display its contents.
14. Check the check box next to the image file uploaded earlier.

15. Click the **More** button, and click **Move to...** in the drop-down menu. The **Move to** dialog box is displayed.

Tip You can also drag and drop files between folders to move them. To copy files between folders, hold the [Ctrl] key as you drag and drop.

16. In the dialog box, expand the folder tree, and select the Documents folder, as shown in **Figure 8-7.**
17. Click the **Move** button to move the file to the selected folder. If a message appears, click the **Move** button to complete the move.

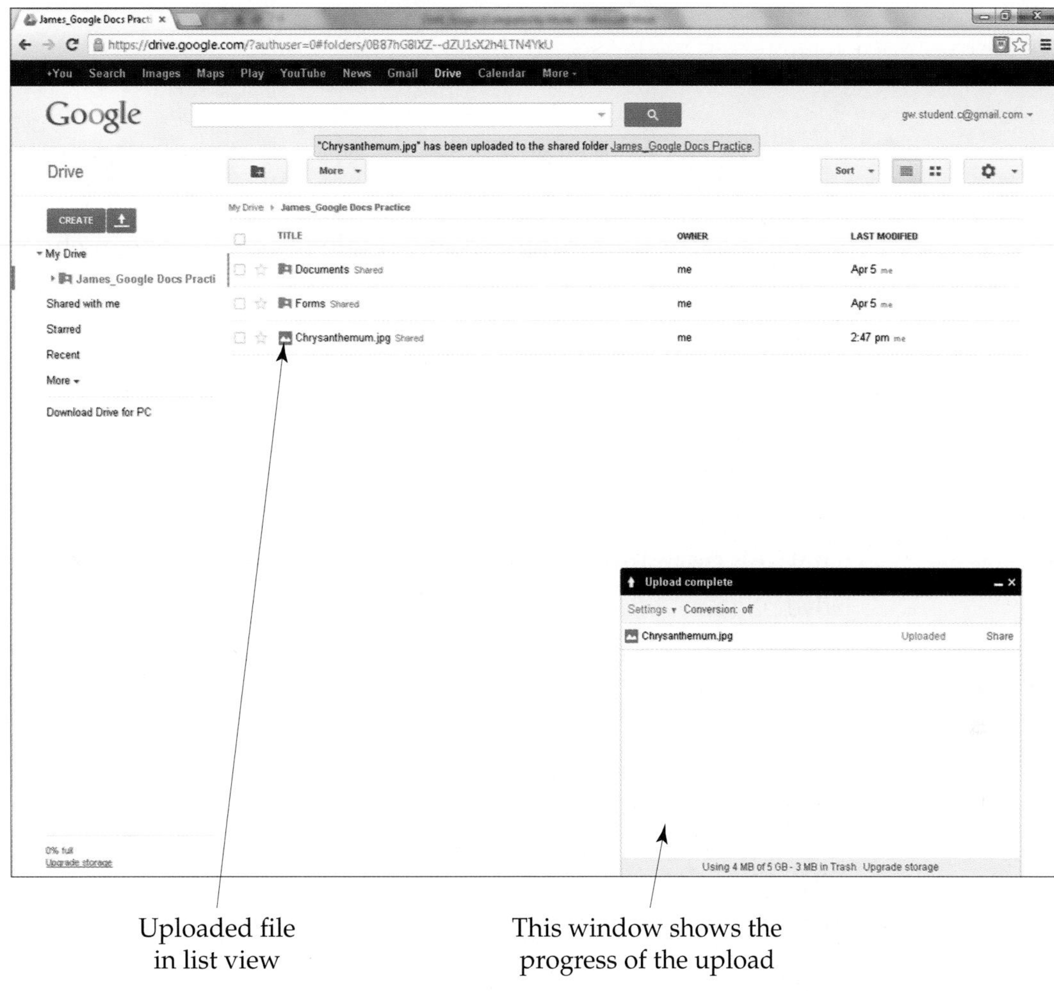

Goodheart-Willcox Publisher

Figure 8-6. Many file types can be uploaded into Google Drive for storage or sharing.

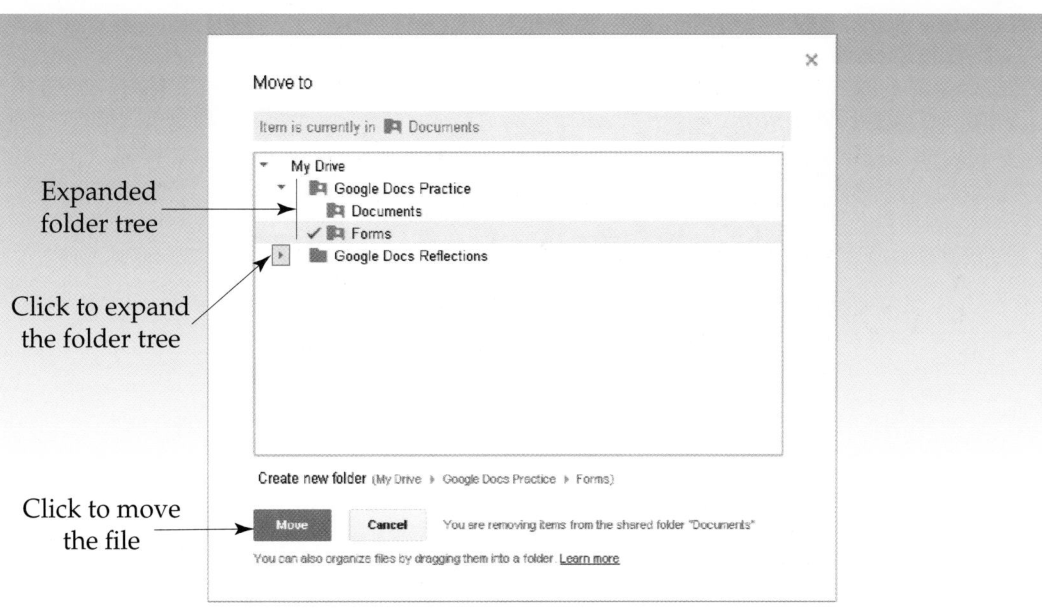

Goodheart-Willcox Publisher

Figure 8-7. Files can be moved between folders.

Lesson 8-4

Searching for Files and Folders

To find files or folders stored in Google Drive, users can choose between using the quick search text box or the advanced search feature. Using search operators with either a quick or advanced search can make a search more effective.

Conducting Basic and Advanced Searches

1. Log in to your Google Mail account.
2. Click the **Drive** link in the menu bar at the top of the page to display the Drive page.

Search

3. Click in the search box at the top of the page, enter Forms, and click the **Search** button. A list is displayed of all matching results. In this case, the Forms subfolder is the only result shown in the list unless you have added other files and folders containing forms in their names.
4. Click in **X** in the quick search text box.
5. Click the **Advanced search options** arrow next to the search text box to display a drop-down menu, as shown in **Figure 8-8.** This menu contains filters for refining the search.
6. In the **Type** area of the drop-down menu, click **Images**. This filters the search results to display only image files. The image files uploaded in Lesson 8-3 are displayed in the search results.

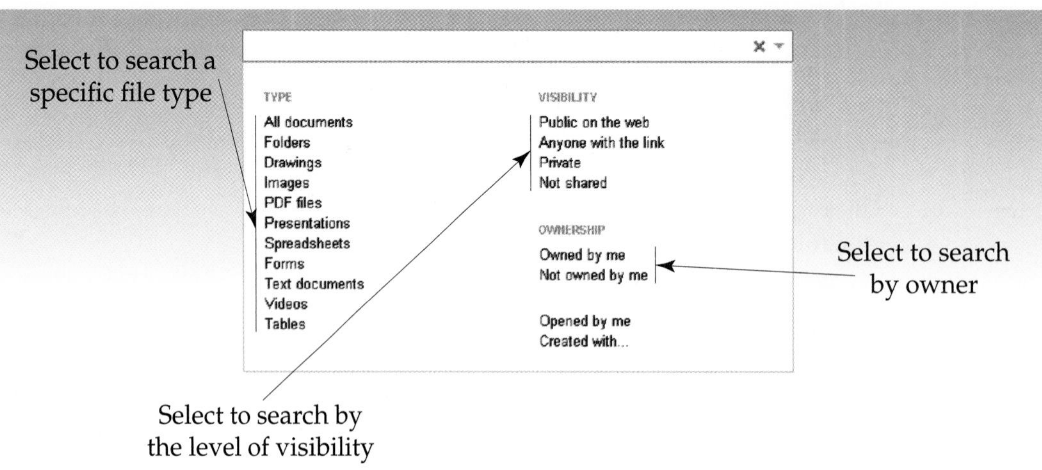

Goodheart-Willcox Publisher

Figure 8-8. Users can select one filter from each category—type, visibility, and ownership—for an advanced search.

Using Search Operators

7. Click the **X** on the filter in the search text box to remove the filter, as shown in **Figure 8-9.**

8. Click in the search text box; enter from: *your e-mail address*, such as from:m&mevents@gmail.com; and click the **Search** button. All files shared by you are displayed in the search results.

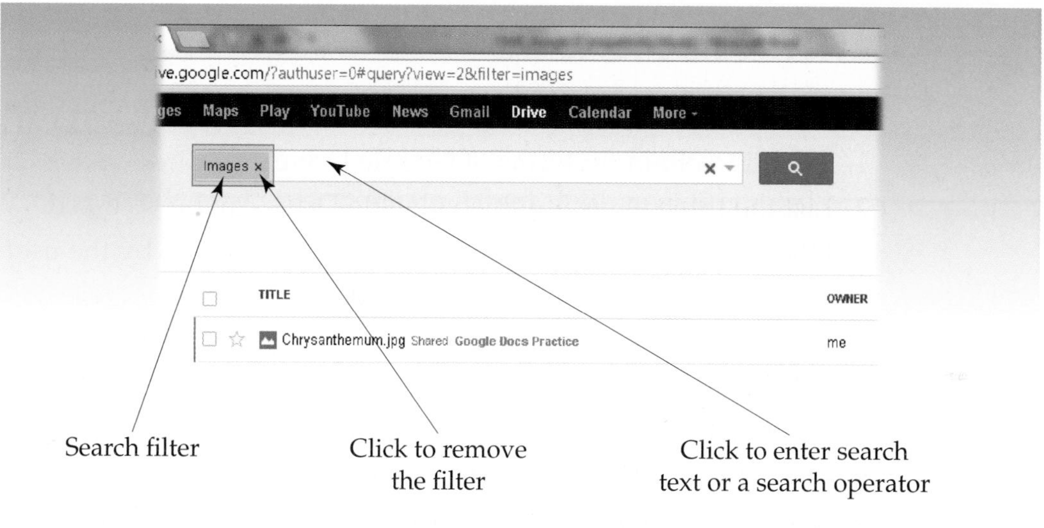

Goodheart-Willcox Publisher

Figure 8-9. Users can click the **X** that is displayed to the right of each filter to remove that filter.

Check Your Google Apps IQ

Now that you have finished this chapter, see what you know about Google Apps by taking the chapter posttest.
www.m.g-wlearning.com
www.g-wlearning.com/informationtechnology/

Skill Review

Answer the following questions on a separate sheet of paper.

1. What is a cloud, in terms of Google Drive?
2. List the three ways in which Google Drive can be accessed.
3. Under which label do the files and folders created by the user appear?
4. What is shown in the **Shared with Me** label?
5. Files and folders can be displayed in a(n) ______ view or a(n) ______ view.
6. What is a subfolder?
7. List the three visibility options for files and folders on Google Drive.
8. How many owners can a document have?
9. If a folder is shared, what is true about the files contained within the folder in terms of visibility?
10. What is the purpose of a filter in an advanced search of the Google Drive?

Lesson Application

These exercises are designed to apply the skills learned in this and previous chapters. General directions are provided, but you will need to draw on your knowledge to determine how to complete each exercise.

Exercise 8-1
Creating Folders

Create a new parent folder in Google Drive named Google Docs Reflections. This folder should be a top-level folder (not a subfolder of any other folder). Within this folder, create a subfolder named Google Documents.

Exercise 8-2
Sharing Folders

Share the Google Doc Reflections folder with two classmates and your instructor. Set their access levels to view only, add a message, and send an e-mail to both the people being added and yourself. For the Google Documents subfolder, remove the two classmates as shared users. Set the access level for your instructor to can edit.

Chapter 9

Google Docs

Objectives

After completing this chapter, you will be able to:

- **Create** a new document.
- **Set** permissions for sharing a document.
- **Format** text in a document.
- **Insert** images and hyperlinks into a document.
- **Use** the research tool from within a document to locate information about a topic.
- **Edit** a shared document.
- **Use** the revision history of a document to revert to a previous version.
- **Download** and print a document.

alexmillos/Shutterstock.com

Check Your Google Apps IQ

Before you begin this chapter, see what you already know about Google Apps by taking the chapter pretest.

www.m.g-wlearning.com
www.g-wlearning.com/informationtechnology/

Using Google Docs

Google Docs is a word processor that allows a user to create and edit documents from any web-enabled device. For example, a Google document created on a school computer could be accessed and revised on a user's home computer with Internet access. Google documents are stored in Google Drive.

Another quality of Google Docs is being able to easily share documents with others. Sharing a document allows others to simply view it, comment on it, or to modify it. The sharing feature allows users to modify documents simultaneously. For example, two users can have a shared document open at the same time, and both can add or change the content of the document. However, care should be taken so simultaneous changes do not become confusing.

Like shared folders, visibility and access are determined by the creator or owner of the document. Google Docs has the same visibility options as folders in Google Drive: visible to the public, visible to anyone with a link, and private. For documents set to be visible to the public or anyone with a link, users are not required to have a Google account to access the document. To access a private document, the user must have a Google account. A document can have the editor, commenter, or viewer access levels assigned. See **Figure 9-1** for access levels. Only in shared documents set as private can the owner transfer ownership to another user. Google limits sharing to 200 viewers and 50 simultaneous editors.

Creating a Document

Documents can be created directly in Google Drive or by uploading and converting a file from another software program. To create a document directly in Google Drive, a user clicks the **Create** button from the Google Drive

Access Level	Convertible File Type
Owner	Has all rights to the document including deleting the file, transferring ownership, and removing access for any collaborator.
Editor	Can edit the document, invite other collaborators, view the collaborator list, and upload or delete file versions.
Commenter	Can use the comments feature to add comments to the document, but cannot change the document.
Viewer	Can make a copy of the document, but cannot make any changes.

Goodheart-Willcox Publisher

Figure 9-1. Access levels are initially set by the creator of the document.

window, then clicks **Document** in the drop-down menu. When creating a new document, the user can set the title, or file name, for the document. Google limits the length of the title to 255 characters. There is no limit to the type of characters used in the title.

To upload a file from another software program, a user clicks the **Upload** button, and then navigates to the desired file. While many file types can be uploaded to Google Drive, the file types that can be converted into Google Docs are Microsoft Word files (DOC and DOCx), HTML, plain text (TXT), and rich text format (RTF). The size of imported document files must be less than two megabytes (MB).

Formatting a Document

Google Docs includes tools to format text and to insert images, tables, and hyperlinks. Many of these options are found on the formatting toolbar, as seen in **Figure 9-2**. By using the formatting toolbar, a user can make various adjustments to the text. Hover the cursor over each button to see the name of command.

Tools allow users to bold, underline, and italicize text. There are options to change the font type, size, and color. Paragraph formatting tools can impact blocks of text, such as text alignment choices, *line spacing*, *bulleted lists*, and *numbered lists*. ***Text alignment*** determines the horizontal placement of text in a document. A user can also insert images, tables, and hyperlinks into a document. To insert an image file, it must be less than 2 MB and one of the following file types: graphics interchange format (GIF), joint photographic experts group (JPG), bitmap (BMP), or portable network graphics (PNG).

Document formatting options, such as headers and footers, footnotes, and page breaks, are also available to Google Docs users in the **Insert** menu. ***Headers*** and ***footers*** are information that will display at the top or bottom of each page in the document. Page numbers are typically added to the header or footer text for a document. ***Footnotes*** are often used to cite sources the user has found during his or her research or while using the research and definition tools. Footnotes are separate from footers and appear above the footer. ***Page breaks*** are used to manually end a page and begin a new one.

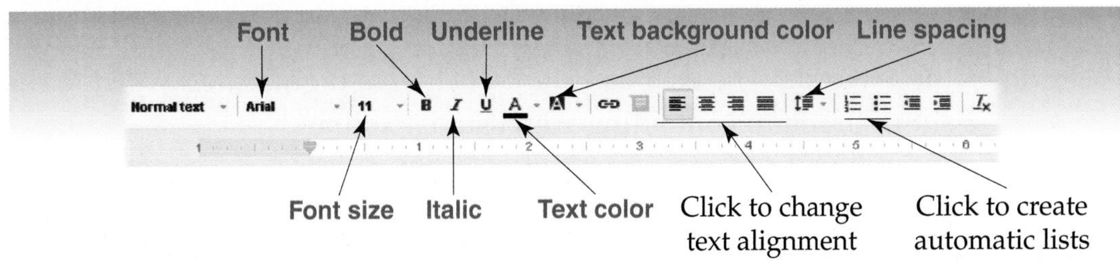

Goodheart-Willcox Publisher

Figure 9-2. The formatting toolbar provides users with many options to make formatting changes to their Google document.

A user can use paragraph styles to be more efficient in his or her application of formatting. ***Paragraph styles*** assign formatting characteristics, typically more than one characteristic, to a paragraph with a single action. For example, a heading paragraph style may be set to 18 point type, bold, and in color. A user can make all of those formatting changes with a single application of the paragraph style. Google Docs includes a set of paragraph styles that can be used as is or modified to suit the needs of the user.

Accessing Reference Information

A user can also access reference material without leaving the document window. The **Tools** menu includes a research tool and a definition tool. A user can click **Research** in the **Tools** pull-down menu to display the **Research** panel. In this panel, a user can choose to search for information or images from the web. Research can also be narrowed to just scholarly writing or quotes. A user can choose to search only in a dictionary or his or her personal files stored on Google Drive from the **Research** panel. If text in the document is highlighted before the **Research** panel is displayed, that text will automatically be researched. New text can be entered into the **Research** panel text box as well. The research results are displayed in the panel in a list format. Depending on the type of research selected, the user can choose to preview the entry, automatically insert a link in the document to any entry, or automatically insert a citation for the entry as a footnote. A footnote entry is shown in **Figure 9-3**.

A user can highlight a word in a document and click **Define** in the **Tools** pull-down menu to display the **Research** panel. The **Research** panel will display definitions for the selected word. A user can choose to highlight a definition, then drag and drop it into the document window to add it.

Revising and Publishing a Document

Once a document is created, there are often revisions. Google automatically saves changes to documents as new data are entered. One of the first steps in revising a document is often checking spelling throughout it. Google Docs approaches *spell check* by highlighting suspicious words with a red-dashed underline. A user can then review his or her document for these words. The user can right-click on a highlighted word to display the shortcut menu containing suggested spellings.

When revising a Google document, a user can easily track what has been changed using the revision history feature. The ***revision history*** is a listing of all changes made to a document. A user clicks the **File** pull-down menu, and then clicks **See revision history** in the menu. The **Revision history** panel is

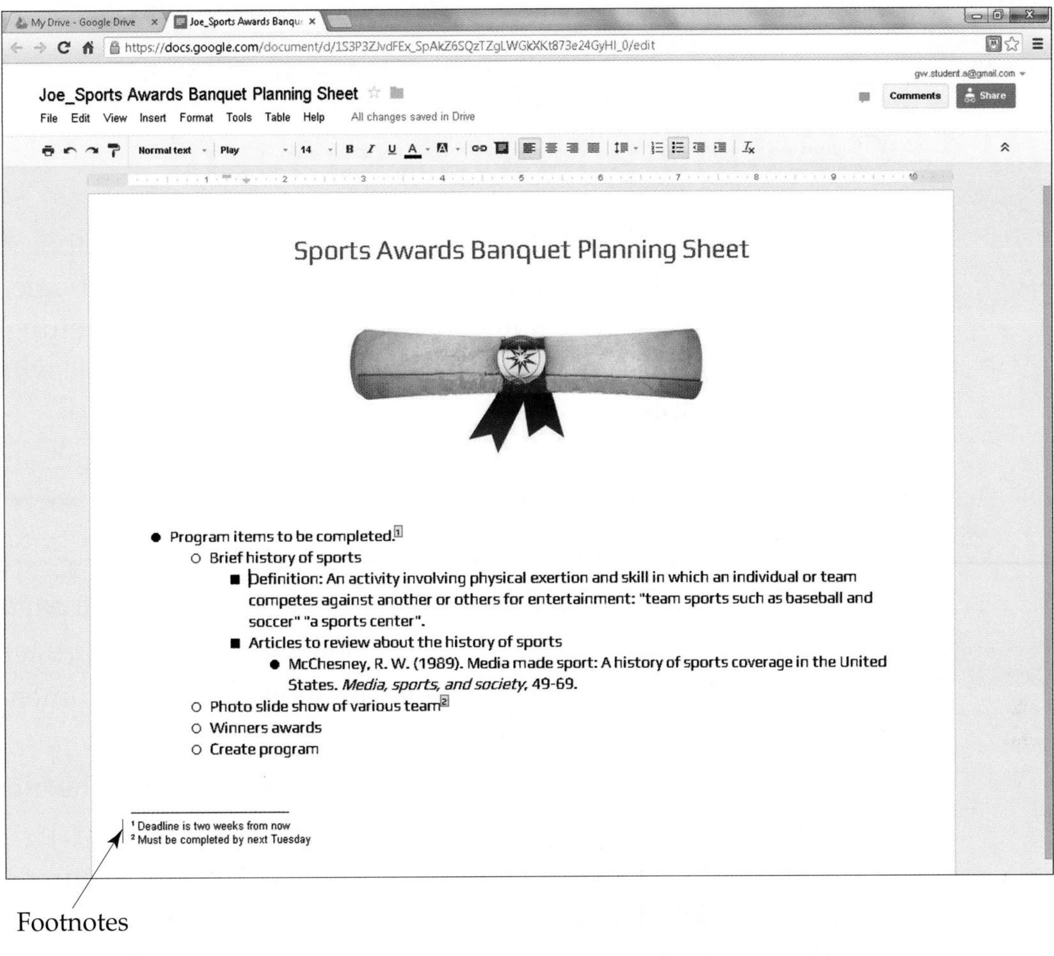

Goodheart-Willcox Publisher

Figure 9-3. Footnotes can be added to a Google document to provide citation information for source materials used or to add a note specific to the content.

displayed on the right side of the page. The list includes when changes were made and which user made the change, if the document is shared. When a user clicks one of the entries, the state of the document at the time of that change is displayed in the document window. The user can then choose to restore that version of the document.

Google documents can be downloaded to use in another software program. Google Documents can be downloaded as a DOCx, open office (ODT), RTF, PDF, TXT, or HTML file. Once downloaded, the document can be opened in an application that supports the file format selected and modified as appropriate.

Printing is also an option with a Google document. A user clicks the **File** pull-down menu, and then clicks **Print** in the menu to display the **Print** window. The user is presented with a few printing options including printing the entire document or specific pages and margins can be adjusted.

Lesson 9-1

Creating a New Document

Documents in Google Docs can be created within the application or imported from other word processing programs. Once in Google Docs, a user can name or rename a document and define the page settings for it. A document can also be moved to a specific folder without leaving the document window.

Creating a Document

1. Log in to your Google Mail account.
2. Click the **Drive** link in the menu bar at the top of the Mail page.

CREATE

3. Click the **Create** button, and click **Document** in the drop-down menu. A new tab or window is opened containing a blank document named Untitled, as shown in **Figure 9-4.**
4. Click the **File** pull-down menu, and click **Rename...** in the menu. The **Rename Document** dialog box is displayed.
5. Click in the **Enter a new document name:** text box, and enter *Your Name_* Sports Awards Banquet Planning Sheet.
6. Click the **OK** button to close the dialog box and rename the document. The new name now appears at the top of the document.

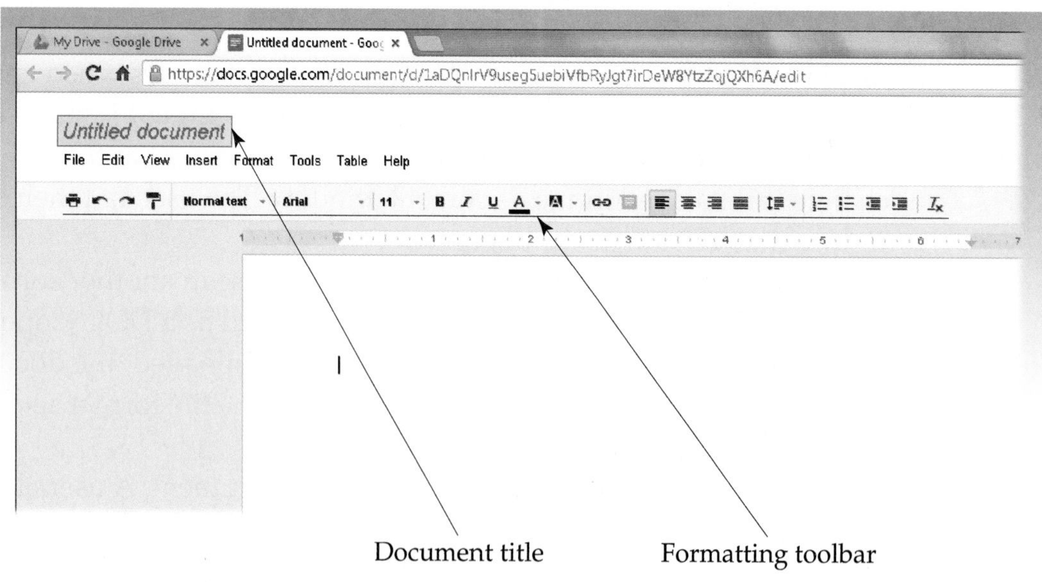

Goodheart-Willcox Publisher

Figure 9-4. When a new document is created, it is automatically named untitled. It can be helpful to rename each document to something that reflects its content.

Setting Page Properties

7. Click the **File** pull-down menu, and click **Page Setup...** in the menu. The **Page Setup** dialog box is displayed, as shown in **Figure 9-5.** This is used to set the page size, orientation, and margins for the document.
8. Click the **Landscape** radio button to change the orientation to wide.
9. Click the **Paper Size** drop-down list, and click **Letter (8.5″ × 11″)** in the list. If this is already selected, as displayed on the button, you can skip this step.
10. In the **Margins** area, click in the **Top**, **Bottom**, **Left**, and **Right** text boxes and enter .5 to set each margin to 1/2″.
11. Click the **OK** button to close the dialog box and change the page properties.

Moving the File into a Google Drive Folder

12. Click the **Folders...** button to the right of the document title. The **Move To** dialog box is displayed, as shown in **Figure 9-6.** The Google Docs Practice folder created in Chapter 8 should be displayed in the dialog box.

Tip Files can be also organized in folders using the drive list.

13. Click the triangle next to the Google Docs Practice folder to expand the folder tree. The subfolders it contains are displayed.
14. Click the Documents folder in the tree. It is highlighted and a check mark appears to the left of its name.

15. Click the **Move** button to move the document into the Documents folder and to close the dialog box.

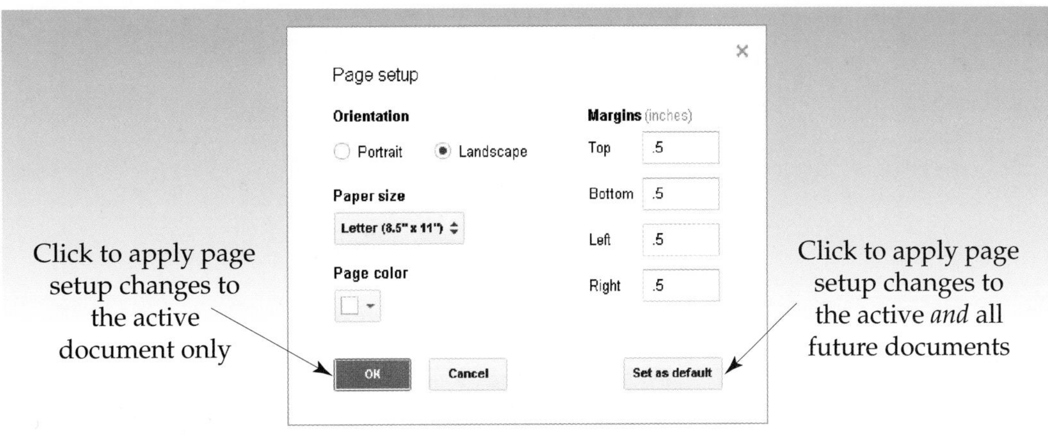

Goodheart-Willcox Publisher

Figure 9-5. In the **Page setup** dialog box, a user can change the page orientation, margins, paper size, and page color.

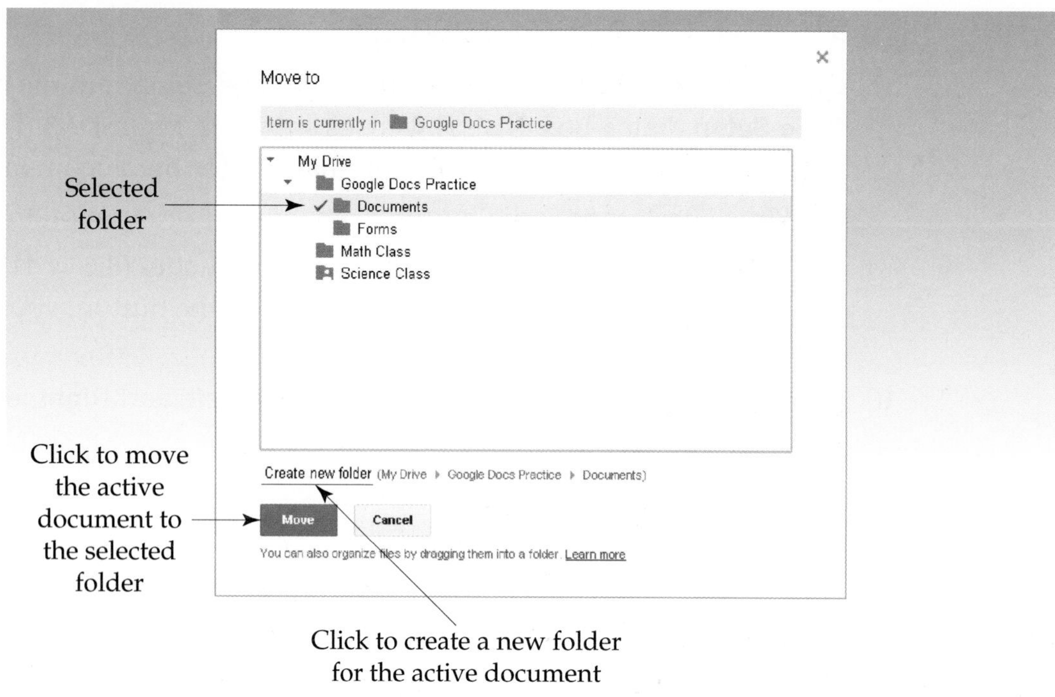

Goodheart-Willcox Publisher

Figure 9-6. In the **Move to** dialog box, a user can select to move his or her active document into another folder.

16. Close the window or tab to close the document. Changes are automatically saved in Google Docs, but if you attempt to close the document while a save is in progress, a message is displayed asking if you want to navigate away from the page. If this occurs, click the **Stay on this Page** button, wait for the save to be completed, and then close the document.

Lesson 9-2

Opening a Document and Setting Its Visibility and Permissions

By default a document's visibility is set to private. A user can change the visibility to allow large or unknown groups of people to access the document. The owner of the document can set the access level of the document with each visibility option.

Opening a Document

1. Log in to your Google Mail account.
2. Click the **Drive** link in the menu bar at the top of the Mail page.
3. On the Drive page, click the triangle next to the **My Drive** label to expand the tree.
4. Continue expanding the tree until the subfolders below the Google Docs Practice folder are displayed.
5. Click the **Documents** label in the folder tree to show the contents of the Documents subfolder. The contents of the folder are displayed in the main window. Since the Sports Awards Banquet Planning Sheet document created in Lesson 9-1 was moved into this folder, its name should appear in the list.
6. Move the cursor over the name of the Sports Awards Banquet Planning Sheet document until the name is displayed as a link. Click the link to open the document.

Setting Visibility

Share

7. Once the document is open, click the **Share** button. The **Sharing settings** dialog box is displayed.
8. Click the **Change...** link in the **Who has access** area of the dialog box. A new dialog box is displayed in which the visibility options can be set, as shown in **Figure 9-7.**
9. Click the **Anyone with the link** radio button. Your instructor may specify a level of visibility.
10. Click the **Access** drop-down list that appears, and click **Can comment** in the list. This specifies that somebody with the link cannot only view the document, but add a comment to it.
11. Click the **Save** button to close the dialog box and return to the previous **Sharing settings** dialog box.

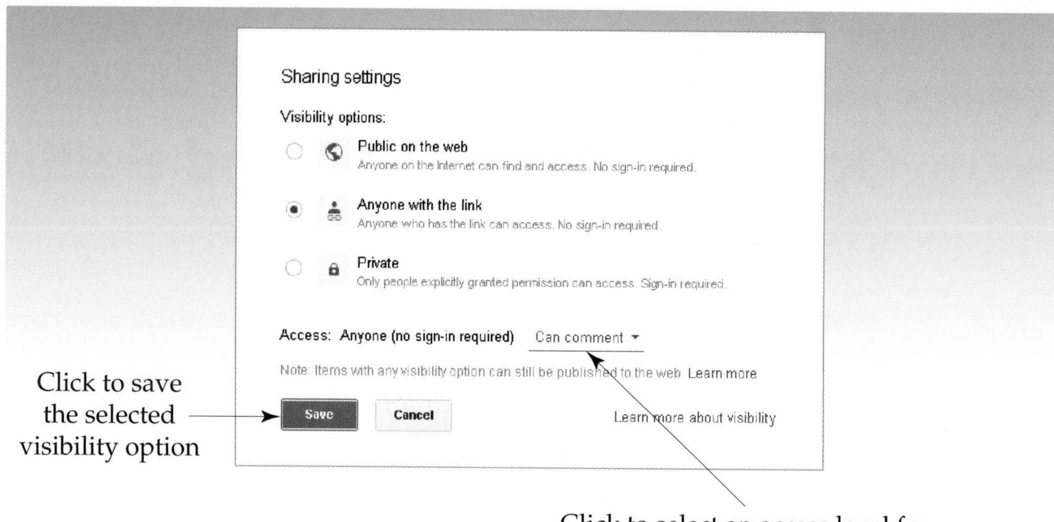

Goodheart-Willcox Publisher

Figure 9-7. When a document is set to the **Public on the web** or **Anyone with the link** visibility options, non-Gmail users can access it.

Set Permissions for Specific Users

12. With the **Sharing settings** dialog box open, click in the **Add people:** text box. The lower part of the dialog box expands with additional options, as shown in **Figure 9-8.**
13. In the text box, enter the name of a classmate, if he or she is a contact, or his or her e-mail address. Multiple addresses can be added, one on each line. Press the [Enter] key to start a new line.

Tip

When more than one person is in a document, profile images appear in the upper-right corner of the document to indicate this. Each person is automatically assigned a different color.

14. Click the drop-down list to the right of the text box, and click the entry for the level of access the person should have.
15. Check the **Notify people via e-mail** check box. When checked, the person being added will receive an e-mail notification that the document has been shared with him or her.
16. Check the **Send a copy to myself** check box. When checked, you will receive the same e-mail notification that the person receives, which can be a useful way to verify that the e-mail was sent.

Share & save

17. Click the **Share & save** button to add the person to the list of people who have access to the document.

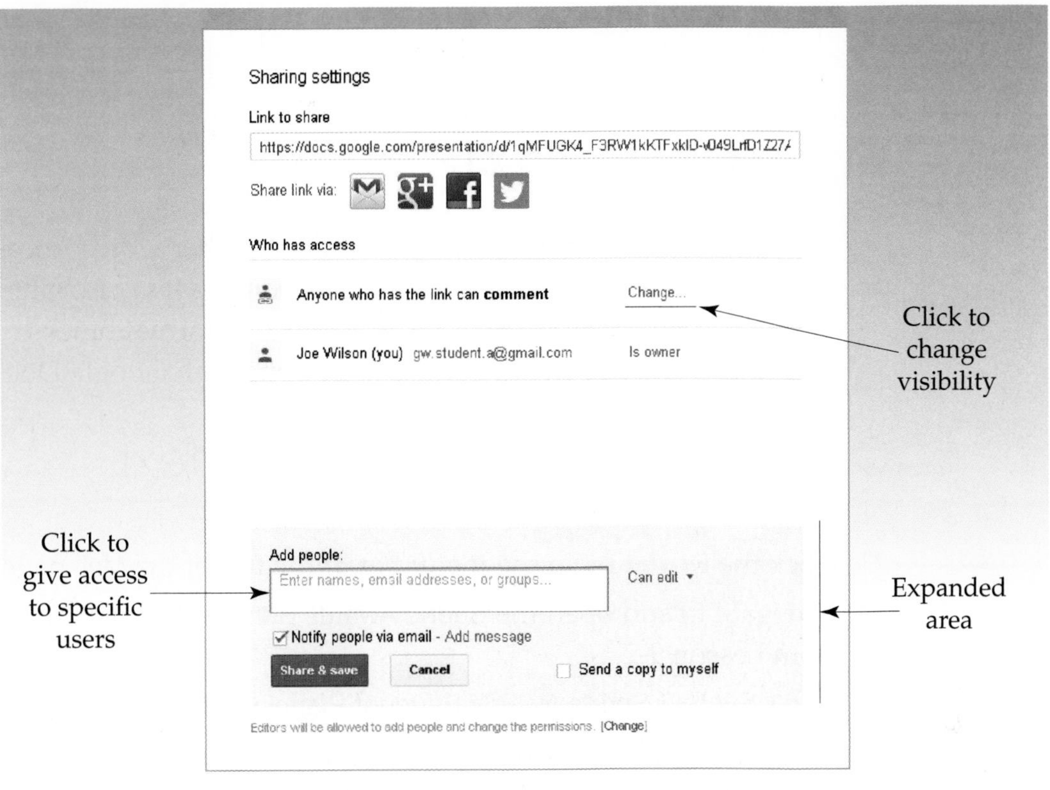

Goodheart-Willcox Publisher

Figure 9-8. Along with setting the visibility of a document, a user can choose to add other users to as an editor, commenter, or viewer of his or her document in the **Sharing settings** dialog box.

18. Click the **Done** button to close the **Sharing settings** dialog box and return to the document.
19. Close the tab or window to close the document.

Lesson 9-3

Formatting Text

Google Docs formatting tools are similar to other word processing programs. Basic formatting options such as bolding text or changing font size are available. Along with those, the ability to format blocks of text such as line spacing and list creation are also options with Google Docs.

Changing the Appearance of Text

1. Log in to your Google Mail account.
2. Click the **Drive** link in the menu bar at the top of the Mail page.
3. Navigate to and open the Sports Awards Banquet Planning Sheet document from Lesson 9-2.
4. Enter the text Sports Awards Banquet Planning Sheet in the document.
5. Select the text by clicking the mouse and dragging over it. When the text is highlighted, release the mouse button.

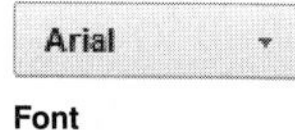

Font

6. Click the **Font** button to display a drop-down list of available fonts, as shown in **Figure 9-9.**
7. Click **Georgia** in the drop-down list, or other font as specified by your instructor. This changes the font of the selected text.

Font Size

8. Click the **Font Size** button to display a drop-down list of point sizes.
9. Click **24** in the drop-down list. This changes the size of the selected text.
10. Click the **Text Color** button to display a color palette.
11. Click a dark green color swatch. This changes the color of the text from black to green.

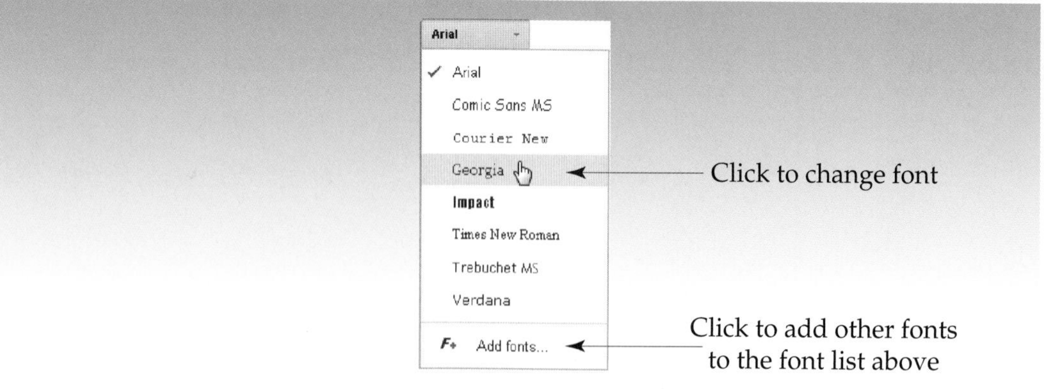

Goodheart-Willcox Publisher

Figure 9-9. The name of each font in the font list is displayed in the font itself, providing users with a preview of what the font will look like.

Making Additional Fonts Available

Arial
Font

12. Click the **Font** button.
13. Click **Add fonts...** in the drop-down list. The **Add fonts** dialog box is displayed, as shown in **Figure 9-10.**

Sort: Popularity

14. Click the **Sort: Popularity** button. The way in which the fonts are sorted is displayed on the button. Sorting the fonts by their popularity is the default. Click **Alphabetical** in the drop-down list. This arranges the list of fonts in the dialog box in alphabetical order.
15. Click the **Lobster**, **Play**, and **Coming Soon** fonts in the list. Selected fonts have a check mark to the left of their names and appear in the **My Fonts** list on the right-hand side of the dialog box. A font can be removed from the **My Fonts** list by clicking the **X** next to its name.
16. Click the **OK** button to close the dialog box and make the selected fonts available for use.

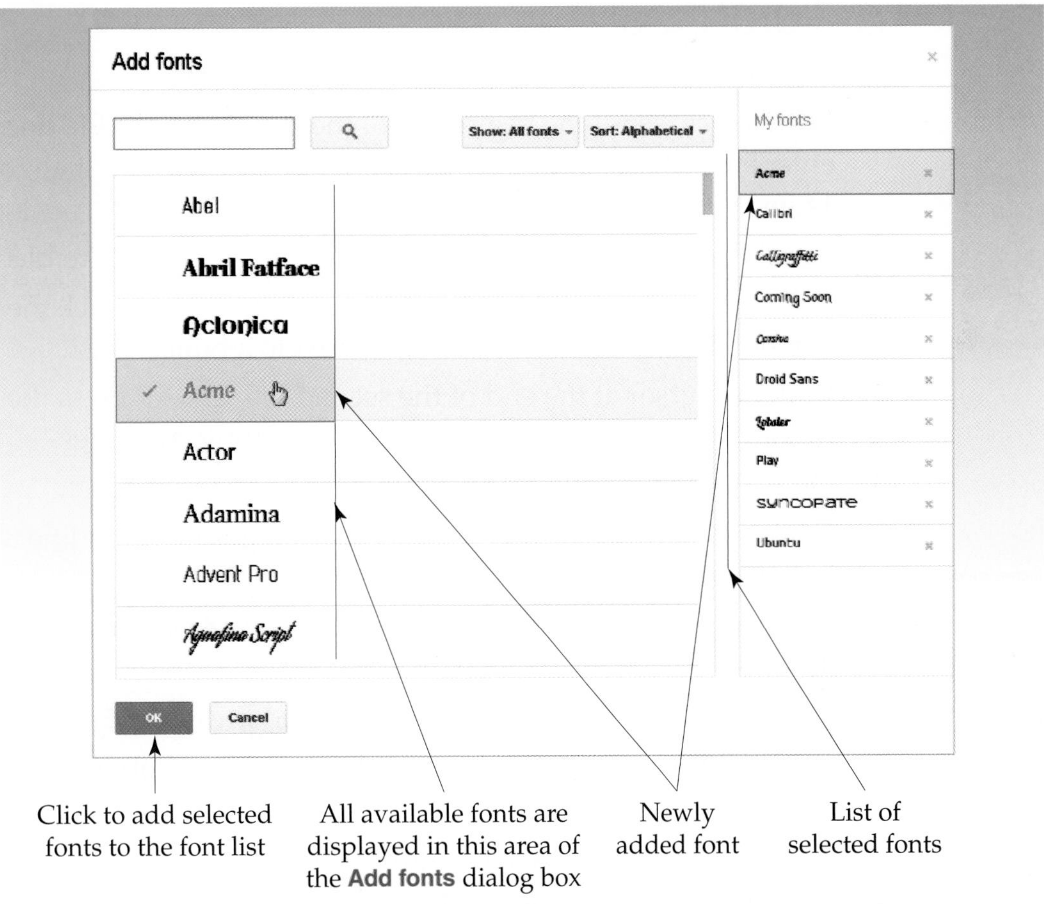

Goodheart-Willcox Publisher

Figure 9-10. Users can make finding available fonts easier by using the search text box, or by selecting to show only a certain category or fonts, or by selecting in what order the fonts will be sorted.

When first made available in the **Font** button drop-down list, an added font is highlighted in yellow. The highlighting is removed the second time the **Font** button is clicked.

17. Select the text in the document.

Font

18. Click the **Font** button, and click **Play** in the drop-down list. The font of the text is changed.

Text Alignment

19. Click anywhere in the line of text in the document.

Center Align

20. Click the **Center Align** button. The text is shifted to the center of the page.
21. Click at the end of the line of text, and press the [Enter] key. This starts a new line in the document.

Left Align

22. Click the **Left Align** button. The cursor is shifted to the left-hand margin. If there was any text on the line, it would be shifted left as well.

Bulleted List

Font Size

23. Click the **Font Size** button, and change the size to 14.
24. With the cursor at the beginning of the second line in the document, enter Program items to be completed. Notice the text is left aligned, in size 14, in the Play font, and in the same green.
25. Select the text on the second line, and change the color to black.

Bulleted List

26. With the cursor anywhere on the second line of text, click the **Bulleted List** button. This changes the line of text to a bulleted list.
27. With the cursor at the end of the second line of text, press the [Enter] key to start a new line. Notice the bullet formatting continues.
28. On the third line, enter Brief history of sports.

Increase Indent

29. Click the **Increase Indent** button. This changes the third line to a sub bullet of the second line.
30. On the fourth line, enter Photo slide show of various teams, and press the [Enter] key.
31. On the fifth line, enter Winners awards, and press the [Enter] key.

Decrease Indent

32. Click the **Decrease Indent** button once to end the sub bulleted list.

Bulleted List

33. Click the **Bulleted List** button to end the bulleted list. The document should appear as shown in **Figure 9-11.**
34. Close the tab or window to close the document.

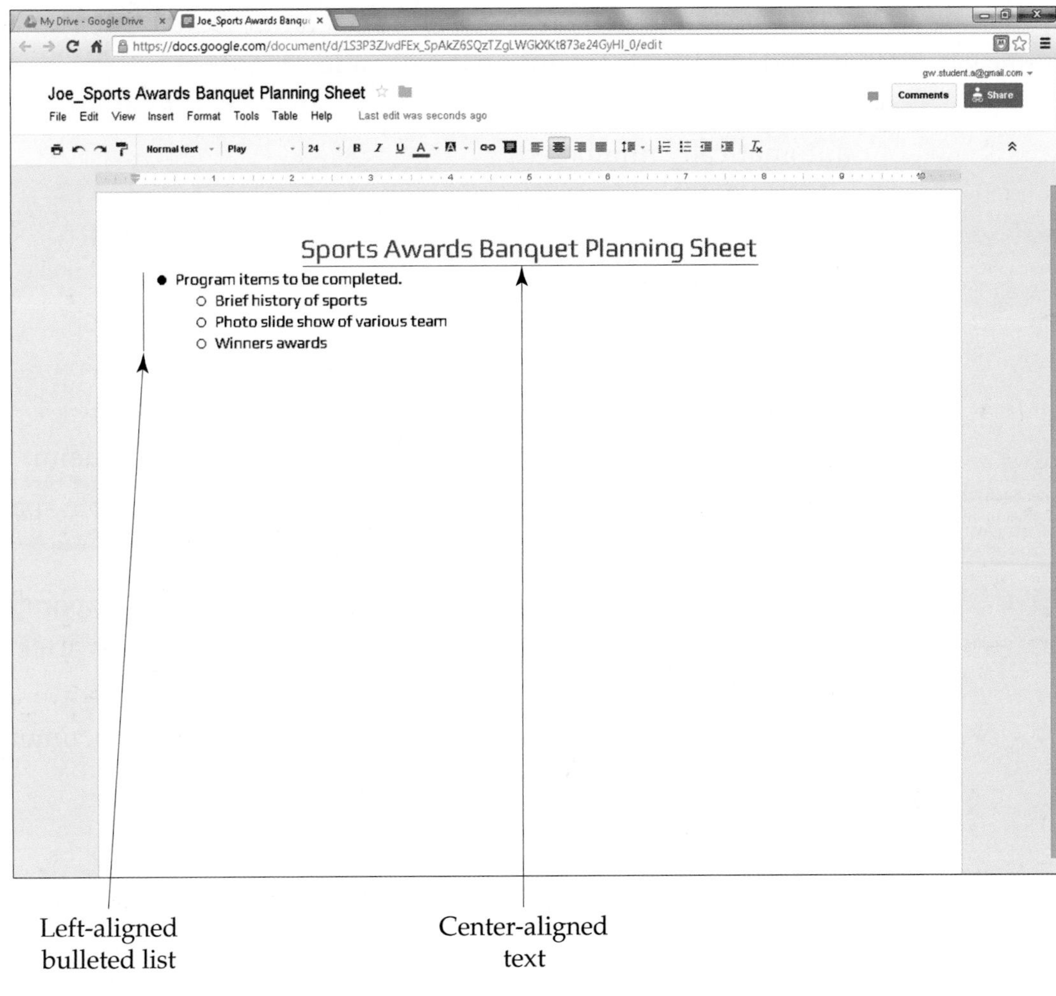

Goodheart-Willcox Publisher

Figure 9-11. Your document should include two levels of bullets along with a title.

Numbered List

35. Switch to the window or tab in which the Drive page is displayed. If needed, open a new window or tab and navigate to the Drive page.
36. Click the **Documents** folder under the **My Drive** label to make the Documents folder the active folder.
37. Click the **Create** button, and click **Document** in the drop-down menu to start a new document. A message may appear asking if you want to create a document in a shared folder. Click the **Create and share** button.
38. Rename the new document as Awardees List.
39. In the document, enter the text Awardees List, and format it the same as the title for the Sports Awards Banquet Planning Sheet.
40. Press the [Enter] key to start a new line.
41. Click the **Left Align** button to align the line to the left-hand margin.
42. Change the text color to black and the font size to 12.

Left Align

43. Click the **Numbered List** button to start a numbered list. The number 1, a period, and a tab are automatically added.
44. Enter the text First place, and press the [Enter] key. Notice the new line is automatically numbered.
45. Enter the text Second place, and press the [Enter] key.
46. Enter the text Third place.

Line Spacing

47. Click and drag over all text in the document to select it.

Line Spacing

48. Click the **Line Spacing** button to display a drop-down menu.
49. Click **2.0** in the menu to change the line spacing to double spaced.
50. Click anywhere in the first line, which is the title.

51. Click the **Line Spacing** button, and click **Add space after paragraph** from the drop-down menu. An additional line space is added after the title, which shifts the numbered list down.
52. Close the tab or window to close the document. This document will be used later in this chapter.

Lesson 9-4

Using Paragraph Styles

Using paragraph styles can make quick work out of formatting a document. Google Docs has default styles that can be changed and used in a new or imported document.

1. Log in to your Google Mail account.
2. Click the **Drive** link in the menu bar at the top of the Mail page.
3. Navigate to the Documents subfolder.

CREATE

4. Click the **Create** button, and click **Document** in the drop-down menu. If prompted, click the **Create and share** button.
5. Click the **File** pull-down menu, and click **Rename...** in the menu. In the **Rename Document** dialog box, name the document Report on Presentations.
6. In the document, enter the text Report on Presentations, and press the [Enter] key.
7. On the next line, enter the text by, and press the [Enter] key.
8. On the next line, enter your name.
9. Click the **Insert** pull-down menu, and click **Page Break** in the menu. This manually ends the page and begins a new one.

Tip The [Ctrl][Enter] key combination can be used to insert a page break.

10. Click anywhere in the first line on the first page (the title).

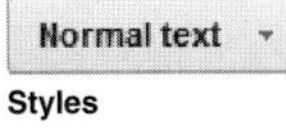

Styles

11. Click the **Styles** button to display a drop-down list. The style of the paragraph in which the cursor is placed is displayed as the name on the **Styles** button. The Normal style is used for basic body text in a document.
12. Click **Title** in the drop-down list. This sets the paragraph style to Title. The text inherits the formatting defined by the paragraph style.
13. Click anywhere in the third line on the first page (your name).

Normal text
Styles

14. Click the **Styles** button, and click **Heading 1** in the drop-down list. The text inherits the formatting of the Heading 1 style.
15. Scroll down, and click on the second page of the document.

Normal text
Styles

16. Make sure the style is set to Normal.
17. Write a couple of paragraphs about various presentations you have given in other classes. Describe any visual aids you used.
18. Click the **Insert** pull-down menu, and click **Page number** in the menu to display a cascading menu.

19. Click **Top of page** in the cascading menu. Page numbers are automatically added to the top-right corner in the header area of each page in the document. As new pages are added, they are automatically numbered as well.
20. Click in front of the page number in the header area on any page.
21. Enter the text Page and a space.
22. Select the text and the page number.
23. Click the **Font Size** button, and change the size to 8. This makes the header, which includes the page number, smaller to minimize its visual impact on the page.

Tip In addition to size, you can change the alignment of page numbers. For example, it is common to have the page number at the bottom of the page and centered.

24. Click anywhere in the document to exit the header area.
25. Proofread your document for proper spelling and grammar.
26. Close the tab or window to close the document.

Lesson 9-5

Inserting Images and Hyperlinks

Documents have several options for inserting images. User can upload an image stored on their computer, or select a picture from their Picasa album, or enter the web address to an image. Hyperlinks can also be inserted into Google Docs.

Inserting an Image

1. Navigate to the student companion website (www.g-wlearning.com/informationtechnology/), and download the Sports Award data file to your working folder.
2. Log in to your Google Mail account.
3. Click the **Drive** link in the menu bar at the top of the Mail page.
4. Open the Sports Awards Banquet Planning Sheet document from Lesson 9-3.
5. Click at the end of the first line, and press the [Enter] key to start a new line.
6. Click the **Insert** pull-down menu, and click **Image...** in the menu. The **Insert Image** dialog box is displayed, as shown in **Figure 9-12.**

Goodheart-Willcox Publisher

Figure 9-12. There are several options for a user looking for an image to use in his or her document including inserting an image from his or her album or entering a URL of an image found online.

7. Click the button **Choose an image to upload** button in the middle of the preview area. A standard file-open dialog box is displayed.
8. Navigate to your working folder, select the Sports Award image file, and click the **Open** button. The image is inserted into the document at the cursor location.
9. Click the image in the document to display the resizing handles, as shown in **Figure 9-13.**
10. Drag one of the corner handles to resize the image until it is an appropriate size that looks good in the document. The four corner handles proportionally resize the image. The handles in the middle of each side resize the image without regard to the original proportions of the image.

Inserting a Hyperlink

11. Switch to the window or tab in which the Drive page is displayed. If needed, open a new window or tab and navigate to the Drive page.

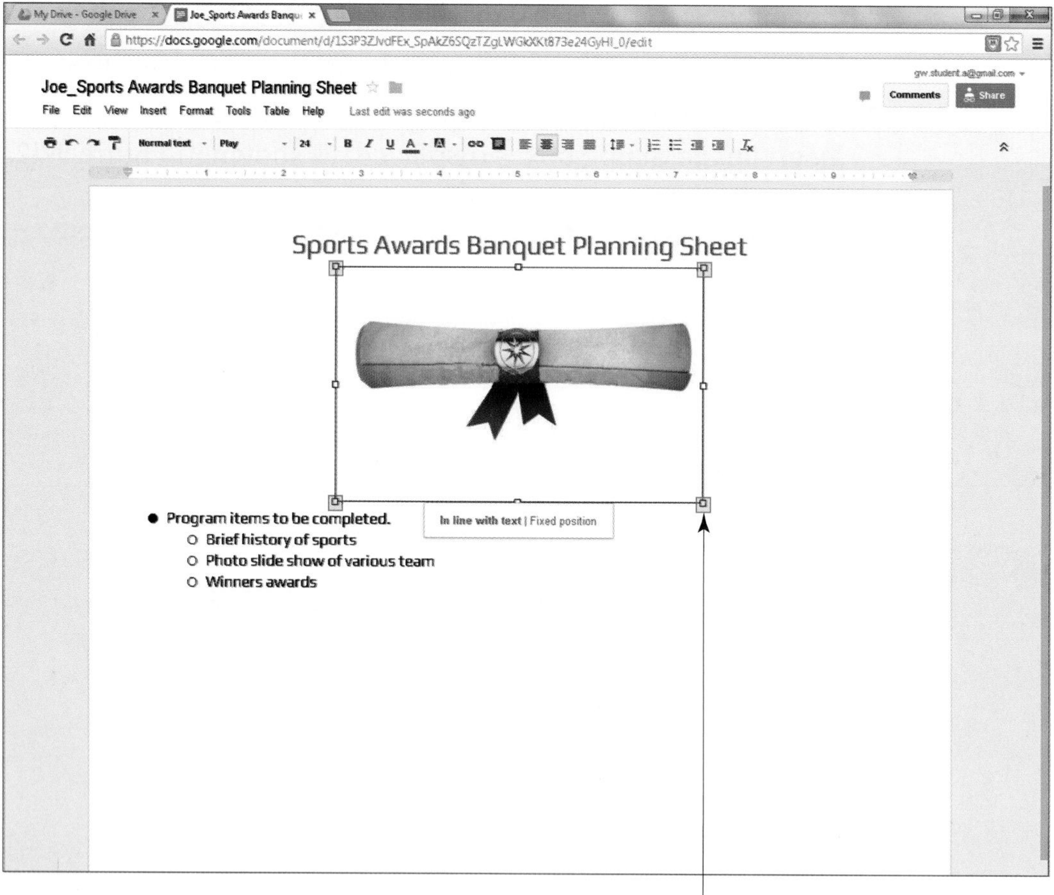

Drag the corner resizing handles to proportionally change the size of the image

Goodheart-Willcox Publisher

Figure 9-13. If an image is resized using the handles at the top, bottom, and sides of the image, the changes will not be proportional.

12. Open the Awardees List document.
13. Click in the address window at the top of the browser, select the entire URL, and press the [Ctrl][C] key combination to copy the address.

If something other than the web address is pasted, return to the **Awardees List** document, and copy the URL again.

14. Close the tab or window to close the document.
15. Switch to the window or tab in which the Sports Awards Banquet Planning Sheet document is displayed or open the document if needed.
16. Click at the end of the text Winners awards to place the cursor there.
17. Press the space bar to add one space at the end of the line.

Insert Link

18. Click the **Insert Link** button. The **Edit link** dialog box is displayed, as shown in **Figure 9-14.**
19. Click in the **Text to display** text box, and enter Awardees List.
20. Click **Web address** in the **Link to** area.
21. Click in the **URL for the link** text box, and press the [Ctrl][V] key combination to paste the web address copied earlier.
22. Click the **Test this link** link to verify the link is to the Awardees List document. The document will be displayed in a new window. Close the window after verifying the document.
23. Click the **OK** button to close the dialog box and set the hyperlink. The display text is added at the cursor location.
24. Close the tab or window to close the document.

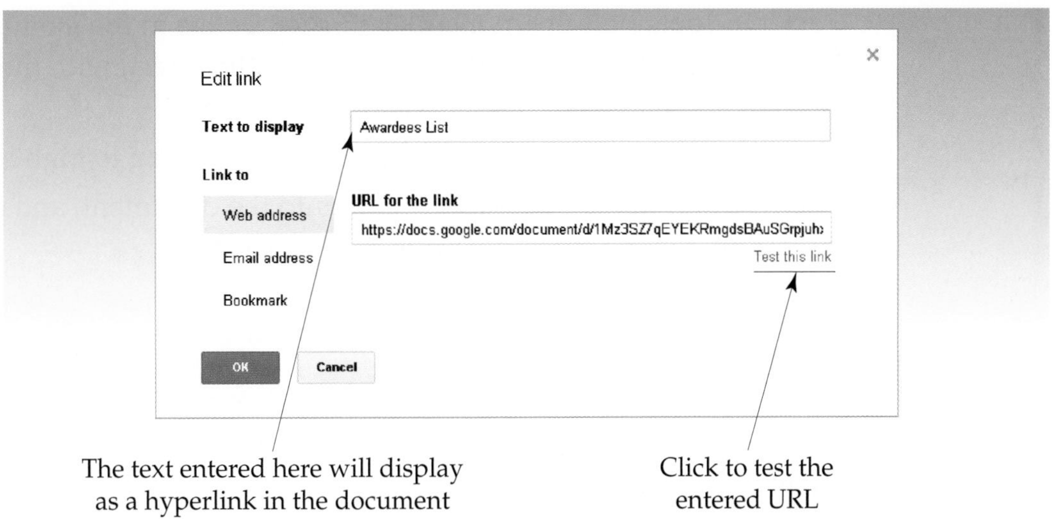

Goodheart-Willcox Publisher

Figure 9-14. In the **Edit link** dialog box, a user can create a link to a website by entering a URL, to a bookmark by selecting one created in the document, or to an e-mail address.

Lesson 9-6

Using the Research Tool

The research tool makes it easy for a user to add resources from the Internet into his or her document. These resources can be in the form of a website, scholarly articles, and dictionary as well as from personal files on his or her Google Drive.

Finding a Definition

1. Log in to your Google Mail account.
2. Click the **Drive** link in the menu bar at the top of the Mail page.
3. Open the Sports Awards Banquet Planning Sheet document from Lesson 9-5.
4. Click after the text Brief history of sports to place the cursor at the end of that line.
5. Press the [Enter] key to add a new line.
6. Press the [Tab] key to indent the new line. This makes the line a sub bullet of the Brief history of sports bullet.

Tip The **Increase Indent** button can also be used to create sub bullets.

7. Enter the text Definition: and a space.
8. Double-click the word sports on the previous line to select it.
9. Click the **Tools** pull-down menu, and click **Define** in the menu. The **Research** panel is displayed on the right of the screen with the selected word in the search box, as shown in **Figure 9-15.**
10. Click at the beginning of the first definition and drag to highlight it.
11. Click the highlighted passage, drag it into the document, and drop it at the end of the line containing the word Definition:

Citing an Article

12. Click at the end of the definition you just dropped into the document, and press the [Enter] key to start a new line. The line is the same sub bullet level as the previous line.
13. Enter the text Articles to review about the history of sports.
14. Press the [Enter] key to start a new line.
15. Press the [Tab] key to make the new line a fourth level of bullets.

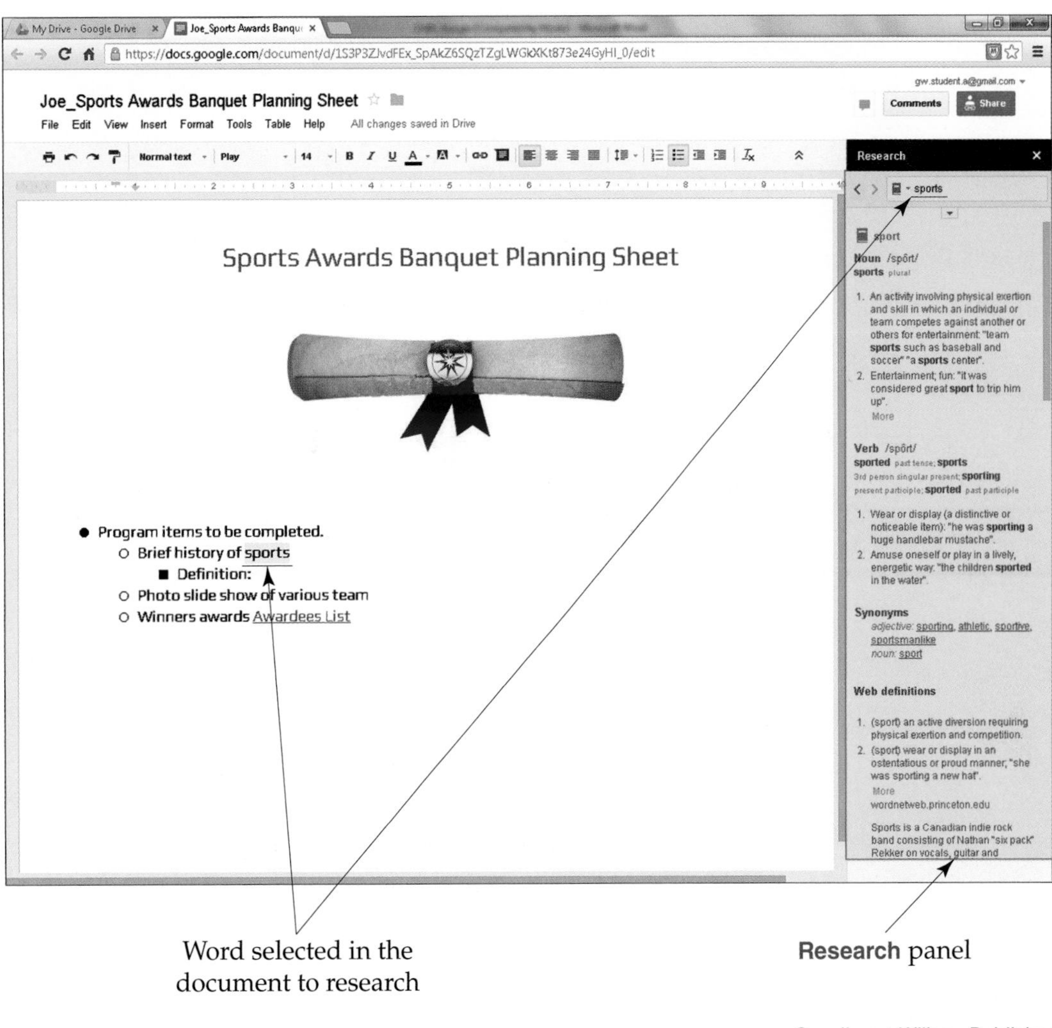

Goodheart-Willcox Publisher

Figure 9-15. The **Research** panel lists research conducted without leaving the document window.

16. In the **Research** panel, click in the text box, and enter history of sports.
17. Click in the text box again to display a drop-down menu, and click **Scholar** in the menu. This changes the search from dictionary definitions to scholarly writings.
18. Click the arrow below the text box and above the search results to display citation options.
19. Click the drop-down list that appears, and click **APA** in the list. This sets the citation format to American Psychological Association (APA) style.
20. Move the cursor over one of the search results. Several options appear for the individual item, as shown in **Figure 9-16.**

Tip To preview the article, click **Web** or **PDF** in the upper, left-hand corner of the options that appear when hovering over a search result.

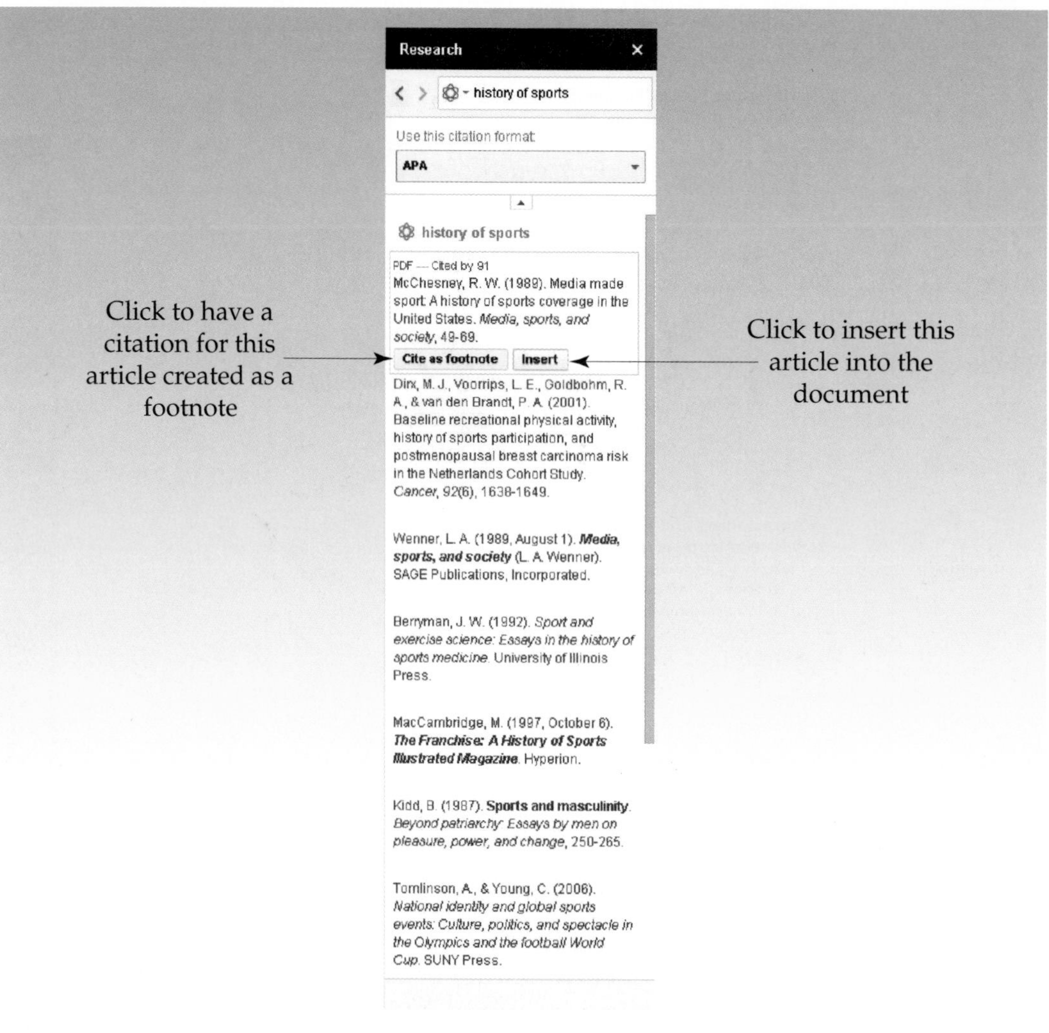

Goodheart-Willcox Publisher

Figure 9-16. For some types of research, users are given the option to preview the research entry as well as the options to cite and insert the data.

Insert

21. Click the **Insert** button to insert a citation of the article at the cursor location.
22. Click the **X** in the upper-right corner of the **Research** panel to close it. Your document should now look like **Figure 9-17,** although your citation will be different.

Inserting a Footnote

23. Click at the end of the line for the first bullet.
24. Click the **Insert** pull-down menu, and click **Footnote** in the menu. A superscript 1 appears at the end of the line and at the bottom of the page below a horizontal line. Footnotes appear at the bottom of the page. Notice the cursor is in the footnote area at the bottom of the page.

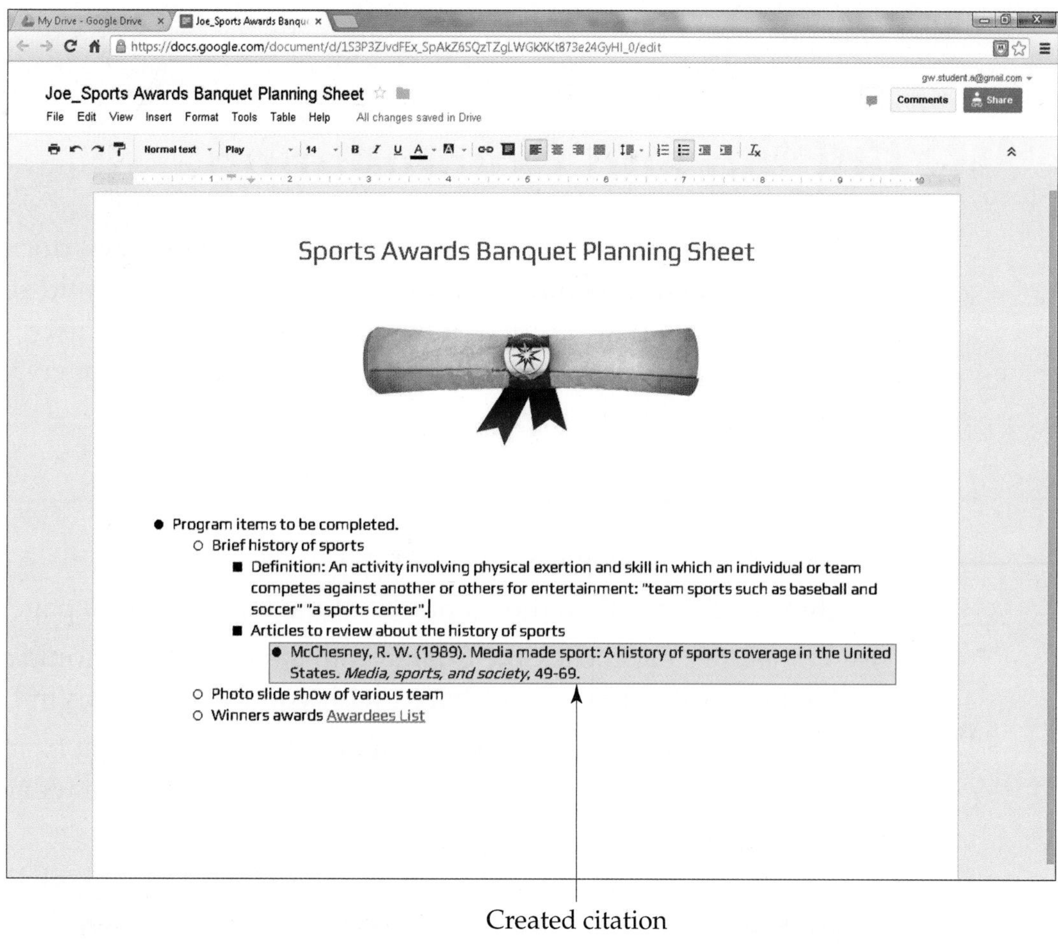

Goodheart-Willcox Publisher

Figure 9-17. The citation inserted into the document is created in APA style as it was selected in the **Research** panel.

25. Enter the text Deadline is two weeks from now as the footnote.
26. Click at the end of the second sub bullet (Photo slide show of various teams).
27. Click the **Insert** pull-down menu, and click **Footnote** in the menu. A superscript 2 appears at the end of the line. All footnotes are sequentially numbered on a given page. Numbering restarts at 1 on each page.
28. Enter the text Must be completed by next Tuesday as the footnote.
29. Close the tab or window to close the document.

Lesson 9-7

Editing and Commenting

Editing a document means making changes to the actual document. Commenting on the document allows a user to make notes and suggestions on the document. In order for a person to make comments, he or she must be the owner of the document or must be assigned editing or commenting access to the document.

Editing a Shared Document

1. Log in to your Google Mail account.
2. Click the **Drive** link in the menu bar at the top of the Mail page.
3. On the Drive page, click the **Shared with me** label. You should see the documents that have been shared with you by classmates in Lesson 9-2.
4. Open the Sports Awards Banquet Planning Sheet document from a classmate as specified by your instructor. This classmate will open your document at this time as well.
5. Click at the bottom of the document. This should be a blank line. If not, press the [Enter] key to create a new line.
6. Click the **Bulleted List** button, if needed to make the line part of the bulleted list.

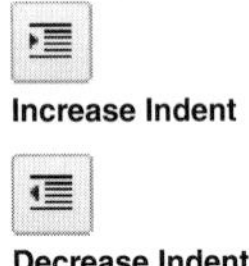

7. The level of bullet should match the line above it. If not, use the **Increase Indent** and **Decrease Indent** buttons so the bullet is the same indent level as the text Winner awards.
8. Enter the text Create program.

Commenting on a Specific Part of the Document

9. Select the text Create program.
10. Click the **Insert** pull-down menu, and click **Comment** in the menu. The selected text is highlighted, and a comment box appears, as shown in **Figure 9-18.**
11. Click in the text box in the comment box, and enter I will begin working on the program.

12. Click the **Comment** button to set the comment. The comment appears to the right side of the page where the comment box was.
13. Close the tab or window to close the document.

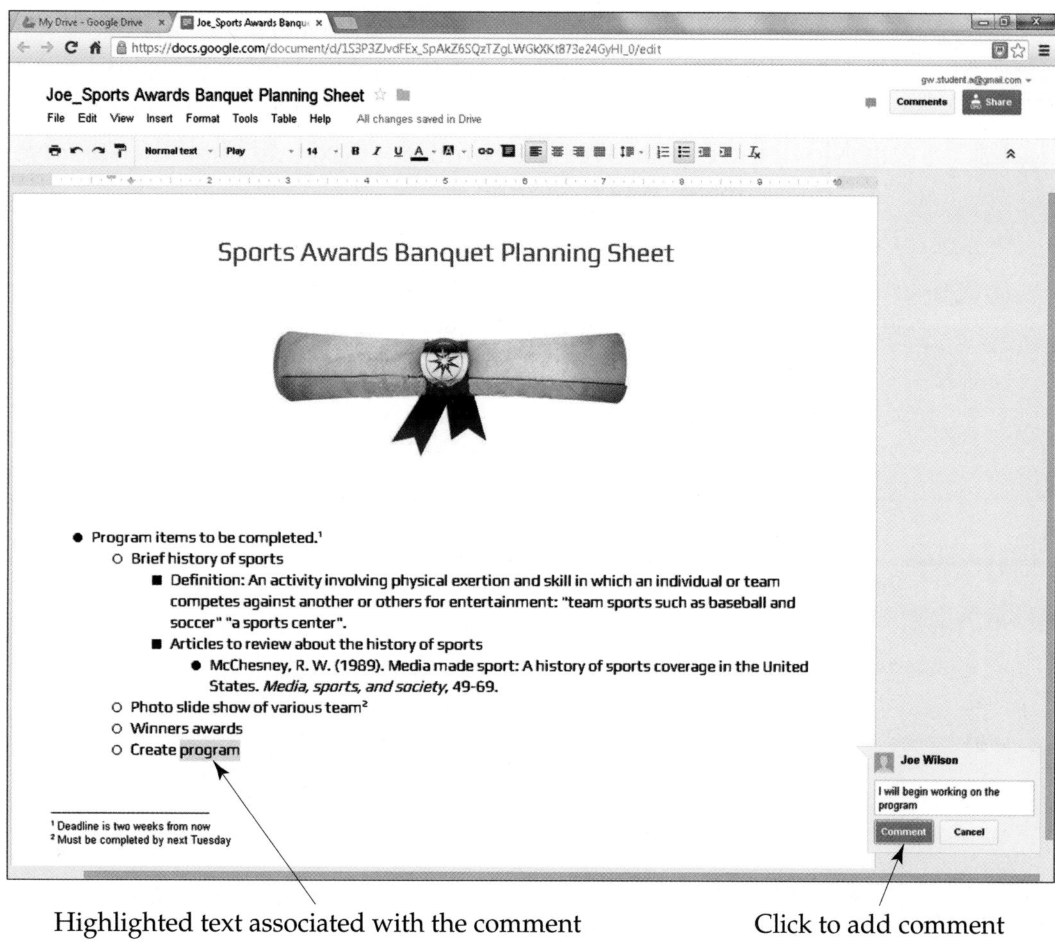

Goodheart-Willcox Publisher

Figure 9-18. When a user has been provided with commenter access, he or she can add comments that are tied to specific parts of the document.

Working with Comments

14. On the Drive page, open your original Sports Awards Banquet Planning Sheet document. This document should have a classmate's comment in it.
15. Click the classmate's comment. A text box appears in the comment box, as shown in **Figure 9-19.**

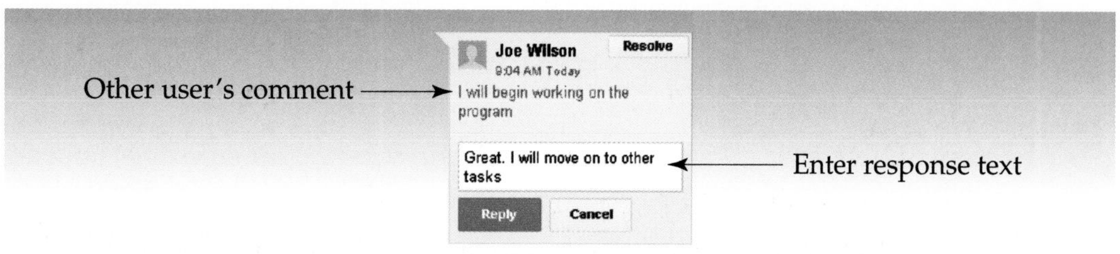

Goodheart-Willcox Publisher

Figure 9-19. A user can respond to another user's comments and, when appropriate, mark them as resolved.

16. Click in the text box, and enter Great, I will move on to other tasks as a reply.

Reply

17. Click the **Reply** button to post the reply. The reply is added to the comment box, similar to how a message is added to a chat.

Resolve

18. Move the cursor over the comment box, and click the **Resolve** button. The comment box is hidden.
19. Click the **Comments** at the top of the document page. All comments in the document are shown in a drop-down window, as shown in **Figure 9-20.**
20. Click the **Re-open** link in the comment you just resolved. The comment is restored to the edge of the document page.
21. Click anywhere in the document to close the drop-down window.
22. Click the comment to display the comment box.
23. In the comment you added, click the **Delete** link. A message appears asking to confirm the deletion.
24. Click the **Delete** button. This permanently removes the comment from the comment box. You can only delete comments that you added.
25. Close the tab or window to close the document.

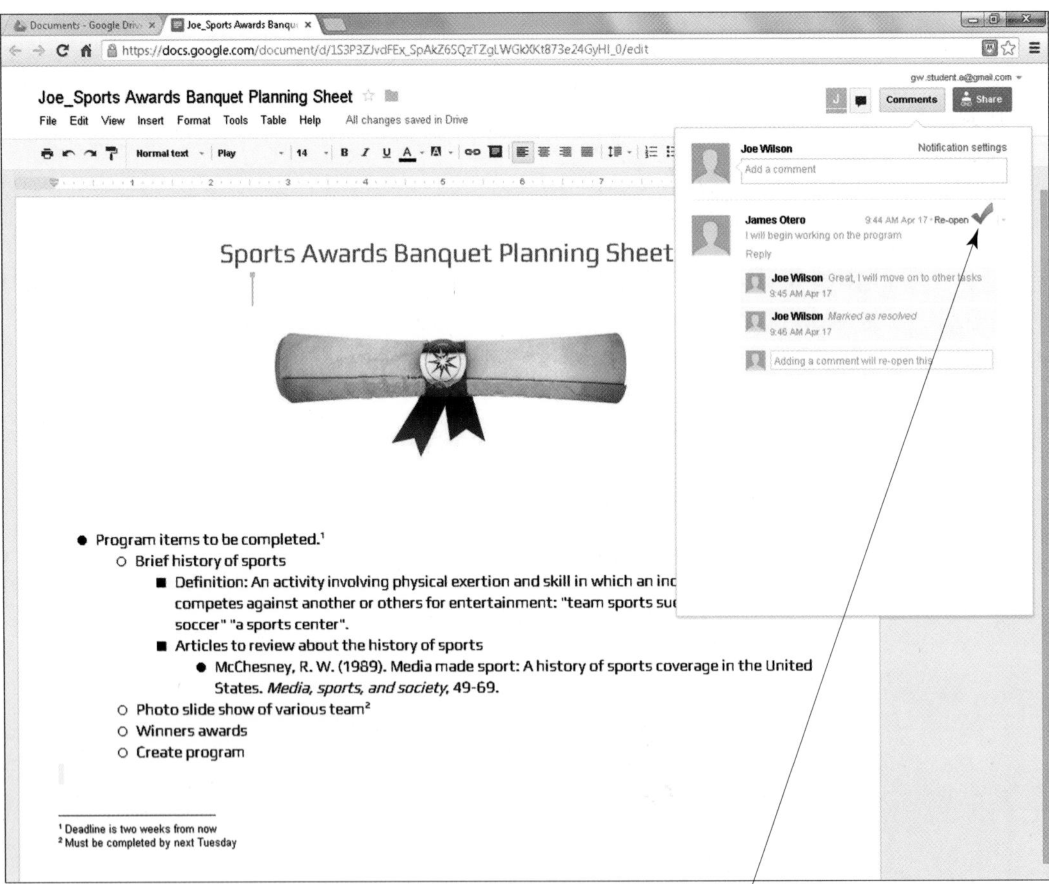

Goodheart-Willcox Publisher

Figure 9-20. To view all of the comments made on a document, a user can choose to display the comments drop-down window.

Lesson 9-8

Using the Revision History

The revision history feature in Google Documents allows a user to see changes made to a document and who made them. A user can also revert to a previous version of a document.

1. Log in to your Google Mail account.
2. Click the **Drive** link in the menu bar at the top of the Mail page.
3. On the Drive page, open your original Sports Awards Banquet Planning Sheet document.
4. Click the **File** pull-down menu, and click **See revision history** in the menu. The **Revision history** panel is displayed on the right side of the page, as shown in **Figure 9-21.** This shows a list of changes that have been made

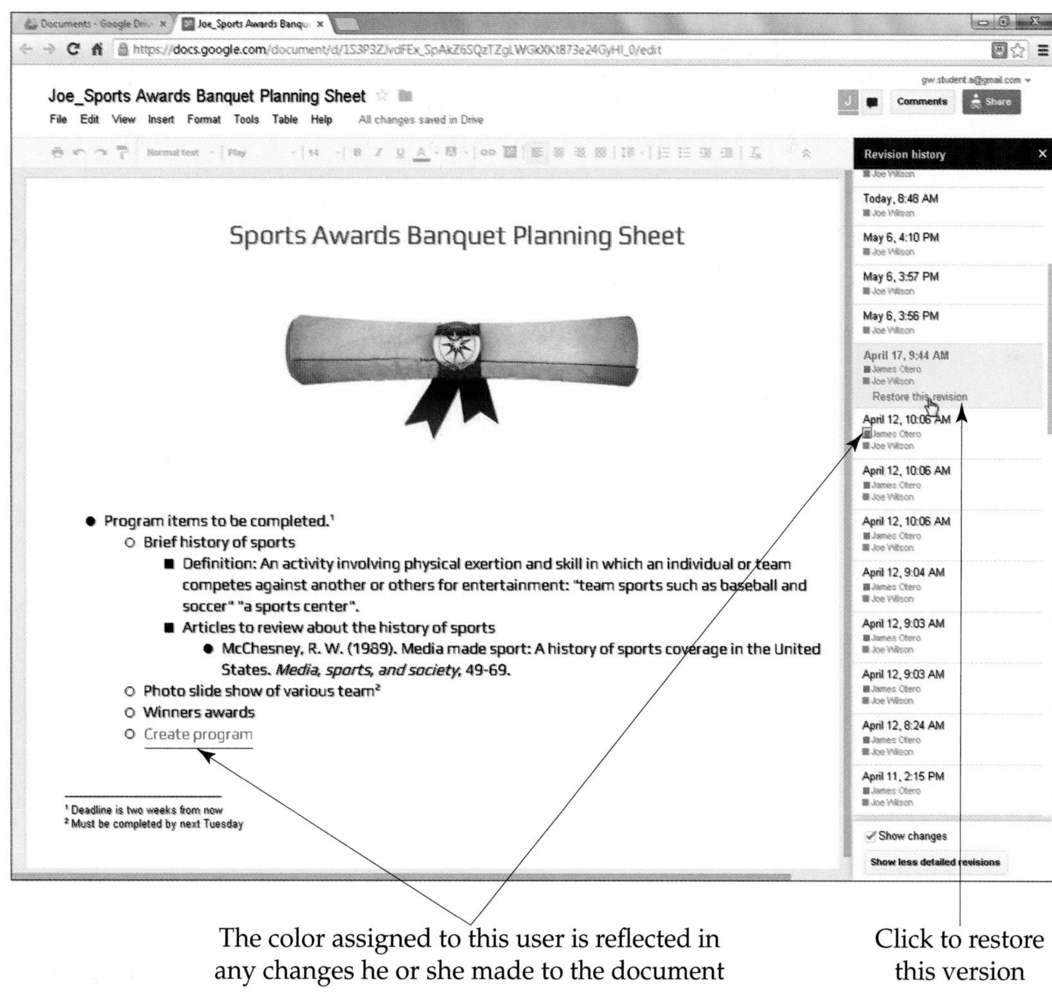

Goodheart-Willcox Publisher

Figure 9-21. The list of revisions can be displayed with less detail for each entry.

to the document with the most recent change at the top of the list. The changes are color coded by person, and each change has a time stamp.

Tip To close the **Revision history** panel, click the **X** in the upper-right corner of the panel.

5. Click an entry in the **Revision history** panel. The person's changes are displayed in the document in the color associated with the person, as shown in **Figure 9-21.** If the changes are not shown in the document, check the **Show changes** check box at the bottom of the **Revision history** panel.
6. By default, a detailed list is of revisions is shown. Click the **Show less detailed revisions** button at the bottom of the **Revision history** panel to view a condensed list.
7. Click the **Show more detailed revisions** button to display the detailed list.
8. Click a change entry. Notice the **Restore this revision** link that appears below the time stamp.
9. Click the **Restore this version** link. This removes all changes made after this time stamp, which are above this time stamp in the list, and closes the **Revision history** panel. Reverting to a previous version does not delete any other versions of the document.
10. Display the **Revision history** panel.
11. Click the second to last version, which is the second to the top of the list.
12. Click the **Restore this version** link. In effect, this undoes the restore completed earlier.
13. Close the tab or window to close the document.

Lesson 9-9

Downloading and Printing a Document

To open a Google Doc document in another software application, the user must download it. During the process, the user must select to which application file type the Google Doc will be converted.

Downloading a Document

1. Log in to your Google Mail account.
2. Click the **Drive** link in the menu bar at the top of the Mail page.
3. On the Drive page, open your original Sports Awards Banquet Planning Sheet document.
4. Click the **File** pull-down menu, and click **Download As** in the menu to display a cascading menu. See **Figure 9-22.**
5. Click **Microsoft Word** in the cascading menu to save the file in DOCx format. The file is saved on your local hard drive. A button also appears at the bottom of the document window for the downloaded document.

Tip The file name for the downloaded document is the same as the document name. If you download the same document more than once, the name is appended with a sequential number in parentheses.

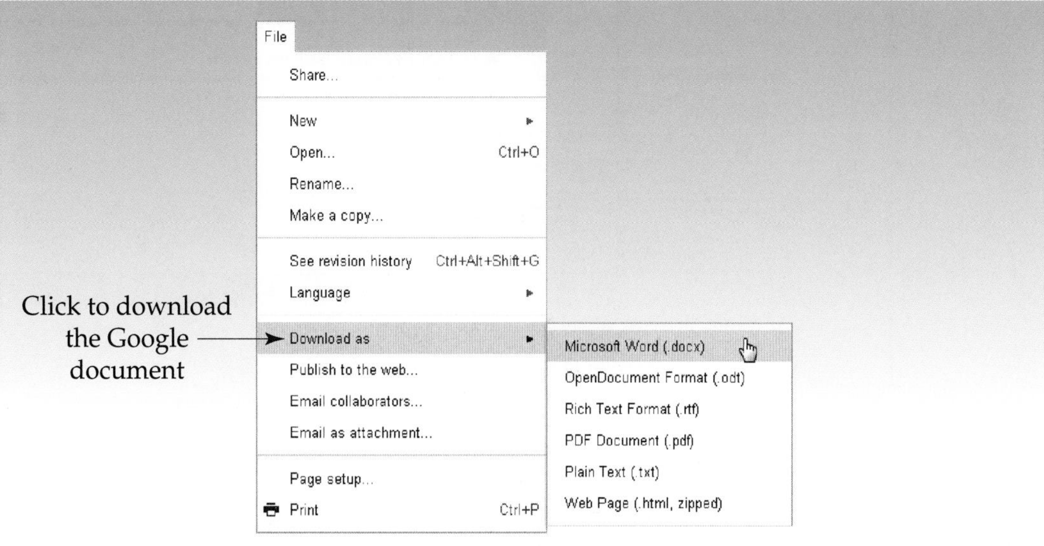

Goodheart-Willcox Publisher

Figure 9-22. Once a document is downloaded, changes made to that document in another software program will not be reflected in the original Google version of the file.

6. Click the arrow on the button for the downloaded document to display a drop-down menu.
7. Click **Show in folder** in the drop-down menu. This displays the folder in which the file was downloaded.
8. Close the folder window, and display the Google document page.
9. Click the button for the downloaded document to open it in the program associated with the DOCx file extension, which is usually Microsoft Word. Once you click this button, it is no longer displayed.
10. Close Microsoft Word, and display the Google document page.

Printing a Document

Print

11. Click the **Print** button on the toolbar. The **Print** dialog box is displayed, as shown in **Figure 9-23.**

You can also click the **File** pull-down menu, and click **Print** in the menu, or press the [Ctrl][P] key combination to print a document.

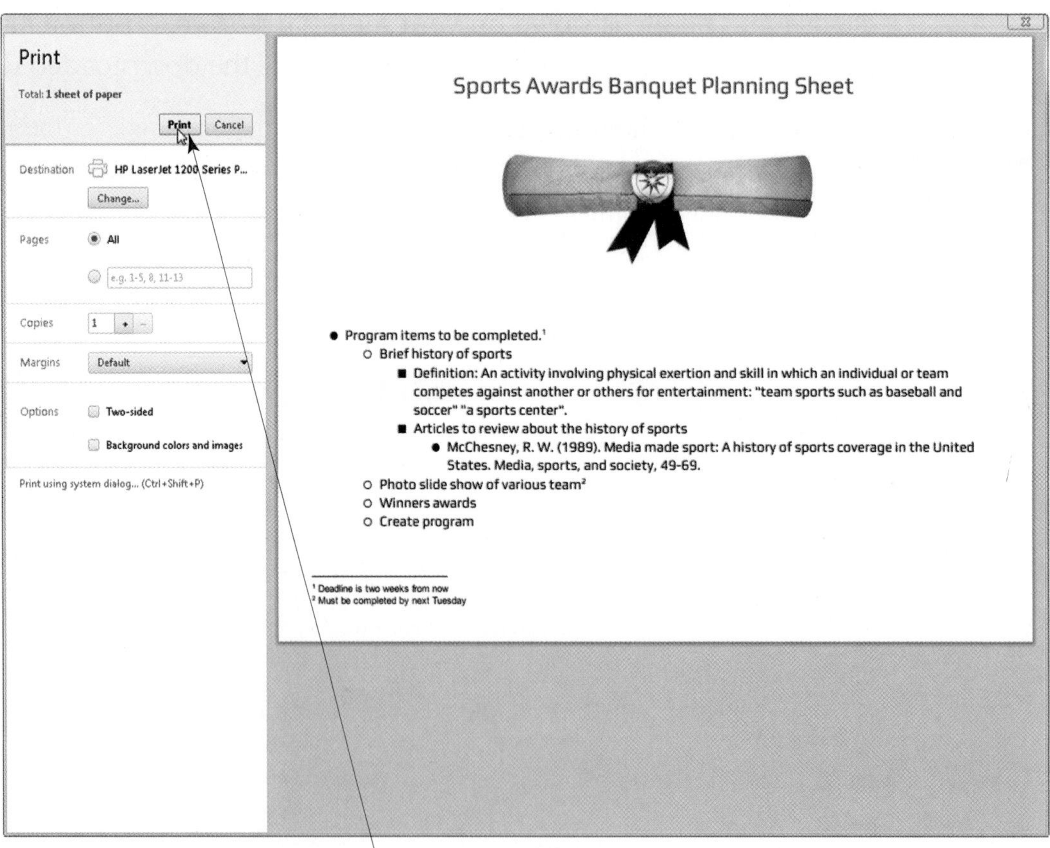

Goodheart-Willcox Publisher

Figure 9-23. The right side of the **Print** dialog box gives the user a preview of what the document will look like when printed.

12. In the **Destination** area of the dialog box, make sure your printer is selected. If necessary, click the **Change...** button, and select the correct printer.
13. In the **Copies** area of the dialog box, click in the text box and enter the number of copies to print.
14. Set any other options in the dialog box as specified by your instructor.
15. Click the **Print** button to send the document to the specified printer. The **Print** dialog box is closed, and the document is printed.
16. Close the tab or window to close the document.

Check Your Google Apps IQ

Now that you have finished this chapter, see what you know about Google Apps by taking the chapter posttest.
www.m.g-wlearning.com
www.g-wlearning.com/informationtechnology/

Skill Review

Answer the following questions on a separate sheet of paper.

1. Where are Google Docs files stored?
2. List the three visibility settings for a document.
3. A document can have up to ______ simultaneous editors.
4. What types of files can be imported into Google Docs?
5. List three types of basic formatting for text in a document.
6. What is the typical use for a footnote?
7. What is a paragraph style?
8. Which tool can be used to locate information about a topic and insert it as a footnote or text in a document?
9. Describe how Google Docs conducts spell checking.
10. Briefly describe how to revert to a previous version of a document.

Lesson Application

These exercises are designed to apply the skills learned in this and previous chapters. General directions are provided, but you will need to draw on your knowledge to determine how to complete each exercise.

Exercise 9-1
Collaborating on a Document

Open the Awardees List document of a classmate as specified by your instructor. Change the title text in the document from Awardees List to Banquet Awards List. Change the font of the title to a font not currently displayed in the **Font** drop-down list. Change the orientation of the page to landscape and all margins to 3/4″. Close the document.

Send the classmate an invitation to an event during the next class period to discuss the banquet awards list. When you receive a similar invitation, accept it.

Exercise 9-2
Formatting Text in a Document

After your classmate has completed Exercise 9-1, open your original Awardees List document. On a new line in the document, enter Basketball Winners, and format it in a color other than black. Set the size of the text to be smaller than the document title. Below this line, create a bulleted list as follows.

- MVP
- Most improved
- Most free throws

On a new line, end the bulleted list. Then, add a hyperlink to the website www.ncaa.org. The text to be displayed for the hyperlink should be College Resources. Close the document, and e-mail your classmate to tell him or her that your stage of the project is completed.

Exercise 9-3
Inserting an Image into a Document

When you receive the e-mail from your classmate indicating he or she is done with Exercise 9-2, open the classmate's Awardees List document. Navigate to the student companion website (www.g-wlearning.com/informationtechnology/), and download the Trophy data file to your working folder. Insert the image under the title Banquet Awards List. Add a comment indicating from where the file was downloaded. Add another comment asking your classmate what he or she thinks about the size of the image and if it should be resized. Close the document, and e-mail your classmate to indicate this stage of the project is completed.

Exercise 9-4
Using the Research Function in a Document

When you receive the e-mail from your classmate indicating he or she is done with Exercise 9-3, open your original Awardees List document. Respond to the comments your classmate added to the document.

On a new line below the College Resources, enter More information: and a space. Use the research tool to locate scholarly writing on the topic basketball in America. Insert the citation following APA style for one of the entries. Add footnotes as appropriate. If a footnote cites a source, be sure to follow the format specified by the style guide you are using (APA, MLA, or Chicago Manual of Style).

Close the document, and e-mail your classmate to indicate this stage of the project is completed. Also, e-mail your instructor.

Exercise 9-5
Using the Revision History

When you receive the e-mail from your classmate indicating he or she is done with Exercise 9-4 and your instructor has approved moving forward with this exercise, open the classmate's Awardees List document. Use the revision history to undo the changes made in Exercise 9-4. Add a comment to the document indicating you have undone this revision.

Close the document. Edit the event created in Exercise 9-1 to change the date of the event to the next time period. Also, invite your instructor to the event. In the next class period, meet with your classmate and instructor to discuss this collaborative project.

Chapter 10

Google Sheets

Objectives

After completing this chapter, you will be able to:

- **Collaborate** with others in a shared spreadsheet.
- **Apply** formatting to cells, including text size and color, background color, and data type.
- **Use** basic formulas to obtain data results in a spreadsheet.
- **Manage** data in a spreadsheet by sorting and filtering.
- **Create** a chart from data in a spreadsheet.

alexmillos/Shutterstock.com

Check Your Google Apps IQ

Before you begin this chapter, see what you already know about Google Apps by taking the chapter pretest.

www.m.g-wlearning.com
www.g-wlearning.com/informationtechnology/

Using Google Sheets

Google Sheets allows users to create and format spreadsheets. A ***spreadsheet*** is a layout of information arranged in rows and columns in a table. Spreadsheets are often used to organize information. People can populate spreadsheets with text-based information. However, one of the biggest advantages of using a spreadsheet is the ability to set it up to calculate numerical information. Spreadsheets are often used to organize information such as financial data, science experiment results, and schedules.

Spreadsheets are tabular with columns and rows, as seen in **Figure 10-1.** ***Columns*** are the vertical spaces running through the table. In Google Sheets and most other spreadsheet software, columns are labeled alphabetically. ***Rows*** are the horizontal spaces running through the table. In most spreadsheet software, rows are labeled numerically. ***Cells*** are the boxes created where the columns and rows meet. Google spreadsheets are limited to 400,000 cells, with a maximum of 256 columns per sheet.

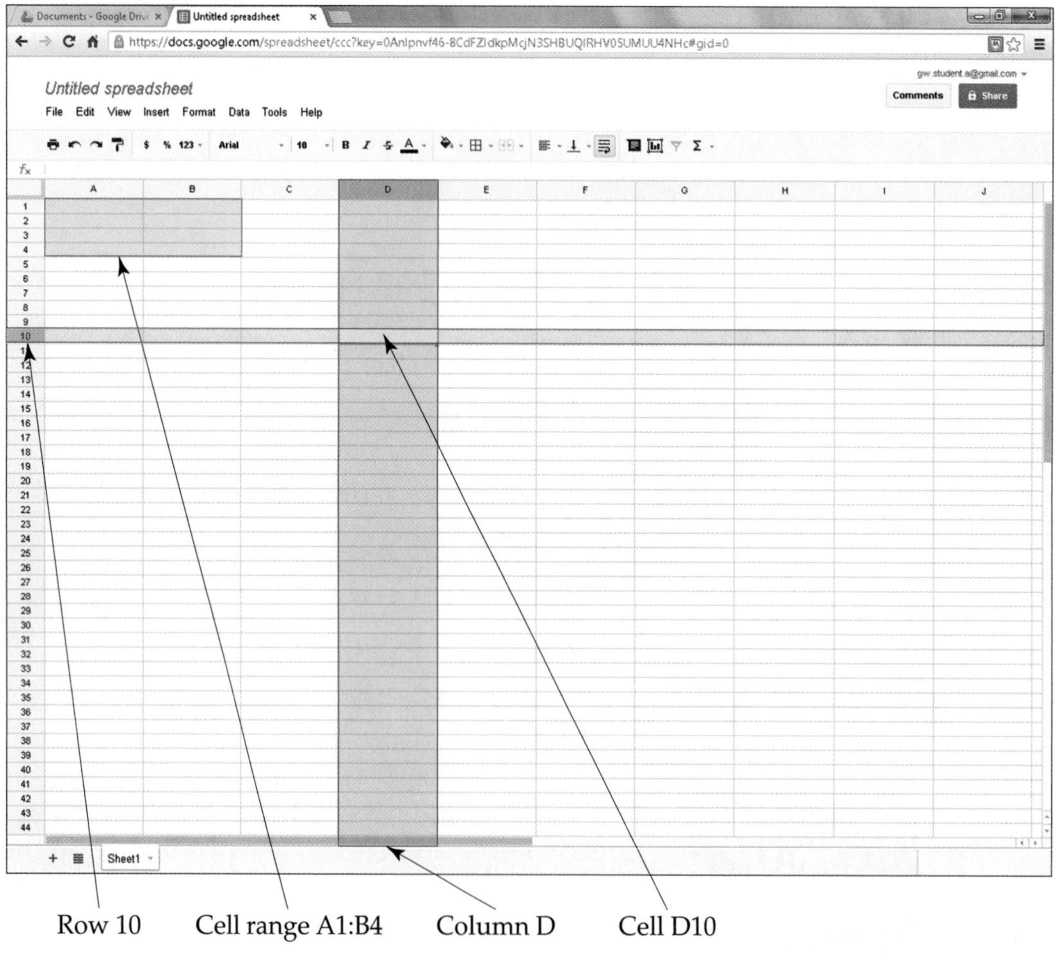

Goodheart-Willcox Publisher

Figure 10-1. A spreadsheet consists of cells arranged in rows and columns.

A cell name consists of the column letter and the row number. For example, cell B16 is found at the intersection of column B and row 16. A range of cells is represented by two cell names separated by a colon. For example, A1:F16 refers to all of the cells in the rectangular area between cells A1 and F16.

Spreadsheets can be created from scratch within Google Sheets or uploaded from other programs and converted into a Google Sheets spreadsheet. File types that can be uploaded and converted are Excel (XLS or XLSx), CSV, TXT, and OpenDocument Spreadsheet (ODS) files. Uploaded spreadsheet files that are to be converted to Google spreadsheets cannot be larger than 20 MB and must be under 400,000 cells and 256 columns per sheet. Once a file is uploaded and converted, it can be used like any other Google spreadsheet.

Sharing Google Sheets

Google Sheets allows users to easily share spreadsheets with others. Shared spreadsheets can be simultaneously viewed and edited by up to 200 users. To share a spreadsheet, the user that created the file, known as the *owner,* can set visibility and access settings, as discussed in Chapters 8 and 9. Care should be taken so simultaneous changes do not become confusing.

When multiple people are editing a spreadsheet simultaneously, everyone participating can identify who is editing. Google automatically assigns a color to each collaborator. The color assigned to each user is displayed. When a collaborator selects a cell to edit, the border of that cell is displayed in the color assigned to that user. Your editing color will always be blue in your view of the spreadsheet.

Formatting Spreadsheets

The usability of spreadsheets can be improved with formatting, as seen in **Figure 10-2.** Because spreadsheets are often used to organize numerical data, there are several numerical formats available for users. Formats such as currency, date, time, and percent automatically change the way the data are displayed.

Borders of rows, columns, or cells can also be formatted. If a user decides to use borders, he or she can determine which sides of the perimeter will have a border. The border line weight, style, and color can also vary. Content of cells can be formatted by changing the font type or size. Data can be bold, italic, underline, and strikethrough. A user can change the color of the data and the background of a cell. Color can be used to convey meaning or help organize information in a spreadsheet.

The format of data can be automatically changed if conditional formatting is used. ***Conditional formatting*** is when the formatting characteristics of a data set changes when user-specified conditions are met. For example, a user can set conditional formatting to change numbers to purple, bold text when the number is more than 50.

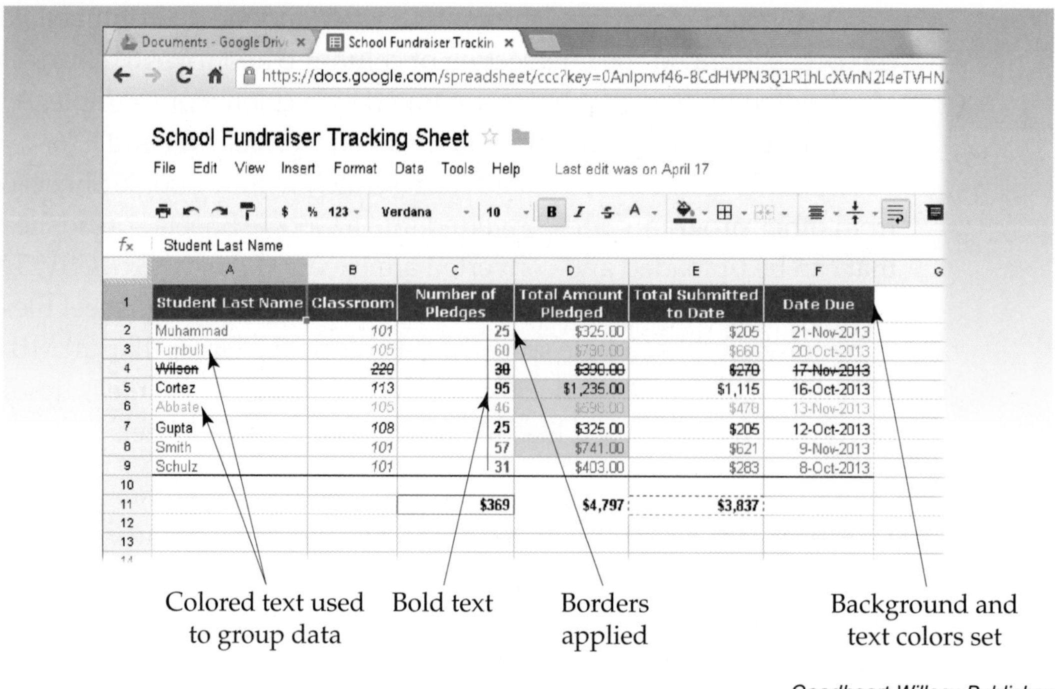

Goodheart-Willcox Publisher

Figure 10-2. Formatting of a spreadsheet can help identify the data it contains.

Often a user will create column or row headers when setting up a spreadsheet. ***Column headers*** or ***row headers*** are cells containing text that informs what data are contained in the rest of the cells in that column or row. For example, a user could create a column header titled Final Grades for a column in which he or she will enter the final grades for each student. In cases like these, it can be helpful to keep the column header in view even when the user needs to scroll down in the spreadsheet. A user can choose to freeze the row with the header. The freeze feature stops the topmost row or rows or the leftmost column or columns from moving as a user scrolls through the spreadsheet.

Columns and rows can be resized by the user. He or she can resize columns or rows manually by dragging the lines between them to the desired size. A column or row can also be automatically resized to fit the cell containing the most data. Additionally, cells can be merged. To ***merge*** a cell is to combine two or more cells within a single rectangular area into a single cell.

Using Formulas and the Auto-Fill Handle

Spreadsheets can be created with ***formulas,*** also called *expressions,* that will perform calculations. The most common formulas can be found in the **Functions** drop-down menu.

- The SUM function adds all of the numbers in a range to provide a total amount.
- The AVERAGE function adds all of the numbers in a range, and then divides the total by the total number of values.

- The COUNT function counts the total number of values in a range.
- The MAX function returns the maximum value in a range.
- The MIN function returns the minimum value in a range.

Basic math operations can be performed as well using the operators + – * and /, as seen in **Figure 10-3.** These formulas that point to cells in the spreadsheet recalculate the data when numbers change. Also, when formulas are copied and pasted, the pattern of the formula is maintained. For example, if the formula in cell E1 reads =SUM(A1,B1,D1), when the formula is copied to cell E2, it will become =SUM(A2,B2,D2).

When formulas or any other data are entered into a cell, they can also be easily copied into horizontally or vertically adjacent cells using auto-fill. In Google Sheets, the ***auto-fill*** feature allows the user to copy data to adjacent cells by selecting the cell, then dragging the auto-fill handle over cells to be filled with the copied content. Auto-fill recognizes patterns and will continue them.

A ***pattern*** is content that repeats in a consistent way. A user must demonstrate a pattern in at least two cells. If auto-fill recognizes the pattern in the selected cells, it will continue it. For example, if a user has entered 1 in a cell and 2 in the next cell, auto-fill will populate the four adjacent cells with the number sequence 3, 4, 5, and 6. Auto-fill recognizes patterns in dates, times, and some text as well. If a user has entered cat, dog, and bird into three adjacent cells, auto-fill will populate the cells with the same three-word pattern. If a pattern is not recognized, the content is simply copied into the other cells.

Sorting and Charting Data

In Google Sheets, a user can sort and chart data to visually organize the information for users. In Google Sheets, to ***sort*** is to rearrange the order of a range of cells or the rows based on alphabetical or numeric values. When sorting, a user can choose to change the order of just the selected cells in a column or all of the rows, too. Also, a user can choose to sort data in ascending

Symbol	Operation
+	Addition (+)
–	Subtraction (–)
*	Multiplication (×)
/	Division (÷)

Goodheart-Willcox Publisher

Figure 10-3. Mathematical operators can be used in formulas in a spreadsheet. The correct symbols must be used.

or descending order. To sort in ***ascending*** order is to begin a list with the lowest number or the first letter in the alphabet in the list and then increase in value for numbers and move toward the end through the alphabet for letters. To sort in ***descending*** order is to begin a list with the highest number or the last letter in the alphabet and then decrease in value for numbers and move toward the beginning through the alphabet for letters.

Creating *charts,* or *graphs,* can be a visually impactful way of displaying data. Google Sheets provides users with several chart types, including line, area, column, bar, scatter, pie, map, and trend, as seen in **Figure 10-4.** A user must be sure that his or her data are correctly set up to create the type of chart desired. Within the available chart types, various styles of each are available to users. Once a chart type and style are selected, the user can customize the chart with a legend and labels for each axis along with color and font types.

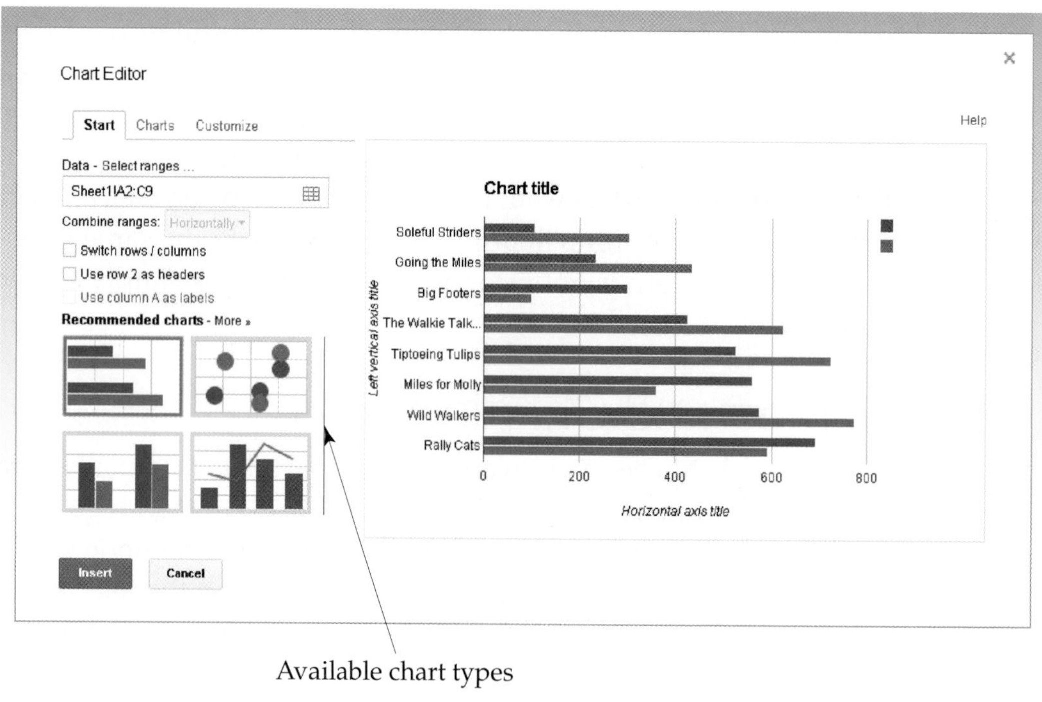

Goodheart-Willcox Publisher

Figure 10-4. Charts can be used to display data in graph form, which can make the data easier to analyze.

Lesson 10-1

Collaborating in a Shared Spreadsheet

The creator, known as the owner, of a Google spreadsheet can determine the visibility and accessibility settings to share it with other users to view, comment, or edit.

Starting a New Spreadsheet

1. Log in to your Google Mail account.
2. Click the **Drive** link in the menu bar at the top of the Mail page.
3. Navigate to the Documents subfolder. You will work with four classmates for this lesson, so make sure this folder is shared with those classmates.
4. Click the **Create** button, and click **Spreadsheet** in the drop-down menu. A new tab or window is opened containing a blank spreadsheet named Untitled, as seen in **Figure 10-5.**
5. Click the **File** pull-down menu, and click **Rename...** in the menu. The **Rename Document** dialog box is displayed.

CREATE

Tip The **Rename Document** dialog box can be quickly displayed by clicking the name of the spreadsheet at the top of the document.

6. Click in the **Enter a new document name:** text box, and enter M&M Events Coverage.
7. Click the OK button to rename the spreadsheet.
8. Click in cell A1, enter Event City, and then press the [Tab] key. Notice that the active cell is now B1, the cell directly to the right of A1.

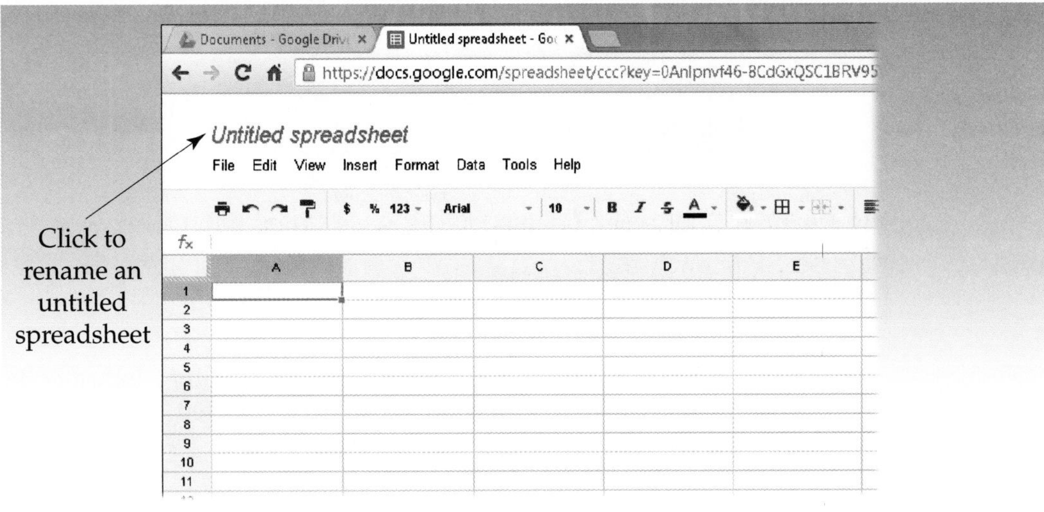

Goodheart-Willcox Publisher

Figure 10-5. Starting a new spreadsheet.

9. Enter Lead Planner in cell B1, and then press the [Tab] key. Enter Catering, Decorating, Entertainment, and Lighting and A/V in the next four adjacent cells to the right.
10. Click in cell A2, enter Chicago, and then press the [Enter] key. Notice that the active cell is now A3, the cell directly below A2. Enter Dallas, New York, Phoenix and Los Angeles in the four adjacent cells below A3. Your spreadsheet should look similar to the spreadsheet in **Figure 10-6.**
11. Close the tab or window to close the spreadsheet.

Collaborating in a Shared Spreadsheet

12. As directed by your instructor, open the M&M Events Coverage spreadsheet on your drive or shared with you by a classmate.
13. Using Google Hangouts, conduct a hangout with your team to determine who will be assigned to lead planner, catering, décor, entertainment, and lighting and audio visual (A/V) at each location. Each team member must be assigned to each type of task only twice.
14. In the spreadsheet, click in the cell corresponding to the task you will be assigned for the first venue (row 2). As you do this, your team will be doing the same thing. Notice that each user is assigned a color, and the cell in which a user is working is highlighted in that color, as shown in **Figure 10-6.**
15. Enter your name in the cell.
16. Continuing entering your name in the cells corresponding to the tasks assigned to you. Your name should appear once in each row and twice in each column.
17. Close the tab or window to close the spreadsheet.

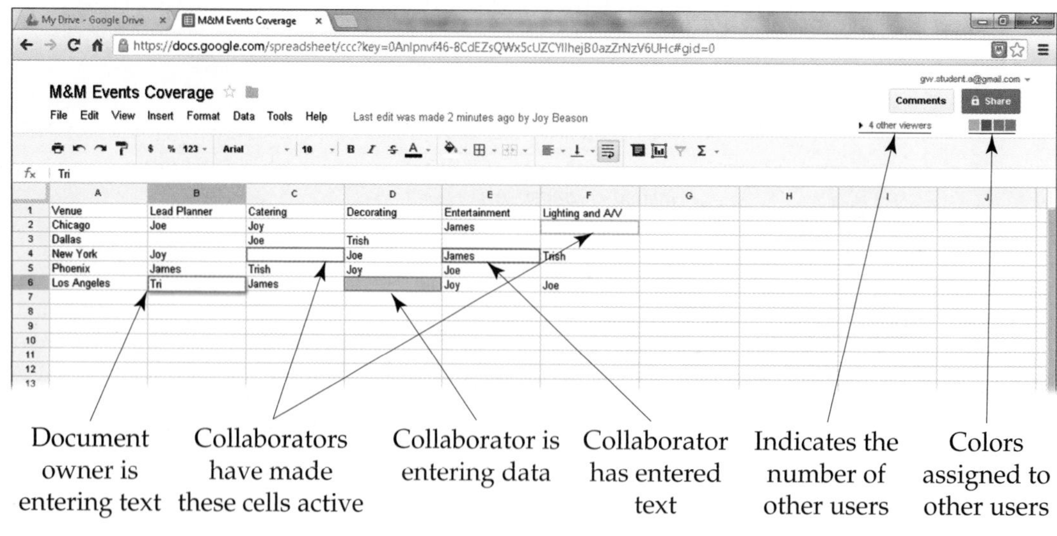

Goodheart-Willcox Publisher

Figure 10-6. When collaborating on a shared spreadsheet, each user is assigned a color.

Lesson 10-2

Formatting Cells

A user can create a spreadsheet or upload an existing one and convert it into a Google spreadsheet. Once the file is a Google spreadsheet a user can format data in spreadsheets. This can be of assistance to the people viewing the content.

Freezing Rows

1. Navigate to the student companion website (www.g-wlearning.com/informationtechnology/), and download the Charity Walk RSVP data file to your working folder. This is a Microsoft Excel file.
2. Log in to your Google Mail account.
3. Click the **Drive** link in the menu bar at the top of the Mail page.
4. Navigate to the Documents subfolder.

Upload

5. Click the **Upload** button, and click **Files...** in the drop-down menu.

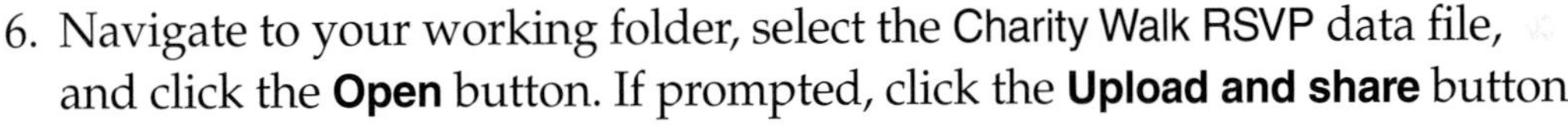

6. Navigate to your working folder, select the Charity Walk RSVP data file, and click the **Open** button. If prompted, click the **Upload and share** button.
7. A dialog box appears showing the status of the upload. When the upload is complete, close the dialog box. The file is now on your Google Drive and available for use.
8. Right-click on the data file in your Google Drive, click **Open With** in the shortcut menu, and click **Google Sheets** in the cascading menu. This converts the Microsoft Excel spreadsheet into a Google spreadsheet. A new file with the same name appears in the Google Drive.
9. On the Drive page, delete the Microsoft Excel (XLSx) spreadsheet.
10. Switch to the tab or window containing the Google spreadsheet. Move the cursor to the upper-left corner of the spreadsheet until it changes into a hand, as shown in **Figure 10-7.**
11. Click, hold, and drag the horizontal dashed line to just below row 1. This freezes the first row, which keeps the header row at the top of the spreadsheet.

Applying Borders

12. Click in cell A1, drag to cell F15, and release the mouse button to highlight (select) the range of cells A1 through F15.

Borders

13. Click the **Borders** button to display a drop-down menu.
14. Click the **All borders** button in the menu. This applies a border on all sides of each selected cell.

All borders

15. Click in any cell to deselect the range of cells and see the borders that were applied, as shown in **Figure 10-8.** Notice the borders are darker than the default lines defining cells.

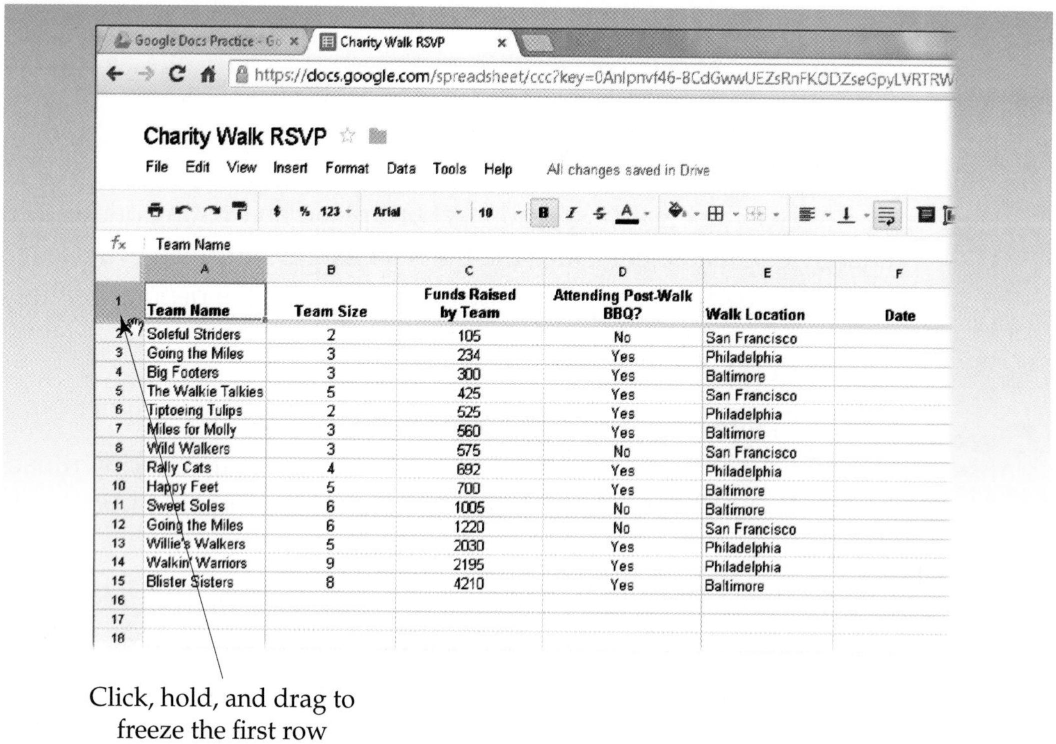

	A	B	C	D	E	F
1	Team Name	Team Size	Funds Raised by Team	Attending Post-Walk BBQ?	Walk Location	Date
2	Soleful Striders	2	105	No	San Francisco	
3	Going the Miles	3	234	Yes	Philadelphia	
4	Big Footers	3	300	Yes	Baltimore	
5	The Walkie Talkies	5	425	Yes	San Francisco	
6	Tiptoeing Tulips	2	525	Yes	Philadelphia	
7	Miles for Molly	3	560	Yes	Baltimore	
8	Wild Walkers	3	575	No	San Francisco	
9	Rally Cats	4	692	Yes	Philadelphia	
10	Happy Feet	5	700	Yes	Baltimore	
11	Sweet Soles	6	1005	No	Baltimore	
12	Going the Miles	6	1220	No	San Francisco	
13	Willie's Walkers	5	2030	Yes	Philadelphia	
14	Walkin' Warriors	9	2195	Yes	Philadelphia	
15	Blister Sisters	8	4210	Yes	Baltimore	

Click, hold, and drag to freeze the first row

Goodheart-Willcox Publisher

Figure 10-7. To freeze a row or column, drag the horizontal or vertical line in the upper-left corner of the sheet.

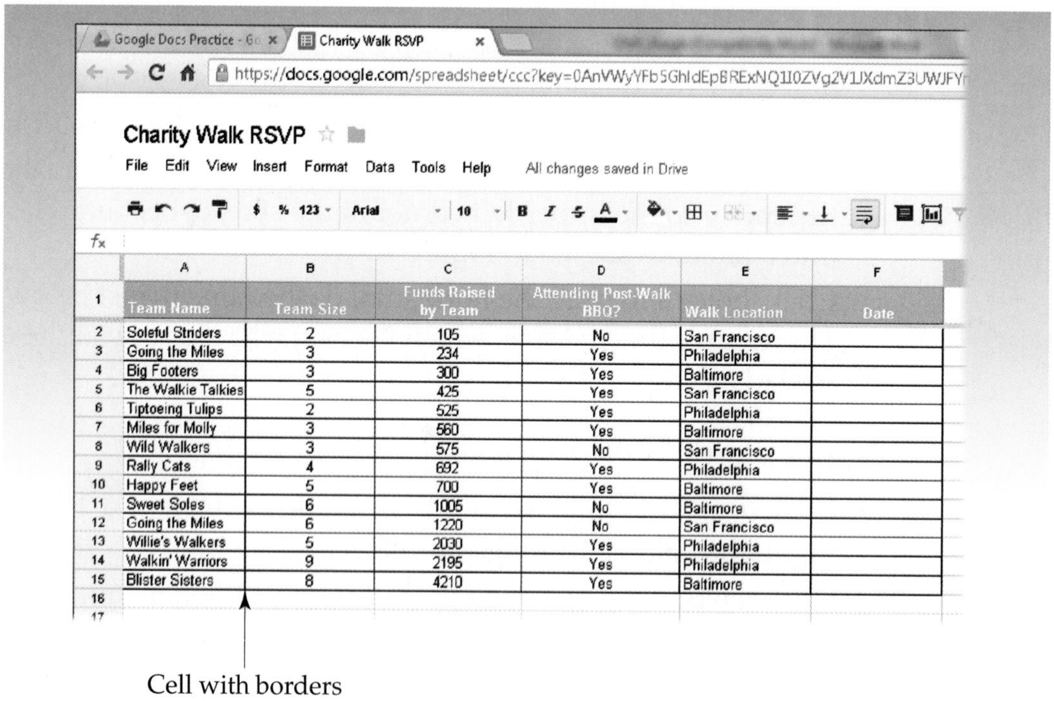

	A	B	C	D	E	F
1	Team Name	Team Size	Funds Raised by Team	Attending Post-Walk BBQ?	Walk Location	Date
2	Soleful Striders	2	105	No	San Francisco	
3	Going the Miles	3	234	Yes	Philadelphia	
4	Big Footers	3	300	Yes	Baltimore	
5	The Walkie Talkies	5	425	Yes	San Francisco	
6	Tiptoeing Tulips	2	525	Yes	Philadelphia	
7	Miles for Molly	3	560	Yes	Baltimore	
8	Wild Walkers	3	575	No	San Francisco	
9	Rally Cats	4	692	Yes	Philadelphia	
10	Happy Feet	5	700	Yes	Baltimore	
11	Sweet Soles	6	1005	No	Baltimore	
12	Going the Miles	6	1220	No	San Francisco	
13	Willie's Walkers	5	2030	Yes	Philadelphia	
14	Walkin' Warriors	9	2195	Yes	Philadelphia	
15	Blister Sisters	8	4210	Yes	Baltimore	

Cell with borders

Goodheart-Willcox Publisher

Figure 10-8. Borders have been applied to some cells in the spreadsheet.

Applying Text and Fill Colors

16. Select cells A1:F1. These cells are column headers. Even though the first row is frozen, action can still be taken on the cells in the row.

17. Click the **Fill color** button to display a drop-down menu.
18. Click a color swatch of your choice. The color is applied as the background color in the selected cells.

19. With the same cells selected, click on the **Text color** button to display a drop-down menu.
20. Click a color swatch of a color that contrasts with the background color you selected. For example, on a dark background, light text provides good contrast.

Automatically Filling Cells

21. Click in cell E2 to select it.
22. Move the cursor over the small square in the bottom-right corner of the cell.
23. Click and hold the small square, and drag it down to cell E5, as shown below in **Figure 10-9.** The content of the originally selected cell (San Francisco) is copied into cells E2, E3, E4, and E5, replacing any existing content.

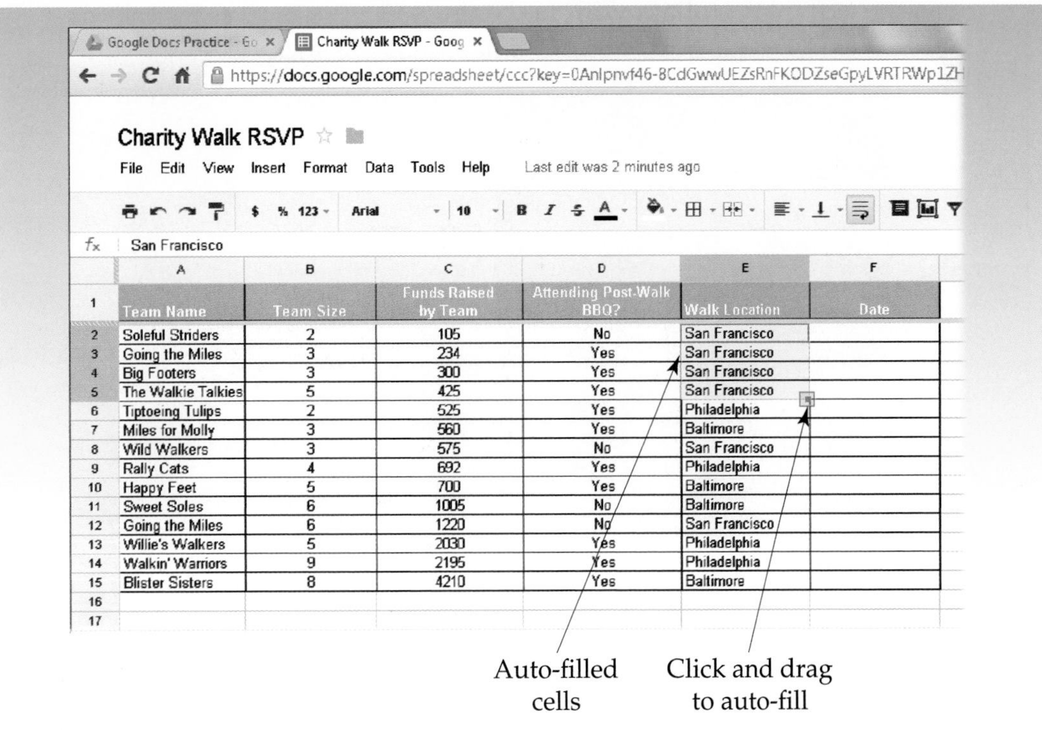

Goodheart-Willcox Publisher

Figure 10-9. The fill handle can be used to automatically copy data to other cells.

To quickly copy the contents of a cell into a series of blank cells below it, double-click the fill handle. The empty cells are filled down to the last cell to the left that contains data.

24. Click in cell F2, and enter Jan 15. Notice that when you press the [Enter] key the date is changed to the format 1/15/201*x*. Unless the cell has been formatted for plain text, Google automatically interprets Jan 15 as a date and uses a default format for it.
25. Enter Feb 15 in cell F3. The date automatically changes format.
26. Select cells F2 and F3.
27. Click the fill handle and drag it down to cell F15. The cells are automatically filled in with sequential months with the date of the 15th. Google uses the pattern established by the data in the selected cells to fill the other cells.

Formatting Data

More formats

28. Click the **C** column header. This selects the entire column.
29. Click the **More formats** button to display a drop-down menu.

The **Format as Currency** button can be used to quickly change the number formatting to the default currency setting of dollars with cents.

30. Click the first currency option in the pull-down menu, as shown in **Figure 10-10.** This sets the format of the cells containing numbers to display dollars with no cents.

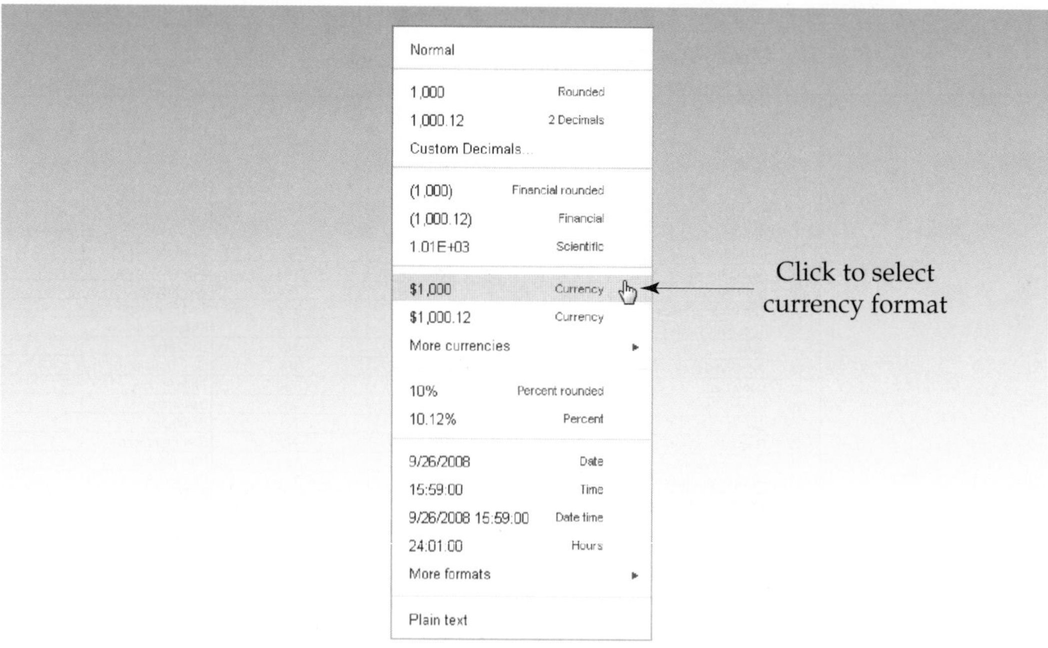

Goodheart-Willcox Publisher

Figure 10-10. Selecting a currency format for data in a cell.

31. Select the range of cells F2:F15. These dates are currently formatted as m/d/yyyy.

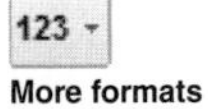

More formats

32. Click the **More formats** button to display a drop-down menu.
33. Click **More formats** in the section of the drop-down menu that contains date formats to display a cascading menu.
34. Click **09-26-2008** in the cascading menu. The dates in the cells are updated to the format mm-dd-yyyy.

Using Conditional Formatting

35. Click the **C** column header. This selects the entire column.
36. Click the **Format** pull-down menu, and click **Conditional formatting...** in the menu. The **Conditional formatting** dialog box is displayed, as shown in **Figure 10-11.**
37. Click the left-hand button to display a drop-down menu, and click **Greater than** in the menu. This sets the conditional operator.
38. In the text box to the left of the conditional operator, enter $999.99. This sets the value being compared.
39. Check the **Text:** check box. A drop-down menu appears.
40. Click the black color swatch in the drop-down menu. This sets the color of text for cells that match the condition.
41. Check the **Background:** check box. A drop-down menu appears.
42. Click a light green color swatch in the drop-down menu. This sets the color of background for cells that match the condition.
43. Click the **Save rules** button to close the dialog box and apply the conditional formatting. All cells in column C that contain a value of $1000 or more are changed to have a green background.

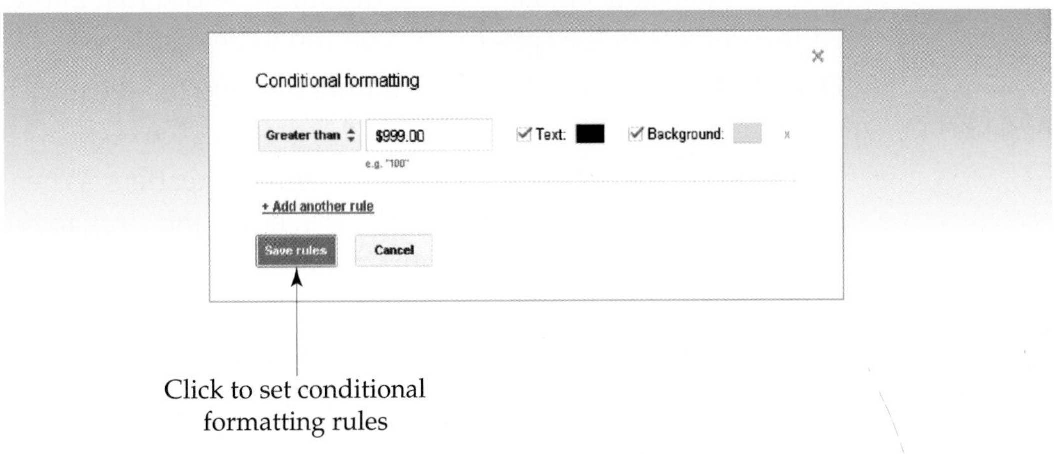

Goodheart-Willcox Publisher

Figure 10-11. Applying conditional formatting.

Merging Cells

44. Click in cell G2, and enter 13:00.

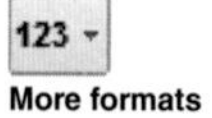
More formats

45. With cell G2 selected, click the **More formats** button, and click **More formats** in the section of the drop-down menu that contains date formats to display a cascading menu.
46. Click **3:59 PM** in the cascading menu. The data in the cell are updated to a 12-hour clock time in the format hour and minute. The data 13:00 are interpreted as a 24-hour clock time and converted to a 12-hour clock time.
47. Use the fill handle to copy the contents of cell G2 into cells G3 through G15.
48. Select cells F1 and G1.

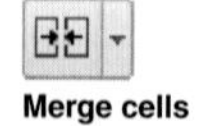
Merge cells

49. Click the **Merge cells** button. The two cells are horizontally combined into one.

If more than one selected cell contains data, only the data in the top-left cell are retained in the merged cells.

50. Select cells E2 through E5. These cells all contain the data San Francisco.

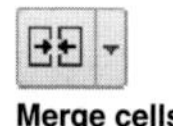
Merge cells

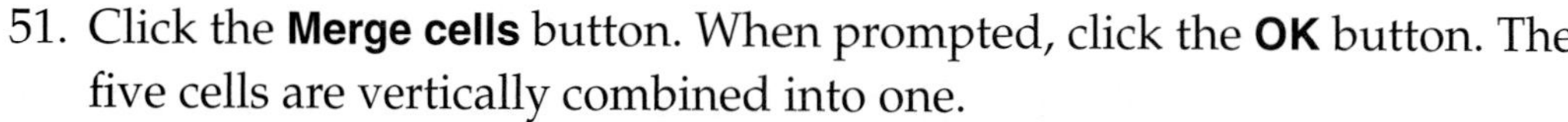

51. Click the **Merge cells** button. When prompted, click the **OK** button. The five cells are vertically combined into one.

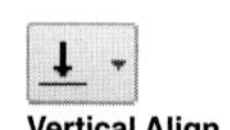
Vertical Align

52. With the merged cell selected, click the **Vertical align** button, and click the **Middle** button in the drop-down menu.

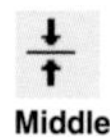
Middle

53. Using this same method, combine other cells in column E that contain the same city name.

Resizing Columns

54. Move the cursor to the vertical line between the **G** and **H** column headers. When the blue line appears, double-click. The width of column G is automatically adjusted to the minimum width that allows for the entire contents of the cells in that column to be displayed.
55. Double-click between the other column headers to adjust each column to the minimum width.
56. Move the cursor between the D and E column headers. When the cursor changes to the resize cursor, click, hold, and drag to the left to manually resize the column. Your spreadsheet should now look similar to **Figure 10-12.**
57. Close the tab or window to close the spreadsheet.

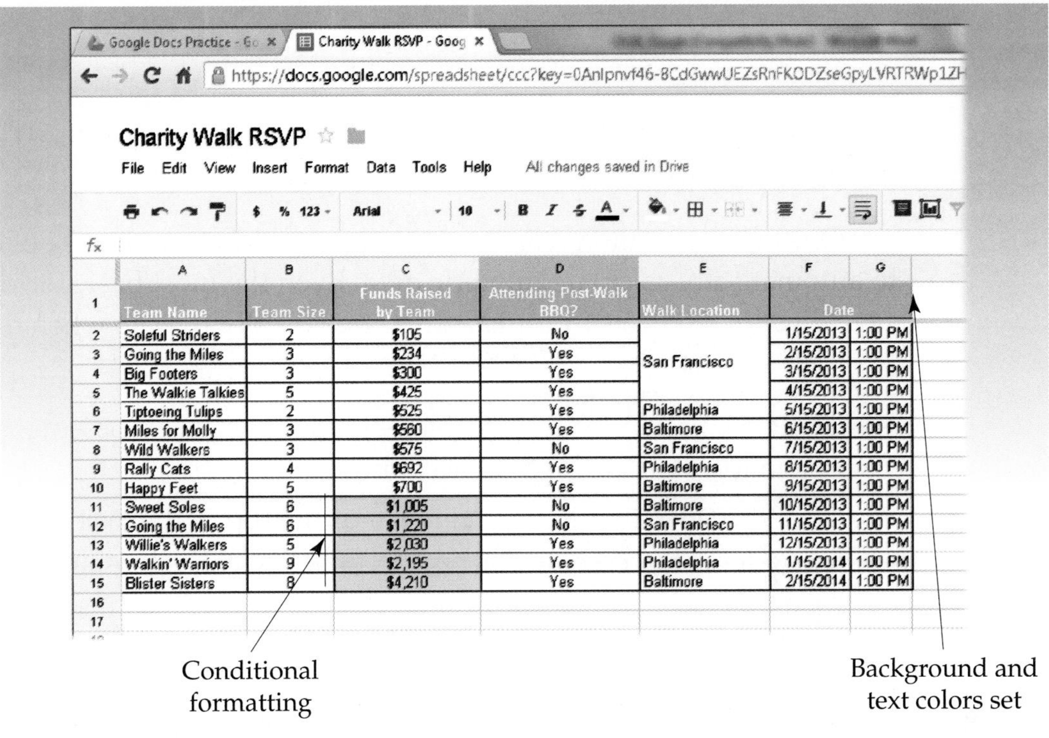

	A	B	C	D	E	F	G
1	Team Name	Team Size	Funds Raised by Team	Attending Post-Walk BBQ?	Walk Location	Date	
2	Soleful Striders	2	$105	No	San Francisco	1/15/2013	1:00 PM
3	Going the Miles	3	$234	Yes		2/15/2013	1:00 PM
4	Big Footers	3	$300	Yes		3/15/2013	1:00 PM
5	The Walkie Talkies	5	$425	Yes		4/15/2013	1:00 PM
6	Tiptoeing Tulips	2	$525	Yes	Philadelphia	5/15/2013	1:00 PM
7	Miles for Molly	3	$560	Yes	Baltimore	6/15/2013	1:00 PM
8	Wild Walkers	3	$575	No	San Francisco	7/15/2013	1:00 PM
9	Rally Cats	4	$692	Yes	Philadelphia	8/15/2013	1:00 PM
10	Happy Feet	5	$700	Yes	Baltimore	9/15/2013	1:00 PM
11	Sweet Soles	6	$1,005	No	Baltimore	10/15/2013	1:00 PM
12	Going the Miles	6	$1,220	No	San Francisco	11/15/2013	1:00 PM
13	Willie's Walkers	5	$2,030	Yes	Philadelphia	12/15/2013	1:00 PM
14	Walkin' Warriors	9	$2,195	Yes	Philadelphia	1/15/2014	1:00 PM
15	Blister Sisters	8	$4,210	Yes	Baltimore	2/15/2014	1:00 PM
16							
17							

Goodheart-Willcox Publisher

Figure 10-12. Columns have been resized in this spreadsheet to create a better visual presentation of the data.

Lesson 10-3

Basic Formulas

One of the common reasons to use a spreadsheet is the use of formulas to automatically calculate numeric data. Even the most basic formulas can save time for users, as formulas can automatically update when data change.

Using the SUM Function

1. Log in to your Google Mail account.
2. Click the **Drive** link in the menu bar at the top of the Mail page.
3. Navigate to the Charity Walk RSVP spreadsheet, and open it.
4. Click in cell C16 to make it active.
5. Click the **Functions** button to display a drop-down menu.

Σ
Functions

6. Click **SUM** in the drop-down menu. The expression =SUM() is automatically entered into the active cell, and the blinking cursor is between the parentheses, as shown in **Figure 10-13.**
7. With the blinking cursor between the parentheses, move the mouse and select cells C2:C15. The range is automatically added to the expression in cell C16 when the mouse button is released, and the range of cells is highlighted.

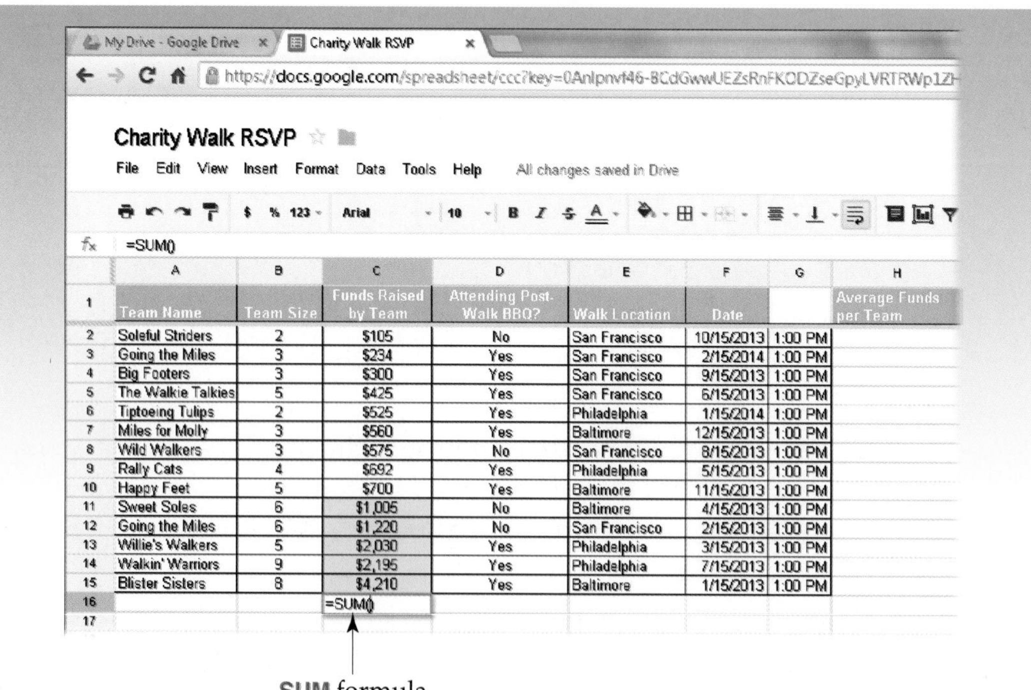

	A	B	C	D	E	F	G	H
1	Team Name	Team Size	Funds Raised by Team	Attending Post-Walk BBQ?	Walk Location	Date		Average Funds per Team
2	Soleful Striders	2	$105	No	San Francisco	10/15/2013	1:00 PM	
3	Going the Miles	3	$234	Yes	San Francisco	2/15/2014	1:00 PM	
4	Big Footers	3	$300	Yes	San Francisco	9/15/2013	1:00 PM	
5	The Walkie Talkies	5	$425	Yes	San Francisco	6/15/2013	1:00 PM	
6	Tiptoeing Tulips	2	$525	Yes	Philadelphia	1/15/2014	1:00 PM	
7	Miles for Molly	3	$560	Yes	Baltimore	12/15/2013	1:00 PM	
8	Wild Walkers	3	$575	No	San Francisco	8/15/2013	1:00 PM	
9	Rally Cats	4	$692	Yes	Philadelphia	5/15/2013	1:00 PM	
10	Happy Feet	5	$700	Yes	Baltimore	11/15/2013	1:00 PM	
11	Sweet Soles	6	$1,005	No	Baltimore	4/15/2013	1:00 PM	
12	Going the Miles	6	$1,220	No	San Francisco	2/15/2013	1:00 PM	
13	Willie's Walkers	5	$2,030	Yes	Philadelphia	3/15/2013	1:00 PM	
14	Walkin' Warriors	9	$2,195	Yes	Philadelphia	7/15/2013	1:00 PM	
15	Blister Sisters	8	$4,210	Yes	Baltimore	1/15/2013	1:00 PM	
16			=SUM()					
17								

Goodheart-Willcox Publisher

Figure 10-13. When a function is selected, the expression is automatically entered, and the cursor is between the parentheses ready for cell names to be entered.

Instead of clicking cells to enter a range in an expression, the cell names can be manually entered between the parentheses. Use a colon to specify a range of cells or a comma to specific individual cells.

8. Press the [Enter] key to set the expression. The data in the cell display the sum of the values of cells C2:C15, which is $14,776.

Using the COUNT Function

9. Click in cell B16 to make it active.

Σ ▾ Functions

10. Click the **Functions** button to display a drop-down menu.
11. Click **COUNT** in the drop-down menu. The expression =COUNT() is automatically entered into the active cell, and the blinking cursor is between the parentheses.
12. With the blinking cursor between the parentheses, move the mouse and select cells B2:B15. The range is automatically added to the expression in cell B16 when the mouse button is released, and the range of cells is highlighted.
13. Press the [Enter] key to set the expression. The data in the cell display the number of cells in the range, which is 14.

Using the AVERAGE Function

14. Click in cell H1 to make it active.
15. Enter the text Average Funds per Team.

Paint format

16. Click in cell E1, and then click the **Paint format** button.
17. Click in cell H1. The formatting applied to E1 is displayed in cell H1.
18. Click in cell H16 to make it active.
19. Format the data as dollars with no cents.

Functions

20. Click the **Functions** button to display a drop-down menu.
21. Click **AVERAGE** in the drop-down menu. The expression =AVERAGE() is automatically entered into the active cell, and the blinking cursor is between the parentheses.
22. With the blinking cursor between the parentheses, move the mouse and select cells C2:C15. The range is automatically added to the expression in cell H16 when the mouse button is released, and the range of cells is highlighted.
23. Press the [Enter] key to set the expression. The data display the average of the selected cells. The result is the same as adding each value and dividing by the total number of values, which could be entered as =SUM(C2:C15)/COUNT(C2:C15), which is $1,055.

Using the MIN and MAX Functions

24. Click in cell I1 to make it active.
25. Enter the text Least Amount Raised.
26. Use the **Paint format** button to format the cell to appear the same as the other cells in the first row.
27. Click in cell J1 to make it active.
28. Enter the text Greatest Amount Raised.
29. Use the **Paint format** button to format the cell to appear the same as the other cells in the first row.
30. Click in cell I16 to make it active.
31. Format the data as dollars with no cents.

Functions

32. Click the **Functions** button to display a drop-down menu.
33. Click **MIN** in the drop-down menu. The expression =MIN() is automatically entered into the active cell, and the blinking cursor is between the parentheses.
34. With the blinking cursor between the parentheses, move the mouse and select cells C2:C15. The range is automatically added to the expression in cell I16 when the mouse button is released, and the range of cells is highlighted.
35. Press the [Enter] key to set the expression. The data display the least value in the selected range of cells, which is $105.
36. Click in cell J16 to make it active.
37. Format the data as dollars with no cents.

Σ Functions

38. Click the **Functions** button to display a drop-down menu.
39. Click **MAX** in the drop-down menu. The expression =MAX() is automatically entered into the active cell, and the blinking cursor is between the parentheses.
40. With the blinking cursor between the parentheses, move the mouse and select cells C2:C15. The range is automatically added to the expression in cell J16 when the mouse button is released, and the range of cells is highlighted.
41. Press the [Enter] key to set the expression. The data display the greatest value in the selected range of cells, which is $4,210.
42. Click in cell C2, enter 265, and then press the [Enter] key. Notice that the formulas in cells C16, H16, and I16 have been updated to reflect the new data.
43. Close the tab or window to close the spreadsheet.

Lesson 10-4

Sorting and Filtering Data

Users can sort data by one or more columns, based on rules they establish. There are several ways to sort data. Filtering allows users to isolate specific rows in their data set based on criteria in one or more columns.

Sorting a Sheet

1. Log in to your Google Mail account.
2. Click the **Drive** link in the menu bar at the top of the Mail page.
3. Navigate to the Charity Walk RSVP spreadsheet, and open it.
4. In column E, select the first set of merged cells.
5. Click the **Merge Cells** button to unmerge the cells. Notice the value (San Francisco) is placed in the topmost cell and the other unmerged cells are empty. Also notice the borders disappeared from the unmerged cells.

Tip A sheet that contains vertically merged cells cannot be sorted.

6. Click in cell E2, and double-click the fill handle to copy San Francisco into the blank unmerged cells.
7. Unmerge the other vertically merged cells in column E, and copy the data into the blank cells.
8. Apply a border to the cells in column E.
9. Move the cursor over the **B** column header. Notice a drop-down arrow appears at the right-hand side of the header, as shown in **Figure 10-14.**
10. Click the arrow to display a drop-down menu.
11. Click **Sort Sheet A → Z** in the drop-down menu. The rows of the spreadsheet are reordered based on the values in column B, from lowest value at the top to highest value at the bottom.

Tip Click **Sort Sheet Z → A** to arrange rows from highest value to lowest value.

Sorting a Range

12. Select the range of cells A1:G15.
13. Click the **Data** pull-down menu, and click **Sort range...** in the menu. The **Sort Range** dialog box is displayed, as shown in **Figure 10-15.**
14. Check the **Data has header row** check box.

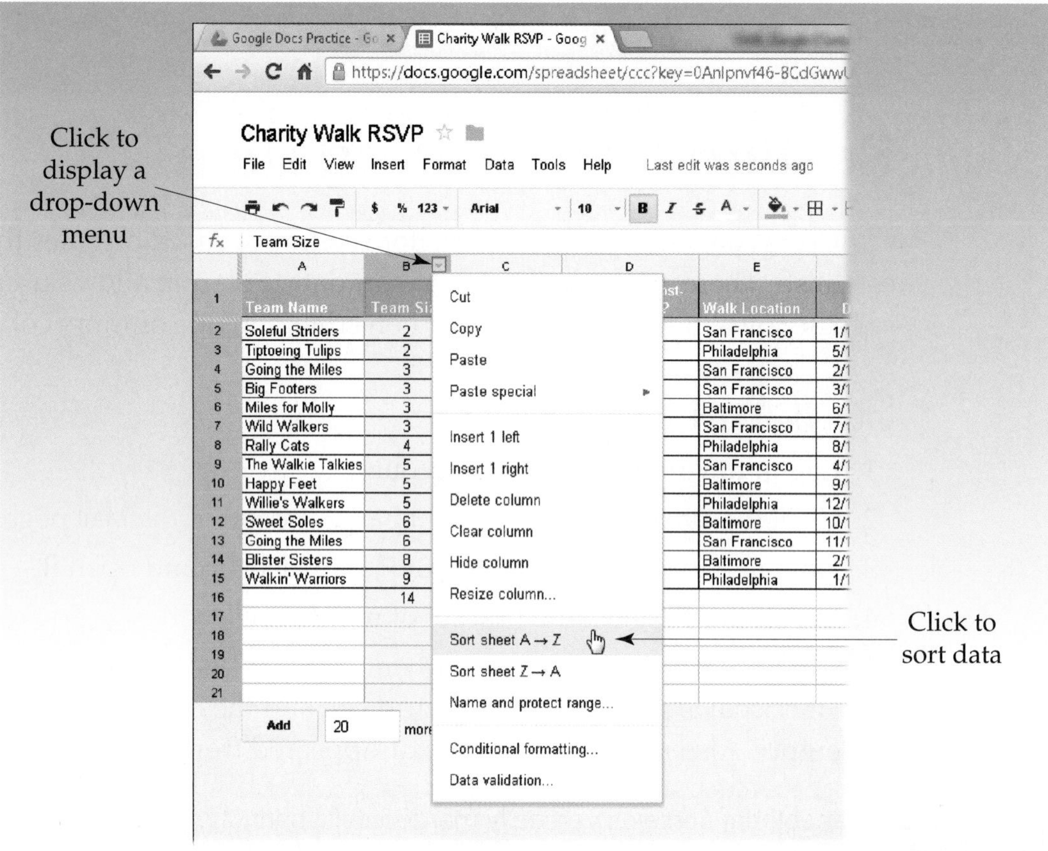

Goodheart-Willcox Publisher

Figure 10-14. The drop-down arrow in a column header displays a menu that contains options for sorting data.

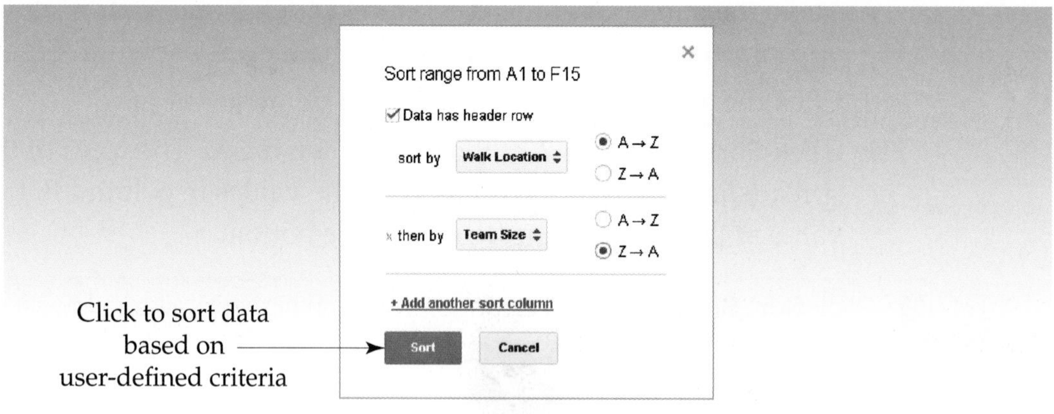

Goodheart-Willcox Publisher

Figure 10-15. The **Sort Range** dialog box is used to specify how a range of cells is sorted.

15. Click the **Sort by** button, and click **Walk Location** in the drop-down menu.
16. Click the **+ Add another sort column** link, click the new button that appears, and click **Team Size** in the drop-down menu.
17. Click the two **Z → A** radio buttons.
18. Click the **Sort** button. The spreadsheet is rearranged first based on the city name, and then by the team size. All of the rows with the city of San Francisco appear at the top, and those rows are then arranged so the largest team is at the top of that group of rows.

Filtering Data

19. Select the range of cells A1:F15, if not already selected.

Filter

20. Click the **Filter** button. Drop-down arrows appear in the top-right corner of each column header, as shown in **Figure 10-16.**
21. Click the drop-down arrow in the Walk Location column (column E). A dialog box is displayed. Notice that the three cities in the column are listed, each with a check mark.

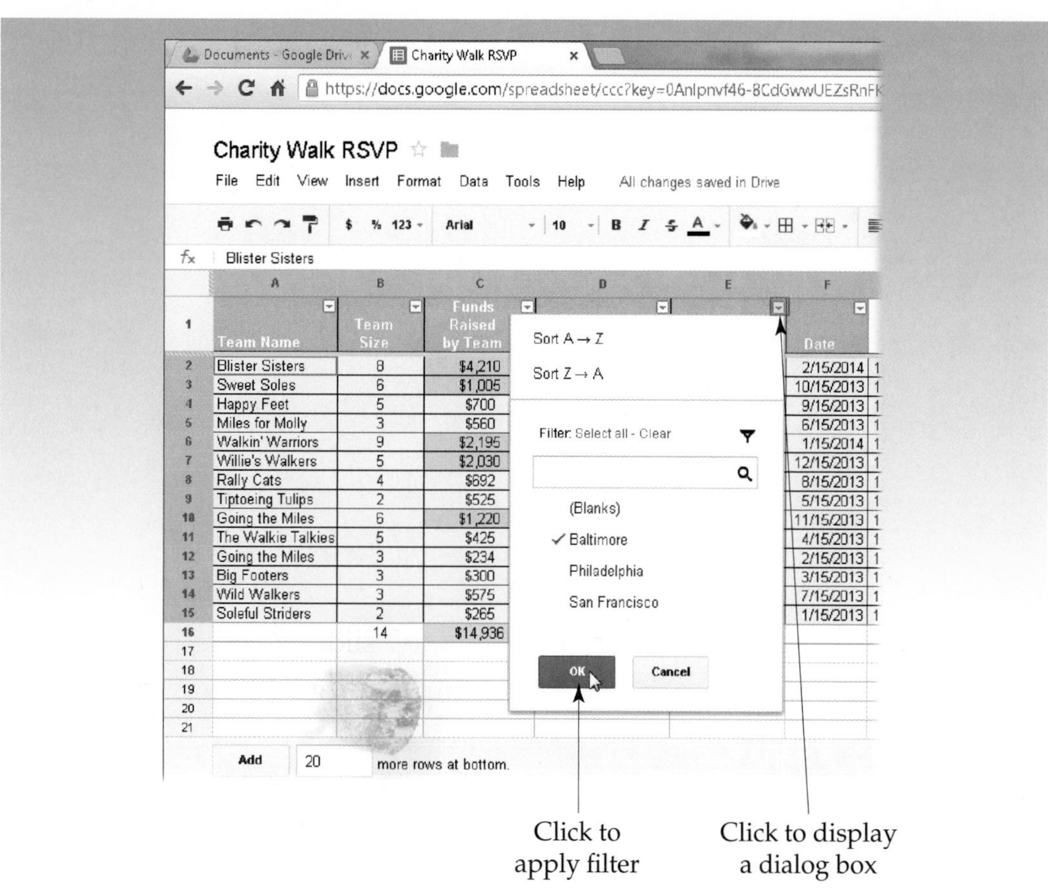

Goodheart-Willcox Publisher

Figure 10-16. When filtering data, the drop-down arrows in the column headers are used to access a menu in which filter settings are made.

22. Click **Blanks**, **Philadelphia** and **San Francisco** in the dialog box to uncheck them.
23. Click the **OK** button. The data in the spreadsheet are filtered so only the rows containing the city Baltimore are displayed. Only **Baltimore** was left checked in the dialog box.
24. Click the **Filter** button. This turns off filtering and displays all data.
25. Close the tab or window to close the spreadsheet.

Lesson 10-5

Creating a Chart and Working with Multiple Sheets

Some data lend themselves to a visual presentation for better understanding by users. In these cases, Google Sheets has several chart types for which a user can choose. It can be helpful to use multiple sheets when creating charts.

Inserting a Chart

1. Log in to your Google Mail account.
2. Click the **Drive** link in the menu bar at the top of the Mail page.
3. Navigate to the Charity Walk RSVP spreadsheet, and open it.
4. Click the **Insert Chart** button. The **Chart Editor** dialog box is displayed, as shown in **Figure 10-17.**

Insert Chart

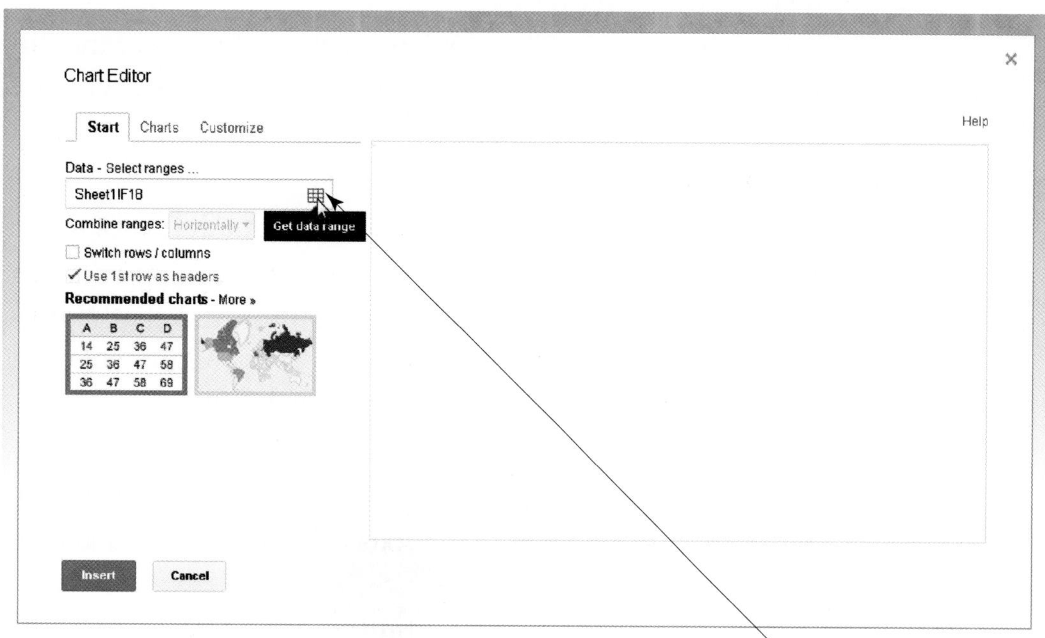

Goodheart-Willcox Publisher

Figure 10-17. Creating a chart in a spreadsheet.

Get Data Range

5. On the **Start** tab of the dialog box, click the **Get Data Range** button at the right-hand end of the **Data—Select ranges...** text box. The **Chart Editor** dialog box is temporarily closed, and the **What Data?** dialog box is displayed. This is a modeless dialog box, which means cells in the spreadsheet can be selected while the dialog box is open.
6. Select the range of cells A2:A15.
7. Click the **Add another range** link in the **What Data?** dialog box. A second text box is added to the dialog box, and it is automatically active, as indicated by the blinking cursor in the text box.

Ranges of cells can be manually added to the text boxes in the **What Data?** dialog box.

8. Select the range of cells C2:C15.
9. Click the **OK** button to close the **What Data?** dialog box and redisplay the **Chart Editor** dialog box. Notice the two selected ranges appear in the **Data—Select ranges...** text box.
10. Click the **Charts** tab in the **Chart Editor** dialog box. This is where the type of chart is selected, although one of the recommended types could be selected on the **Start** tab.
11. Click **Bar** in the list at the left of the **Charts** tab. Samples of two types of bar charts are displayed.
12. Click the top sample. The preview on the right side of the dialog box changes to represent the selected data in the selected type of chart.
13. Click the **Customize** tab in the dialog box. The settings on this tab vary, depending on the type of chart selected.
14. Click in the **Title** text box and replace the default text Chart title with Team Progress.
15. In the **Legend** area, click the left-hand button and click **None** in the drop-down list. The options in this list set the alignment of the legend or, as in this case, turns off the display of the legend.
16. Click the button in the **Axis** area—you may need to scroll down to have this area displayed—and click **Horizontal** in the drop-down list.
17. Click in the **Title** text box in the **Axis** area, and enter Funds Raised. This is the title for the horizontal axis.
18. In the **Bars** area, click the **Color** button, and click a green color swatch in the drop-down menu.
19. Click the **Insert** button to insert the chart.

Tip If the data in the chart range change, the chart will be automatically updated.

20. Click anywhere on the chart to display the header area above it, as shown in **Figure 10-18.**
21. Move the cursor to the header area until it changes to a hand.
22. Click and hold, then drag the chart to the right so it is not covering any of the cells containing data. You may need to position it beyond the right edge of the visible screen. Also, notice how the bottom of the chart extends below the bottom of the sheet.

Tip The chart cannot be moved into the first row because that row is frozen.

Editing a Chart

23. Scroll the spreadsheet to the right, if needed, so the entire chart is visible.

Quick Edit Mode

24. Display the header area, if it is not already displayed, and click the **Quick Edit Mode** button. This turns on edit mode for the chart. A message appears in the header bar of the chart as well.
25. Click title of the chart. A pop-up box appears above the title.

Font Color

26. Click the **Font Color** button, and click a dark blue color swatch in the drop-down menu.

Tip Additional chart settings, such as the data ranges or chart type, can be modified by selecting the **Advanced Edit...** button.

View Mode

27. Click the **View Mode** button in the header area. This turns off editing mode.

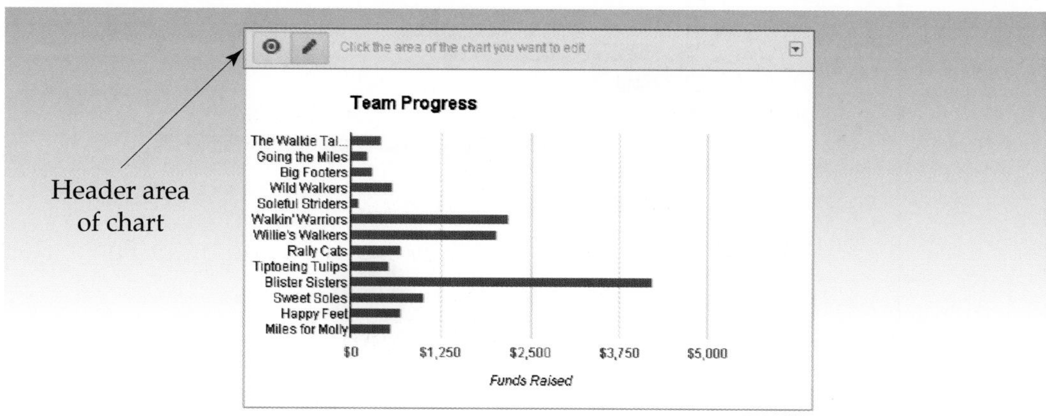

Goodheart-Willcox Publisher

Figure 10-18. Clicking on a chart displays a header bar above the chart that contains options for working with the chart.

Using Multiple Sheets

28. Display the header area, if it is not already displayed, and click the drop-down arrow on the right-hand end of the header area to display a drop-down menu.
29. Click **Move to own sheet...** in the drop-down menu. A new tab is added to the spreadsheet, and the chart is moved to that tab, as shown in **Figure 10-19.**
30. Click the tab name, and click **Rename...** in the drop-down menu.
31. Eenter Team Progress.
32. Press the [Enter] key.
33. Click the **Sheet 1** tab to display that sheet.
34. Click the tab name again, and click **Rename...** in the drop-down menu.
35. Enter Team Data as the sheet name.
36. Close the tab or window to close the spreadsheet.

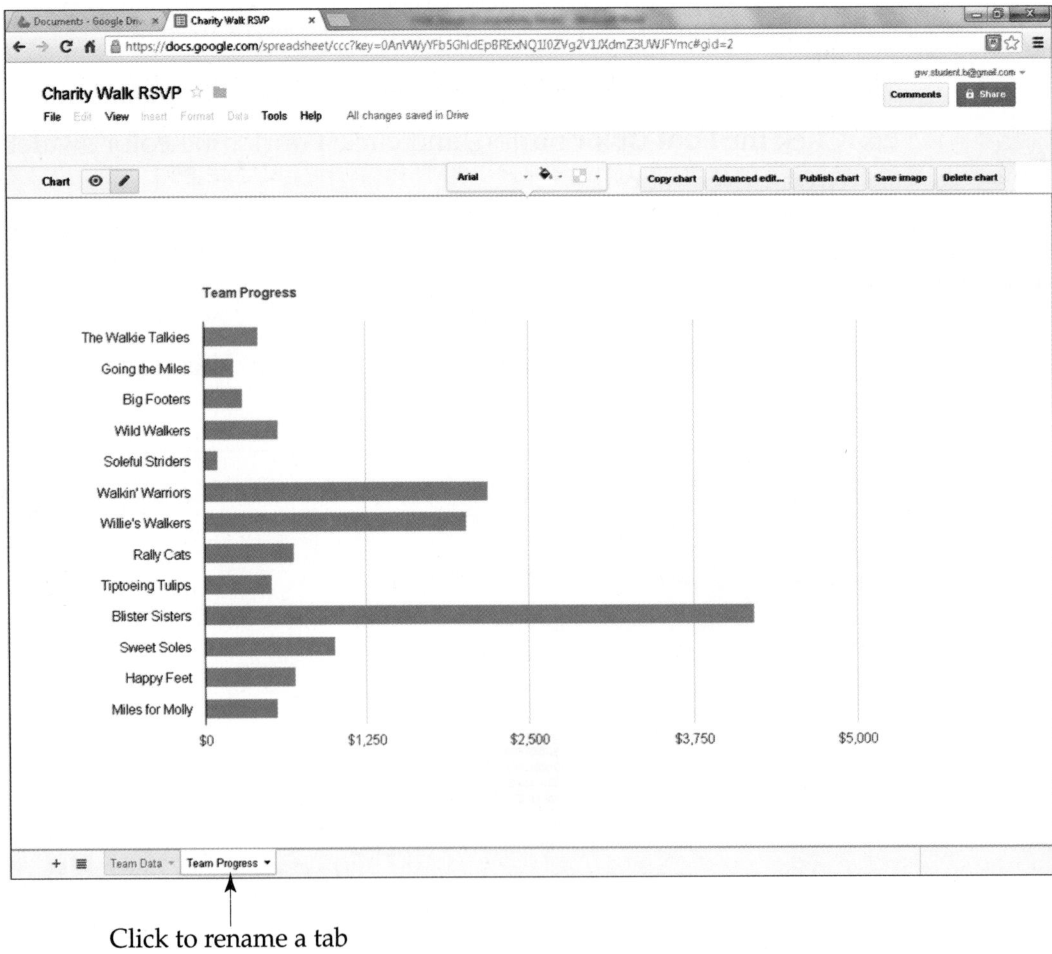

Goodheart-Willcox Publisher

Figure 10-19. A chart has been moved to its own sheet. Click the tab for each sheet to navigate between sheets.

Lesson 10-6

Printing and Publishing a Spreadsheet

Print options for spreadsheets include controlling the number of pages on which the spreadsheet will print. Publishing a spreadsheet allows a user to share it with others via a direct link, or by embedding it in a website.

Printing a Spreadsheet

1. Log in to your Google Mail account.
2. Click the **Drive** link in the menu bar at the top of the Mail page.
3. Navigate to the Charity Walk RSVP spreadsheet, and open it. The Team Data sheet is displayed.

4. Click the **Print** button on the toolbar. The **Print Settings** dialog box is displayed, as shown in **Figure 10-20.**
5. Click the **Current Sheet** radio button in the **Options** area of the dialog box.
6. Make sure the size listed in the **Paper Size** area matches your printer.
7. Click the **Fit to Width** and **Landscape** radio buttons in the **Layout** area. This forces the spreadsheet to be reduced if needed to fit on the page, and also sets the page to print wide instead of tall.

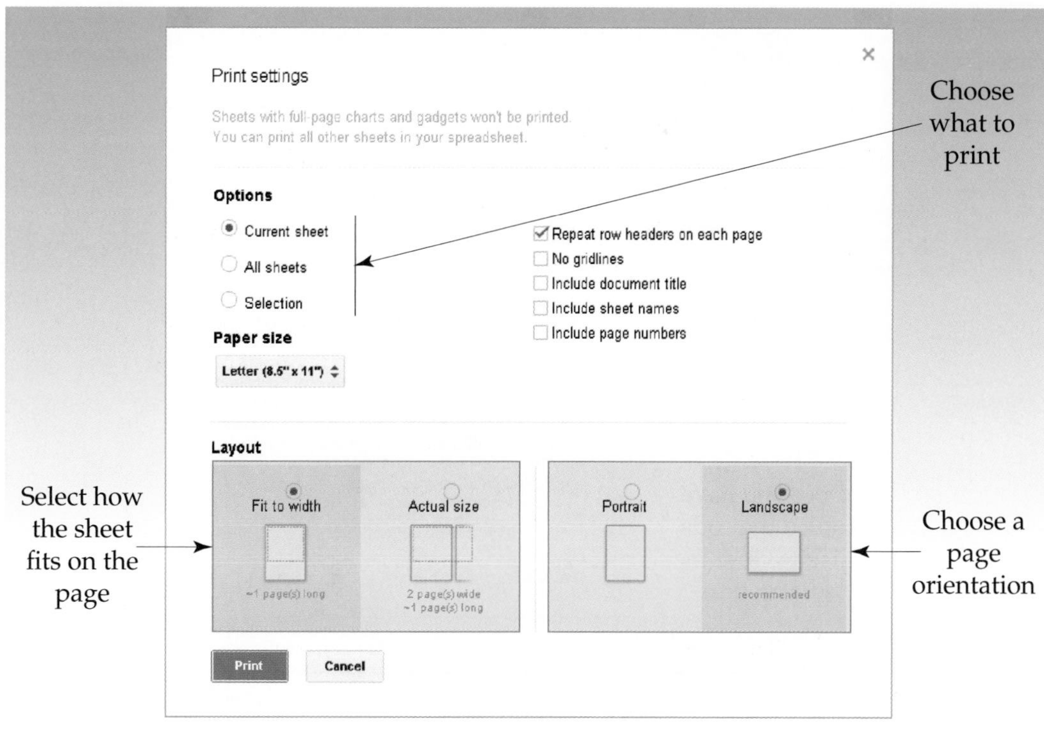

Goodheart-Willcox Publisher

Figure 10-20. When printing a spreadsheet, certain options must be set.

8. Click the **Print** button. The **Print** dialog box is displayed, and a new tab or window is opened showing a layout preview of the spreadsheet, which is behind the dialog box.
9. In the **Destination** area of the **Print** dialog box, make sure your printer is selected. If necessary, click the **Change...** button, and select the correct printer.
10. In the **Copies** area of the dialog box, click in the text box and enter the number of copies to print.
11. Set any other options in the dialog box as specified by your instructor.
12. Click the **Print** button to send the document to the specified printer. The **Print** dialog box is closed, and the spreadsheet is printed.
13. Close the layout preview tab or window.

Publishing a Chart

14. Click the **Team Progress** tab to display the sheet that contains the chart.

Publish chart

15. Click the **Publish Chart** button. A message appears indicating that to publish the chart, all sheets must be published.
16. Click the **OK** button. The **Publish Chart** dialog box is displayed, as shown in **Figure 10-21.** In the middle of the dialog box is the HTML code that can be copied and pasted into a web page definition to display the chart on the web page.
17. Click the **Done** button to close the dialog box.
18. Close the tab or window to close the spreadsheet.

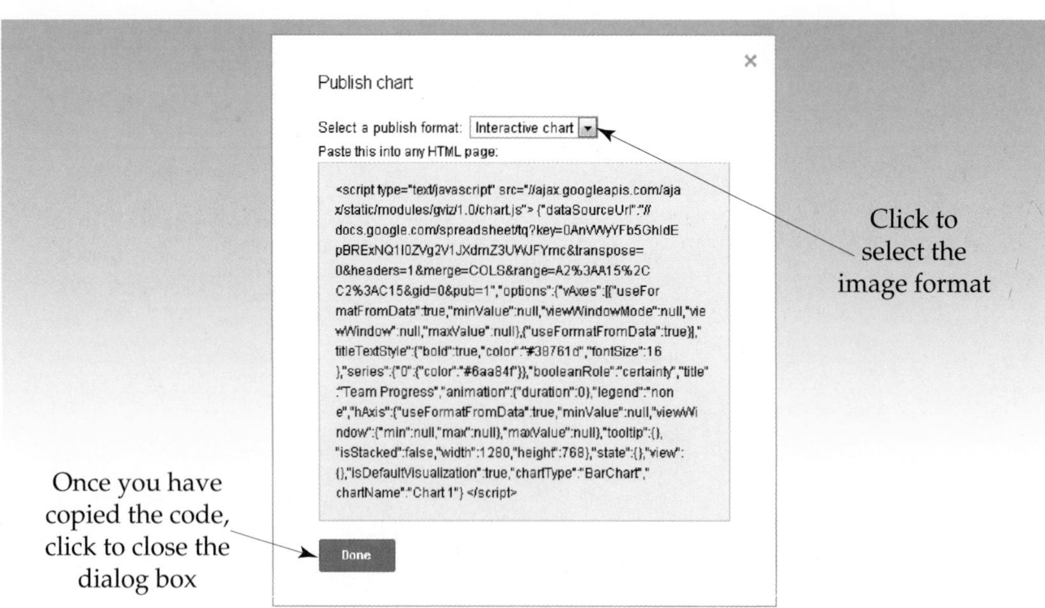

Goodheart-Willcox Publisher

Figure 10-21. The HTML code in this dialog box is used to add the chart to a web page. This code must be pasted into the HTML code that defines the web page on which the chart will appear.

Check Your Google Apps IQ

Now that you have finished this chapter, see what you know about Google Apps by taking the chapter posttest.
www.m.g-wlearning.com
www.g-wlearning.com/informationtechnology/

Skill Review

Answer the following questions on a separate sheet of paper.

1. What is a spreadsheet?
2. How are cells in a spreadsheet named?
3. When a spreadsheet is shared, who sets the visibility and access settings?
4. Briefly describe conditional formatting.
5. What does it mean to merge cells?
6. When the character / is entered in a cell, what is the mathematical operation that will be performed?
7. Briefly describe how to use the auto-fill function to copy a pattern of data.
8. What is sorting?
9. What are the two orders in which data can be sorted?
10. List three types of charts that can be created in Google Sheets.

Lesson Application

These exercises are designed to apply the skills learned in this and previous chapters. General directions are provided, but you will need to draw on your knowledge to determine how to complete each exercise.

Exercise 10-1
Formatting a Spreadsheet

Navigate to the student companion website (www.g-wlearning.com/informationtechnology/), and download the Individual Practice data file to your working folder. This is a Microsoft Excel file. Upload the file to your Google Drive in the Documents folder. Convert the file to a Google Sheet, and delete the Microsoft Excel file from your Google Drive. Open the Google Sheet spreadsheet, and rename it as *Your Name*—Individual Practice.

Freeze the first row. Also, add a background color to the cells in the first row, bold the text, and change the color of the text to a color that contrasts with the background color. Format the cells in column F as dollars with cents. Apply a border to all of the cells in the spreadsheet that contain data. Take the steps needed to automatically apply a red background to the cells in column E corresponding to events with more than 200 expected attendees. Share the spreadsheet with your instructor, and send an e-mail indicating the spreadsheet is shared.

Exercise 10-2
Sorting Data

Open the Individual Practice spreadsheet from Exercise 10-1. Sort the events in ascending order based on the number of attendees. Which will be the three largest events? Invite your instructor to a hangout, and report your answer.

Filter the data to display only events that occur in December. Which city has more than one event in December? Which project manager has more than one event? Report your answers to your instructor in a hangout.

Exercise 10-3
Using Formulas

Open the Individual Practice spreadsheet from Exercise 10-2. Use a formula to determine the average cost per attendee for all events. Use a formula to calculate which event will cost the least per attendee. Use the formula *=cost per event*number of attendees*, where cost per event and number of attendees are replaced with cell names, to calculate the total cost of events. Enter the formula into the first blank cell in column G, and then automatically apply the formula in the remaining blank cells in the column. Use the data in column G and a formula to calculate which event will have the highest overall cost. Compose and send an e-mail to your instructor reporting the results of this exercise.

Exercise 10-4
Creating a Chart

Open the Individual Practice spreadsheet from Exercise 10-3. Create a column-type chart that displays the event names and the total cost per event. Include a chart title and a label for the horizontal axis. Take the steps needed to place the chart on a sheet by itself. Rename the sheets to be descriptive of what they contain. Invite your instructor to a hangout and inform him or her that the spreadsheet is complete.

Chapter 11

Google Slides

Objectives

After completing this chapter, you will be able to:

- Convert a presentation from an uploaded file.
- Insert images and video onto slides in a presentation.
- Insert tables onto slides in a presentation.
- Draw shapes on slides in a presentation.
- Add animations to objects and transitions to slides in a presentation.
- Add a theme to a presentation.
- Present a Google Slides slide show.
- Download a presentation.

alexmillos/Shutterstock.com

Check Your Google Apps IQ

Before you begin this chapter, see what you already know about Google Apps by taking the chapter pretest.

www.m.g-wlearning.com

www.g-wlearning.com/informationtechnology/

Using Google Slides

A user can create electronic slide show presentations with Google Slides. A ***slide show*** is a collection of pages containing text and images typically presented on screen. Google provides users with many options to develop dynamic and colorful slide show presentations. Along with text and images, a user can embed videos in his or her Google presentation. A user can include tables on slides and can draw shapes on slides.

Slide show elements can be animated. Also, transitions can be assigned to the slides themselves. A user can choose a theme for his or her slide show from the variety of styles available. A user can also choose a personal background to create a custom slide show design. Like other Google files, presentations can be shared with collaborators who can edit simultaneously, comment, and chat with each other.

Creating a Presentation

A user can create a new Google presentation in Google Drive or upload a presentation created in Microsoft PowerPoint (PPT, PPS, or PPTx). To modify a PowerPoint presentation in Google, it must be converted to the Google format. Files uploaded and converted to the Google format must be less than 50 MB. A user can also import and incorporate individual PowerPoint slides into a Google presentation.

Presentation software has two modes: edit mode and presentation mode. When a user creates a presentation, he or she mostly works with it in edit mode. ***Edit mode*** is where a user builds the presentation: adding and editing text, incorporating visuals, and assigning animation and transitions. ***Presentation mode*** is used to show the slides to the audience. In this mode, each slide is displayed without the navigation panel, toolbar, or speaker notes. Google Slides cycles through the slides in the show. It can be helpful to view a slide show in presentation mode a couple of times during the development process before considering it final to see how the slides and transitions are coming together.

Navigating Google Slides

The Google Slides page has three main sections: the slide navigation panel, the active slide section, and the speaker notes section, as seen in **Figure 11-1.** The slide navigation panel is on the left side of the page and displays thumbnails of all of the slides in the presentation file. A user can quickly see and move through all of the slides by scrolling up and down in this panel. Slides can be added or deleted from within this panel. Also, some modifications can be made to slides from within the navigation panel. A

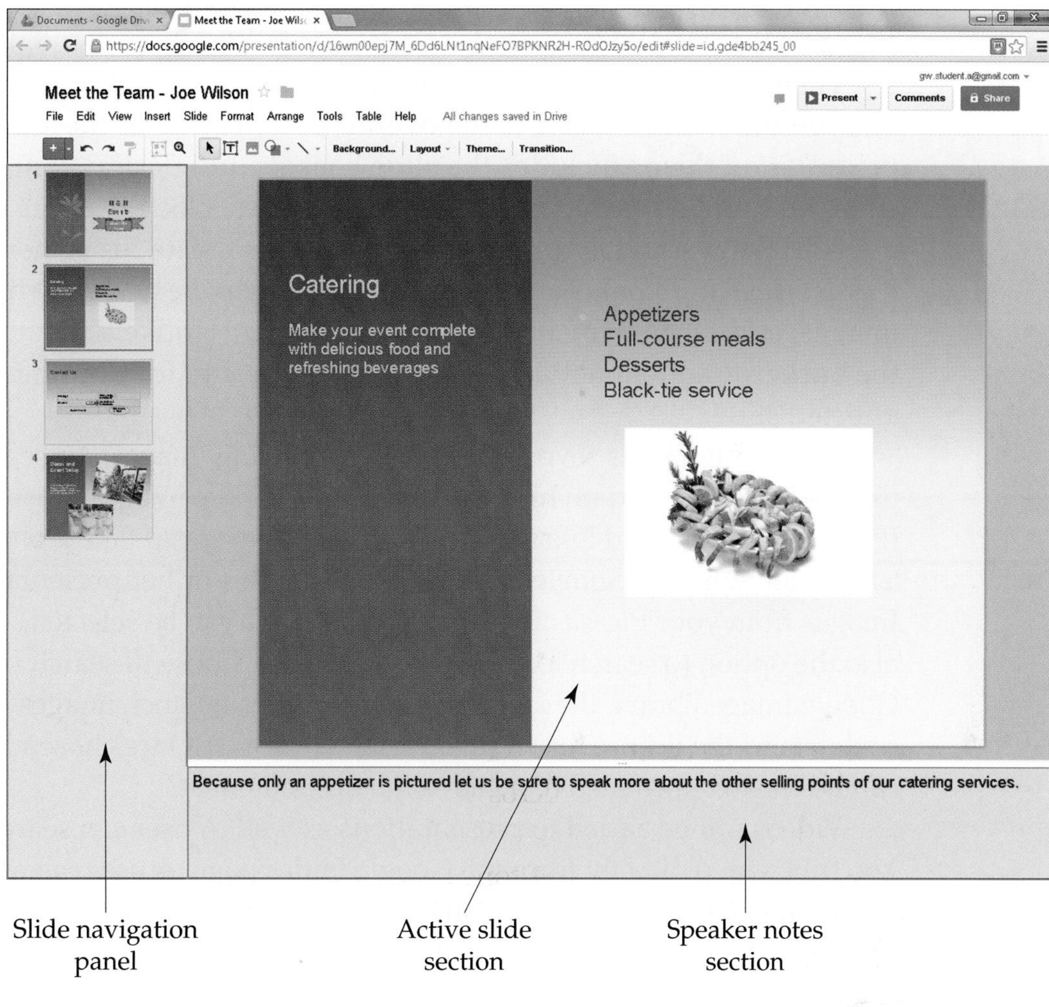

Goodheart-Willcox Publisher

Figure 11-1. The Google Slides window contains three main areas.

user can change the layout selection of a slide and the order in which slides appear. Also, a user can click on a slide in the navigation panel to display that slide in the active slide section. The navigation panel is not seen in presentation mode.

The active slide section is where a user can add or modify the content of an individual slide. Text and images can be added or changed. Text boxes on the ***layout*** of the slide indicate where text can be added. A layout is the composition of the text, images, and shapes, and other elements on the slide. When a user clicks the designated text box, he or she can enter text. The active slides are seen in presentation mode.

The speaker notes section of the slide page allows the user to add notes to each slide. A user can add notes about key points or details related to an individual slide. By default, the notes section is not seen in presentation mode.

Adding Visuals to Presentations

Themes and backgrounds allow a user to enhance the appearance of a presentation. A ***theme*** is the overall design of all of the slides. The presentation theme includes the slide background design, font style, font color, and font sizes that will apply to all slides. Google Slides provides users with several theme options or a user can create his or her own theme. A ***background*** is a color or image that can be added behind text, images, and other elements on one or all slides. Unlike a theme, changing the background will not automatically change any font settings on the affected slide.

Google Slides has several options for inserting images. A user can upload images stored on his or her computer. These images must be PNG, JPEG, or GIF files and less than 2 MB in size. A user can take a photo with a web cam while in Google Slides and use it in his or her presentation. Images from your Picasa album or Google Drive can be selected. There is also the option to search for images. A user can choose to search within the Google Image library, the Life magazine archive, or stock images. Be sure to understand the license for an image before using it. Once chosen, an image can be resized or rotated to achieve the desired effect.

Videos can be added to presentations as well. A user can search for a YouTube video directly from the Google Slides page. A user can also simply enter the URL for the desired YouTube video. Check the license information to ensure appropriate use of a video in presentations.

Some data, especially complex data, are easier to present and view if they are displayed in a table. A table can be added to a Google presentation. A user can determine the number of rows and columns and the format of the text within the cells.

A user can also draw shapes to add to a slide. There are several shapes from which a user can choose. Once added, a user can customize the look of the shape. The size and placement of the shape is also decided by the user. There are options as to the weight and color of the outline of the shape. A user can choose the fill color feature to change the background color of the selected shape. Text can be added to shapes as well, as seen in **Figure 11-2.** This work can be completed within Google Slides or Google Drawing. Google Drawing is a separate program that allows users to create drawings or modify images. A Google Drawing file can be downloaded as a PNG or a JPEG and placed on a slide like any other image.

Adding Movement to Presentations

Animations and transitions are two effects that add movement to a slide show in presentation mode. ***Animations*** affect the way an element on a slide appears on or disappears from the slide. ***Transitions*** control

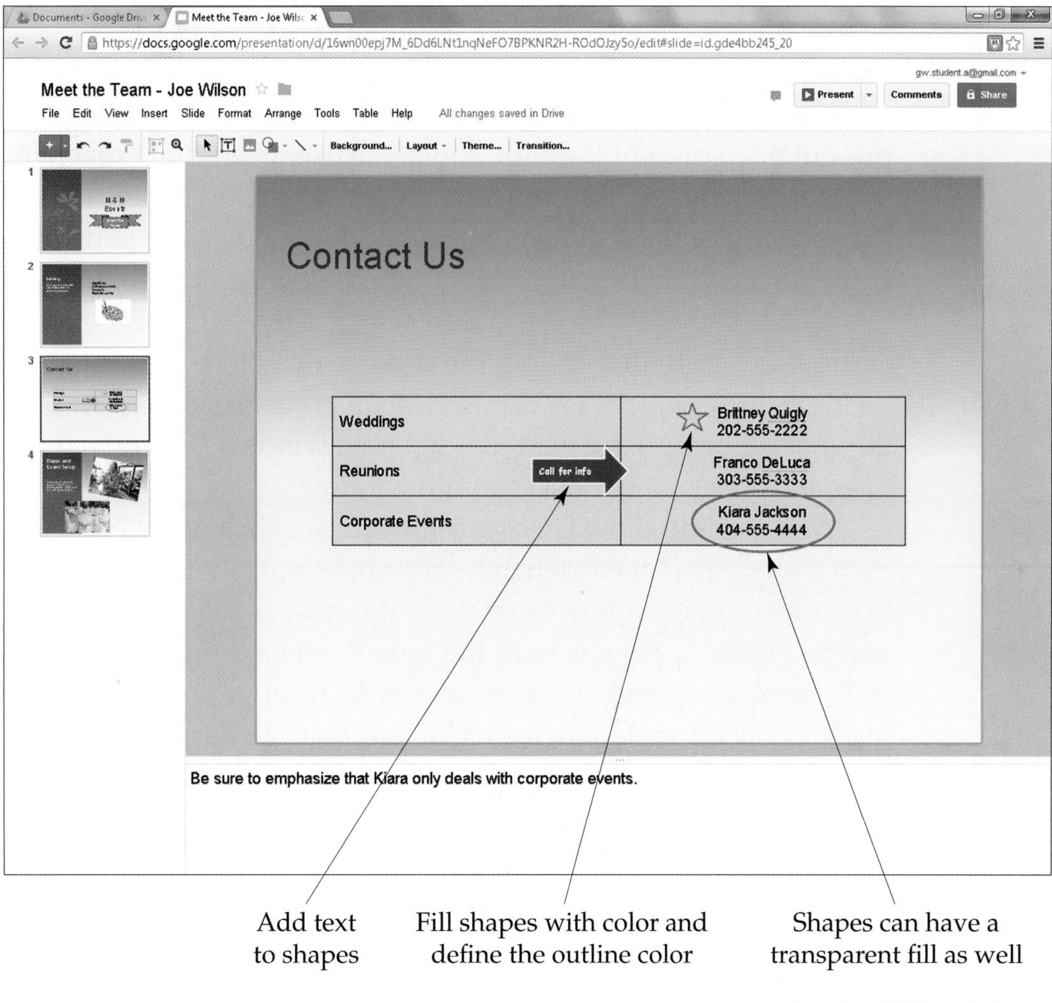

Goodheart-Willcox Publisher

Figure 11-2. Shapes can be drawn on slides and edited as needed.

how the presentation changes from one slide to the next. Animations are assigned to the elements on a slide, whereas a transition is attached to the slide itself.

There are three actions that can start an animation: on click, after previous, and with previous. ***On click*** animations are triggered when the user clicks the mouse button. Animations set to ***after previous*** will start after another effect is finished. An element set as ***with previous*** will be animated at the same time as the element immediately before it in the animation list. There are seven animation styles from which to choose. A user can also determine the speed with which the animation occurs.

A transition can be applied to specific slides or to the entire presentation. Slide transitions can be selected from the six available options: fade, slide in from the right, slide in from the left, flip, cube, and gallery. Like animation options, a user can assign a speed to the transition.

Presenting and Publishing

When a slide show is complete and the user is ready, he or she can present it. To present the slide show, the user clicks the **Present** button to enter presentation mode. Click the arrow next to the button to display presentation options. When in presentation mode, each slide occupies the entire screen with a small presentation toolbar near the bottom of the page.

A slide show can be set to start with the first slide and cycle through the entire show. With this option, the slide show will be presented from within the same browser window. A user can also choose to present the slides with the speaker notes displayed in a separate window. The final option is to open the presentation in a separate window.

When a slide show is *presented,* the user is in control of the file and when each slide is displayed. When a slide show is *published,* a user allows people to access and view the presentation. It is assigned a unique web address and will be visible to anyone with the link. Published presentations appear in full-screen mode and automatically cycle through the slides. If changes are made to the presentation, they will automatically appear in the published version. A user can also choose to stop publishing at any time.

Lesson 11-1

Automatic Conversion on Upload

PowerPoint files can be uploaded and converted for use as a Google presentation. A user can set his or her Google Drive to automatically convert compatible uploaded documents into the Google equivalent.

Upload Settings

1. Navigate to the student companion website (www.g-wlearning.com/informationtechnology/), and download the M&M Events Presentation data file to your working folder. This is a Microsoft PowerPoint file.
2. Log in to your Google Mail account.
3. Click the **Drive** link on the bar at the top of the Mail page.

Settings

4. Click the **Settings** button, and click **Upload Settings** in the drop-down menu to display a cascading menu, as shown in **Figure 11-3.**
5. Click **Convert uploaded files to Google Docs format** in the cascading menu so it is checked.
6. Click the **Settings** button again, click **Upload settings** in the drop-down menu, and click **Confirm settings before each upload** in the cascading menu so it is checked.

If the **Convert uploaded files to Google Docs format** option is not checked, uploaded files will not be automatically converted, but can still be manually converted, as demonstrated in Chapter 10.

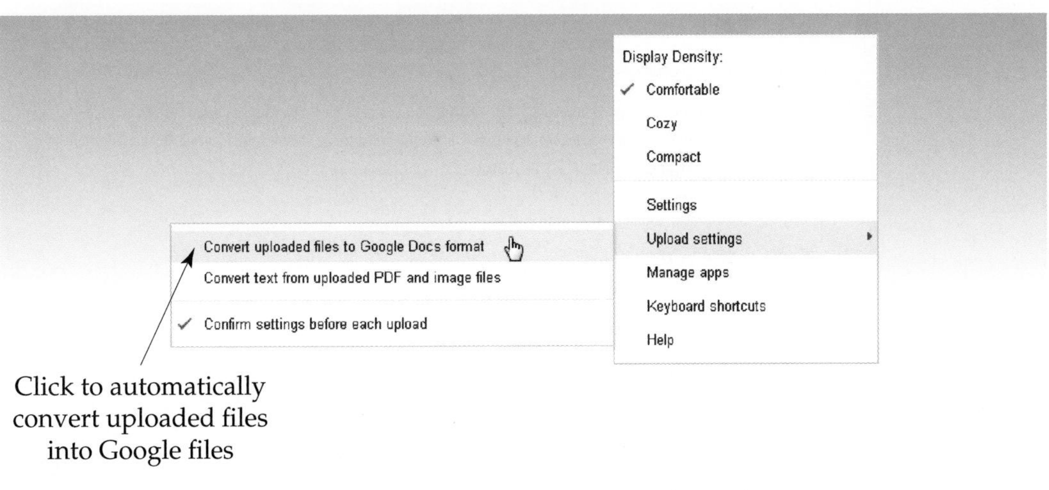

Goodheart-Willcox Publisher

Figure 11-3. Setting automatic conversion for uploaded files.

Automatically Converting on Upload

7. Navigate to the Documents subfolder.

Upload

8. Click the **Upload** button, and click **Files** in the drop-down menu. A standard file-open dialog box is displayed.
9. Navigate to your working folder and select the M&M Events Presentation data file. Since the **Confirm settings before each upload** option is on, the **Upload settings** dialog box is displayed, as shown in **Figure 11-4.**
10. Confirm the settings in the dialog box, and then click the **Start upload** button. When the file is uploaded, close the upload status dialog box. The Microsoft PowerPoint file is now uploaded and in Google Slides format.
11. Click the M&M Events Presentation file name to open the presentation document.
12. Click the **File** pull-down menu, and click **Rename...** in the menu.
13. In the **Rename document** dialog box, change the name of the file to Meet the Team—*Your Name*.
14. Close the **Rename document** dialog box.

Inserting and Deleting Slides

New slide

15. Click the arrow to the right of the **New slide** button to display a drop-down list, as shown in **Figure 11-5.** This list contains the names of layouts that can be used for slides.
16. Click **Title and Content with Caption** in the drop-down list. The new slide is added after the current slide. This specific slide layout contains three text boxes, one for a title, one for a caption, and one for content.

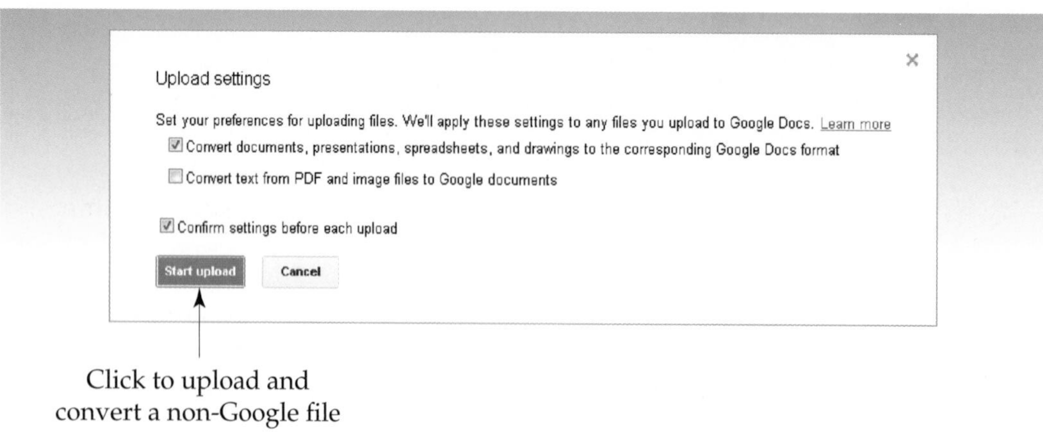

Goodheart-Willcox Publisher

Figure 11-4. Confirming a file conversion as it is uploaded.

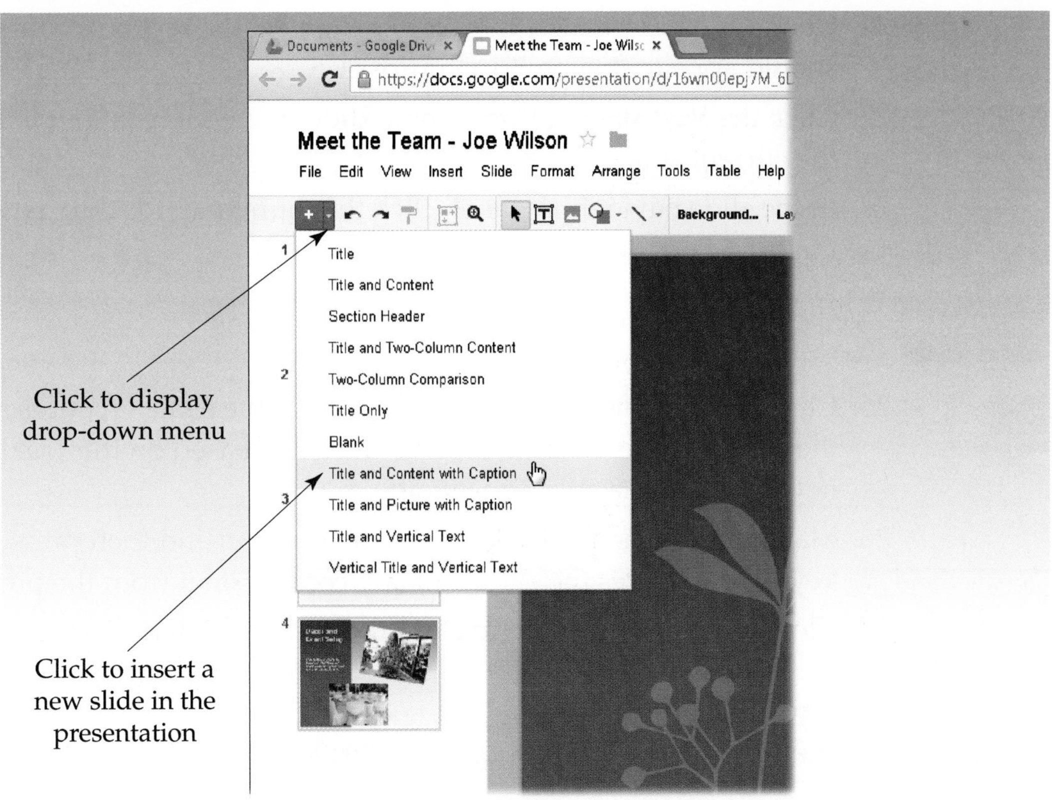

Goodheart-Willcox Publisher

Figure 11-5. Selecting a layout to use for a new slide.

Tip The layout of an existing slide can be changed by clicking the **Layout** button on the toolbar and selecting the name of a new layout in the drop-down list.

17. Click in the text box containing the default text Click to add title, and enter Catering.
18. Click in the text box below the title containing the default text Click to add text, and enter Make your event complete with delicious food and refreshing beverages.
19. Click in the text box to the right of the title containing the default text Click to add text, and press the [Enter] key twice to add two blank lines.

Bulleted list

20. Click the **Bulleted list** button on the formatting toolbar to start a bulleted list.
21. Add the following bullet points.

- Appetizers
- Full-course meals
- Desserts
- Black-tie service

22. Click anywhere just off the slide to deselect the text box. The slide should appear as shown in **Figure 11-6.**

23. Click the **New slide** button. A new slide of the same layout is added after the current slide.
24. In the slide navigation panel, click the thumbnail for the first slide to make that slide active.

Slides can be rearranged by dragging and dropping.

25. Click the **New slide** button. A new slide of the same layout is added after the current slide. Since the active slide was based on the Title layout, the new slide also has the Title layout.
26. Make sure the new (blank) title slide is active, and then press the [Delete] key. This removes the slide and any content on it from the presentation.
27. Close the window or tab to close the presentation document.

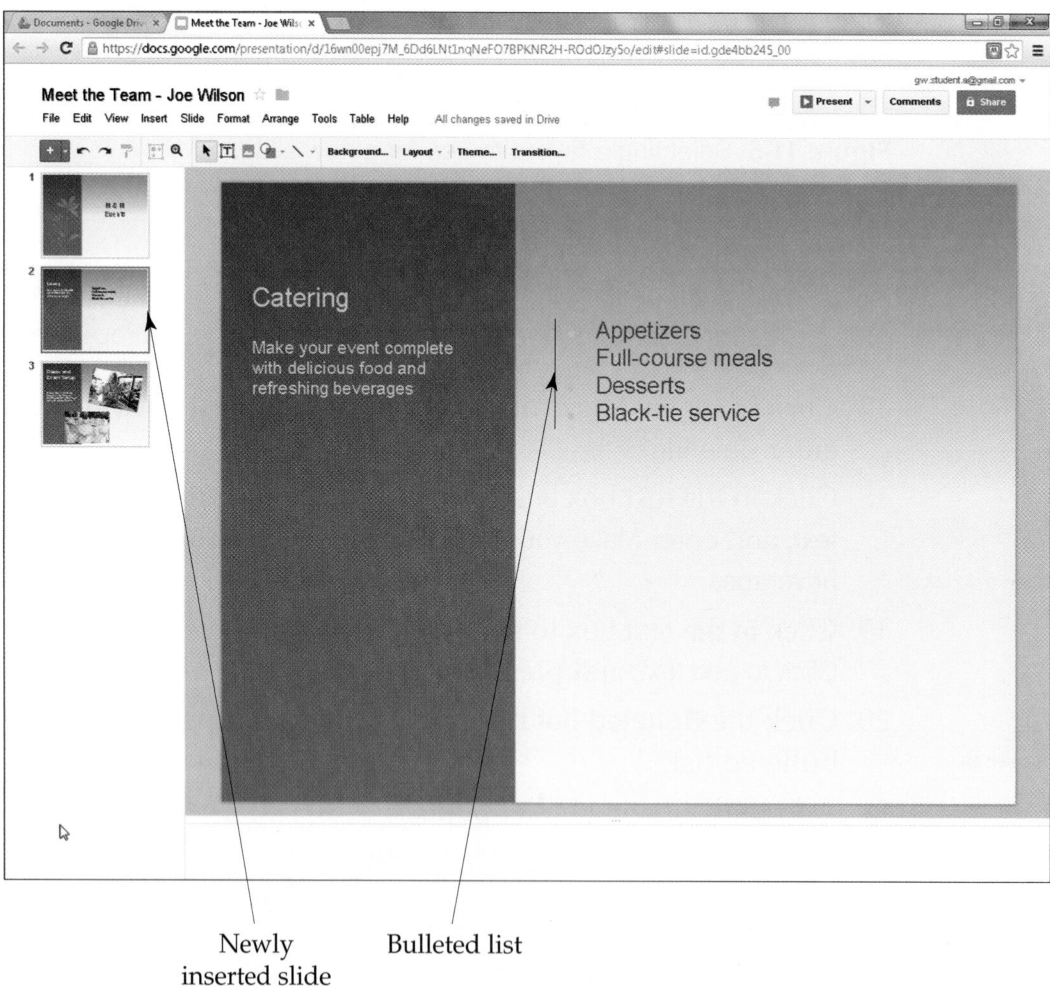

Goodheart-Willcox Publisher

Figure 11-6. The slide should appear similar to the one shown here.

Lesson 11-2

Adding Images and Video

Images or video can help an audience better understand the content being presented. Google provides several options to incorporate images into slides. Also, videos from YouTube can be inserted into a presentation.

Inserting an Image

1. Log in to your Google Mail account.
2. Click the **Drive** link in the menu bar at the top of the Mail page.
3. Navigate to the Meet the Team presentation, and open it.
4. Click on the slide thumbnail for the second slide. This is the slide with the bulleted list.

5. Click the **Image...** button on the toolbar. The **Insert image** dialog box is displayed, as shown in **Figure 11-7.**
6. Click **Search** on the left side of the dialog box.
7. Click **Stock Images**.
8. Click in the search box, and enter food.

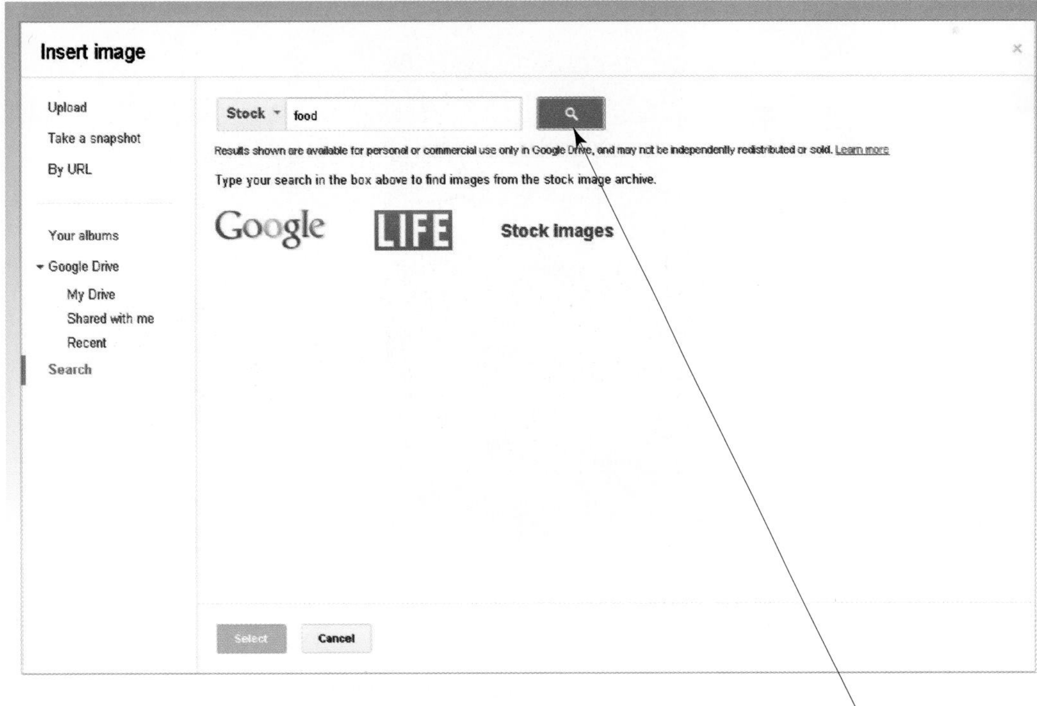

Goodheart-Willcox Publisher

Figure 11-7. Inserting an image onto a slide.

9. Click the **Search** button to search for stock images that match the keyword.
10. Scroll through the list of results to find an appropriate image of your choice. Click the image to highlight it.
11. Click the **Select** button to insert the image onto the slide.

Resizing and Rotating an Image

12. If the handles are not displayed on the image, click the image.
13. Click and drag one of the corner handles to proportionally resize the image. The image should be small enough to fit on the right side of the slide below the bulleted list.
14. Click anywhere on the image and drag to move it, as seen in **Figure 11-8**. Notice as the image is moved that red alignment lines appear at key points on the slide. For example, one appears at the center of the right side of the slide when the image is horizontally centered in that area.

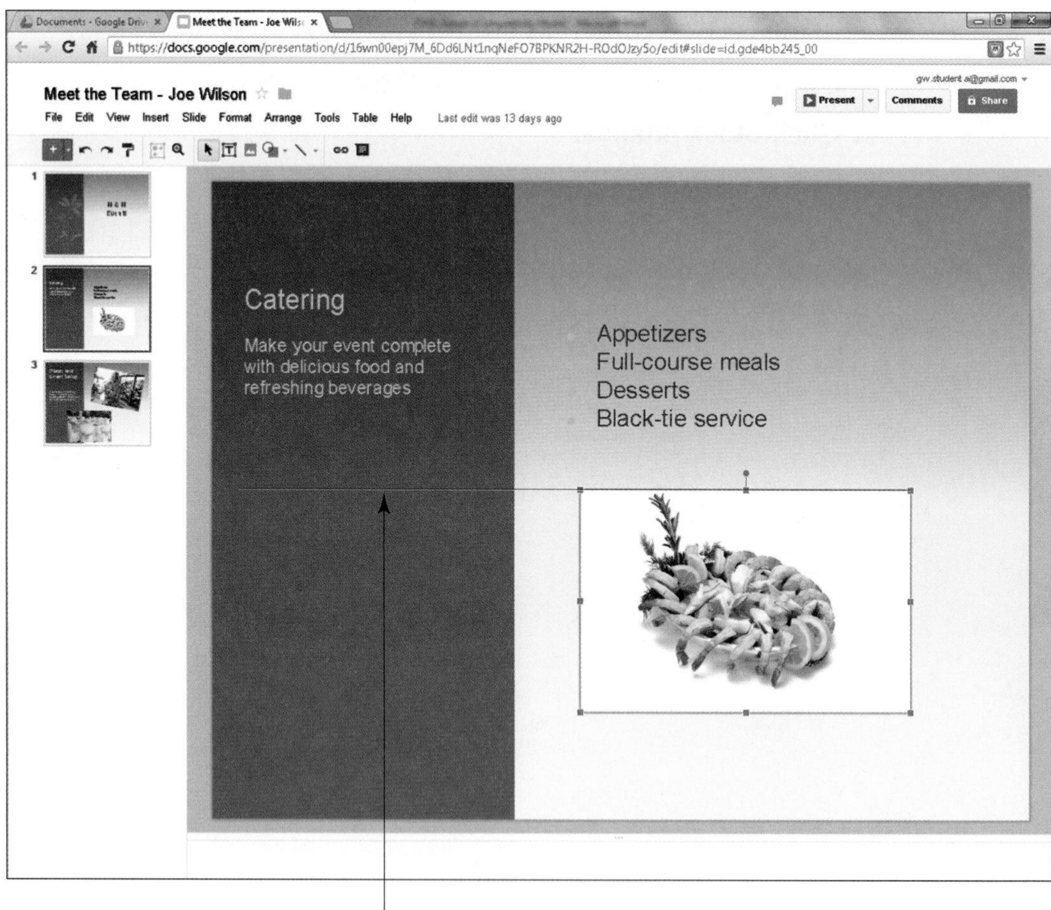

Goodheart-Willcox Publisher

Figure 11-8. Moving an image on a slide.

When the image is horizontally centered on the right side of the slide, release the mouse button to reposition it.

15. Move the cursor to the round handle at the top of the image. This handle is used to rotate the image.
16. Click and drag the handle. As the image is rotated, the number of degrees of rotation is displayed next to the cursor.
17. When the image is rotated to an appropriate angle, release the mouse button.
18. Click off of the image to deselect it.

Inserting a Video

19. Click the thumbnail for the third slide. This is the blank slide.
20. Click the **Insert** pull-down menu, and click **Video...** in the menu. The **Insert Video** dialog box is displayed, which is similar to the **Insert image** dialog box.
21. Click in the search text box, and enter wedding planning. Note: your instructor may provide a different search term or the URL of a video to use; if a URL is provided, click **URL** and enter the address in the text box.
22. Scroll through the list of results to find an appropriate video of your choice. Click the video thumbnail to highlight it.

Tip The thumbnail for a video can be clicked to preview the video.

23. Click the **Select** button to insert the video onto the slide.
24. Resize and move the video as needed in the same way an image is resized and moved. A video cannot be rotated.
25. Close the window or tab to close the presentation document.

Lesson 11-3

Inserting a Table

Presenting complex content in a table can make it clearer for the audience. A user can create a table and then format it and the content within it.

1. Log in to your Google Mail account.
2. Click the **Drive** link in the menu bar at the top of the Mail page.
3. Navigate to the Meet the Team presentation, and open it.
4. Click the thumbnail for the last slide to make the slide active.
5. Click the **New Slide** button to insert a new slide after the current slide.

New slide

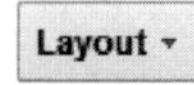

6. With the new slide active, click the **Layout** button on the toolbar, and click **Title Only** in the drop-down list. This changes the slide to a different layout.
7. Click in the text box on the slide, and enter Contact Us.
8. Click anywhere on the slide to deactivate the text box.
9. Click the **Table** pull-down menu, and click **Insert table** in the menu to display a cascading menu, as shown in **Figure 11-9.**
10. Move the cursor in the cascading menu until two cells across and two cells down are highlighted, and then click. This creates a blank 2 × 2 table on the slide.

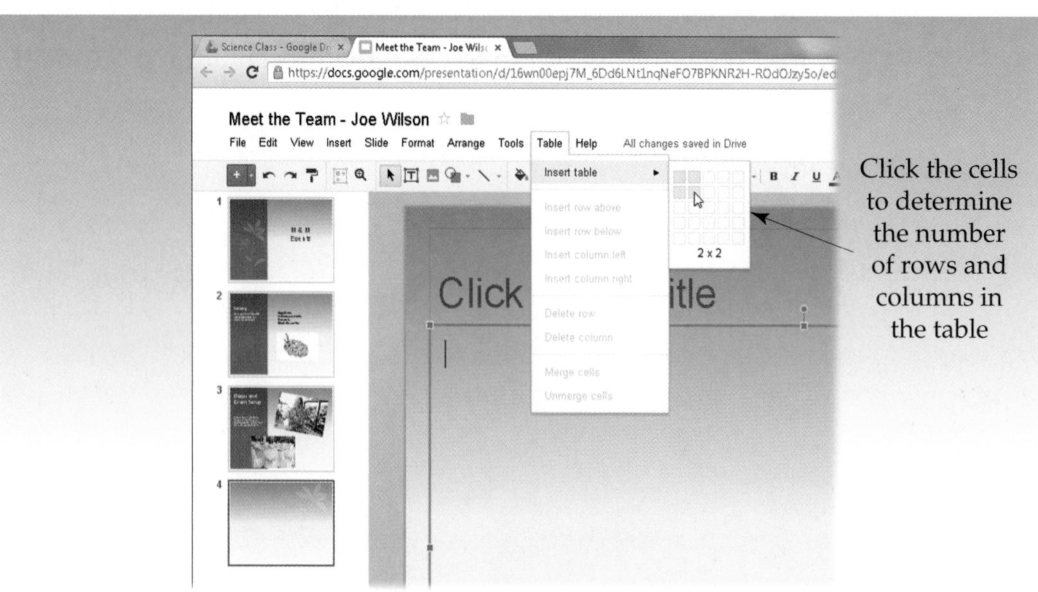

Goodheart-Willcox Publisher

Figure 11-9. Inserting a table onto a slide.

11. Click and hold the blue outside border of the table, and move the table to the center of the slide. Use the red alignment lines to find the center.
12. Enter the following text in the table. Press the [Enter] key to start a new line within a cell.
    - Top-left cell: Weddings
    - Top-right cell: Brittney Quigly
      202-555-2222
    - Bottom-left cell: Reunions
    - Bottom-right cell: Franco De Luca
      303-555-3333

Use the [Tab] key to navigate between cells in a table.

13. Click in the upper-left cell, hold, and drag to the bottom-right cell to highlight all cells.

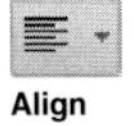

14. Click the **Align** button on the formatting toolbar to display a drop-down menu, as shown in **Figure 11-10.**

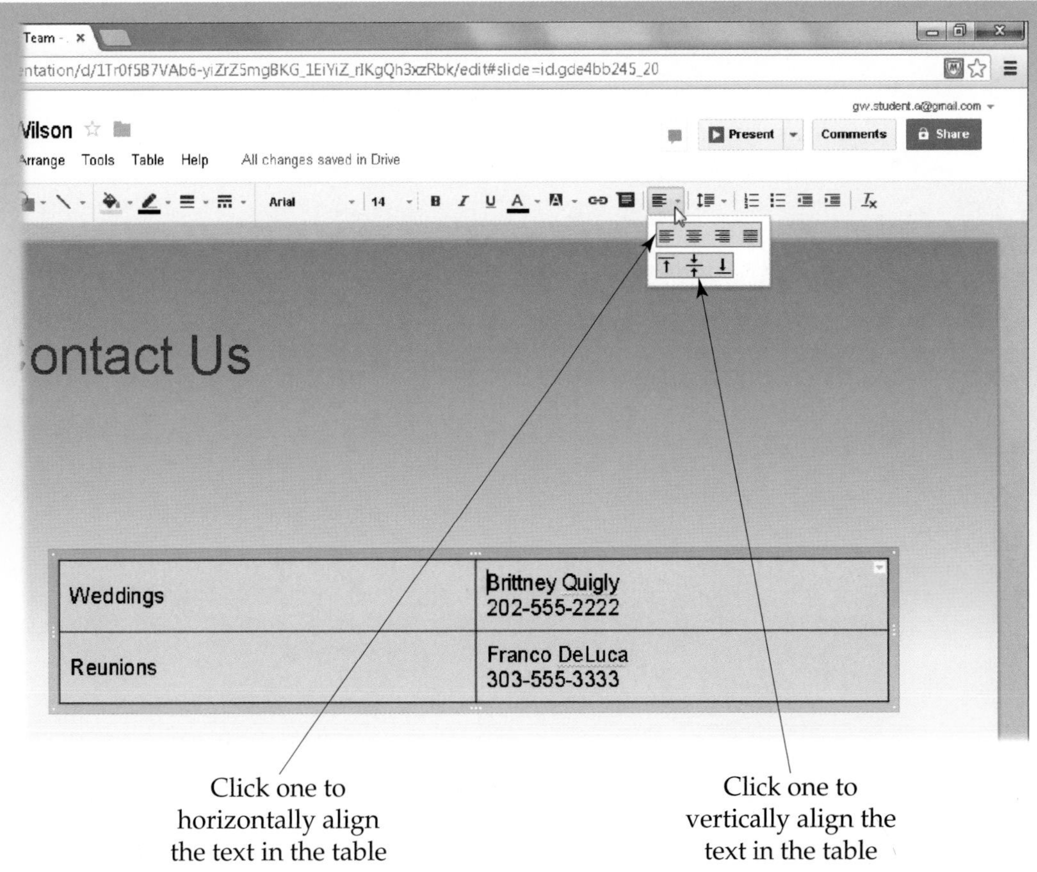

Goodheart-Willcox Publisher

Figure 11-10. Selecting alignment for cells in a table.

Center

15. Click the **Center** button in the drop-down menu. This horizontally centers the text in each cell.
16. Click the **Align** button again, and click the **Middle** button in the drop-down menu. This vertically centers the text in each cell.

Fill Color

17. With all cells highlighted, click the **Fill Color** button on the formatting toolbar to display a drop-down menu.
18. Click a light blue color swatch in the drop-down menu.
19. Click in one of the cells on the bottom row.
20. Click the **Table** pull-down menu, and click **Insert row below** in the menu. A new row is added to the table.
21. In the new row, enter Corporate Events in the left-hand cell and Kiara Jackson and 404-555-4444 in the right-hand cell.

Center

22. Select the two cells in the bottom row, and center align the text.
23. Close the window or tab to close the presentation document.

Lesson 11-4

Drawing Shapes

Shapes include basic geometric shapes, arrows, callouts, and mathematic symbols. Once added to a slide, the size and color of the shape can be changed to meet the needs of the presentation.

1. Log in to your Google Mail account.
2. Click the **Drive** link in the menu bar at the top of the Mail page.
3. Navigate to the Meet the Team presentation, and open it.
4. Click the thumbnail for the first slide to make it the active slide, unless it is already active.

Shape

5. Click the **Shape** button to display a drop-down menu.
6. Click **Callouts** in the drop-down menu to display a cascading menu, as shown in **Figure 11-11.**

Down Ribbon

7. Click the **Down Ribbon** button in the cascading menu. The cursor changes to crosshairs.
8. Click on the slide below the title, hold, and drag to create a drawing shape in the form of a ribbon.

Fill color

9. With the shape selected, click the **Fill color** button to display a drop-down menu.

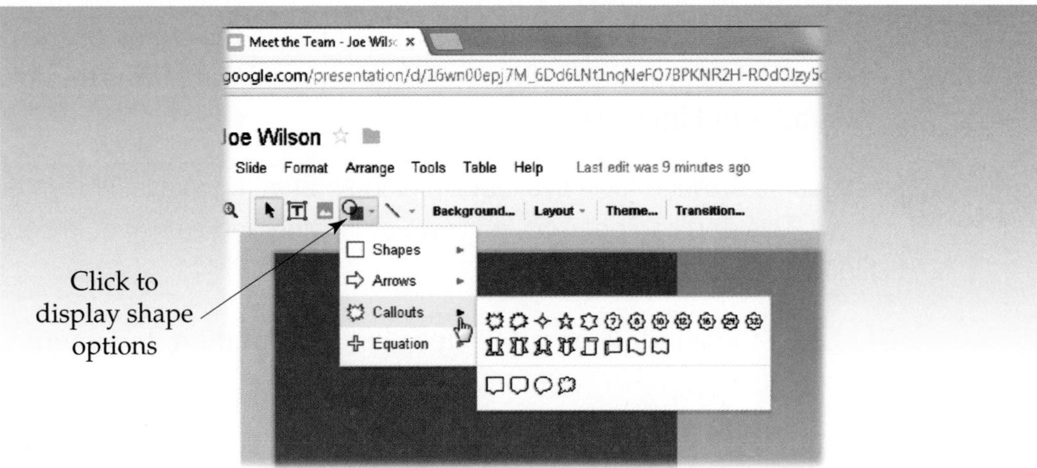

Goodheart-Willcox Publisher

Figure 11-11. Selecting a shape to draw on a slide.

10. Click a color swatch in the drop-down menu that contrasts with the background color of the slide. The filled-in areas of the shape are changed to that color.

Line color

Line weight

11. Click the **Line color** button, and click a color swatch that is a darker version of the fill color. The lines in the shape are changed to that color.
12. Click the **Line weight** button, and click **4px** in the drop-down menu. The lines in the shape are set to four points in width.

Line Dash

13. Click the **Line Dash** button, and click the long dash entry (second from the bottom) in the drop-down list. The lines in the shape are changed to dashed.
14. Double-click on the new shape. A blinking cursor appears in the middle of the shape, similar to a text box.
15. Enter Meet the Team.

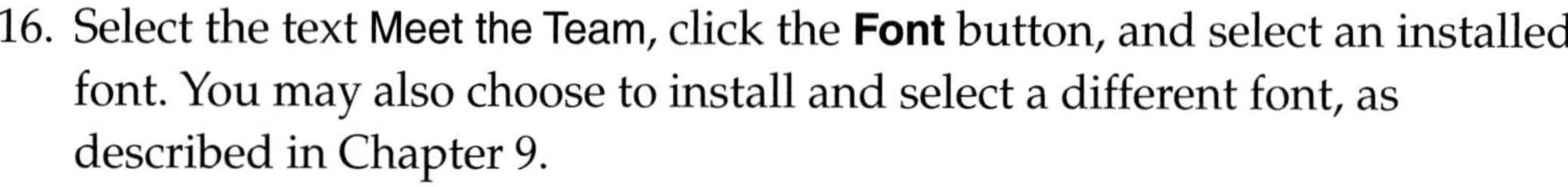

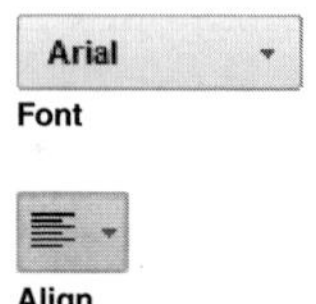
Font

Align

Center

Font size

Text color

16. Select the text Meet the Team, click the **Font** button, and select an installed font. You may also choose to install and select a different font, as described in Chapter 9.
17. Click the **Align** button, and click the **Center** button in the drop-down menu. This horizontally centers the text in the shape.
18. With the text selected, click the **Font size** button, and click **30** in the drop-down menu. This sets the point size to 30.
19. With the font selected, click the **Text color** button, and click a color swatch in the drop-down menu that contrasts with the fill color of the shape.
20. Use the resizing handles to enlarge or reduce the shape until the text just fits in the middle part of the shape. You may use the side, top, and bottom handles to nonproportionally resize the shape or the corner handles to proportionally resize the shape. Your slide should appear similar to **Figure 11-12.**

The same drawing tools available in Google Sheets are available in Google Draw. This app can be used to create a drawing and save it as a separate file in Google Drive.

21. Close the window or tab to close the presentation document.

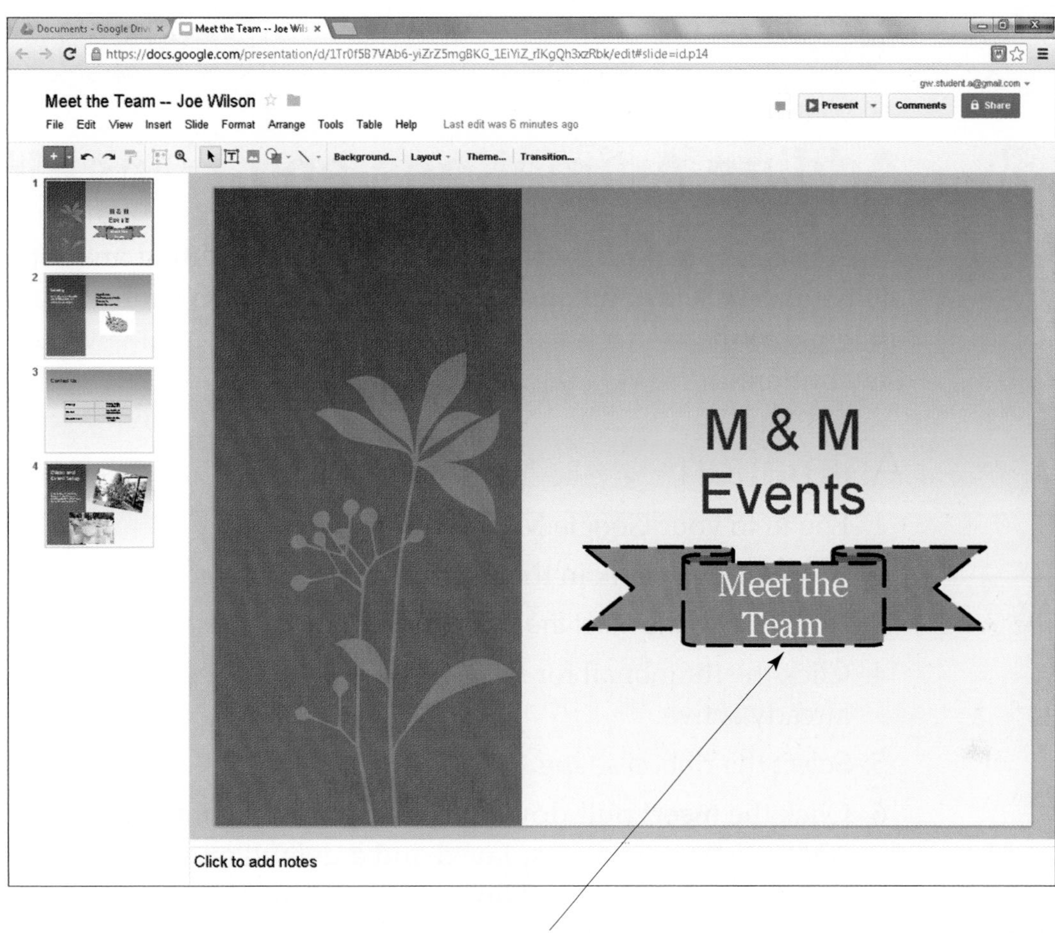

Goodheart-Willcox Publisher

Figure 11-12. After the shape is added to the slide, the slide should appear similar to the one shown here.

Lesson 11-5

Adding Animations and Transitions

A user can make a presentation dynamic by adding animation to the elements on a slide and adding transitions between slides. The speed assigned to these effects can be checked in editing mode by clicking the **Play** button.

Animation

1. Log in to your Google Mail account.
2. Click the **Drive** link in the menu bar at the top of the Mail page.
3. Navigate to the Meet the Team presentation, and open it.
4. Click the thumbnail for the first slide to make the slide active, unless it is already active.
5. Select the ribbon shape.
6. Click the **Insert** pull-down menu, and click **Animation** in the menu. The **Animations** panel is displayed and a default animation is assigned to the shape, as shown in **Figure 11-13.** A thumbnail of the shape appears in the panel.

Tip To display the **Animations** panel without assigning a default animation, click the **View** pull-down menu, and click **Animations** in the menu. You can also press the [Ctrl][Alt][Shift][B] key combination.

7. Click the name of the animation in the **Animations** panel. The properties of the animation are displayed in an expanded area below the animation name.
8. Click the **Animation type** drop-down list (top), and click **Zoom in** in the list. This animation type makes the shape appear on the slide starting small and increasing in size to its final size, like zooming in on the object.
9. Click the **Start condition** drop-down list (bottom), and click **After previous** in the list. This sets the animation to start automatically after the previous animation. In this case, there is no previous animation, so the animation will start automatically when the slide is displayed.
10. Drag the **Duration** slider toward the middle near the **Medium** label. As you drag the slider, the duration in seconds is displayed by the cursor. With the slider near the middle, the animation will take about two and one-half seconds to complete.

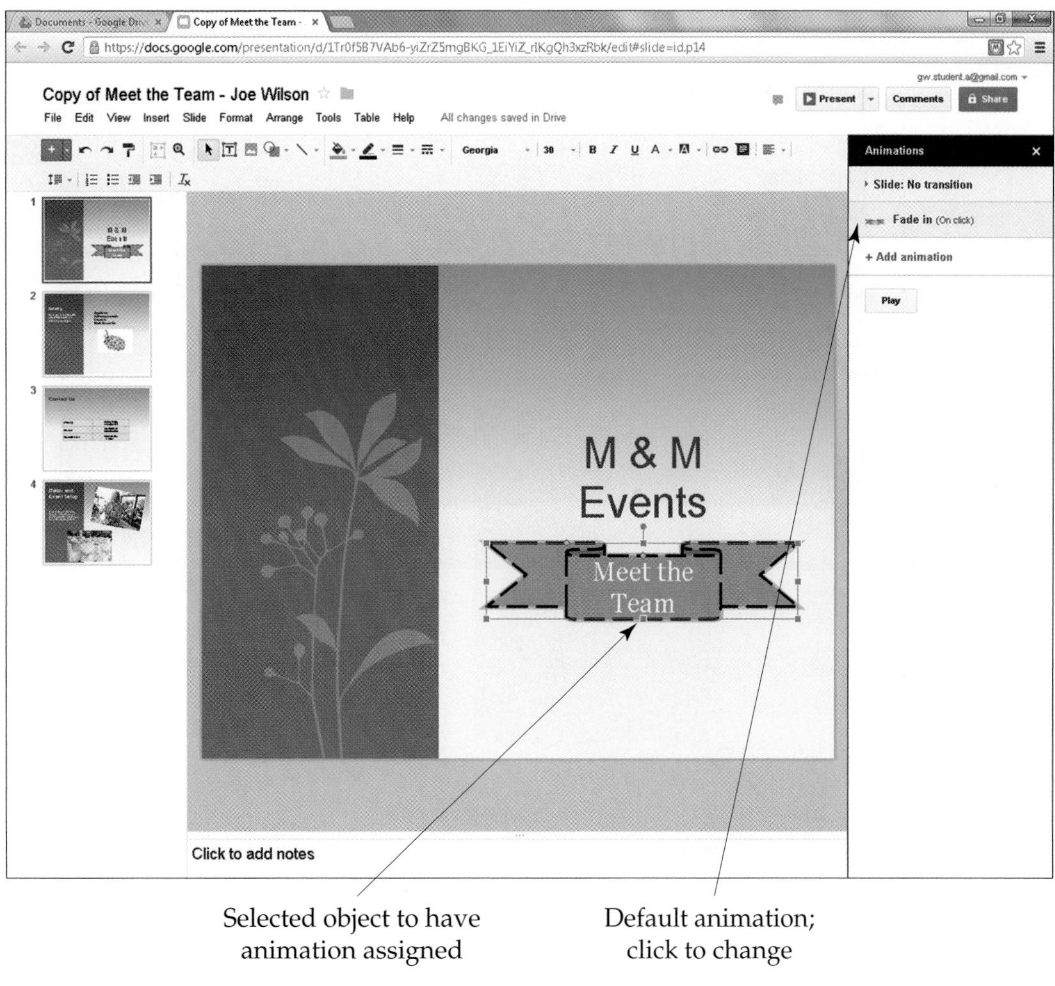

Goodheart-Willcox Publisher

Figure 11-13. The **Animations** panel is used to add animations to objects and transitions to slides.

11. Click the **Play** button on the **Animations** panel to preview the animation. The preview is played in the main slide area. While this preview is playing, a pointer moves along the **Animations** panel to show the step currently displayed.
12. Click the **Stop** button in the **Animations** panel to end the preview.

Transitions

13. In the **Animations** panel, click the **Slide: No transition** label. The panel is expanded to show options for adding a transition, as shown in **Figure 11-14.** As indicated by the label, there is currently no transition applied to the slide.

Tip To display the **Animations** panel with the transition area automatically expanded, click the **Slide** pull-down menu, and click **Change transition** in the menu.

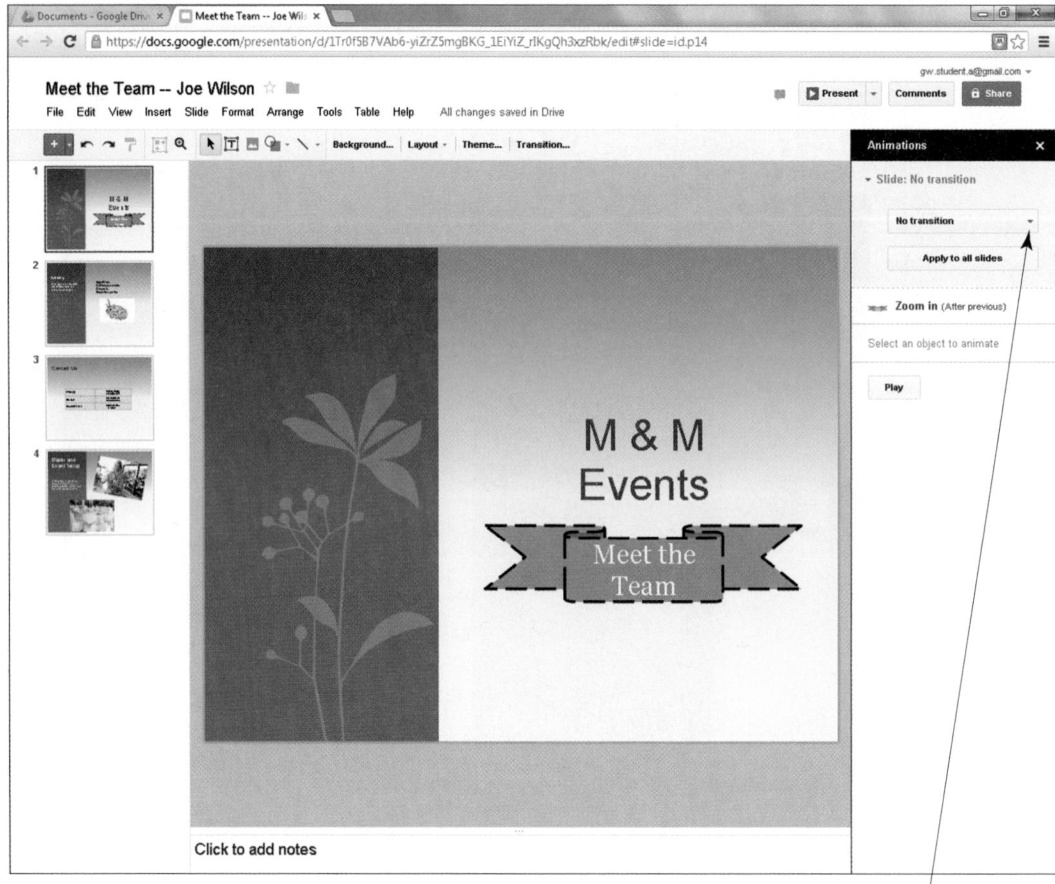

Goodheart-Willcox Publisher

Figure 11-14. Adding a transition to a slide.

14. Click the **Transition type** drop-down list (top), and click **Fade** in the list. This sets the slide to gradually appear when the presentation is played.
15. Drag the **Duration** slider toward the middle near the **Medium** label. This sets the transition to occur over about two and one-half seconds.
16. Click the **Apply to all slides** button. All slides in the presentation will have this same transition.
17. Click the **Play** button to preview the transition on the slide. All animations on the slide are also previewed, so the shape is animated as well.
18. Click the **Stop** button to end the preview.
19. Click the **X** on the **Animations** panel to close it.
20. Close the window or tab to close the presentation document.

Lesson 11-6

Using Themes, Backgrounds, and Speaker Notes

When using a theme for a slide show, text, bullets or numbers in automatic lists are formatted to match the color and font of the theme. The theme formatting is not applied to text added to the speaker notes section of a slide show.

Starting a New Presentation

1. Log in to your Google Mail account.
2. Click the **Drive** link in the menu bar at the top of the Mail page.
3. CREATE Click the **Create** button, and click **Presentation** in the drop-down menu. A new Google Sheets presentation is opened in a new tab or window, and the **Choose a theme** dialog box is displayed (unless it has been disabled), as shown in **Figure 11-15.**

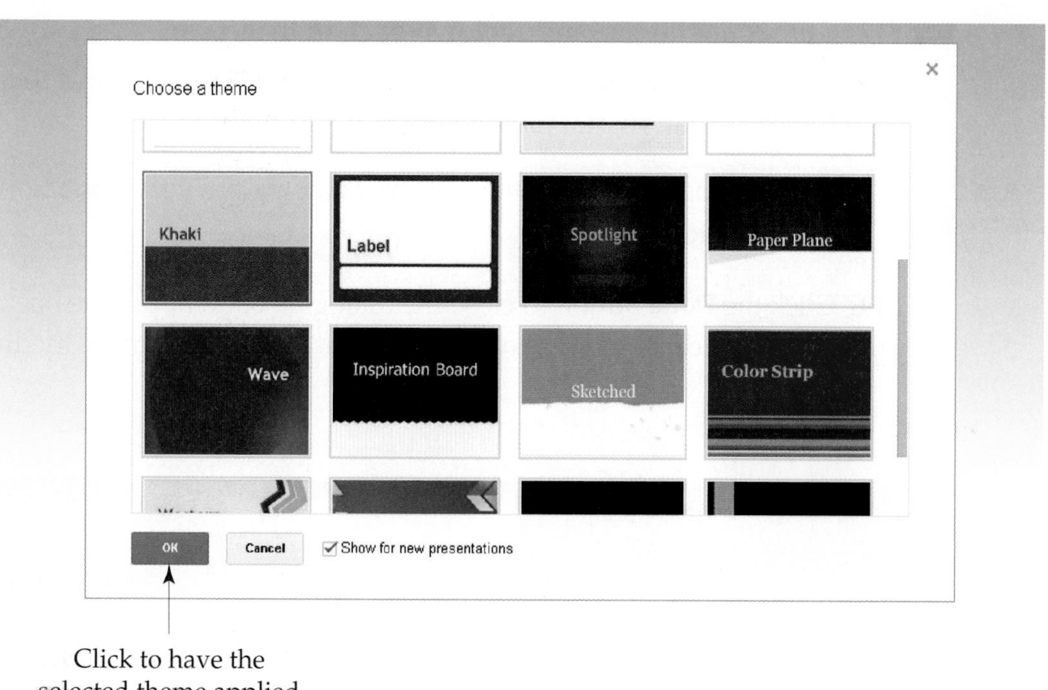

Goodheart-Willcox Publisher

Figure 11-15. Selecting a theme for a presentation.

4. In the **Choose a theme** dialog box, scroll through the list of thumbnail previews, click the Khaki preview, and click the **OK** button. The theme is applied to the presentation.
5. Click the **File** pull-down menu, and click **Rename...** in the menu.
6. In the **Rename document** dialog box, enter the name *Your Name*'s Presentation.

Applying a Theme

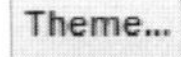

7. Make sure no objects are selected, and click the **Theme...** button on the toolbar. The **Choose a Theme** dialog box is displayed.
8. Scroll through the list of thumbnail previews, and click the **Inspiration Board** preview.
9. Click the **OK** button. The selected theme is applied to the presentation, replacing the previously applied theme. Note that a theme is applied to the entire presentation, not individual slides.

Applying a Background

10. Click the **Background...** button on the toolbar. The **Background** dialog box is displayed, as shown in **Figure 11-16.**
11. Click the **Color** button to display a drop-down menu.
12. Click a medium orange color swatch in the menu.
13. Click the **Apply to all** button. This applies the background to all slides in the presentation, not just the current slide.

Tip To apply the background to the current slide only, click the **Done** button instead of the **Apply to all** button.

14. Click the **Done** button to close the dialog box and apply the background color. Notice the portion of the slide that was white is now medium orange.

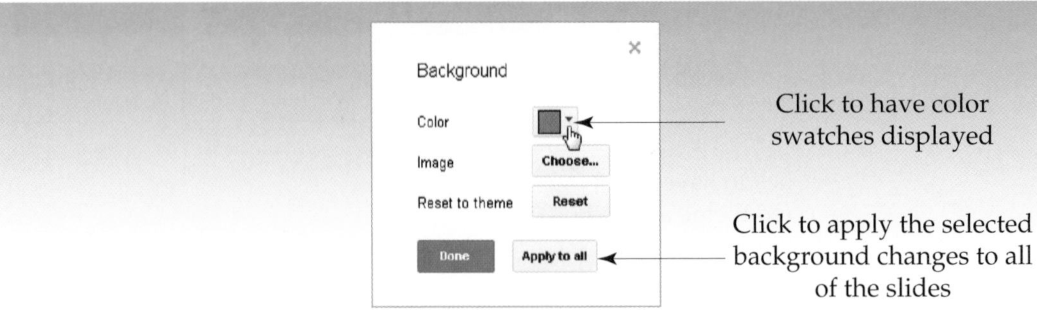

Figure 11-16. Adding a background to a slide.

Speaker Notes

15. Click in the notes section at the bottom of the screen. The default text in the notes section is Click to add notes.
16. Enter the text Full service planning: catering, music, decor, stationery.

Tip Notes are visible in published presentations, so they can be used as transcripts for viewers.

17. Close the window or tab to close the presentation document.

Lesson 11-7

Presenting a Slide Show

After the slide show is completed, the user is ready to present it to an audience. In presentation mode, the audience will see only the slides, not the editing tools.

1. Log in to your Google Mail account.
2. Click the **Drive** link in the menu bar at the top of the Mail page.
3. Navigate to the Meet the Team presentation, and open it.
4. Add speaker notes to each slide. Enter the text of your choice for each note, but relate it to what the slide shows.

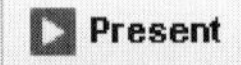

5. Click the **Present** button. The slide show is played from the *current* slide. A toolbar is displayed in the bottom-left corner of the screen as the show is played, as shown in **Figure 11-17.** A message is also displayed at the top of the screen indicating Google Drive is in full-screen mode.

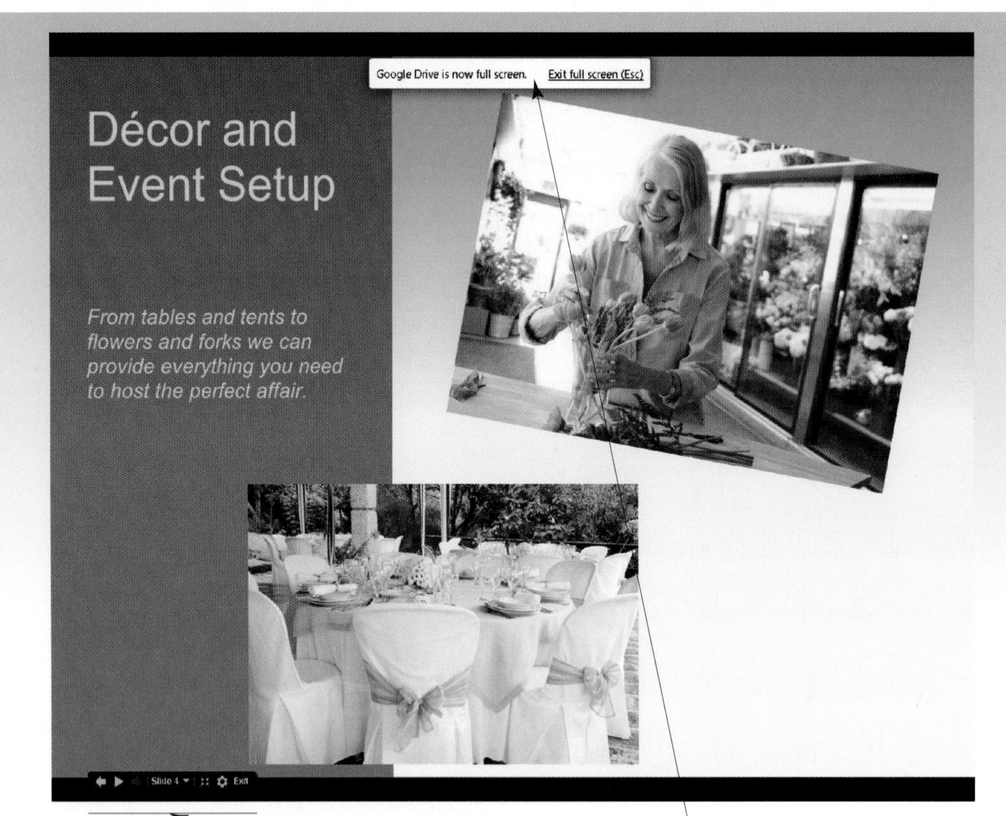

Use this toolbar to navigate through slides while in presentation mode

Full screen message is only displayed for a short time

Goodheart-Willcox Publisher

Figure 11-17. Playing a Google Slides presentation.

6. Click the **Allow** button in the message at the top of the screen to permit Google Drive to be displayed in full-screen mode, if needed. The toolbar in the bottom-left corner will be hidden when there is a period of inaction, but is displayed by moving the mouse or using the keyboard.

Use the arrow keys or [Page Up] and [Page Down] keys on the keyboard, the buttons on the toolbar, or the mouse button or wheel to move from one slide to the next.

Options

7. Click the **Options** button on the toolbar to display a drop-down menu.
8. Click **Open speaker notes** in the menu. A new window is opened containing the speaker notes for the slide, as shown in **Figure 11-18.** A timer is also included to show how long the slide show has been running.
9. Navigate through the presentation by clicking on the **Previous** and **Next** thumbnails in the **Speaker Notes** window.
10. Click the **X** in the **Speaker Notes** window to close it.
11. Click the **Exit** button on the toolbar or press the [Esc] to close the slide show.
12. Close the window or tab to close the presentation document.

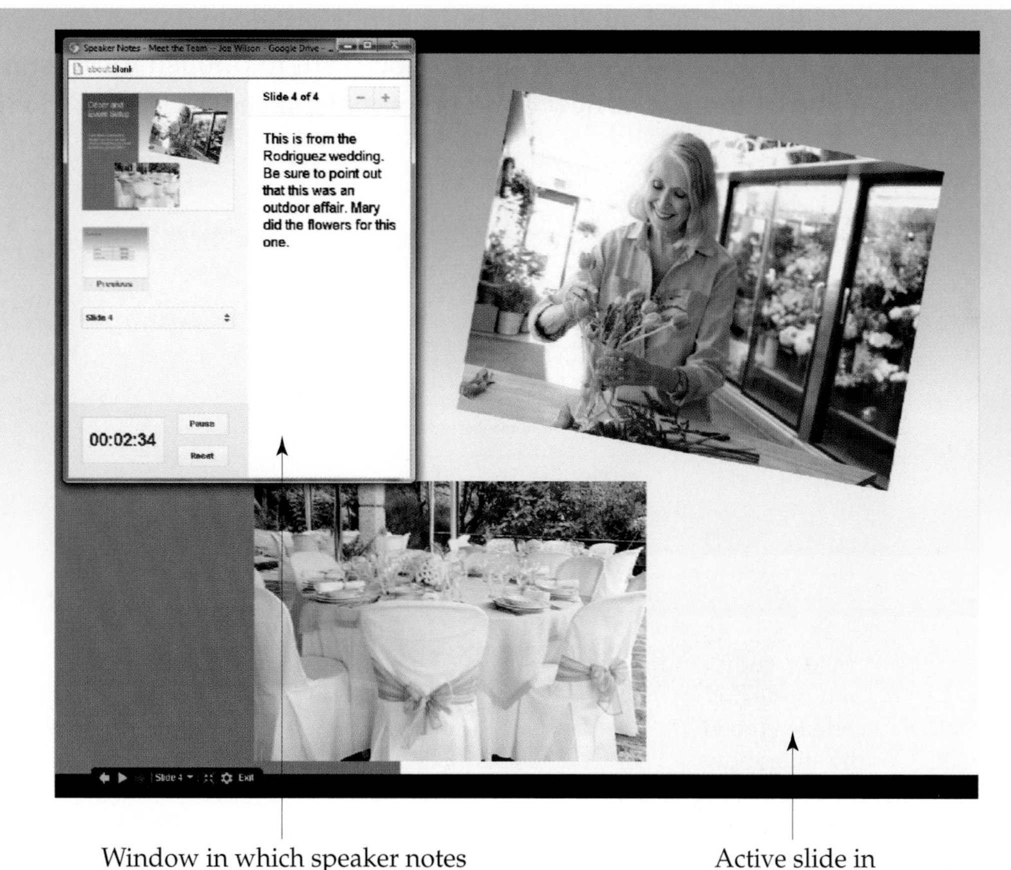

Goodheart-Willcox Publisher

Figure 11-18. The **Speaker Notes** window can be used to advance the presentation, track the time for the presentation, and view speaker notes.

Lesson 11-8

Publishing, Sharing, and Downloading a Presentation

A user can share a slide show with others to help during the creation of it. Once complete, a slide show can also be published so others can view it in presentation mode. A Google Slide file can also be downloaded and converted into a PowerPoint file for use in that program.

Publishing

1. Log in to your Google Mail account.
2. Click the **Drive** link in the menu bar at the top of the Mail page.
3. Navigate to the Meet the Team presentation, and open it.
4. Click the **File** pull-down menu, and click **Publish to the web...** in the menu. The **Publish to the web** dialog box is displayed.
5. Click the **Start publishing** button in the dialog box.
6. If a message appears asking if you want to publish the document, click the **OK** button. A new dialog box is displayed, as shown in **Figure 11-19.**

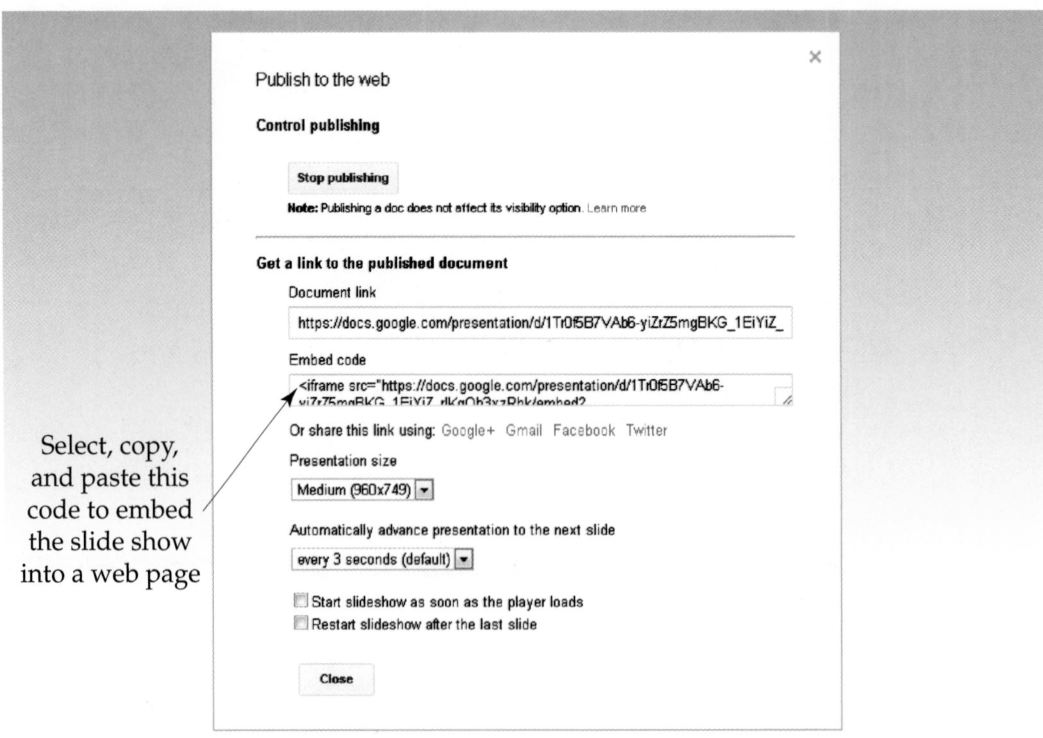

Goodheart-Willcox Publisher

Figure 11-19. Publishing a Google Slides presentation.

In the **Document link** text box in the middle of the dialog box is the URL that can be provided to others so they may access the presentation. In the **Embed code** text box is HTML code that can be pasted into a web page definition to link to the presentation.

Tip A presentation can be unpublished at any time by clicking the **Stop publishing** button in the **Publish to the web** dialog box.

7. Click the **Close** button to close the **Publish to the web** dialog box.

Sharing

Share

8. Click the **Share** button.
9. Click the **Change...** link in the **Who has access** area of the dialog box. A new dialog box is displayed in which the visibility options can be set.
10. Click the **Anyone with the link** radio button. Your instructor may specify a level of visibility.
11. Click the **Access** drop-down list that appears, and click **Can comment** in the list. This specifies that somebody with the link cannot only view the document, but add a comment to it.
12. Click the **Save** button to close the dialog box and return to the previous **Sharing settings** dialog box.
13. With the **Sharing settings** open, click in the **Add people:** text box. The lower part of the dialog box expands with additional options.
14. In the text box, enter the name of a classmate, if he or she is a contact, or his or her e-mail address. Multiple addresses can be added, one on each line. Press the [Enter] key to start a new line.
15. Click the drop-down list to the right of the text box, and click the entry for the level of access the person should have.
16. Check the **Notify people by email** check box. When checked, the person being added will receive an e-mail notification that the document has been shared with him or her.
17. Check the **Send a copy to myself** check box. When checked, you will receive the same e-mail notification that the person receives, which can be a useful way to verify that the e-mail was sent.

Share & save

18. Click the **Share & save** button to add the person to the list of people who have access to the document.

Done

19. Click the **Done** button to close the **Sharing settings** dialog box and return to the document.

Downloading a Presentation

20. Click the **File** pull-down menu.
21. Click **Download as** to display a cascading menu.

22. Click **Microsoft PowerPoint (.pptx)** in the cascading menu. The file is saved on your local hard drive in your My Documents\Downloads folder. A button also appears at the bottom of the document window for the downloaded document, as shown in **Figure 11-20.**
23. Click the arrow on the button for the downloaded document to display a drop-down menu.
24. Click **Show in folder** in the drop-down menu. This displays the folder in which the file was downloaded.
25. Close the folder window, and display the Google document page.
26. Click the button for the downloaded document to open it in the program associated with the PPTx file extension, which is usually Microsoft PowerPoint. Once you click this button it is no longer displayed.
27. Close Microsoft PowerPoint, and display the Google document page.
28. Close the window or tab to close the presentation document.

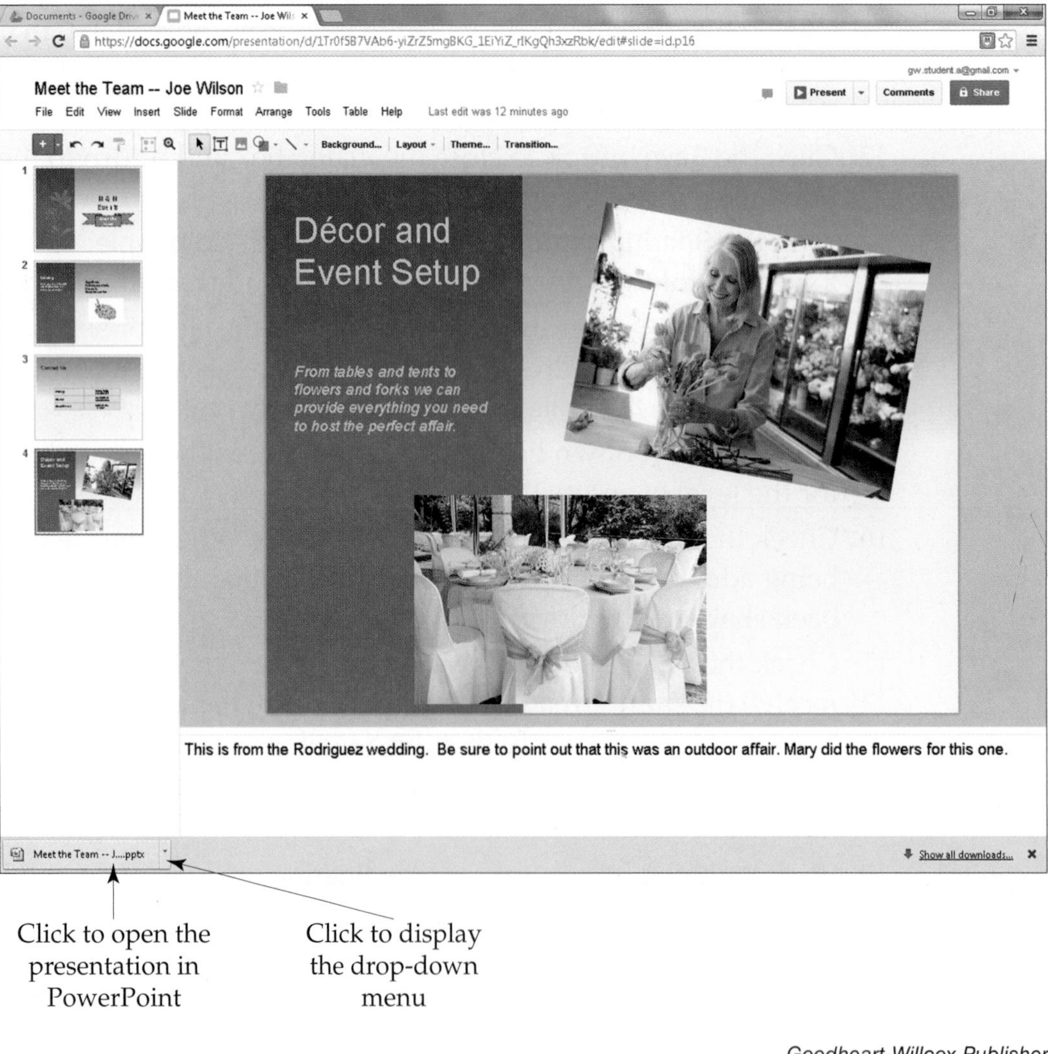

Goodheart-Willcox Publisher

Figure 11-20. When a presentation is downloaded, a message appears in a bar at the bottom of the screen.

Check Your Google Apps IQ

Now that you have finished this chapter, see what you know about Google Apps by taking the chapter posttest.
www.m.g-wlearning.com
www.g-wlearning.com/informationtechnology/

Skill Review

Answer the following questions on a separate sheet of paper.

1. What is the name of the mode in which a slide show is created?
2. When is presentation mode primarily used?
3. List the three main sections of the Google Slides page.
4. What is a theme?
5. What can be used as a background?
6. List the image file types that can be imported into Google Slides.
7. What must be checked for appropriateness of use before adding an image or video from the web to a slide?
8. How is a Google Drawing file added to a Google Slides presentation?
9. Describe the basic difference between an animation and a transition in Google Slides.
10. What is the difference between presenting a slide show and publishing it?

Lesson Application

These exercises are designed to apply the skills learned in this and previous chapters. General directions are provided, but you will need to draw on your knowledge to determine how to complete each exercise.

Exercise 11-1 Uploading and Converting a Presentation

Navigate to the student companion website (www.g-wlearning.com/informationtechnology/), and download the Our Services data file to your working folder. This is a Microsoft PowerPoint file. Upload the file to your Google Drive in the Documents folder. Convert the file to a Google Slides presentation, and delete the Microsoft PowerPoint file from your Google Drive. Open the Google Slides presentation, and rename it as *Your Name*-Our Services. Share the presentation with your instructor, and send an e-mail indicating the presentation is shared.

Exercise 11-2
Editing and Formatting a Presentation

Open the Our Services presentation from Exercise 11-1. Select and apply a theme for the presentation. Insert a new slide using the Title and Content layout. Enter the title Weddings. For the content, write a catchy intro sentence that an event planner may use to entice potential clients. Conduct a Google hangout with a classmate to brainstorm services the event planner may offer. Create a bulleted list on the slide to outline at least four of these services.

Exercise 11-3
Adding Images, Transitions, and Animations to a Presentation

Open the Our Services presentation from Exercise 11-2. Add two new slides. Select a layout that will be appropriate for including images and a brief bulleted list on each. Use the search function within Google Slides to locate wedding-themed images. Insert at least three images on the two slides. Add animation to each image. Add a final slide, and enter contact information in a table. Apply a different transition to each slide in the presentation.

Exercise 11-4
Publishing a Presentation

Open the Our Services presentation from Exercise 11-3. Publish the presentation. Compose an e-mail to your instructor describing the process used to create the presentation. Follow an appropriate writing structure, and use proper grammar and spelling. Include the URL for the published presentation, and send the e-mail to your instructor.

Chapter 12

Google Forms

Objectives

After completing this chapter, you will be able to:

- Create a Google form.
- Distribute a Google form to collect responses.
- Manage response data.
- Edit a form.

alexmillos/Shutterstock.com

Check Your Google Apps IQ

Before you begin this chapter, see what you already know about Google Apps by taking the chapter pretest.

www.m.g-wlearning.com
www.g-wlearning.com/informationtechnology/

Using Google Forms

Google Forms are an easy way to collect and analyze information. They can be used to conduct a survey or give an online quiz. A ***survey*** is a poll or questionnaire distributed to a group of people with the intent of collecting data related to a specific topic. All of the responses to a form are gathered and documented. The response information can remain private or shared with others. There is not a limit to the number of questions in a Google form or the number of people that can respond. A Google account is not required in order to receive and complete a Google form.

Information from completed forms can be collected in a Google spreadsheet or saved in Google Forms. There are some limitations with regard to how much response information can be captured in a spreadsheet. As discussed in Chapter 10, each Google spreadsheet has a maximum of 400,000 cells. If a user expects a higher number of responses, he or she can choose to have the responses saved in Google Forms. Then the responses can be downloaded as a CSV file, which can hold more data than a Google spreadsheet. Keep this in mind as you plan your questions and the number of people who will be completing the form.

Creating and Distributing a Form

Forms must be created, as opposed to importing other file types. A title or file name and descriptive text about the form can be added. Questions can then be added by the user, also known as the ***form creator*** or owner. There are several question types available in Google Forms, as seen in **Figure 12-1.** The user can also set up questions as required. This setting requires the form respondent to answer these questions before he or she can submit the form. Once created, questions can be edited, duplicated, or deleted. All of this work is done in the Google Forms edit mode. A form creator can view the live form at any time during the editing process.

Every form has a default confirmation message that will be displayed when a form has been submitted. A user can customize this message for his or her audience. The confirmation page section of the form includes other options to present after a form has been submitted.

By enabling the **Show link to submit another response** option, a link to the same form invites the respondent to submit another response. There is also the option to allow form respondents to see the responses of anyone else that has completed the form. The form creator can even allow respondents to go back and change their responses after submitting the form.

Google provides various themes for forms. Like the themes available for Google Slides, the ***theme*** determines the overall design of the form. The background and header color or image, the font type and color, the use and style of rules, and the spacing are all set by the theme. The theme is only visible when the form is viewed live.

Question Types	Description
Text	Respondents enter a word or short phrase in response.
Paragraph	Respondents enter an extended response; this is longer than the text type.
Multiple choice	Respondents are provided with options as defined by the form creator. Users can only select one of the options provided.
Checkboxes	Respondents are provided with options as defined by the form creator. Users can select one or more of the options provided.
Choose from a list	Respondents are provided with options in a drop-down list. Users can only select one of the options provided.
Scale	Respondents choose a number between 0 and 10 in response. Users can only select one of the number options provided. The form creator can label one or more of the numbers to communicate what each number indicates.
Grid	Respondents choose a response on a two-dimensional grid or table. The columns in the grid refer to the response options, which are often ratings. The rows in the grid refer to the items being responded to or, in many cases, rated.

Goodheart-Willcox Publisher

Figure 12-1. These are some of the types of questions available for a Google form.

A form creator can share his or her form with others to collaborate on the development of the form. Like other Google applications, the owner can determine visibility and accessibility settings, as discussed in Chapters 8 and 9. Collaborators can access the form before it is sent out to be completed by respondents.

Once it is final, the user can e-mail the form to its intended audience. E-mail addresses can be entered manually or selected from the user's Google Contacts. A link to the form will be included in the e-mail for the recipient to use to access the form. The user can also choose to include the form in the e-mail message. The version in the e-mail will not be displayed with the theme applied. Recipients invited to complete the form are not required to have a Google account.

Managing Form Data

A form creator can choose how he or she is notified that people have completed a Google form. When a user opens a form that has been sent, a number in parentheses is displayed to the right of the **Responses** pull-down menu. This reflects the number of responses the form has received. However, a user is not required to open the form file to know how many responses his or her form has received. Notification options allow the form creator to receive an e-mail when someone submits a form. E-mail notification can also be limited to a single summary e-mail sent once per day.

Once responses are received, a user can view the data by opening the responses spreadsheet or downloading the CSV file. Google creates a chart for each question that summarizes the response data, as seen in **Figure 12-2.** Text and paragraph questions are not shown in a chart. A user can access these charts directly in the **Responses** pull-down menu. The charts automatically change as more people submit responses. However, to see the complete response data or to organize the data differently, a user must select a response destination.

A user can choose to have the response data stay with the form or collected in a Google spreadsheet. Response data that stay with the form can be downloaded as a CSV file. To view responses in a Google spreadsheet, a user can open the spreadsheet file from Google Drive or from within the form window.

Goodheart-Willcox Publisher

Figure 12-2. Response data for a form are summarized in a chart.

With the data in a Google spreadsheet, the data can be organized to help in analysis. Data can be sorted or formatted to improve usability. The Google spreadsheet that is displayed includes each form question in the top row of the spreadsheet. The responses fill the remaining rows. The time and date of each form response, called a ***time stamp,*** is automatically entered into Column A. Response data can also be shared by accessing the **Sharing settings** dialog box in the spreadsheet file and setting the visibility and accessibility options.

Lesson 12-1

Creating a Form

Google provides users with several question types to use when creating a form. Users can check the spelling and grammar of their questions. It can be helpful to do this when previewing the live form.

Creating a New Form

CREATE

1. Log in to your Google Mail account.
2. Click the **Drive** link in the menu bar at the top of the Mail page.
3. Navigate to the Forms subfolder.
4. Click the **Create** button, and click **Form** in the drop-down menu. A new form is opened, and the **Choose title and theme** dialog box is displayed (unless it has been disabled), as shown in **Figure 12-3.**
5. In the **Title** text box, enter *Your Name*_Customer Satisfaction to rename the form. The **Default** theme is highlighted.
6. Click the **OK** button in the dialog box to display the new form. The **Default** theme is applied. Notice that the name of the document is also displayed at the top of the form.
7. Click in the **Form description** text box below the form title, and enter Thank you for taking the time to complete this survey; your feedback is important to us. This message will be visible to the person filling out the form.

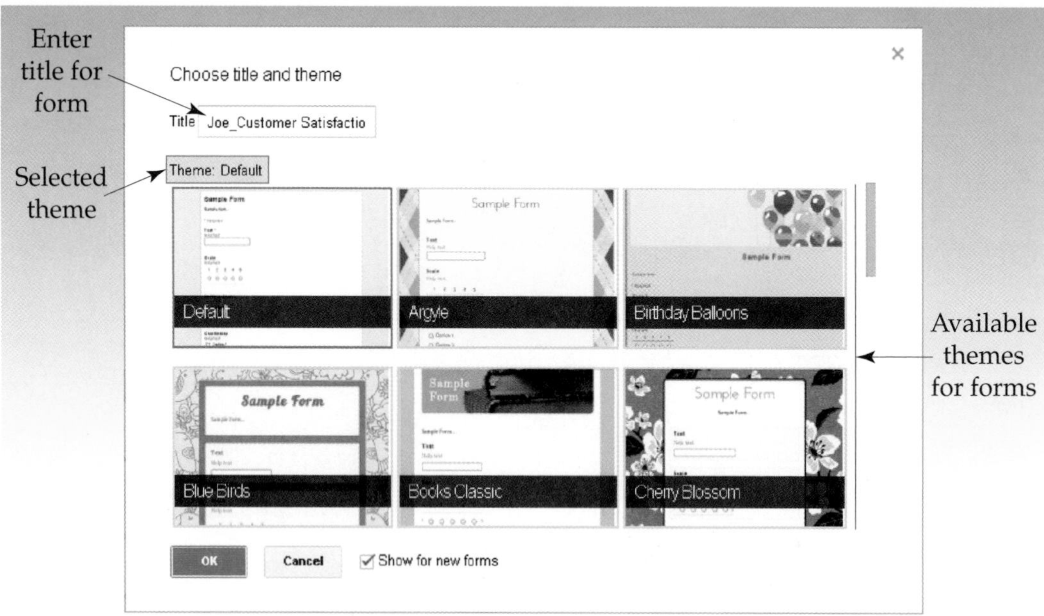

Goodheart-Willcox Publisher

Figure 12-3. Selecting a theme for a new form.

Adding Questions

8. Click in the **Question Title** text box, and enter What is your overall satisfaction rating with our company?, as shown in **Figure 12-4.** This is the question that will be presented to the respondent.
9. Click the **Question Type** button to display a drop-down menu.
10. Click **Scale** in the drop-down menu. This changes the type of question to a rating scale, and the options in the question area change to reflect this type. Leave the range as the default of 1 to 5.
11. Click in the **1:** text box, and enter Very Dissatisfied.
12. Click in the **5:** text box, and enter Very Satisfied.
13. Check the **Required question** check box. This means that the respondent cannot skip this question.
14. Click the **Done** button to end creation of this question.

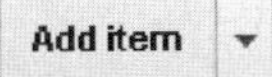

15. Click the drop-down arrow next to the **Add item** button, and click **Paragraph text** in the drop-down list. This adds a new question of the paragraph text type, which presents the respondent with a text box to enter a long response.

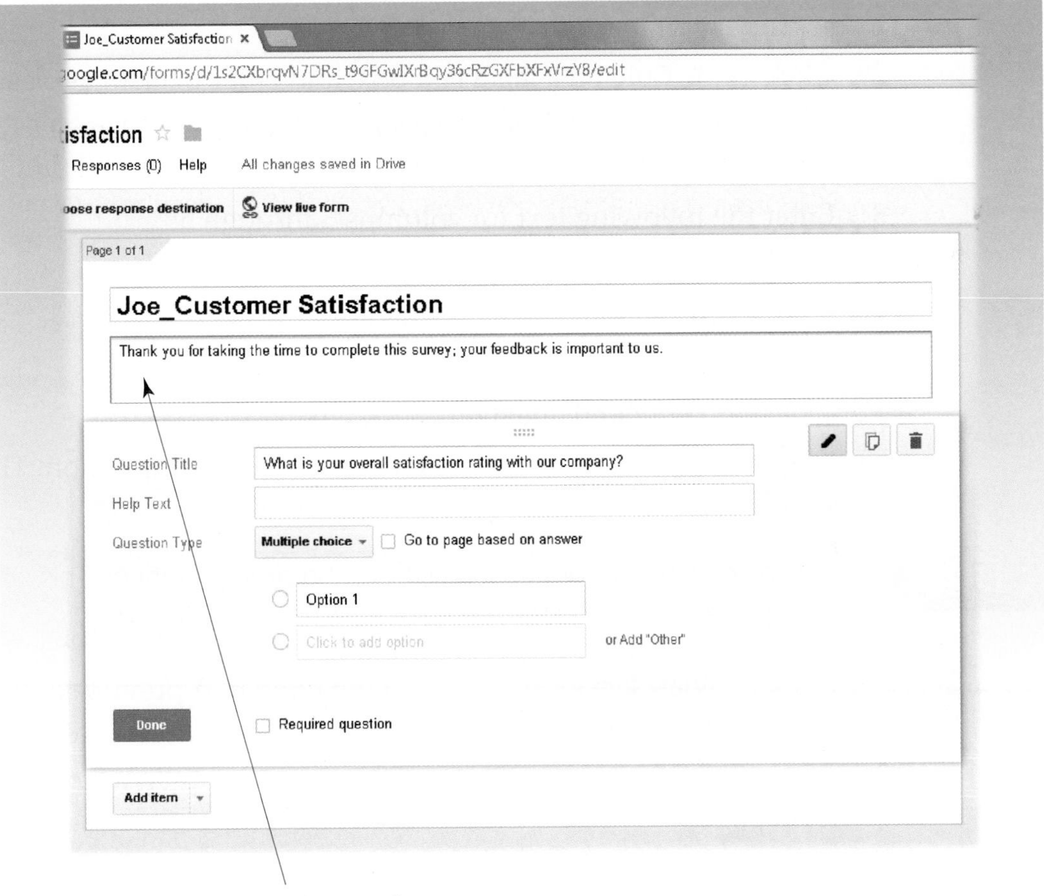

Goodheart-Willcox Publisher

Figure 12-4. Adding a question to a form.

16. In the **Question Title** text box for the new question, enter Please tell us why you feel that way.
17. Check the **Required question** check box.
18. Click the **Done** button to end creation of the second question.
19. Click the drop-down arrow next to the **Add item** button, and click **Grid** in the drop-down list. This adds a new question of the grid type.
20. In the **Question Title** text box for the new question, enter Please rate your satisfaction with our customer service in the following areas.
21. Click in the **Help Text** text box, and enter Please reflect on your most recent visit.
22. Click in the **Row 1 label** text box, and enter Responsiveness.
23. Click the entry Click to add a row next to **Row 2 label** to add a second row.
24. Click in the **Row 2 label** text box, and enter Professionalism.
25. Click the entry Click to add a row next to **Row 3 label** to add a third row.
26. Click in the **Row 3 label** text box, and enter Understanding of My Needs.
27. Click in the **Column 1 label** text box, and enter Very Dissatisfied.
28. Click the entry Click to add a column next to **Column 2 label** to add a second column.
29. Click in the **Column 2 label** text box, and enter Somewhat Dissatisfied.
30. Click the entry Click to add a column next to **Column 3 label** to add a third column.
31. Enter the following text for columns 3 through 5:
    - Column 3: Neither Dissatisfied nor Satisfied
    - Column 4: Somewhat Satisfied
    - Column 5: Very Satisfied
32. Check the **Required question** check box.
33. Click the **Done** button to end creation of the third question. The form should look like the one shown in **Figure 12-5.**

Questions can be rearranged by clicking and dragging them. This will not rearrange the order of questions in the spreadsheet of results.

34. Click the **View live form** button on the toolbar. A preview of the form is displayed in a new tab or window.
35. Close the preview tab or window to close the preview and return to the form page.

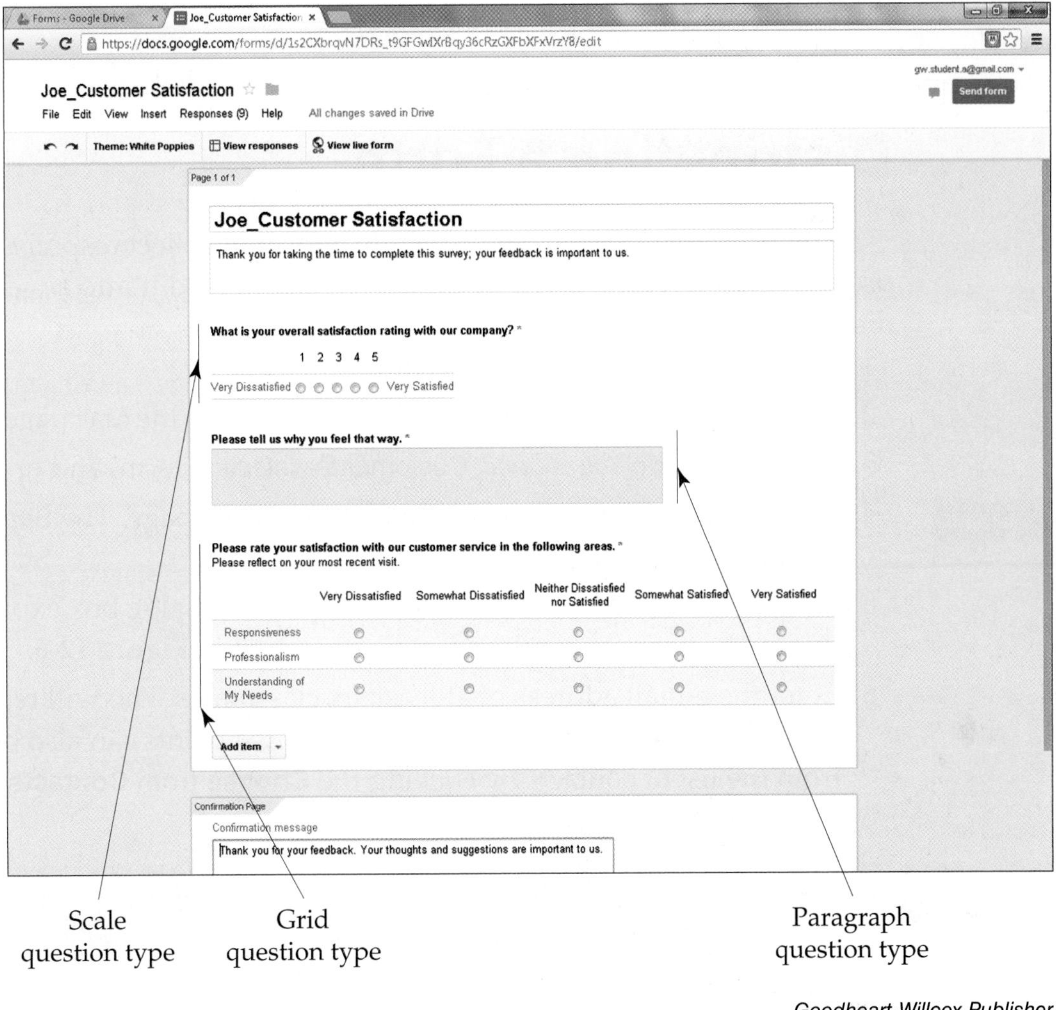

Figure 12-5. The form after three questions have been added.

Applying a Theme

Theme...

36. On the form page, click the **Theme...** button. The **Choose Theme** dialog box is displayed. This is the same dialog box displayed when starting a new form.
37. Scroll through the list of thumbnails, and click the thumbnail of the theme you want to use.
38. Click the **OK** button to apply the theme. The theme is only visible when you view it live.
39. Click the **View live form** button on the toolbar. A preview of the form with the selected theme is displayed in a new tab or window.
40. Close the window or tab to close the form. This does *not* send the form.

Lesson 12-2

Distributing a Form

There are several ways to distribute a form to collect responses. A user can e-mail it directly from Google Forms, embed it into a website, or distribute the link to the form via e-mail or a website.

1. Log in to your Google Mail account.
2. Click the **Drive** link in the menu bar at the top of the Mail page.
3. Navigate to the *Your Name*_Customer Satisfaction form, and open it.
4. Click the **Send form** button at the bottom of the page. The **Send form** dialog box is displayed.
5. Click in the **Send form via email:** text box. The dialog box expands to display options for sending e-mail, as shown in **Figure 12-6.**
6. Enter the e-mail address of at least six classmates who will receive the form. Separate addresses with a comma. Recipients can also be selected from the list of contacts by clicking the **Choose from Contacts** link, if available.

Send form

Tip At the top of the **Send Form** dialog box is the **Link to share** text box. This contains the URL that can be e-mailed or included in a web page definition.

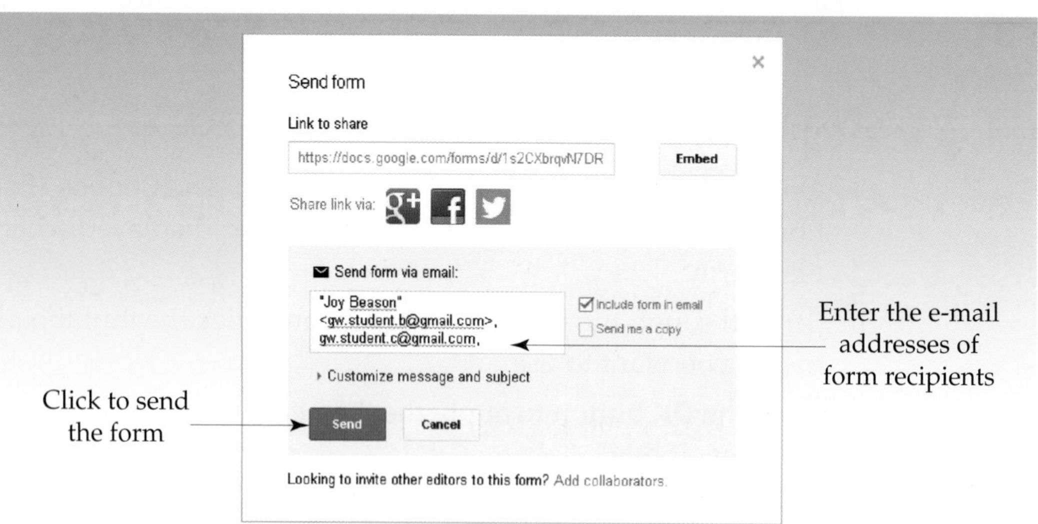

Goodheart-Willcox Publisher

Figure 12-6. Options for sending a form via e-mail.

7. Uncheck the **Include form in email** check box. When this is unchecked, the recipient is e-mailed a link that must be clicked to get to the form. If the form is included in the e-mail, the applied theme is not included.
8. Click the **Send** button to send the form to each e-mail address that was entered. If you receive an e-mail from a classmate with a link to his or her survey, be sure to complete and submit it. The **Choose response destination** dialog box is displayed, as shown in **Figure 12-7.**
9. Click the **New spreadsheet** radio button. This means the responses to the form will be entered into a new spreadsheet that is saved on your Google Drive.
10. Click in the text box below the **New spreadsheet** radio button, and enter Responses from Customer Satisfaction Survey. This is the name of the spreadsheet that will be created.

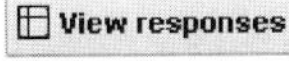

11. Click the **Create** button to set the destination for responses to this form. It may take a minute or two for Google to set up the spreadsheet. When the spreadsheet is set up, the **View responses** button appears on the form page.

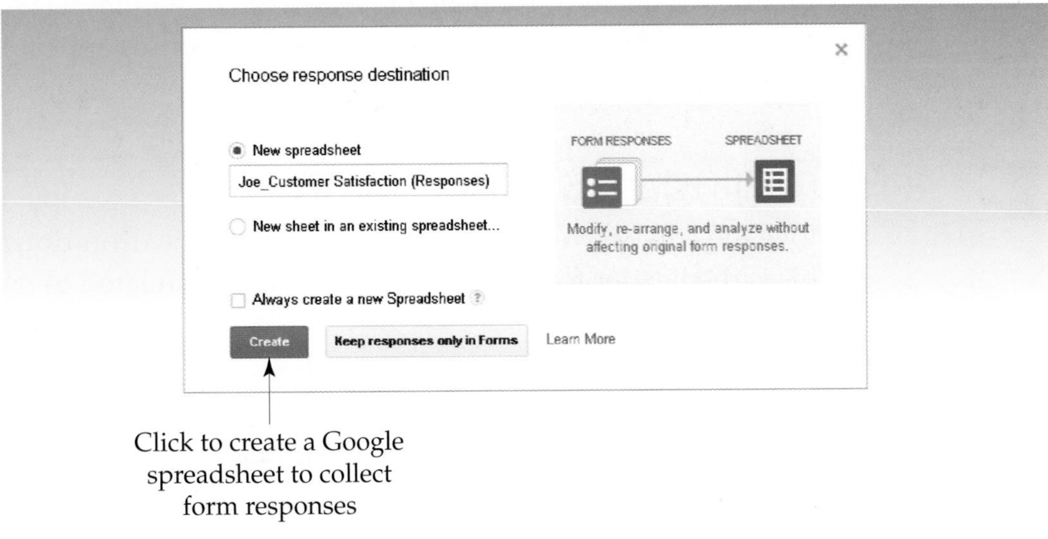

Goodheart-Willcox Publisher

Figure 12-7. When a form is sent, the destination for the responses must be set.

Lesson 12-3

Viewing and Managing Responses

When a user creates a form, he or she is the only person that can view the results. When the responses are collected in a Google spreadsheet, the file can be shared by changing the visibility and accessibility settings.

Viewing Responses

1. Log in to your Google Mail account.
2. Click the **Drive** link in the menu bar at the top of the Mail page.
3. Navigate to the Customer Satisfaction form, and open it. Make sure your six classmates have responded to the form, as indicated by the number in parentheses next to the **Responses** pull-down menu.

The spreadsheet containing responses to a form can be opened directly from Google Drive.

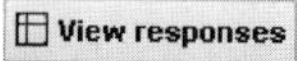

4. Click the **View responses** button. The spreadsheet containing all responses to the form is opened in a new tab or window. The questions appear in the first row of the spreadsheet. Responses appear in the cells below each heading.

Managing Response Data

5. Move the cursor over the **B** header to display the drop-down arrow. This is the header for responses to the question related to overall satisfaction.
6. Click the sort ascending option in the drop-down list, as shown in **Figure 12-8.** The sheet is sorted based on ascending values in column B.
7. Move the cursor to the upper-left corner of the sheet, above and to the left of cell A1, and click. This selects the entire sheet.
8. Right-click anywhere in the sheet, and click **Sort range...** in the shortcut menu that is displayed. The **Sort range** dialog box is displayed.
9. Check the **Data has header row** check box.
10. Click the **Sort by** button, and click **What is your...** in the drop-down list. This entry is the first three words from the header cell in column B.
11. Click the **+ Add another sort column** link, click the new button that appears, and click **Please tell...** in the drop-down menu. This entry is the first two words from the header cell in column C.
12. Click the two **Z → A** radio buttons.

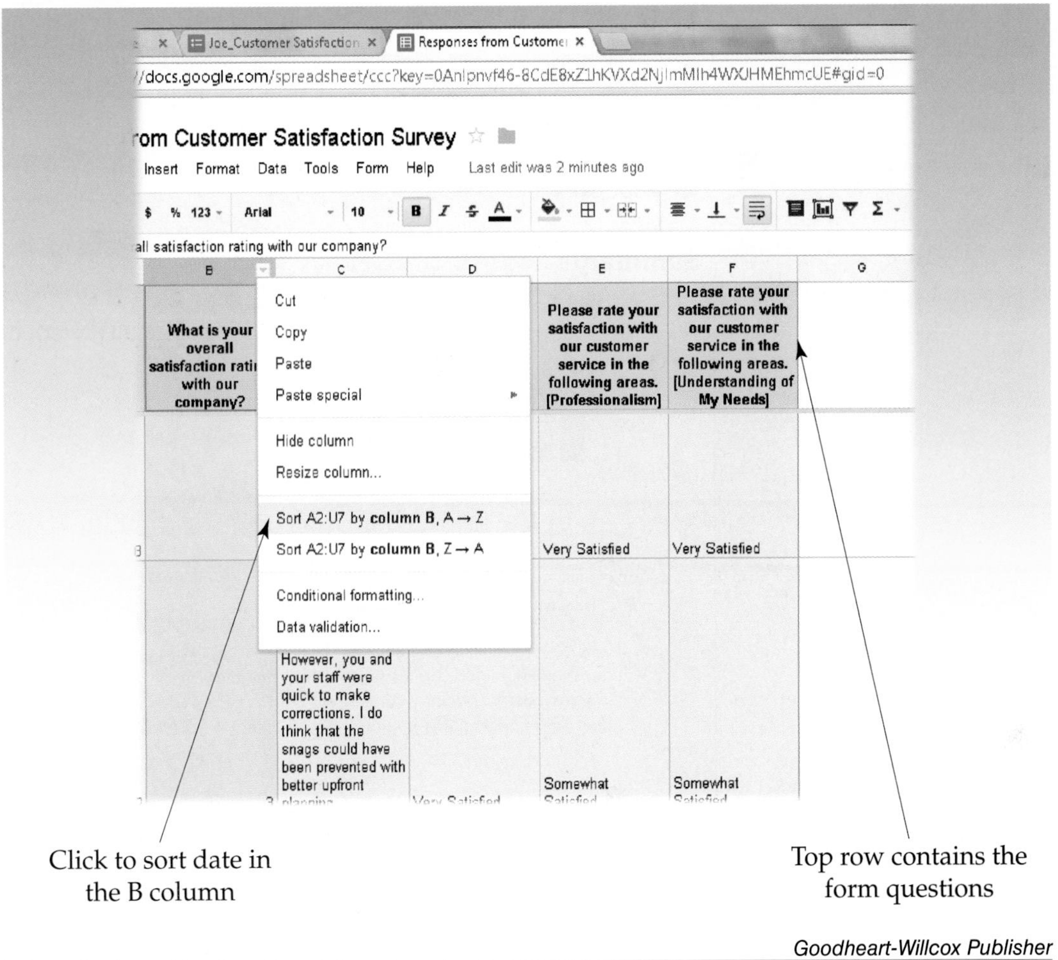

Goodheart-Willcox Publisher

Figure 12-8. Sorting response data in ascending order.

13. Click the **Sort** button. The spreadsheet is rearranged first based on the value for the overall satisfaction question, and then alphabetical by the response entered.
14. Click the **Form** pull-down menu, and click **Show summary of responses** in the menu. A new tab or window is displayed that illustrates the responses in charts, as shown in **Figure 12-9.**

To print the summary of responses, right-click on the summary and select **Print...** from the shortcut menu.

15. Close the tab or window to close the summary and return to the spreadsheet.

Sharing Response Data

16. Click the **Share** button in the upper-right corner of the spreadsheet window. The **Sharing settings** dialog box is displayed.
17. Click in the **Add people:** text box, and enter the e-mail address of your instructor.

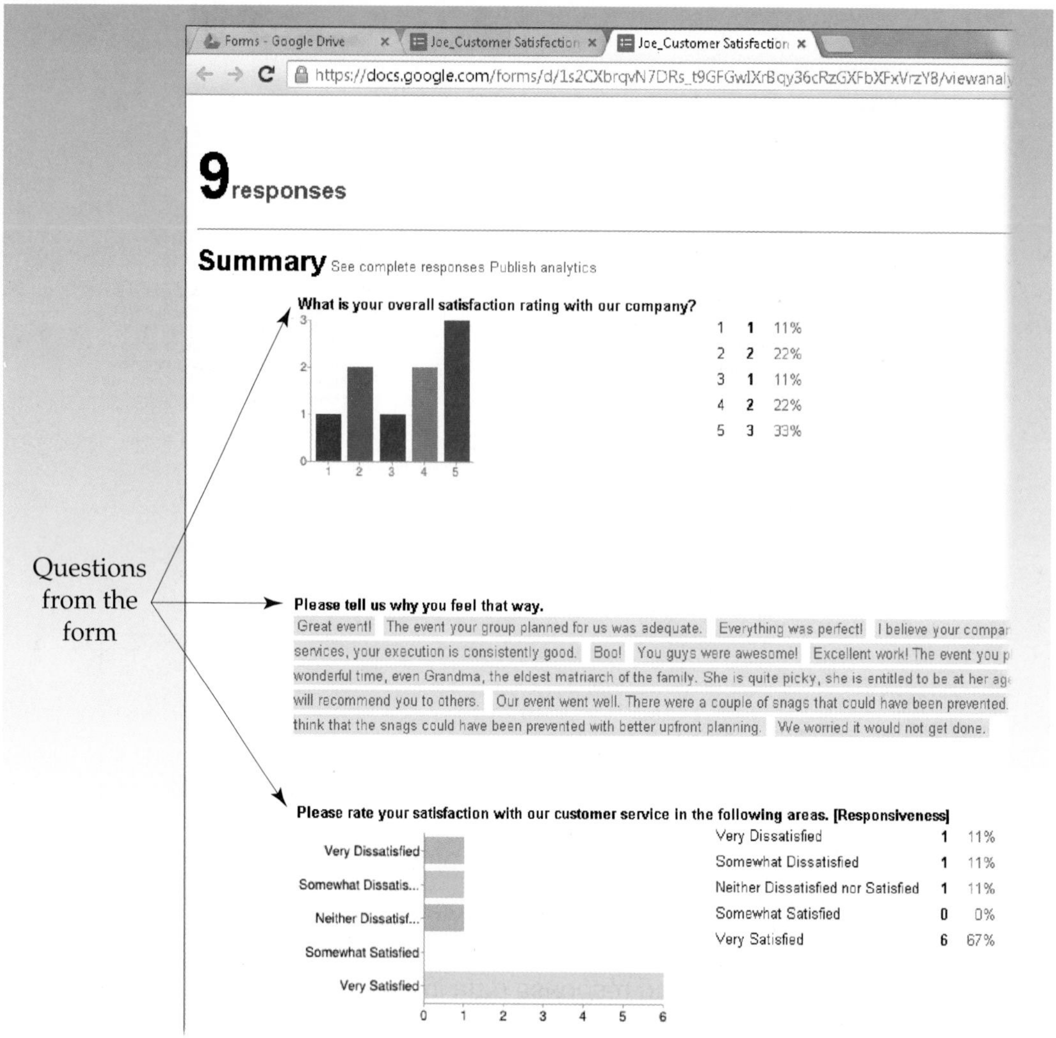

Forms - Google Drive | Joe_Customer Satisfaction | Joe_Customer Satisfaction

https://docs.google.com/forms/d/1s2CXbrqvN7DRs_t9GFGwlXrBqy36cRzGXFbXFxVrzY8/viewanal

9 responses

Summary See complete responses Publish analytics

Questions from the form

What is your overall satisfaction rating with our company?

1	1	11%
2	2	22%
3	1	11%
4	2	22%
5	3	33%

Please tell us why you feel that way.

Great event! The event your group planned for us was adequate. Everything was perfect! I believe your compar services, your execution is consistently good. Boo! You guys were awesome! Excellent work! The event you p wonderful time, even Grandma, the eldest matriarch of the family. She is quite picky, she is entitled to be at her ag will recommend you to others. Our event went well. There were a couple of snags that could have been prevented. think that the snags could have been prevented with better upfront planning. We worried it would not get done.

Please rate your satisfaction with our customer service in the following areas. [Responsiveness]

Very Dissatisfied	1	11%
Somewhat Dissatisfied	1	11%
Neither Dissatisfied nor Satisfied	1	11%
Somewhat Satisfied	0	0%
Very Satisfied	6	67%

Goodheart-Willcox Publisher

Figure 12-9. A summary of responses is displayed in chart form in a new tab or window.

18. Click the drop-down list to the right of the text box, and click **Can view** in the list.
19. Check the **Notify people via email** check box.
20. Click the **Add message** link, and enter Here are the results of our customer service survey. Overall they are positive. in the text box that appears.
21. Check the **Send a copy to myself** check box.

Share & save

22. Click the **Share & save** button to add your instructor to the list of people who have access to the document.

23. Click the **Done** button to close the **Sharing settings** dialog box and return to the spreadsheet.
24. Close the window or tab to close the spreadsheet, and display the form page.
25. Close the window or tab to close the form.

Lesson 12-4

Editing a Form

After a form has been created, a user can apply advanced features including custom confirmation messages for form respondents. When people respond to the form, a user can receive notification as set up within the form itself. A user can also close a form to responses.

Adding a Custom Confirmation Message

1. Log in to your Google Mail account.
2. Click the **Drive** link in the menu bar at the top of the Mail page.
3. Navigate to the Customer Satisfaction form, and open it.
4. In the **Confirmation Page** area at the bottom of the form, click in the **Confirmation message** text box, and enter Thank you for your feedback. Your thoughts and suggestions are important to us.
5. Make sure the **Publish and show a link to the results of this form** check box is not checked. If checked, the summary of results is displayed to the respondent when the form is submitted. Since this form asks for personal information, it is not appropriate to share the results with anyone.

Send form

6. Click the **Send form** button, and send the form to three classmates who have not received the form. When your classmates submit the form, they should receive the new confirmation message.

Setting Notification Behavior

View responses

7. Click the **View responses** button. The spreadsheet containing all responses to the form is opened in a new tab or window.
8. Click the **Tools** pull-down menu, and click **Notification rules...** in the menu. The **Set notification rules** dialog box is displayed, as shown in **Figure 12-10.**
9. Check the **A user submits a form** check box. This tells Google to monitor when a form response is submitted.
10. Check the **Email—right away** check box. This tells Google that as soon as the action occurs to send you an e-mail.
11. Click the **Save** button. The **Set notification rules** dialog box changes to display the notification that was set, as shown in **Figure 12-11.**
12. Click the **Done** button to close the **Set notification rules** dialog box.
13. Close the tab or window to close the spreadsheet and return to the form page.

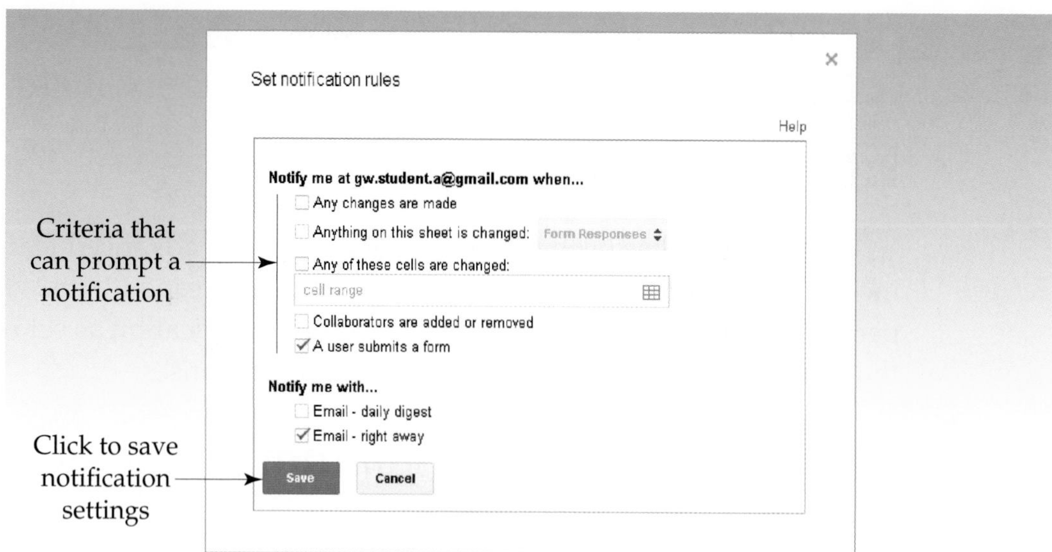

Goodheart-Willcox Publisher

Figure 12-10. Creating a notification rule.

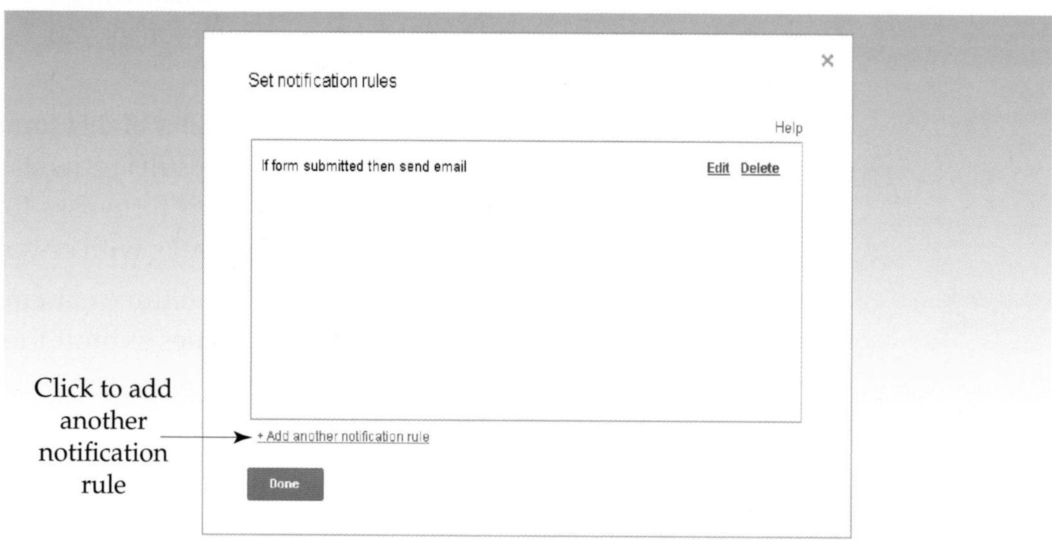

Goodheart-Willcox Publisher

Figure 12-11. After a notification rule has been set, it is displayed in the **Set Notification Rules** dialog box.

Closing a Form to Responses

14. Click the **Responses** pull-down menu.
15. Click **Accepting responses** in the pull-down menu to remove the check mark. Unchecking this turns off the form. No one will be able to view the questions or submit responses.
16. Close the window or tab to close the form.

Tip To open a form to responses, check **Accepting responses** in the **Responses** pull-down menu.

Check Your Google Apps IQ

Now that you have finished this chapter, see what you know about Google Apps by taking the chapter posttest.
www.m.g-wlearning.com
www.g-wlearning.com/informationtechnology/

Skill Review

Answer the following questions on a separate sheet of paper.

1. What is a survey?
2. What is the limit on the number of questions that can be in a Google Form?
3. Give the two locations in which information gathered from a form can be stored.
4. What is the limit on the number of cells in a Google spreadsheet?
5. What term is associated with the person who creates a form?
6. How many types of questions are available for a form?
7. What does a theme control for a form?
8. What are the two ways a form can be presented to a recipient?
9. How does Google summarize the response data for each question in a form?
10. If response data for a form are displayed in a spreadsheet, what does the top row in the spreadsheet contain?

Lesson Application

These exercises are designed to apply the skills learned in this and previous chapters. General directions are provided, but you will need to draw on your knowledge to determine how to complete each exercise.

Exercise 12-1
Creating a Form

Create a new form named Employee Satisfaction Survey. Select an appropriate theme. Enter a description for the survey. Conduct a Google hangout with a classmate to brainstorm at least five questions to ask employees related to job satisfaction. For example, one question may ask how long the employee has been working for the company. The questions should include one of these types: choose from list, multiple choice, scale, grid, and paragraph text. Enter the questions into the form. Preview and proofread the form.

Exercise 12-2
Editing a Form

Edit the Employee Satisfaction Survey form created in Exercise 12-1. Add a custom confirmation message to the form. Work with the classmate from Exercise 12-1 to brainstorm the message. After the message is entered, take the steps needed to prevent recipients from seeing the responses to the form. Select at least five classmates and send the form to them.

Exercise 12-3
Viewing/Sharing Data

Ensure the classmates have responded to the form sent in Exercise 12-2. Open the spreadsheet of responses to the form. Sort the data by years at the company and then overall satisfaction. If your form does not include these two questions, select two similar questions. View the summary of results and print it. Share the spreadsheet with your instructor. Include a message when sharing the spreadsheet to indicate you have completed the exercises in this chapter.

Unit 3 Review

Scenario

The Jackson County school system has hired M&M Event Planning to organize a college fair. You have been put in charge of this event. Use Google Docs to view information and collaborate with the various committees working on this project. Use the information learned in this unit to complete the activities. As much as possible, these activities should be completed without referring to the chapters for information.

Activities

1. Create a brainstorming sheet to plan for the college fair. Create this sheet as a document. Name the file College Fair Brainstorming Ideas. Include a formatted title in the file. Include an image to represent colleges and a section titled Resources. Use the research tool to find and add links to three college fair resources to the planning sheet. Share the document with at least four classmates. As classmates are commenting in your document, comment in the documents provided to you by classmates. Use comments to discuss how you can use the resources you have found.
2. Create a form for people to sign up to attend the college fair. Include questions for name; grade level; high school; workshop interest, such as workshops for financial aid, essay writing, and college tours; and additional comments. Add a custom confirmation, and collect responses from five classmates. Share the form results with your instructor.
3. Create a presentation to highlight three colleges that will attend the fair. Use a theme and other formatting to make the presentation attractive. Provide the following content about each school: name, location, tuition cost, and a statement describing the school. Also, include an image, table, or drawing on at least three slides. Add animations and transitions to the presentation. Publish the completed presentation to the web, and send the link to your instructor.

4. Navigate to the student companion website (www.g-wlearning.com/informationtechnology/), and download the College Fair Registration data file from the Chapter 12 area to your working folder. This is an Excel file. Upload the file, and convert it to a Google spreadsheet. Format the spreadsheet so the header row is frozen and has a background. Use a formula to calculate the average GPA of students attending the fair. Share the spreadsheet with your instructor.
5. Create a folder in Google Drive named Google Docs Review. Create these subfolders below it: Documents, Spreadsheets, Presentations, and Forms. Move the files for the college fair to the appropriate folder. Share the Google Docs Review folder and its subfolders with your instructor.

Unit 4

Google Sites

Google Sites is a collaborative tool for creating customized websites. A user can choose from several page templates to create basic web pages or specific pages types, such as announcement-style pages, file cabinet pages, or list pages. Web pages created in Google Sites can include text, images; files; content from other Google tools such as Drive, Calendar, and Picasa; and other media, like video. Sites can be edited in any browser. The user controls who can access to the site, so it can be private where only a few people have access or public where anybody can access it. Google users can be invited to collaborate on the creation or management of the entire site or just specific pages. The best part is that you do not need to have any special web-development training or know how to program HTML code.

Chapters

Chapter 13

Creating and Managing a Site

Objectives

After completing this chapter, you will be able to:

- Create a Google site.
- Edit pages on a Google site.
- Create an announcements page.
- Manage posts on an announcements page.
- Manage files on a file cabinet page.
- Populate a list page with entries.
- Collaborate with others to manage a Google site.

alexmillos/Shutterstock.com

Check Your Google Apps IQ

Before you begin this chapter, see what you already know about Google Apps by taking the chapter pretest.

www.m.g-wlearning.com
www.g-wlearning.com/informationtechnology/

Using Google Sites

Google Sites provides users with tools to develop websites without requiring the knowledge of web scripting or programming languages. The site can be a ***public site,*** in which case it is open to anyone with access to the Internet. A user can also create a ***private site*** limiting access to just specific people. Similarly, a user can choose to invite others to collaborate on the creation of the site.

There are many reasons to create a website. A user working on a project with several classmates can create a private site for the group. The group can use the site to store and share the work of each member. An individual could create a personal portfolio site to keep a copy of his or her work throughout a course or an entire school career. The site could be used as a convenient, private place to house all of the data, or it could be shared as part of an application for a job or internship. On the other hand, a school club, such as a soccer club, could create a public site to share its team schedule and stats, as well as images and videos from past matches.

Creating a Website

Websites are created with main pages and sub pages. The main pages are the top level of the hierarchy of a website. ***Hierarchy*** is when things are placed in an order according to ranks. The sub pages are typically related to and linked from one of the main pages. The hierarchy of a Google website is reflected on the navigation panel, which is displayed in the sidebar on the left side of the website window. The ***navigation panel*** consists of a list of the links to the pages in the website, as seen in **Figure 13-1**. It is the main method of moving through the site. If a sub page is listed, it is typically indented under its related main page listing.

To create new pages in Google Sites, a user names the page, and then selects the page template and the level of the new page. ***Top-level pages*** exist at the same level as the home page, and are often reserved for main categories of the site's content. These pages often contain the most frequently accessed data.

The user that creates the site is the site owner. The owner determines the visibility of the website, just as discussed with a Google document or spreadsheet. The site owner can also invite other Google users to collaborate with him or her in the creation and management of the site. Through the accessibility settings, as discussed in Chapters 8 and 9, the site owner can allow other users to edit, view, or comment on a site.

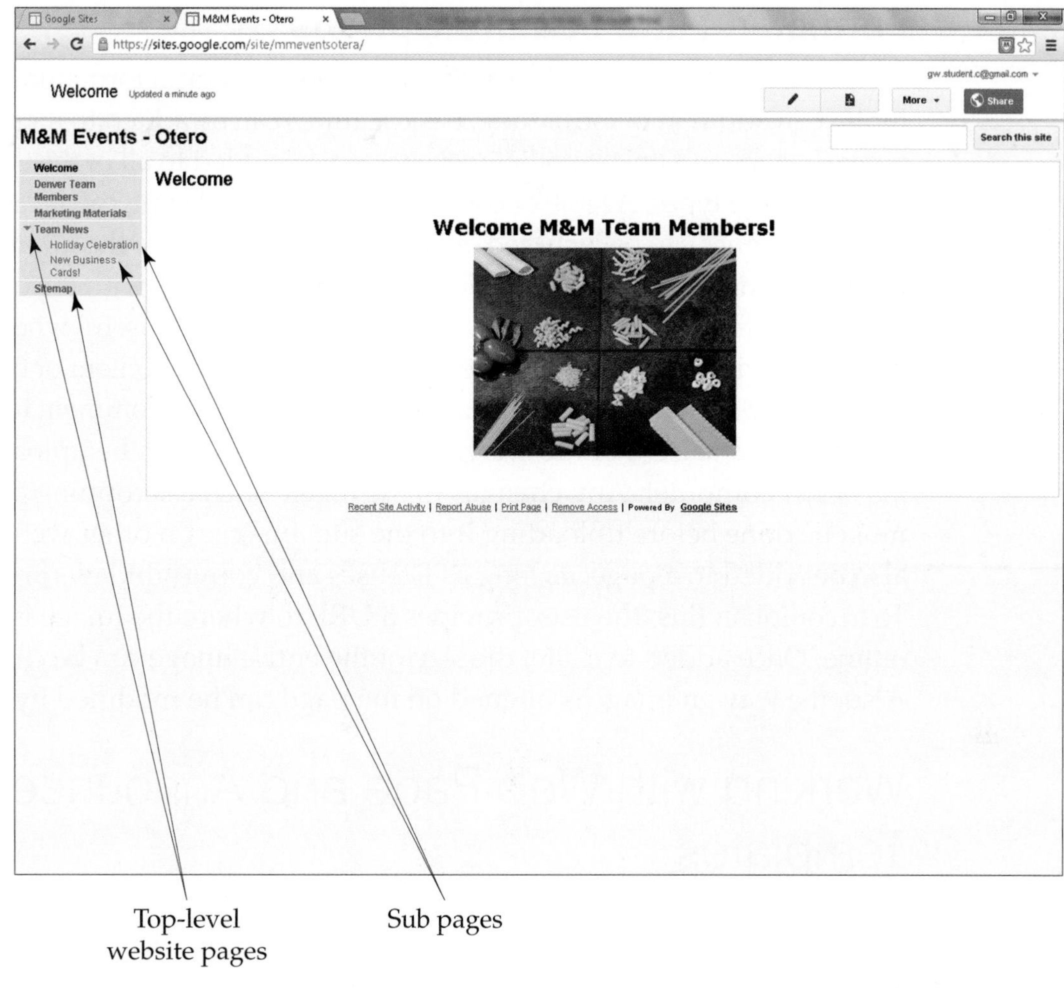

Goodheart-Willcox Publisher

Figure 13-1. The navigation panel is the basic way to move through a Google site.

Types of Web Pages

There are four standard page templates in Google Sites: web page, announcements page, file cabinet page, and list page. Each template has a specific purpose and contains features that support its purpose.

- ***Web page template*** is a basic page that can be customized and is the default template for new pages.
- ***Announcements template*** is a page for users to posts on a specific topic.
- ***File cabinet template*** is a page that stores uploaded files and links to other websites.
- ***List template*** is a page to organize information in columns and rows that can be sorted by the viewer.

Formatting and Feature Options

Each page template includes character and paragraph formatting options for text. In addition to formatting, basic features can be added to most page types. Images and links to other websites can be added to all of the Google Site web page types. A table of contents or a sub page listing can be added. Horizontal lines can be included on a page to help organize the information presented. Most page types in a Google Site provide users with the option of attaching files to the bottom of the page. Attachments are useful when you only need to provide a few files that are directly related to the content of the page. A user can also include an area that allows visitors to add a comment to the page.

A user can also include images on pages. Images can be uploaded from his or her computer. Any changes to the image such as cropping or rotating must be done before uploading it to the site. Images on other websites can also be added to a page, as long as licenses and copyright laws are followed. To accomplish this, the user provides a URL to where the image is stored online. Once added to a site, the size of the entire image can be changed. Also, the way an image is aligned on the page can be modified by the user.

Working with Web Page and Announcement Templates

When a user begins creating a site, the home page is automatically created using the web page template. The name of the page, Home, also automatically appears in the navigation panel. This name can be changed during the editing process. Text, images, video, gadgets, and other content can be added to the page. A user can modify the layout of the web page template for better organization of his or her content. The web page template includes several layout options, as seen in **Figure 13-2.**

Layout Option	Visual of Layout
One column (simple)	
Two column (simple)	
Three column (simple)	
One column	
Two column	
Three column	
Left sidebar	
Right sidebar	
Left and right sidebars	

Goodheart-Willcox Publisher

Figure 13-2. The layout options for the web page template.

Posts on an announcement page are created using the **New Post** button. Each post is a sub page of the main announcement page. Because each post is a new page in the site, the process for deleting a post is the same as deleting any page in the site.

There are two saving options when creating an announcement post: save and save draft. The save draft option allows the user to save the content of the post without making it visible to the audience. This is helpful if a user is interrupted while working or is creating posts to be shared at a future date. Draft posts are only visible to the person who created them. Even other editors of the site will not see them. When a user chooses the regular save option, the post is immediately automatically published and visible to all viewers of the site. Once a post has been saved, it can no longer be saved as a draft.

Working with File Cabinet and List Templates

File cabinet pages provide files and web links for site visitors to view or download. File cabinet pages are displayed as a list of folders, files, and links. Files have an icon to the left of the file name that indicates the file type. Many types of files can be previewed in the browser by clicking on the **View** link. This will open a read-only version of the file. To make any changes to the file or to view it offline, the file must be downloaded. Web links do not have an icon and can be viewed by clicking the **View** link. The target link will open in a new tab or window, depending on your browser's settings.

The site creator and any Google user with edit-level access to the site can upload files and add web links on a file cabinet page. Individual files cannot be larger than 20 MB. When content is added, it is automatically listed at the top of the page in chronological order. Files and links that are not organized in folders will appear above the folder list. Folders are displayed open by default, but a user can collapse them. A file cabinet page is similar to a file-storage software program, but has some limitations. The tips in **Figure 13-3** can help work around some of these limitations.

File Cabinet Rules	Suggested Work Around
Folders cannot be renamed once they are created.	If a folder name needs to be changed, a user can create a new folder with an appropriate name, move the contents of the existing folder to the new folder, and then delete the old folder.
Subfolders cannot be created.	A user that needs to organize content into many folders can create several file cabinet folders.
Folders will always be displayed in alphabetical order.	A user can add a numerical prefix, such as 01, 02, to the folder name to force a different order.

Goodheart-Willcox Publisher

Figure 13-3. Workarounds for the limitations of a file cabinet page.

List pages allow a user to organize information in a table format that spans the main section of the web page window. There are three basic templates for list pages and the option to create a custom list: action items, issue list, and unit status. Creating a custom list allows the user to determine how many columns are needed and what each one will be titled.

Managing a Site

The site creator can rename, copy, or a delete a Google site. For example, the name of a site can be updated to reflect a new company or club name. It can also be helpful to update the name to reflect a new focus of the content of the site. A user can update the name of the site from the Manage Site page. It is important to note that the URL of the site cannot be changed except when the site is created.

Creating a copy of a Google site is useful if the site creator wants to change the URL. Also, if a user is planning to create another site that is similar, copying an existing site can expedite the development process. Only a site creator can delete a site. When a site is deleted, all viewers and editors automatically lose access to it. Deleted sites can be restored to active status within thirty days of being deleted. The options to copy or delete a site are also available from the Manage Site page.

Lesson 13-1

Creating a New Site

A user has several options when he or she is ready to create a Google site. Google provides a blank template containing blank versions of the web page, announcement, file cabinet, and list page types. A user can also choose from designed templates with a theme, layout, navigation, and often content placeholders.

1. Log in to your Google Mail account.
2. Click the **More** link, and click **Even More** in the drop-down list.
3. On the new tab or window that is opened, scroll down and click **Sites** in the **Home & Office** area. You may be asked to enter your password on a new page. If so, enter your password to continue to the Sites page, as shown in **Figure 13-4.**

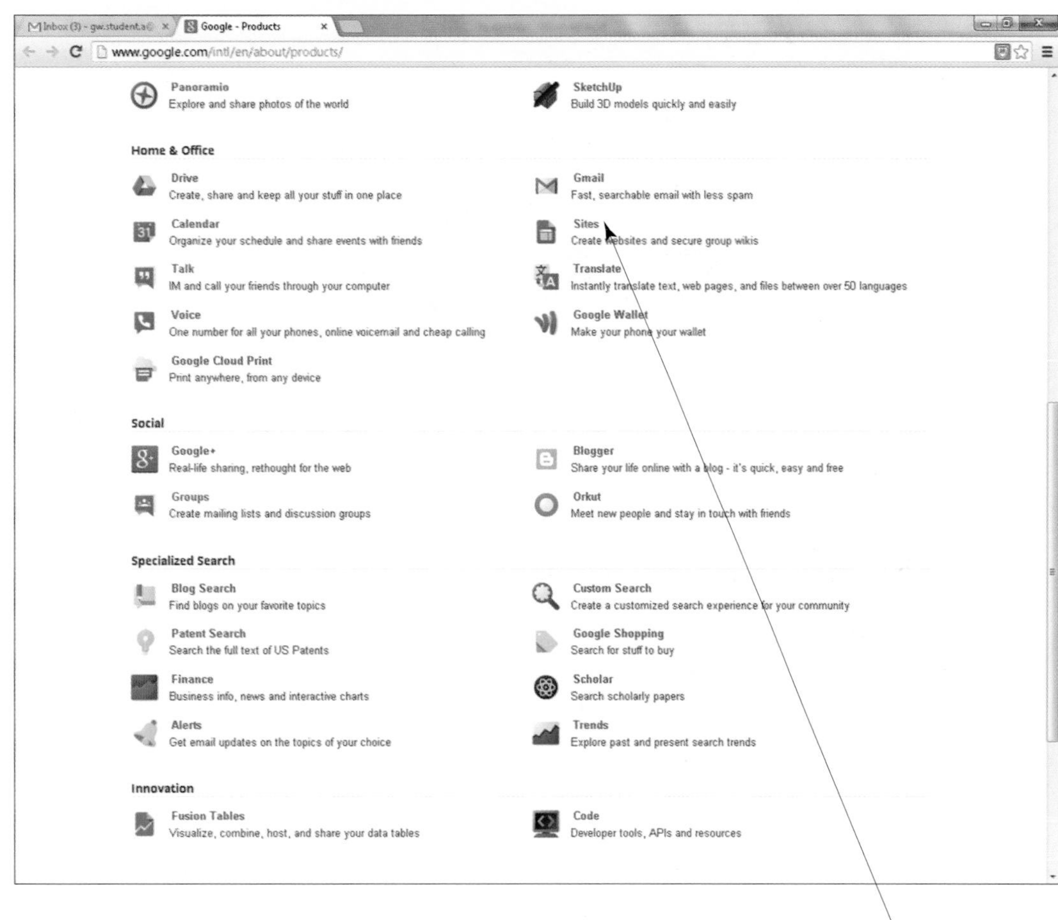

Goodheart-Willcox Publisher

Figure 13-4. This Sites page lists any sites in which you are a member. If you are not a member of any sites, the page appears as shown here.

4. Click the **Create** button. A new page is displayed on which to define the site, as shown in **Figure 13-5.**
5. Click the **Blank template** thumbnail in the **Select a template to use:** area. The site will be created with a single, empty page.

To select a template not shown as a thumbnail in the **Select a template to use:** area, click the **Browse the gallery for more** link.

6. Click in the **Name your site:** text box and enter M&M Events—*Your Last Name*. The site name can be changed later if desired.
7. Click in the **Site location** text box. The default URL in the text box is based on the name of the site. The URL enter in this text box is the permanent URL for the site, so change it as needed now. For example, you may decide to shorten the URL to make it easier for someone to enter. The complete URL for the site will be http://sites.google.com/site/Your URL.

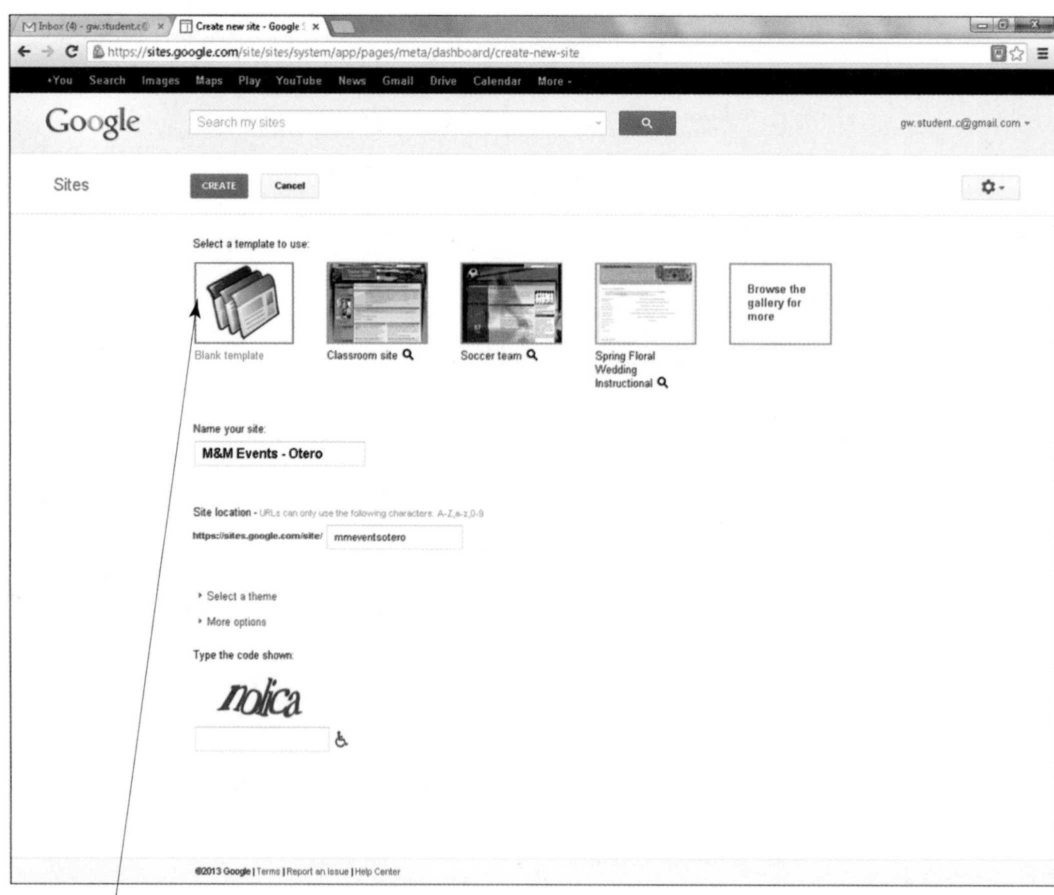

Goodheart-Willcox Publisher

Figure 13-5. Defining a new Google site.

8. Click the **Select a theme** link. The page expands, and a list of thumbnails of available themes is displayed. Click a thumbnail to select that theme.
9. Click the **More options** link. The **Site description** text box is displayed, along with a check box.
10. Click in the **Site description** text box, and enter a phrase that summarizes the content on the site. The description can be used by people searching for sites to identify what the site contains. For this site, enter This site is a sample event planning site as part of *Your Instructor*'s class.
11. In the text box at the bottom of the page, enter the security code shown above the text box. If you require audio assistance with the code, click the button to the right of the text box. The security code is required to ensure a human is creating the site, not a software robot.

CREATE

12. Click the **Create** button at the top of the page. After the security code is verified, the site is created and displayed.
13. Close the tab or window displaying the site.

Lesson 13-2

Editing a Site

After creating a site, a user might want to make changes, such as adding more text, modifying the original text, or adding images. The content on an existing page can be changed or an entire page can be added or deleted.

Editing a Web Page on a Site

1. Log in to your Google Mail account.
2. Click the **More** link, and click **Even More** in the drop-down list.
3. Click **Sites** in the **Home & Office** area of the new tab or window to display the Sites page. The site created in Lesson 13-1 should be displayed on the Sites page.
4. Click the name of the M&M Events site to display it in a new tab or window.
5. Click the **Edit Page** button. The page is displayed in editing mode, as shown in **Figure 13-6.**

Edit Page

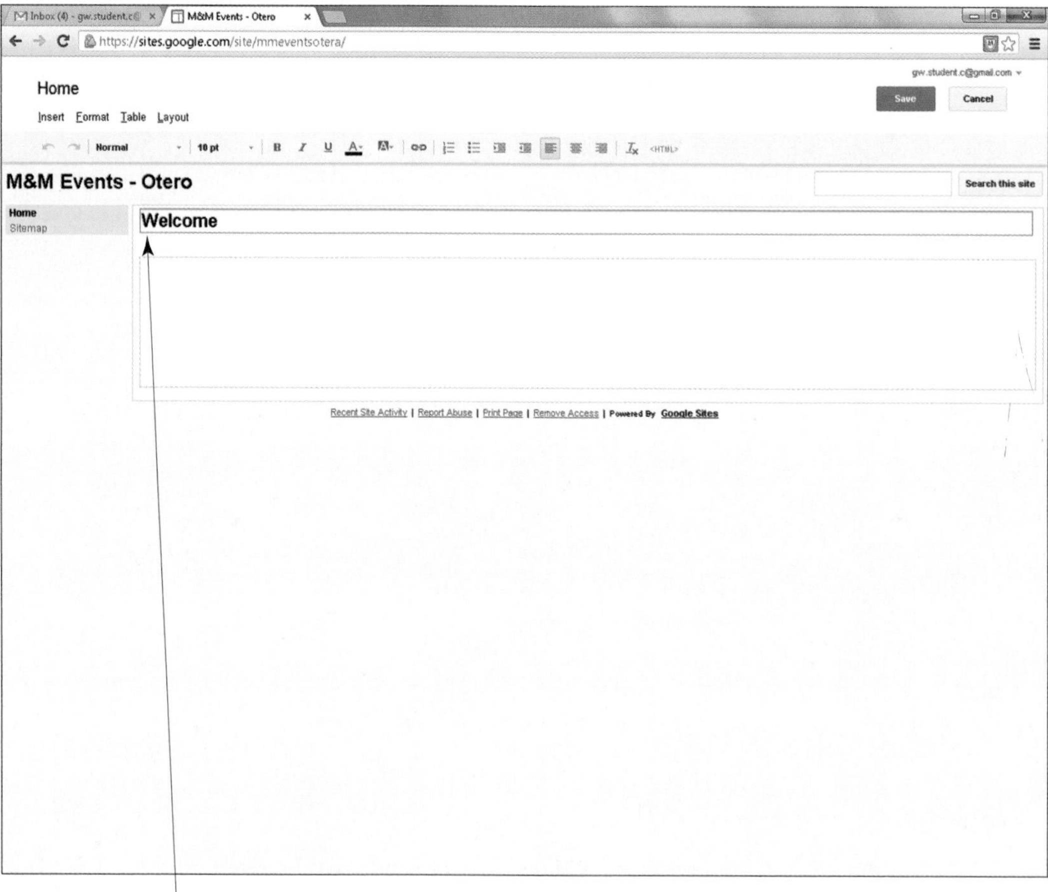

Goodheart-Willcox Publisher

Figure 13-6. Editing mode allows the page to be modified.

6. Click in the title text box, which contains the default text Home.
7. Enter Welcome. This is the new title for the page, but the page title will not change in the sidebar navigation pane until the page is saved.

Changing the Layout of a Web Page

8. Click the **Layout** pull-down menu. This menu contains a list of layouts that can be applied to the web page, as shown in **Figure 13-7.** Each menu entry has a thumbnail that represents the way the content area will be divided. The current layout is checked in the menu.
9. Click **Two column**, not **Two column (simple)**, in the pull-down menu. The content area below the page title now contains text boxes for header, left and right columns, and a footer instead of a single text box.
10. Click in the header text box, and enter Welcome M & M Team Members!
11. Select the text, and click the **Bold** button on the formatting toolbar.

B
Bold

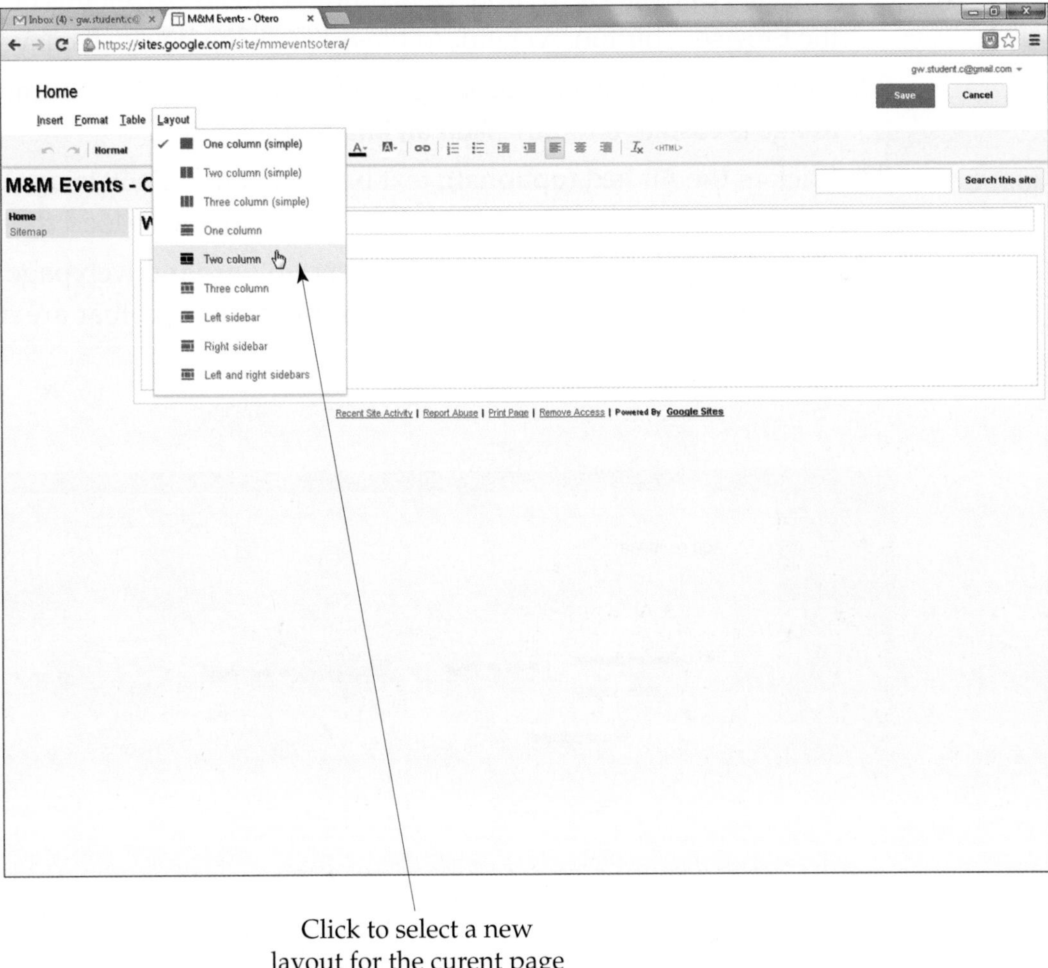

Goodheart-Willcox Publisher

Figure 13-7. A page can be arranged in one of several different layouts.

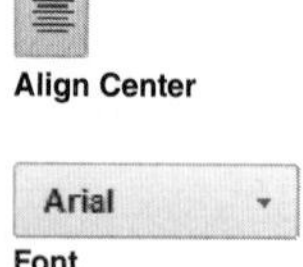

Align Center

Font

Font Size

12. Click the **Align Center** button to center justify the text.
13. Click the **Font** button, and click **Verdana** in the drop-down list.
14. Click the **Font Size** button, and click **18 pt** in the drop-down list.
15. Click the **Save** button. This not only saves the changes, but exits editing mode.

Inserting an Image onto a Web Page

16. Navigate to the student companion website (www.g-wlearning.com/informationtechnology/), and download the Homepage Image data file to your working folder. This is a JPEG image file.

Edit Page

17. On the site page, click the **Edit Page** button.
18. Click in the left-hand text box in the content area.
19. Click the **Insert** pull-down menu, and click **Image** in the menu. The **Add an Image** dialog box is displayed, as shown in **Figure 13-8.**
20. Click the **Uploaded images** radio button.
21. Click the **Choose File** button. Depending on the browser, this button may be the **Browse...** button. A standard file-open dialog box is displayed.
22. Navigate to the Homepage Image.jpg file and select it. A thumbnail of the image is displayed in the **Add an Image** dialog box.
23. Click in the **Alt text (optional):** text box, and enter Food Image. This text will be displayed to users if the browser is unable to load the image.
24. Click the **OK** button. The image is inserted onto the web page. It is automatically selected, and the image properties toolbar are displayed, as shown in **Figure 13-9.**

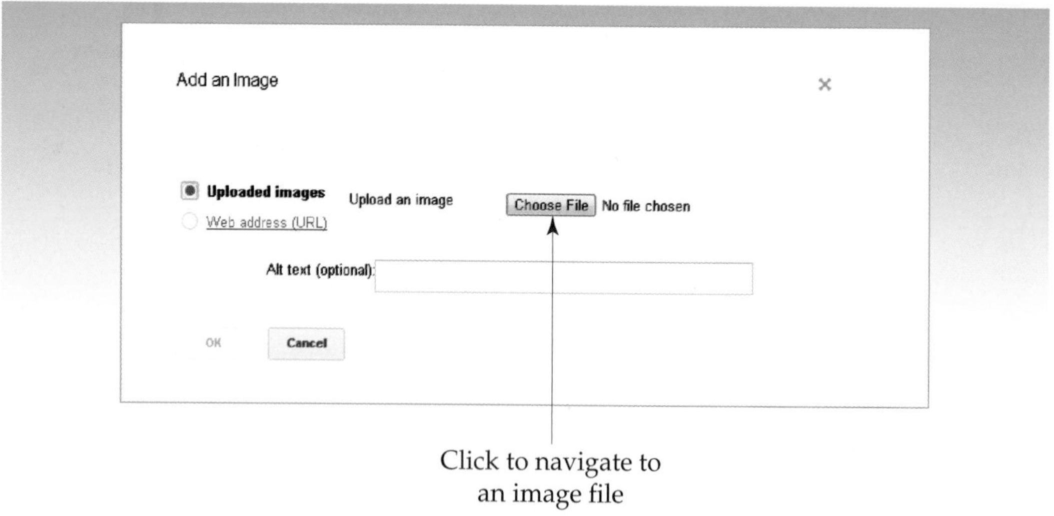

Goodheart-Willcox Publisher

Figure 13-8. Adding an image to a page.

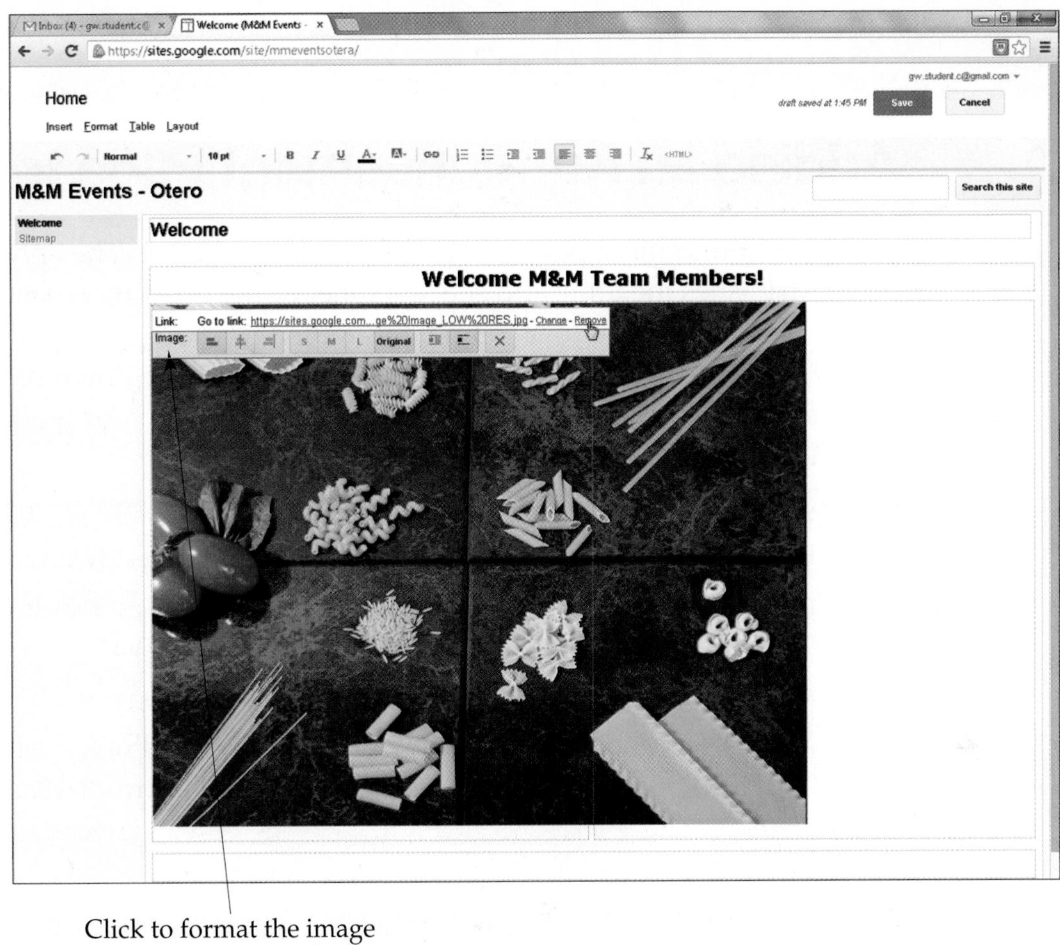

Goodheart-Willcox Publisher

Figure 13-9. The image properties toolbar is displayed when an image is selected.

25. Click the **Remove** link in the **Link:** (top) row of the image properties toolbar. By default, an image can be clicked to display a full-size version. Clicking the **Remove** link prevents this action, and the **Link:** row is no longer displayed in the toolbar.

Instead of removing the link, it can be redirected to a different website using the **Change:** link in the **Link:** row of the image properties toolbar.

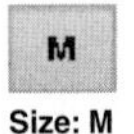

Size: M

26. Click the **Size: M** button on the image properties toolbar. This sets the size of the image to medium. In some browsers, handles are displayed on the image when it is selected, and these can be used to manually resize the image.

Align Center

27. Click the **Align Center** button on the image properties toolbar. This aligns the image left-to-right in the text box.

28. Click the **Save** button to save the page and exit editing mode.
29. Close the tab or window displaying the site.

Lesson 13-3

Adding an Announcement Page to a Site

An announcement page is typically a top-level page. The announcement page establishes the topic and sets the tone for the posts it contains.

1. Navigate to the student companion website (www.g-wlearning.com/informationtechnology/), and download the Announcement Image and Business Card data files to your working folder. These are JPEG image and PPTx presentation files.
2. Log in to your Google Mail account.
3. Click the **More** link, and click **Even More** in the drop-down list.
4. Click **Sites** in the **Home & Office** area of the new tab or window to display the Sites page.
5. Click the name of the M&M Events site to display it in a new tab or window.

New Page

6. Click the **New Page** button. A new page is displayed on which details of the page being added are entered, as shown in **Figure 13-10.**

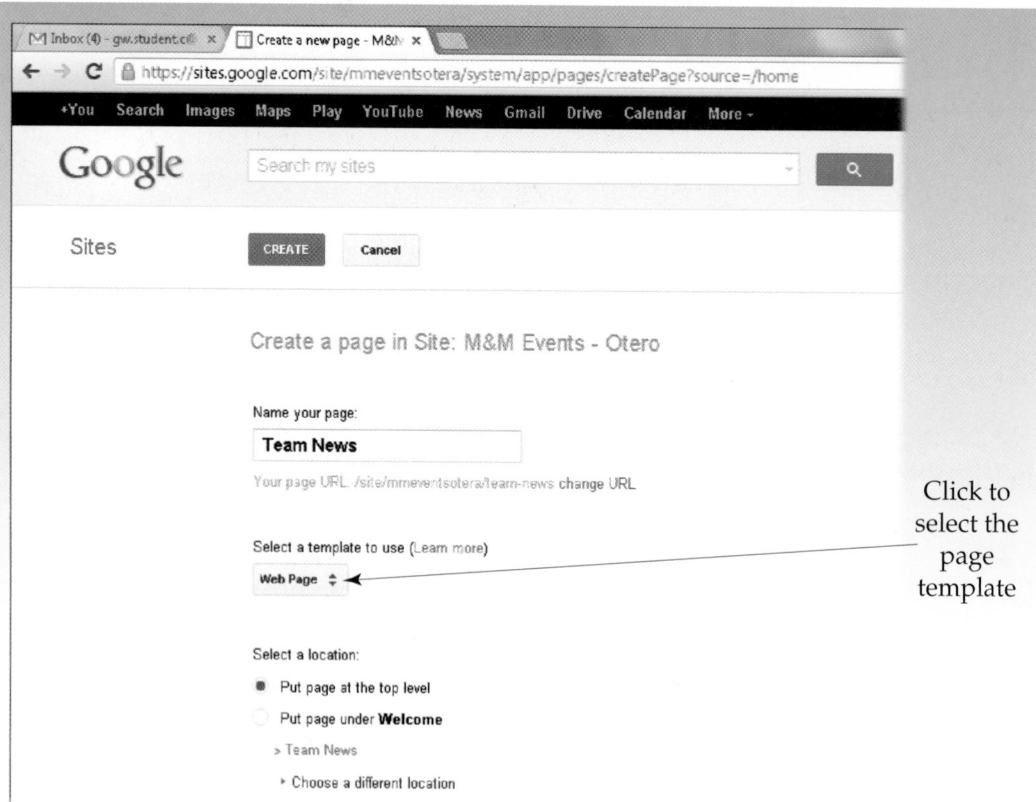

Goodheart-Willcox Publisher

Figure 13-10. Creating an announcement page.

7. Click in the **Name your page:** text box, and enter Team News.

> **Tip**
> The URL for the new page is automatically generated and displayed below the **Name your page:** text box, but it can be changed by clicking the **Change URL** link.

8. Click the **Select a template to use** button to display a drop-down menu, and click **Announcements** in the menu. This sets the type of page being created to a list of posts.
9. In the **Select a location** area, click the **Put page at top level** radio button. This makes the page the same level as the Welcome page in the navigation panel on the site.

CREATE

10. Click the **Create** button to add the page.

Creating an Announcement Post with an Image

New post

11. Make sure the Team News page is displayed, and click the **New Post** button on the page. A new page is displayed for composing a post, as shown in **Figure 13-11.**
12. Click in the title text box, delete the default text Untitled Post, and enter Holiday Celebration.

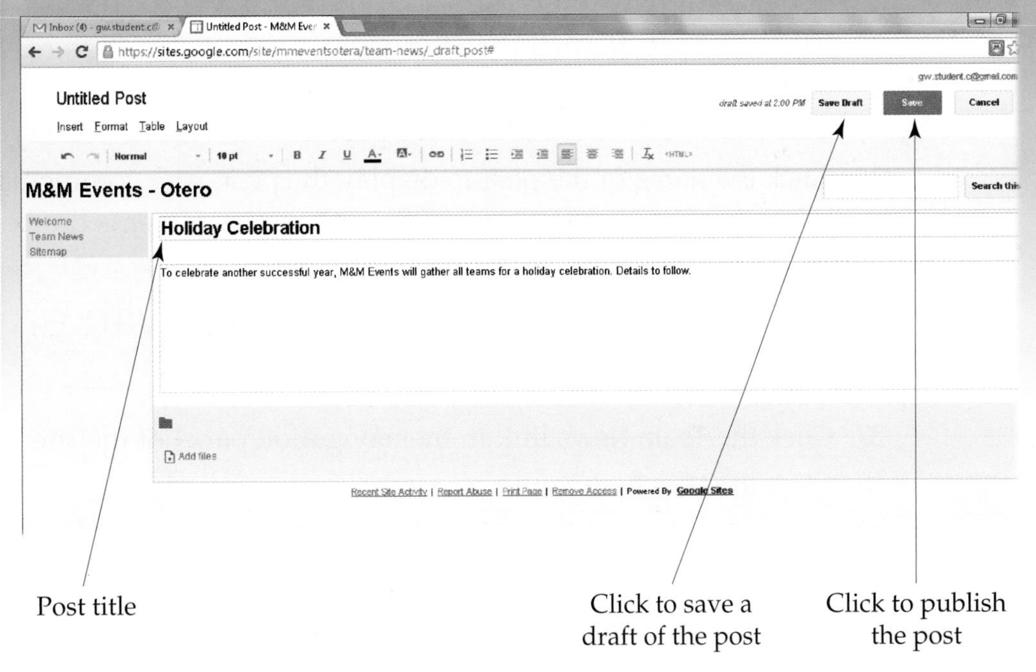

Goodheart-Willcox Publisher

Figure 13-11. Composing a post on an announcement page.

13. Click in the main message text box, and enter To celebrate another successful year, M & M Events will gather all teams for a holiday celebration. Details to follow.
14. Select the text in the main message text box.

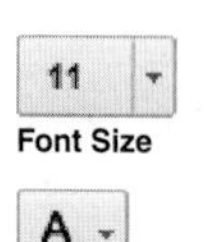
Font Size
Text Color

15. Use the **Font Size** and **Text Color** buttons to increase the size of the text and change its color.
16. Click in front of the first word of the text in the main message text box to place the cursor there.
17. Click the **Insert** pull-down menu, and click **Image** in the menu. The **Add an Image** dialog box is displayed.
18. Click the **Choose File** (or **Browse...**) button, navigate to the Announcement Image.jpg file, and select it. A thumbnail of the image is displayed in the **Add an Image** dialog box.
19. Click in the **Alt text (optional):** text box, and enter Food Image.
20. Click the **OK** button to close the **Add an Image** dialog box and insert the image.

Size: S

21. Click the **Size: S** button on the image properties toolbar to set the image at the smallest size.

Align Left

22. Click the **Align Left** button on the image properties toolbar. This places the image on the left-hand side of the text box.

Wrap On

23. Click the **Wrap On** button. This forces the words on the same line as the image to wrap around the image instead of below it.

24. Click the **Save** button to publish the post. The post should appear similar to that shown in **Figure 13-12.**
25. Click the **Team News** link in the navigation panel of the site. All posts on that page are displayed, which is currently only one post. Notice the time stamp below the title of the post. This is visible to everyone.
26. Click the name of the post to display the post. Any comments that have been added to the post are visible, and new comments can be added.

Create an Announcement Post with an Attachment

27. Click the **Team News** link in the navigation panel of the site.
28. Click the **New Post** button.
29. Name the new post New Business Cards!
30. Enter The template for our new business cards is here. Download the attachment, customize it, and print! as the text for the post.

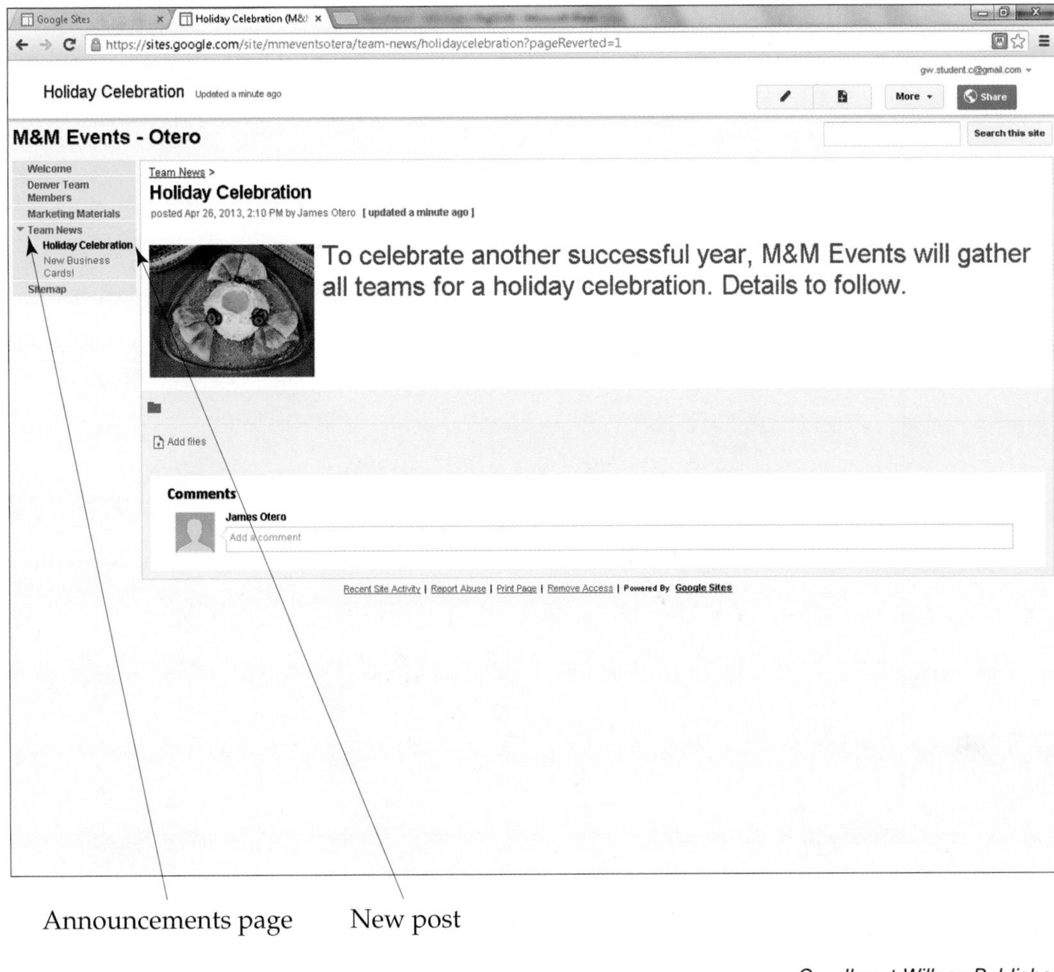

Goodheart-Willcox Publisher

Figure 13-12. A published post appears similar to that shown here.

31. Format the text as needed.
32. Click the **Add files** link at the bottom of the post. A standard file-open dialog box is displayed.
33. Navigate to the Business Card.pptx file, and select it. A status of the upload is displayed until the file is uploaded.

Save

34. Click the **Save** button to publish the post.
35. Click the name of the file at the bottom of the post, as shown in **Figure 13-13.** If the file can be displayed by Google, which is true of a PowerPoint file, the content of the file is displayed.
36. Click the browser's back button to return to the post.

37. Click the **Download** button on the far right of the line displaying the file name. The file is downloaded to your local hard drive.
38. Close the tab or window to close the site.

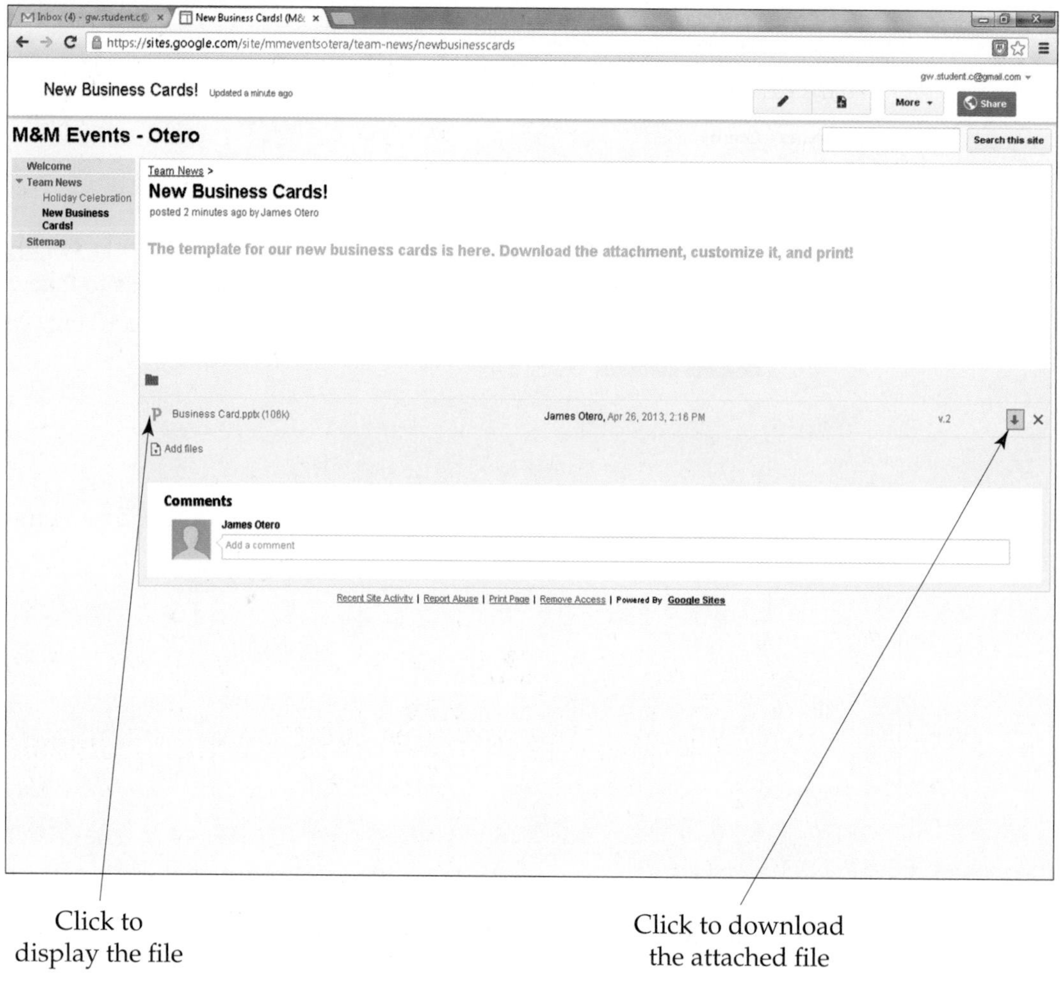

Goodheart-Willcox Publisher

Figure 13-13. Attached files are listed at the bottom of a post.

Lesson 13-4

Managing Posts

As a sub page to its parent announcement page, a post can be edited or deleted like any other web page in the site. Also, a user can access the revision history for the announcement page to revert to a previous version.

Editing a Post

1. Log in to your Google Mail account.
2. Click the **More** link, and click **Even More** in the drop-down list.
3. Click **Sites** in the **Home & Office** area of the new tab or window to display the Sites page.
4. Click the name of the M&M Events site to display it in a new tab or window.
5. Click the arrow next to the **Team News** link in the navigation panel of the site to see all posts in a tree format below it. If the tree is already displayed, clicking the arrow will hide it.
6. Click the **Holiday Celebration** link in the tree to display that post.
7. Click the **Edit Page** button to enter edit mode.

Tip Edit mode can also be entered by pressing the [E] key on the keyboard.

Save

8. Click the image to select it and display the image properties toolbar.
9. Click the **Remove** button on the image properties toolbar to delete the image.
10. Change the text Details to follow. to Details are:, and press the [Enter] key to start a new line.
11. Click the **Bullet List** button to start a bulleted list.
12. Enter Meet at the convention center restaurant, and press the [Enter] key.
13. Enter After lunch, a bus will take us to the show.
14. Click the **Save** button to update the post.

Modifying Post Settings

More ▾

15. With the Holiday Celebration post displayed, click the **More** button to display a drop-down menu.
16. Click **Page Settings** in the menu. The **Page Settings** dialog box is displayed, as shown in **Figure 13-14.**

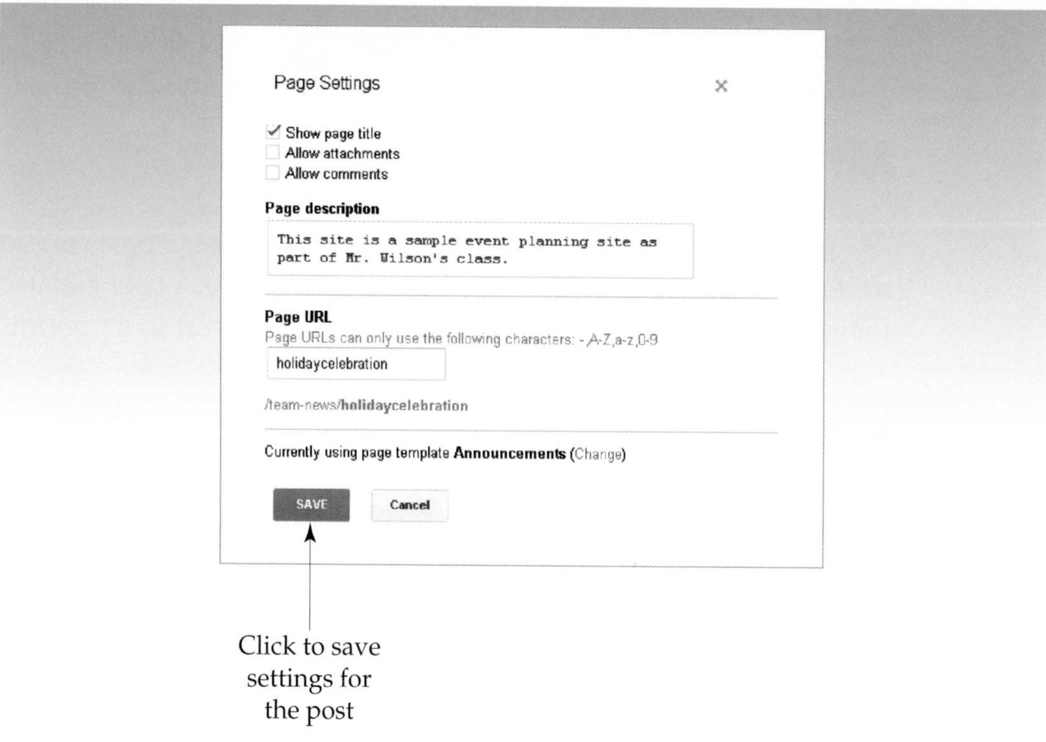

Goodheart-Willcox Publisher

Figure 13-14. The **Page Settings** dialog box is used to modify the settings of a page.

17. Uncheck the **Allow attachments** check box. This prevents viewers of the page from being able to attach files to the post.
18. Uncheck the **Allow comments** check box. This removes the comment section from the post so viewers are unable to leave a comment on the post.
19. Click the **Save** button to update the settings for the post. Notice that the post now just provides information, and there is no way to interact with the post through comments or attaching files.

Deleting a Post

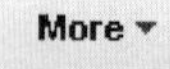

20. With the Holiday Celebration post displayed, click the **More** button to display a drop-down menu.
21. Click **Delete page** in the menu. A dialog box appears asking to confirm the deletion, as shown in **Figure 13-15.** Displayed in the dialog box is a list of items that will be removed, which includes any inserted images or attached files.
22. To remove the current page (post), click the **Delete** button in the dialog box, but for this example, click the **Cancel** button to keep the page.

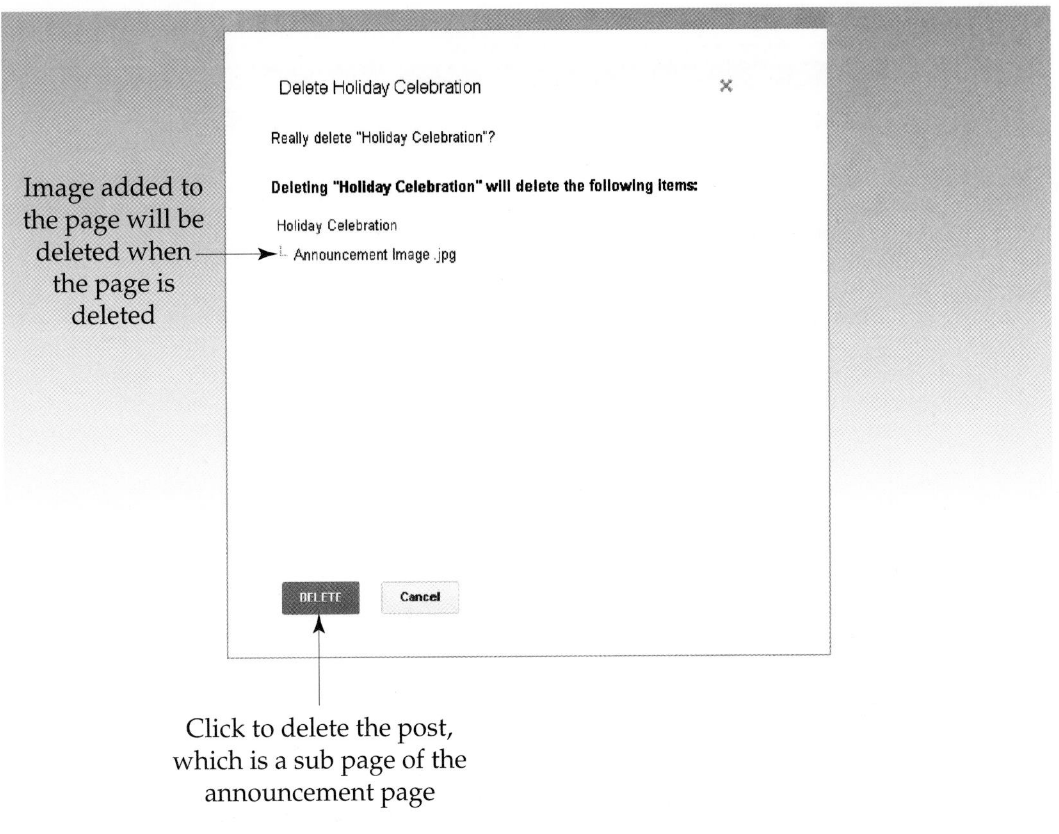

Goodheart-Willcox Publisher

Figure 13-15. When deleting a page, you are asked to confirm the deletion.

Using the Revision History

23. With the Holiday Celebration post displayed, click the **More** button to display a drop-down menu.
24. Click **Revision History** in the menu. The Manage Site page is displayed that contains a list of all versions of the page (post), as shown in **Figure 13-16.**
25. Click the **Version 1** listing to view how the page (post) looked in that version.

Tip A version can be restored without first viewing it by clicking the **Revert to this version** link on the Manage Site page.

26. To revert to this version, click the **Revert to this version** link. The page (post) is restored to that state, but all versions created *after* it are still available.
27. Close the tab or window to close the site.

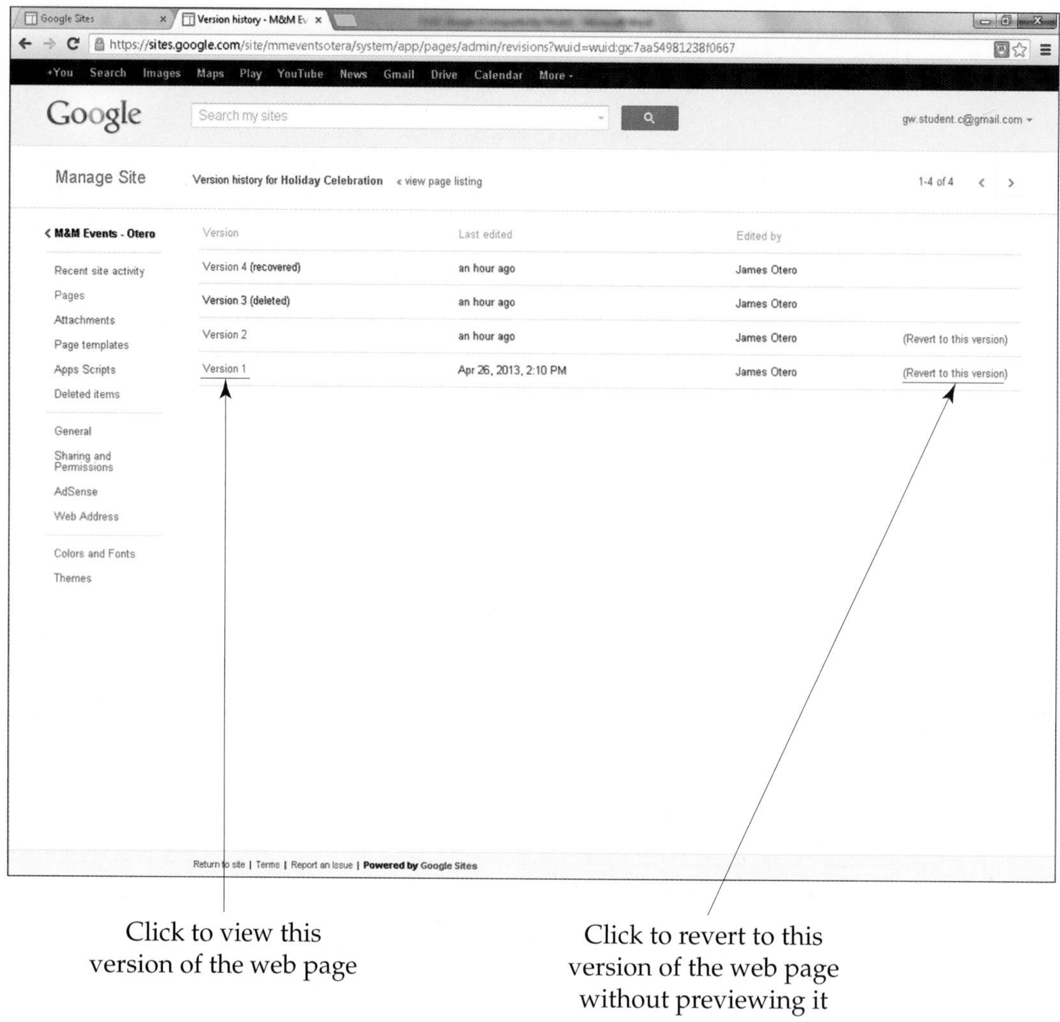

Goodheart-Willcox Publisher

Figure 13-16. The revision history of a page is shown in the Manage Site page.

Lesson 13-5

File Cabinet Pages

When a user needs to share more than three files on his or her website, a file cabinet page can be helpful. Also, if he or she needs to share files on multiple topics, a file cabinet page can be a good addition to the site.

Creating a File Cabinet Page

1. Navigate to the student companion website (www.g-wlearning.com/informationtechnology/), and download the Brochure data file to your working folder. This is a PDF document file.
2. Log in to your Google Mail account.
3. Click the **More** link, and click **Even More** in the drop-down list.
4. Click **Sites** in the **Home & Office** area of the new tab or window to display the Sites page.
5. Click the name of the M&M Events site to display it in a new tab or window.

New page

6. Click the **New page** button.
7. Name the new page Marketing Materials.
8. Click the **Select a template to use** button, and click **File cabinet** in the drop-down menu.
9. Click the **Put page at the top level** radio button.

CREATE

10. Click the **Create** button to create the page. The page appears similar to that shown in **Figure 13-17.**

Adding Content

+ Add file

11. Click the **+ Add file** button on the Marketing Materials page. A standard file-open dialog box is displayed.
12. Navigate to the Brochure.pdf file, and select it. A status of the upload is displayed until the file is uploaded. Once the file is uploaded, it is listed on the file cabinet page.

+ Add link

13. Click the **+ Add link** button. The **Add Link** dialog box is displayed, as shown in **Figure 13-18.**
14. Click in the **Add file from web** text box, and enter http://eventplannersassociation.com/. Any URL can be entered in this text box, not only a URL of a file.
15. Click in the **Text to display:** text box, and enter Event Planners Organization. This is the text that is displayed on the file cabinet page, similar to a file name.

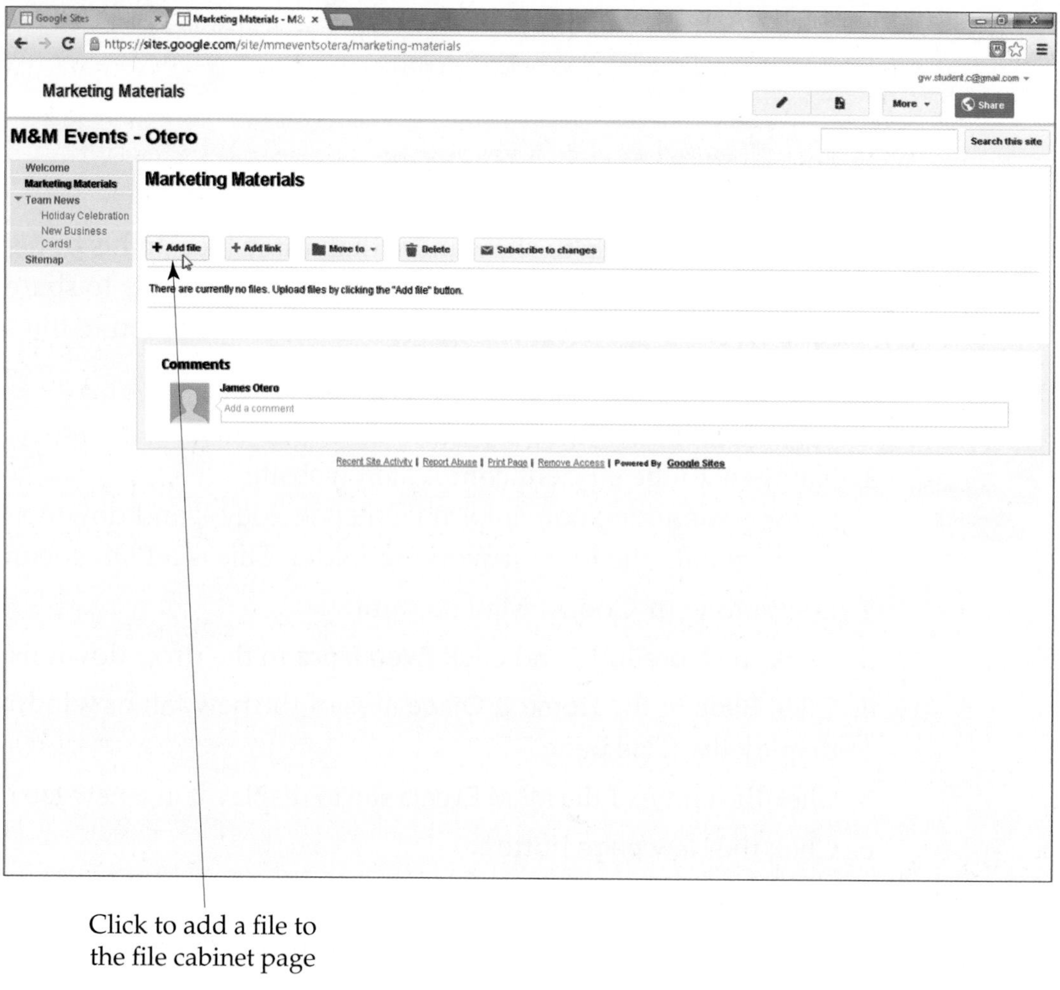

Goodheart-Willcox Publisher

Figure 13-17. Creating a file cabinet page.

Add Link

Add a file from the **web** (paste in URL)

http://eventplannersassociation.com/

Text to display:

Event Planners Organization

Link description:

A good resource for sample materials.

Click to add the link to the file cabinet page

ADD Cancel

Goodheart-Willcox Publisher

Figure 13-18. Adding a link to a file cabinet page.

16. Click in the **Link Description:** text box, and enter A good resource for sample materials. This description is optional, but can be useful to those viewing the file cabinet page.
17. Click the **Add** button. The resource is added to the file cabinet page. Clicking the **View** link displays the website entered in the **Add Link** dialog box.

Organizing Content

18. Click the **Move to** button to display a drop-down menu. Since there are currently no subfolders, the only entry is for creating a new folder.
19. Click **New Folder...** in the menu. The **New Folder** dialog box is displayed.
20. Click in the **Enter a name for the folder:** text box, and enter Weddings .
21. Click the **Save** button to create the folder. The Weddings folder appears below the list of files, as shown in **Figure 13-19.**
22. Check the check box to the left of the Brochure.pdf file.

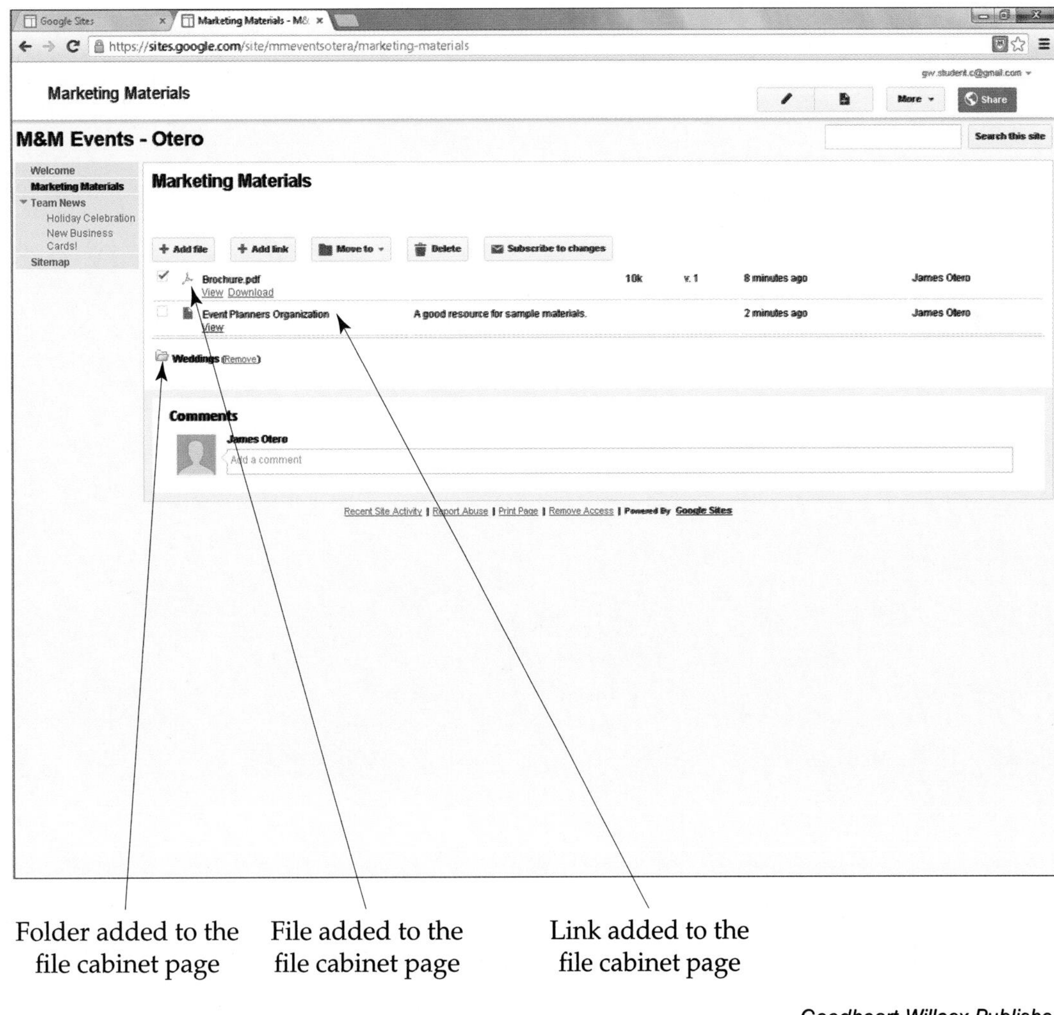

Figure 13-19. Folders can be added to a file cabinet page.

Move to

23. Click the **Move to** button. The new folder appears in the drop-down menu along with the option to create a new folder.
24. Click **Weddings** in the menu. The file is moved to the Weddings folder.

Comments

25. Click in the text box at the bottom of the Marketing Materials page that contains the default text Add a comment.
26. Enter When will these be updated?, and click the **Comment** button. The comment is posted at the bottom of the page.
27. Click the **Reply** link below the posted comment.

To edit, delete, or link to a comment, click the drop-down arrow to the right of a comment's time stamp.

28. Click in the text box that appears, enter Very soon, and click the **Reply** button.
29. Close the tab or window to close the site.

Lesson 13-6

Creating a List Page

The list template creates a page that organizes information in columns that can be presorted by the site creator and resorted by the viewer. A user can employ an existing list template or create a custom one.

Creating a List Page

1. Log in to your Google Mail account.
2. Click the **More** link, and click **Even More** in the drop-down list.
3. Click **Sites** in the **Home & Office** area of the new tab or window to display the Sites page.
4. Click the name of the M&M Events site to display it in a new tab or window.

New page

5. Click the **New page** button.
6. Name the new page Denver Team Members.
7. Click the **Select a template to use** button, and click **List** in the drop-down menu.
8. Click the **Put page at the top level** radio button.

CREATE

9. Click the **Create** button to create the page. The page appears similar to that shown in **Figure 13-20.**

Customizing a List

10. Click the **Use template** button in the **Create your own** area of the Denver Team Members page. The **Customize Your List** dialog box is displayed.
11. Click in the **Column name:** text box, and replace the default text with Team Member.
12. Click the **Add a column** link. A new column is added as a row above the link, and the **Column/Fields Details** area of the dialog box is reset to default settings, as shown in **Figure 13-21.** The contents of this area are for the column currently selected on the left side of the dialog box.
13. Click in the **Column name:** text box, and replace the default text with Member Since.
14. Click the **Type:** drop-down list, and click **Date** in the list. This sets the entry for the column to a date, which is selected in a minicalendar.
15. Click the **Add a column** link.

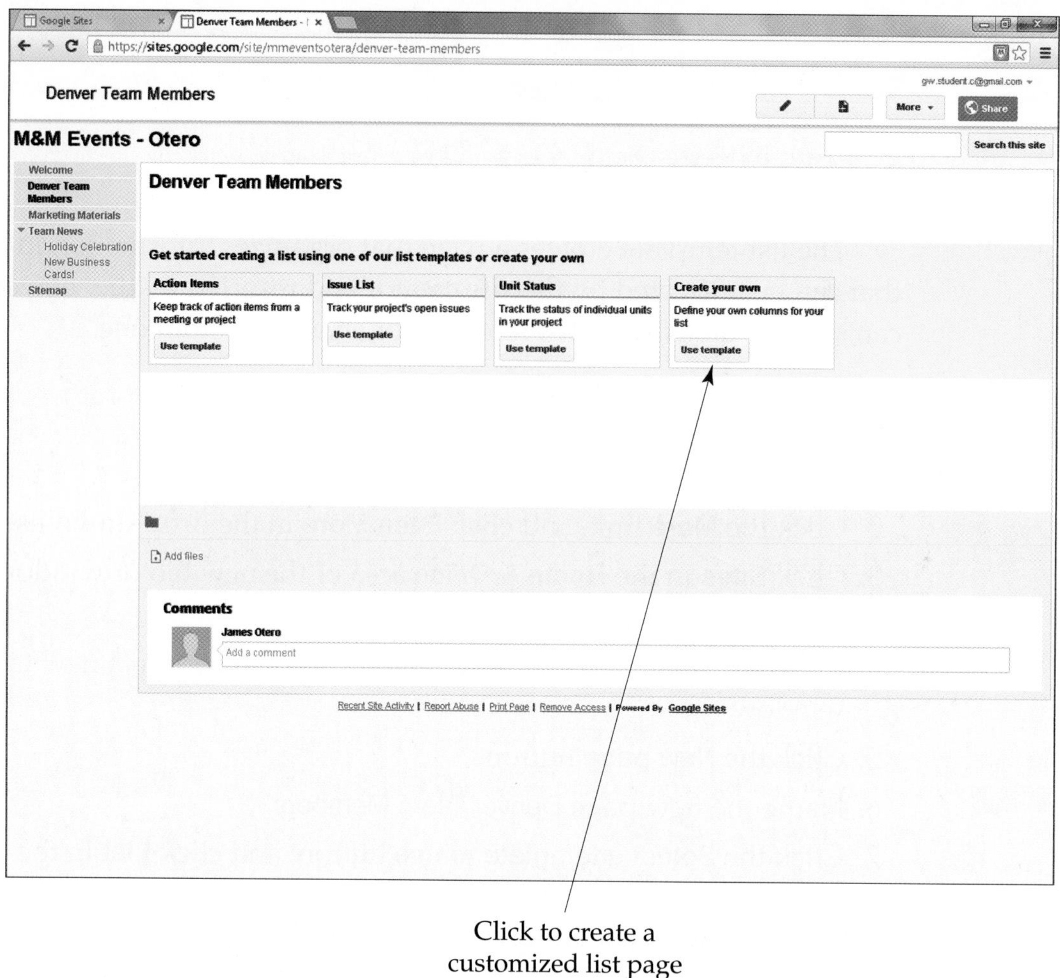

Goodheart-Willcox Publisher

Figure 13-20. Creating a list page.

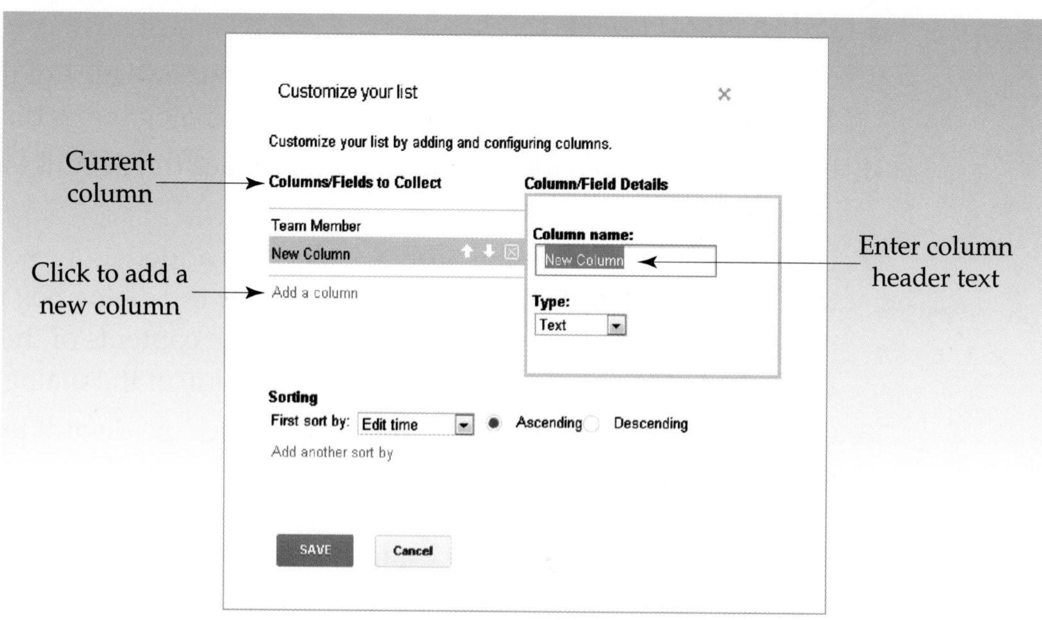

Goodheart-Willcox Publisher

Figure 13-21. Defining columns in a list page.

16. Click in the **Column name:** text box, and replace the default text with Department.
17. Click the **Type:** drop-down list, and click **Dropdown** in the list. The **Column/Fields Details** area of the dialog box expands to include the **Options** text box.
18. Click in the **Options** text box, and enter Marketing.
19. Click the **Add another** link below the **Options** text box. A new **Options** text box appears.
20. Click in the **Options** text box, and enter Sales. There are now two options for this list.
21. In the list of columns, click the upward-pointing arrow to the right of **Department** to move the column up one. It will appear between the Team Member and Member Since columns (which are rows in this dialog box).
22. Click the **First sort by:** drop-down list in the **Sorting** area of the dialog box, and click **Department** in the list. This specifies the list will be sorted by entries in the Department column.
23. Click the **Save** button to updated the page.

Adding an Item to a List

24. Click the **Add item** button on the Denver Team Members page. The **Add Item** dialog box is displayed as shown in **Figure 13-22.** Notice that the labels in this dialog box match the column names.
25. Click in the **Team Member:** text box, and enter Tyler Jackson.
26. Click the **Department:** drop-down list, and click **Sales** in the list.

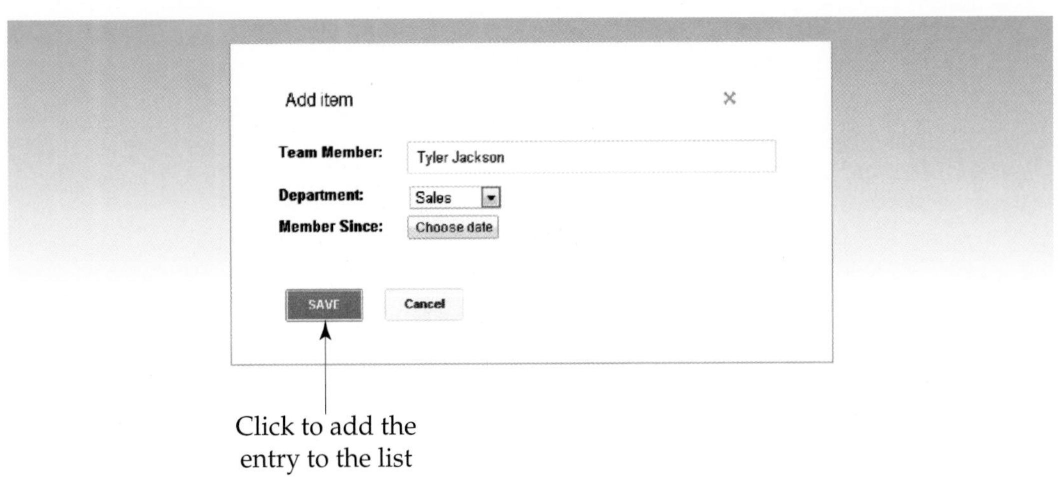

Figure 13-22. Adding an item to a list page.

27. Click the **Choose Date** button, and in the minicalendar choose a date in 2013.
28. Click the **Save** button to add the entry to the list.
29. Add two more entries to the list. Use the names of two classmates, and assign them both to the marketing department.
30. Refresh the web browser. Notice the entries are rearranged to be grouped by department name, with marketing first.
31. Click **Sort** under the **Team Member** column heading, and click **Ascending** in the drop-down menu. Notice that the list is reorganized in alphabetical order by first name.
32. Close the tab or window to close the site.

Lesson 13-7

Managing a Site through Collaboration

The settings in Google Sites allow the owner to invite other Google users to manage the website. Unlike other Google programs, the settings in Google Sites allow the owner to specify the accessibility by page within the site. For example, a user can be provided with access to edit the announcement page, but only comment on the home page.

1. Log in to your Google Mail account.
2. Click the **More** link, and click **Even More** in the drop-down list.
3. Click **Sites** in the **Home & Office** area of the new tab or window to display the Sites page.
4. Click the name of the M&M Events site to display it in a new tab or window.
5. Click the **More** button, and click **Manage Site** in the drop-down menu. The **Manage Site** page is displayed.
6. Click **Sharing and Permissions** in the navigation panel. The permissions settings for the site are displayed, as shown in **Figure 13-23.**

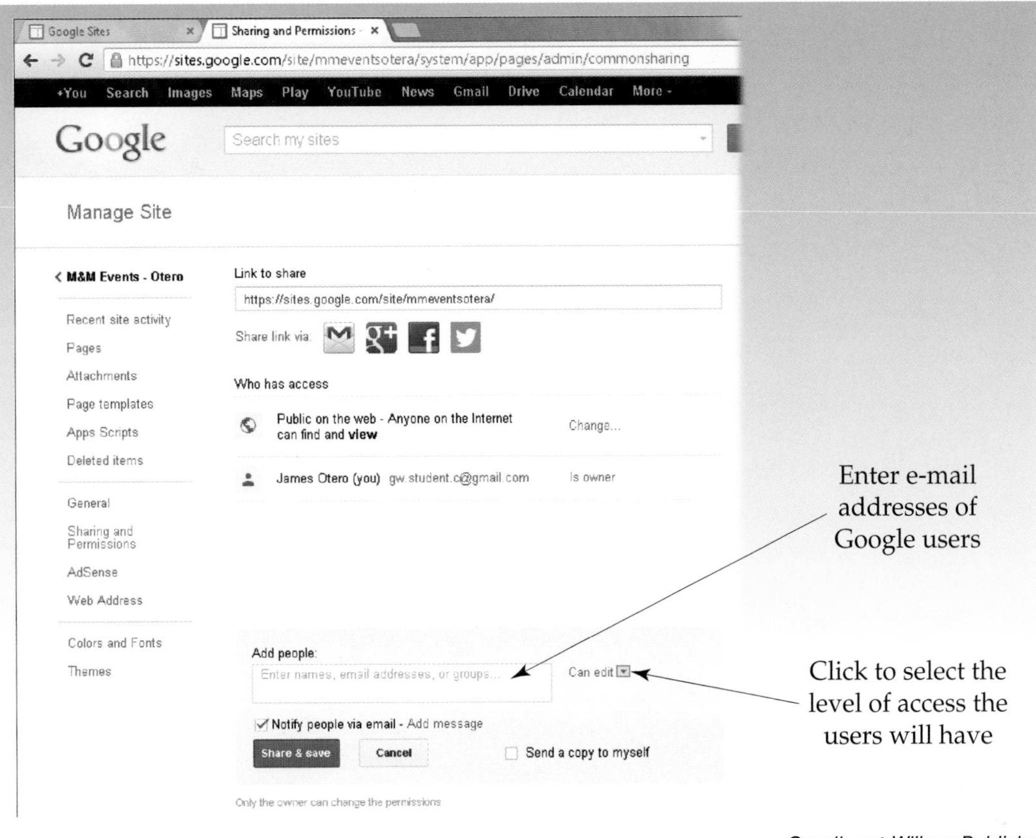

Goodheart-Willcox Publisher

Figure 13-23. Setting permissions that allow others to collaborate on the management of a site.

7. Click in the **Add people:** text box.
8. Enter the e-mail address of a classmate.
9. Make sure **Can edit** is selected in the drop-down menu to the right of the text box.
10. Click the **Share & Save** button. The classmate can now collaborate with you in managing the site.
11. Close the tab or window to close the site.

Lesson 13-8

Renaming a Site

From time to time a user may need to modify the name of his or her site. Visitors will use the same URL to access the site, but will see the new name when the site is displayed.

1. Log in to your Google Mail account.
2. Click the **More** link, and click **Even More** in the drop-down list.
3. Click **Sites** in the **Home & Office** area of the new tab or window to display the Sites page.
4. Click the name of the M&M Events site to display it in a new tab or window.
5. Click the **More** button, and click **Manage site** in the drop-down menu. The Manage Site page is displayed with general site information, as shown in **Figure 13-24.**

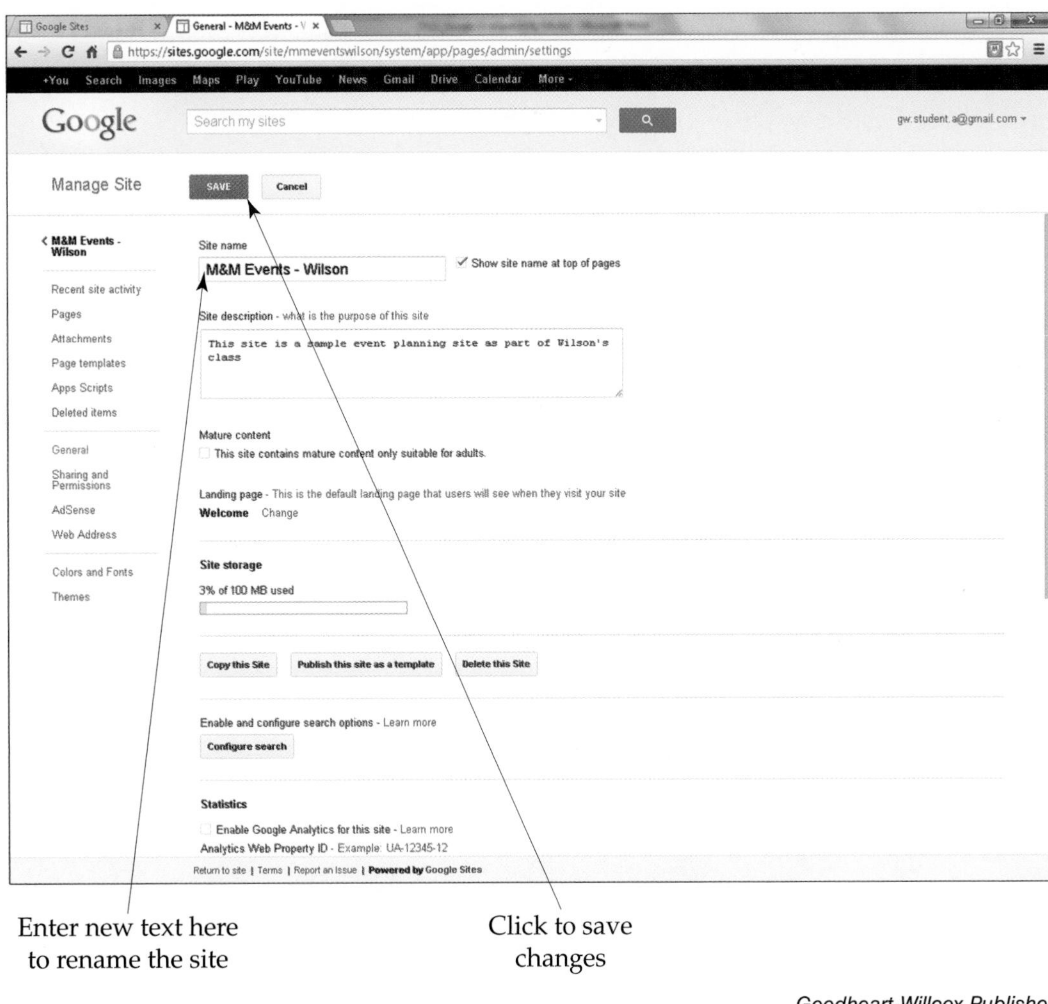

Goodheart-Willcox Publisher

Figure 13-24. When a user renames a site, the site URL does not change.

To access the general settings with another view of the **Manage Site** page displayed, click the **General** link.

6. Click in the **Site name** text box, and change the name to M & M Events, Inc—*Your Last Name*.

Save

7. Click the **Save** button to save the changes.
8. Click the name of the site in the navigation panel to return to the site.
9. Close the page or tab to close the site.

Lesson 13-9

Copying or Deleting a Site

Access and visibility settings, revision history, and page comments can be included when copying a site. When a user deletes a site, it will remain recoverable for 30 days unless deleted permanently before then.

Copying a Site

1. Log in to your Google Mail account.
2. Click the **More** link, and click **Even More** in the drop-down list.
3. Click **Sites** in the **Home & Office** area of the new tab or window to display the Sites page.
4. Click the name of the M&M Events site to display it in a new tab or window.
5. Click the **More** button, and click **Manage site** in the drop-down menu. The Manage Site page is displayed with general site information.
6. Click the **Copy this Site** button. A new page is displayed, as shown in **Figure 13-25.**

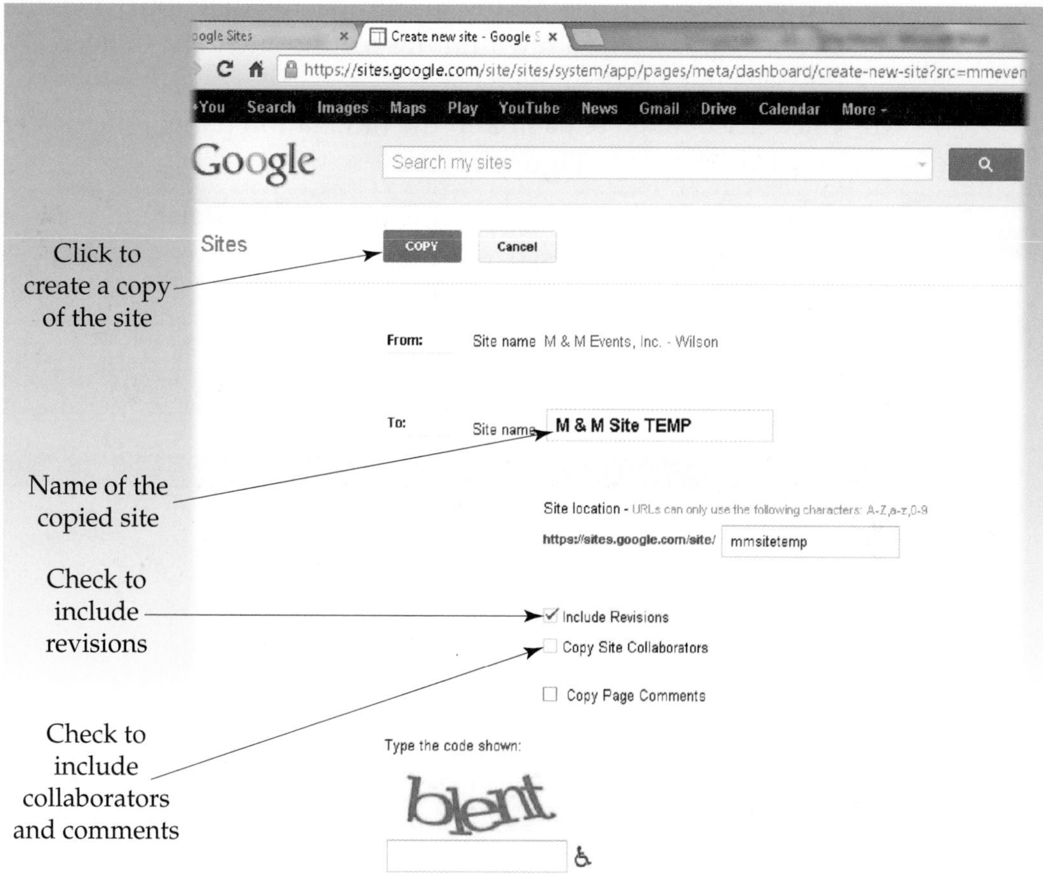

Goodheart-Willcox Publisher

Figure 13-25. The collaborators and their comments can be included when a site is copied.

7. Click in the **Site name** text box, and enter M & M Site TEMP. This is the name of the new site.
8. Uncheck the **Include Revisions** check box. This prevents the revision history from being included in the new site.
9. Uncheck the **Copy Site Collaborators** check box. This means the new site will have no viewers or editors. They will have to be added.
10. Uncheck the **Copy Page Comments** check box. No comments will be copied to the new site, so none of the pages will have comments.
11. In the text box at the bottom of the page, enter the security code shown above the text box. If you require audio assistance with the code, click the button to the right of the text box. The security code is required to ensure a human is creating the site, not a software robot.
12. Click the **Copy** button. The new site is displayed. Notice the title on the site reflects the new site name.

Deleting a Site

13. With the new site displayed, click the **More** button, and click **Manage site** in the drop-down menu. The Manage Site page is displayed with general site information.
14. Click the **Delete this Site** button.
15. A dialog box appears asking to confirm the deletion. Click the **Delete** button. It may take a few minutes for the site to be deleted. When it is, the Sites page is displayed.
16. Click the **Deleted sites** link in the navigation panel. The deleted site is listed, as shown in **Figure 13-26**.

Tip Click **Restore Site** to return it to active status. Click **Delete Permanently** to completely remove the site, which cannot be undone. A deleted site is automatically removed after 30 days.

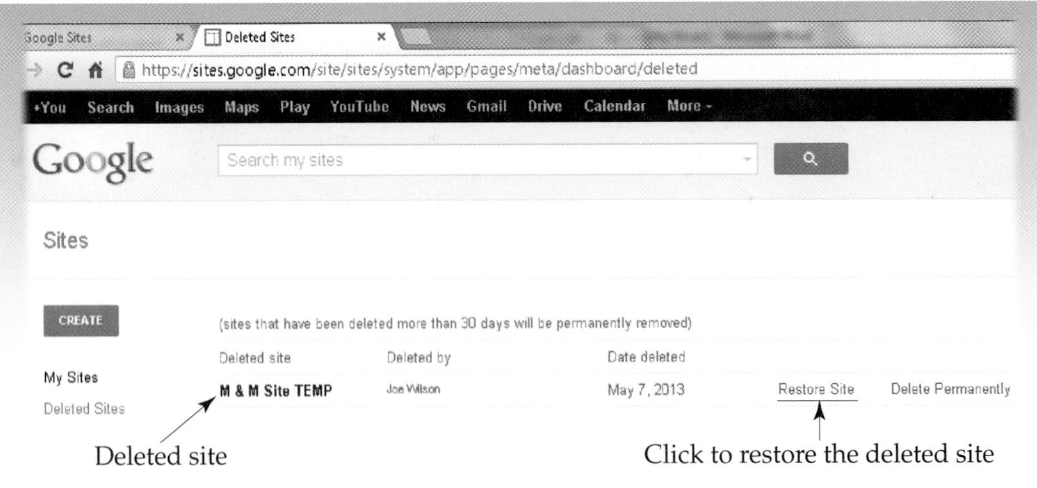

Goodheart-Willcox Publisher

Figure 13-26. When a site is deleted, it can be restored, but this must be done within 30 days.

Check Your Google Apps IQ

Now that you have finished this chapter, see what you know about Google Apps by taking the chapter posttest.
www.m.g-wlearning.com
www.g-wlearning.com/informationtechnology/

Skill Review

Answer the following questions on a separate sheet of paper.

1. Describe the difference between a public site and a private site.
2. What is the main method for moving through a site?
3. Which pages are often reserved for the main categories of a site's content?
4. Who controls the visibility and accessibility settings of a Google site?
5. List the four standard page templates for a Google site.
6. Which page template would be best suited for:
   A. weekly updates?
   B. an archive of the PDF version of the company newsletter?
   C. information about how to contact M & M events?
   D. links to vendor websites and contact information, grouped by type of product?
7. List four formatting functions that can be changed for text on a site.
8. When creating a new announcement post, if it is not ready to publish, use the ______ option to save it.
9. What is the limit on the size of files uploaded to a file cabinet page?
10. A site can be renamed, copied, or deleted on the ______ page.

Lesson Application

These exercises are designed to apply the skills learned in this and previous chapters. General directions are provided, but you will need to draw on your knowledge to determine how to complete each exercise.

Exercise 13-1
Creating an Announcement Page and Posts

Create a new announcement page entitled Fundraising Competition. Add three posts to the page. All posts should be related to the topic of the page. For one post, include an image. Be sure to include alternate text for the image in case a user's browser cannot display the image. For another post, attach a word processing document that describes the competition (you will need to create this document). For the third post, reply to one of the other two posts. Send your instructor an e-mail with a link to the page, and indicate the exercise is complete.

Exercise 13-2
Creating and Populating a List Page

Create a new list page that contains columns for Class Name, Period, and Instructor Name. Take the steps needed to make the Class Names column a text-box entry, the Period column a drop-down list that contains the times for class periods, and the Instructor Name column a text-box entry. Add each class of your schedule to the list page, including the appropriate information. Share the page with your instructor, and send an e-mail to indicate it is shared.

Exercise 13-3
Creating a File Cabinet Page

Work with three classmates as assigned by your instructor. Brainstorm ideas for files that should be stored in a common location related to operating a small business. Create examples of these files, such as a memo template, expense form, marketing brochure, and so on. Create a file cabinet page, and take the steps needed to allow all team members to collaborate on the management of the site. Upload the example files. As a team, compose an e-mail describing the files located on the file cabinet page, and send it to your instructor.

Chapter 14

Embedding Google Drive App Files and Gadgets

Objectives

After completing this chapter, you will be able to:

- **Insert** an existing Google Drive app file onto a Google Sites page.
- **Add** a Google-created gadget containing site information onto a Google Sites page.
- **Locate** third-party gadgets to insert onto a Google Sites page.

alexmillos/Shutterstock.com

Check Your Google Apps IQ

Before you begin this chapter, see what you already know about Google Apps by taking the chapter pretest.

www.m.g-wlearning.com
www.g-wlearning.com/informationtechnology/

Google Drive App Files and Gadgets on Google Sites

In addition to text and images, a user can embed rich content into a Google site. ***Rich content*** is information that includes a combination of elements such as images, audio, video, and animation, as well as interactive elements. This can include content from Google Drive apps, such as Docs, Sheets, Slides, Forms, and Drawings. Google gadgets can also be incorporated. In terms of a website, a ***gadget*** is an application that performs simple tasks and is small enough to be added to and run directly from a web page. Google gadgets fall into two main categories. There are Google-created gadgets that display content pulled from other pages on a site. There are also third-party gadgets; these vary greatly in their functionality. A ***third-party gadget*** is developed by someone outside of Google. For example, there is a dictionary gadget, a calculator gadget, and a gadget that provides up-to-the-minute weather conditions.

Each Google gadget will have different properties that a user may need to set. These properties are specific to the gadget, but often include determining the size of the gadget along with a title for it. Often there are not directions explaining what the specific gadget properties are. Sometimes trial and error is the best way to figure them out.

There are also some formatting options for all types of rich-content elements. These options can be set to best incorporate the elements into the overall design of the website. The user can choose where on the page to add the file or gadget. Once these elements are placed, their alignment on the page can be set. The user can also choose whether or not textual content (words) on the web page will wrap around the gadget or file.

Adding Google Drive App Files to Google Sites

To ***embed*** a file means to make the file appear as part of the page, as seen in **Figure 14-1.** In order to do this, coding is added to the web page definition to make the file appear. Any Google Drive file—document, spreadsheet, slide, form, or Google Calendar—can be embedded into a site as an object. To set up a Google Drive app file to be embedded into a site, the file owner must make sure that the file is published, or that the visibility setting on the file is either set to **Public on the web** or shared with the specific people who have access to the site.

Goodheart-Willcox Publisher

Figure 14-1. A Google Drive app file can be embedded into a Google site.

Adding Google-Created Gadgets to Google Sites

A user can embed a Google-created gadget that displays content from other pages in the site. When updates are made to the content of the other pages, those changes are automatically updated in the gadget. This can provide a user with an opportunity to highlight information found on another page without having to create and update the same data in two places. Embedding these gadgets can also help a user encourage people to visit other pages in the site. For example, the ***recent posts gadget*** displays posts from an announcement page. The ***recently updated files gadget*** displays files or links recently added to a file cabinet page. The ***recent list items gadget*** displays items recently added to a list page.

Adding Third-party Gadgets to Google Sites

In addition to Google-created gadgets, there are third-party gadgets that can be embedded in a web page. Third-party gadgets can be added to enhance the existing content on a site. For example, there are third-party gadgets that provide current sporting news. This type of gadget could enhance the content of the soccer club's website.

Google provides a few ways to search for third-party gadgets in the **Add a gadget to your page** dialog box. A user can review a list of gadgets featured by Google. The featured apps represent a small portion of those available. A user can also enter a keyword to search for gadgets in this dialog box. A user can search the web and provide a URL to link to a gadget on another website. When selecting a third-party gadget, be sure to fully evaluate it before using it. For example, some of these may have advertisements that appear with the gadget.

Lesson 14-1

Inserting a Google Drive App File on a Site

Adding Google Drive app files to a website allows visitors of the site to view these files as read-only objects on the site. Including files on a site allows the user to make the content easily visible. As the file is updated, and remains published, the version on the site will automatically update to reflect the changes.

Inserting a Slides Gadget

1. Log in to your Google Mail account.
2. Click the **More** link, and click **Even More** in the drop-down list.
3. Click **Sites** in the **Home & Office** area of the new tab or window to display the Sites page. The site created in Lesson 13-1 should be displayed on the Sites page.
4. Click the name of the M&M Events site created in Chapter 13 to display it in a new tab or window.
5. Click the name of the Denver Team Members page created in Chapter 13.
6. Click the **Edit Page** button to enter edit mode.

Edit Page

7. Click the **Insert** pull-down menu, and click **Presentation** in the menu. The **Insert...** dialog box is displayed, as shown in **Figure 14-2.** The presentations on your Google drive are shown in the dialog box.
8. Locate the thumbnail for the Meet the Team presentation created in Chapter 10, and select it.
9. Click the **Select** button. The **Insert Google Presentation** dialog box is displayed, as shown in **Figure 14-3.**
10. Click in the **Include title:** text box. The default title is the name of the presentation file. Enter Our Team as the new title. Make sure the **Include title:** check box is checked so the title will be displayed.
11. Check the **Start slideshow as soon as player loads** check box. This makes the presentation start automatically after the page loads the presentation player.
12. Check the **Restart slideshow after last slide** check box. This makes the presentation loop.

Goodheart-Willcox Publisher

Figure 14-2. The **Insert...** dialog box is used to select a gadget to insert onto a web page.

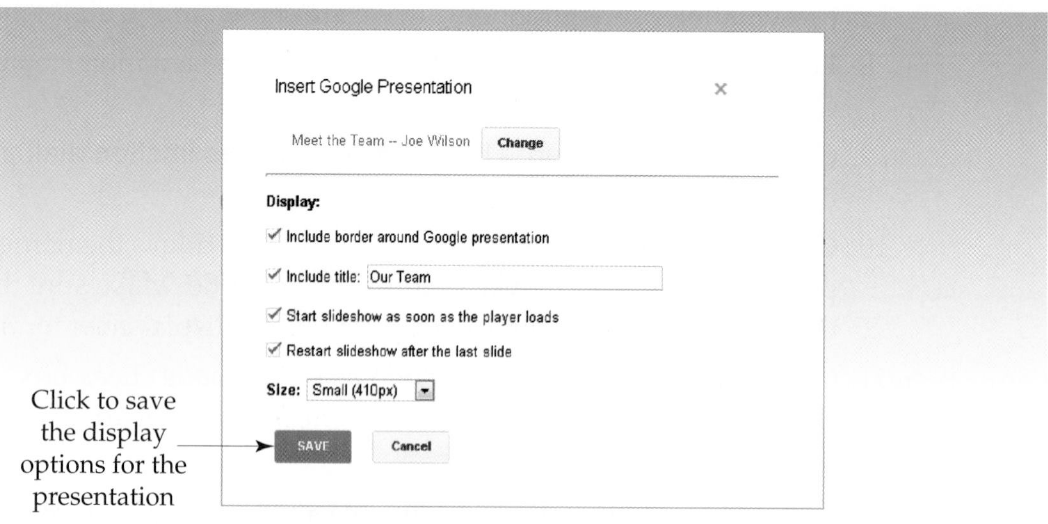

Goodheart-Willcox Publisher

Figure 14-3. Inserting a **Google Slides** presentation onto a web page.

13. Click the **Size:** drop-down list, and click **Medium (555px)** in the list. This sets the size of the presentation on the page. The pixel dimension is the width of the presentation.

Since the layout and purpose of every site varies, it is often easiest to save the gadget with the default settings, view the saved page, and then determine if the gadget should be larger or smaller.

14. Click the **Save** button to add the presentation to the page. A gadget placeholder (gray box) is displayed and selected, as indicated by the display of the properties toolbar.
15. Select the **Align Center** button on the properties toolbar. This centers the presentation in the text box.
16. Click the **Save** button to update the page. The presentation is visible on the live page, and begins playing as soon as the live page is displayed.

Align Center

Editing the Properties of a Gadget

Edit Page

Properties

17. Click the **Edit Page** button to enter edit mode.
18. Click the gadget placeholder to select it. The properties toolbar is displayed on the placeholder.
19. Click the **Properties** button on the properties toolbar. The **Google Presentation Properties** dialog box is displayed. This is the same dialog box displayed when adding the gadget.
20. Uncheck the **Include border around Google presentation** check box. This removes the thin line surrounding the presentation on the web page.
21. Click the **Save** button in the dialog box to update the gadget settings.
22. Click the **Save** button to save the page and see it live with the updated gadget.

Inserting a Form Gadget

Edit Page

23. Click the **Edit Page** button to enter edit mode.
24. Click after the current gadget, and press the [Enter] key to start a new line.
25. Click the **Insert** pull-down menu, and click **Spreadsheet form** in the menu. The **Insert...** dialog box is displayed.
26. Click the thumbnail image of the Customer Satisfaction survey created in Chapter 12.
27. Click the **Select** button. The **Insert Google Spreadsheet Form** dialog box is displayed.
28. Click in the **Include title:** text box, and enter Customer Satisfaction Survey. Make sure the check box next to **Include title:** is checked.

29. Click the **Save** button to add the gadget to the page below the presentation gadget.

Align Center

30. Click the **Align Center** button on the properties toolbar for the gadget to center the gadget in the text box.

Save

31. Click the **Save** button to save the page and see it live with the updated gadget.
32. Close the tab or window to close the site.

Lesson 14-2

Inserting a Gadget Containing Site Information

Embedding gadgets that contain site information can help a user encourage people to visit other pages in the site. Multiple gadgets can be inserted onto any page.

1. Log in to your Google Mail account.
2. Click the **More** link, and click **Even More** in the drop-down list.
3. Click **Sites** in the **Home & Office** area of the new tab or window to display the Sites page.
4. Click the name of the M&M Events site to display it in a new tab or window.
5. With the home page displayed, click the **Edit Page** button to enter edit mode.
6. Click in the right-hand text box next to the one containing the image.
7. Click the **Insert** pull-down menu, and click **Recent posts** in the menu. The **Insert Recent Announcements** dialog box is displayed, as shown in **Figure 14-4.**

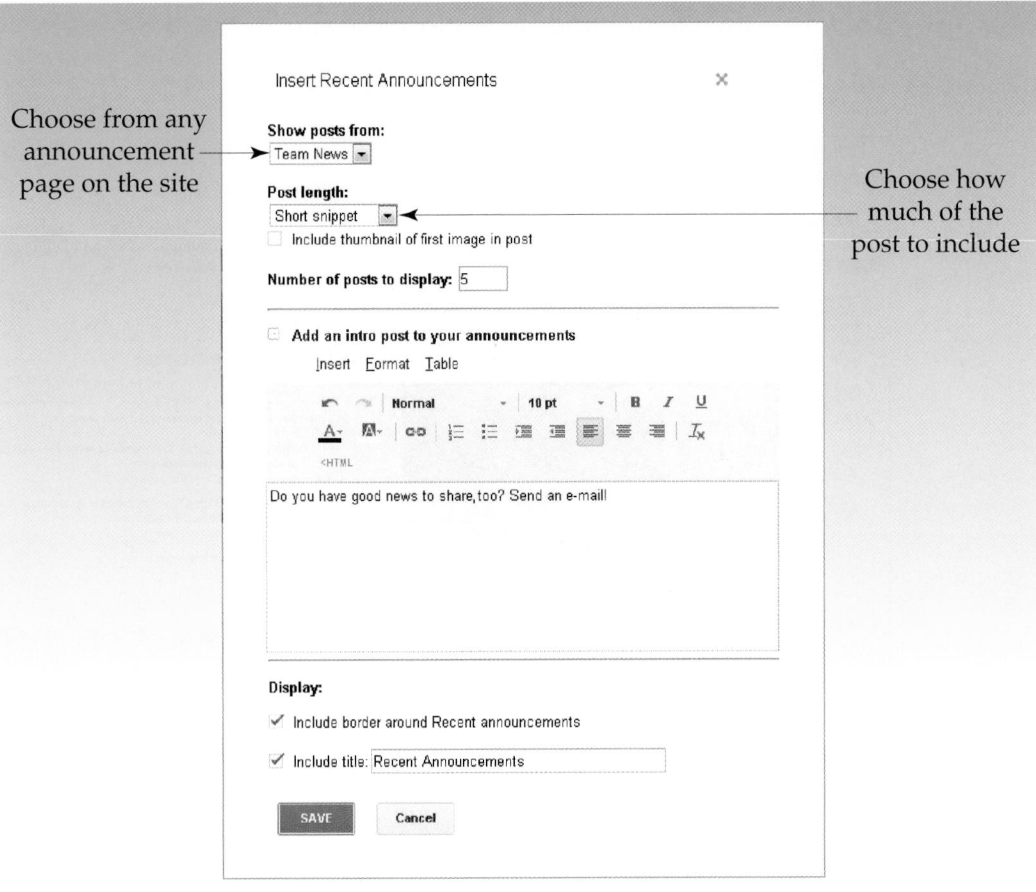

Goodheart-Willcox Publisher

Figure 14-4. Inserting a gadget that contains site posts onto a web page.

8. Click the **Show posts from:** drop-down list, and select which page will feed this gadget. Since there is only one page on the site that contains posts, Team News, it is the only option in the list.
9. Click the **Post length:** drop-down list, and click **Medium snippet** in the list. This specifies the preview of the post will be of medium length.
10. Click the plus sign next to the **Add an intro post to your announcements** label. An expanded area appears below the label.
11. Click in the text box in the expanded area, and enter a message to display above the posts.

Tip The formatting tools can be used to change the appearance of the introduction post.

12. Click in the **Include title:** text box in the **Display:** area, and enter Good News. This is the title for the gadget. Make sure the check box next to **Include title:** is checked.
13. Click the **Save** button to add the gadget. A gray box placeholder is displayed in the right-hand text box.
14. Click the **Save** button to save the page and see it live with the updated gadget. The page should appear similar to that shown in **Figure 14-5.**
15. Close the tab or window to close the site.

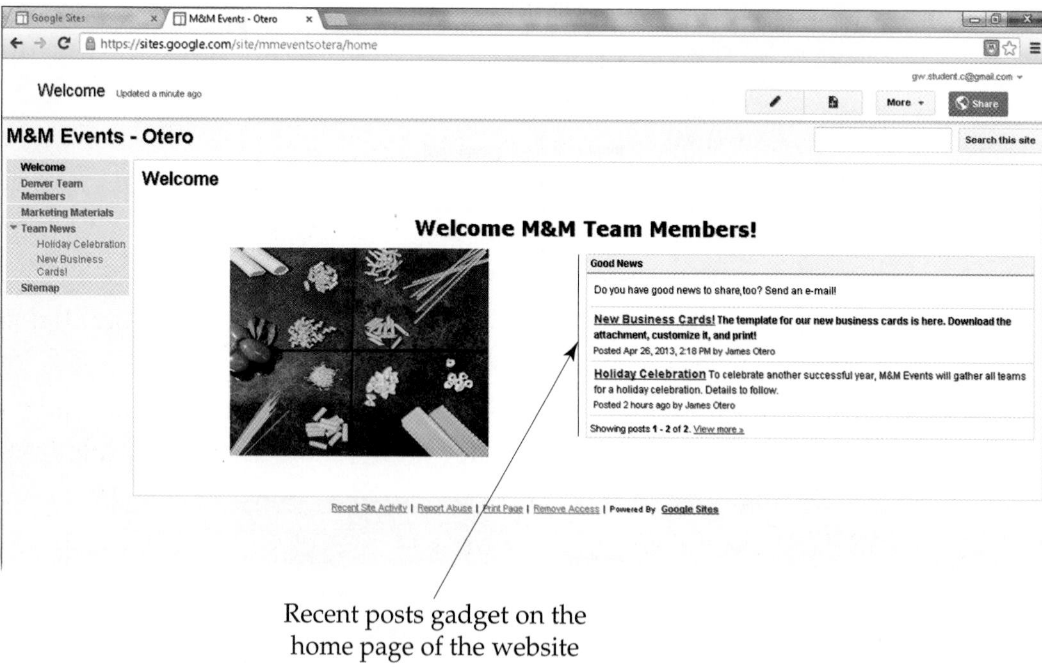

Goodheart-Willcox Publisher

Figure 14-5. The site should appear similar to this once the posts gadget is added.

Lesson 14-3

Inserting Other Gadgets on a Site

There are many third-party gadgets available. Some gadgets are chosen as a convenience to site visitors such as time and date or weather gadgets. Game gadgets are often selected to keep people at the site longer than they would be otherwise.

Adding a Dictionary Gadget

1. Log in to your Google Mail account.
2. Click the **More** link, and click **Even More** in the drop-down list.
3. Click **Sites** in the **Home & Office** area of the new tab or window to display the Sites page.
4. Click the name of the M&M Events site to display it in a new tab or window.
5. Click the name of the Marketing Materials page to display it.

Edit Page

6. Click the **Edit Page** button to enter edit mode.
7. Click the **Insert** pull-down menu, and click **More gadgets...** in the menu. The **Add a gadget to your page** dialog box is displayed. By default, featured gadgets are displayed.
8. Click **Public** on the left side of the dialog box.

Search Gallery

9. Click in the search box that is displayed, enter dictionary, and click the **Search Gallery** button, as shown in **Figure 14-6.** Only gadgets matching the search criterion are displayed.
10. Click on the first result, as shown in **Figure 14-6.** Information about the gadget is displayed.
11. Click the **Select** button. The **Add a gadget to your page** dialog box is redisplayed with properties for the selected gadget.
12. Click the drop-down list next to the **Width:** text box, and click **pixels** in the list. This sets the measurement to pixels instead of a percentage.
13. Click in the **Width:** text box, and enter 400.

Tip

Width is entered as either pixels or percentage. If set to a percentage and the **Width:** text box is left blank, the gadget will take up the entire width of the section in which it is placed.

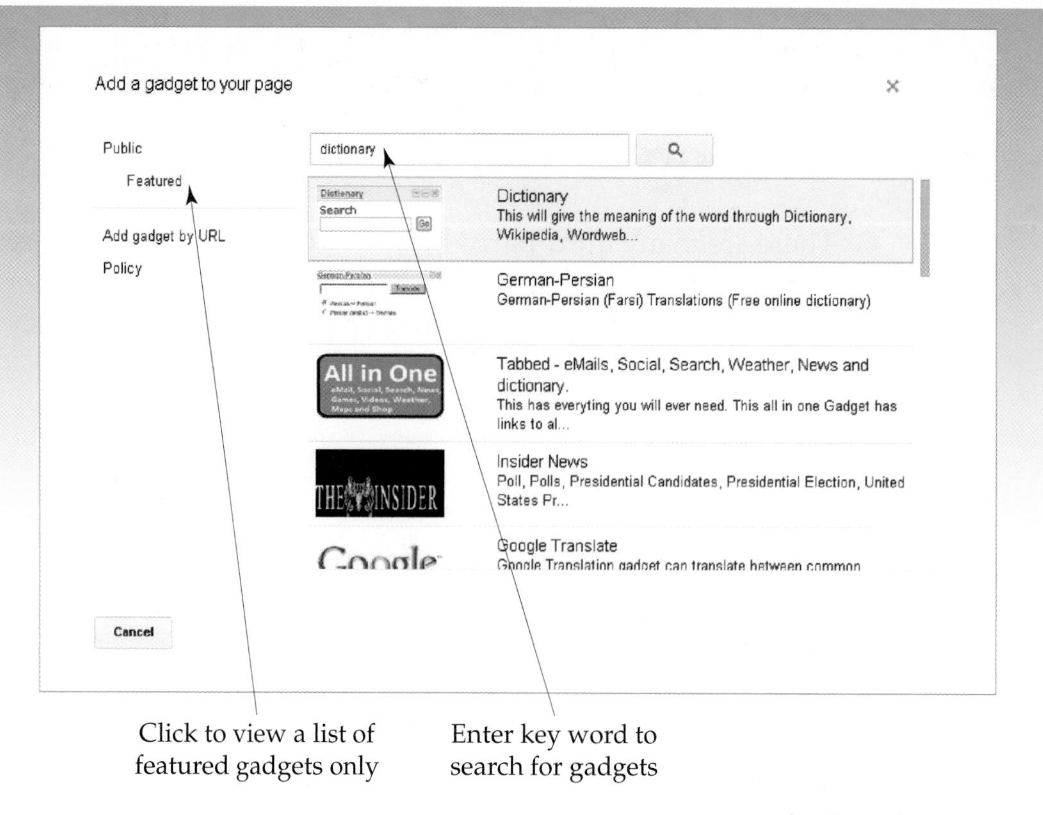

Goodheart-Willcox Publisher

Figure 14-6. Searching for a dictionary gadget to add to a web page.

14. Click in the **Height:** text box, and enter 200.
15. Click the **OK** button to add the gadget to the page. The gadget placeholder is inserted into the main text box on the page.

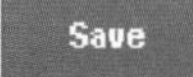

16. Click the **Save** button to save the page and see it live with the updated gadget.

Adding a Map Gadget

17. Click the **Edit Page** button to enter edit mode.
18. Click after the current gadget to place the cursor there.
19. Click the **Insert** pull-down menu, and click **Map** in the menu. The **Insert...** dialog box is displayed.
20. Click in the search box at the top of the dialog box, and enter your town and zip code, and press the [Enter] key. The map preview changes to your town, as shown in **Figure 14-7.**

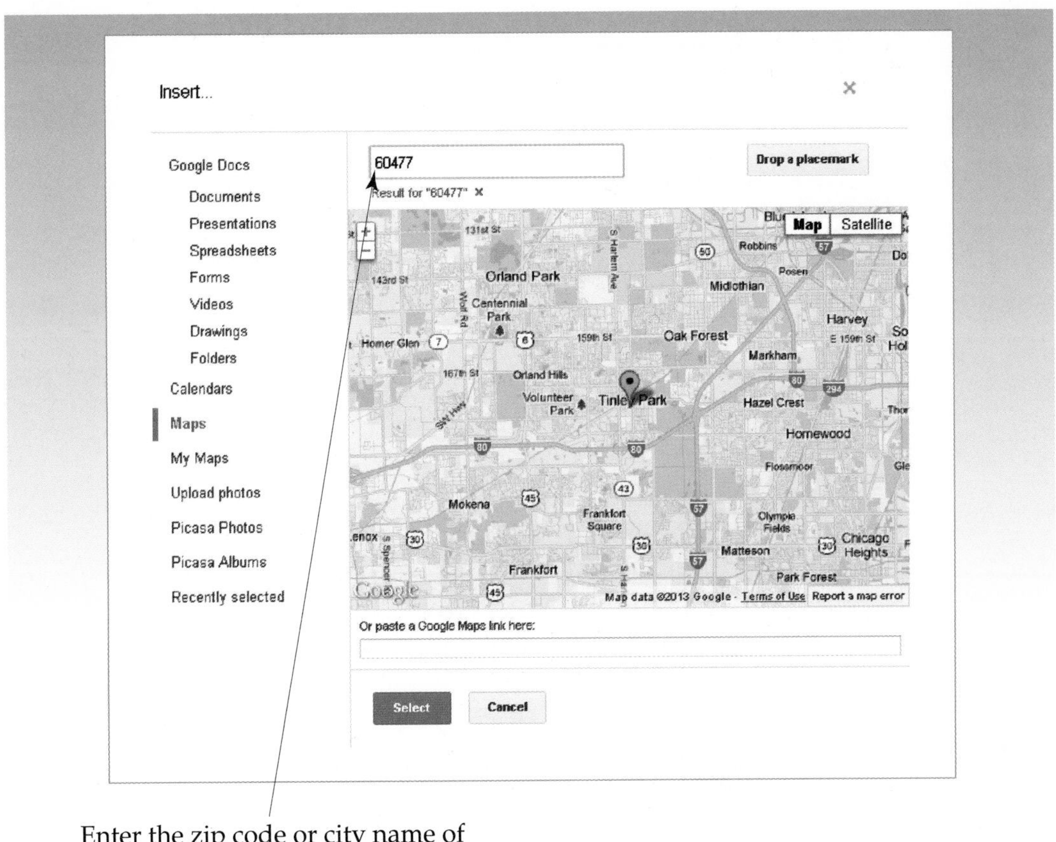

Goodheart-Willcox Publisher

Figure 14-7. Selecting a map view for a map gadget to be added to a web page.

21. Click the **Select** button. The **Insert Google Map** dialog box is displayed.
22. Click in the **Include title:** text box, and enter Our Location. Make sure the check box next to **Include title:** is checked.
23. Click in the **Height:** text box, and enter 400.
24. Click in the **Width:** text box, and enter 400. If this text box is left blank, the gadget will be as wide as the available space.
25. Click the **Save** button to add the gadget. A gray box placeholder is displayed in the right-hand text box.

Save

26. Click the **Save** button to save the page and see it live with the updated gadget. The page should appear similar to that shown in **Figure 14-8.**
27. Close the tab or window to close the site.

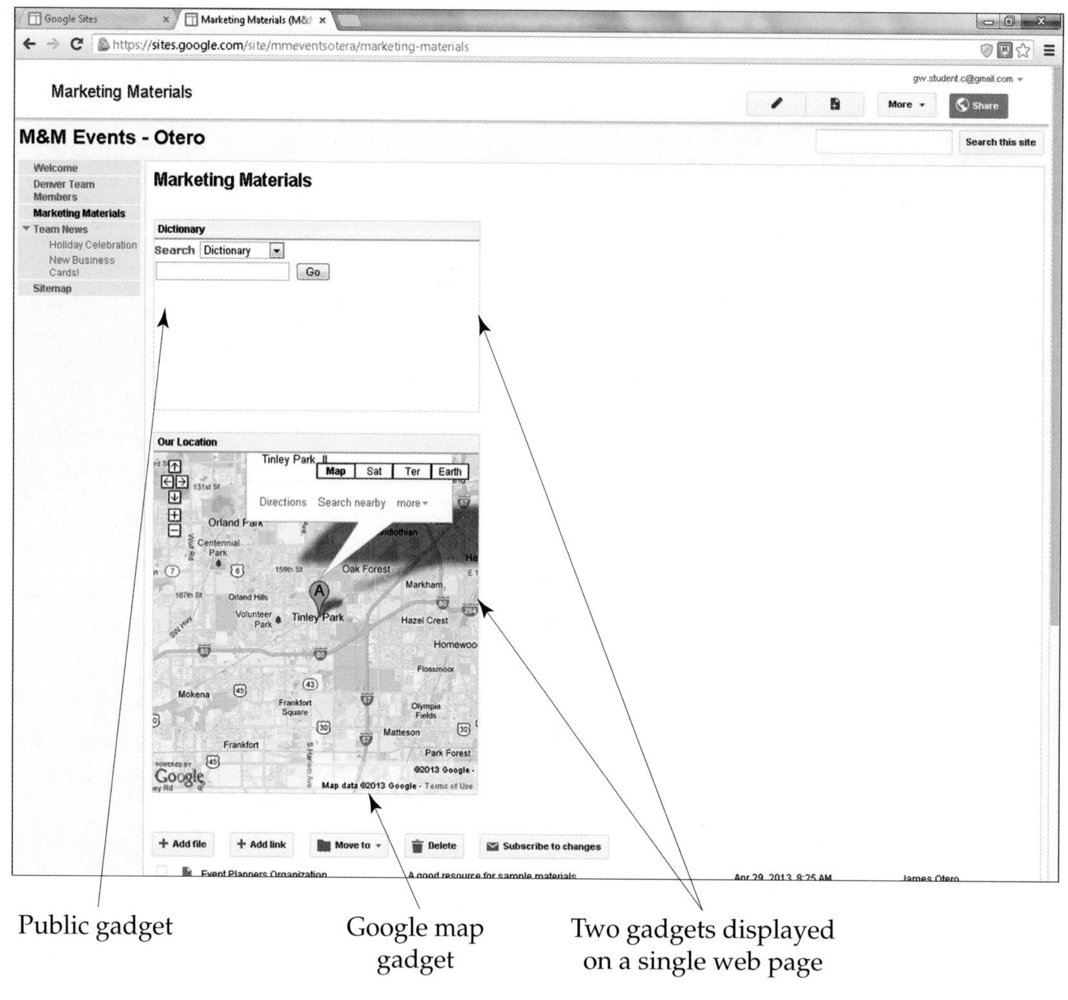

Goodheart-Willcox Publisher

Figure 14-8. The site should appear similar to this once the map gadget is added.

Check Your Google Apps IQ

Now that you have finished this chapter, see what you know about Google Apps by taking the chapter posttest.
www.m.g-wlearning.com
www.g-wlearning.com/informationtechnology/

Skill Review

Answer the following questions on a separate sheet of paper.

1. What is rich content?
2. Describe what a gadget is.
3. List the two basic types of gadgets.
4. What does it mean to embed a file?
5. Which type of gadget can pull information from other pages on a Google site?
6. Which gadget displays posts from an announcement page on a Google site?
7. Which gadget displays content recently added to a file cabinet page on a Google site?
8. Which gadget displays items recently added to a list page on a Google site?
9. Describe a third-party gadget.
10. What is one reason why it is a good idea to evaluate a third-party gadget before using it?

Lesson Application

These exercises are designed to apply the skills learned in this and previous chapters. General directions are provided, but you will need to draw on your knowledge to determine how to complete each exercise.

Exercise 14-1
Inserting a Google Form

Edit the M&M Events site, and add a new page entitled Employee Survey. Insert the Employee Satisfaction survey created in Exercise 12-2. Set the form to display at 100 percent of the available width. View the form on the live page to see if the height needs to be adjusted. The entire form, including the submit button, must be displayed. Edit the form properties as needed so the height allows the entire form to be displayed. Share the page with your instructor, sending an e-mail when sharing the page.

Exercise 14-2
Embedding a Google Gadget

Edit the Welcome page on the M&M Events site. Add a map Google-created gadget below the image. The default location on the map should be the address of your school. Include an appropriate title for the map. The map should be approximately the same width as the image, and it should be square.

Use what you have learned in this chapter to add a recently updated files gadget below the recent announcements gadget. Set the gadget to display the four most-recently updated files. Include a border around the gadget, and include an appropriate title for the gadget. Save the page, and compose an e-mail to your instructor explaining how you adjusted the size of the map to match the image.

Chapter 15

Site Composition

Objectives

After completing this chapter, you will be able to:

- **Modify** the order of the page links on the sidebar.
- **Add** gadgets to the sidebar.
- **Modify** the horizontal navigation bar.
- **Edit** the site header and footer.
- **Modify** the site appearance including theme, fonts, and colors.

alexmillos/Shutterstock.com

Check Your Google Apps IQ

Before you begin this chapter, see what you already know about Google Apps by taking the chapter pretest.

www.m.g-wlearning.com
www.g-wlearning.com/informationtechnology/

Customizing the Site Composition

Once the content of a site is set, a user can modify the composition of the site. ***Site composition*** includes setting up or changing the elements of the website that are common to all of the pages on the site. These elements include the sidebar, header and footer, use of a horizontal navigation bar, theme, and use of specific colors and fonts on the site, as seen in **Figure 15-1**. While all of this can be done at any time, these changes are best made when the content of the site is close to final because they will impact most of the pages on a site.

A user should be sure of the purpose and the audience for the site before customizing its composition. The purpose of the site could be to persuade a private group to take a certain position or to inform the public on a certain issue. When evaluating the audience for a website, it can be important to keep in mind what technology skills people who visit the site are likely to have. These considerations should be reflected in the overall composition of the site. The checklist shown in **Figure 15-2** can help a user ensure that the content, layout, and appearance of the site serve its purpose and audience.

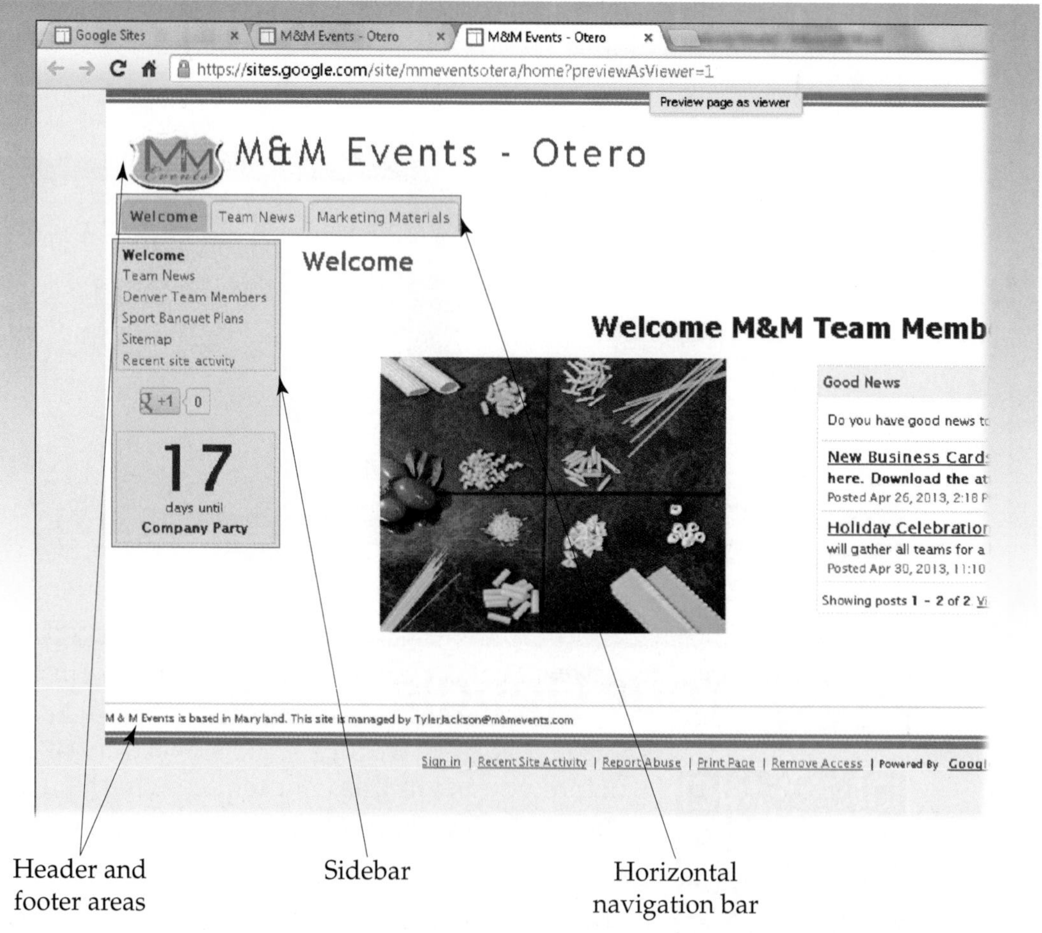

Goodheart-Willcox Publisher

Figure 15-1. Various elements of a Google site can be customized.

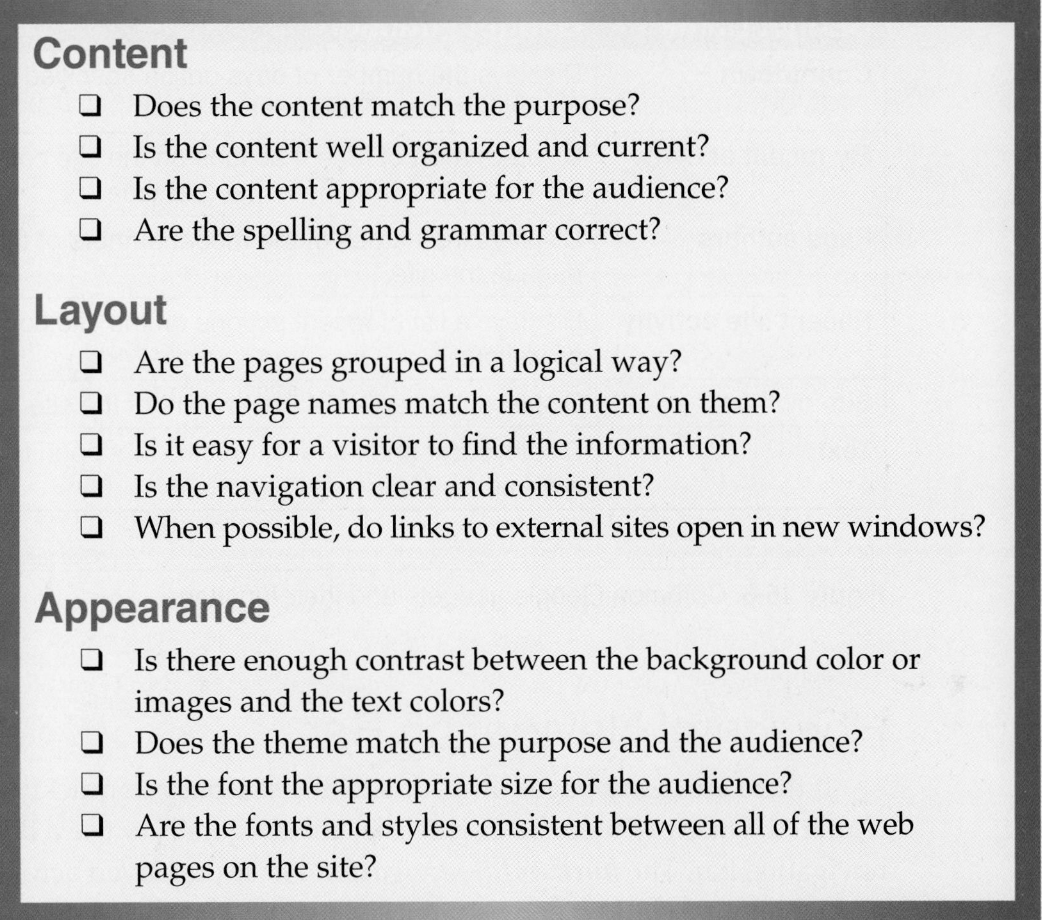

Content

- ❑ Does the content match the purpose?
- ❑ Is the content well organized and current?
- ❑ Is the content appropriate for the audience?
- ❑ Are the spelling and grammar correct?

Layout

- ❑ Are the pages grouped in a logical way?
- ❑ Do the page names match the content on them?
- ❑ Is it easy for a visitor to find the information?
- ❑ Is the navigation clear and consistent?
- ❑ When possible, do links to external sites open in new windows?

Appearance

- ❑ Is there enough contrast between the background color or images and the text colors?
- ❑ Does the theme match the purpose and the audience?
- ❑ Is the font the appropriate size for the audience?
- ❑ Are the fonts and styles consistent between all of the web pages on the site?

Goodheart-Willcox Publisher

Figure 15-2. Use this check sheet when planning and designing a website.

Customizing Common Elements of a Google Site

The navigation of a site can be improved by refining the sidebar. As discussed in Chapter 13, the ***sidebar*** is displayed on every web page of a site. By default the navigation panel gadget is part of the sidebar. As new pages are created, they are automatically added to the navigation panel gadget on the sidebar in alphabetical order. However, a user can customize which pages are listed in the sidebar and in what order they appear.

In addition to the default navigation panel gadget, a user can add other gadgets to the sidebar. The gadgets that can be used by anyone with a Google account are listed in **Figure 15-3**. Once gadgets are added to the sidebar, the user can change the order in which they appear. For example, the user may want to keep the navigation panel gadget at the top of the sidebar. The sidebar is displayed on the left side of the page by default. It can be moved to the right side of the page. A user can also modify the width of the sidebar from its default setting.

Gadget Name	Gadget Function
Countdown	Displays the number of days until a specified date; usually the date is associated with an event.
My recent activity	Displays a list of recent actions on the site completed by the visitor that is signed-in at that time.
Page authors	Displays the names of the recent authors of the active page in the site.
Recent site activity	Displays a list of recent actions on the site completed by all visitors.
Site owners	Displays the names of the owners of the site.
Text	Displays text and images, or links that open in a new window.

Goodheart-Willcox Publisher

Figure 15-3. Common Google gadgets and their functions.

Horizontal Navigation Bar

If there are many pages on your site, the sidebar can quickly become cluttered. One way to make a site easier to navigate is to use a horizontal navigation bar. The ***horizontal navigation bar*** is displayed across the width of the browser window between the site header and the content of the specific page. The user can customize which pages appear in the bar and in what order they are displayed. There are three styles for the horizontal navigation bar: boxes, tabs, and links.

When a user chooses to have sub pages associated with a page listed in the horizontal navigation bar, Google creates a drop-down menu associated with the parent page. The sub pages are automatically added to the drop-down list under the parent page. Drop-down menus work best when there is more than one sub page. Like customizing the sidebar, the pages must be created before organizing them.

Customizing the Header and Footer

The ***header*** section of site is displayed at the top of each page. The ***footer*** section is displayed at the bottom of each page. The content in the header and footer of a site should be information that needs to be easily accessible, but will not interfere with the content of the site. The header can be a good place to include a company or organization name and logo. The footer can be a good place to put contact information for the company or information about who maintains the site. This footer is different from the default footer that appears on all Google sites, which cannot be changed.

Customizing the Appearance of a Google Site

The *theme* impacts the font style and color as well the overall color scheme of the site. These selections are reflected in all of the areas of each page on the site, including the content area, header, footer, sidebar, and horizontal navigation bar. A user can select a new theme at any time from the theme gallery. Applying a new theme to an existing site will not add new content; it will only change the appearance.

Although themes are a quick way to set the appearance of a site, there may be colors and fonts associated with the theme that a user would like to change. Google allows users to change the colors and fonts of most website elements. Changes to the fonts and colors are selected for an area of the page: the entire page, site header, content area, content area gadgets, sidebar gadgets, navigation gadget, horizontal navigation, and the horizontal navigation drop-down menu. Some themes do not allow a user to change certain elements, so it is better to select a theme, and then customize the colors and fonts.

Lesson 15-1

Modifying the Sidebar

Reorganizing the sidebar can improve the navigation of a website. Top level and second level pages are displayed by default, but a user can change this. Pages must already exist to be included in the sidebar.

1. Log in to your Google Mail account.
2. Click the **More** link, and click **Even More** in the drop-down list.
3. Click **Sites** in the **Home & Office** area of the new tab or window to display the Sites page.
4. Click the name of the M&M Events site created in Chapter 13 to display it in a new tab or window.

More ▾

5. Click the **More** button, and click **Edit site layout** in the drop-down menu. A toolbar appears at the top of the page, as shown in **Figure 15-4.** The depressed buttons indicate the site elements that are currently enabled.

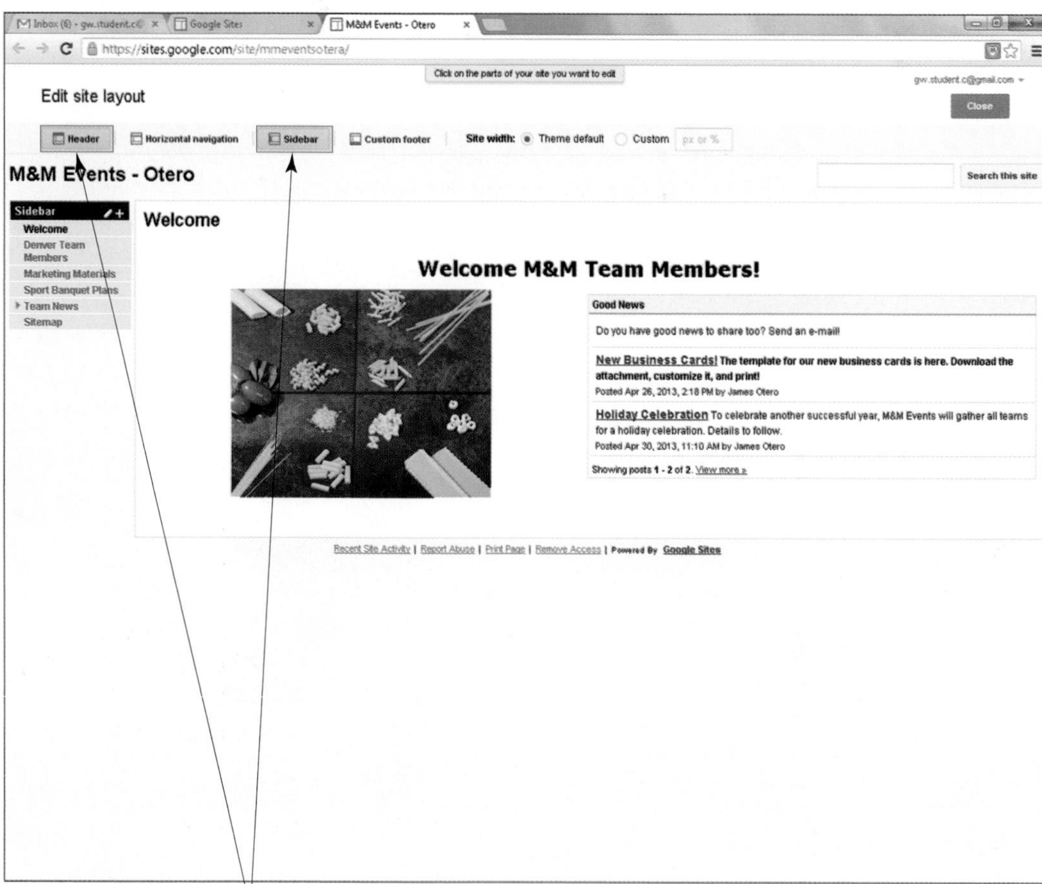

Goodheart-Willcox Publisher

Figure 15-4. Editing the layout of a site.

Tip The [Ctrl][L] key combination can be used to enter edit mode for the site layout.

6. Hover the cursor over the navigation panel gadget. It is highlighted as shown in **Figure 15-5.** Click anywhere in the box to edit the gadget. The **Configure navigation** dialog box is displayed.
7. Click the **Level of pages to show:** drop-down list, and click **1** in the list. This will prevent the individual announcement pages from being displayed in the navigation panel gadget.

Tip The sitemap displays a list of all of the pages in your site. To remove the sitemap from the navigation panel gadget, uncheck the **Sitemap** check box in the **Configure navigation** dialog box.

8. Click the **OK** button to apply the change. Notice how the navigation panel gadget now shows only the top-level pages.
9. Click the navigation panel gadget to edit it. The **Configure navigation** dialog box is again displayed.
10. Uncheck the **Automatically organize my navigation** check box. The dialog box expands below the check box to include the **Select pages to show** list box, as shown in **Figure 15-6.**

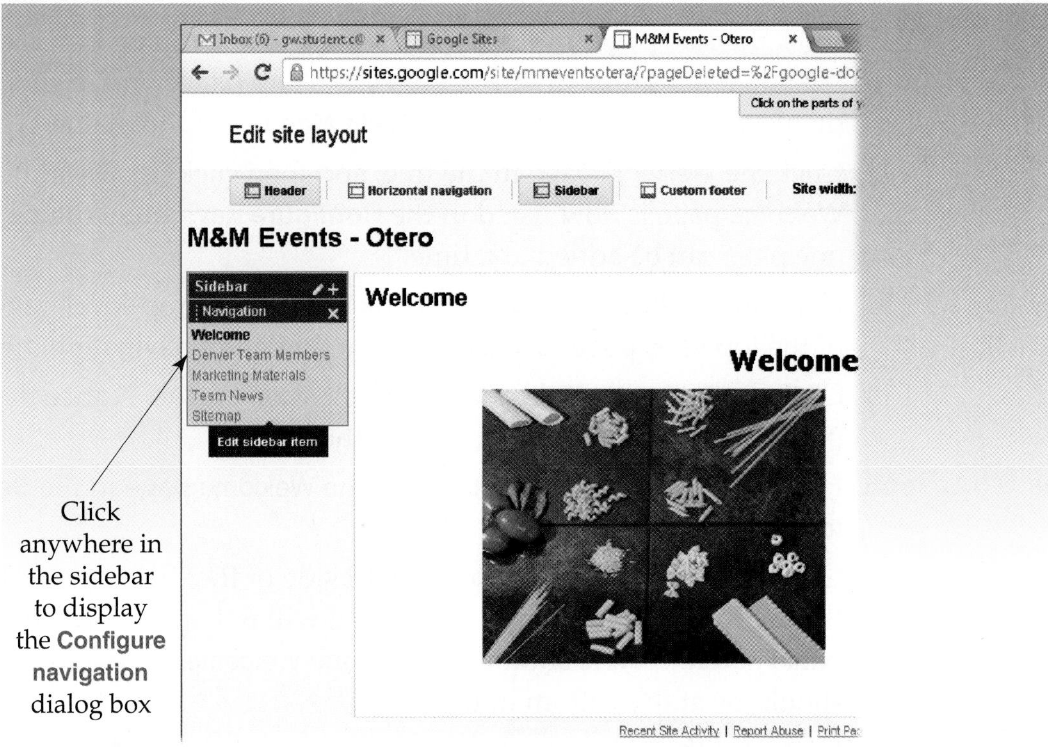

Goodheart-Willcox Publisher

Figure 15-5. When editing the layout of a site, hover the cursor over the gadget to edit and click to edit it.

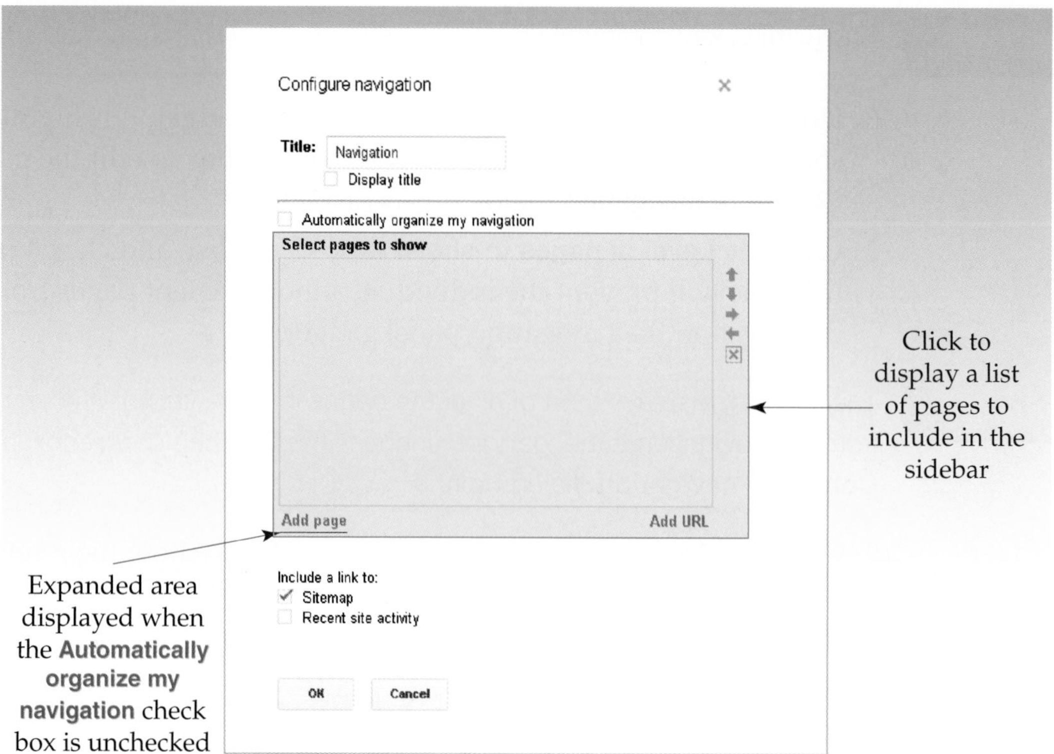

Goodheart-Willcox Publisher

Figure 15-6. Editing the navigation panel gadget.

11. Click the **Add page** link. The **Select page to add** dialog box is displayed, as shown in **Figure 15-7.** The pages and sub pages on the site are displayed in a tree format on the **Site Map** tab of the dialog box.
12. Click the Welcome page in the tree, and then click the **OK** button. The Welcome page is now listed in the **Configure navigation** dialog box. Only one page can be added at a time.
13. Continue clicking the **Add page** link and adding top-level pages until all of the top level pages are listed in the **Configure navigation** dialog box.
14. Click the **Add page** link, and add the Welcome page. Notice that the same page can appear more than once in the list.
15. Highlight the first (top) instance of the Welcome page in the **Select pages to show** list box.

Remove

16. Click the **Remove** button on the right side of the dialog box. This deletes the highlighted page from the list so it will not appear in the navigation panel gadget. There should be only one Welcome page in the list, and it should be at the bottom of the list.

Move Up

17. Highlight the Welcome page in the list, and click the **Move up** button on the right side of the dialog box. Continue clicking the button until the Welcome page is at the top of the list.

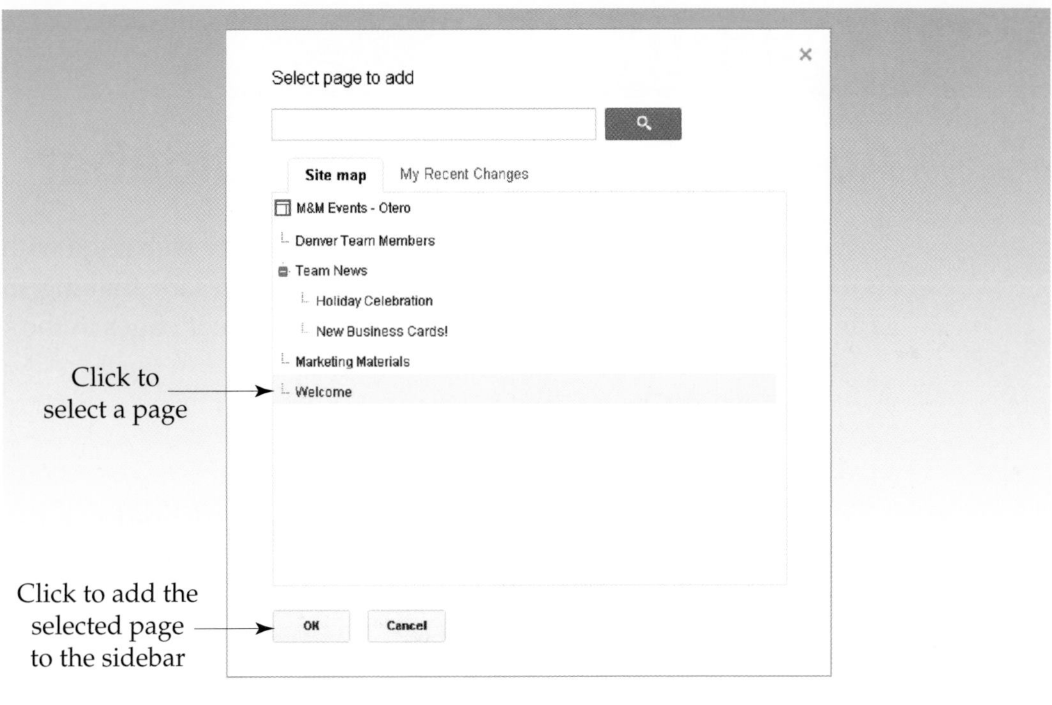

Goodheart-Willcox Publisher

Figure 15-7. Specifying pages to include in the navigation panel gadget.

Move Down

18. Use the **Move up** and **Move down** buttons to arrange the pages in the list in this order: Welcome, Team News, Denver Team Members, and Marketing Materials.
19. Highlight the Denver Team Members page in the list.
20. Click the **Indent** button on the right side of the dialog box. This moves the page down one level, and it will no longer be a top-level page.
21. Click the **OK** button to update the navigation panel gadget. Notice that the Denver Team Members page becomes a sub page of Team News. Also notice that it is the only sub page displayed because no other sub pages were manually added to the list.
22. Click the **Close** button to exit edit mode for the site layout.
23. Close the page or tab to close the site.

Indent

Close

Lesson 15-2

Adding Gadgets to the Sidebar

Gadgets in the sidebar will be displayed on every web page within the site. As a result, a user should select sidebar gadgets with care, making sure that the gadgets will not distract from the content of individual pages in the site.

Adding a Countdown of Days

1. Log in to your Google Mail account.
2. Click the **More** link, and click **Even More** in the drop-down list.
3. Click **Sites** in the **Home & Office** area of the new tab or window to display the Sites page.
4. Click the name of the M&M Events site to display it in a new tab or window.
5. Click the **More** button, and click **Edit site layout** in the drop-down menu.
6. Click the **+** button on the sidebar, as shown in **Figure 15-8.** The **Choose a New Sidebar Item** dialog box is displayed.
7. Scroll to Countdown, and click the **Add** button. The gadget is immediately added to the bottom of the sidebar.
8. Click the countdown gadget in the sidebar to edit its properties. The **Configure Countdown** dialog box is displayed.

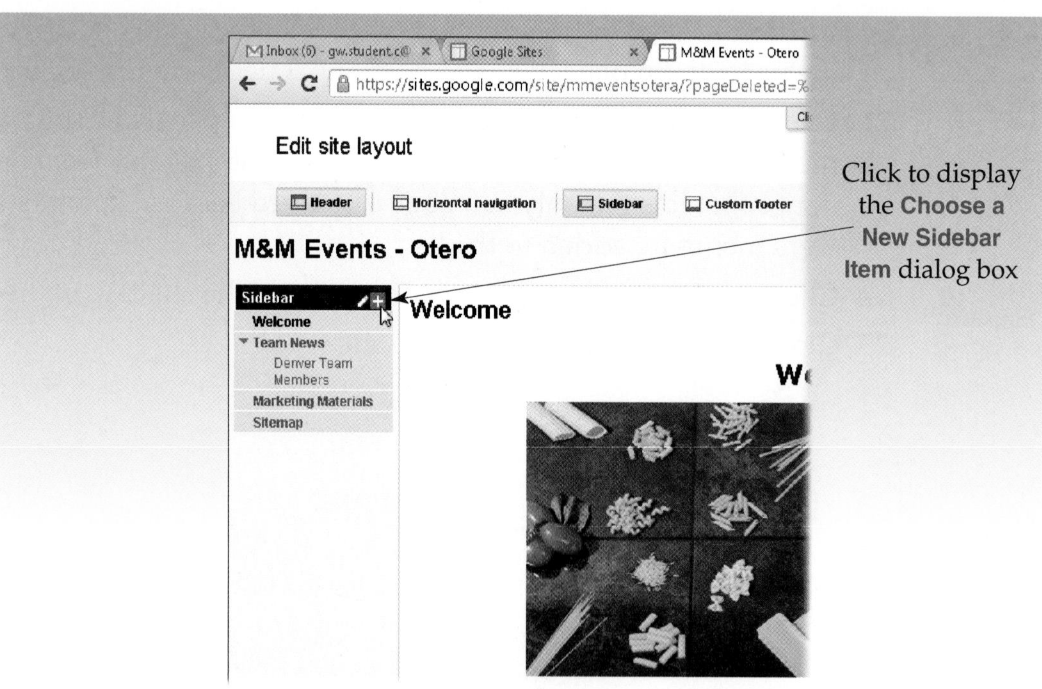

Goodheart-Willcox Publisher

Figure 15-8. To edit the sidebar or to add an item to it, click the **+** button.

9. Click in the **Event:** text box, and enter Company Retreat.
10. Click the **Choose date** link next to **Event date:**. A minicalendar is displayed.
11. Click a date that is no more than three weeks from today.
12. Click the **OK** button to update the gadget. The countdown displays the number of days until the date selected.

Tip After the event has occurred, the countdown will display the number of days *since* the event. To prevent the site from appearing outdated, change the countdown to a new event or remove it from the sidebar after the event has occurred.

Adding Text

13. Click the **+** button on the sidebar to display the **Choose a New Sidebar Item** dialog box.
14. Scroll to Text, and click the **Add** button. The text gadget is immediately added to the bottom of the sidebar gadget. Since it is currently empty, the gadget will be very small.
15. Hover the cursor over the text gadget. When it is highlighted, click to edit the gadget. The **Configure Text Box** dialog box is displayed, as shown in **Figure 15-9.**
16. Click in the **Title:** text box, and enter Remember… as the title.

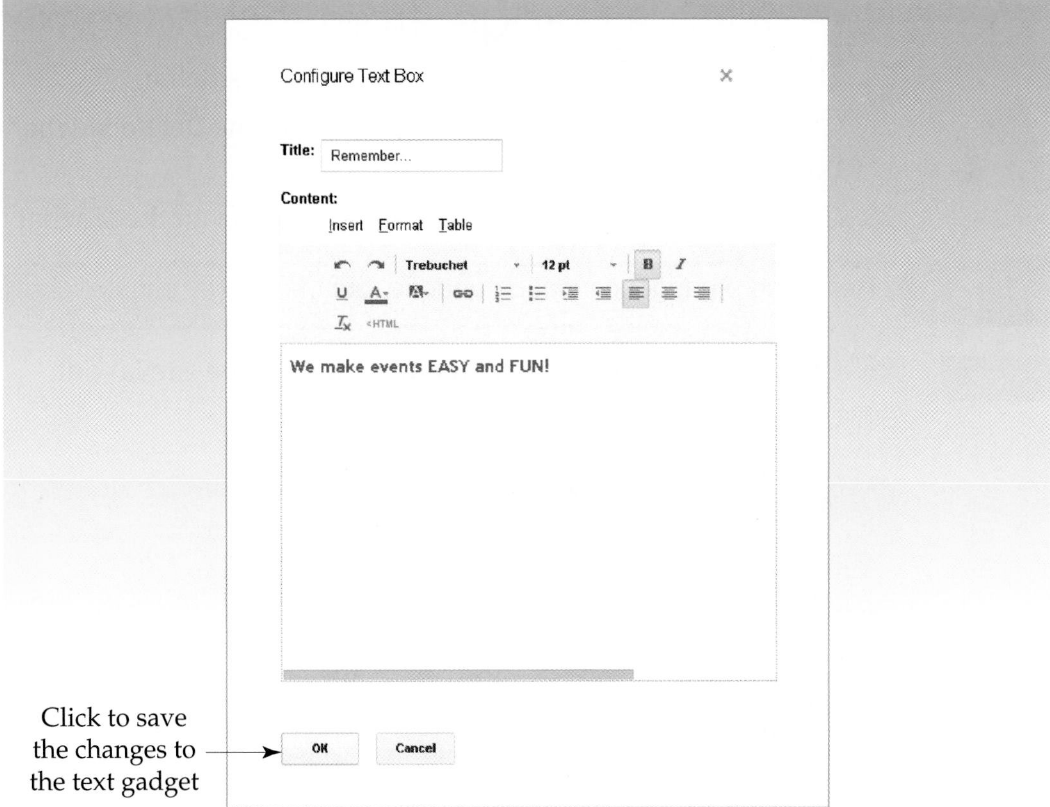

Goodheart-Willcox Publisher

Figure 15-9. Adding a text box gadget to the sidebar.

17. Click in **Content:** text box, and enter We make events EASY and FUN!.
18. Use the text formatting tools to format the text as needed.
19. Click the **OK** button to update the gadget.

Rearranging Gadgets on the Sidebar

20. Hover the cursor over the text gadget.
21. When the gadget is highlighted, click and hold, then drag the gadget to the top above the navigation panel gadget.
22. Release the cursor to relocate the gadget.

Tip If you have trouble moving a gadget to the top location, try moving down the gadgets that appear above the one you are trying to move.

Changing the Location of the Sidebar

23. Click the pencil button on the sidebar to display the **Edit sidebar** dialog box, as shown in **Figure 15-10.**
24. Click the **On the right** radio button. This places the sidebar on the right-hand side of the site page.
25. Click the **OK** button to reposition the sidebar.

Removing a Gadget from the Sidebar

26. Hover the cursor over the text gadget in the sidebar.
27. Click the **X** that is on the gadget's title bar. The **Delete sidebar item** dialog box is displayed.
28. Click the **OK** button. The gadget is removed from the sidebar.

Tip Removing a gadget cannot be undone, but the gadget can be recreated.

29. Click the **Close** button to exit edit mode for the site layout.
30. Close the page or tab to close the site.

Goodheart-Willcox Publisher

Figure 15-10. Setting the location for the sidebar.

Lesson 15-3

Horizontal Navigation Bar

A horizontal navigation bar can replace the sidebar as the navigation tool for a website. It can also be used in conjunction with the sidebar. If both are used, it can be helpful to include pages in just the navigation bar.

Adding a Horizontal Navigation Bar

1. Log in to your Google Mail account.
2. Click the **More** link, and click **Even More** in the drop-down list.
3. Click **Sites** in the **Home & Office** area of the new tab or window to display the Sites page.
4. Click the name of the M&M Events site to display it in a new tab or window.
5. Click the **More** button, and click **Edit site layout** in the drop-down menu.
6. Click the **Horizontal Navigation** button on the site layout toolbar. This enables the horizontal navigation bar gadget on the site. The bar appears below the site name.
7. Hover the cursor over the horizontal navigation bar gadget until it is highlighted and click. The **Configure navigation** dialog box is displayed, which is similar to the one used to modify the navigation panel gadget in the sidebar.
8. Click the **Add page** link. The **Select page to add** dialog box appears. This is the same dialog box used to add pages to the navigation panel gadget.
9. Select the Denver Team Members page, and then click the **OK** button.
10. Click the **Add page** link, select the Team News page, and click the **OK** button.
11. Click the **OK** button to close the **Configure navigation** dialog box. There are three navigation buttons at the top of the page, as shown in **Figure 15-11.**

Tip In most cases, the same pages are not listed in the sidebar *and* the horizontal navigation bar.

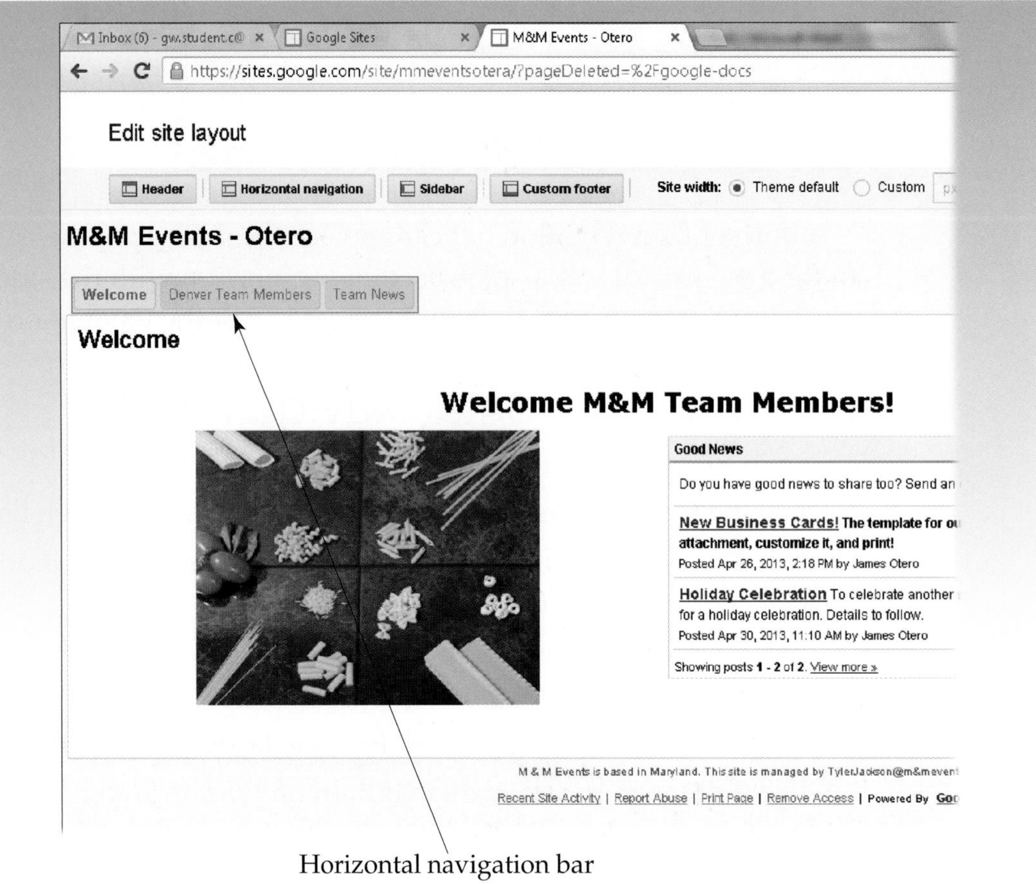

Goodheart-Willcox Publisher

Figure 15-11. The horizontal navigation bar has been enabled for the site.

Customizing the Navigation Bar Look

12. Click the navigation bar gadget to display the **Configure navigation** dialog box.
13. Click the **Tabs** radio button in the **Style** area at the bottom of the dialog box.
14. Click the **OK** button to update the gadget. The page links in the horizontal navigation bar now appear as tabs instead of buttons. Functionality is the same.
15. Click the **Close** button to exit edit mode for the site layout.
16. Close the page or tab to close the site.

Close

Lesson 15-4

Custom Site Header and Footer

Adding a company name and logo to the site header area can ensure that visitors will know which company's site they are visiting even if they begin on a page other than the home page. Text, images, or links can be added to the footer area of the site as well.

Adding a Header to a Google Site

1. Navigate to the student companion website (www.g-wlearning.com/informationtechnology/), and download the M-M Logo data file to your working folder. This is a PNG image file.
2. Log in to your Google Mail account.
3. Click the **More** link, and click **Even More** in the drop-down list.
4. Click **Sites** in the **Home & Office** area of the new tab or window to display the Sites page.
5. Click the name of the M&M Events site to display it in a new tab or window.
6. Click the **More** button, and click **Edit site layout** in the drop-down menu.
7. Hover the cursor over the header until it is highlighted and click. The **Configure site header** dialog box is displayed, as shown in **Figure 15-12.**

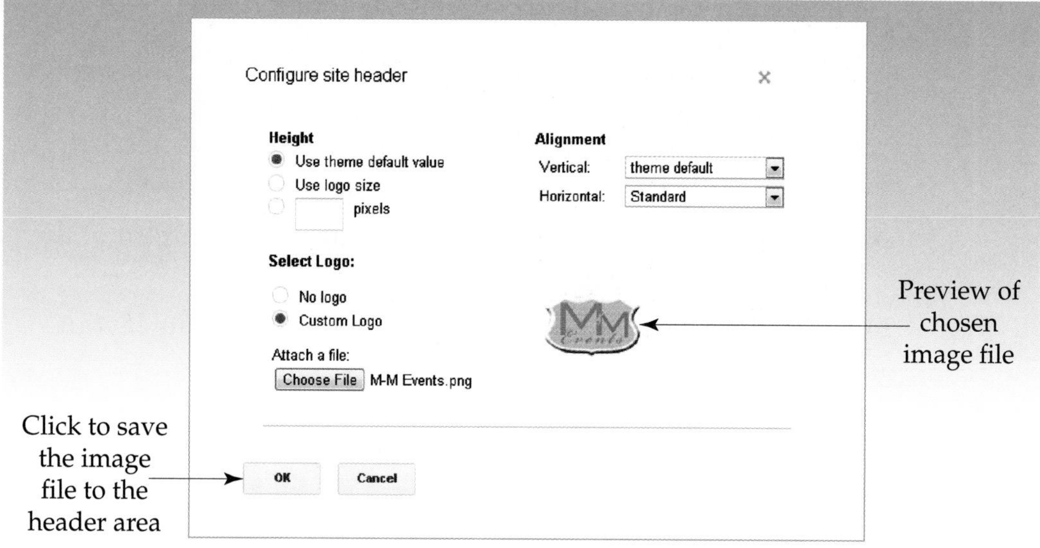

Goodheart-Willcox Publisher

Figure 15-12. Adding a logo image to the site header.

8. Click the **Custom Logo** radio button.
9. Click the **Choose File** button. A standard file-open dialog box is displayed.
10. Navigate to your working folder, select the M-M Logo.png data file, and open it. A preview of the file appears in the **Configure Site Header** dialog box.

Tip To remove an existing image, click the **No logo** radio button in the **Configure Site Header** dialog box.

11. Click the **OK** button. The logo is added to the site header.

Close

12. Click the **Close** button to exit edit mode for the site layout.
13. Close the page or tab to close the site.

Adding a Footer to a Google Site

14. Log in to your Google Mail account.
15. Click the **More** link, and click **Even More** in the drop-down list.
16. Click **Sites** in the **Home & Office** area of the new tab or window to display the Sites page.
17. Click the name of the M&M Events site to display it in a new tab or window.
18. Click the **More** button, and click **Edit site layout** in the drop-down menu.
19. Click the **Custom Footer** button on the site layout toolbar. This enables the footer gadget on the site.
20. Move the cursor to the bottom of the page where the Click to edit custom footer text is displayed until the footer area is highlighted, as shown in **Figure 15-13,** and click. The **Edit site footer** dialog box is displayed.
21. Click in the text box, and enter M & M Events is based in Maryland. This site is managed by TylerJackson@m&mevents.com.
22. Use the text-formatting tools to format the text as needed. For example, a footer is often set in a small type size.
23. Click the **OK** button. The footer appears at the bottom of the page, just above the Google footer.

Close

24. Click the **Close** button to exit edit mode for the site layout.
25. Close the page or tab to close the site.

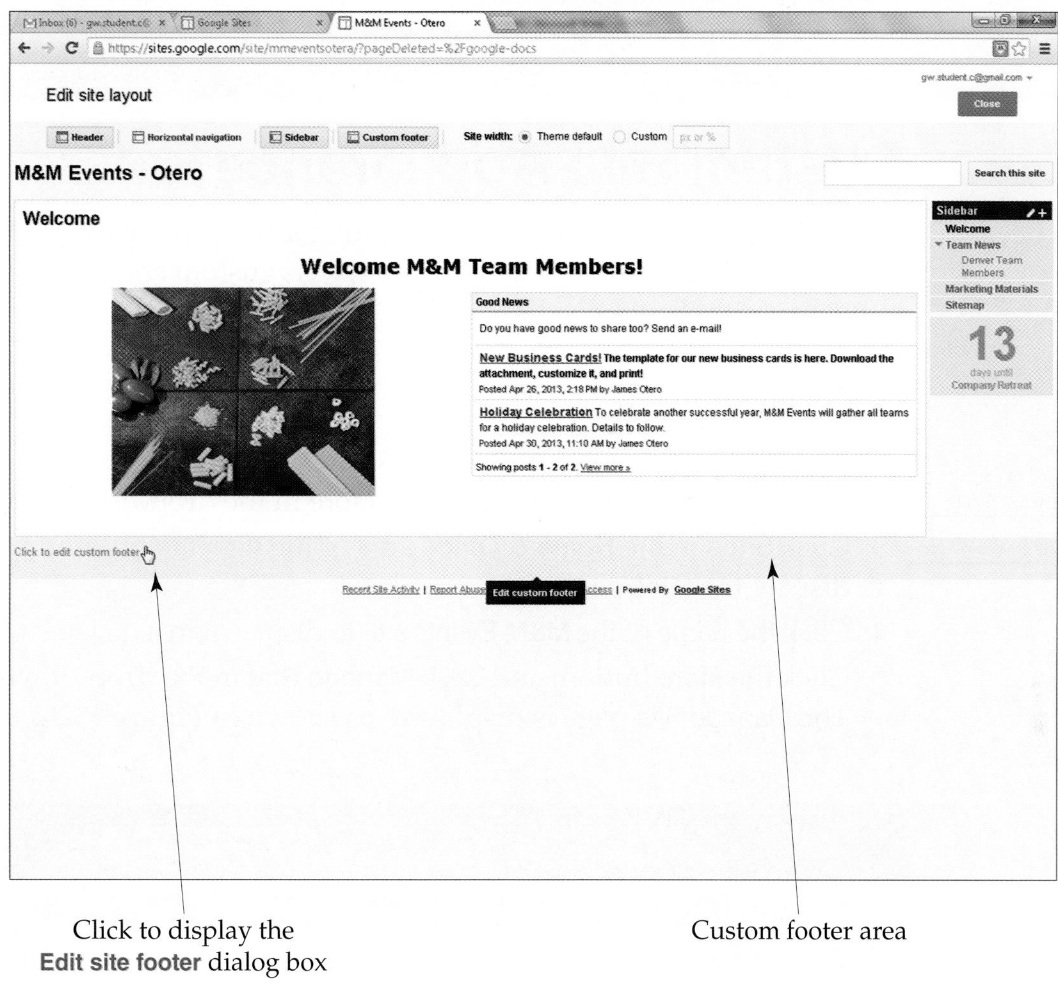

Goodheart-Willcox Publisher

Figure 15-13. Editing the footer for the site.

Lesson 15-5

Custom Site Appearance

A user can select a theme when creating a site. Once chosen, the colors and fonts can be customized. As a user selects custom colors and fonts, a preview of the changes is displayed.

Site Themes

1. Log in to your Google Mail account.
2. Click the **More** link, and click **Even More** in the drop-down list.
3. Click **Sites** in the **Home & Office** area of the new tab or window to display the Sites page.
4. Click the name of the M&M Events site to display it in a new tab or window.
5. Click the **More** button, and click **Manage Site** in the drop-down menu. The Manage Site page is displayed, as shown in **Figure 15-14.**

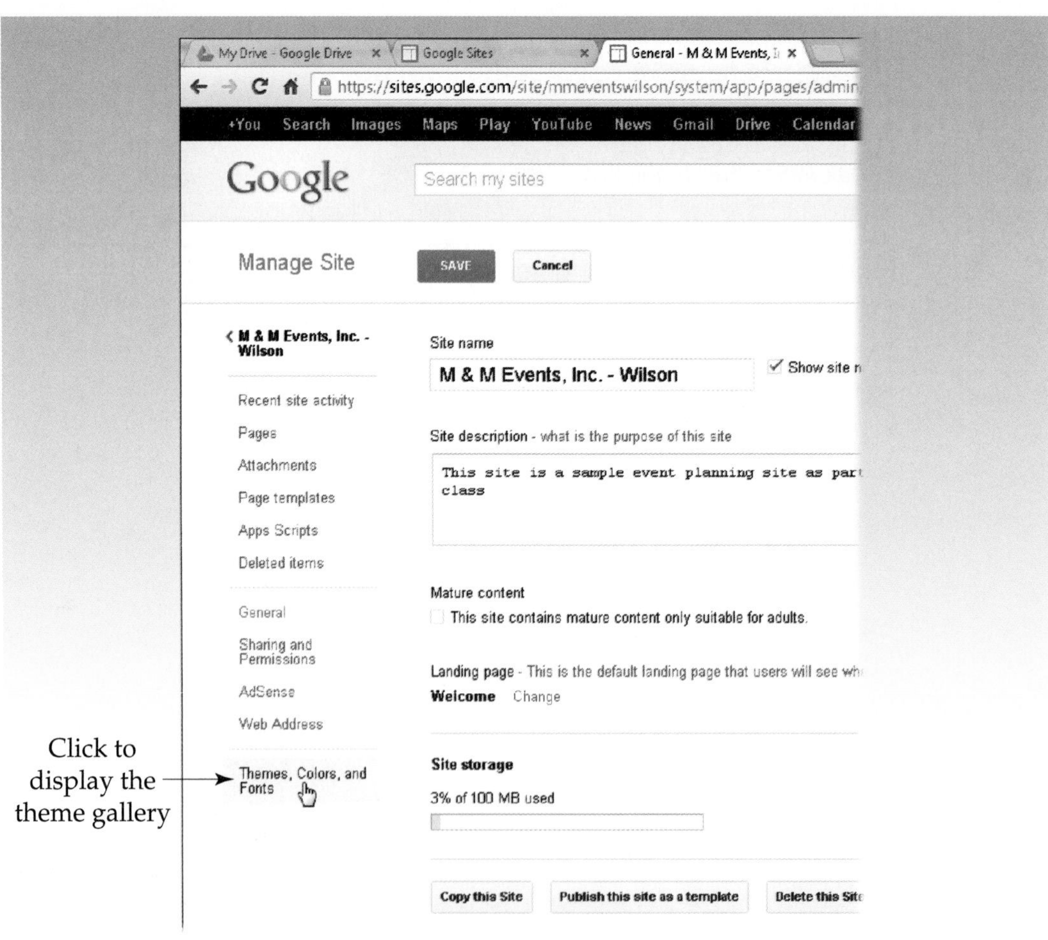

Goodheart-Willcox Publisher

Figure 15-14. Using the **Manage Site** page to select a theme for the site.

6. Click the **Themes, Colors, and Fonts** link in the navigation panel.
7. Click the **Base theme:** button to display a gallery of built-in themes in a pop-up list.
8. Click the thumbnail for the theme to use.

Custom Colors and Fonts

9. Click **Site Header** in the list, and click **Title**. The settings of the header title font are shown to the right of the list, as shown in **Figure 15-15.**
10. In the **Font:** row, click the button next to the right-hand radio button to display a list of fonts.
11. Select a font from the list. The preview automatically updates to reflect the change.

Tip When selecting a font for a site, avoid ones that are too fancy. Simple fonts are easier to read.

12. In the **Color:** row, click the button next to the right-hand radio button to display a color palette.

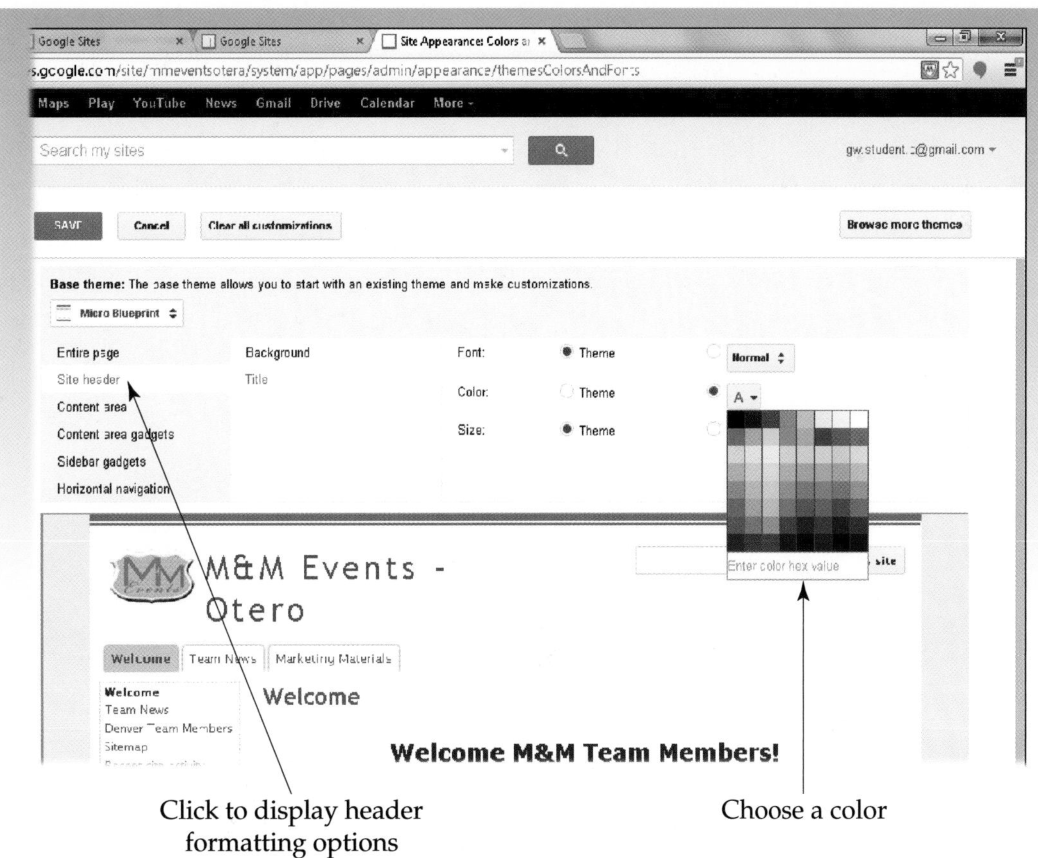

Goodheart-Willcox Publisher

Figure 15-15. Changing the appearance of fonts and colors on a site.

13. Click a color swatch to set the font color. The preview automatically updates to reflect the change.
14. In the **Size:** row, click the button next to the right-hand radio button to display a list of font sizes.
15. Click a size in the list. The preview automatically updates to reflect the change.

SAVE

16. Click the **Save** button to apply the changes. A message appears at the top of the page to confirm the change is saved.
17. Click the site name in the navigation panel to return to the site.
18. Close the page or tab to close the site.

Check Your Google Apps IQ

Now that you have finished this chapter, see what you know about Google Apps by taking the chapter posttest.
www.m.g-wlearning.com
www.g-wlearning.com/informationtechnology/

Skill Review

Answer the following questions on a separate sheet of paper.

1. List elements that encompass the composition of a Google site.
2. What two things should be determined before customizing a site's composition?
3. What is the default gadget contained in the sidebar?
4. Where is the sidebar displayed by default?
5. Describe the horizontal navigation bar.
6. List the three styles for the horizontal navigation bar.
7. How are sub pages displayed in the horizontal navigation bar?
8. Where is the footer section displayed on a Google site?
9. Briefly describe what type of information should be contained in a header or footer on a site.
10. What is a theme, as applied to a Google site?

Lesson Application

These exercises are designed to apply the skills learned in this and previous chapters. General directions are provided, but you will need to draw on your knowledge to determine how to complete each exercise.

Exercise 15-1
Adding Sidebar Gadgets

Edit the M&M Events site. Add the recent site activity gadget to the sidebar. Place the gadget at the top of the sidebar. Arrange the gadgets in the sidebar from the top as: recent site activity, countdown, and text. Remove the navigation panel gadget from the sidebar.

Exercise 15-2 Modifying Page Navigation

Edit the M&M Events site. Add all top level pages to the horizontal navigation bar. Add the announcement post pages below the Team News page, and take the steps necessary to specify them as sub pages on the horizontal navigation bar. Arrange the pages from left to right as: Welcome, Marketing Materials, Team News, and Denver Teams. Set up the horizontal navigation bar to be either boxes or tabs. Compose an e-mail to your instructor explaining how sub pages are displayed.

Exercise 15-3 Changing the Site Appearance

Edit the M&M Events site. Change the selected theme. Customize all of the options in the site header area. Make sure that the font selections and background colors complement the selected theme.

Scenario

The senior class at Wilkins High School needs a website to keep the students and community informed about upcoming events, such as the senior prom and the upcoming college fair. You will build on the work already completed for Wilkins High School in Unit 2. Use the information learned in this unit to complete the activities. As much as possible, these activities should be completed without referring to the chapters for information.

Activities

1. Create a new Google Site named Wilkins Senior Class: *your name*. Choose a template that you feel is appropriate for a high school senior class. Make sure your home page is engaging. Apply and modify a theme as needed. Include an image of the school (you may use an image of your school).
2. Create a What's New announcements page with at least two announcements, one about the prom and one about the college fair. Embed the college fair presentation created at the end of Unit 3 in the announcement. Create a list page to organize information about academic advisors. Include names, office hours, office phone numbers, and grade levels served. Add at least two items to your list. Create a file cabinet page with three folders: Prom, Fair, and Yearbooks. Include at least one link or document on the page and in each folder.
3. Create a new page, and insert the college fair form created at the end of Unit 3. Adjust the size of the gadget to make sure the entire form is visible. Create a new page, and insert the Wilkins School calendar created at the end of Unit 2.
4. Design an appropriate navigation system for the site using a combination of the sidebar and the horizontal navigation bar. Do not display the individual announcements in the navigation system. Add a public dictionary gadget to the sidebar. In the site footer, enter This site is maintained by *your full name*.
5. Customize the colors and fonts used in the site header. Add a countdown to the sidebar. Count down to either the prom or to the college fair. Make sure a label is included to indicate what the countdown shows. Share the completed site with your instructor.

Other Google Tools

Google Apps includes other tools to complete many types of tasks, including the well-known Google search engine. Google Photos allows a user to upload images, organize them in albums, and share them with other users. Using Google Maps and Google Earth, people can explore places all around the world. Google Maps allows users to get directions to or from or general information about places. With Google Earth, users can view a three-dimensional version of a place. There are even apps that allow users to explore the Moon and Mars. Google News and Google Alerts can help users stay informed. Google News is a single, customizable web page that provides news from many sources. Google Alerts sends e-mail to users whenever new information about specific topics is posted on the web. People can use SketchUp to develop three-dimensional models.

Chapters

Chapter 16

Google Photos

Objectives

After completing this chapter, you will be able to:

- **Upload** images to a Google Photos album.
- **Use** basic editing tools, such as cropping and rotating, on images in a Google Photos album.
- **Add** captions and details to images in a Google Photos album.
- **Manage** a Google Photos album, including organizing images and playing a slide show.
- **Share** albums and individual images.

alexmillos/Shutterstock.com

Check Your Google Apps IQ

Before you begin this chapter, see what you already know about Google Apps by taking the chapter pretest.

www.m.g-wlearning.com
www.g-wlearning.com/informationtechnology/

Using the Google Photos

Google Photos is a free tool that allows people to upload and share images and videos. Images can be organized into albums that can be kept private or shared with specific people. Images can be edited as well. A user can also add captions and tags to images. A user can add the images in Google Photos to other Google Drive apps files, such as slide shows, documents, and Google Sites.

To access Google Photos, a user first logs into his or her Gmail account. The user must click the **More** link at the top of the Mail page, then **Photos** in the drop-down list. Then the Google Photos home page is displayed. You must be a member of Google+ to access Google Photos.

The Google Photos home page includes three main tabs, as seen in **Figure 16-1: Highlights**, **Photos**, and **Albums**. Google automatically adds images to the **Highlights** tab based on an analysis of the quality of the images and the people in the images. The **Photos** tab includes all of the images the user has uploaded to Google Photos. The **Albums** tab is a collection of all of the Google Photos albums created by the user.

Goodheart-Willcox Publisher

Figure 16-1. The Google Photos home page consists of three basic sections.

Working with Images

A user can upload images to Google Photos that are stored on a computer or a device. Devices include digital cameras, CDs, DVDs, and memory cards. Uploaded images can be edited. Metadata can be added to uploaded images.

Editing Images

A user can make edits to images, from a few small changes to many large alterations. Along the top of the image-editing window are four tabs—**Basic Edits**, **Effects**, **Decorate**, and **Text**—each containing a group of editing tools.

The **Basic Edits** tab is displayed by default when the image-editing window is displayed. In this tab, a user can crop, rotate, and resize images. To ***crop*** an image is to trim it outside of a specified rectangular area. The basic editing tools also include the ability to adjust the exposure and colors of an image and to work with the sharpness of the image.

The options in the **Effects** tab are applied to the entire image. An ***effect,*** sometimes called a *filter,* is applied to an image to alter the visual appearance. The effects available include the option to convert a color image to black and white, apply a tint, or even make it look like a heat map. There are more than 20 different effects available. A user can apply multiple effects to a photo, but they must be applied one at a time.

Using the **Decorate** tab, a user can introduce elements to an image. To ***decorate*** an image in Google Photos is to add drawings, paint, and similar elements to the image. For example, masks, mustaches, and speech bubbles can be added to an image. The options are grouped by category.

The **Text** tab provides users with the ability to add text directly to the image. The user enters the desired text, and then can move the text to the appropriate space on the image, the border of the image, or a decoration element such as a speech bubble. The **Text** tab includes many font options. The color and size of the text and each decoration element can be changed by the user.

Adding Metadata to Images

Each photo in an album can be annotated with several details that will be displayed on the **Photo details** panel, as seen in **Figure 16-2.** This information is called metadata. ***Metadata*** are any information attached to the image beyond the data needed to create the image. Some metadata are automatically added to an image by the digital camera used to capture the image. Other metadata can be added. Basic data, such as the file name and the number of pixels that make up an image, are stored when the photo is uploaded. A user can add a caption and locational information to each image.

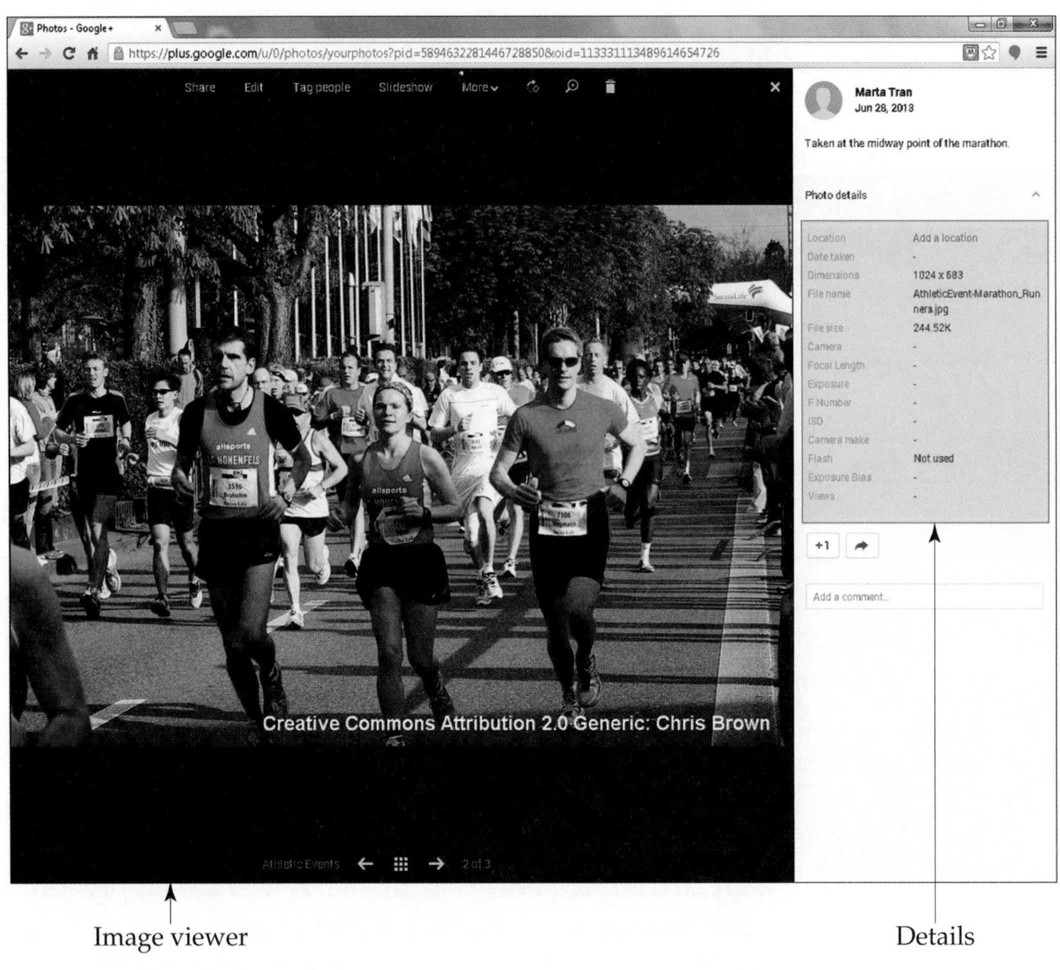

Goodheart-Willcox Publisher

Figure 16-2. The **Photo details** panel contains information, or metadata, about the image.

The intention of a ***caption*** is to describe what is happening in the image. A caption can also include other details that might not be obvious to the viewer. Once added, the caption is displayed under the image whenever it is viewed in a slide show.

A user can tag people in images. To ***tag*** a person in an image means to associate the name of a person with a face in an image. A user can select an appropriate place on an image, such as the person's face, to add a tag. Once added, the name of the person is displayed when a user hovers over the tagged place on the image. Also, the person's name is displayed in the **Photo details** panel.

A location can be associated with an image as well. Using the map tool within Google Photos, a user can search for a location as specific as a street address or as broad as a continent. A user can also search for landmarks such as the White House or the Taj Mahal. Once found, the location can be associated with the image. A minimap is displayed in the **Photo details** panel with the location identified by a red marker.

Working with Albums

Albums are used in Google Photos to organize images. When a user selects an album, thumbnails of each image it contains are displayed. Information about the album is visible above the thumbnails. Options are displayed on the upper-right side of the window. These provide a user with several options to take action on the group of images.

The **Share** button allows a user to provide access for specific people to view his or her album. People in images can also be tagged at the album level using the **Tag people** button. Within an album, a user can further organize his or her images. The **Organize** button provides a user with the option to rearrange the order of the images in an album. Also, images can be uploaded from a computer or other device to that specific album.

A drop-down menu to the right-hand side of the **Add photos** button includes several options that will impact all of the images in the album. The **Slideshow** option can be used to display all of the images in an album as a slide show. All of the images from an album can be downloaded from this menu. Also, an album can be deleted by selecting the **Move album to the trash** option in the menu.

Sharing Albums and Images

A user can share entire albums or individual images. When a user decides to share an album, Google automatically suggests recipients. The **Share Album** dialog box includes groups of potential recipients. A user can choose from these groups. Contact groups from the user's Google Contacts are listed as suggested recipients. Any people identified in the image with tags are automatically included as suggested recipients. A user can also enter the e-mail addresses of others not listed in the suggestions.

An album can be set up to receive images from others. A user can invite the people with whom he or she has shared an album to contribute images to it. This can be helpful if several people are taking photographs for a single event, for example.

Licenses for Images and other Creative Works

Copyright is automatically assigned to a work as soon as it is in tangible form, including an image, whether it is in print, on the Internet, or in any other form or media. A ***copyright*** acknowledges ownership of a work and specifies that only the owner has the right to sell or use the work or to give permission for someone else to sell or use it. A copyright statement or symbol is *not* required for a work to be copyrighted, and lack of a symbol does *not* mean the work is free to use. Most information on the Internet is copyrighted, including images, documents, music, and videos. If someone shares an image with you, it does not give you the right to use that image without getting permission from the owner.

In many cases, an image may have one of several Creative Commons licenses assigned to it. ***Creative Commons licensing*** allows a user to maintain his or her copyright and grant permission for others to change, share, or reuse it for commercial purposes. A user can also allow reuse with attribution. ***Attribution*** is a statement of copyright ownership for the work. This license means that the image can be used by others as long as the owner is given credit for it.

Lesson 16-1

Uploading Images

A new album can be created as an image is uploaded. If a name is not given to the album, it is named with today's date. An image can also be uploaded to an existing album.

1. Navigate to the student companion website (www.g-wlearning.com/informationtechnology/), and download the Chapter 16 data file to your working folder. This is a ZIP file. Unzip the contents of the file into your working folder.
2. Log in to your Google Mail account.
3. Click the **More** link, and click **Photos** in the drop-down list. The Photos page is displayed.
4. Click the **Upload Photos** link. A dialog box appears for uploading images, as shown in **Figure 16-3.**

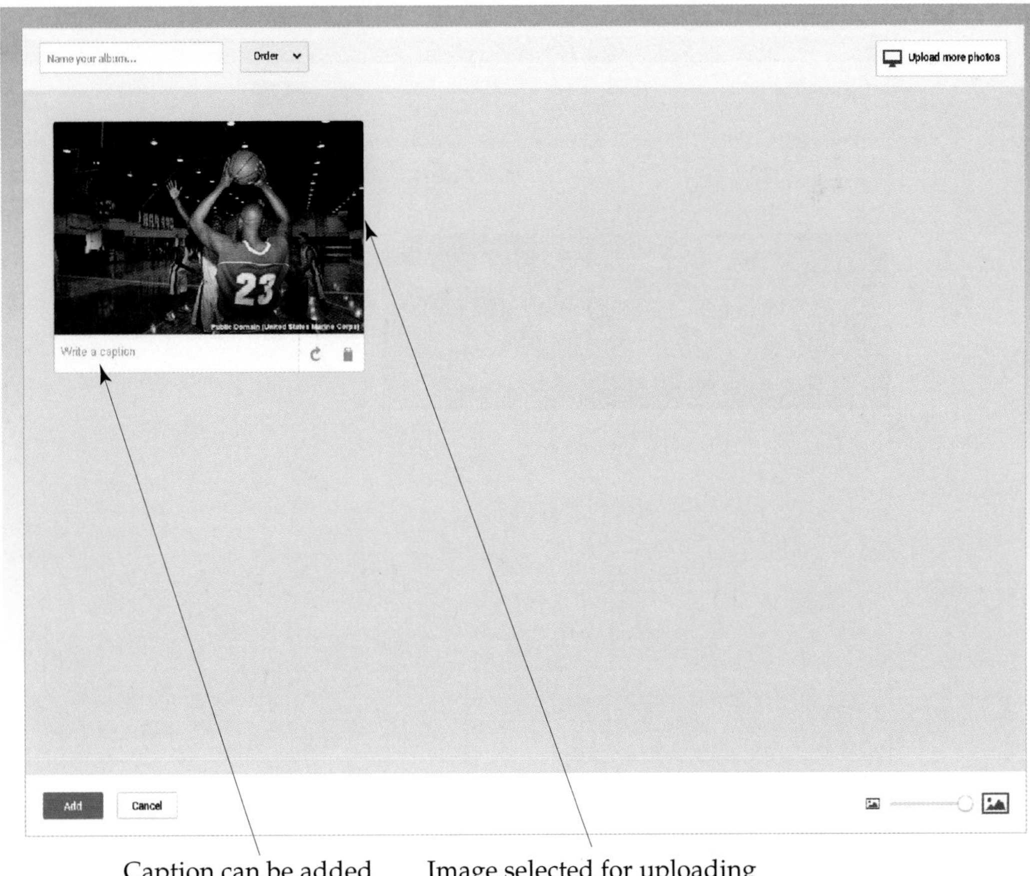

Goodheart-Willcox Publisher

Figure 16-3. Photos can be uploaded by dragging and dropping them into this dialog box.

5. Click anywhere in the middle of the dialog box to display a standard file-open dialog box.
6. Navigate to your working folder. Hold the [Ctrl] key, select AthleticEvent-basketball.jpg and AthleticEvent-Marathon_Runners.jpg, and click the **Open** button. The image files are uploaded and displayed as thumbnails.
7. Click in the text box that appears at the top of the dialog box, and enter Athletic Events as the name of the new album.

Add

8. Click the **Add** button. A new album named Athletic Events is created and displayed, as shown in **Figure 16-4.**
9. A dialog box is displayed offering the opportunity to tag the images. Click the **Skip Tagging** button; tagging images is covered later in this chapter.
10. A dialog box is displayed offering the opportunity to share the album. Click the **Cancel** button so the album is not shared.
11. Click the **Albums** tab. The Athletic Events album is displayed on the tab.

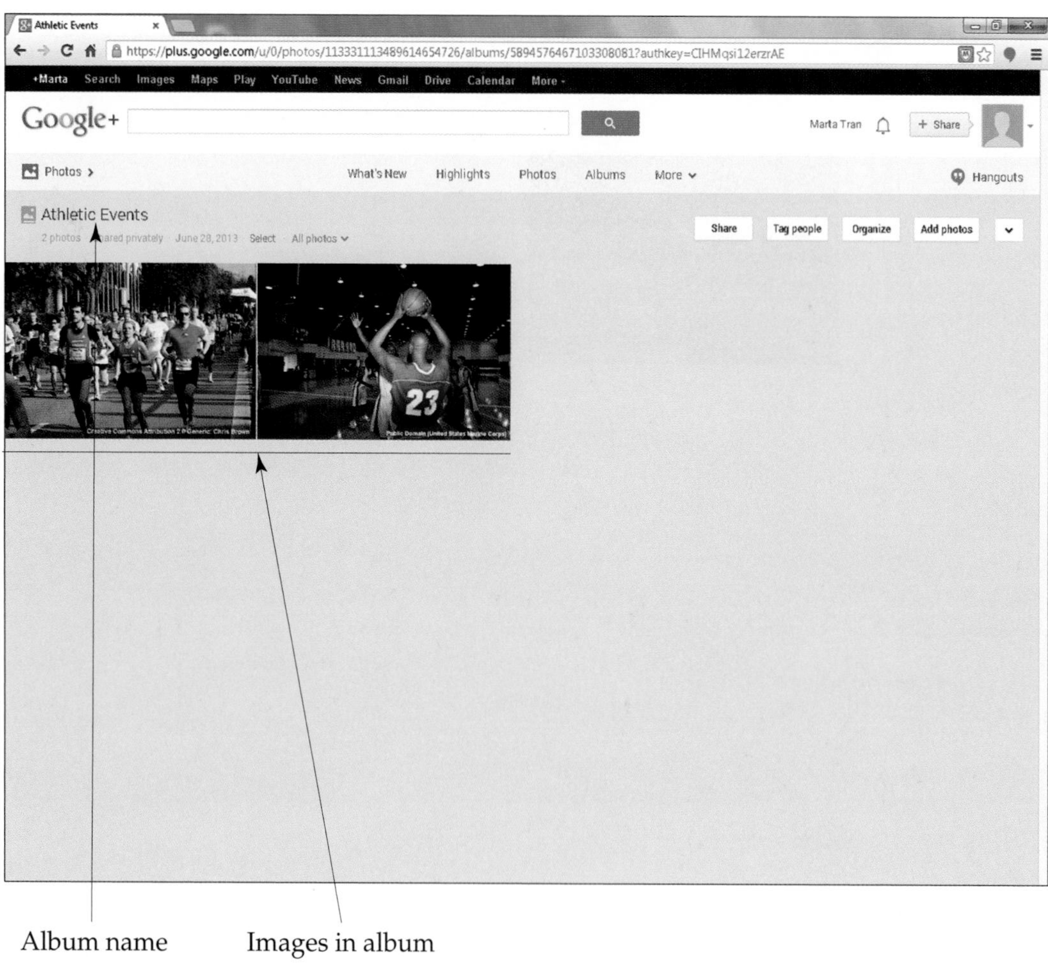

Goodheart-Willcox Publisher

Figure 16-4. The new album is created, and the photos have been added to it.

12. Click the album to display its contents.
13. Close the tab or window to close Google Photos.

Tip

Images can be uploaded directly to an album by displaying the album, clicking the **Organize** button, and then clicking the **Add More Photos** button.

Lesson 16-2

Editing Images

Editing tools available include those that correct or enhance the image itself. There are also tools that allow the user to introduce images or text to the image. Edits to an image permanently alter the image when saved.

Performing Basic Edits on Images

1. Log in to your Google Mail account.
2. Click the **More** link, and click **Photos** in the drop-down list.
3. Click the **Upload Photos** link, and upload the AthleticEvent-finishingline.jpg image file from your working folder. The photo is added to an album named with today's date.
4. Click the **Photos** tab. All images uploaded to your Google Photos are displayed.
5. Click on the image of the marathon finishing line. It is displayed in a viewer.
6. Click the **Edit** link at the top of the viewer. The image is loaded into an image-editing window.

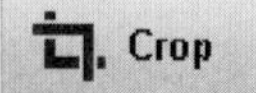

7. Make sure the **Basic Edits** tab is displayed, and click the **Crop** button. A box with circular handles is displayed on top of the image. The portion of the image inside the box will remain after cropping.
8. Drag the handles to resize the box.

The cropping box can be set to standard dimensions, such as 4 × 6 or 5 × 7, by selecting the dimensions from the drop-down menu below the **Crop** button.

9. Click, hold, and drag the box to the section of the image you want to remain, as shown in **Figure 16-5.**
10. Click the **Apply** button below the **Crop** button to apply the cropping.

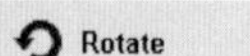

11. Click the **Rotate** button.
12. Click the mouse near the lower-right corner of the image, drag to the upper-left corner, and release. The image is straightened to the line drawn by the mouse and cropped. The **Straighten:** slider below the **Rotate** button indicates the number of degrees of rotation. The slider can be dragged to change the setting.

Goodheart-Willcox Publisher

Figure 16-5. Cropping a photo removes the portion of the image outside of the crop box.

Tip The image can be rotated 90° left or right, or flipped horizontally or vertically using the buttons above the **Straighten:** slider.

13. Click the **Apply** button to apply the change in rotation.

Adding an Effect to an Image

14. Click the **Effects** tab.
15. Click the Polaroid® Plus effect to preview the image with the effect. An expanded area containing settings for the effect also appears below the effect name.
16. Click the **Fade** slider below the effect name, and drag it right and left. The fading effect on the image changes in the preview. Each effect has different options; experiment with some to get the image just right.
17. Click the **Apply** button to add the effect to the image.

Decorating an Image

18. Click the **Decorate** tab.
19. Click **Speech Bubbles** to display thumbnails of the types of speech bubbles.
20. Click the last speech bubble. The sticker is applied to the image, and the **Sticker Properties** dialog box is displayed, as shown in **Figure 16-6.**
21. Click the slider on the color palette, and drag it down to change the color of the sticker to black.

Tip A color can also be selected by dragging the circular node on the color palette.

22. Click the sticker, and drag it to the bottom white border created by the Polaroid effect.
23. Drag the handles to resize the speech bubble. Keep it within the white border.
24. Click anywhere off of the sticker to deselect it.

Text

25. Click the **Text** tab.
26. Click in the text box at the top, and enter a short phrase about the image. For example, Running Wild! may be a good fit for the marathon.
27. Click a font name in the list. Select a font that looks like handwriting.
28. Click the **Add** button. The text is added to the image, and the **Text Properties** window is displayed, as shown in **Figure 16-7.**
29. Click the slider on the color palette, and drag it down to change the color of the text to black.
30. Click the text, and drag it to the bottom white border created by the Polaroid effect. Place it next to the speech bubble sticker.

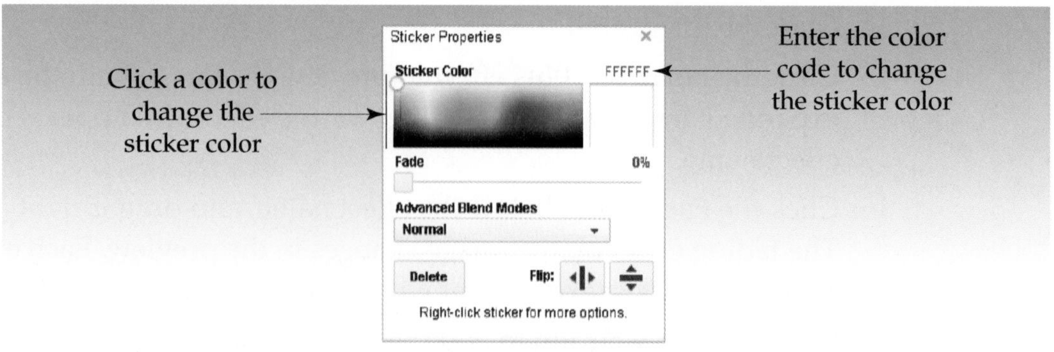

Goodheart-Willcox Publisher

Figure 16-6. Adding a sticker to an image is a way to personalize the image.

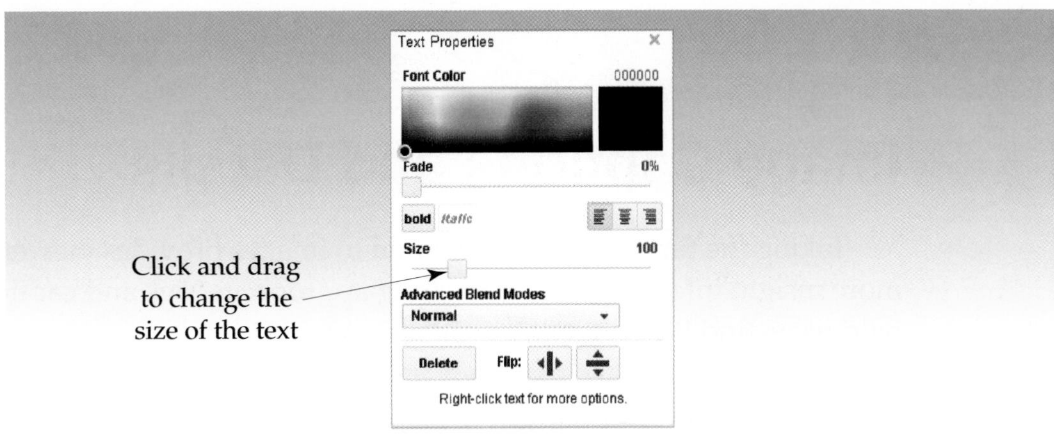

Goodheart-Willcox Publisher

Figure 16-7. Text can be added to an image as a way to personalize the image or add a description.

31. Click the rotation handle in the top-middle, and drag to rotate the text.
32. Drag the **Size** slider in the **Text Properties** dialog box left or right to change the size of the text.

Tip The sizing handles on the text object can be used to resize the text.

Save Your Photo

33. Click the **Save** button. A dialog box appears asking to confirm the action.
34. Click the **Replace** button. This saves the changes in the original image file and closes the image-editing window.
35. Click the close button (**X**) to close the image viewer.
36. Click the **Albums** tab, and open the Athletic Events album. The updated image appears in the album.
37. Close the tab or window to close Google Photos.

Lesson 16-3

Image Captions and Details

Taking the time to add information to images provides viewers with more insight into the image. Attaching appropriate tags and captions can help users find the image.

Adding a Caption to an Image

1. Log in to your Google Mail account.
2. Click the **More** link, and click **Photos** in the drop-down list.
3. Click the **Albums** tab. The Athletic Events album is displayed as a thumbnail.
4. Click the Athletic Events album to open it.
5. Click one of the marathon photos to display it in the viewer.
6. Click the **Add caption** link in the right-hand panel. The link changes to a text box.
7. Enter Taken at the midway point of the marathon. as the caption.
8. Click the close button (**X**) to close the image viewer.

Tagging Images

9. Click the unedited marathon image to display it in the viewer.
10. Click the **Tag people** link at the top of the viewer. A circular region appears around the cursor as you move the mouse.
11. Move the mouse over a face in the image, and click. A dialog box is displayed for entering a name.
12. Click in the text box in the dialog box, and enter your name, as shown in **Figure 16-8.** The names of tagged faces are added to the right-hand panel below the caption.
13. Click the **Done** button to finish tagging.
14. Move the cursor over the image. When the cursor is over the face that was tagged, a label appears with the name.
15. Click the **X** that appears in the label displayed when hovering the cursor over a tagged face. A message appears asking to confirm the deletion.
16. Click the **Yes** button to remove the tag.

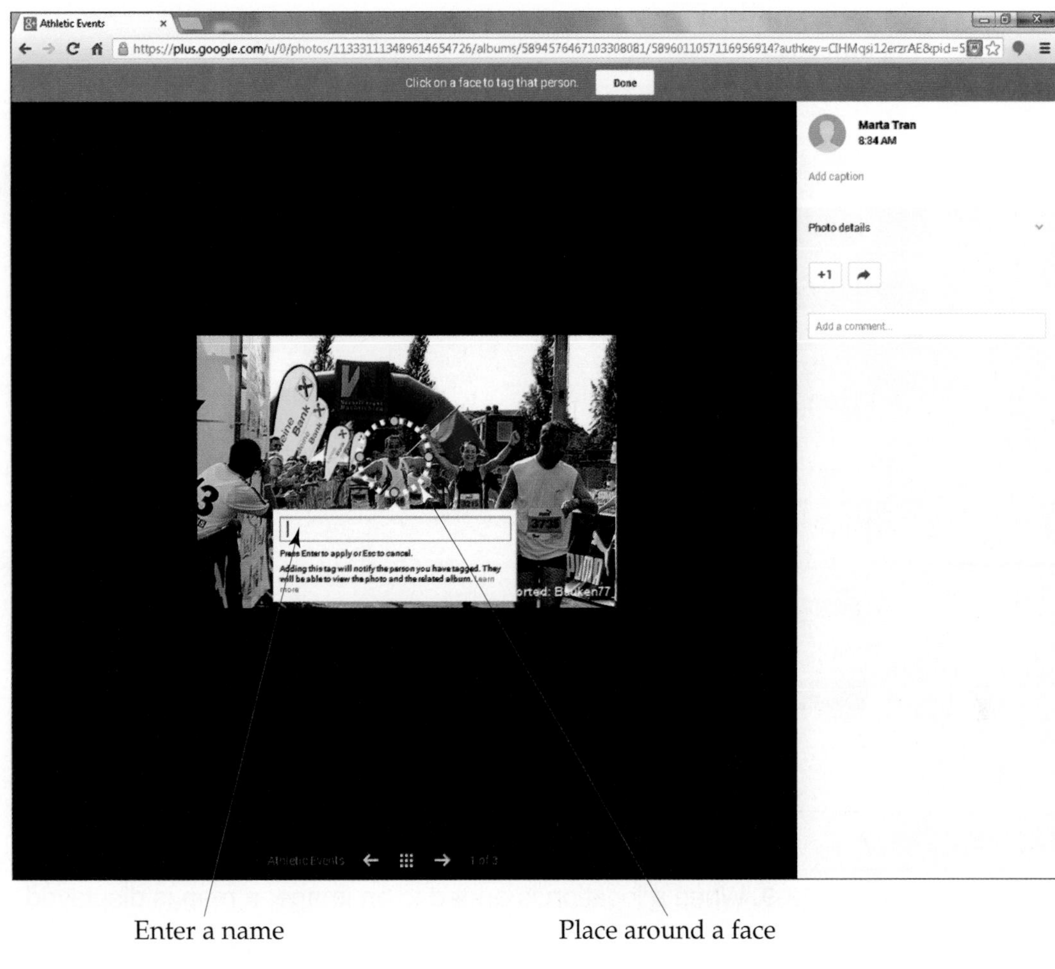

Goodheart-Willcox Publisher

Figure 16-8. A tag for a person can be added to an image. The tag will be visible when a viewer moves the cursor over the area that is tagged.

Adding a Location to an Image

17. Click **Photo details** in the right-hand panel to expand the **Photo details** panel.
18. Click the **Add a location** link. The **Add location** dialog box is displayed, as shown in **Figure 16-9.**
19. Click in the text box at the top of the dialog box, and enter the ZIP code for your city.
20. Click the **Save** button to assign the location to the image. A minimap is displayed in the **Photo details** panel.

Tip To edit the photo location, click the **Edit** link that appears on the minimap.

22. Click the close button (**X**) to close the image viewer.
23. Close the tab or window to close Google Photos.

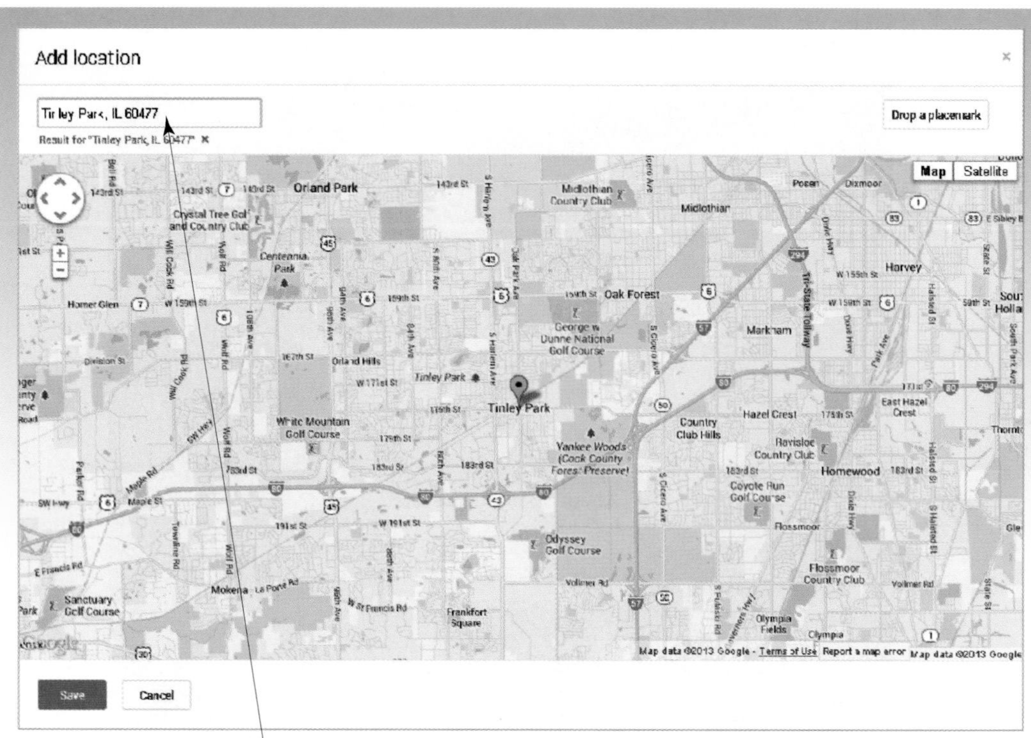

Enter an exact address
or a broad description

Goodheart-Willcox Publisher

Figure 16-9. When a location is added to an image, a map is displayed showing the location.

Lesson 16-4

Working with Albums

The images in an album can be automatically organized, or the user can manually organize the images. Also, all images in an album can be displayed in a slide show.

Organizing an Album

1. Log in to your Google Mail account.
2. Click the **More** link, and click **Photos** in the drop-down list.
3. Click the **Albums** tab. The Athletic Events album is displayed as a thumbnail.
4. Click the Athletic Events album to open it.

Organize

5. Click the **Organize** button. A new page is displayed that is used to sort images, as shown in **Figure 16-10.**

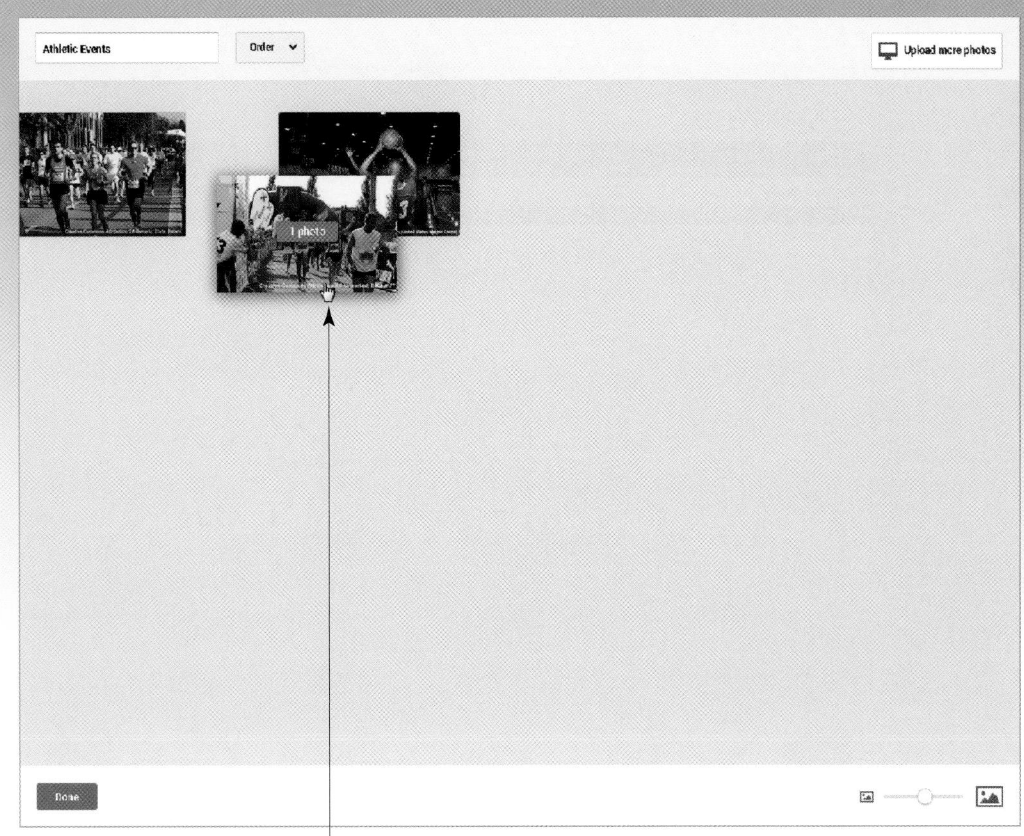

Goodheart-Willcox Publisher

Figure 16-10. The images within an album can be rearranged.

6. Click the last image, drag it to between the other two images, and drop. This rearranges the order of the images.

Tip Hold down the [Ctrl] key to select more than one image to move.

7. Click the **Order** button, and click **By name** in the list. The images are arranged in alphabetical order based on the name of each file. The first (upper-left) image is used as the album cover.
8. Click the **Done** button to close the organizer.
9. Click the **Photos** tab. All images that have been uploaded are displayed.
10. Click any image to display it in the viewer.
11. Click the **More** link to display a drop-down list, and click **Add to album** in the list. The **Copy your photo to...** dialog box is displayed, as shown in **Figure 16-11.**
12. Click in the **New album** text box, and enter My New Album.

To copy an image to an existing album, click the album thumbnail in the **Copy your photo to...** dialog box.

Goodheart-Willcox Publisher

Figure 16-11. Images can be copied between albums. An image can appear in more than one album.

13. Click the **Copy** button. The new album is created, and the image is copied into the album.
14. Click the close button (**X**) to close the image viewer.

Slide Shows

15. Click the **Albums** tab. The Athletic Events album is displayed as a thumbnail.
16. Click the Athletic Events album to open it.
17. Click the down arrow button in the upper-right corner of the page, and click **Slideshow** in the drop-down list that is displayed. The images in the album are displayed in a slide show format, as shown in **Figure 16-12.** Captions, if entered, appear at the bottom of the screen for each image.

Goodheart-Willcox Publisher

Figure 16-12. The images in an album can be viewed as a slide show.

18. Move the cursor to the bottom of the slide show screen. A toolbar is displayed.

19. Click the **Pause** button.

20. Click the **Resume** button. The slide show resumes.
21. Click the **Exit** button to end the slide show.
22. Close the tab or window to close Google Photos.

Lesson 16-5

Sharing Albums and Images

When an album is shared, an e-mail is sent with the album cover and a link to the rest of the album. An individual image can be shared instead of an entire album.

Sharing Albums

1. Log in to your Google Mail account.
2. Click the **More** link, and click **Photos** in the drop-down list.
3. Click the **Albums** tab. The Athletic Events album is displayed as a thumbnail.
4. Click the Athletic Events album to open it.
5. Click the **Share** button, and click **Album** in the drop-down list that is displayed. The **Share album** dialog box is displayed, as shown in **Figure 16-13.**

Share

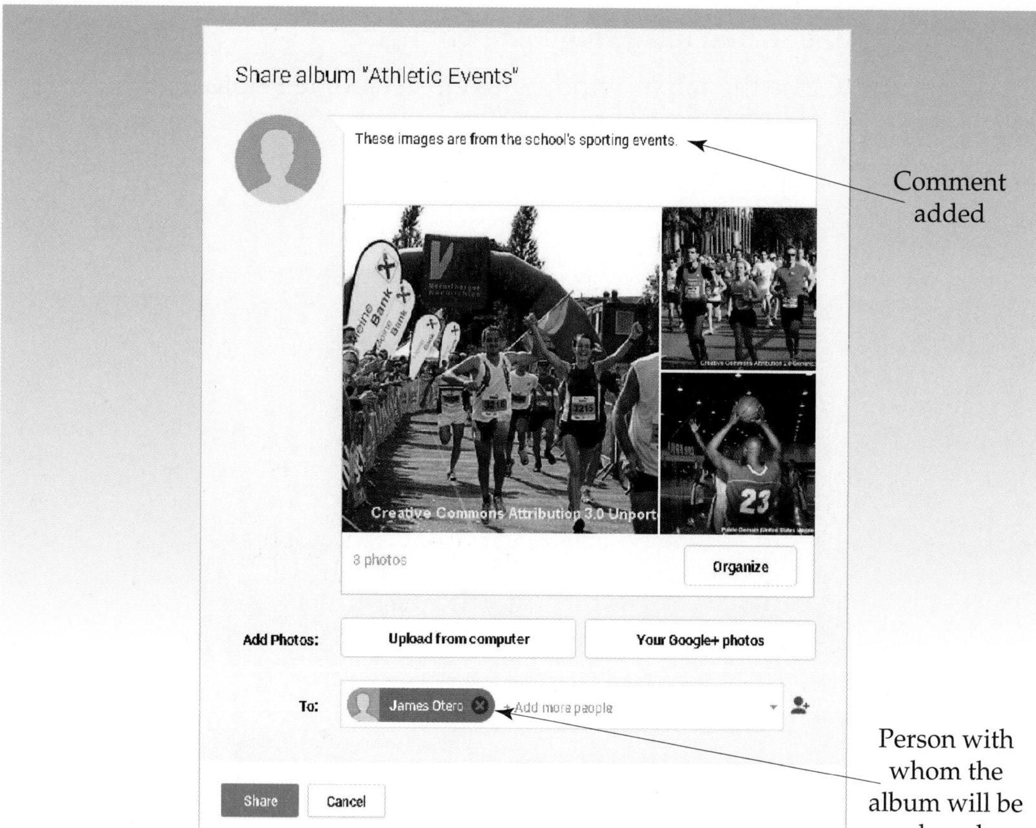

Goodheart-Willcox Publisher

Figure 16-13. An album can be shared with others.

6. Click in the text box at the top of the dialog box, and enter These images are from the school's sporting events.
7. Click in the **To:** text box, and enter the name of your instructor. If your instructor is not a contact, enter his or her e-mail address.

Share

8. Click the **Share** button. An e-mail is sent to everyone listed in the **To:** text box. The e-mail contains a link that can be used to access the shared album.

Sharing an Individual Image

9. Click the **Photos** tab. All images that have been uploaded are displayed.
10. Click any image to display it in the viewer.
11. Click the **Share** link at the top of the viewer.
12. The **Share this photo** dialog box is displayed.
13. Click in the text box at the top of the dialog box, and enter a description of the image.
14. Click in the **To:** text box, and enter the name of your instructor. If your instructor is not a contact, enter his or her e-mail address.

Share

15. Click the **Share** button. An e-mail is sent to everyone listed in the **To:** text box. The e-mail contains the image and a link that can be used to access the shared image for commenting.
16. Close the tab or window to close Google Photos.

Check Your Google Apps IQ

Now that you have finished this chapter, see what you know about Google Apps by taking the chapter posttest.
www.m.g-wlearning.com
www.g-wlearning.com/informationtechnology/

Skill Review

Answer the following questions on a separate sheet of paper.

1. Briefly describe the purpose of Google Photos.
2. What type of Google account must a user have in order to use Google Photos?
3. What does it mean to crop an image?
4. A(n) ______, sometimes called a filter, is applied to an image to alter the visual appearance.
5. What does it mean to decorate an image in Google Photos?
6. Define metadata.
7. What are tags on images in Google Photos?
8. Describe the purpose of an album in Google Photos.
9. Define copyright.
10. Briefly describe Creative Commons licensing.

Lesson Application

These exercises are designed to apply the skills learned in this and previous chapters. General directions are provided, but you will need to draw on your knowledge to determine how to complete each exercise.

Exercise 16-1
Uploading Photos

Before beginning this exercise, navigate to the student companion website (www.g-wlearning.com/informationtechnology/), and download the Exercises Chapter 16 data file to your working folder. This is a ZIP file. Unzip the contents of the file into your working folder. Upload the Wedding-Bouquet.jpg and Wedding-CeremonySite.jpg photographs to a new album named Wedding Highlights. Create the album as part of the uploading process. Once the album is created, add the Wedding-Cake.jpg and Wedding-Rings.jpg images to it.

Using a digital camera, take a photograph of a group of at least four classmates. Download the image to your working folder, and name the file Wedding-Guests.jpg. Upload this image to the Wedding Highlights album.

Organize the images so they appear in this order from left to right: Wedding-CeremonySite, Wedding-Guests, Wedding-Bouquet, Wedding-Cake, Wedding-Rings. Set the cover photo of the album to be the image of wedding rings.

Exercise 16-2
Editing a Photo

Open the Wedding Highlights album, and open the Wedding-Cake image for editing. Rotate the image so the cake is vertical.

Open the Wedding-CeremonySite image for editing. Apply decoration to the image. Select a decoration that will emphasize the area of the image where the ceremony platform is located.

Open the Wedding-Bouquet image for editing. Use the exposure tool to lighten the image. Record the process and settings you used to correct the photo. Compose an e-mail to your instructor describing the exposure tool, how it functions, and what settings you used to correct the photo.

Add captions to all images in the Wedding Highlights album. Add a location to the Wedding-CeremonySite image. Use your town as the location. Tag your classmates in the Wedding-Guests image.

Exercise 16-3
Sharing an Album

Edit the information for the Wedding Highlights album. Share the album with all classmates in the Wedding-Guests image. Select one photo in the album, and share it with your instructor. Compose an e-mail to your instructor listing and describing at least three ways you could use a Google Photos album for personal or educational use.

Chapter 17

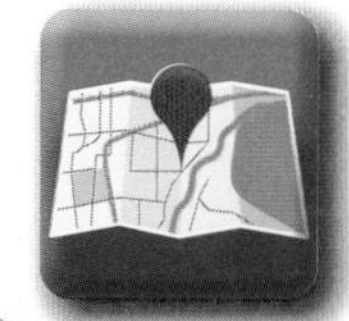

Google Maps

Objectives

After completing this chapter, you will be able to:

- **Search** for and view locations on a map.
- **Use** a map to create travel directions.
- **Create** a custom map.
- **Save** locations and directions to My Maps.
- **Edit** location details in My Maps.
- **Add** lines and shapes to a map.
- **Collaborate** on a map.

alexmillos/Shutterstock.com

Check Your Google Apps IQ

Before you begin this chapter, see what you already know about Google Apps by taking the chapter pretest.

www.m.g-wlearning.com
www.g-wlearning.com/informationtechnology/

Using Google Maps

Google Maps is a service that allows users to search and view basic maps, generate driving directions, and create custom maps that can be shared and edited by others. Maps can also be used to locate and find contact information for local business and landmarks.

The Google Maps page includes three elements: the search text box, the panel, and the map window, as seen in **Figure 17-1.** Users can enter information in the ***search text box*** to get information about locations. The ***panel*** displays textual information and links regarding the searched location. For example, if museums near Chicago, IL is entered in the search text box, a list of museums in Chicago will be displayed in the panel. The panel can also be hidden. The ***map window*** displays the map for the selected location.

Goodheart-Willcox Publisher

Figure 17-1. There are three basic elements to the Google Map page.

Searching in Google Maps

There are multiple ways to search for a location in Google Maps. The search criteria can be specific or general. In any case, a map will be displayed in the map window as a result of a search. An exact street address can be used or two streets that intersect can be entered as well. A user can also enter the name of a city, country, or a continent. For these broader searches, links to places within the search will appear in the panel to encourage further exploration. A user can search the name of a landmark or a business. For example, a user can enter the name of his or her favorite restaurant to have a map to it displayed. While entering criteria in the search text box, autocomplete suggestions appear based on what has been entered. For some landmarks, an exact street address will be displayed in autocomplete that can focus a user's search.

Search results will appear as a marker on the map in the map window and as locational information on the panel. The locational information includes a marker containing a letter to the left of the listing to match a corresponding marker on the map. This is helpful when a search returns more than one result. Depending on the specificity of the location, the location information on the panel can include an exact street address, a website, a phone number, keywords that describe the place, the number of reviews about the place, and a brief portion of a review.

The map window displays locations in three views: map view, satellite view, and street view. The ***map view*** looks like a traditional map, a representation of an area including streets, buildings, parks, and bodies of water. The ***satellite view*** is a satellite image of an area. In both views, the user can pan or zoom into the location using the navigation controls. A user can make additional data visible on maps, including traffic, photographs, weather, videos, and transit information, as seen in **Figure 17-2.**

From either the map or satellite view, a user can get a closer view of a location using the street view. The ***street view*** is an image of a location taken from the point of view of a person standing on the sidewalk. Using the street view, a user can pan the location 360 degrees. In some cases, a user can explore the inside of a building using street view.

Maps can be shared using a link created in Google Maps. The link can be copied and pasted into an e-mail or a text message. The recipient simply clicks the link to display the map.

Getting Directions in Google Maps

Google Maps is often used to get directions between a starting point and a single destination. The ***destination*** is the ending point. A user can add multiple destinations to a single set of directions. Directions can be created as well to reflect the user's mode of transportation including driving, taking public transportation, walking, or biking.

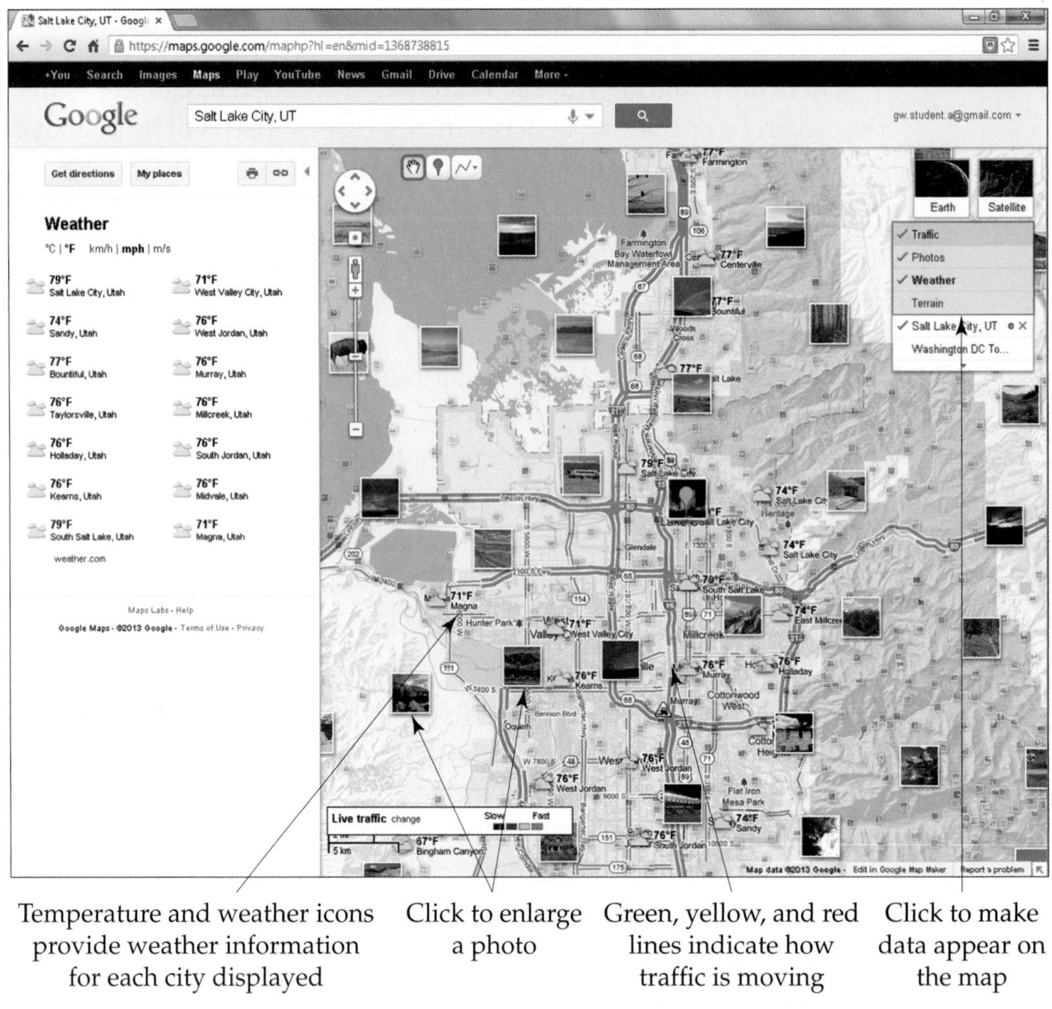

Goodheart-Willcox Publisher

Figure 17-2. Several types of additional information can be displayed on a map.

To get directions, a user clicks the **Get directions** button near the top of the panel. A user enters the address of the starting location in **Start address** text box and the address of the destination in the **End address** text box. Often, the **End address** text box is automatically completed to reflect the location currently displayed in the map window. Autocomplete suggestions will display as a user enters text in the starting and ending address text boxes.

Once the user clicks the **Get Directions** button under the **End address** text box, the directions are displayed in list form in the panel. The route is displayed as a blue line in the map window. Before the first step of the directions, the total miles and trip duration are displayed.

Directions can be printed. Printing a map includes the option of how to show the steps in the directions. Steps are displayed as text by default, but can also appear in a map or street view. A user can choose a view for all of the steps or choose to have certain steps displayed in one view and others in another view. If a part of the directions is especially complex, it can be helpful to include the map or street view for that step or groups of steps.

A user can also choose to include the large map with the route line in the printed map as well.

If the directions have multiple destinations, the destinations can be reordered. This is done by dragging and dropping the destinations in the list. The steps in the directions are automatically adjusted to reflect the new order.

Directions can be shared using a link created in Google Maps. The link can be copied and pasted into an e-mail or a text message. The recipient simply clicks the link to display the directions.

Creating and Sharing Custom Maps and Directions

Google Maps allows for the creation of a custom map that has specific places of interest to a user. A ***custom map*** is one saved by a Google user to his or her account. The custom maps can be shared with others so they can collaborate on the map. Custom maps are only available if you have a Google account.

Once a user creates a map or directions to a location, there is an option to save it to My Maps in the panel. Custom maps can be created from within My Maps as well. A user can log into his or her Google account and access custom maps and directions. The user clicks the **My places** button to have the list of saved custom maps and directions displayed, as seen in **Figure 17-3.**

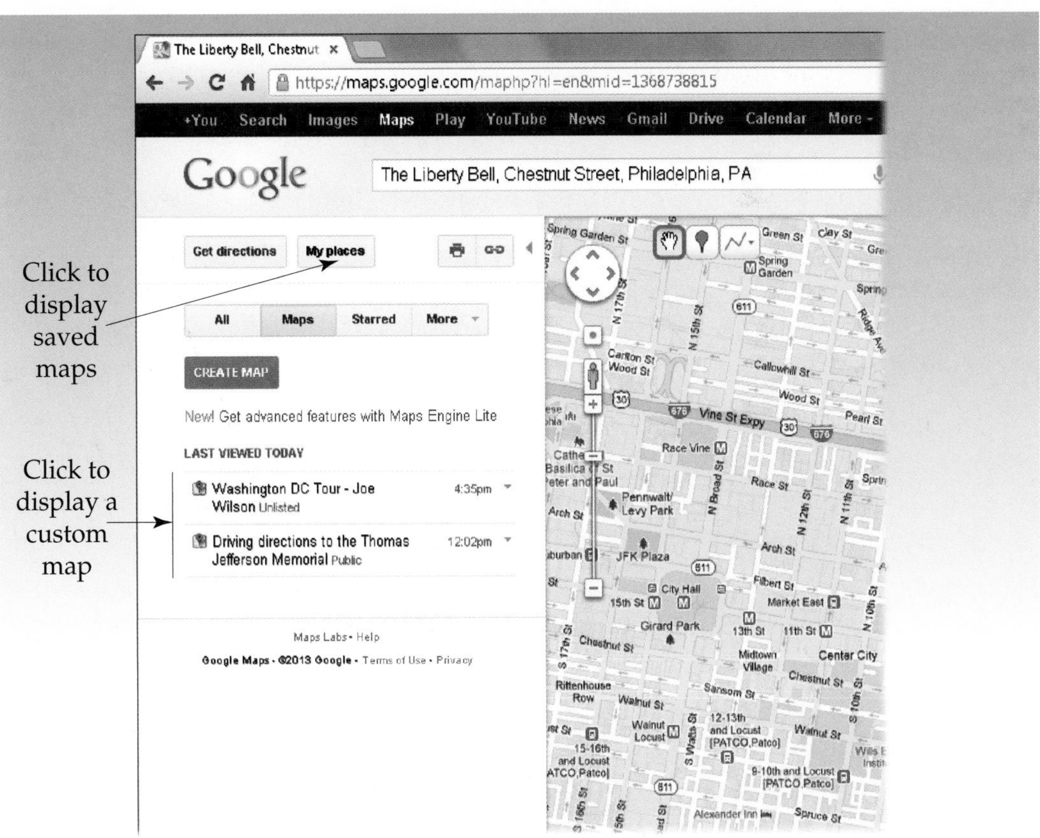

Goodheart-Willcox Publisher

Figure 17-3. A user can save custom maps, which can be restored at any time.

Markers, lines, and shapes can be added to a custom map. A ***marker*** is an icon that is placed on the map to indicate a specific location, and it appears in the panel as well. Lines and shapes can be added to a map as well. When a user adds a marker, line, or shape detailed information can be added in the details window. A title and description can be added to the details window. The description area provides a user with the opportunity to add formatted text, a photograph, a link, and a video to the details window.

A user can choose to share custom maps and directions with others. The **Collaborator** link in the panel provides a user with sharing options. A user can provide a collaborator with the ability to view and edit the map and to invite others to share the map. A person must have a Google account to edit a map or invite others to share it. Anyone can view a custom map. Collaborators receive invitations through e-mail. The e-mail will include a link to the map and can include a custom message from the user.

Lesson 17-1

Map Locations

Google Maps can provide a user with maps as large as cities or countries or as small as a single neighborhood. A user can also find a park or a local business with Google Maps.

Accessing and Searching Google Maps

Search

1. Log in to your Google Mail account.
2. Click the **More** link, and click **Even More** in the drop-down list.
3. Click **Maps** in the **Geo** section of the page that is displayed. The maps page is displayed with a default location based on your ISP.
4. In the search box at the top of the page, enter presidential houses in DC.
5. Click the **Search** button.
6. Click the **The White House** link to identify it on the map, as shown in **Figure 17-4.**

Click to display detailed locational information

Goodheart-Willcox Publisher

Figure 17-4. Clicking the link in the search results displays a marker on the map.

7. In the search box at the top of the page, enter **1600 Pennsylvania Ave NW, Washington, DC.**

Search

8. Click the **Search** button. There should be one returned result.

For the best results, when searching by address use one of these formats: ***street, city, state*** or ***street, city, zip code***. If the location is a landmark, include the name of place with the address to narrow the results.

9. Click the **more** link in the returned result, and click **Zoom here** in the drop-down menu. The map is zoomed in to the White House location on the map.

Viewing the Map

10. Click on the **Satellite** link in the map menu, as shown in **Figure 17-5.** The map view changes from a rendered map to a view of satellite photographs.

Goodheart-Willcox Publisher

Figure 17-5. The satellite view is a composite view of satellite photos.

Satellite and Google Earth images are usually one to three years old.

11. Move the cursor over the layers drop-down menu, and click **Photos** in the menu. A check mark appears next to the active layer. Locations for which photographs have been assigned are shown on the map, as shown in **Figure 17-6.**
12. Click any photo thumbnail on the map to display it in a pop-up window. Click the **X** in the pop-up window to close it.
13. Click and hold anywhere on the map, then drag the mouse to move around. Place the White House in the middle of the screen.

Street View

14. Click and hold the **Street View** button in the navigation controls, and drag and drop it on top of the marker for the White House. The street view of the inside of the White House is displayed.

Street view is only available for certain locations. It usually shows the outside view of a location, not the inside view.

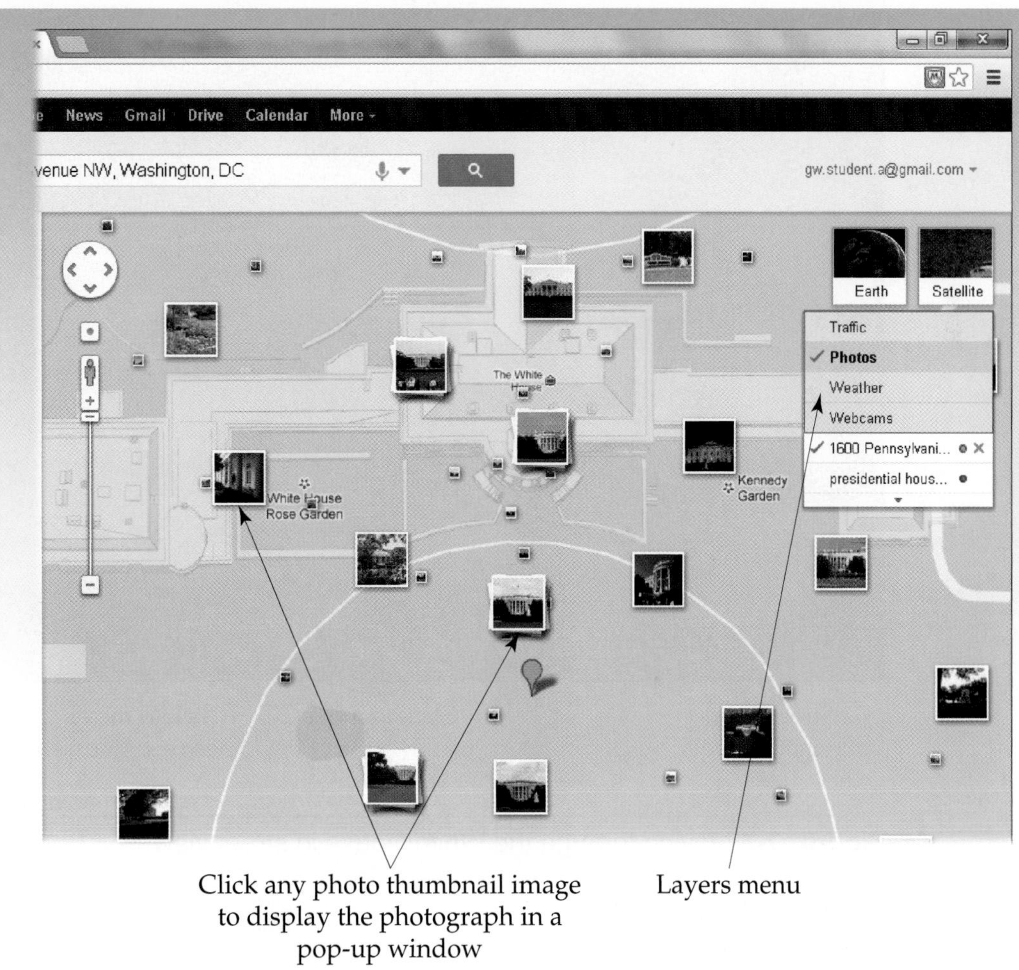

Goodheart-Willcox Publisher

Figure 17-6. Locations for which photographs have been assigned appear as icons.

Full screen

15. Click the **Full screen** button. The street view is displayed in full-screen mode.
16. Click the street view navigation tools to move around the White House, as shown in **Figure 17-7.**
17. Use the floor navigation buttons to move between the first and second floors of the White House.
18. Press the [Esc] key to exit full-screen mode.

Exit Street View

19. Click the **Exit Street View** button or zoom out to return to the map or satellite view.
20. Close the tab or window to close the map page.

Goodheart-Willcox Publisher

Figure 17-7. Moving through the White House in street view.

Lesson 17-2

Travel Directions

Once a user has found a location using Google Maps, he or she can get directions there as well. Directions are provided as step-by-step instructions. The suggested route is also drawn on the map.

Getting Directions

1. Log in to your Google Mail account.
2. Click the **More** link, and click **Even More** in the drop-down list.
3. Click **Maps** in the **Geo** section of the page that is displayed. The maps page is displayed with a default location based on your ISP.

Get directions

4. Click the **Get Directions** button. The directions are displayed in the panel.

By Car

5. Click the **By Car** button to specify driving directions.

Directions can be displayed for walking, bicycling, or taking public transit by clicking the **Walking**, **Bicycling**, or **By Public Transit** button.

6. Click in the **Start address** text box, labeled **A**, and enter your home address.
7. Click in the **End address** text box, labeled **B**, and enter the White House.

Get directions

8. Click the **Get Directions** button. Directions are shown in the directions panel, as shown in **Figure 17-8,** and a view of the route is shown on the map or satellite view. The total mileage is calculated and displayed next to the suggested route. In some cases, more than one route is suggested.
9. If there are multiple suggested routes, click the **Suggested routes** label to show only the directions.
10. Move the cursor over each step in the directions. The location of that step is highlighted on the map or satellite image.

Adding Destinations

11. Click the **Add Destination** link below the address text boxes. A third text box is added to the list.
12. In the new **End address** text box, labeled **C**, enter Lincoln Memorial, Washington DC.

Get directions

13. Click the **Get Directions** button to update the directions.

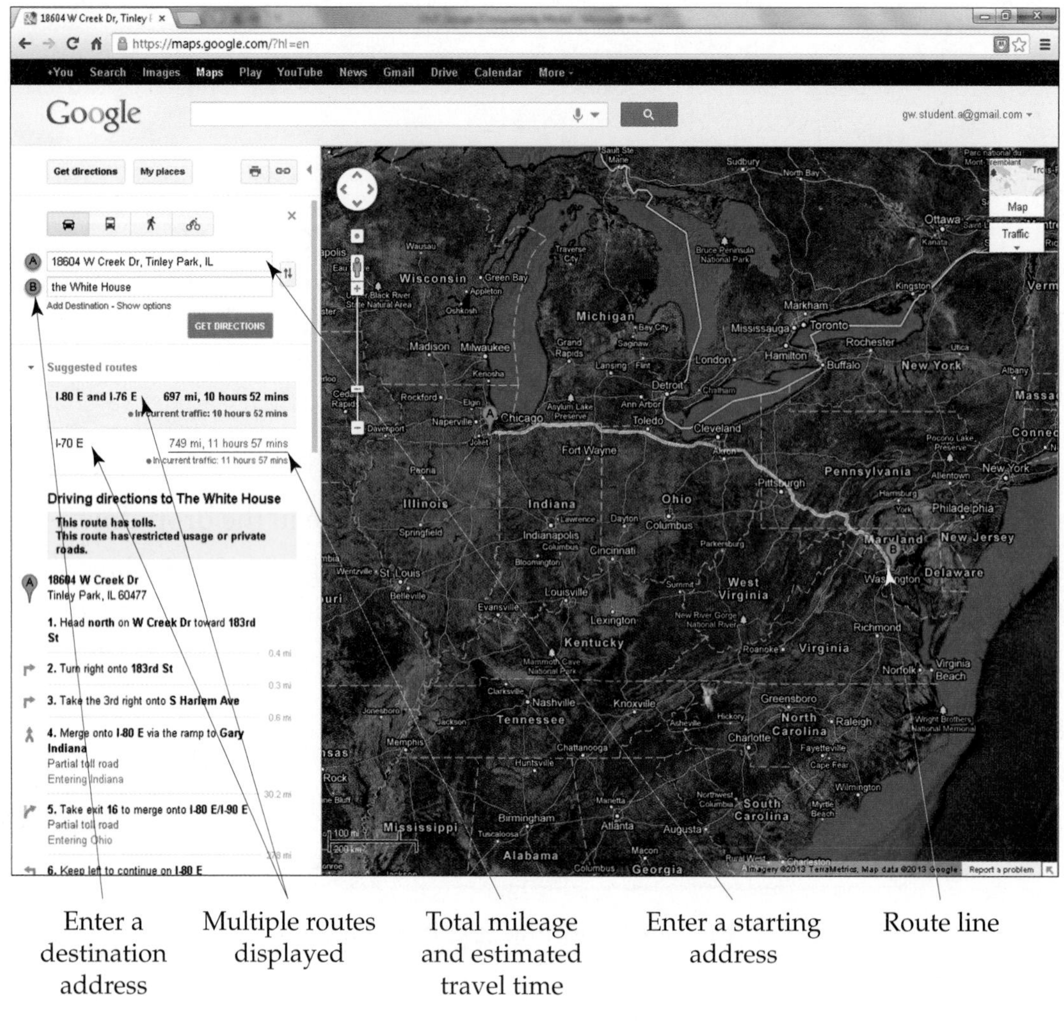

Goodheart-Willcox Publisher

Figure 17-8. Directions are displayed in the panel.

14. Click the **Add Destination** link, and in the new **End address** text box (**D**), enter Jefferson Memorial, Washington DC.

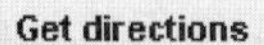

15. Click the **Get Directions** button to update the directions. The directions reflect a starting point and three destinations.

Rearranging or Deleting Destinations

16. Hover the cursor over the **D** in the list of destinations. The cursor changes to a hand.
17. Click, hold, and drag the **D** to under the **A**. The order of destinations is changed, and the directions are automatically updated. The first destination is now the Jefferson Memorial.
18. Click the **X** to the right of the Lincoln Memorial destination. The destination is removed from the directions, which are automatically updated. There are now only two destinations.

Printing or Sharing Directions

Print

19. Click the **Print** button in the directions panel. A new page is displayed showing only the directions.
20. Hover the cursor over a step in the directions. The step is highlighted, and links are displayed.
21. Click the **Map link** to include a map for the step.
22. Hover the cursor over another step in the directions, and click the **Street View** link. A street-view image is included in the step. See **Figure 17-9.**

Print

23. Click the **Print** button. The **Print** dialog box is displayed.
24. Verify the settings, and click the **Print** button in the dialog box.
25. Close the tab or window containing the list of directions for printing.
26. In the directions panel, click the **Link** button. A dialog box is displayed for sharing the directions, as shown in **Figure 17-10.**

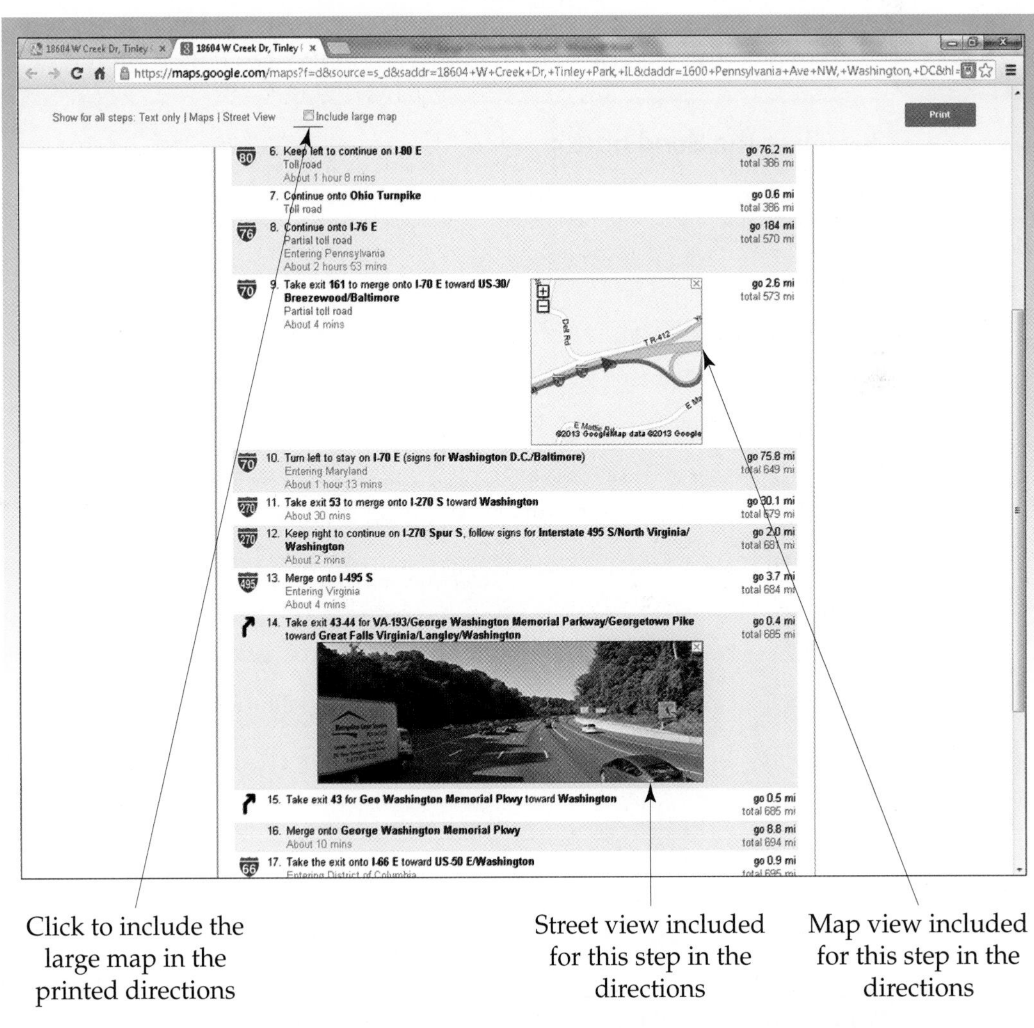

Goodheart-Willcox Publisher

Figure 17-9. A street-view image can be included in directions.

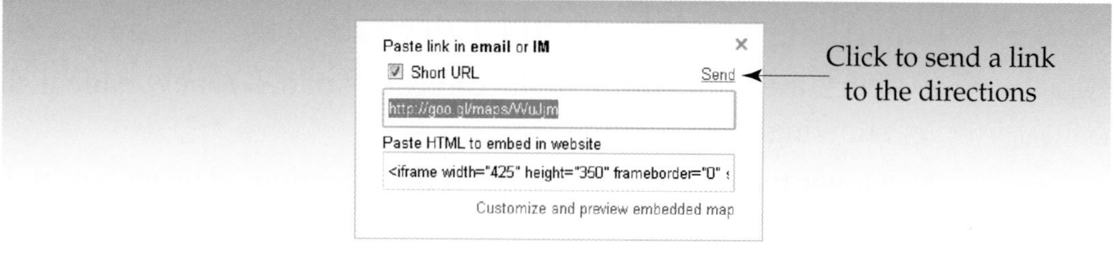

Goodheart-Willcox Publisher

Figure 17-10. Directions can be shared with others.

27. Check the **Short URL** check box. The full URL for directions can be very long, so the use of a URL shortener makes it a length that can easily be copied and pasted into another document.
28. Click the **Send** link. A dialog box is displayed in which a destination is entered, as shown in **Figure 17-11.**
29. Click in the **To:** text box, and enter the e-mail address of the person with whom to share the directions.

Tip Directions can also be sent to certain models of cars and GPS units.

30. Click the **Send** button.
31. Close the tab or window to close the map page.

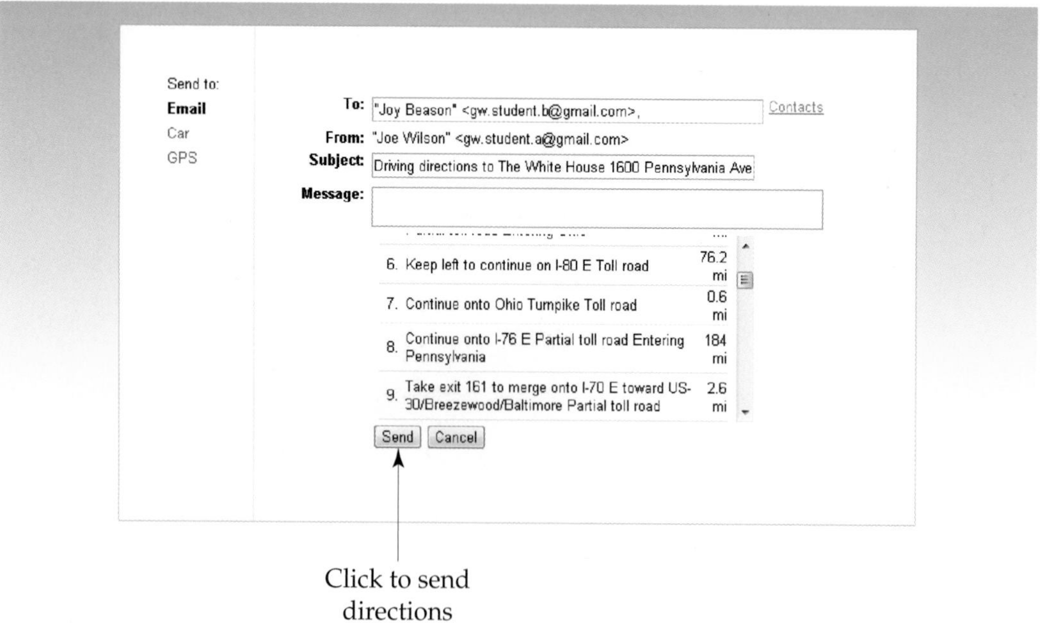

Goodheart-Willcox Publisher

Figure 17-11 Directions can be e-mailed to others.

Lesson 17-3

Custom Maps

Creating a map that is unique to the user can be helpful when planning a road trip, for example. A user can add details that are specific to the trip.

1. Log in to your Google Mail account.
2. Click the **More** link, and click **Even More** in the drop-down list.
3. Click **Maps** in the **Geo** section of the page that is displayed. The maps page is displayed with a default location based on your ISP.
4. Click in the search text box, enter the White House, and click the **Search** button. The map or satellite view should center and zoom on the White House.
5. Click the **My places** button.
6. Click the **Create Map** button. The panel changes, as shown in **Figure 17-12.**

Search

My places

CREATE MAP

Goodheart-Willcox Publisher

Figure 17-12. Creating a custom Google map.

7. Click in the **Title** text box, and enter Washington DC Tour—*Your Name*.
8. Click in the **Description** text box, and enter Possible stops for the DC tour.
9. Click the **Unlisted** radio button. This makes the map private, not public.

Add a Placemark

10. Click the **Add a Placemark** button. A marker is attached to the cursor.
11. Click on the White House to add the marker to the map. A pop-up window is displayed in which information about the location can be added.
12. Click in the **Title** text box in the pop-up window, and enter The White House.
13. Click the **OK** button in the pop-up window to add the information to the marker.
14. Click the **Done** button. The map is saved and displayed in the list whenever the **My places** button is clicked.

Search

15. Close Google Maps and restart the browser. This is sometimes required for a custom map to properly restore.

16. Click the **My places** button.

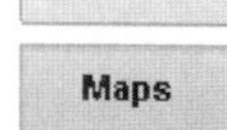

17. Click the **Maps** button. The list displays only custom maps that have been saved.
18. Click the name of the Washington DC Tour map in the list. The custom map is restored.
19. Close the tab or window to close the map page.

Saving to My Maps

A user can access locations he or she has created by saving them to My Maps. This can be important when working with custom maps, so changes are captured and do not need to recreated.

Saving a Location

1. Log in to your Google Mail account.
2. Click the **More** link, and click **Even More** in the drop-down list.
3. Click **Maps** in the **Geo** section of the page that is displayed. The maps page is displayed with a default location based on your ISP.

Search

4. Click in the search text box, enter the Washington Monument, and click the **Search** button. The map or satellite view should center and zoom on the Washington Monument.
5. Click the **Save to map** link in the search results. An expanded area appears below the search result, as shown in **Figure 17-13.**

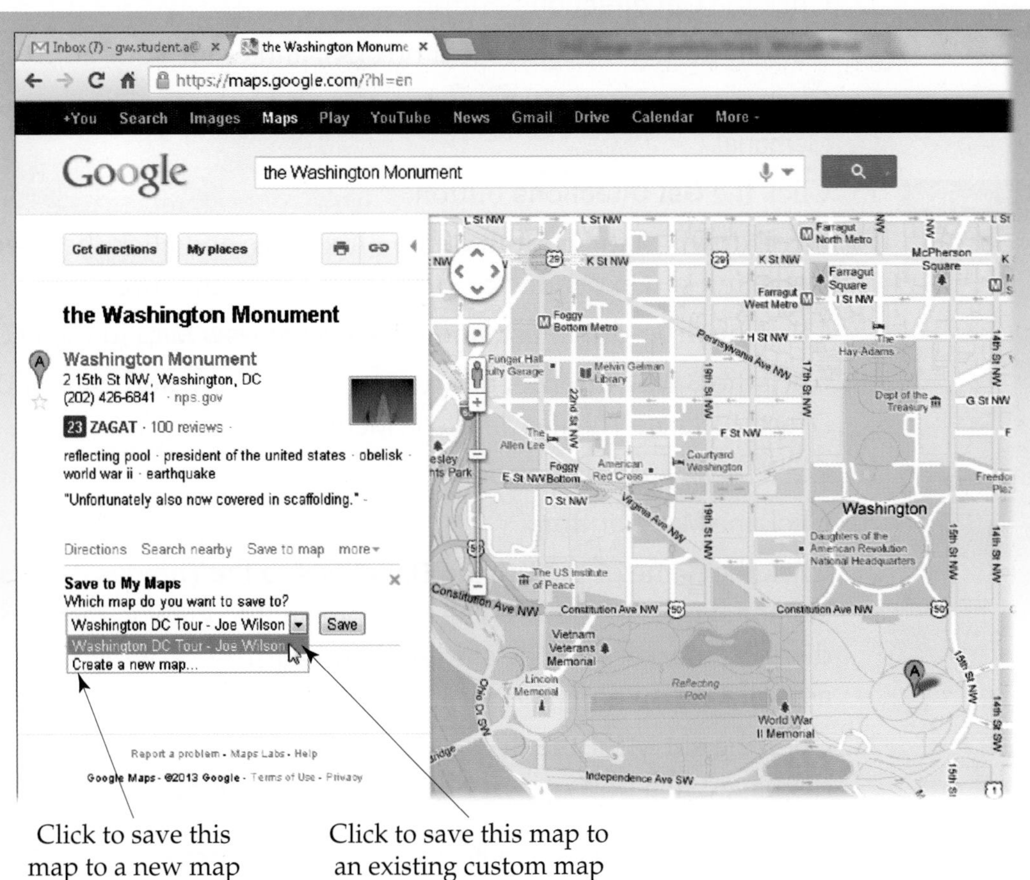

Goodheart-Willcox Publisher

Figure 17-13. A location can be saved to a custom map.

6. Click the drop-down list in the expanded area, and click **Washington DC Tour** in the list. This is the custom map created in Lesson 17-3.

To add the location to a new custom map, click **Create a new map...** in the drop-down list.

7. Click the **Save** button. A save confirmation will appear at the top of the map to show the location has been saved.

Search

8. Click in the search text box, enter the Lincoln Memorial, and click the **Search** button. The map or satellite view should center and zoom on the Lincoln Memorial.
9. Click the **Save to Map** link in the search results.
10. Click the drop-down list in the expanded area, and click **Washington DC Tour** in the list.
11. Click the **Save** button. The custom map created in Lesson 17-3 is now updated to include not only the White House, but the Washington Monument and Lincoln Memorial locations.

Saving Directions

Get directions

12. Click the **Get directions** button.
13. Click in the **Start address** text box (**A**), and enter your address.
14. Click in the **End address** text box (**B**), and enter the Thomas Jefferson Memorial.

GET DIRECTIONS

15. Click the **Get Directions** button.
16. Scroll down to the bottom of the directions, and click the **Save to My Maps** link. An expanded area appears below the directions.
17. Click the drop-down list, and click **Create New Map** in the list.
18. Click the **Save** button. A new custom map is created named Driving Directions to the Thomas Jefferson Memorial.

My places

19. Click the **My places** button.

Maps

20. Click the **Maps** button.
21. Click the name of the **Driving Directions to the Thomas Jefferson Memorial** map in the list. The map or satellite view is restored. The panel displays markers for the start and end addresses, which are on the map as well, and an entry for the driving direction.
22. Click the entry for the driving directions in the panel. The directions are displayed in a pop-up window, as shown in **Figure 17-14.**

Tip

You can also click the blue route line on the map to view the directions.

23. Close the tab or window to close the map page.

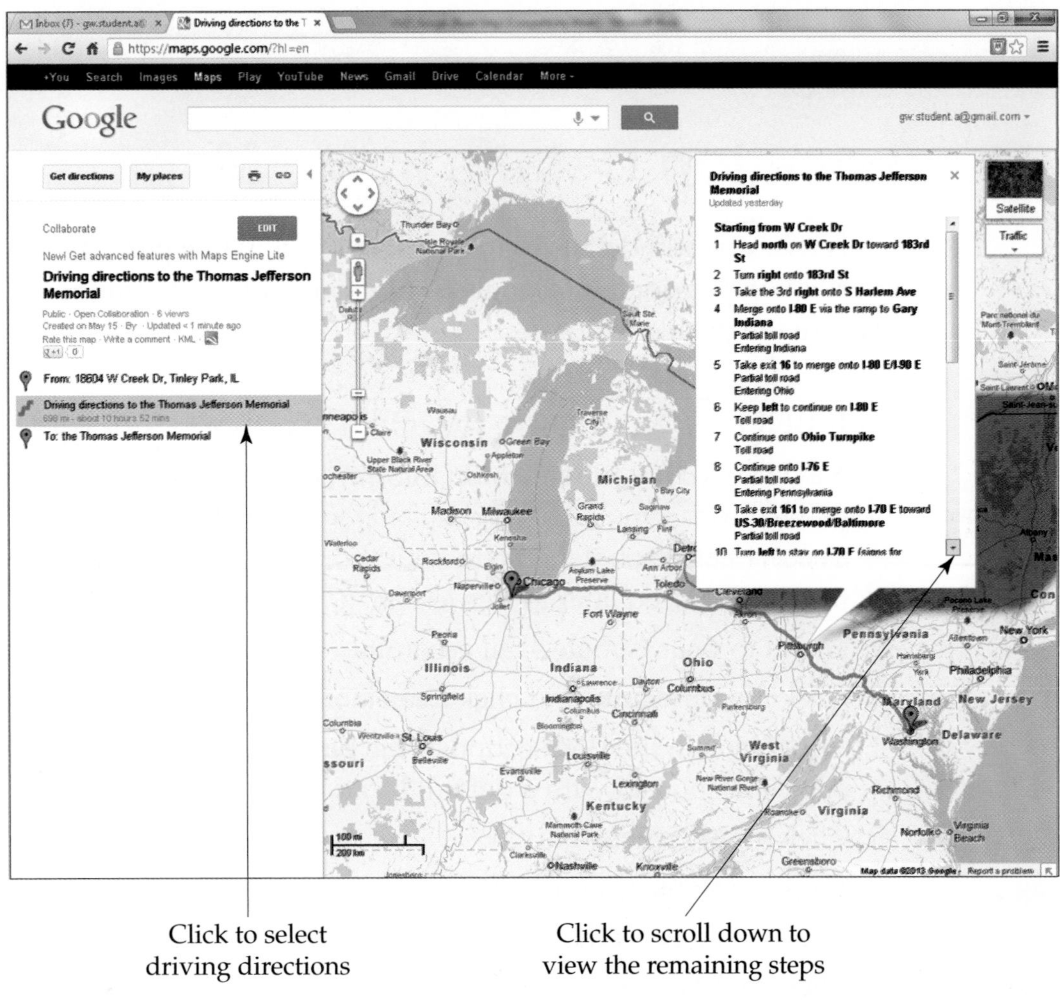

Goodheart-Willcox Publisher

Figure 17-14. Clicking the directions in the panel displays the directions in a pop-up window.

Lesson 17-5

Location Details in My Maps

A user can add details to maps that would not be part of the general information provided by Google. A user can add photographs, links, and video to the details window.

Adding Text and Hyperlinks to a Map

1. Navigate to the student companion website (www.g-wlearning.com/informationtechnology/), and download the Lincoln Photograph data file to your working folder. This is a JPEG file that will be used later in this lesson.
2. Log in to your Google Mail account.
3. Click the **More** link, and click **Even More** in the drop-down list.
4. Click **Maps** in the **Geo** section of the page that is displayed. The maps page is displayed with a default location based on your ISP.
5. Click the **My places** button.
6. Click the **Maps** button.
7. Click the name of the Washington DC Tour map to restore it.

8. Click the **Edit** button.
9. Click the marker for the Lincoln Memorial in the map window. The details pop-up window is displayed, as shown in **Figure 17-15.**

If the **Edit** button is not clicked first, the details pop-up window is displayed, but the details cannot be edited.

10. Click the **Rich Text** link in the pop-up window.

Bold

11. Click in the **Description** box, click the **Bold** button, and enter Abraham Lincoln was the 16th President of the United States.
12. Press the [Enter] key to start a new line, and enter For more information click here.
13. Select the text click here.

Link

14. Click the **Link** button. A dialog box is displayed in which a URL can be entered.
15. Click in the **Enter a URL:** text box, and enter www.history.com/topics/abraham-lincoln.
16. Click the **OK** button to close the dialog box.
17. Click the **OK** button to close the details window. The added details appear below the marker in the list in the panel.

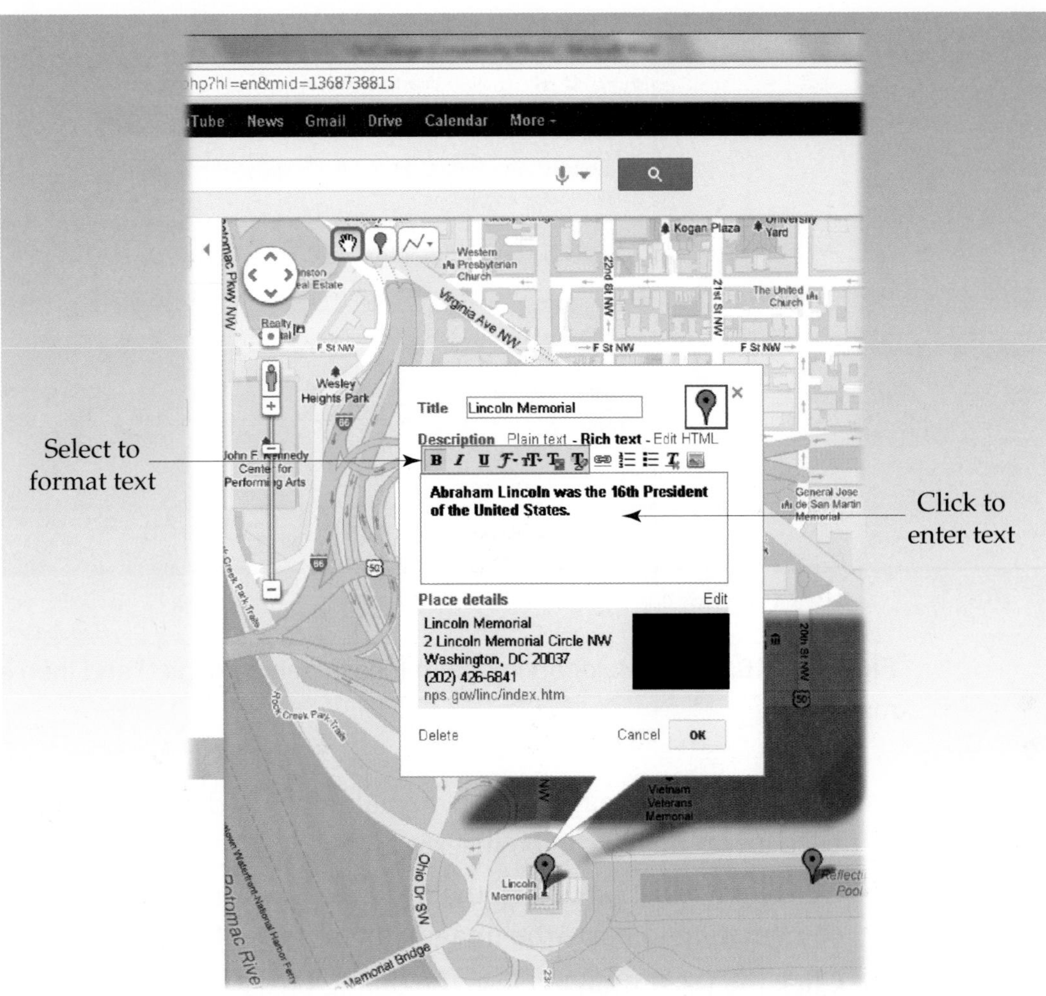

Goodheart-Willcox Publisher

Figure 17-15. Specifying details for a marker after it has been added to the map.

Adding Photos to a Map

18. Open a new tab or window and launch Picasa. Refer to Chapter 16 for information on using Picasa.
19. Upload the Lincoln Photograph image file from your working folder. It can be added to an existing album or to a new album.
20. Right-click on the image, and click **Copy Image URL** in the shortcut menu that is displayed, as shown in **Figure 17-16.**
21. Switch to the tab or window containing Google Maps. This should still be in edit mode. If not, click the **Edit** button.
22. Click the placemark for the Lincoln Memorial to display the details pop-up window for editing.
23. Click after all of the text in the text box. If needed, press the [Enter] key to start a new line.

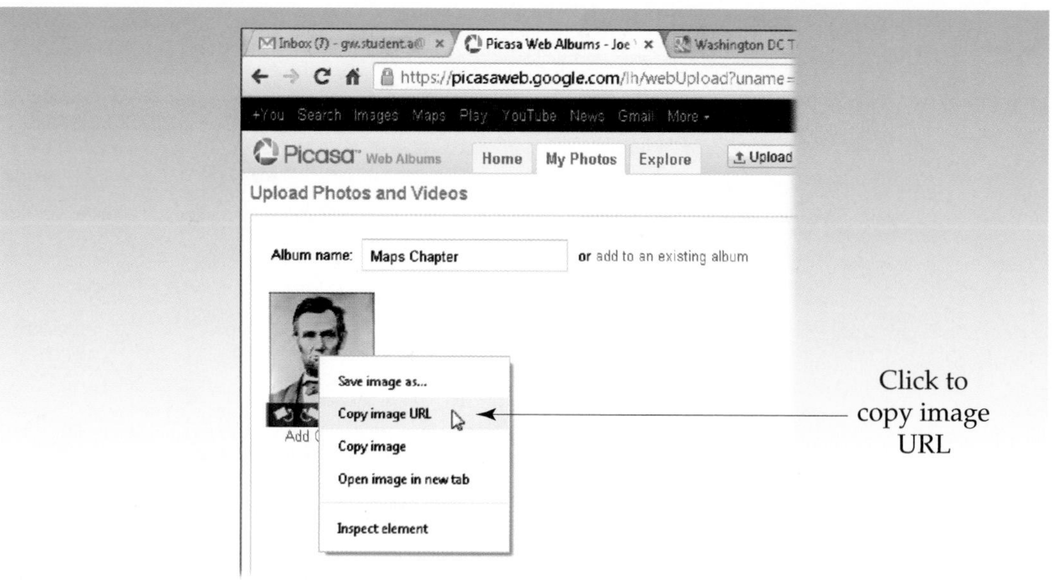

Goodheart-Willcox Publisher

Figure 17-16. The URL for an image in Picasa can be copied and then added to a map.

Insert Image

24. Click the **Insert Image** button. A dialog box is displayed in which the URL for an image can be inserted.
25. Delete any existing text in the text box, then press the [Ctrl][V] key combination to paste the image link in the text box.
26. Click the **OK** button to close the dialog box.
27. Click the **OK** button to close the details pop-up window.
28. Click the **Done** button to exit edit mode. The image is now shown in the details pop-up window when the marker is clicked, as shown in **Figure 17-17.**

Adding Videos to a Map

29. Open a new tab or window, and navigate to www.youtube.com. Your instructor may provide an alternate address to locate videos.
30. On the YouTube page, search for the video A New Way to Tour the White House. Click the link for the video with this name.
31. On the video page, click the **Share** link, as shown in **Figure 17-18.**
32. Click the **Embed** link, and copy the code in the text box.
33. Display the tab or window containing Google Maps. The Washington DC Tour map should be displayed. If not, display it.

34. Click the **Edit** button to enter edit mode.
35. Click the marker for the White House. The details pop-up window is displayed.

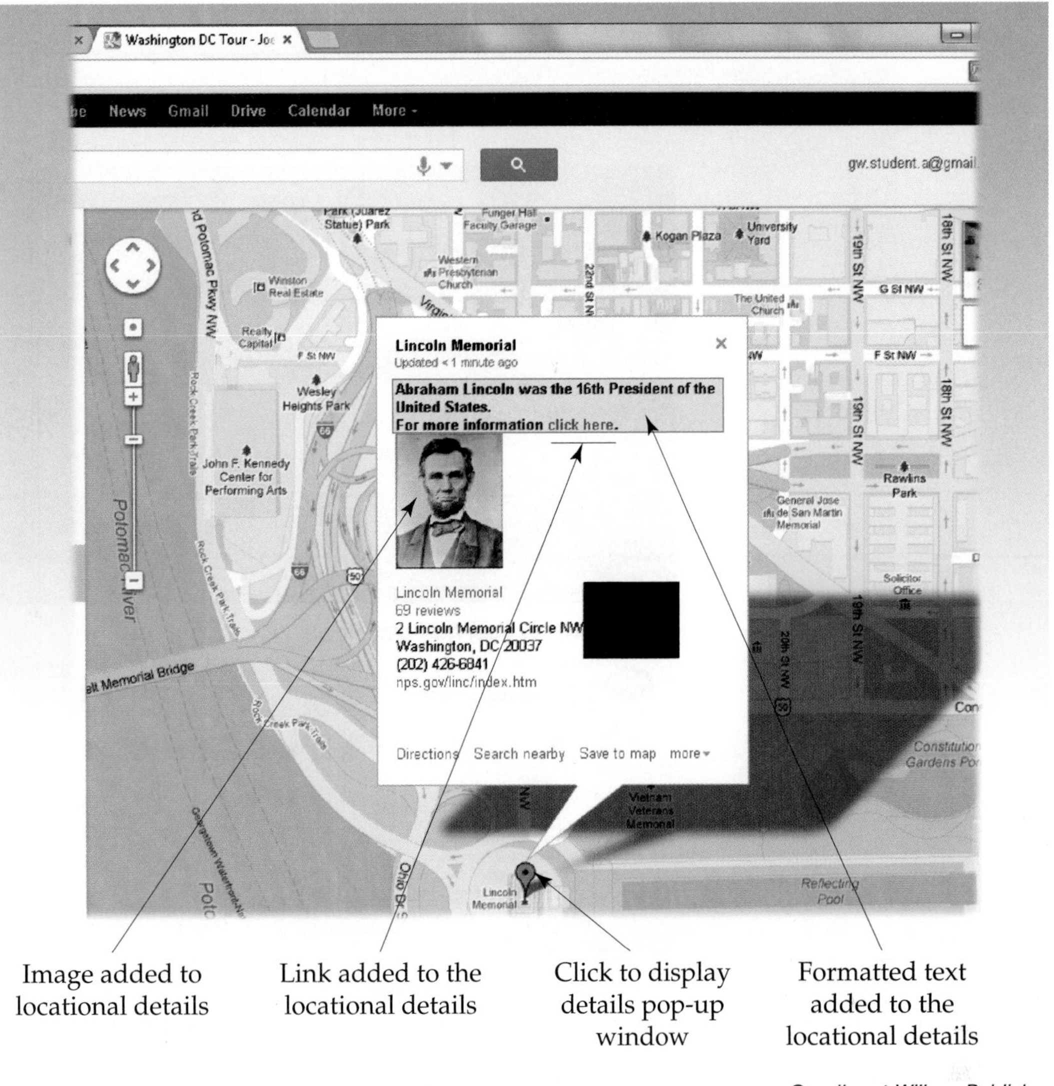

Goodheart-Willcox Publisher

Figure 17-17. When an image is added to the details of a marker, it appears in the details pop-up window.

36. Click the **Edit HTML** link in the pop-up window.
37. Click in the text box, and press the [Ctrl][V] key combination to paste the code for the video link.
38. Click the **OK** button to close the details pop-up window.
39. Click the **Done** button. The video is now available in the details pop-up window for the White House marker.
40. Click the marker for the White House. The first frame of the video appears in the details pop-up window.
41. Click anywhere on the video frame to play the video.
42. Close the details pop-up window.
43. Close the tab or window to close the map page.

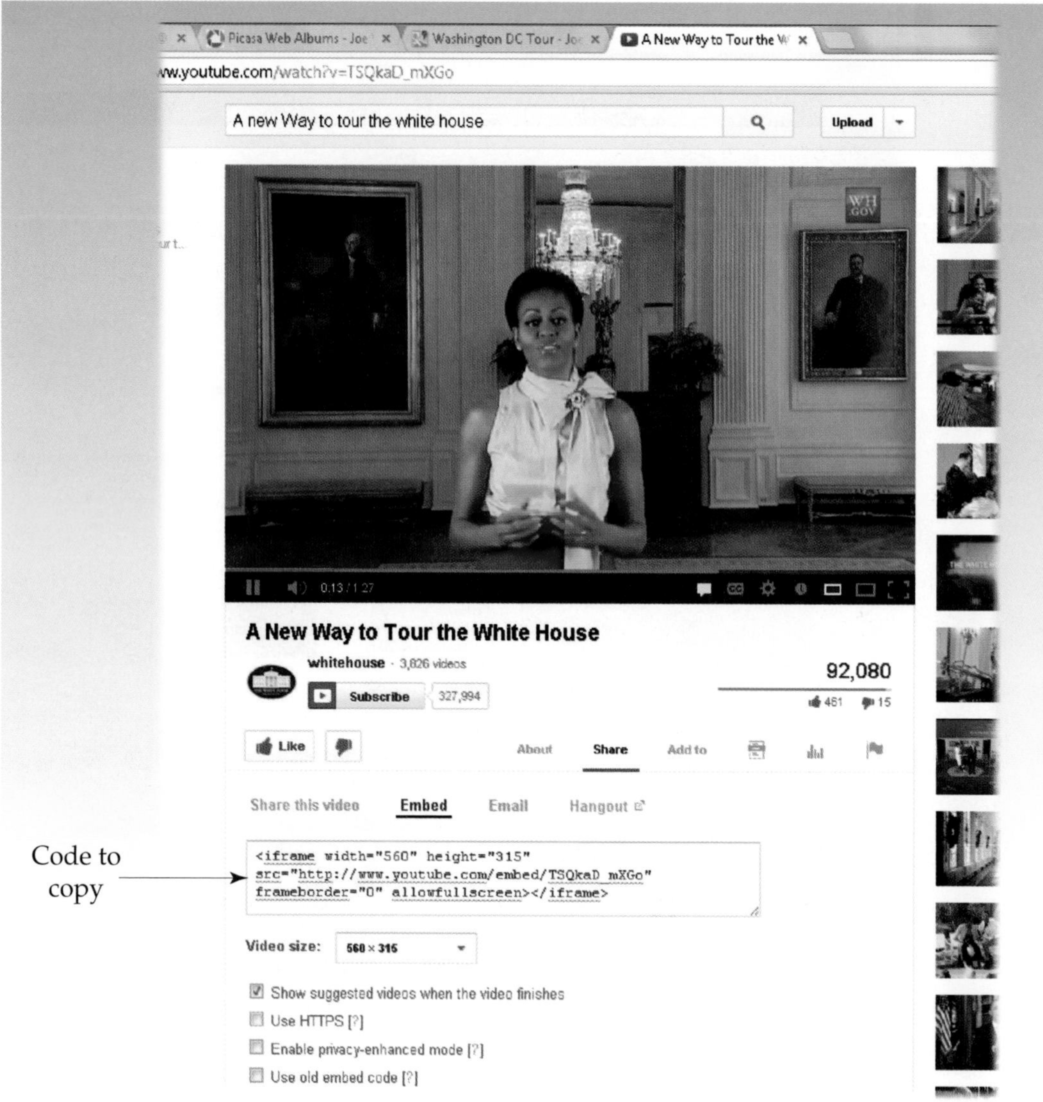

Goodheart-Willcox Publisher

Figure 17-18. Videos from YouTube can be included in the details for a marker.

Lesson 17-6

Lines and Shapes

Google provides users with the ability to add lines and shapes to custom maps. Users can draw lines along roads or freehand. The line style can be selected as well.

Adding Lines to a Map

1. Log in to your Google Mail account.
2. Click the **More** link, and click **Even More** in the drop-down list.
3. Click **Maps** in the **Geo** section of the page that is displayed. The maps page is displayed with a default location based on your ISP.

4. Click the **My places** button.
5. Click the **Maps** button.
6. Click the name of the Washington DC Tour map to restore it. Display the map view if the satellite view is displayed. If possible, have all locations displayed in the map window.

Draw a Line

7. Click the **Edit** button.
8. Click the **Draw a Line** button. The cursor changes to an X.

Tip To draw a shape or to draw along roads, click the arrow next to the **Draw a Line** button to display a drop-down menu, and then click the appropriate option. To cancel the operation, press the [Esc] key.

9. Move the cursor next to the White House. Do not place the cursor directly over the marker.
10. Click the mouse once. This starts the line.
11. Drag the line from the White House to the Lincoln Memorial and double-click. Double-clicking ends the line, and the details pop-up window is displayed, as shown in **Figure 17-19.**
12. Click in the **Title** text box in the details pop-up window, and enter Distance to Lincoln Memorial. The distance is displayed at the bottom of the pop-up window.

Line Style

13. Click the **Line Style** button in the details pop-up window. The pop-up window changes, as shown in **Figure 17-20.**
14. Click the **Line color** swatch, and click a color in the palette that is displayed.
15. Check the **Snap to Roads** check box. This forces the line to follow roads instead of being a straight line between the two points.
16. Click the **OK** button in the pop-up window to set the details. Directions are automatically added to the details pop-up window, and a distance is displayed at the bottom of the directions.

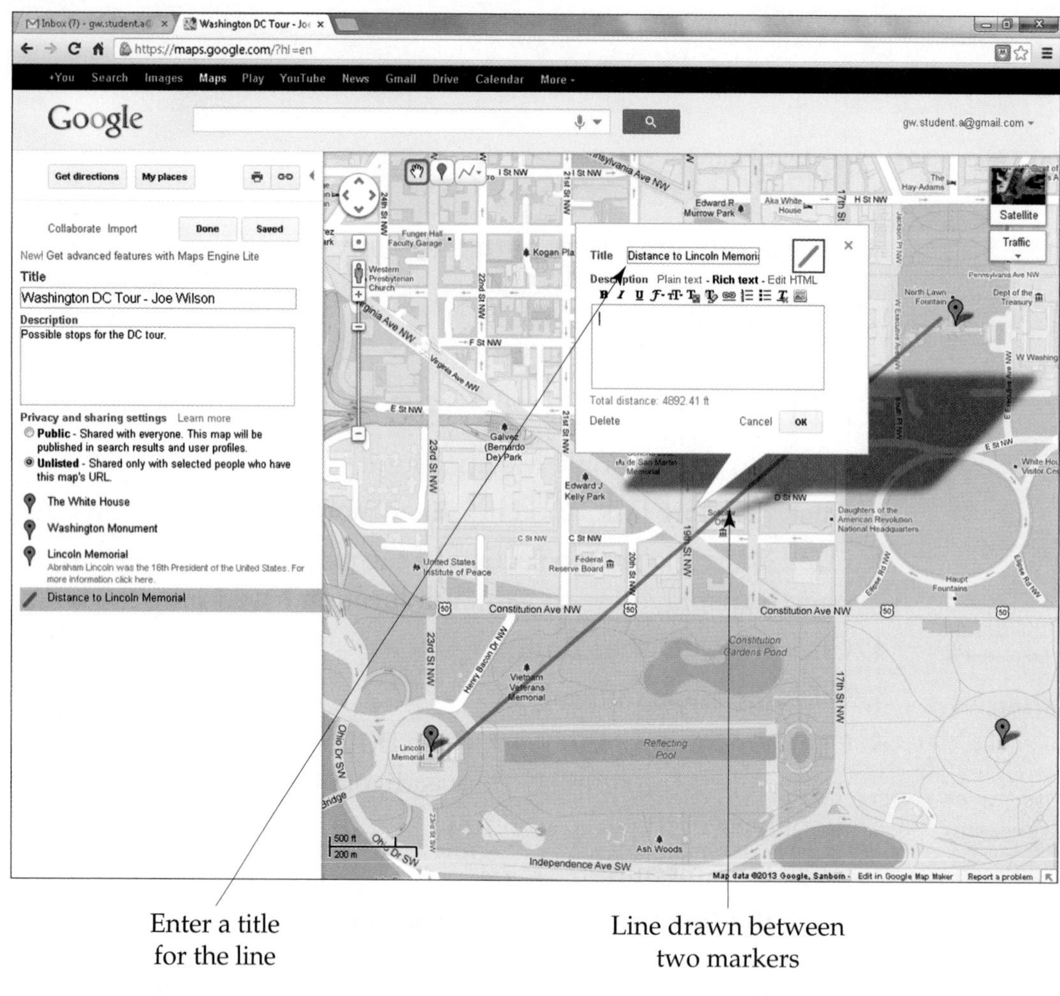

Goodheart-Willcox Publisher

Figure 17-19. A line can be added to a map, and details added to the line.

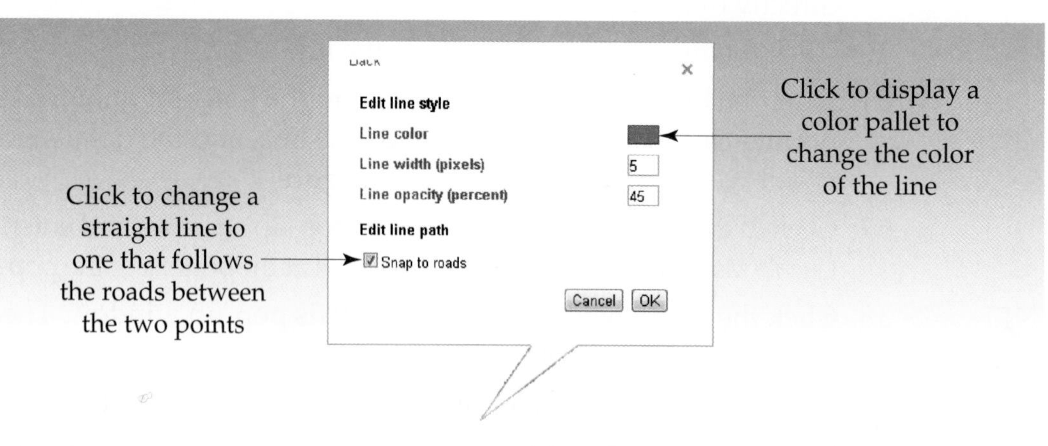

Goodheart-Willcox Publisher

Figure 17-20. The style of a line added to a map, including its color, can be changed.

To move a line, click the starting or ending point and drag it to a new location. To delete a line, click the **Delete** link in the details pop-up window.

17. Click the **OK** button to close the details pop-up window.

Adding Shapes to a Map

Draw a Shape

18. Click the arrow next to the **Draw a Line** button to display a drop-down menu, and then click **Draw a Shape** in the menu. The button changes to the **Draw a Shape** button.
19. Locate a place on the map somewhere between the White House and the Lincoln Memorial, and click the mouse once. This starts the shape.
20. Draw a rectangular shape by clicking three more times, once at each remaining corner.
21. Move the cursor over the first corner and click. This ends drawing the shape, and the details pop-up window is displayed, as shown in **Figure 17-21.**

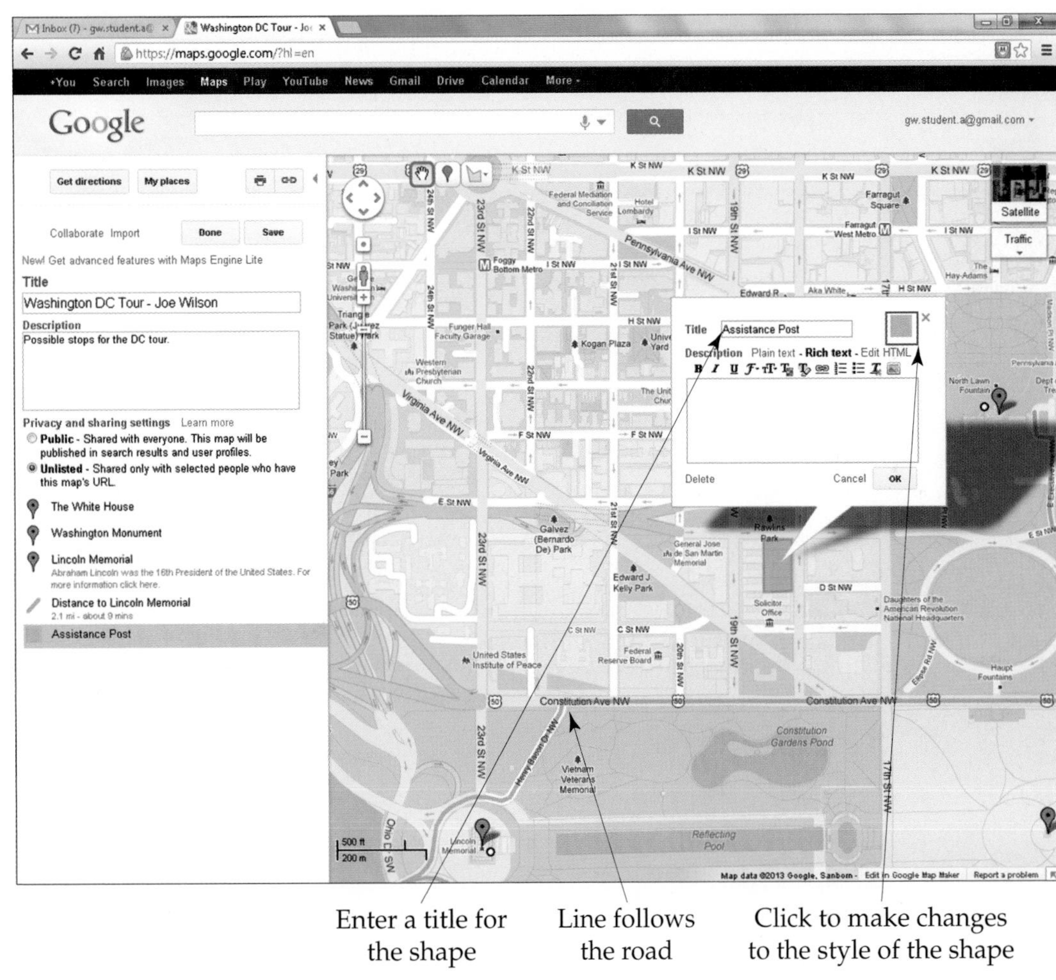

Goodheart-Willcox Publisher

Figure 17-21. A shape can be added to a map, and details added to the shape.

22. Click in the **Title** text box in the details pop-up window, and enter Assistance Post.

Shape Style

23. Click the **Shape Style** button in the details pop-up window.
24. Click the **Line color** swatch, and click a color in the palette that is displayed.
25. Click the **OK** button to set the details.
26. Click the **OK** button to close the details pop-up window. The shape is now available in the list in the panel.
27. Click the **Done** button.

Tip To move a shape, click on each point to drag and drop it in the new location. To delete a shape, click delete in the details window.

28. Close the tab or window to close the map page.

Lesson 17-7

Collaborate on Maps

Google Maps allows users to share maps with other people or give them collaborator rights so they can add information to a map. People must have a Google account to add information to a map.

Sharing

1. Log in to your Google Mail account.
2. Click the **More** link, and click **Even More** in the drop-down list.
3. Click **Maps** in the **Geo** section of the page that is displayed. The maps page is displayed with a default location based on your ISP.

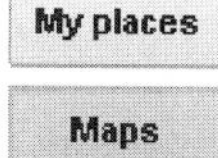

4. Click the **My places** button.
5. Click the **Maps** button.
6. Click the name of the Washington DC Tour map to restore it. Display the map view if the satellite view is displayed.

Link

7. Click the **Link** button. A dialog box is displayed that contains the URL and HTML code for the map.
8. Click the **Send** link. A dialog box is displayed in which an e-mail address can be entered.
9. Click in the **To:** text box, and enter the e-mail address for your instructor.
10. Click the **Send** button. The full URL for the map is e-mailed to the recipient.
11. Close the dialog box containing the URL and HTML code for the map.

Collaborate

12. Click the **Collaborate** link in the panel. A dialog box is displayed in which collaborators can be invited and managed, as shown in **Figure 17-22.**
13. Click in the **Invite people as collaborators** text box, and enter a classmate's e-mail address.
14. Click in the **Message:** text box, and enter Please add possible points of interest.
15. Check the **Send me a copy of this invitation** check box. This will send yourself a copy of the e-mail invitation.
16. Click the **Send invitations** button. A message appears indicating collaborators have been invited.
17. Click the **OK** button to dismiss the message.
18. Close the tab or window to close the map page.

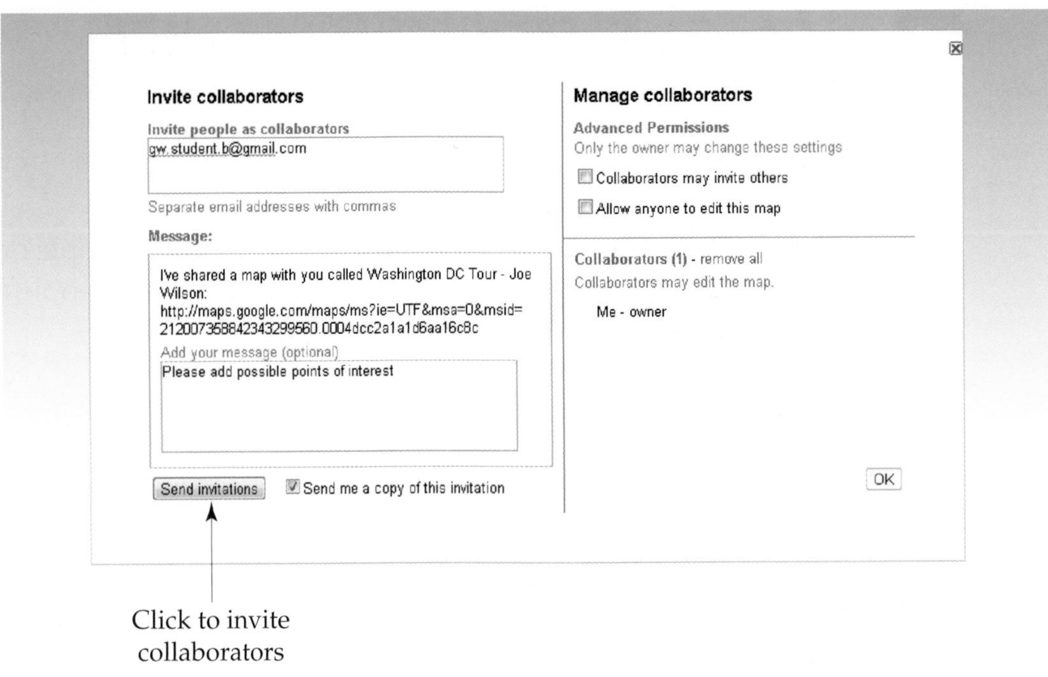

Goodheart-Willcox Publisher

Figure 17-22. Maps can be shared with others who can then collaborate on the map.

Editing a Shared Map

19. Log in to your Google Mail account, or switch to the tab or window containing your Gmail.
20. Open the e-mail from your classmate sharing his or her map, and click the link to the map in the e-mail. The map is displayed in a new tab or window.
21. Click the **Save to My Places** link in the panel. Your classmate's custom map is now available whenever you click the **My places** button.

22. Click the **Edit** button.

Search

23. Click in the **Search** text box, enter Martin Luther King Jr. Memorial, and click the search button.
24. Click the **Save to map** link in the search results for the memorial, and save the location to your classmate's Washington DC Tour map.

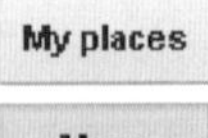

Maps

25. Click the **My places** button, and then click the **Maps** button.
26. Click the name of your classmate's Washington DC Tour map.
27. Click the marker for the Martin Luther King, Jr. Memorial in the list in the left-hand pane.
28. In the details pop-up window that is displayed, enter I would like to visit this memorial in the **Description** text box.
29. Click the **OK** button to close the pop-up window.
30. Click the **Done** button to finish editing the map.
31. Close the tab or window to close the map page.

Check Your Google Apps IQ

Now that you have finished this chapter, see what you know about Google Apps by taking the chapter posttest.
www.m.g-wlearning.com
www.g-wlearning.com/informationtechnology/

Skill Review

Answer the following questions on a separate sheet of paper.

1. List the three basic elements of the Google Maps page.
2. What are the two views in which a location can be viewed, not including the street view?
3. Briefly describe the street view.
4. What are the modes of transportation for which directions can be found?
5. In addition to the steps between the starting and ending points, what do directions display?
6. What are the three ways in which steps in directions may appear?
7. When directions have multiple destinations, how can the order of destinations be changed?
8. What is a custom map?
9. What is a marker?
10. How are collaborators given access to a shared map?

Lesson Application

These exercises are designed to apply the skills learned in this and previous chapters. General directions are provided, but you will need to draw on your knowledge to determine how to complete each exercise.

Exercise 17-1
Editing Markers

Using Google Maps, search for your school address. Create a new custom map called My School. Save the school location to that map. Edit the marker for the school, or add a marker if needed. Enter the school name as the name of the marker. Add a picture of the school and a link to the school's website to the details.

If your school has a YouTube channel, search for a video of an outdoor event, such as a football game or soccer match. Add a marker outside the school where the event occurred. Add the video to the marker details.

Exercise 17-2
Directions

Create driving directions from your home, to school, and back to your home. Save the directions to the My School map created in Exercise 17-1. Make sure the map is unlisted and not shared with anybody. Identify the mileage and estimated driving time for the round-trip. Compare the driving time with the estimated time for public transit, walking, and bicycling. Compose an e-mail to your instructor comparing and contrasting the times.

Exercise 17-3
Collaborating on Maps

Create a new custom map called School Fieldtrip. Locate two landmarks in your state, and add markers to the map. Make one of your classmates a collaborator. Ask him or her to choose one of the landmarks, draw a shape around the landmark, and explain in the details why he or she would like to visit this landmark. Another classmate should make you a collaborator on his or her map. Select a landmark you would like to visit, add a shape, and explain why. Also, add two additional landmarks to the map. Create driving directions to one of the added landmarks, and save the directions in the School Fieldtrip map. When you and your classmates are done editing maps, share your custom map with your instructor in an e-mail.

Chapter 18

Google Chrome and Google Search

Objectives

After completing this chapter, you will be able to:

- **Use** Google Chrome to navigate the World Wide Web.
- **Manage** bookmarks for web pages.
- **Perform** basic keyword searches.
- **Conduct** a web search for images.
- **Filter** search results.
- **Manage** a library of online e-books.
- **Translate** words and phrases between various languages.

alexmillos/Shutterstock.com

Check Your Google Apps IQ

Before you begin this chapter, see what you already know about Google Apps by taking the chapter pretest.

www.m.g-wlearning.com
www.g-wlearning.com/informationtechnology/

Using Google Chrome

A ***web browser*** is a software application that allows a user to find and review information on the Internet, including the World Wide Web. Google Chrome is one of several web browsers currently available and, based on several indicators, is the choice for most users worldwide.

Most Google tools make user-specific information portable or available from one computer and one device to another. Google Chrome provides users with this feature as well. When a user logs into Google Chrome with his or her Google account information, the user's bookmarks and the browser settings, for example, are made available. Also unique to Chrome are automatic updates to the browser software. Most often Google provides updated versions of Chrome without requiring user interaction.

When a user launches Google Chrome, the default Chrome home page is displayed. A user can enter a URL in the address text box, which Google calls the ***omnibox***, to have a specific website displayed. A ***URL*** is the abbreviation for uniform resource locator and is the address for websites or documents available on the Internet. The default Chrome home page includes buttons to other Google apps such as Search, Drive, and Gmail. A user can click on one of these buttons to begin. A user can also access a website by clicking a bookmark link. The default Chrome home page is a gray bar along the top of the website window with links to bookmarks the user has created. ***Bookmarks*** allow a user to tag a web page so that exact location is saved for future navigation.

Google Chrome Interface

One of the unique features of Google Chrome is its simple interface. The ***interface*** is the general display of a program for a user when it is launched, including the menus and toolbars. Chrome has a single toolbar that is displayed

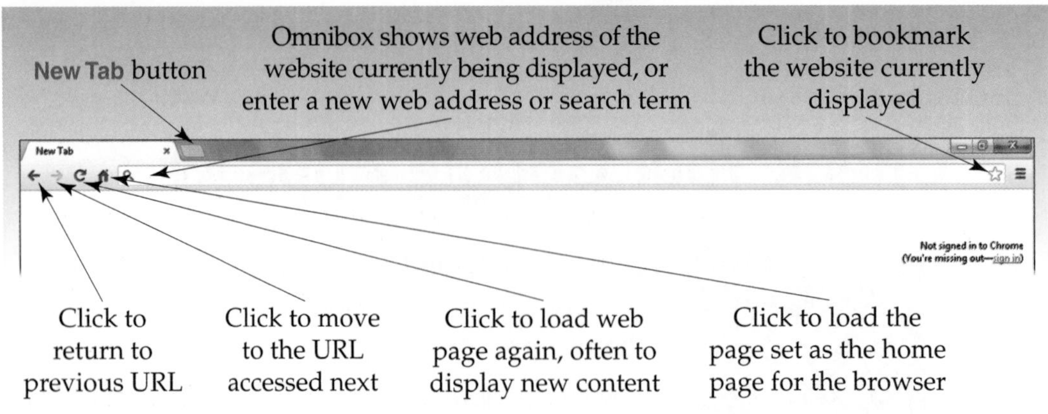

Goodheart-Willcox Publisher

Figure 18-1. Google Chrome has some basic tools on a toolbar at the top of the screen.

along the top of the browser window, as seen in **Figure 18-1.** The toolbar includes the following options: the **Click to go back** button, the **Click to go forward** button, the **Reload this page** button, the **Open the home page** button, the omnibox, the **Bookmark this page** button, and the **Customize** button.

When a user clicks the **Customize** button, a drop-down menu appears. From this menu a user can open a new tab, window, or incognito window. An ***incognito window*** allows the user to view websites, download files, and otherwise browse the web without a record of the user's activity being saved in his or her browser or search history. A user can view a listing of all websites he or she has bookmarked from this drop-down menu. Web pages can be saved or printed, and a user can use the **Find** option to locate text on a page from this menu. Browser history and downloads can be deleted as well. Chrome settings can be modified by clicking **Settings** in the drop-down menu.

The default download location is specified in the Chrome settings. On the Settings page, click the **Show advanced settings...** link at the bottom of the Settings page. On the expanded page, click the **Change...** button next to the **Download location:** text box, browse to the new folder, select it, and click the **OK** button. Then, close the Settings page.

Above the toolbar to the right of the tab is the **New Tab** button. A user clicks it to have a new tab displayed. By default, Chrome features tab browsing. ***Tab browsing*** is when web pages are displayed in a separate tab of one browser window rather than in a new browser window.

Managing Bookmarks and History

Some people have many bookmarks and use them often. With Google's Bookmark Manager, a user can organize bookmarks. A user can create folders for bookmarks to group them into general categories to make them easier to find. For example, a user could create a folder specific to a school project containing all bookmarks for that project. Using the Bookmark Manager, bookmarks can be deleted, renamed, and sorted. A user can also import bookmarks created in another browser or export Chrome bookmarks into an HTML file. The export feature might be useful to provide a list of sources used for a project, for example.

The Google Chrome history tracks websites visited. The date and the time of the visit and the exact URL are recorded. From the History page accessed with the **Customize** button, a user can select a page to revisit, search for a specific page, remove selected items, or clear the entire history.

Using Google Search

A ***search engine*** is a program used to search the Internet for information. Google Search is used to conduct more searches than any other engine available. A person can conduct a simple keyword search or use Google tools to conduct a targeted and complex search for data including web pages, documents, images, or videos. A ***keyword search*** is when a user enters text, a word or phrase, to find files that contain the specified text.

To conduct a simple keyword search, a user enters a word or phrase in the search text box on the Google Search home page and clicks the **Google Search** button. The results page is then displayed. Depending on the keywords entered, there could be millions of returned results. A user can click the **I'm Feeling Lucky** button, rather than the **Google Search** button. This option will display what would have been the first page in the returned results rather the results page with a list of all of the results.

A user can search without entering search terms using a keyboard. Google's voice search allows users to speak search terms. Using a computer equipped with a microphone, a person clicks the **Search by Voice** button at the end of the search box, then says the search terms. The keywords are displayed in the search box as the user speaks. When the user stops speaking, the results are displayed.

Google Returned Results

After the **Search** button is clicked, the results page is displayed. The total number of returned results appears followed by the list of results. The results can include links to websites, files, and images relevant to the search terms provided. A user can click the link of any result in the list to display the suggested website.

Result entries, as seen in **Figure 18-2,** include a title for the site, which is also a link to it. The URL for the link is displayed below the title. A snippet follows the URL. A ***snippet*** is a short description of the web page. The search terms used are in bold text anywhere they appear in the result entry. In the list of results, Google displays the most relevant page first. Indented result entries are separate pages in the same website.

Sponsored results are also displayed in the returned results list. A ***sponsored result*** is an ad or a returned result that has been included because a company has paid to have it included. Shading behind the result can

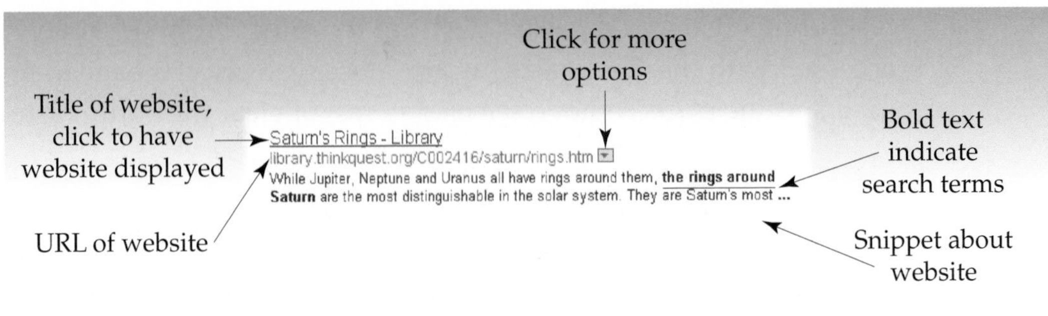

Goodheart-Willcox Publisher

Figure 18-2. An individual result appears similar to the one shown here.

signify that the result is a sponsored result. Some sponsored results are displayed in an ad listing that may not have shading, but that is separate from the returned results list.

When a user searches for a person, place, or thing, a summary including facts, photos, and links may be displayed to the right of the returned results list. A list of related searches is displayed at the bottom of the results page. Also, if the number of returned results are too numerous to fit on a single page, links to additional pages of results will appear at the bottom of the page.

Search Tips and Tools

A search that provides millions of fair results can be less helpful than a search that yields twenty results with the exact information needed. There are many tips and tools available to help a user focus a search to get better results.

Basic search tips include carefully choosing keywords. It can be helpful to start a search using the name, place, or concept and then add words that convey key details. Considering how the information would be phrased on a web page and constructing the search phrase in a similar manner can provide more useful results. Also, entering just the keywords rather than an entire sentence can produce better search results.

Using Search Operators

A user can add Boolean and other search operators to search terms as another way to improve a search, as seen in **Figure 18-3.** A ***Boolean operator*** is a logical connector, such as **OR** and **NOT**, added to a search phrase to typically either narrow or broaden the search results.

Using operators often requires the user to be exact with regard to using all uppercase or lowercase letters. Punctuation and spacing can also make a difference in whether the operator will work properly. For example, the file name operator only works if there is no space or punctuation between filename: and the file extension.

Google Search Filters and Tools

Once a user has conducted an initial search, he or she can refine the search using filters, search tools, or an advanced search. A ***filter*** can limit a search to a specific criterion, such as a subject area, web page type, or file type. Google Search filters include images, videos, news, books, blogs, discussions, recipes, applications, shopping, flights, and patents. When the results page is displayed after an initial search, a search text box appears containing the original search terms. A subset of filter types is visible under the search text box. Google varies the filters it displays under the search text box based on the original search term. The remaining filters are available from a drop-down menu.

Search Operator	Description	Example
Quotes ("")	Searches for the exact phrase within the quotation marks.	"weather on Jupiter" Results will contain this exact phrase rather than just information about weather or just information about Jupiter.
Dash (–)	Searches for results that do not include the word immediately following the operator.	interplanetary weather information –Jupiter Results will not include Jupiter.
site:	Searches only the specified website for the search term.	site:nytimes.com Jupiter Results of this search will only be from nytimes.com.
Asterisk (*)	Searches for keywords and adds a word or words in place of the operator.	"the * around Saturn" Results of this search will include phrases where the asterisk has been replaced with a word or words, such as "the rings around Saturn," "the atmosphere around Saturn," and "the way around Saturn."
number...number	Searches for a number range.	1...4 Jupiter Results will include one, four, and any number in between one and four.
filetype:	Searches for specified file extension containing the search term.	weather filetype:PDF Results will be limited to PDF files.
OR	Searches for one word or the other word per result. This is a Boolean operator.	weather on Jupiter OR Mars Each result will contain information about weather on Jupiter or Mars, or both in the same result.
AND	Searches for both words per result. This is a Boolean operator.	weather on Jupiter AND Mars Each result will contain information about both Jupiter and Mars.
NOT	Searches for results that do not include the word immediately following the operator. This is a Boolean operator that is similar to the dash operator.	weather on Jupiter NOT Mars Each result will contain information about Jupiter, but not Mars.

Goodheart-Willcox Publisher

Figure 18-3. Google searches can be filtered and refined.

The **Search tools** button is displayed to the right of the filters. The search tools allow a user to guide returned results by adding time, location, and other requirements, such as reading level, on to search criteria. A user can specify that he or she only wants to see results that have been posted to the web within a select time period. A zip code or city can be entered as well and results close to that location will be displayed. This can be helpful when searching for a local news article or a place of business, for example.

Google Search includes an advanced search function. After an initial search, a user can access the Advanced Search page from the results page by clicking the **Options** button. The top portion of the page allows a user to specify which search terms should or should not be included in the search results. The bottom portion allows a user to narrow search results based on specific parameters. Many of the options on the Advanced Search page are also achieved using search operators, filters, and tools. Unique to the Advanced Search page, a user can search by language and by usage rights to find works that are in the public domain or that have been labeled for reuse under Creative Commons.

Another way a Mac user can search is using the Google Quick Search Box program. ***Google Quick Search Box*** is a program that searches the web and the user's computer. Returned results include links to websites and files stored on the user's computer relevant to the search terms.

Lesson 18-1

Using Google Chrome to Navigate the World Wide Web

Using Google Chrome, a person can enter a URL in the omnibox to view a website. A user can also access the browser history to revisit specific web pages.

Using Google Chrome to Access a Website

1. Launch Google Chrome.
2. Click in the omnibox at the top of the screen.
3. Enter www.usa.gov as the URL of the site you want to go to, and press the [Enter] key. The official website for the US government is loaded into the browser window, as shown in **Figure 18-4.**

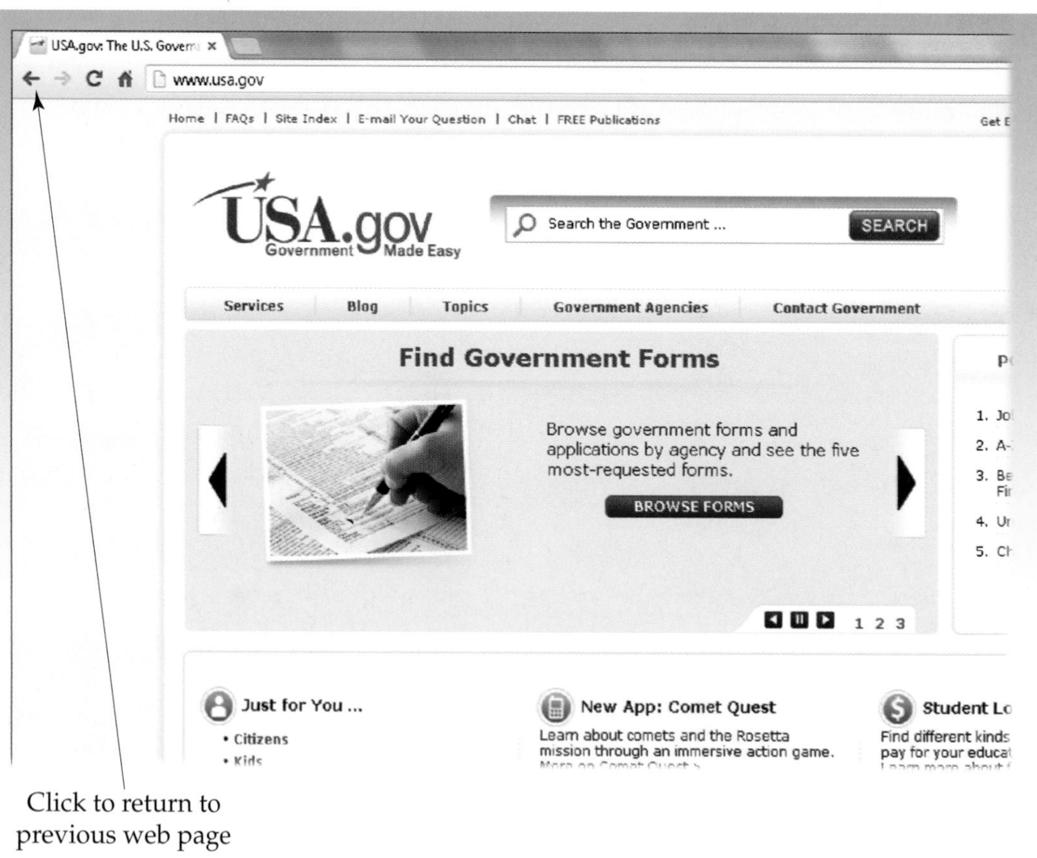

Goodheart-Willcox Publisher

Figure 18-4. When navigating to a web page, the page is displayed in the browser window.

4. Click the **Click to go back** button. The previous web page is displayed, which in this case should be the default Google Chrome page.
5. Click the **Click to go forward** button. The US government page is redisplayed.
6. Click the **About Us** link at the bottom of the US government page. A different page on the US government website is displayed.
7. Locate the **USA.gov Fact Sheet** link on the page, and click it. If this link is unavailable, click on any other link on the page.

Using the Quick History

8. Click and hold the **Click to go back** button. A drop-down list is displayed that contains the URLs visited in this session with the most recent one listed at the top, as shown in **Figure 18-5.**
9. Click the entry in the drop-down list for USA.gov. The home page for the website is displayed. This allows you to skip over the About USA.gov page that is the previously viewed page.

10. Click and hold the **Click to go forward** button. A quick history is displayed for moving forward in navigation.
11. Click the entry in the drop-down list for the fact sheet PDF (or whichever link you clicked on the About USA.gov page). The PDF is displayed in the browser window, skipping over the About USA.gov page.

Using the Full History

12. Click the **Customize and control Google Chrome** button, to display a drop-down menu.
13. Click **History** in the drop-down menu. The full history is shown in a new tab, as seen in **Figure 18-6.** The websites that have been visited over the past several days are displayed in a list along with the date and time when pages were accessed. Sites that are bookmarked have a yellow star next to them.

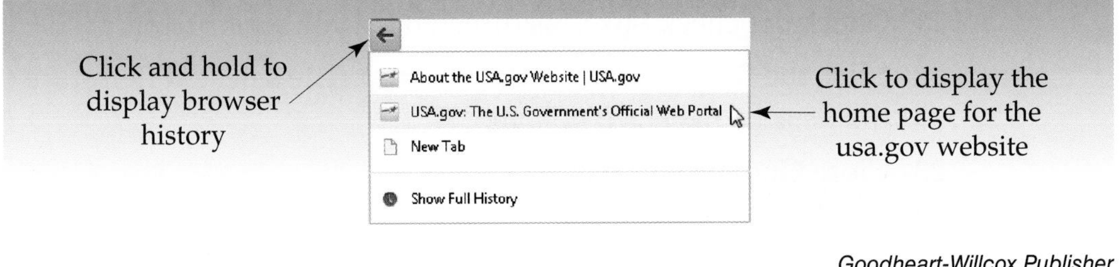

Goodheart-Willcox Publisher

Figure 18-5. The quick history is a convenient way to navigate to viewed pages.

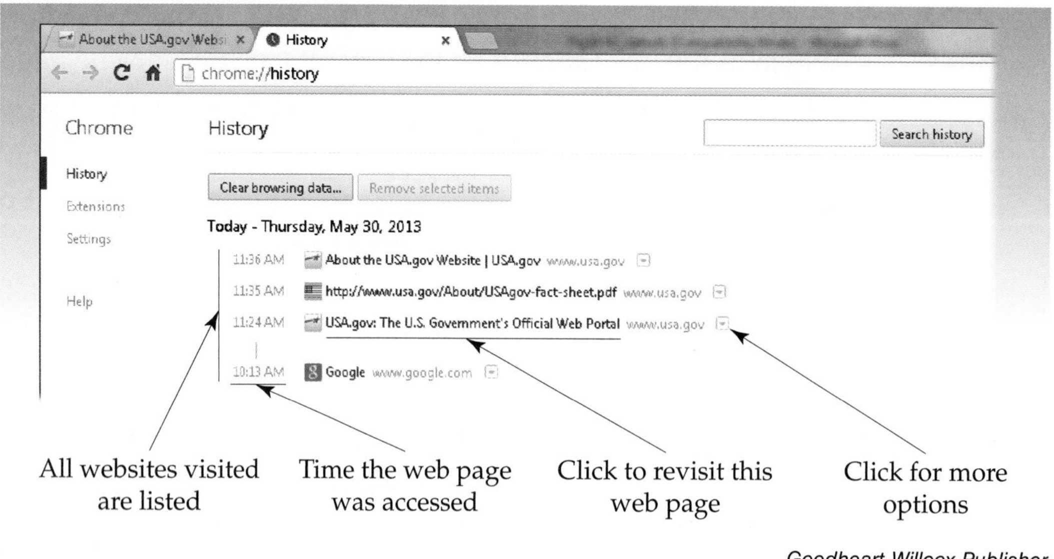

Goodheart-Willcox Publisher

Figure 18-6. The full history is displayed in a new tab or window.

Tip The full history can also be displayed by clicking **Show Full History** in the quick history drop-down list.

Search history

14. Click in the **Search History** text box, enter USA, and click the **Search history** button. All entries in the history that contain USA are displayed.
15. Locate the entry for the USA.gov fact sheet PDF, hover the cursor over it, and check the check box that appears to the left of the entry.

Remove selected items

16. Click the **Remove selected items** button. A message appears asking you to confirm the deletion.
17. Click the **OK** button in the confirmation message. The entry is removed from the history. It will not appear in the quick history either.
18. Click the **X** on the **Search History** text box to clear the search and display the full history.

Clear browsing data...

19. Click the **Clear browsing data...** button. The **Clear Browsing Data** dialog box is displayed, as shown in **Figure 18-7.**
20. Click the drop-down button, and click **the beginning of time** in the drop-down list. Your instructor may specify a different entry to click.
21. Check the check boxes as directed by your instructor.
22. Click the **Clear Browsing Data** button. The selected items are cleared, and the Settings page is displayed.
23. Close Google Chrome.

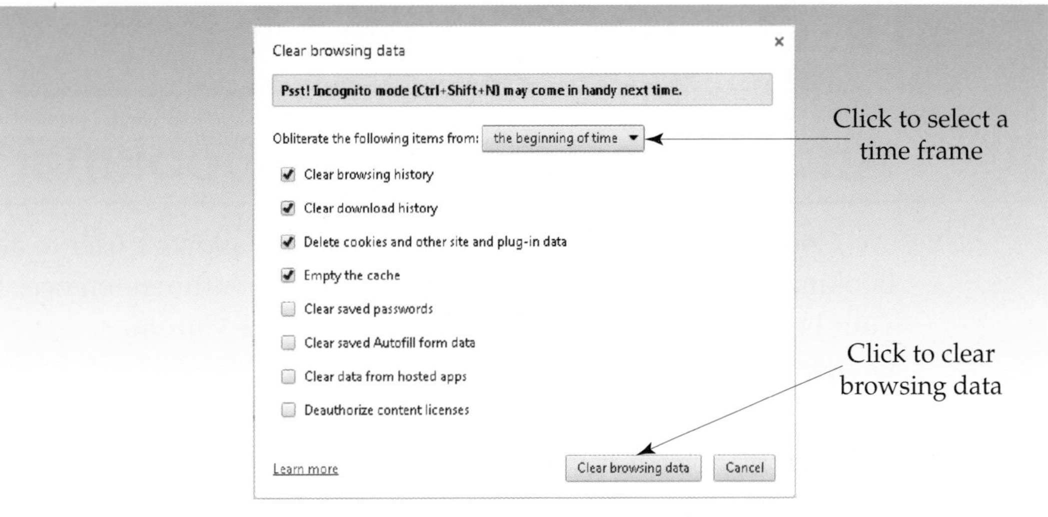

Goodheart-Willcox Publisher

Figure 18-7. Browsing data can be cleared to remove the browsing history.

Lesson 18-2

Adding and Managing Bookmarks

Google Chrome, like many other browsers, allows a user to add bookmarks to pages he or she wants to save for future reference. To access your bookmarks on any computer or device, use Chrome to log into your Google account.

Adding a Bookmark

1. Launch Google Chrome.
2. Log in to your Google Mail account.
3. Click in the omnibox at the top of the screen, enter www.usa.gov as the URL, and press the [Enter] key. The official website for the US government is loaded into the browser window.

Bookmark this page

4. Click the **Bookmark this page** button. The **Bookmark** pop-up window is displayed, as shown in **Figure 18-8.**
5. Click in the **Name:** text box, and enter Official Website of the Federal Government. This changes the name from name provided by the site.
6. Click the **Done** button to add the bookmark to the default location.

Using Bookmarks

Customize and control Google Chrome

7. Click the **Customize and control Google Chrome** button.
8. Click **Bookmarks** in the drop-down menu, and click **Show bookmarks bar** in the cascading menu. The **Bookmarks** toolbar is displayed below the omnibox.
9. Click in the omnibox, and enter www.google.com. The Google search page is displayed.

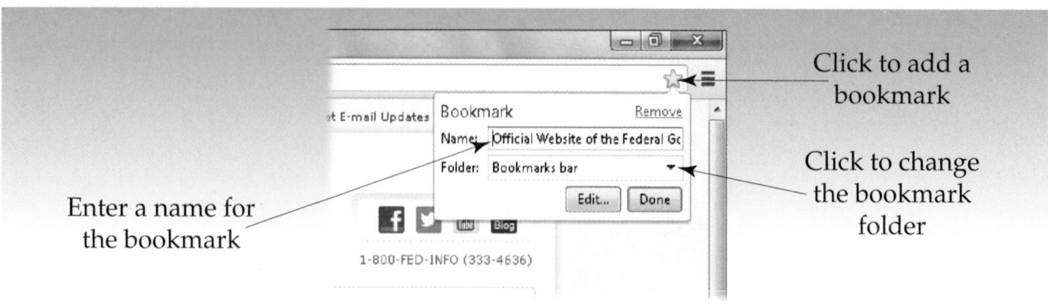

Figure 18-8. Creating a bookmark for a web page.

10. Click the **Official Website of the Federal Government** button on the **Bookmarks** toolbar. That page is loaded in the browser window.

If the desired bookmark is in a folder, the folder appears as a button on the **Bookmarks** toolbar. Clicking the folder button displays a drop-down list containing the bookmarks in the folder.

Editing and Managing Bookmarks

11. Right-click on the **Official Website of the Federal Government** button on the **Bookmarks** toolbar, and click **Edit...** in the shortcut menu. The **Edit Bookmark** dialog box is displayed, as shown in **Figure 18-9.**
12. Highlight the Bookmarks bar folder, and click the **New folder** button. A new subfolder is added below the Bookmarks bar folder.
13. Name the new subfolder My Class Bookmarks.
14. Select the new subfolder, click the **Save** button. This moves the bookmark being edited to the new subfolder and closes the **Edit Bookmark** dialog box.
15. Right-click on any button on the **Bookmarks** toolbar, and click **Bookmark manager** in the drop-down menu. The Bookmark Manager page is displayed in a new tab, as shown in **Figure 18-10.**
16. Click the **Organize** link to display a drop-down menu, and click **Add page...** in the menu. A new blank entry is added to the list of bookmarks.
17. Click in the **Name** text box, and enter Social Security Administration.

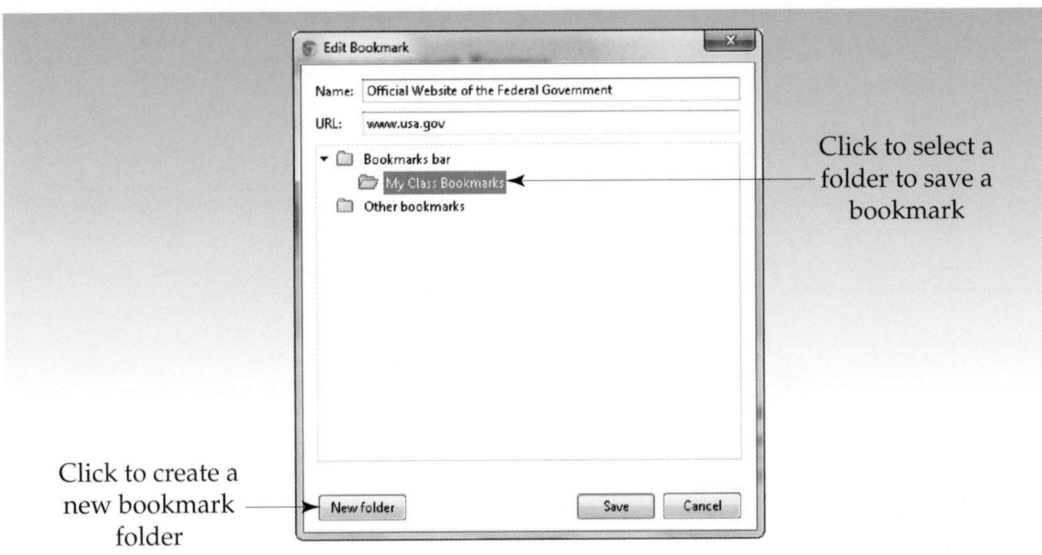

Goodheart-Willcox Publisher

Figure 18-9. A bookmark can be edited after it has been created.

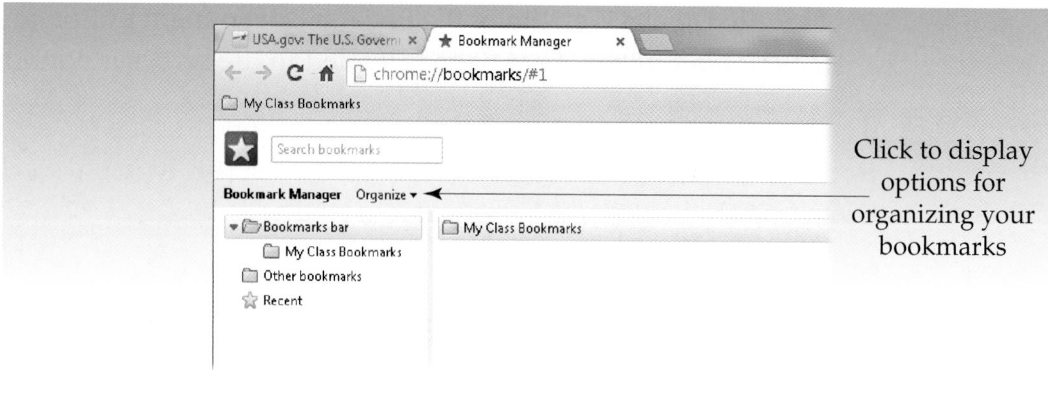

Goodheart-Willcox Publisher

Figure 18-10. Bookmarks can be edited and managed using the Bookmark Manager page.

Tip To rename an existing bookmark, right-click on it, and select **Edit...** from the shortcut menu.

18. Click in the **URL** text box, and enter www.ssa.gov. Press the [Enter] key to add the bookmark.
19. Select the Bookmarks bar folder, click the **Organize** link, and click **Add folder...** in the drop-down menu.
20. Name the new folder My Governmental Sites.
21. Select the My Class Bookmarks folder to display the bookmarks it contains.
22. Hold the [Ctrl] key, and click both bookmarks to select them.
23. Drag both bookmarks to the My Governmental Sites folder, and drop them. The bookmarks are moved to that folder.
24. Close the tab to end managing bookmarks.
25. Close Google Chrome.

Lesson 18-3

Keyword Search

Most Google searches start with keywords or search terms. Search or Boolean operators can be added to better focus a search.

Conducting a Basic Search

1. Launch Google Chrome.
2. Click in the omnibox at the top of the screen, enter www.google.com as the URL, and press the [Enter] key. The Google Search page is displayed.

A search term can aslo be entered directly in the omnibox.

3. Click in the search text box, enter dog bath, and click the **Google Search** button. The search results are displayed, as shown in **Figure 18-11.**

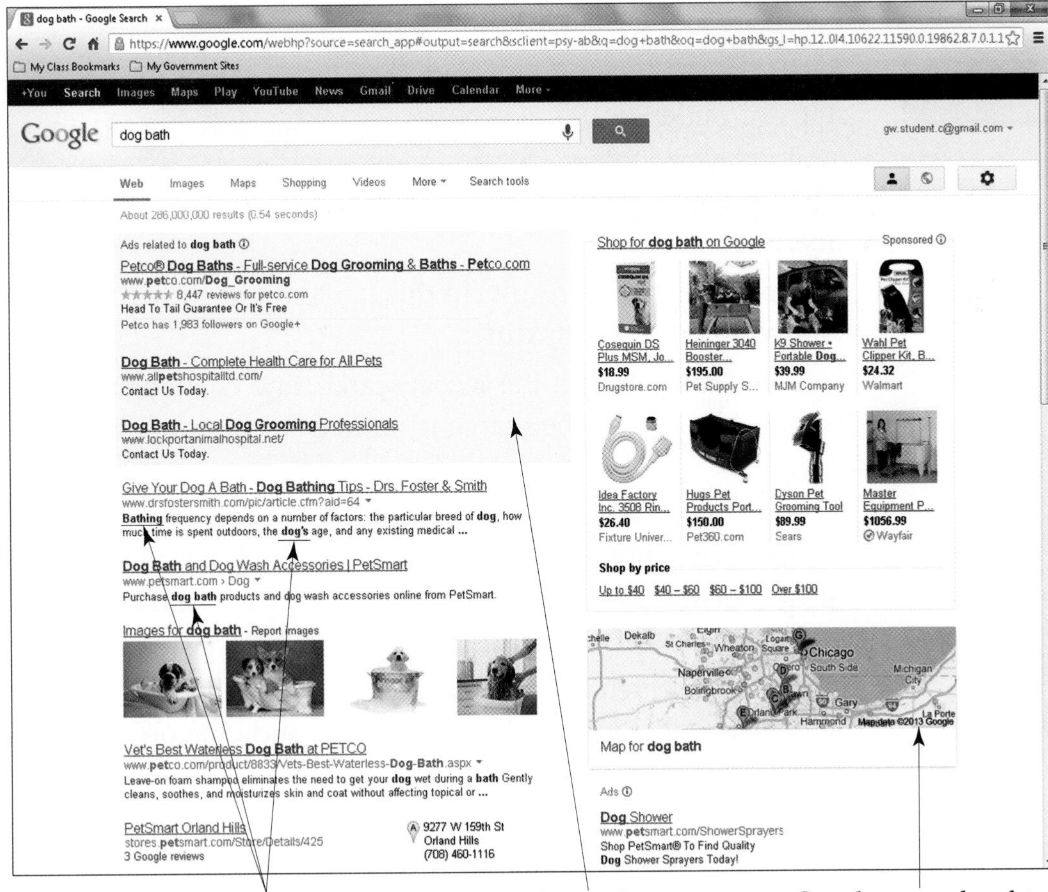

Goodheart-Willcox Publisher

Figure 18-11. Search results for a basic Google search.

Notice the results include bathtubs for dogs, places to take your dog for a bath, and other information. Also notice that related words such as *groomer* and *grooming* appear several times.

4. Click in the search text box, enter tips dog grooming, and click the **Google Search** button. Did this return results about how to groom your dog?
5. Click in the search text box, enter dog grooming tips, and click the **Google Search** button. How do the results differ from the previous search? The order of words in the search text box can make a difference in the results that are displayed.

Refining the Search

6. Click in the search text box, enter lincoln, and click the **Google Search** button. Identify at least three different Lincoln-related topics found in the search results.
7. Click the **New tab** button at the top of the screen. A new tab is opened with the default Chrome home page displayed.
8. Navigate to the Google search page.

Tip You can display the Google Search page by selecting the **Search** link at the top most Google App pages, such as your Gmail page or Calendar page.

9. Click in the search text box, enter "abraham lincoln", and click the **Google Search** button.
10. Compare the search results in this tab to those shown in the other tab. Notice how the results differ.
11. Switch to the tab with the lincoln search, and change the search to lincoln –movie. Notice that the search is refined so no search results related to movies are displayed.
12. Change the search to lincoln nebraska OR oregon. How do these results compare to the previous ones? By using the Boolean operator **OR**, the results include both Nebraska and Oregon. There is a Lincoln, Nebraska and a Lincoln City, Oregon.
13. Change the search to lincoln nebraska AND oregon. The search displays only results that include both Nebraska and Oregon.

Using Google Chrome's Speech Recognition to Search the Web

14. Make sure a microphone is plugged into your computer and fully functional.
15. Open a new tab, and navigate to the Google Search page.

Search by Voice

16. Click the **Search by Voice** button at the right of the search text box. A message appears at the top of the browser window indicating Google wants to use the microphone, as shown in **Figure 18-12.** This message may not always appear.
17. Click the **Allow** button to continue. A new page is displayed that indicates to start speaking.
18. Clearly speak abraham lincoln into the microphone. When you stop speaking, the search results are displayed.

Depending on the search words spoken, audio information may be played through the computer speakers when the search results are displayed. This can be especially useful if you speak a question, such as **what time is it?**

19. Compare the search results of this audio search to the search conducted by entering "abraham lincoln". The results should be similar; however, note that the quotation marks are not included in the spoken search.
20. Use the mouse to click on a search result. The web page is displayed in the browser.
21. Close Google Chrome.

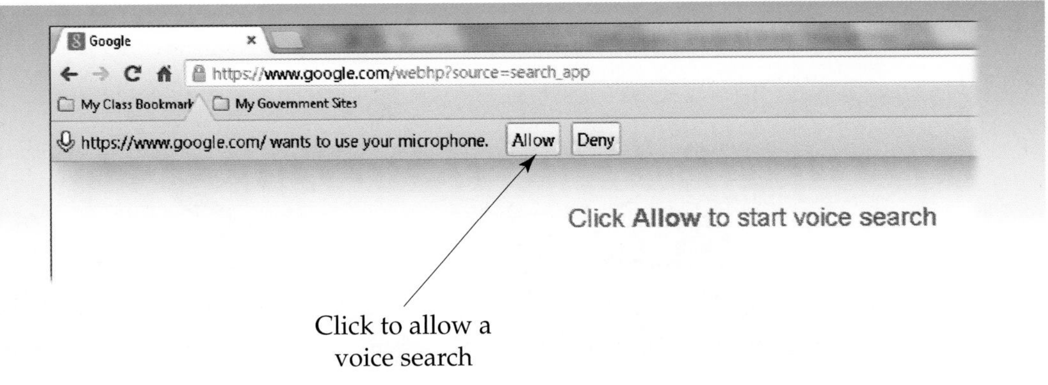

Goodheart-Willcox Publisher

Figure 18-12. To use the microphone for a search, you must allow it.

Lesson 18-4

Image Search

Although image results sometimes appear in regular search results pages, you can search for images only. Also, a search can start with an image instead of a keyword. This may happen when a user finds an image, but wants more options.

Searching for Images by Keyword

1. Launch Google Chrome.
2. Click in the omnibox at the top of the screen, enter www.google.com as the URL, and press the [Enter] key. The Google Search page is displayed.
3. Click the **Images** link in the navigation bar. The Google Image Search page is displayed.

4. Click in the search text box, enter grand opening, and click the **Google Search** button. The search results appear as thumbnails of the images, as shown in **Figure 18-13.**

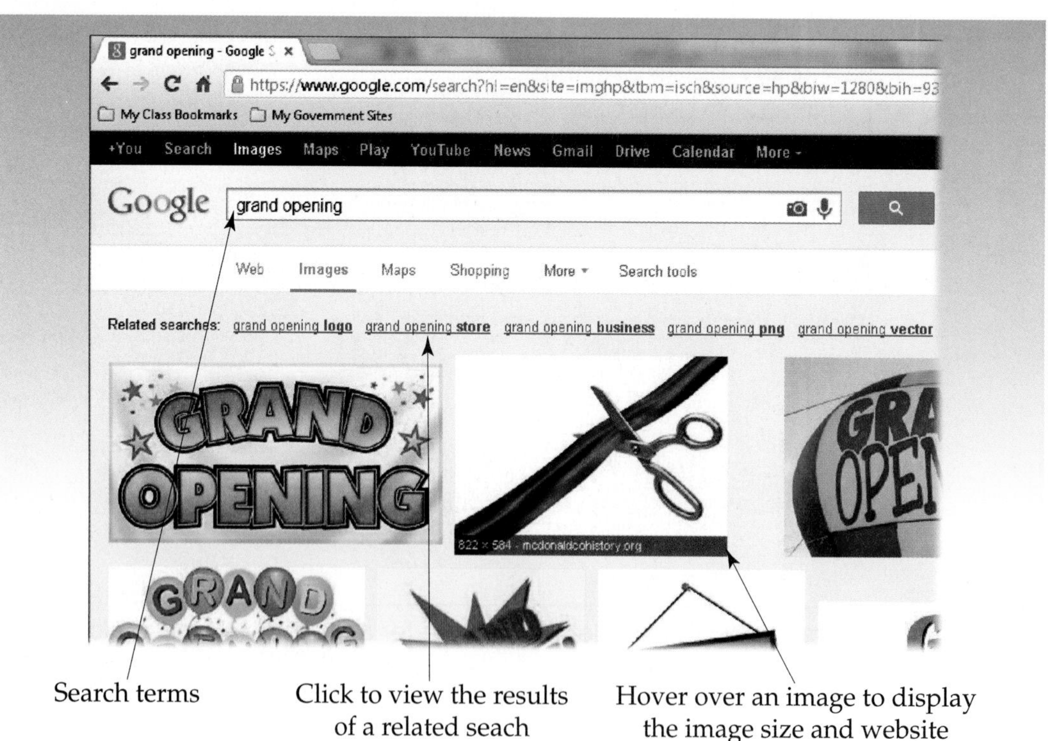

Goodheart-Willcox Publisher

Figure 18-13. The results for an image search appear as thumbnail images.

Tip For image searches, links to related searches are displayed at the top of the page between the search box and the results. These suggestions may help refine the search.

5. Hover the cursor over a thumbnail image. The size of the image and the web page for the image are displayed on the thumbnail.
6. Click on one of the search results. A pop-up window is displayed containing a larger version of the image and additional information, links to the web page where the image is, and suggestions for visually similar images. See **Figure 18-14.**
7. Right-click on the image in the pop-up window, and click **Save Image As...** in the shortcut menu. A standard file-save dialog box is displayed.
8. Navigate to your working folder, name the file, and click the **Save** button. The image is saved in its original file format.
9. Close the pop-up window.

Goodheart-Willcox Publisher

Figure 18-14. Clicking on a thumbnail image in an image search displays the image in a pop-up window.

Searching for Images by Image

Search by Image

10. Click the **Search by Image** button on the right of the search text box. The **Search by Image** dialog box is opened, as shown in **Figure 18-15.**

A URL for the image to search by can be entered in the text box in the **Search by Image** dialog box.

11. Click the **Upload an image** link.
12. Click the **Choose File** button that is displayed. A standard file-open dialog box is displayed.
13. Navigate to the image to search by, select it, and click the **Open** button. The file is uploaded, and a search is initiated. The results page displays the uploaded image at the top, followed by a best guess of the content of the image in words and then the list of results.
14. Close Google Chrome.

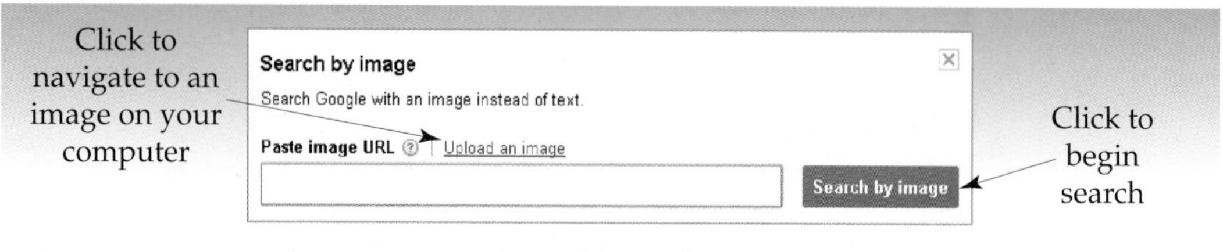

Goodheart-Willcox Publisher

Figure 18-15. An image can be uploaded to search for similar images.

Lesson 18-5

Search Tools and Filters

A search can be refined using search terms and operations; however, you may need to narrow your results even further. This can be done through the search tools and filters displayed above the search results.

Filtering Keyword Searches

1. Launch Google Chrome.
2. Click in the omnibox at the top of the screen, enter www.google.com as the URL, and press the [Enter] key. The Google Search page is displayed.
3. Click in the search text box, enter eagles, and click the **Google Search** button. The search results are displayed. Between the search box and the search results are several filter links and the **Search Tools** button, as shown in **Figure 18-16.**
4. Click the **Shopping** filter link. The results are filtered to show only shopping results. The page also changes to allow the search to be further filtered by category, price, brand, and other criteria.

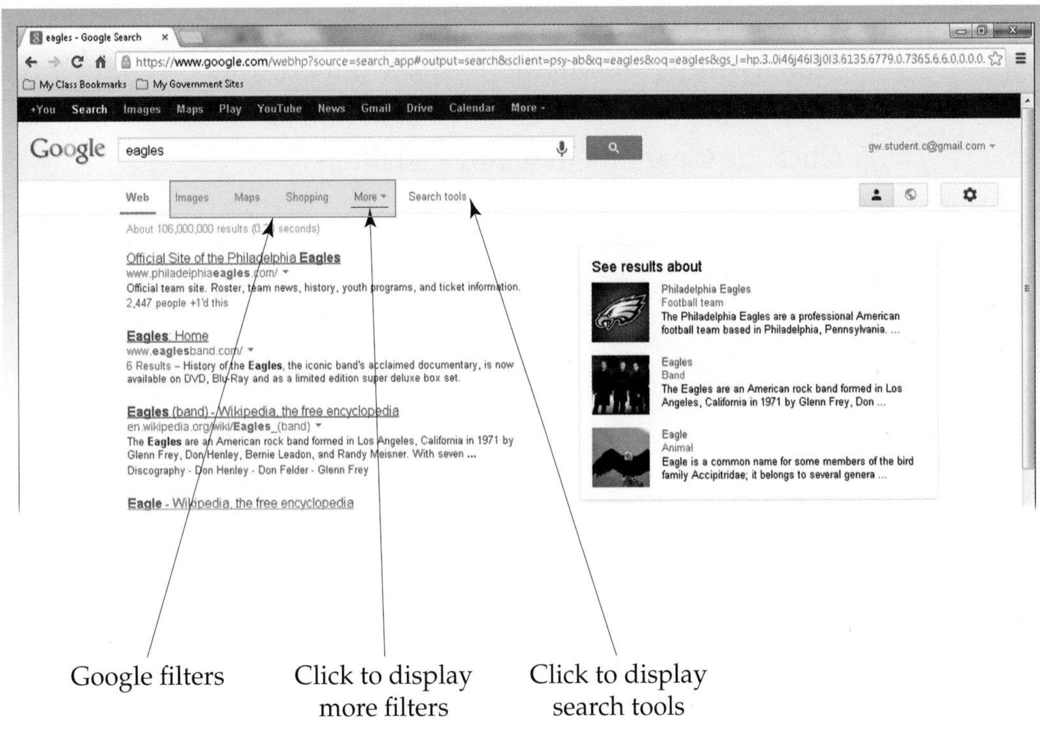

Goodheart-Willcox Publisher

Figure 18-16. Filter links appear between the search text box and the search results.

Click to go back

5. Click the **Click to Go Back** button to redisplay the original search.
6. Click the **More** link to display a drop-down menu, and click **Videos** in the menu. The search results are filtered to show primarily videos.
7. Click the **Click to Go Back** button to redisplay the original search.

Search tools

8. Click the **Search Tools** button. Three links for drop-down lists are displayed above the search results.
9. Click the **Any Time** link to display the drop-down list, and click **Past Year** in the list. The search results are refined to show only results posted within the past 12 months. The published date or, in some cases, time is included at the beginning of each website description.
10. Click the date filter link again, which is now **Past Year**, and click **Custom Range...** in the drop-down list. The **Custom Date Range** dialog box is displayed, as shown in **Figure 18-17.**
11. Click in the **From** text box, and enter 01/01/2013 or other date specified by your instructor. Be sure to enter four digits for the year (2013).
12. Click in the **To** text box, and then click on today's date in the minicalendar.
13. Click the **Go** button. The results are filtered to show only results posted within the specified range.
14. Click the **Clear** link to remove all filters. The full search results for eagles are displayed, and the filter links are hidden.

Search tools

15. Click the **Search Tools** button.
16. Click the **All results** link, and click **Verbatim** in the drop-down list. The search results are filtered to show only results containing the exact word eagles.
17. Click the **Clear** link to remove all filters.

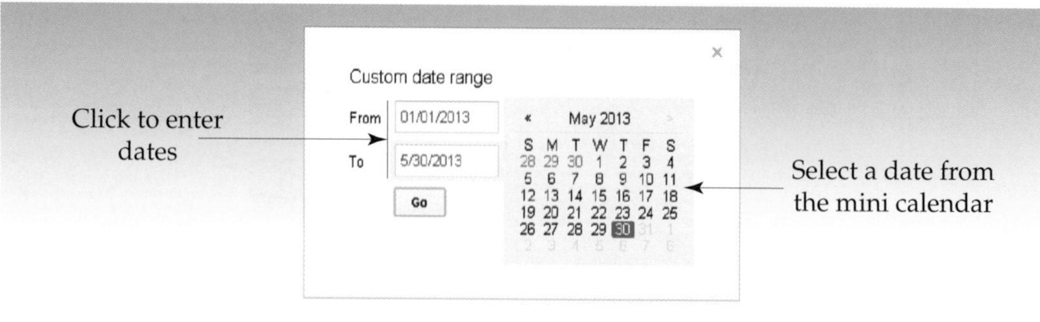

Goodheart-Willcox Publisher

Figure 18-17. A search can be filtered by date, including setting a custom range of dates.

Advanced Search Options

18. Click the **Options** button to display a drop-down menu, and click **Advanced Search** in the menu. The Advanced Search page is displayed, as shown in **Figure 18-18.** Notice the current search phrase is entered in the first text box.
19. Click in the **Any of these words:** text box, and enter birds OR flight.
20. Click in the **None of these words:** text box, and enter –football, –team.

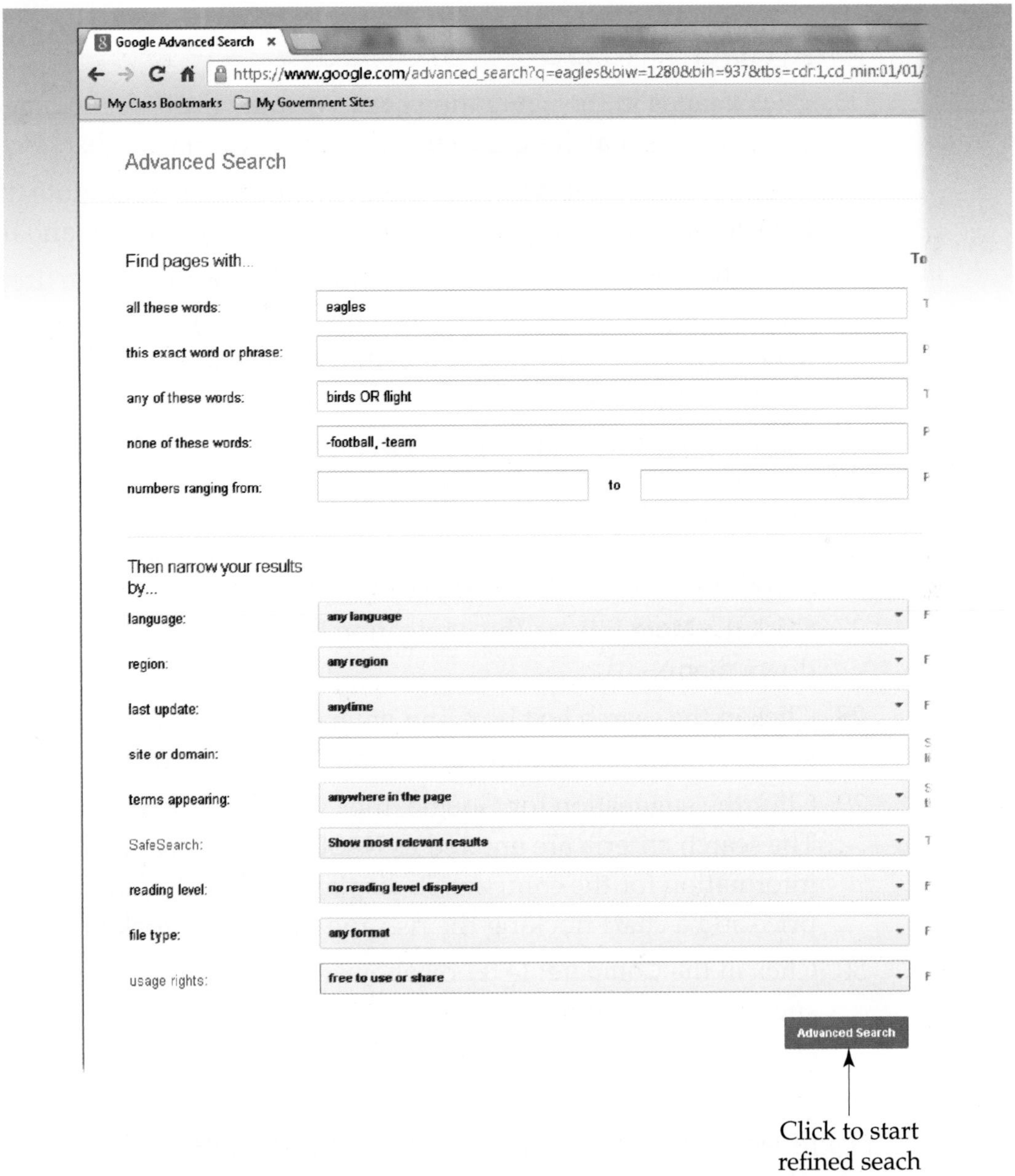

Click to start refined seach

Goodheart-Willcox Publisher

Figure 18-18. An advanced search can be conducted when a basic search is insufficient.

The entries in the text boxes at the top of the page can be directly entered on the Google Search page. It is the options at the bottom of the page that create an advanced search.

21. Click the **Usage rights:** button to display a drop-down list, and click **Free to use or share** in the list.

Advanced Search

22. Click the **Advanced Search** button. The search results display links to articles that have been marked as free to use or share under Creative Commons that contain the words eagles, birds, or flight, but excludes articles that contain the word football or team.

Filtering Image Searches

23. Click **Images** in the navigation bar to display the Google Images search page. Images matching the current search criteria are displayed.
24. Click on **Search Tools** button to display the filter links. Note that the links for an image search are different from those for a standard search.
25. Click the **Color** link, and click the blue color swatch in the drop-down menu. The results are filtered to show only images that are mainly blue in color. In this case, most of the images probably will be of eagles flying against a blue sky.
26. Click the **Type** link, and click **Clip art** in the drop-down list. The results are filtered to show primarily images that are clipart.

Conducting a Financial Search

27. Click the **More** link on the navigation bar, and click **Finance** in the drop-down menu.
28. Click in the search text box, and enter google. Notice that suggestions for stock symbols are displayed, as shown in **Figure 18-19.**
29. Click the suggestion for Google, Inc., which is stock symbol GOOG. The search criteria are entered as NASDAQ:GOOG, and various financial information for the company is displayed, including the current stock price and a chart tracking the rise and fall of the stock price.
30. Click in the **Compare:** text box above the chart, enter yahoo, and click the suggestion for Yahoo!, Inc., which is stock symbol YHOO. The search criteria are entered as NASDAQ:YHOO.
31. Click the **Add** button. The chart changes to a comparison of the stock prices for the two companies, as shown in **Figure 18-20.**
32. Close Google Chrome.

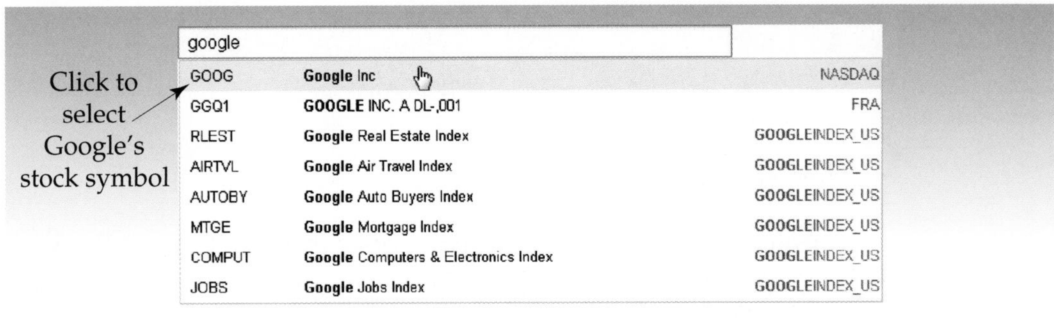

Goodheart-Willcox Publisher

Figure 18-19. When something is entered in the search text box, suggestions are provided.

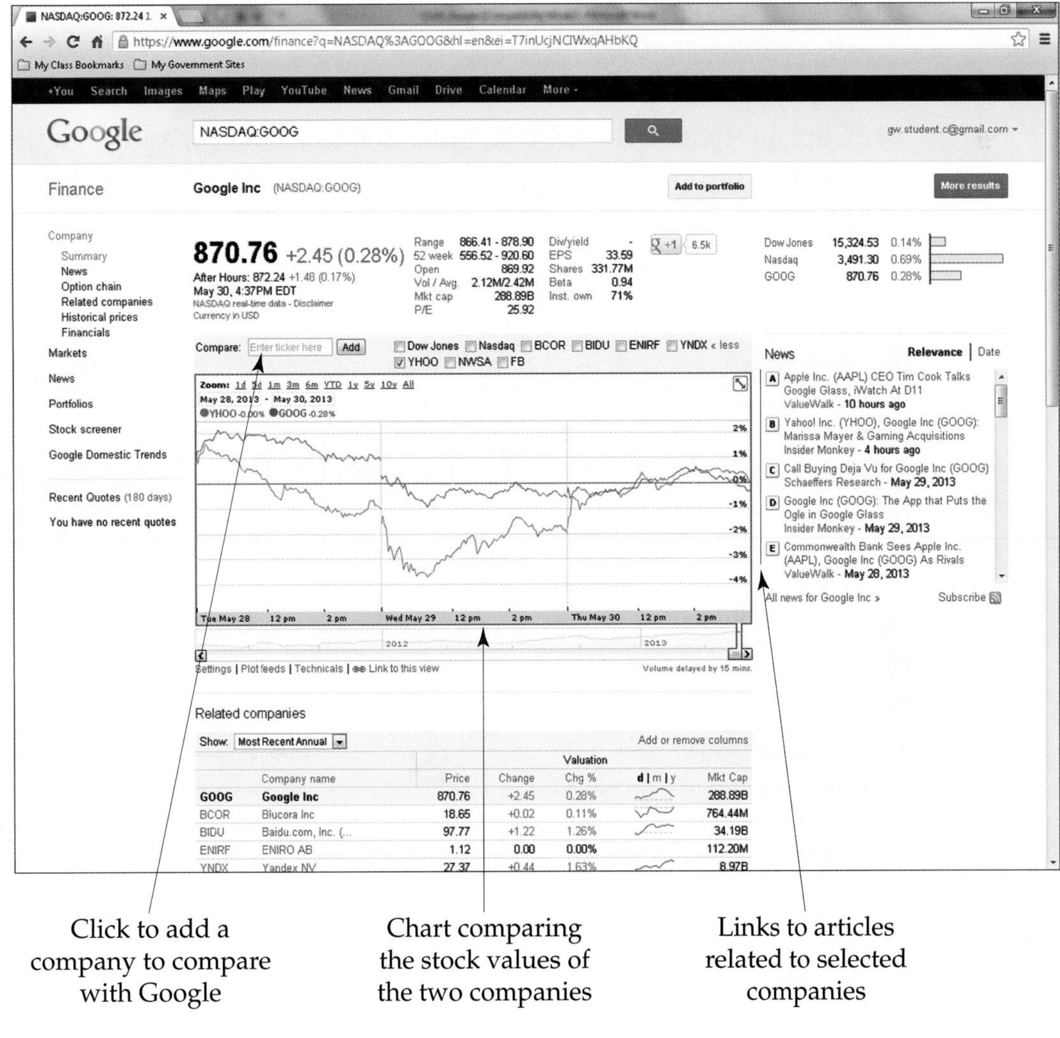

Goodheart-Willcox Publisher

Figure 18-20. In this example, the chart displays a comparison of stock prices for two companies.

Lesson 18-6

Google Books

A user can search, save, and read books through Google Books. This includes some free e-books and previews of other books that can be purchased. To save an e-book, the user must log into his or her Google account, and then books can be saved to categories within the user's Google library.

1. Launch Google Chrome.
2. Click in the omnibox at the top of the screen, enter www.google.com as the URL, and press the [Enter] key. The Google Search page is displayed.
3. Click the **More** link in the navigation bar, and click **Books** in the drop-down menu. The Google Books page is displayed, as shown in **Figure 18-21.**
4. Click in the search text box, enter sherlock holmes, and click the **Search Books** button. The results displayed are books related to Sherlock Holmes.

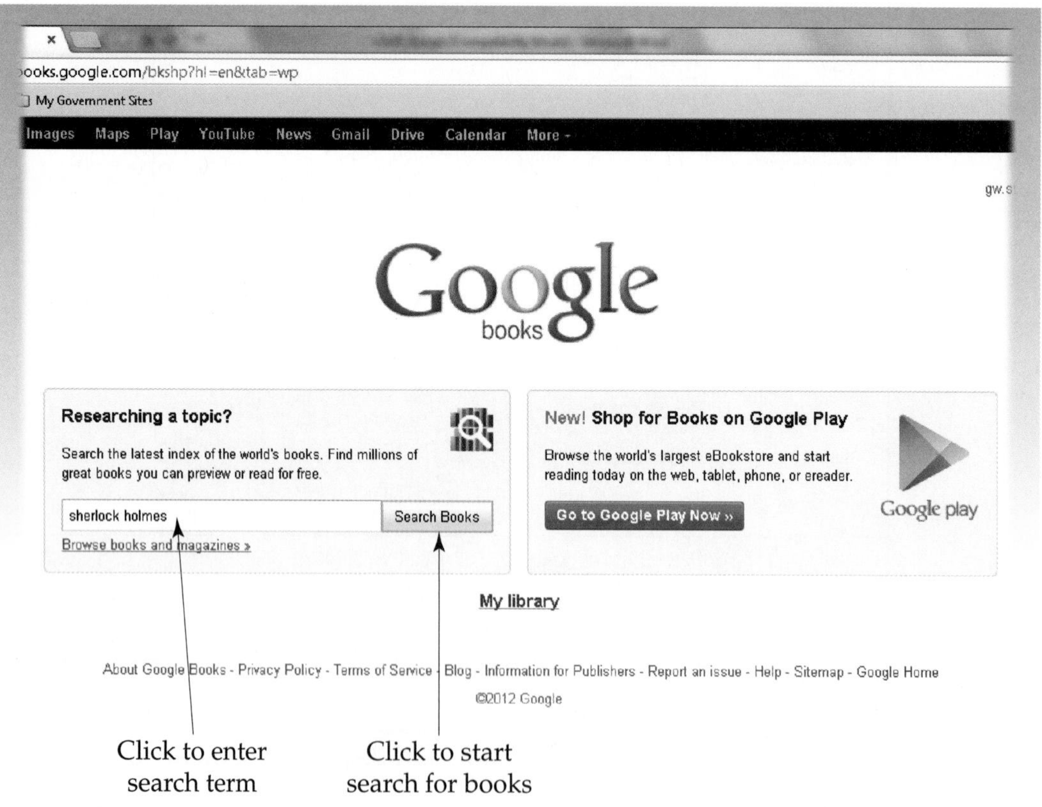

Goodheart-Willcox Publisher

Figure 18-21. Searching for books using Google.

Search tools

5. Click the **Search tools** button to display the filter links.
6. Click the **Any books** link, and click **Free Google eBooks** in the drop-down list. The results are filtered to show only books available for free on Google.
7. Click a link in the results. The book is displayed in an online reader, as shown in **Figure 18-22.**
8. Click the **Sign In** button.
9. Enter your user name and password. Once signed in, the book is redisplayed.

Add to my library

10. Move the cursor over the **Add to my library** button to display a drop-down list. This button is not available for all books, so if it is not displayed, select a different book.

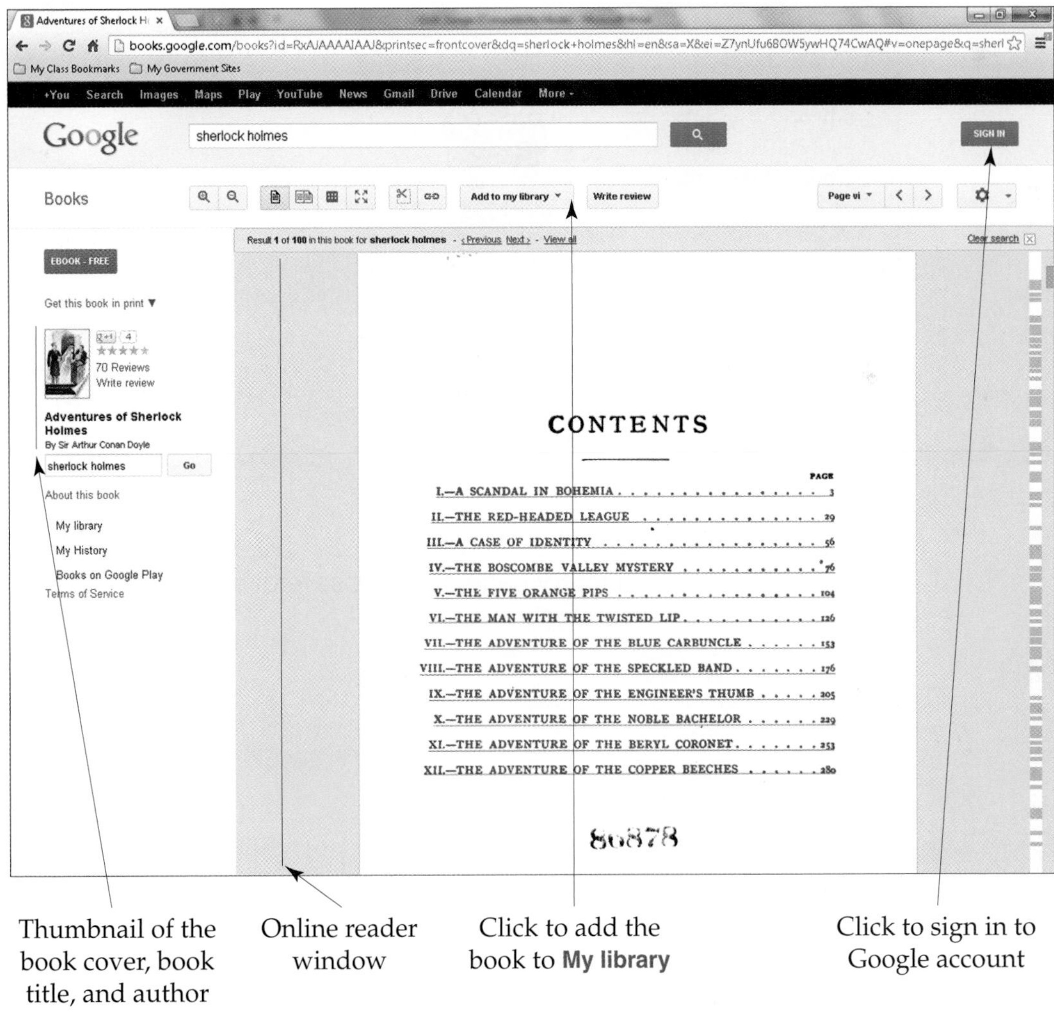

Goodheart-Willcox Publisher

Figure 18-22. When a book is selected from the search results, it is displayed in an online reader.

11. Click **Favorites** in the drop-down list. The book is added to the Favorites shelf in your My Library.
12. Click the **My Library** link. The bookshelves in your My Library are displayed, as shown in **Figure 18-23.**
13. Scroll down to the Favorites shelf.
14. Click the cover of the book just added to the Favorites shelf. A details page for the book is displayed.
15. Click the front cover for the book on the details page. The book is displayed in the reader.
16. Close Google Chrome.

Goodheart-Willcox Publisher

Figure 18-23. The My Library page contains several shelves on which books can be stored.

Lesson 18-7

Using Google Translate

Small blocks of text can be translated into many languages using Google's translation tool. Google will attempt to automatically detect the language entered. A user can choose from more than 60 different languages in which to translate the entered text.

1. Launch Google Chrome.
2. Click in the omnibox at the top of the screen, enter www.google.com as the URL, and press the [Enter] key. The Google Search page is displayed.
3. Click the **More** link in the navigation bar, and click **Translate** in the drop-down menu. The Google Translate page is displayed, as shown in **Figure 18-24.**
4. Click in the left-hand text box, and enter Me gusta estudiar para esta clase. The translation appears in the right-hand text box. Google detects the language as Spanish, and the translation is in English by default.
5. Click the **To:** button to display a drop-down list, and click **French** in the list. The translation is changed to French.

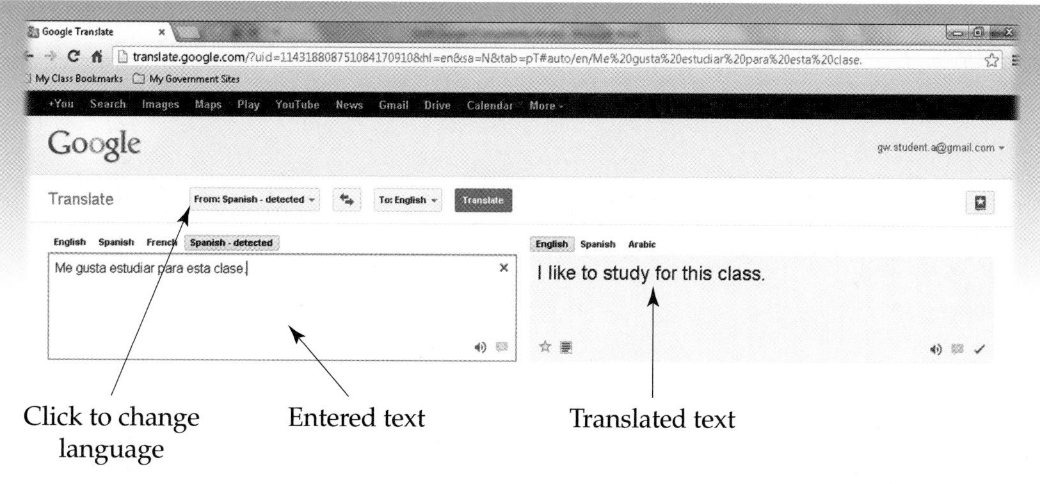

Goodheart-Willcox Publisher

Figure 18-24. Google can be used to translate words and phrases between several languages.

6. Click the **To:** button, and click **Japanese** in the drop-down list. The translation is changed to Japanese.

Read Phonetically

7. Click the **Read Phonetically** button. Words appear below the translation that represent how the characters are pronounced.
8. Make sure the sound is on, and click the **Listen** button. The translation is spoken.
9. Close Google Chrome.

Check Your Google Apps IQ

Now that you have finished this chapter, see what you know about Google Apps by taking the chapter posttest.
www.m.g-wlearning.com
www.g-wlearning.com/informationtechnology/

Skill Review

Answer the following questions on a separate sheet of paper.

1. What software applications allow you to find and review information on the Internet?
2. A ______ is a page that has been tagged by the user so the exact location of the page is saved.
3. What is URL an abbreviation for?
4. Describe an incognito window.
5. What is the term for the basic program used to seek information on the Internet?
6. Searching for information based on specific words is known as a(n) ______ search.
7. What is a Boolean operator?
8. Briefly describe what is shown in an individual search result in a basic search.
9. What is the purpose of a search filter?
10. How are search results ordered on the results page?

Lesson Application

These exercises are designed to apply the skills learned in this chapter. General directions are provided, but you will need to draw on your knowledge to determine how to complete each exercise.

Exercise 18-1
Keyword Searches

Using Google Chrome, search for an author about whom you would like to know more. Start by searching for the author's name. Select a page that contains biographical information for the author, and bookmark the page.

Return to the Google Search page, change to a book search, and see if there are any free Google e-books by the author. If so, add one to your My Library. If not, search for any free Google e-book, and add it to your My Library.

Exercise 18-2 Search Filters

Using Google Chrome, search for your school. Use Boolean operators as needed to limit the search results to primarily your school. Filter the search to display only results for the current school year. Locate your school's home page or another page related to activities in your school. Bookmark the page.

Exercise 18-3 Image Searches

Using Google Chrome, perform an image search for an artist who you like. Select the image that shows what you think is the greatest work by this artist, and display it in the preview window. Save the image to your working folder. Use the links in the preview window to visit the site where the image is found.

Exercise 18-4 Books and Translations

Using Google Chrome, perform a book search to find a book in a foreign language. This may be a book written in the language, or a book that teaches the language. Display the book. Select a passage or phrase from the book that is in the foreign language. Open a new tab, navigate to the Google Translate page, and translate the word or phrase into English.

Use the Google Translate page to find out how to write have a nice day in three different languages. Enter the three translations into an e-mail, and send the e-mail to your instructor. Include the language next to each translation. Use the **Listen** feature to learn how to pronounce the phrase, and then say the phrase to your instructor.

Chapter 19

Google Alerts

Objectives

After completing this chapter, you will be able to:

- **Create** an alert for specified search criteria.
- **Modify** an existing alert.
- **Delete** an alert.

alexmillos/Shutterstock.com

Check Your Google Apps IQ

Before you begin this chapter, see what you already know about Google Apps by taking the chapter pretest.

www.m.g-wlearning.com
www.g-wlearning.com/informationtechnology/

Using Google Alerts

Google Alerts is a tool that gathers online data and sends them to the user's e-mail. An ***alert*** in terms of Google is a notification that is e-mailed to you providing results to a saved search. The user defines what data are gathered and how and when they are delivered. Once set up, the alerts will automatically arrive in the user's e-mail. A user can create multiple alerts, to keep track of various topics. Alerts can be created for a company name, a sports team, or even your name.

Creating Alerts

Creating a new alert begins with choosing a topic for which you would like to receive an alert and then the best search terms for it. The search terms are entered into the **Search query:** text box. A ***query*** is a question or inquiry on specific criteria. The search terms determine what content will be included in the alert. It can be helpful to use the search tips discussed in Chapter 18 when selecting the search terms for a new alert. Also, some search operators can be used to further focus the content of an alert.

The result type and the frequency for an alert are also set by the user. The result type allows the user to filter for a specific type of data. Results can be in the form of news, blogs, videos, discussions, or books. If the result type is set to **Everything**, all types of results will be included in the alert.

An alert e-mail can be delivered once a day, once a week, or as it happens. If the user selects **as-it-happens**, the alert will be sent as soon as updated data that match the search terms are posted online and located by Google. Google Alerts can send all of the data that match the search terms. However, a user can choose to have Google apply a filter to the data so only the most relevant are included in an alert. This is done by selecting **Only the best results** in the **How many:** text box. Alerts are sent to the Gmail address the person used to log in to Google Alerts.

Managing Alerts

Google provides tools to manage alerts. Alerts can be modified or deleted. Once a user receives a few alert e-mails, he or she may decide to change the settings. A user could find, for example, that the search terms need to be more or less precise or that receiving the alert once a day is too often. Any of the alert settings can be modified by clicking the **Manage your alerts** button from the Alerts page. A user can also make some changes to alerts from the alert e-mail he or she receives.

The format of all e-mail alerts can be changed from the HTML default to text only. ***HTML*** stands for hypertext markup language. The HTML default will include formatted text and images. Text only e-mail will be strictly text based. Selecting the text only e-mail format could result in the content loading faster.

An alert can also be deleted. An alert is immediately and permanently removed when a user chooses to delete it. To restore an alert, it must be recreated from scratch.

Lesson 19-1

Creating an Alert

A user can keep up-to-date on a particular news story or monitor new online information about a favorite author by creating Google Alerts. Once set, relevant online data will be automatically compiled and delivered to your e-mail inbox.

1. Log in to your Google Mail account.
2. Click the **More** link in the navigation bar, and click **Even More** in the drop-down list.
3. Click to **Alerts** in the **Specialized Search** area. The Alerts page is displayed, as shown in **Figure 19-1.**

Goodheart-Willcox Publisher

Figure 19-1. The form used to create an alert.

4. Click in the **Search query:** text box, and enter your school's name. A preview of the latest results for the current day appears on the right-hand side of the page.

Search operators can be used to make the results more precise. For example, use quotation marks around a group of words to search for an exact phrase.

5. Click the **Result type:** drop-down button, and click **News** in the list.
6. Click the **How often:** drop-down button, and click **As-it-happens** in the list.
7. Make sure your e-mail appears on the **Deliver to:** button. If not, click the button, and click your e-mail address in the drop-down list.

CREATE ALERT

8. Click the **Create Alert** button. An alert is created that will send you e-mail every time a new news result for your school is found. The Alerts page is displayed, as shown in **Figure 19-2.**

CREATE A NEW ALERT

9. Click the **Create a New Alert** button on the Alerts page. The form for creating an alert is displayed.
10. Click in the **Search query:** text box, and enter engineering college scholarships.
11. Click the **Result type:** drop-down button, and click **Everything** in the list.
12. Click the **How often:** drop-down button, and click **Once a week** in the list.

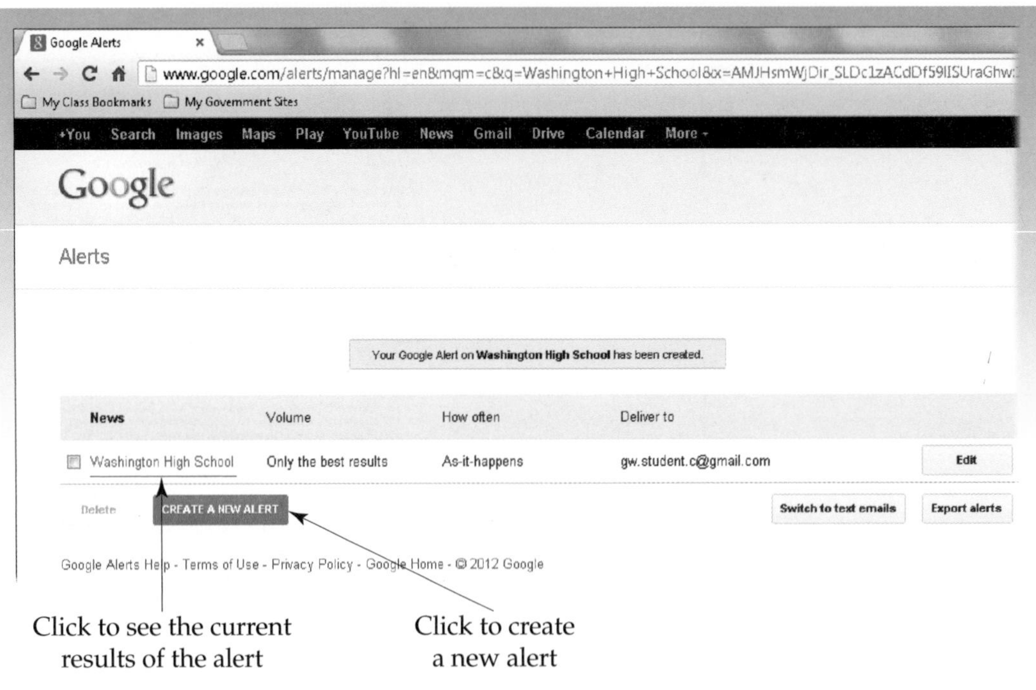

Goodheart-Willcox Publisher

Figure 19-2. The Alerts page contains all alerts that have been created and is where alerts are managed.

13. Make sure your e-mail appears on the **Deliver to:** button. If not, click the button, and click your e-mail address in the drop-down list.
14. Click the **Create Alert** button. A new alert is created that will send you e-mail once a week showing the search results.
15. Close Google Chrome.

Lesson 19-2

Modifying an Alert

A user can modify alert settings at any time. Alerts can also be exported into a CSV file that can be opened in a spreadsheet program. The data can then be sorted and organized.

1. Log in to your Google Mail account.
2. Click the **More** link in the navigation bar, and click **Even More** in the drop-down list.
3. Click **Alerts** in the **Specialized Search** area to display the Alerts page.
4. Click the **Manage your alerts** button. The Alerts page displays the currently saved searches, as shown in **Figure 19-3.**
5. Click the **Edit** button for the alert for your school. The elements of the search are activated for editing.
6. Click the **How often** button, and click **Once a day** in the drop-down list.
7. Click the **Save** button for the alert row. The alert is changed to send e-mails once a day instead of as soon as results are located.
8. Click the **Edit** button for the alert for scholarships.

Manage your alerts

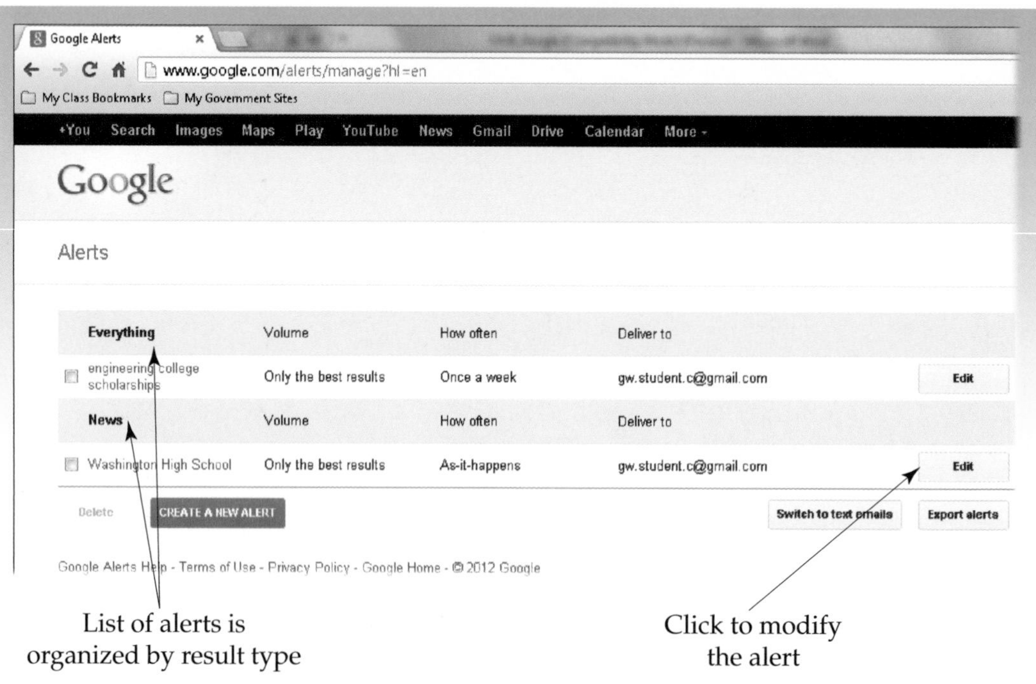

Goodheart-Willcox Publisher

Figure 19-3. When editing an alert, the elements of the alert are enabled for changes.

9. Click in the text box, and change the search query to medical scholarships.
10. Click the **Save** button for the alert row. The alert is changed to search for medical scholarships instead of engineering scholarships.
11. Click the **Export alerts** button. The alerts are saved to a CVS file in your My Documents/Downloads folder.

Export alerts

12. Close Google Chrome.

Lesson 19-3

Deleting an Alert

If an alert is no longer relevant for the user, it can be deleted. To delete an alert, a user will navigate to the page where he or she manages created alerts.

1. Log in to your Google Mail account.
2. Click the **More** link in the navigation bar, and click **Even More** in the drop-down list.
3. Click **Alerts** in the **Specialized Search** area to display the Alerts page.
4. Click the **Manage your alerts** button.
5. Check the check box to the left of the alert for your school.
6. Click the **Delete** button. The alert is removed.

Alerts can also be deleted by clicking on the remove link at the bottom of the e-mail received from an alert.

7. Close Google Chrome.

Check Your Google Apps IQ

Now that you have finished this chapter, see what you know about Google Apps by taking the chapter posttest.
www.m.g-wlearning.com
www.g-wlearning.com/informationtechnology/

Skill Review

Answer the following questions on a separate sheet of paper.

1. What is an alert in terms of Google?
2. What is a query?
3. List the three options for when an alert is delivered.
4. Which button is clicked to start modifying an alert?
5. Once an alert is deleted, how is it restored?

Lesson Application

These exercises are designed to apply the skills learned in this and previous chapters. General directions are provided, but you will need to draw on your knowledge to determine how to complete each exercise.

Exercise 19-1
Creating Alerts

Conduct a text hangout with the classmate assigned by your instructor. Brainstorm ideas for alerts that can be created related to your school or town. Select four ideas. Create a Google Doc that outlines each of the selected ideas, what the alert is to show, and the reason for selecting each alert. Create an alert for each idea using the default settings for each alert. Share the Google Doc with your instructor, sending an e-mail to indicate the document is shared and ready for review.

Exercise 19-2
Modifying Alerts

Conduct a video hangout or, if the equipment for a video hangout is not available, a text hangout with your teammate. Discuss how frequently you should be notified of each alert created in Exercise 19-1. Also discuss whether or not the search criteria is sufficient or if they should be modified with Boolean operators to produce better results. Edit the four alerts created in Exercise 19-1 based on your discussion. Once the alerts are modified, export the alerts to a file, and e-mail the file to your instructor.

Chapter 20

Google News

Objectives

After completing this chapter, you will be able to:

- **Search** for news topics.
- **Add** a custom section to the Google News page.
- **Adjust** the frequency for news feeds on the Google News page.

alexmillos/Shutterstock.com

Check Your Google Apps IQ

Before you begin this chapter, see what you already know about Google Apps by taking the chapter pretest.

www.m.g-wlearning.com
www.g-wlearning.com/informationtechnology/

Overview of Google News

Google News is a free news aggregator with Google's search functionality. A ***news aggregator*** compiles articles from thousands of sources around the world and displays them on one site. When you access Google News, the standard news page is displayed, which includes top current news articles arranged by relevance and popularity as well as eight other news sections. Users can personalize the news page to show topics according to their interest.

Google News Page

The Google News page displays a small amount of information about many news articles with the opportunity to get more information about each. Each news article listed includes the headline of the article, news source, time the article was posted or updated, and lead paragraph of the article. The headline of each article is a link to the site that published the article.

A user can also display the story box by clicking the **Click to see related articles** button to the right of the headline. A ***story box*** is a cluster of listings and links about or related to the same news topic from various news sources, as seen in **Figure 20-1.** The story box can also include other features related to the original headline. Images, videos, and live video coverage can be included in a story box. Different types of articles can be included as well.

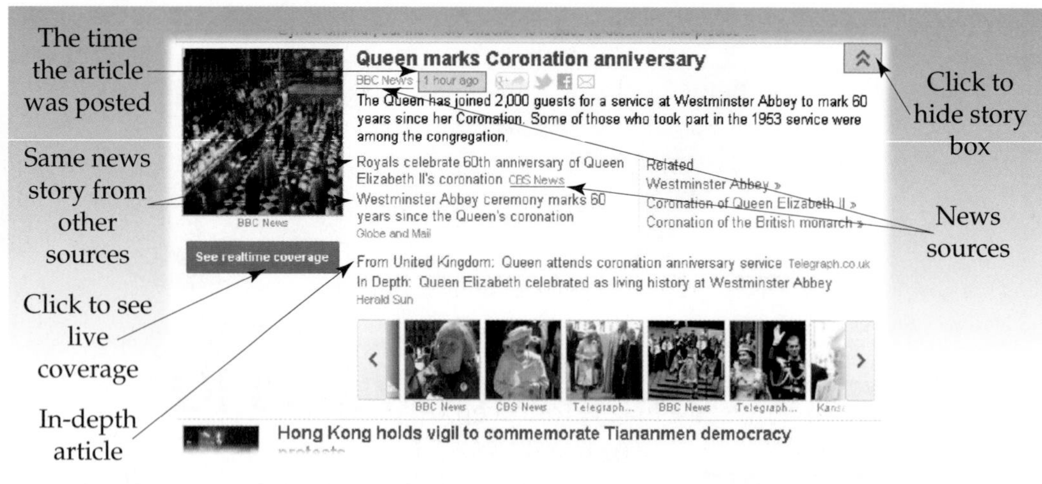

Goodheart-Willcox Publisher

Figure 20-1. A story box contains links to articles related to a single topic.

Google News labels these articles, which include in-depth articles, opinion pieces, satire pieces, or highly cited articles. A ***highly cited article*** is an article that has been frequently referenced by other articles.

The Google News page includes three main areas. The news entries are listed in the center of the page. Links to the news sections are listed on the left side of the window. The right side of the window includes links to recent new articles and can include information specific to the user's location, such as weather.

Searching Google News

News articles included on the main Google News page are selected using computer algorithms based on how often and where a news topic has been posted online. An ***algorithm*** is a step-by-step process for solving a problem within a specific number of steps. If a certain news article is not displayed, a user can search for it. The articles available from the main Google News page have been posted or updated within 30 days. A user can search the site for older articles.

The main news page includes a search text box. By entering a search term or phrase a user can conduct a simple search. By clicking the **Advanced news search** button on the right end of the search text box, a user can conduct a more advanced search from the Google News page. The standard Google Search results page displays with the **News** filter enabled. A user can click on the link of any site listed to display the site that published the article.

Personalizing Google News

With Google News, a user can personalize what news sections are shown, how frequently each section is shown, and how the news page is displayed according to his or her interests. These personal settings can transfer to other computers or devices as long as the user is logged into his or her Google account when selections are made.

A user can modify which news sections are shown on the Google News page. The top news is a section that cannot be moved or deleted. However, a user can remove any of the other eight sections. By default, world news and US news are listed, followed by articles on business, technology, entertainment, sports, science, and health.

Google offers many preset custom sections in addition to the default sections, such as sections for space, mobile technology, and US equity markets. These sections can be added to the news page. A user can also create a custom section for a topic. A custom section can be private and viewed only by the user or published so that it will appear in the directory of preset custom sections.

A user can customize how frequently news will be displayed for each news section selected. When customizing news content, a slider is displayed to the right of each section, as seen in **Figure 20-2**. The default setting is **Sometimes**. A user moves the slider between the plus and minus signs to customize how much news will be shown for each section. The choices are rarely, occasionally, sometimes, often, and always.

Google News can also be personalized for different regional and language preferences. There are more than 60 different regional editions of Google News. Different editions will often display different news articles. The news articles displayed in each section are included because they are especially relevant to people from or interested in that region of the world. Also the language of everything on the news page, including buttons and menus, may change to reflect the language of the region selected.

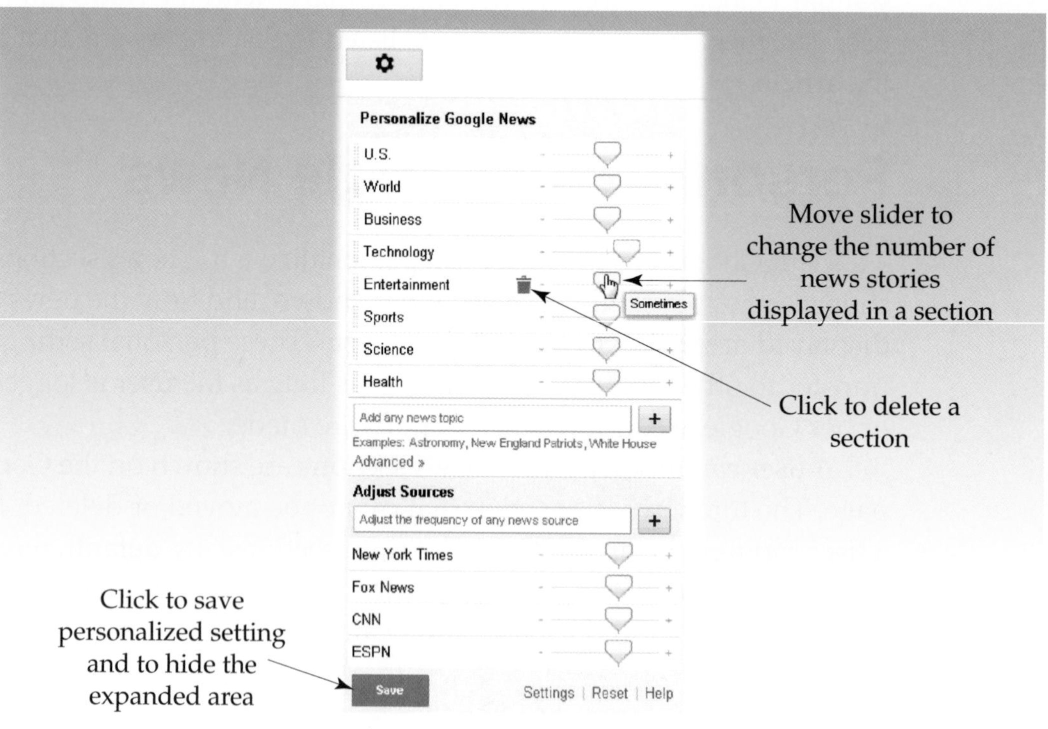

Goodheart-Willcox Publisher

Figure 20-2. The amount a source contributes to the results on the news page can be adjusted, as can the sources.

The view of the news page can also be customized. There are four options: **Modern**, **Headlines**, **Compact**, and **Classic**. Each view slightly changes the layout of the news page to emphasize or de-emphasize elements of the page. For example, the **Headlines** view excludes all images from the news page.

Lesson 20-1

Searching for Topics

Along with viewing headlines from thousands of news sources, Google News users can access Google's search functionality to find specific news articles from the news page. An extension of Google News is the Google Newspaper Archive, which includes scanned newspapers from as far back as the 1800s.

1. Log in to your Google Mail account.
2. Click the **News** link in the navigation bar. The News page is displayed showing the top stories, as shown in **Figure 20-3.**

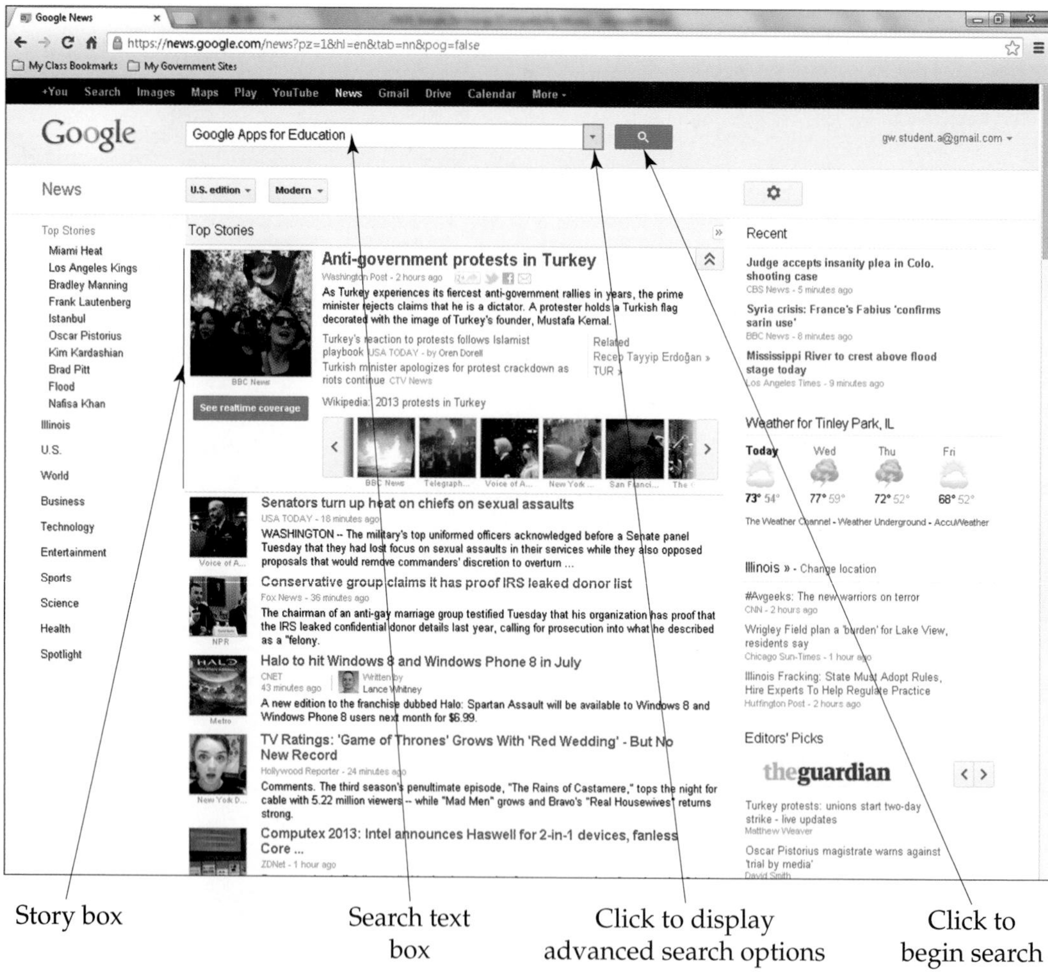

Goodheart-Willcox Publisher

Figure 20-3. Results are shown on the News page in a format similar to a standard search.

Search

3. Click in the search text box, enter Google Apps for Education, and click the **Search** button. The results appear in a list similar to a standard Google search. Click on the title of an article to view it.
4. Click in the address text box, and enter news.google.com/newspapers. The Google News archive page is displayed, which contains the archive search text box and a list of archived newspapers.

Tip: The newspaper archive can also be searched by entering a search term in the omnibox, and, once the results are displayed, clicking **Search tools>Any time>Archive**.

Search Archive

5. Click in the archive search text box (next to Google News), enter d-day, and click the **Search Archive** button. A list of results is displayed, and the **Search Tools** button is automatically on to display links for search filters.
6. Click the **Archives** link, and click **Custom range...** in the drop-down list. The **Custom date range** dialog box is displayed, as shown in **Figure 20-4.**
7. Click in the **From** text box, and enter 6/1/1944.
8. Click in the **To** text box, and enter 6/10/1944.
9. Click the **Go** button. The results are filtered to show only newspaper articles in the specified range of dates.
10. Locate an article discussing D-Day that is not a pay-per-view article, and click the link. The scanned newspaper is displayed in an online reader, as shown in **Figure 20-5.**

Full Screen

11. Click the **Full Screen** button to display the newspaper in an enlarged viewer.
12. Move the mouse over the newspaper. The cursor changes to a hand.
13. Click and hold, then drag to move the newspaper around to read the entire article.

Tip: The mouse wheel can be used to move the newspaper up and down.

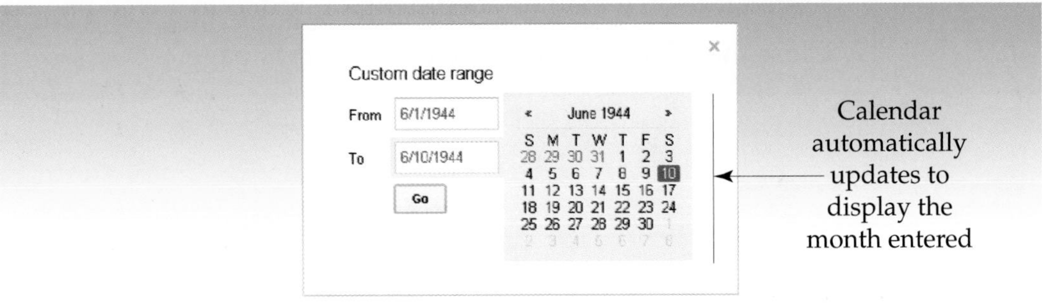

Goodheart-Willcox Publisher

Figure 20-4. Specifying a custom range of dates for articles in the newspaper archive.

Goodheart-Willcox Publisher

Figure 20-5. Newspapers in the archive are displayed in an online reader.

14. Click the **Link to article** link. A pop-up window is displayed.
15. Click on the article in the newspaper to create a hyperlink.
16. Copy the code for the hyperlink in the pop-up window. It can now be pasted into an e-mail or document, or added to a web page definition.
17. Close the tab or window to close the news page.

Lesson 20-2

News Sections

A user can have easy access to topics of interest by adding news sections to his or her news page. The added news sections can be a topic you create or a preset custom section created by Google or other Google News users.

Adding a Custom Section

1. Log in to your Google Mail account.
2. Click the **News** link in the navigation bar.

3. Click the **Personalize your news** button. An expanded area appears below the button, as shown in **Figure 20-6.**

+ Add

4. Click in the **Add any news topic** text box, and enter Fashion, and click the **Add** button to the right of the text box. A **Fashion** entry is added to the list of sections in the expanded area.

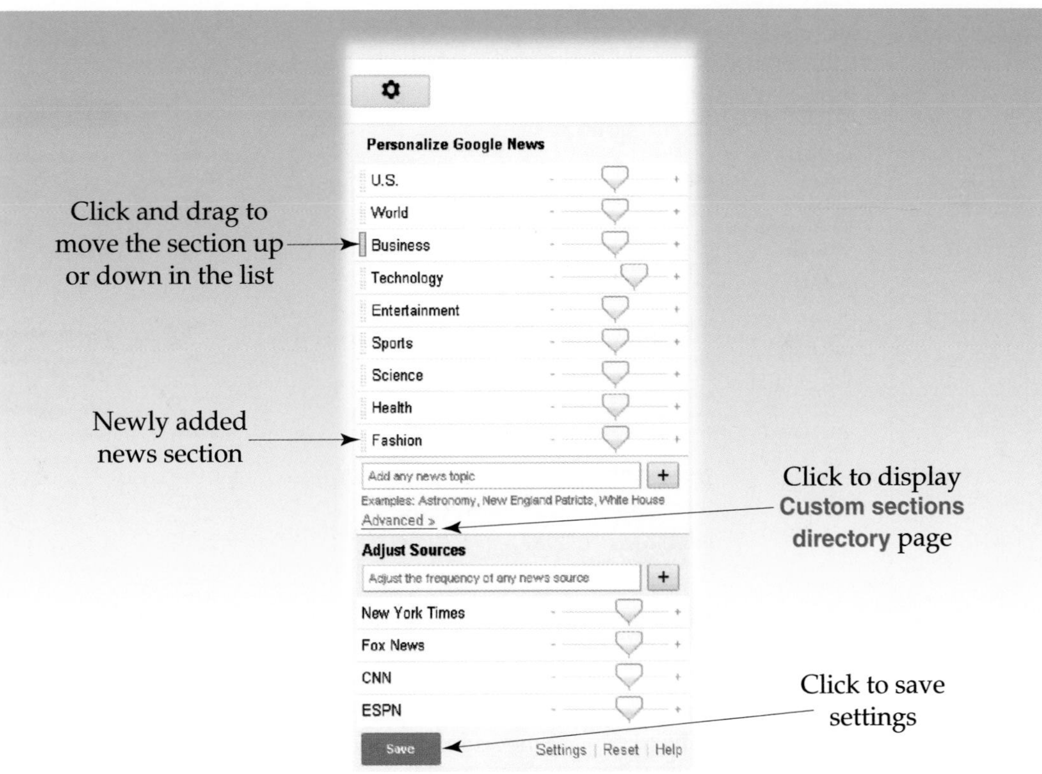

Goodheart-Willcox Publisher

Figure 20-6. The News page can be personalized by adding custom sections and adjusting the news feeds.

5. Click the **Save** button at the bottom of the expanded area. The expanded area is hidden, and the Fashion section is added to the bottom of the list on the left-hand side of the page.
6. Click **Fashion** in the list on the left-hand side of the page. News related to fashion is displayed in the main area of the page.

Adding a Preset Custom Section

7. Click the **Personalize your news** button to display the expanded area.
8. Click the **Advanced** link in the expanded area. The Custom sections directory page is displayed, as shown in **Figure 20-7.** Each preset custom section is displayed with a title, description, category, who created the section, number of users, and rating.

Goodheart-Willcox Publisher

Figure 20-7. There are many preset custom sections that can be added to a News page.

9. Click the **Technology** link in the **Narrow by Category** list on the left-hand side of the page.
10. Scroll through the list to find the **Video Games** custom section.
11. Click the title of the **Video Games** custom section. The news related to that section is displayed.
12. Return to the Custom sections directory page.

Add this section

13. Locate the **Video Games** custom section, and click the **Add this section** button. The news page is displayed, and the custom section is added to the list.
14. Return to the Custom sections directory page.
15. Click in the **Search for sections** text box, enter college, and click the **Search** button. A list of custom sections associated with college is displayed.
16. Locate a custom section related to a college topic you are interested in, and click the **Add this section** button.

Creating a Custom Section

17. Return to the Custom sections directory page.
18. Click the **Create a custom section** link. A new page is displayed on which a custom section can be created, as shown in **Figure 20-8.**
19. Click in the **Section title:** text box, and enter College Scholarships.
20. Click in the **Search terms:** text box, and enter colleges, financial aid, scholarships, college life. A preview of results meeting these criteria appears on the right-hand side of the page.
21. Click in the **Source location:** text box, and enter USA. This limits the results to those originating in the United States.

Tip Checking the **Publish this section to the directory** check box makes the custom section available to the public. A description must be entered and a category selected.

22. Click the **Create** button. The new section is created and the results displayed.
23. Close the tab or window to close the news page.

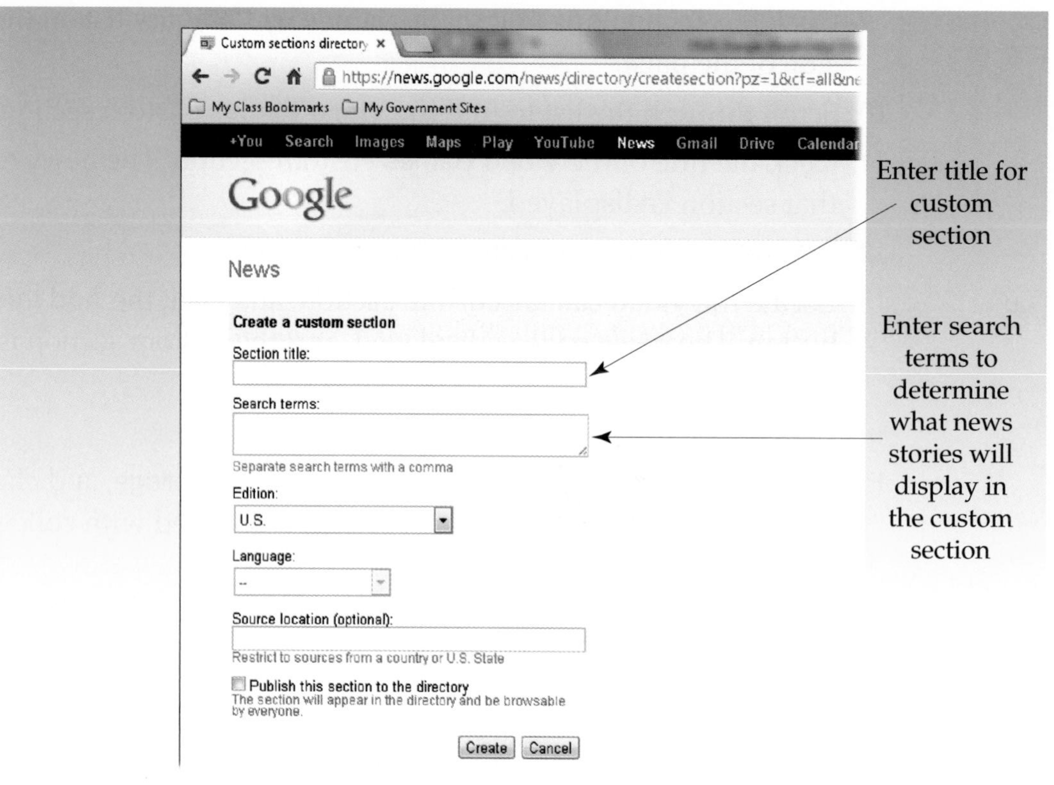

Goodheart-Willcox Publisher

Figure 20-8. A custom section can be created. It can be added to the public directory or left private.

Lesson 20-3

Personalizing the News Page

Personalizing the Google News page allows the user to select which news sections are visible on the news page and to reorder the sections. A user can also adjust amount of news viewable in a section.

1. Log in to your Google Mail account.
2. Click the **News** link in the navigation bar.

3. Click the **Personalize your news** button. An expanded area appears below the button.
4. Click and hold the slider next to the **College Scholarships** custom section, and drag it to the **Often** setting. The name of the setting appears as help text as the slider is moved. See **Figure 20-9.**

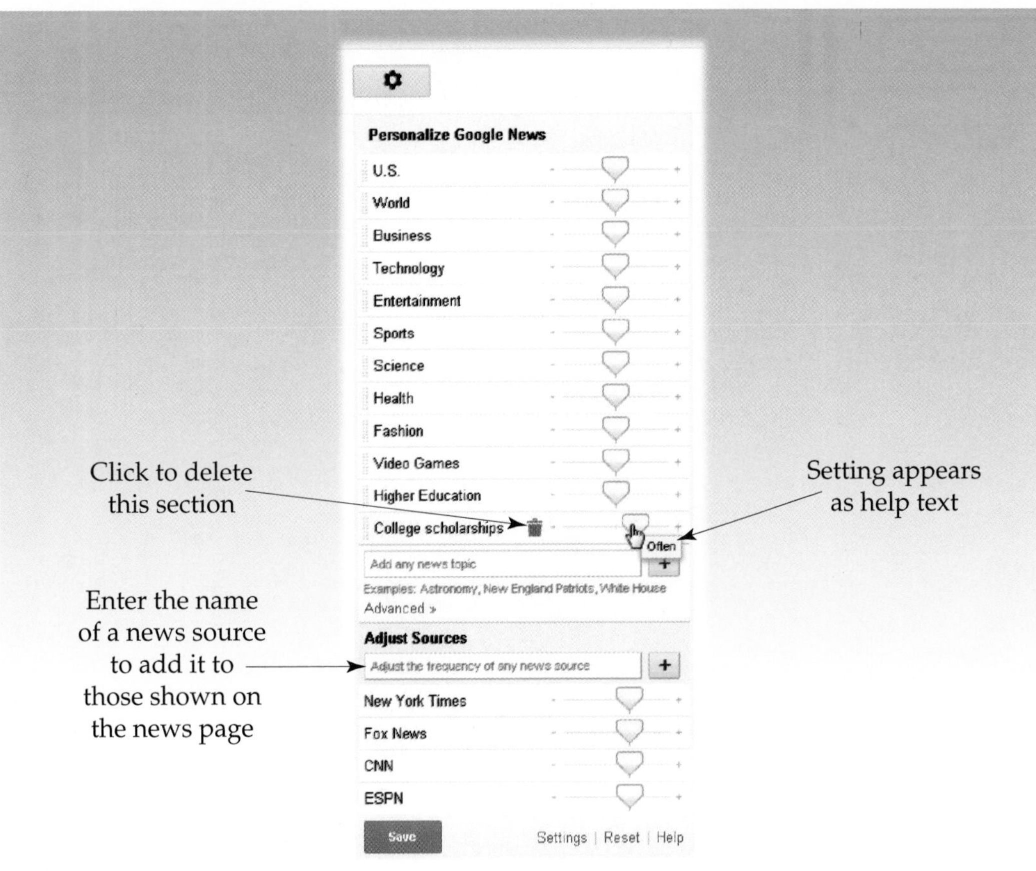

Goodheart-Willcox Publisher

Figure 20-9. Adjusting the amount a news feed contributes to the results on the News page.

5. Click and hold anywhere on the **Fashion** custom section, drag it to below the **College Scholarships** custom section, and drop. The order of the sections is changed.

6. Move the cursor over the **Video Games** custom section to display the **Delete this section** button.
7. Click the **Delete this section** button to remove the **Video Games** custom section.

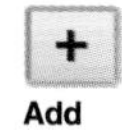

8. Click in the **Adjust Sources** text box, enter Washington Post, and click the **Add** button.
9. Click and hold the slider next to the Washington Post source, and drag it to the **Rarely** setting.

10. Click the **Save** button.
11. Close the tab or window to close the news page.

Check Your Google Apps IQ

Now that you have finished this chapter, see what you know about Google Apps by taking the chapter posttest.
www.m.g-wlearning.com
www.g-wlearning.com/informationtechnology/

Skill Review

Answer the following questions on a separate sheet of paper.

1. Describe a news aggregator.
2. What is a story box?
3. An article that has been frequently referenced by other articles is called a(n) ______.
4. Describe the three main areas of the Google News page.
5. What is an algorithm?
6. What is the time span for articles available in the main Google News page?
7. List three things that can be personalized on the Google News page.
8. List the types of articles that appear on the Google News page by default.
9. What are the choices for how frequently a news section contributes to the postings?
10. List the four views in which the Google News page can be displayed.

Lesson Application

These exercises are designed to apply the skills learned in this and previous chapters. General directions are provided, but you will need to draw on your knowledge to determine how to complete each exercise.

Exercise 20-1
Adding a Preset Custom Section

Working in a team of three or four as assigned by your instructor, conduct a text hangout to discuss a common area of interest for which you would like to receive news. Identify why each team member would like to receive the news. Everybody on the team must agree to the topic. Additionally, the topic must be available in the preset custom sections. Identify which preset custom section will be added to your news page, and add it.

Exercise 20-2
Creating a Custom Section

Working with the team from Exercise 20-1, conduct a text hangout to discuss a second area of common interest related to your school or town. Create a custom section for this news. Be sure to use search terms and operators to focus the search as needed on the specific news you seek. Do not publish the section to the directory. Send your instructor an e-mail outlining the section you added, the reason it was selected, and the specific search terms used.

Chapter 21

Google Earth

Objectives

After completing this chapter, you will be able to:

- Create a virtual field trip or sightseeing tour.
- Create and edit markers.
- Add text, links, and images to markers.
- Use layers to access multiple features and views.
- Navigate through Google Sky, Google Moon, and Google Mars.

alexmillos/Shutterstock.com

Check Your Google Apps IQ

Before you begin this chapter, see what you already know about Google Apps by taking the chapter pretest.

www.m.g-wlearning.com
www.g-wlearning.com/informationtechnology/

Introducing Google Earth

Google Earth is a virtual globe. Satellite images, maps, terrain, and three-dimensional structures provide users with the opportunity to learn and share information about most any location on Earth. A user can take a virtual tour of a location or create a tour to share with others. Markers can be added to specific locations in Google Earth to provide a user with a quick and easy way to return to the locations. Layers of data can be made visible to provide additional information about a location. A user can also explore space, the Moon or Mars through Google Earth.

Google Earth is a separate application from the Google Chrome browser that must be downloaded and installed. When a user logs in using Google account information, additional options are made available. When logged in, a user can access markers, create tours, or other personalized Google Earth information from other computers or devices with Google Earth installed. Also logged-in users can share images or created tours with all Google account holders.

There are two main components to the Google Earth window: the map display and sidebar containing information panels, which appear in the left sidebar of the window, as seen in **Figure 21-1.** A toolbar spans the map in the viewer window. Some of these tools allow a user to add a marker, polygon, plot path, or image to a map. A user can also create a tour, see historical imagery on the map, and show sunlight on the map using the toolbar buttons. A map can be e-mailed, printed, or saved. The **Tour Guide** panel spans the bottom of the map display. It includes available images and tours.

There are three information panels in the sidebar: **Search**, **Places**, and **Layers**. The **Search** panel includes a search text box as well as a list of recent searches and the ability to view a complete history. A user can also choose to get directions from one location to another in this panel. The **Places** panel includes a list of markers that have been added as well as tours the user has created. The **Layers** panel is a list of all of the data layers that can be turned on or off using the check boxes.

Viewing and Creating Tours in Google Earth

Google Earth can be used to explore locations of interest. Like Google Maps, exact addresses or names of locations can be entered into the search text box to find a specific spot on the virtual globe. Once a location is displayed, tours appear in the **Tour Guide** panel that are specific to the location. ***Tours*** are short videos that show the movement from one location to another during which facts about the location are displayed. Tours can also be static images related to the location. By accessing available tours, Google Earth users can tour the Grand Canyon in Arizona, as seen in **Figure 21-2,** the Eiffel Tower in France, the Leaning Tower of Pisa in Italy, the Victoria Falls in Zimbabwe, Mount Fuji in Japan, and many other locations.

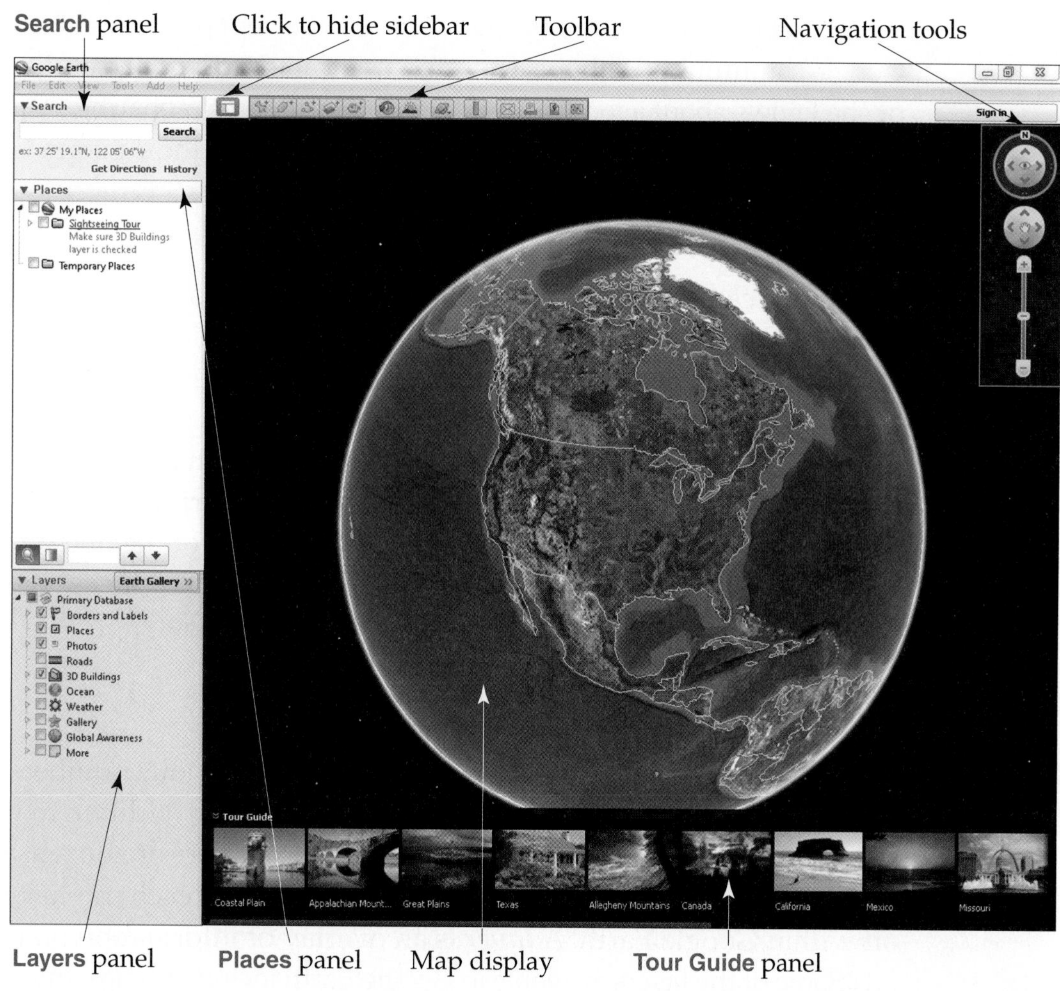

Goodheart-Willcox Publisher

Figure 21-1. The Google Earth interface consists of two main components, the map display and the information panels.

Goodheart-Willcox Publisher

Figure 21-2. A tour of the Grand Canyon is just one of the many available in Google Earth.

A user can create tours as well. Tours can be kept private or shared with the Google community. With this feature, a user can share with an audience what he or she knows about a location. For example, a student preparing a presentation on the Sahara Desert could create a virtual field trip to the desert in Google Earth.

Working with Markers

A user can add **markers** to save a specific location or several locations. A ***marker*** is an icon that is placed on the map to indicate a specific location. Once markers are placed, the user can quickly and easily return to these places. The markers can also be used to create tours or to save certain views of an area. Once a marker has been inserted, it can be repositioned or edited to give it a different label or enhance its description. Also, by default, the marker is a yellow pushpin. However, the style of the marker can be changed. A user can choose from a gallery of available choices or create a custom icon. Markers can also be organized into folders.

Using Layers

When viewing Google Earth, there are an enormous number of choices for what data are displayed at any given location. In addition to roads, state and country borders, and locational labels, there are dozens of options available. Each option is referred to as a layer—and each can be turned on or off within Google Earth. A ***layer*** is an overlay of information on the view.

Some of the layers available in Google Earth include photos, three-dimensional buildings, weather, and traffic information, as seen in **Figure 21-3.** There are also layers for parks and recreation areas, including golf courses, national parks, visitor facilities, park descriptions, and trails. There are layers for governmental information such as postal code boundaries, congressional districts, and school districts. The Ocean layer will add icons to the map indicating animal tracking, shipwrecks, and protected marine areas among other information.

In addition to the layers, there are also choices for the position from which the user views Google Earth. By default, the view is from above with the ability to zoom in or out. The user also has the option to use the ground-level or, in certain areas, the street view. With these options, a user can view a location as if he or she were walking through it. You can even stay in one spot and turn around 360 degrees to see everything around you. This is called a ***panoramic view.***

Using Google Sky, Google Moon, and Google Mars

A user can see things beyond Earth with Google Sky, Moon, and Mars. Google Sky is a celestial viewer. It allows the user to see stars, constellations, galaxies, moons, and planets. The **Layers** panel for Google Sky includes

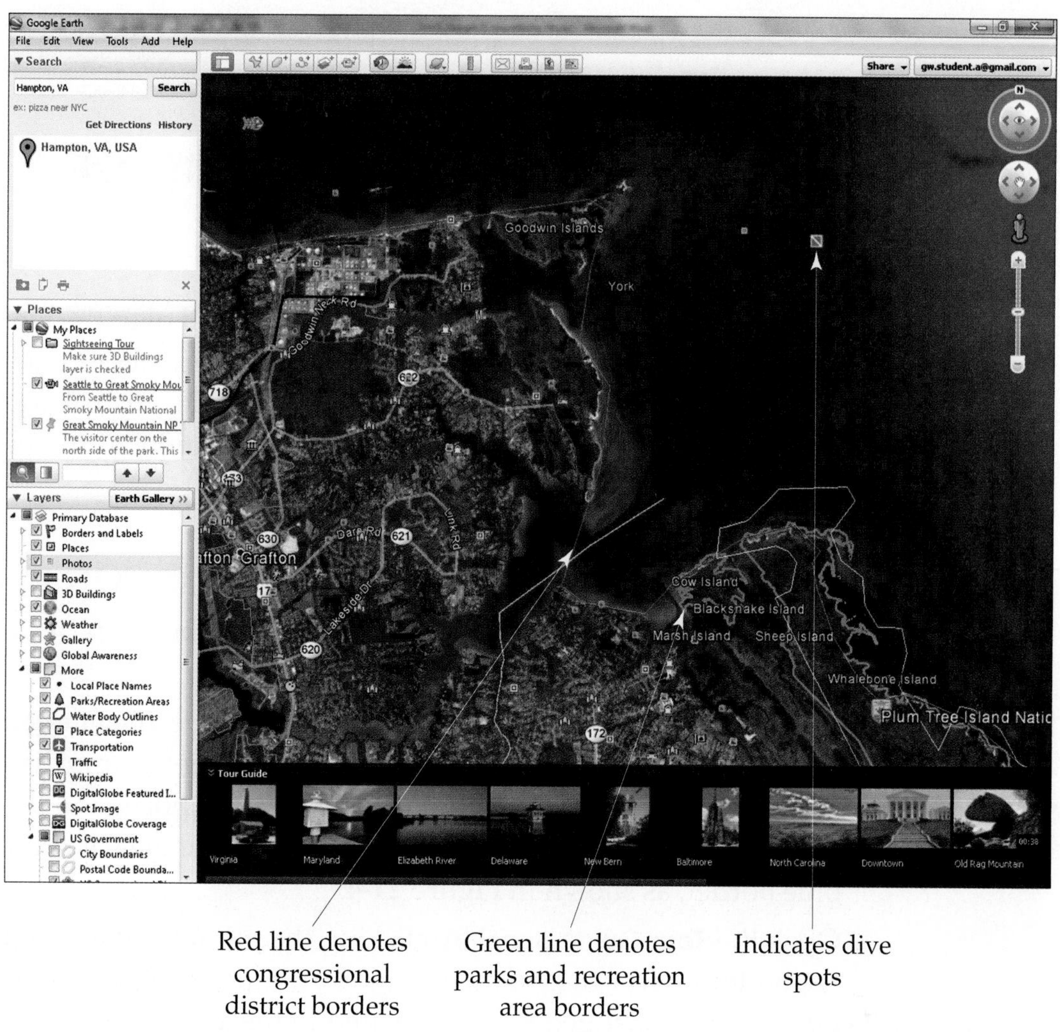

Goodheart-Willcox Publisher

Figure 21-3. Layers can be turned on or off to display or hide information available in Google Earth.

different options than Google Earth. Among other things, a user can see overlays of the constellations on real images of the sky or view images from the Hubble telescope.

Google Moon, as the name implies, provides tools for exploring Earth's Moon. It shows satellite images of the Moon and allows the user to pan and zoom. Guided tours are also provided. A user can also choose a colorized terrain view, which illustrates the differing elevations of the Moon.

Google Mars uses information collected from the 2010 Mars Global Surveyor and the 2001 Mars Odyssey, both NASA Mars missions, to provide views of Mars. A user can change from the default view to colorized terrain for elevation data, daytime or nighttime infrared data, or several other image options. Additionally, there are layers of information on the Mars rovers and landers as well as historic maps of Mars.

Lesson 21-1

Creating a Virtual Field Trip or Sightseeing Tour

Using Google Earth, a person can view places all over the world. In addition to looking around a place, a user can learn about places by accessing the tours that are available through Google Earth. A user can also share his or her knowledge and experience of a location with other Google Earth users by creating tours.

Using Tours and Navigating in Google Earth

1. Launch Google Earth. If the **Start-Up Tip** dialog box appears, click the **Close** button.
2. Scroll through the **Tour Guide** panel, and click the **Washington** tour or other entry as specified by your instructor. A brief tour is displayed in which the view zooms into the northwestern portion of the United States. The state of Washington is centered in the view surrounded by a blue border, as shown in **Figure 21-4**.
3. Open the **Tour Guide** panel by clicking the minimized **Tour Guide** in the bottom-left corner of the Google Earth viewer. Notice that the tour options have changed to those related to the area of Washington. Many tours have a tag that tells you how long the tour is.
4. Click on the **Mount Rainier** tour. A tour that shows the view from atop Mount Rainier is displayed in the viewer.
5. Click on one of the photographs in the view. A new window opens that shows an image of Mount Ranier and provides some information about the location.
6. Click the **X** to close the image window.
7. Click and hold the left arrow in the **Click to look around** tool in the upper-right corner of the viewer. The point from which you are seeing the view remains stationary while the view pans about that point. Clicking the button without holding it pans the view in increments.

Click to look around

Tip Notice that the upper **Click to look around** tool has an N on it. This can be dragged around the circle in the tool to reorient the view.

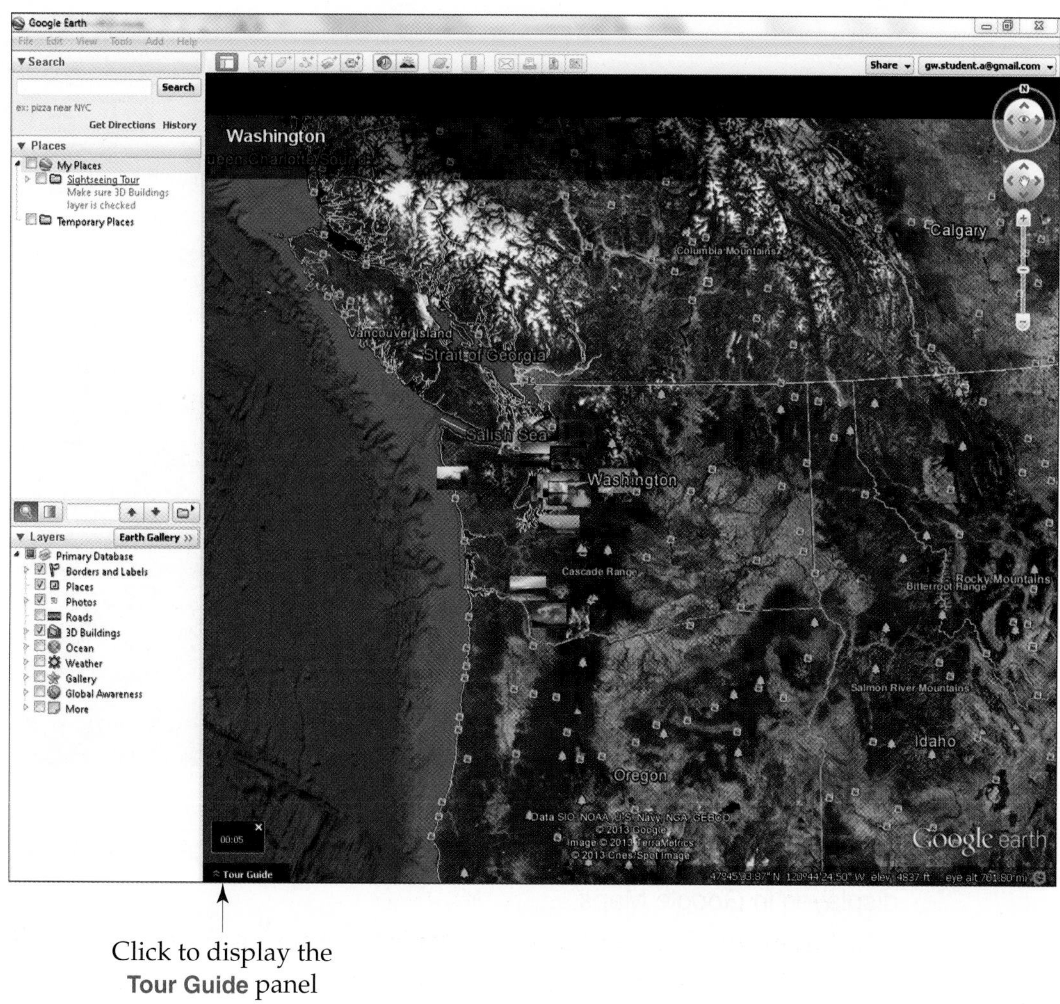

Goodheart-Willcox Publisher

Figure 21-4. A tour of the state of Washington has been selected and played.

8. Move the cursor over the Google Earth image, click and hold, and drag the view. This allows you to "fly" around within Google Earth. As you move to different areas, other overlaid features may show up, such as the names of peaks in the mountain range, campgrounds, or visitor centers.
9. Click the – button on the **Zoom** slider. The view is zoomed out.

Tip The mouse wheel can be used to zoom in and out.

10. Zoom out and pan the view as needed so Seattle is visible.

Street View

11. Click the **Drag to enter Street View** button and drop it someplace in Seattle. Google Earth zooms in to that location and provides a view appearance of standing on the ground, as shown in **Figure 21-5.**
12. Use the **Click to look around** button to rotate the view.
13. Click the **Exit Street View** button to return to the Google Earth view.

Goodheart-Willcox Publisher

Figure 21-5. Google Earth can display a street view, similar to what can be displayed in Google Maps.

Creating a Virtual Field Trip

14. Minimize the **Tour Guide** panel.

Record a Tour

15. Click the **Record a Tour** button in the toolbar. The recording toolbar is displayed.
16. Click in the **Search** text box in the **Search** panel, and enter Great Smoky Mountains National Park, but do not click the **Search** button.

Begin Recording

17. Click the **Begin Recording** button on the recording toolbar, and then click the **Search** button in the **Search** panel. The view is centered on the Great Smoky Mountains National Park, and the navigation is recorded.

Tip A voiceover can be added when recording a tour. Rehearse what you are going to say about the trip before recording so the audio will match the video.

Stop Recording

18. Click the **Stop Recording** button to end the tour. The entire tour is automatically replayed, and the recording toolbar changes to a progress meter, as seen in Figure 21-6.
19. Click the **Save** button in the recording toolbar. The **New Tour** dialog box is displayed.

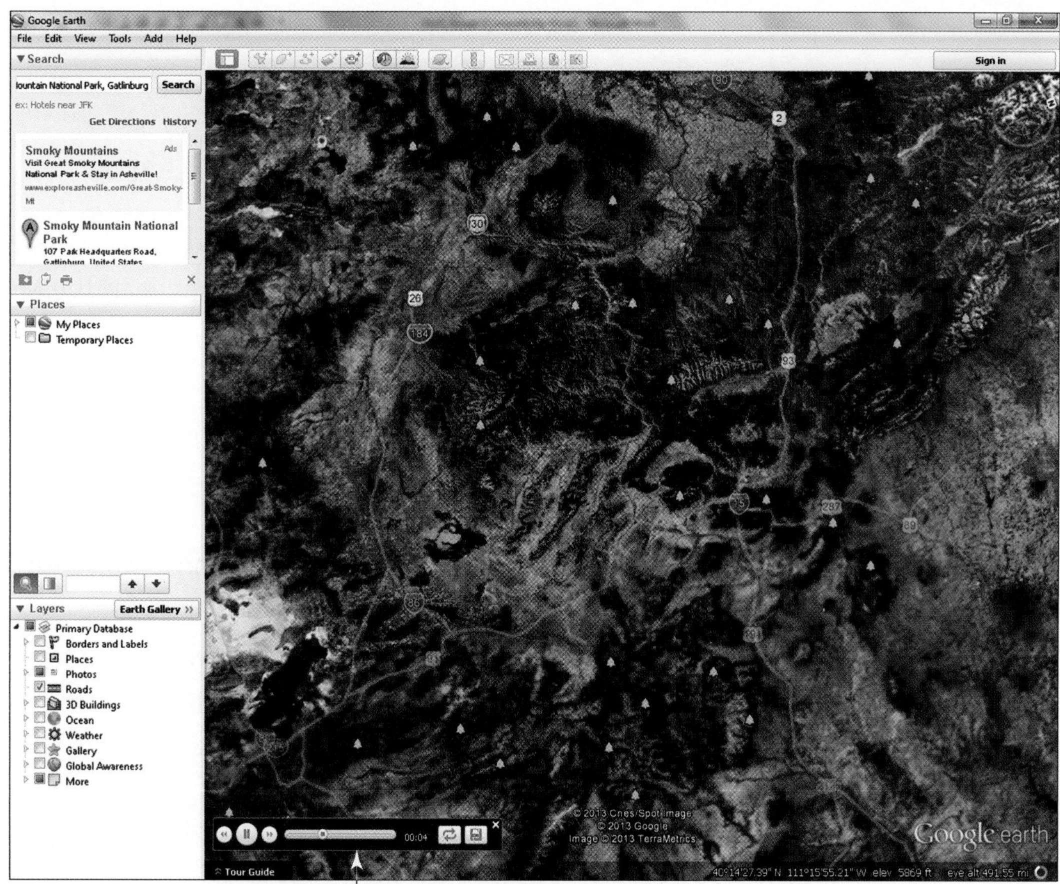

Goodheart-Willcox Publisher

Figure 21-6. The recording toolbar changes to a progress meter once the **Stop Recording** button is clicked.

20. Click in the **Name:** text box, enter Seattle to Great Smoky Mountains National Park, and click the **OK** button. The tour is added to the My Places branch of the tree in the **Places** panel.
21. Double-click on the Seattle to Great Smoky Mountains National Park branch in the **Places** panel. The tour is replayed from beginning to end.
22. Close Google Earth.

Lesson 21-2

Creating and Editing Markers

Markers can be used to denote any place in the world—from your backyard to the highest mountain peak. Markers appear in the My Places branch in the **Places** panel.

Creating a Marker

1. Launch Google Earth. If the **Start-Up Tip** dialog box appears, click the **Close** button.
2. Replay the Seattle to Great Smoky Mountains National Park tour. At the end of the tour, the park should be centered in the view.
3. Close the playback toolbar, which is displayed while the tour is active, to exit the tour. This toolbar must be closed to enable other tools on the main toolbar.
4. Use the navigation tools to show a clear view of the Sugarland Visitor Center in the north-central part of the park near Gatlinburg. If needed, use the **Search** panel to search for the Sugarland Visitor Center.

Add Placemark

5. Click the **Add Placemark** button in the toolbar. The **New Placemark** dialog box is displayed, as shown in **Figure 21-7.** A marker also appears in the viewer window and is flashing.

A marker can be added by clicking **Placemark** in the **Add** pull-down menu.

6. Click the marker in the viewer window and drag it on top of the visitor center building.
7. In the **New Placemark** dialog box, click in the **Name:** text box, and enter Great Smoky Mountain National Park Visitor Center. The label on the marker in the viewer window changes to match.
8. Click the **OK** button to set the mark and close the dialog box. The marker appears as a branch under My Places in the **Places** panel.

Unchecking the check mark next to an item in the **Places** panel turns off the display of that item.

9. Use the **Search** panel to locate and display another location, such as your home or school.
10. Double-click on the Great Smoky Mountain National Park Visitor Center branch in the **Places** panel. The view in the viewer window flies to the marker.

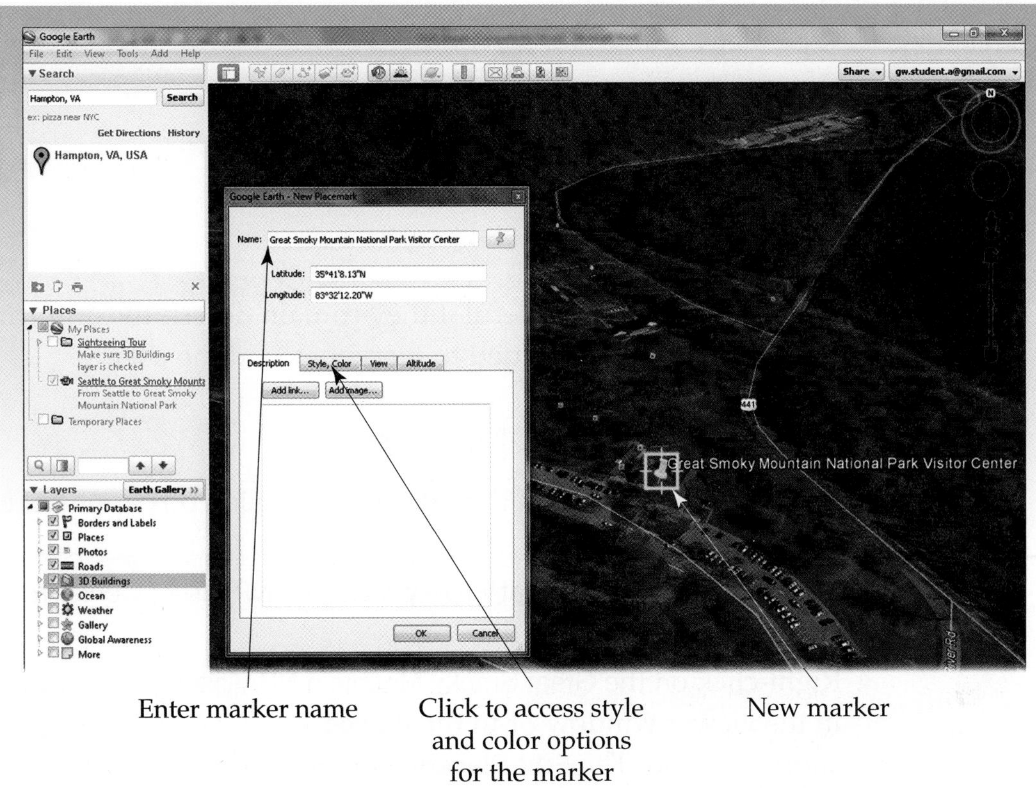

Goodheart-Willcox Publisher

Figure 21-7. Adding a marker to Google Earth.

Editing a Marker

11. Right-click on either the marker in the viewer window or its branch in the **Places** panel and click **Properties** in the shortcut menu. The **Edit Placemark** dialog box is displayed. This is the same dialog box used to create the marker, just with a different name.
12. Click and drag the mark to a different location, perhaps the parking lot instead of on top of the building.
13. Click in the **Name:** text box in the dialog box, and change the text to Great Smoky Mountain NP Visitor Center.
14. Click the **OK** button. The marker is updated.
15. Use the navigation tools to display the exact view of the visitor center you want to show.
16. Right-click on the marker in the viewer window or in the **Places** panel, click **Snapshot View** in the shortcut menu. The current view is the view that will be displayed each time the marker is restored.
17. Close Google Earth.

Lesson 21-3

Adding Text, Links, and Images to Markers

Markers can be more useful if they contain descriptive information. Links and images can be added to markers to aid the user.

Adding Text to a Marker

1. Launch Google Earth. If the **Start-Up Tip** dialog box appears, click the **Close** button.
2. Double-click on the Great Smoky Mountain NP Visitor Center marker in the **Places** panel to display that view.
3. Right-click on the Great Smoky Mountain NP Visitor Center marker either in the viewer window or in the **Places** panel, and click **Properties** in the shortcut menu. The **Edit Placemark** dialog box is displayed.
4. Click the **Description** tab, click in the text box on the tab, and enter The visitor center on the north side of the park. This is a great place to pick up maps of the best hiking trails.
5. Click the **OK** button to update the marker.
6. Single-click on the marker in either the viewer window or **Places** panel. A pop-up window appears by the marker in the viewer window displaying the description and offering options to get directions to or from the location, as shown in **Figure 21-8.** The description also appears in the marker's branch in the **Places** panel.
7. Click the **X** button to close the pop-up window.

Tip The pop-up window will not appear if the marker does not contain information beyond just a name.

Adding Links and Images to a Marker

8. Open the **Edit Placemark** dialog box for Great Smoky Mountain NP Visitor Center marker.
9. In the **Description** tab, click at the end of the description to place the cursor there, and press the [Enter] key to start a new line.
10. Click the **Add link...** button. The **Link URL:** text box appears below the button.

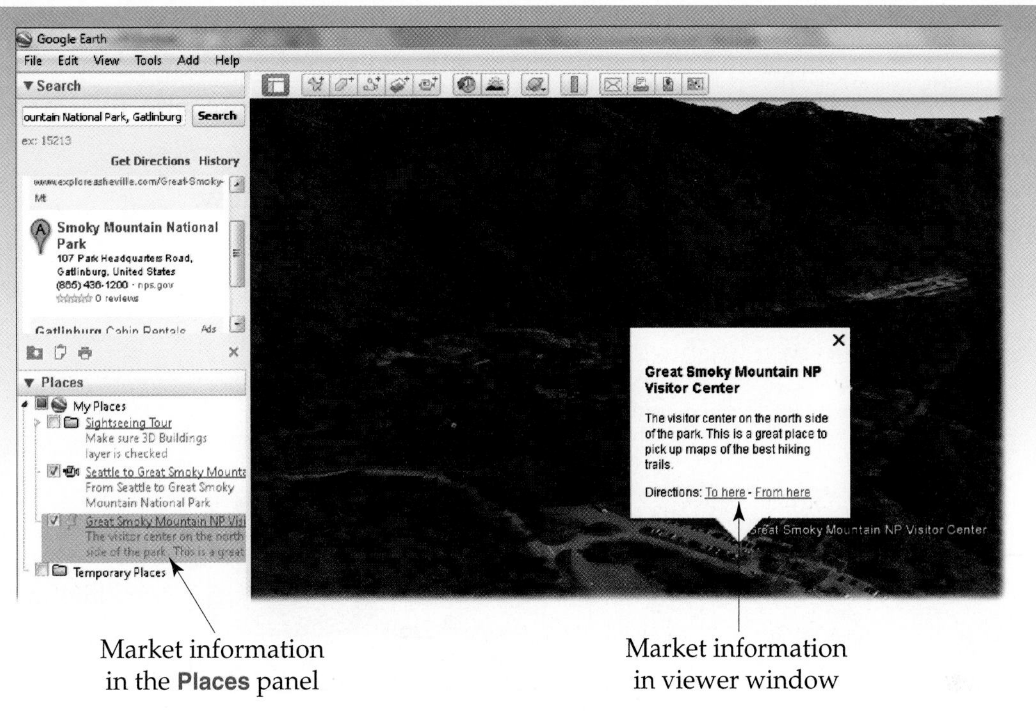

Goodheart-Willcox Publisher

Figure 21-8. Once details are added to a marker, a pop-up window can be displayed to view the details.

11. Click in the **Link URL:** text box, enter www.nps.gov/grsm, and click the **OK** button to the right of the **Link URL:** text box. HTML code for the URL is added to the description.
12. Launch an Internet browser, and navigate to www.nps.gov/grsm.
13. Click the site's Photos and Multimedia link or use the site's search function.
14. Locate an image you would like to add to the marker, display the image, and determine the URL of the photo. Generally, the URL can be found by right-clicking on the image, selecting **Properties** from the shortcut menu, and copying the address in the **Properties** dialog box that is displayed.
15. In Google Earth, click the **Description** tab in the **Edit Placemark** dialog box.
16. Click after the HTML code for the URL entered earlier, and press the [Enter] key to start a new line.
17. Click the **Add image...** button. The **Image URL:** text box appears below the button.
18. Paste the URL for the image you located on the National Park Service website, and click the **OK** button to the right of the **Image URL:** text box. HTML code for the image's URL is added to the description.
19. Click the **OK** button to close the **Edit Placemark** dialog box and update the marker.

20. Single-click on the marker to display the details pop-up window. The name and description you entered appears, followed by a link to the Great Smoky Mountain National Park website, and the image to which you linked, as shown in **Figure 21-9.**
21. Click the **X** button to close the pop-up window.
22. Close Google Earth.

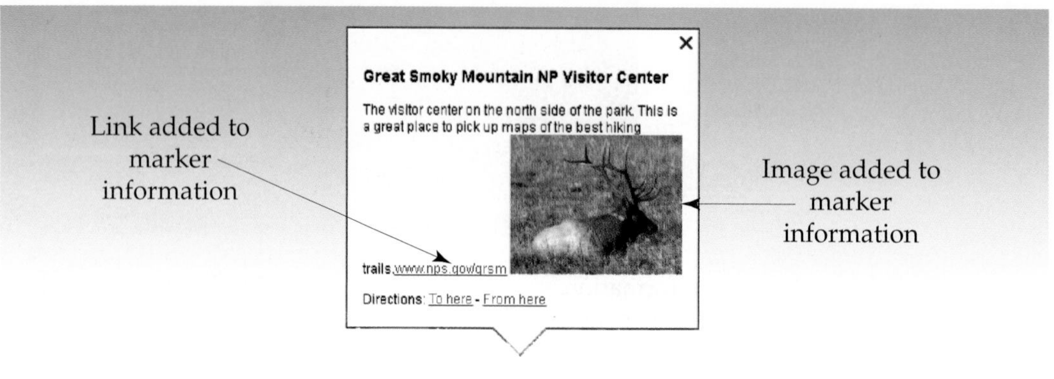

Goodheart-Willcox Publisher

Figure 21-9. An image and a link have been added to the details in this pop-up window.

Lesson 21-4

Using Layers to Access Multiple Features and Views

Google Earth provides users with the flexibility to display a great deal of data on a map, or none, using layers. Some layers, such as the 3D Buildings layer, must be turned on to properly display certain tours.

1. Launch Google Earth. If the **Start-Up Tip** dialog box appears, click the **Close** button.
2. Use the **Search** panel to locate and navigate to New Orleans.
3. In the **Layers** panel, uncheck the check box to the left of each branch. This turns off every layer and leaves just the satellite image in the viewer window along with the marker and label for the search (New Orleans).
4. Check the check box to the left of the Roads branch in the tree to turn on that layer. Roads are displayed in the viewer window as yellow lines, and interstates are identified with shields and numbers.
5. Expand the More branch. Other layers are displayed.
6. Check the check box to the left of the Local Place Names branch below the More branch to turn on that layer. Labels are added to the viewer window for local places, as shown in **Figure 21-10.**
7. Expand the Parks/Recreation Areas branch below the More branch to display other layers.
8. Check the check box to the left of the Parks branch to turn on that layer. All parks in the view are outlined in green.
9. Expand the Photos branch to display other layers.
10. Check the check box to the left of the 360 Cities branch. Icons are added to the view indicating where other Google Earth users have added photographs using 360 Cities. While zooming does not make the icons larger, this action can make additional icons visible.

Goodheart-Willcox Publisher

Figure 21-10. The Local Name Place layer has been turned on in this view.

11. Click one of the photo icons in the viewer window. The photograph is displayed in a pop-up window, as shown in **Figure 21-11.**
12. Click the image in the pop-up window. The viewer window is zoomed into the location and displays a panoramic view, similar to a street view.
13. Click and hold on the view, and drag to rotate the view. The position from where the image is viewed does not change, but the image is a 360 degree sphere.

Tip The mouse wheel can be used to zoom in and out in the panoramic view.

14. Click the **Exit Photo** button to exit the panoramic view. The viewer window displays a satellite view of the location.
15. Close Google Earth.

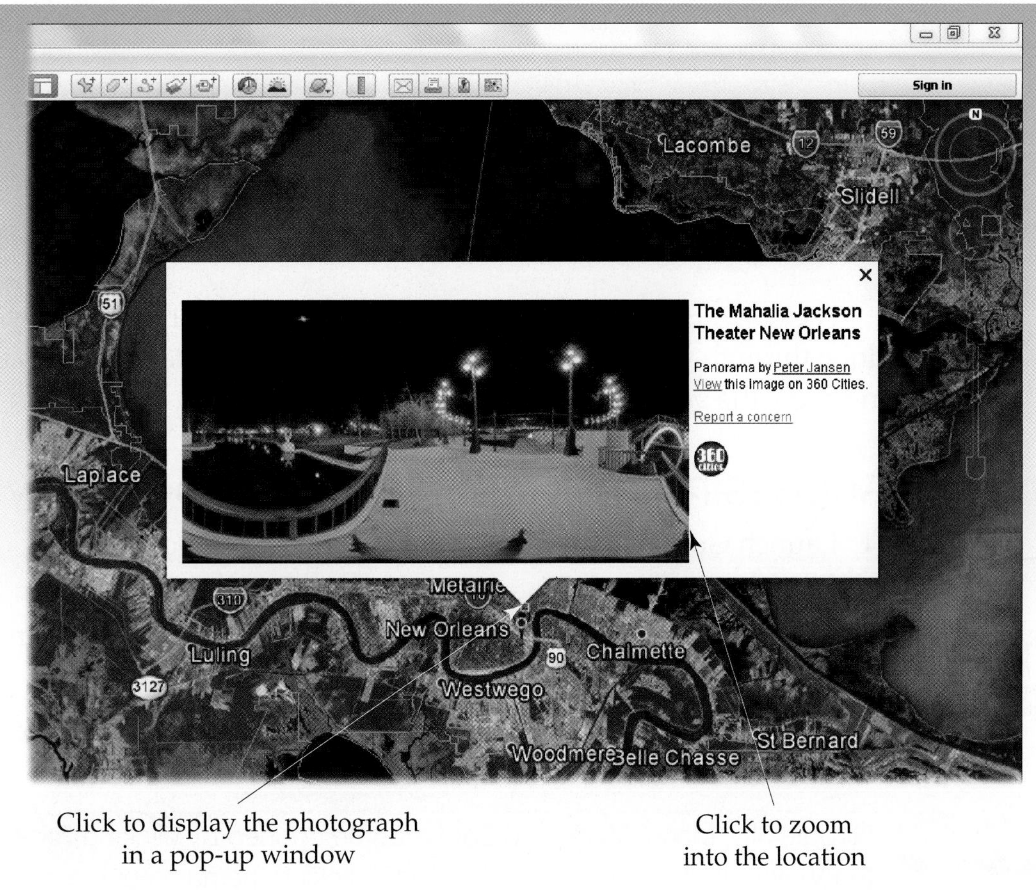

Goodheart-Willcox Publisher

Figure 21-11. Photos that have been added to Google Earth can be displayed in a pop-up window.

Lesson 21-5

Google Sky, Google Moon, and Google Mars

A Google Earth user can expand his or her exploration to beyond the globe through Google Sky, Moon, and Mars. A user can see stars in the sky and view the surface of the Moon and Mars.

Accessing and Navigating Google Sky

1. Launch Google Earth. If the **Start-Up Tip** dialog box appears, click the **Close** button.

Switch between Earth, Sky, and other planets

2. Click the **Switch between Earth, Sky, and other planets** button on the main toolbar. A drop-down menu is displayed.
3. Click **Sky** in the drop-down menu. The default Google Sky view is displayed in the viewer window, as shown in **Figure 21-12.**

Tip Google Sky, Moon, Mars, and Earth can be opened by clicking **Explore** in the **View** pull-down menu bar, and then clicking the name of the viewer in the cascading menu.

4. Click the **Welcome to Sky** feature in the viewer window. A pop-up window is displayed.
5. Click the **Getting to Know Sky** link in the pop-up window. The first of a series of views is displayed in the viewer window.
6. Click the **Getting to Know Sky** feature in the view. A pop-up window is displayed containing details about how to use Google Sky.
7. Read the information in the pop-up window, and then click the **Next** button. The next view in the tutorial is displayed in the viewer window.
8. Continue reading the content in the pop-up windows and clicking the **Next** button to move through the tutorial. There are a total of eight views in the tutorial. This will provide a quick and thorough overview of what things are available in Google Sky.
9. Click the **X** button to close the final pop-up window in the tutorial.
10. In the **Layers** panel, uncheck the check box to the left of the Welcome to Sky branch. This turns off the tutorial layer.

Tip The tutorial features can be accessed at any time by turning on the tutorial layer.

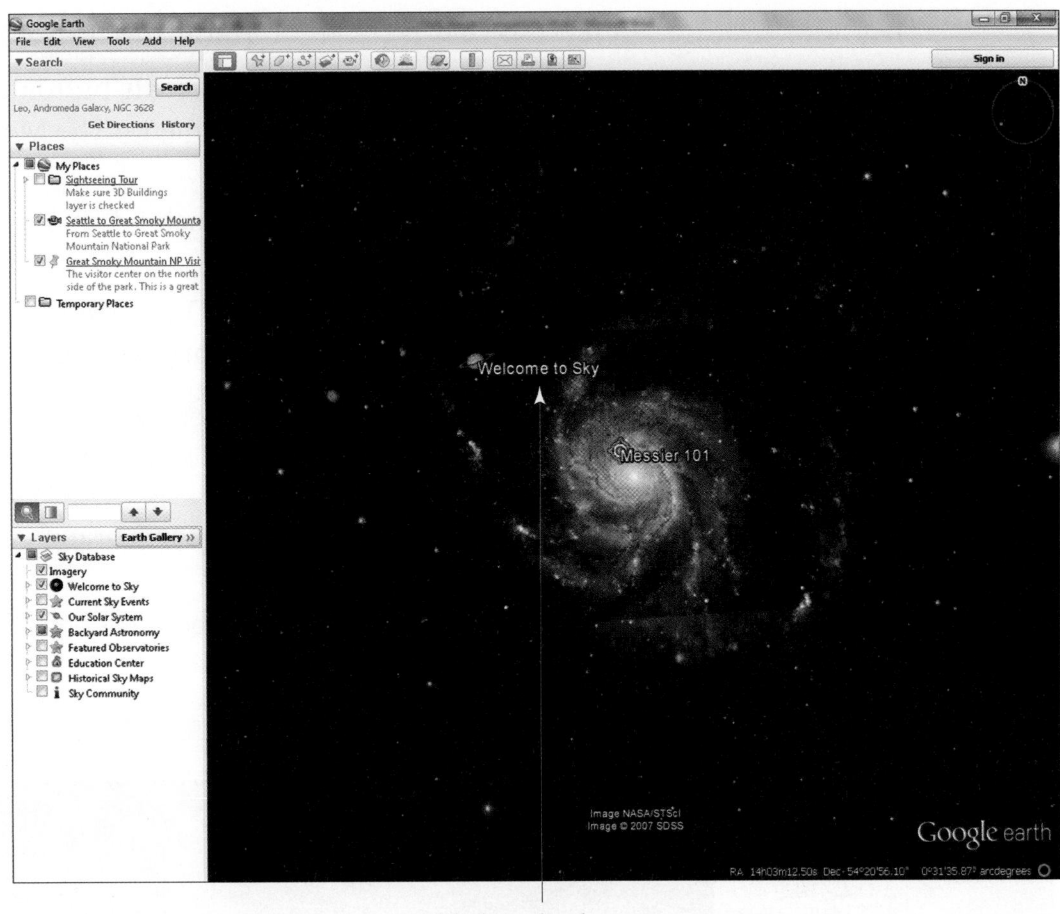

Goodheart-Willcox Publisher

Figure 21-12. Google Sky allows you to explore the stars and planets.

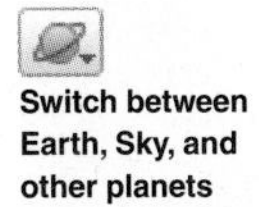
Switch between Earth, Sky, and other planets

11. Click the **Switch between Earth, Sky, and other planets** button on the main toolbar, and click **Earth** in the drop-down menu.
12. Using the **Search** panel, locate and navigate to your home address.

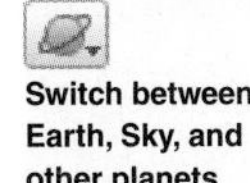
Switch between Earth, Sky, and other planets

13. Click the **Switch between Earth, Sky, and other planets** button on the main toolbar, and click **Sky** in the drop-down menu. A view of the sky as it currently appears from the current Google Earth location is displayed in the viewer window.
14. In the **Layers** panel, uncheck all branches.
15. Expand the Sky Database branch, if it is not already expanded. This is the top branch.
16. Expand the Backyard Astronomy branch, and check the Constellations branch below it. The outline of the constellations is displayed in the viewer window along with the names of the constellations.

Accessing and Navigating Google Moon

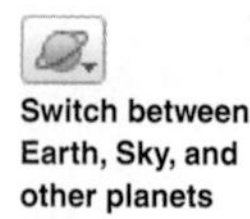

Switch between Earth, Sky, and other planets

17. Click the **Switch between Earth, Sky, and other planets** button on the main toolbar, and click **Moon** in the drop-down menu. The Moon appears as shown in **Figure 21-13.**
18. In the **Layers** panel, expand the Global Maps branch if it is not already expanded.
19. Click the radio button to the left of the Colorized Terrain branch. The different elevations of the Moon are shown in varying colors.

The branches within the **Global Maps** branch are controlled by radio buttons instead of check boxes because only one of these branches can be active at a time.

20. Click the radio button to the left of the Visible Imagery branch to return to the original, default view.
21. Expand the Moon Gallery branch, and then the Apollo Missions branch.

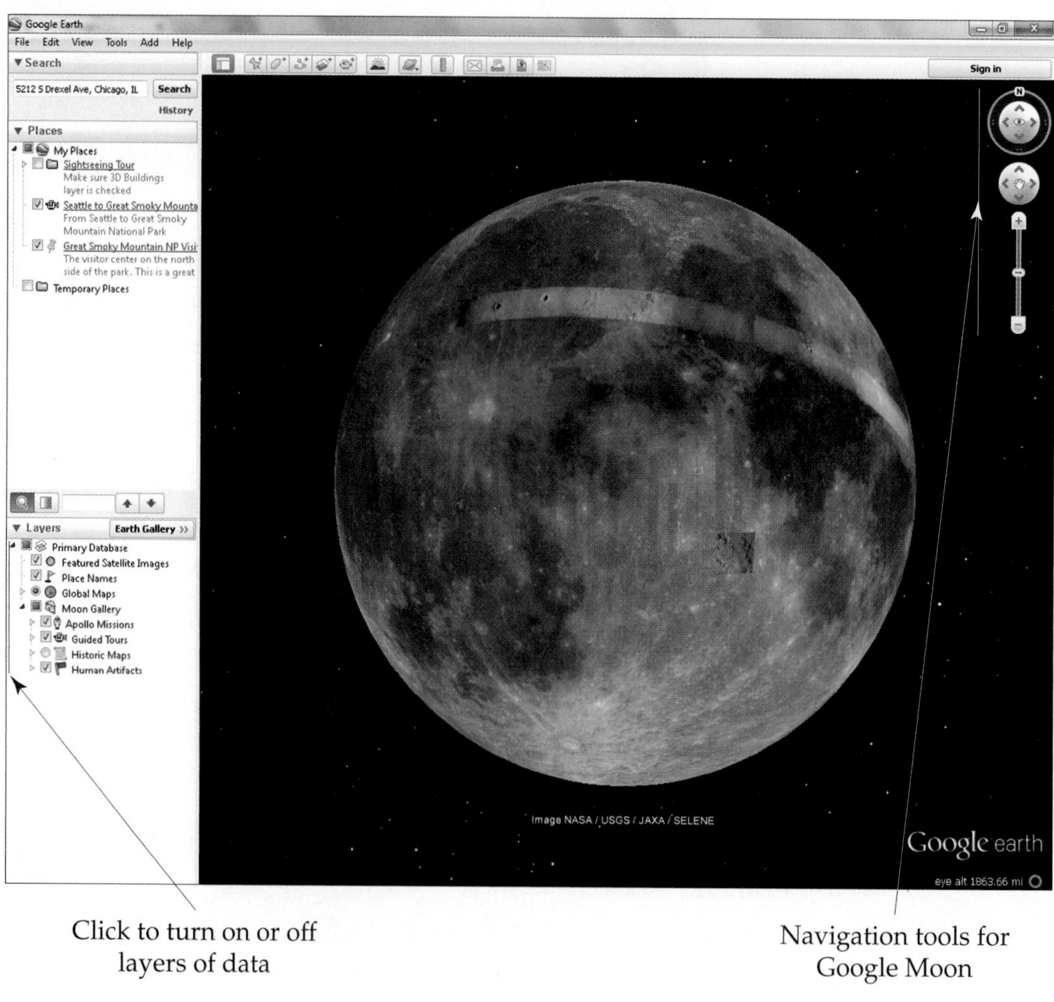

Goodheart-Willcox Publisher

Figure 21-13. Google Moon allows you to explore the Moon, just as Google Earth allows you to explore Earth.

22. Click the branch (link) for one of the Apollo missions. A pop-up window is displayed in the viewer window containing information about the mission.
23. Click the **X** button to close the pop-up window.
24. Expand the Guided Tours branch in the **Layers** panel.
25. Click the Apollo 11: Buzz Aldrin branch (link) to display a pop-up window.
26. Click the **Play this tour** link in the pop-up window. An animation of the Apollo 11 mission is overlaid on the satellite images of the Moon. This is about 12 minutes in length.
27. Close the replay toolbar when the animation is finished.

Accessing and Navigating Google Mars

Switch between Earth, Sky, and other planets

28. Click the **Switch between Earth, Sky, and other planets** button on the main toolbar, and click **Mars** in the drop-down menu. Mars appears as shown in **Figure 21-14.**

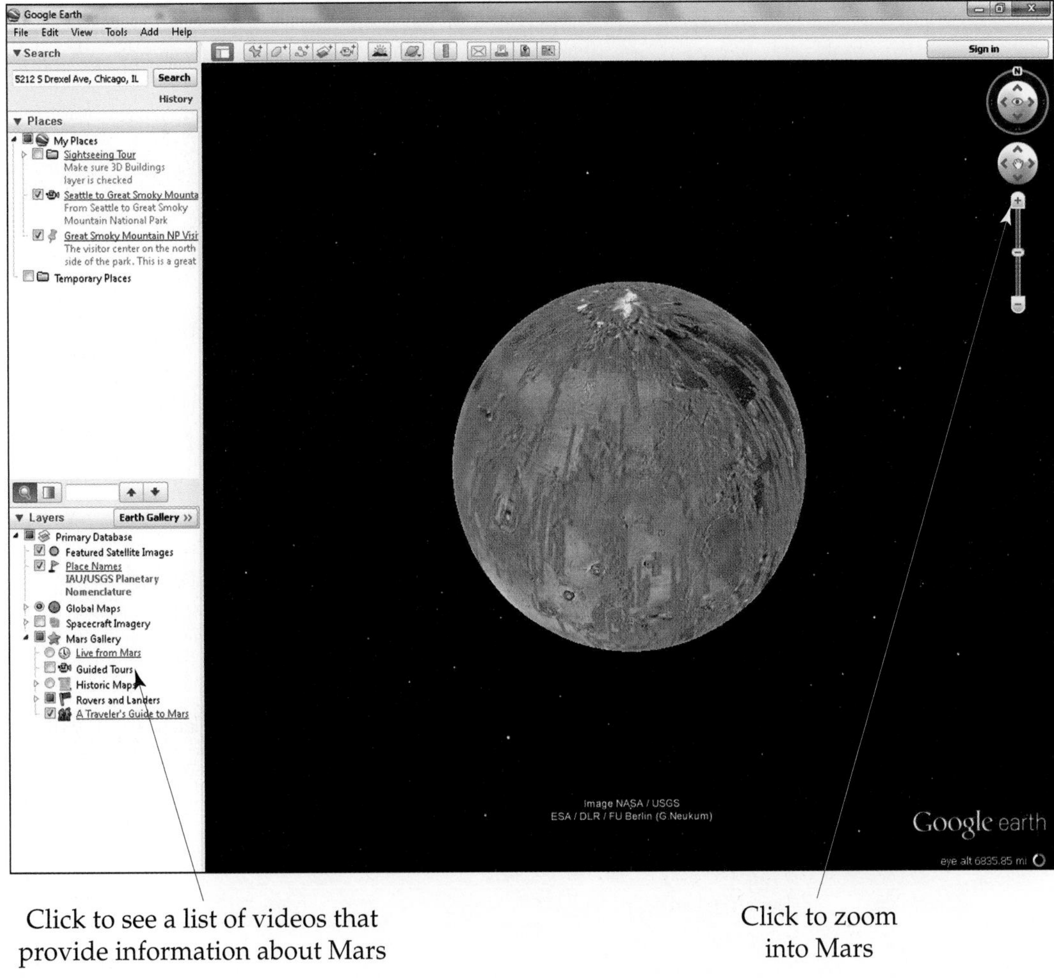

Goodheart-Willcox Publisher

Figure 21-14. Google Mars allows you to explore the planet Mars.

29. In the **Layers** panel, expand the Global Maps branch if it is not already expanded.
30. Click the radio button to the left of the Colorized Terrain branch. The different elevations of Mars are shown in varying colors.
31. Click the radio button to the left of the Visible Imagery branch to return to the original, default view.
32. Expand the Mars Gallery branch, if it is not already expanded, and then expand the Guided Tours branch.
33. Double-click the Mars Exploration branch. Watch the tour of Mars, narrated by Bill Nye. This is about eight minutes in length.
34. Close the replay toolbar when the tour is finished.
35. Close Google Earth.

Check Your Google Apps IQ

Now that you have finished this chapter, see what you know about Google Apps by taking the chapter posttest.
www.m.g-wlearning.com
www.g-wlearning.com/informationtechnology/

Skill Review

Answer the following questions on a separate sheet of paper.

1. ______ is a virtual globe.
2. A(n) ______ allows you to save a specific location and quickly return to that location in the future.
3. In Google Earth, look for a specific place or address by using the ______ panel.
4. What is the relationship between Google Earth and Google Chrome?
5. A(n) ______ is a preset experience where you move from one location to another following a specific path.
6. In what ways can a marker be altered once it is set?
7. The options that allow you to pick and choose what you see overlaying the satellite images in Google Earth, Sky, Moon, and Mars are referred to as ______.
8. What is a panoramic view?
9. What software application would you use to obtain a view of the sky above your home?
10. How was the imagery data for Google Mars collected?

Lesson Application

These exercises are designed to apply the skills learned in this and previous chapters. General directions are provided, but you will need to draw on your knowledge to determine how to complete each exercise.

Exercise 21-1
Finding Your Home with Google Earth

Using Google Earth, locate your home. Set a marker at that location, and label it My Home. Adjust the view around the marker, using the street or ground view if possible. Set this view as the default for the marker.

Exercise 21-2
Creating a Tour with Google Earth

Choose a region where you have never been, such as a rain forest, and explore it using Google Earth. View the pictures that are available and determine what you would like to see and do if you have the opportunity to go there. Set markers for each specific thing you would like to see in that region. Then, create a sightseeing tour of the region using your markers to navigate the region. If you have a microphone, record a voiceover for the tour to explain what is being shown.

Exercise 21-3
Learning from Google Sky

Using Google Sky, view the stars above your home. Display the constellations. Turn on the Virtual Tourism layer (Education Center>Virtual Tourism), locate a tour, and play the video in the pop-up window. Compose an e-mail to your instructor that summarizes the virtual tour and how it impacts what you see as you look up from your backyard.

Chapter 22

SketchUp

Objectives

After completing this chapter, you will be able to:

- **Visualize** geometry and other mathematical concepts.
- **Demonstrate** architectural concepts.
- **Design** a full-scale 3D building.
- **Collaborate** with others on building designs.

alexmillos/Shutterstock.com

Check Your Google Apps IQ

Before you begin this chapter, see what you already know about Google Apps by taking the chapter pretest.

www.m.g-wlearning.com
www.g-wlearning.com/informationtechnology/

Introduction to SketchUp

SketchUp is a three-dimensional (3D) modeling application. The basic versions of the program are available as a free download, while a more full-featured professional version is available for purchase. In this text, you will work with SketchUp Make, which is one of the free versions. Despite being free, this is an advanced 3D modeling application. Many people in a variety of careers, such as architects and product designers, design things they intend to build as 3D models. Modeling programs are also used by people designing virtual worlds, such as video game developers.

Three-Dimensional Modeling

Three-dimensional modeling is creating a virtual object using computer-aided drafting and design (CAD) software. Space in a 3D model is based on the standard Cartesian coordinate system used in math classes. The ***Cartesian coordinate system*** consists of three axes—X, Y, and Z—to represent three-dimensional space. Any point in space can be located using X, Y, and Z coordinates. For example, the intersection of the three axes is called the ***origin,*** and its coordinates are (0,0,0), as shown in **Figure 22-1.**

A ***plane*** is flat and has no height. It is defined by two axes. Only two coordinates are required to locate a point on a plane. The Cartesian coordinate system has XY, XZ, and YZ planes. Shapes, such as rectangles and circles, are called two dimensional because they lay flat on a plane.

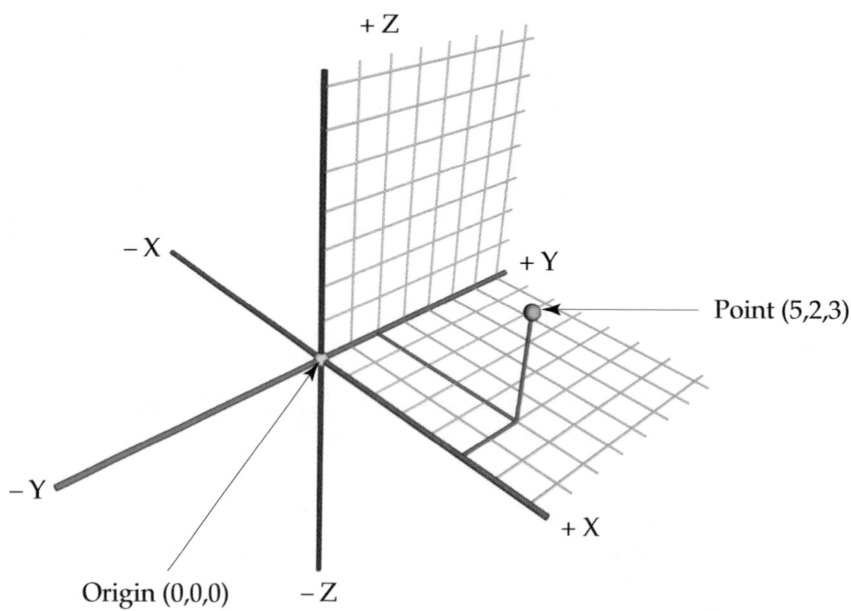

Goodheart-Willcox Publisher

Figure 22-1. Any point in space can be located with three dimensions on the Cartesian coordinate system.

A ***rectangle*** is a shape made up of four right angles and sides of unequal length. To add volume to a 2D shape, a third dimension is added by extruding or lofting.

Navigating SketchUp

There are several templates from which to choose when SketchUp is launched. The choices include simple templates for basic modeling and an architectural design template to use for architecture and interior design. Also included is a Google Earth modeling template to create models for use in Google Earth, along with an engineering template and a product design and woodworking template for smaller projects. Each of these templates has a version that uses the metric system of measurement and a version that uses the US customary system of measurement.

The SketchUp workspace is a user-friendly interface with simple, intuitive tools. The default workspace includes an image of a person standing in the middle of the workspace. This helps orient the workspace. Red, green, and blue lines show the X, Y, and Z axes, respectively. A toolbar extends across the top of the workspace. Buttons on the toolbar include those that allow a user to create shapes, manipulate shapes, measure shapes, fill shapes, and move around the workspace.

Using SketchUp

With SketchUp, a user can create precise geometric shapes using the **Circle**, **Rectangle**, **Polygon**, and **Arc** tools. These shapes can be made into three-dimensional objects with the **Push/Pull** tool. Using this tool, a circle becomes a cylinder and a rectangle becomes a box. These 3D objects can be rotated, moved, and scaled to better represent parts of a building, for example.

Using SketchUp, simple shapes can quickly be developed into buildings. Everything from a basic house to a replica of the Empire State Building, to new and complex designs can be drawn with SketchUp. In addition to three-dimensional models of buildings, a user can also create detailed floor plans in SketchUp. Spatial models can also be created in SketchUp. A ***spatial model*** is created, often in architectural planning, to project space requirements using basic shapes to represent objects and structures.

Developing Architectural Concepts Using SketchUp

Exact measurements needed in creating building models are provided with SketchUp. The dimensions of each created object can be displayed to determine the surface area and volume of shapes, as seen in **Figure 22-2.**

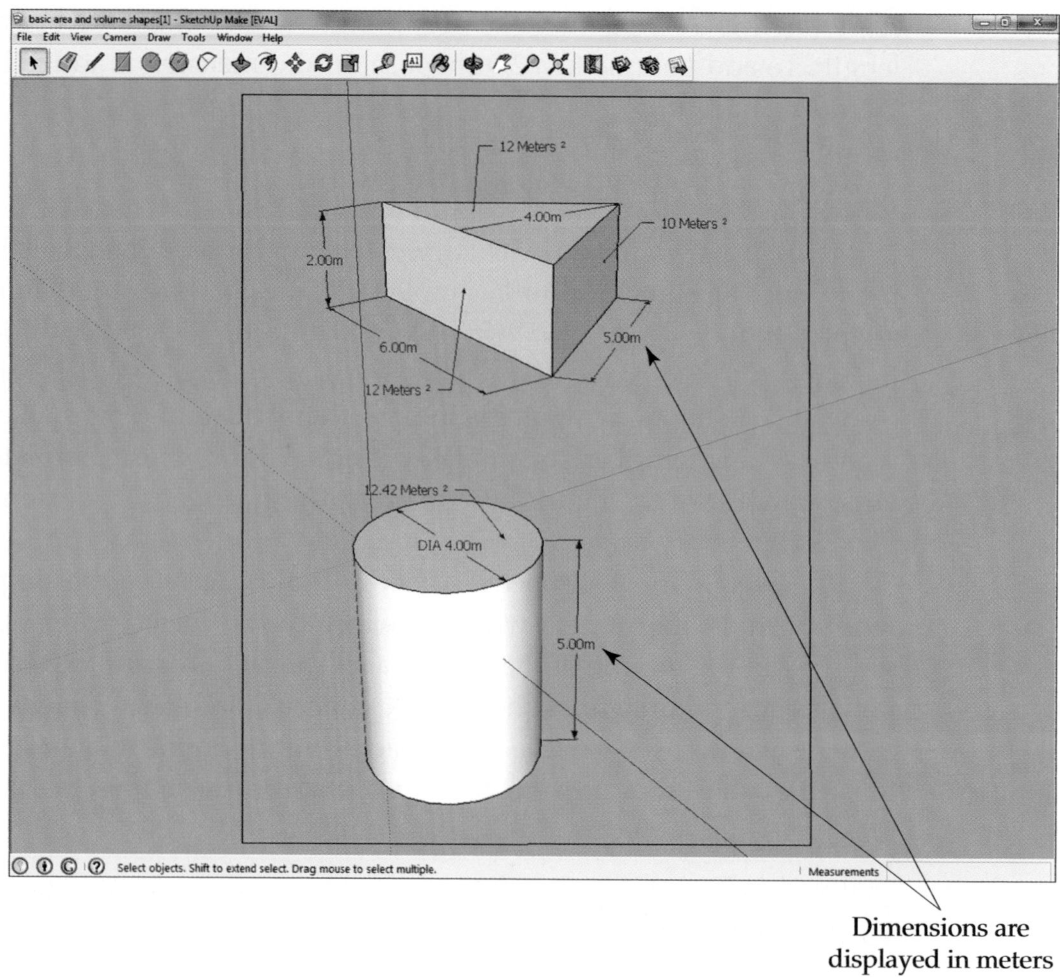

nvboettcher

Figure 22-2. Two basic geometric shapes have been drawn in SketchUp.

At the basic level, when drawing a simple rectangle, help text displays when the user has drawn a square as well as a golden section. A ***square*** is a rectangular shape having four equal sides and four right angles. A ***golden section*** occurs when the dimension of the short side of the rectangle is two-thirds of the dimension of the long side. The golden section, also known as the golden ratio or rule of thirds, has long been used to determine aesthetically pleasing proportions.

SketchUp allows more than just draw a building floating in space, as seen in **Figure 22-3**. Using the tools available, it is possible to create interesting and dynamic 3D buildings as well as the environments around them. Landscaping can be added to develop an entire architectural and aesthetic concept. Additionally, because SketchUp has tools integrated with Google Earth, geo-data from a specific location in Google Earth can be incorporated into a model. This allows the SketchUp models to include actual terrain information.

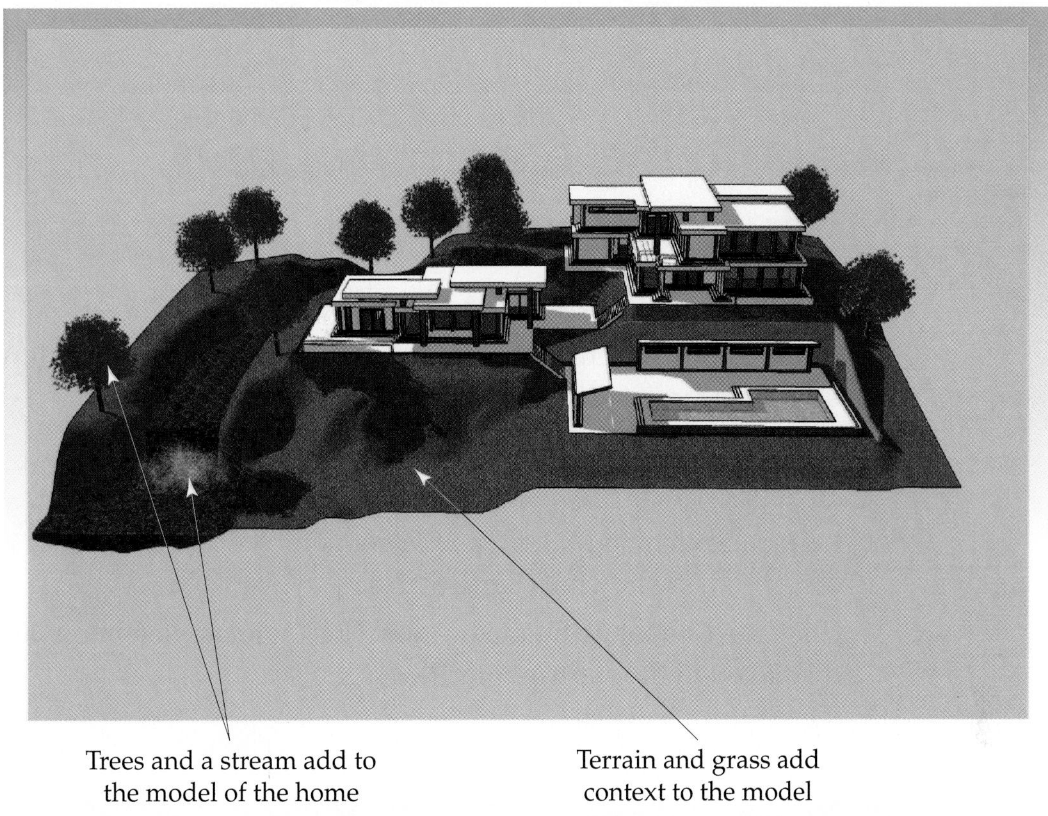

Adam

Figure 22-3. Environmental elements, such as trees and landscaping, can be added to a SketchUp model.

Collaborating with Others

Through the 3D Warehouse, a SketchUp user can download the shared work of others as well as upload his or her own work. As the name implies, the 3D Warehouse is cloud-based storage for models of all sorts. A shared model could be a basic shape to illustrate a point, such as a tree, shrub, or a piece of furniture, or it could be a very detailed model of a structure. A user can find items in the 3D Warehouse by conducting a keyword search or by searching through categories or collections.

A model can be private and only shared with collaborators as well. Like other Google programs, a user can choose to share a SketchUp file with specific people. When sharing, other SketchUp users can be given the ability to change a file or just to view it. The creator of the file is the owner by default and has the ability to invite others to collaborate on it.

Lesson 22-1

Visualizing Geometry and Mathematical Concepts

Creating geometric shapes for visualizing mathematical concepts is a useful feature of SketchUp. Shapes can be created freely or with precise measurements in mind.

Getting Started with SketchUp

1. Launch SketchUp Make. The **Welcome to SketchUp** window is displayed, as shown in **Figure 22-4.**
2. Click the **Choose Template** button. The **Template Selection:** area is displayed in the startup window.

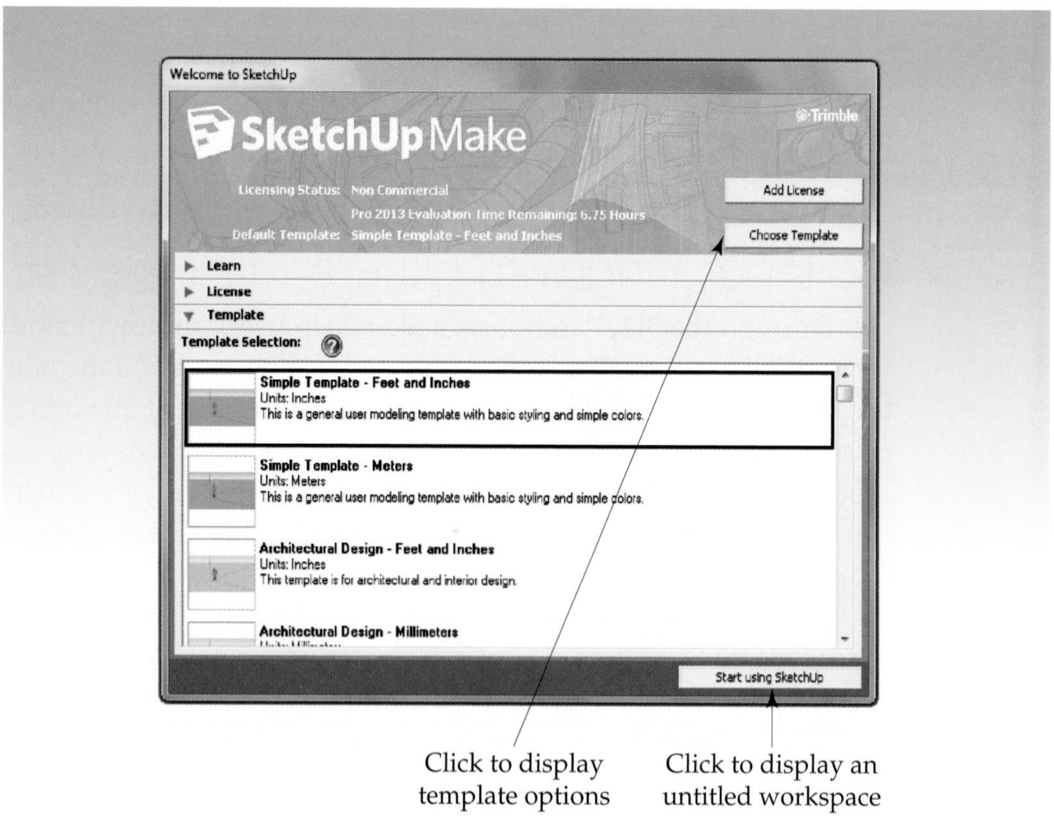

Goodheart-Willcox Publisher

Figure 22-4. When SketchUp is launched, you must select a template on which to base the model.

3. Click the **Simple Template – Meters** template, and then click the **Start using SketchUp** button. An untitled SketchUp workspace is displayed, as shown in **Figure 22-5.** If the **Instructor** window is displayed, close it.

Orbit

4. Click the **Orbit** button on the toolbar. The cursor changes to the orbit cursor.
5. Click and hold anywhere on the screen, and drag the mouse. As you drag, the view is rotated about the origin (center point) of the coordinate system.

Pan

6. Click the **Pan** button on the toolbar. The cursor changes to the pan cursor.
7. Click and hold anywhere on the screen, and drag the mouse. As the view is panned, your vantage point of the scene moves.

Zoom

8. Click the **Zoom** button on the toolbar. The cursor changes to the zoom cursor.

Tip
The mouse wheel can be scrolled to zoom the view.

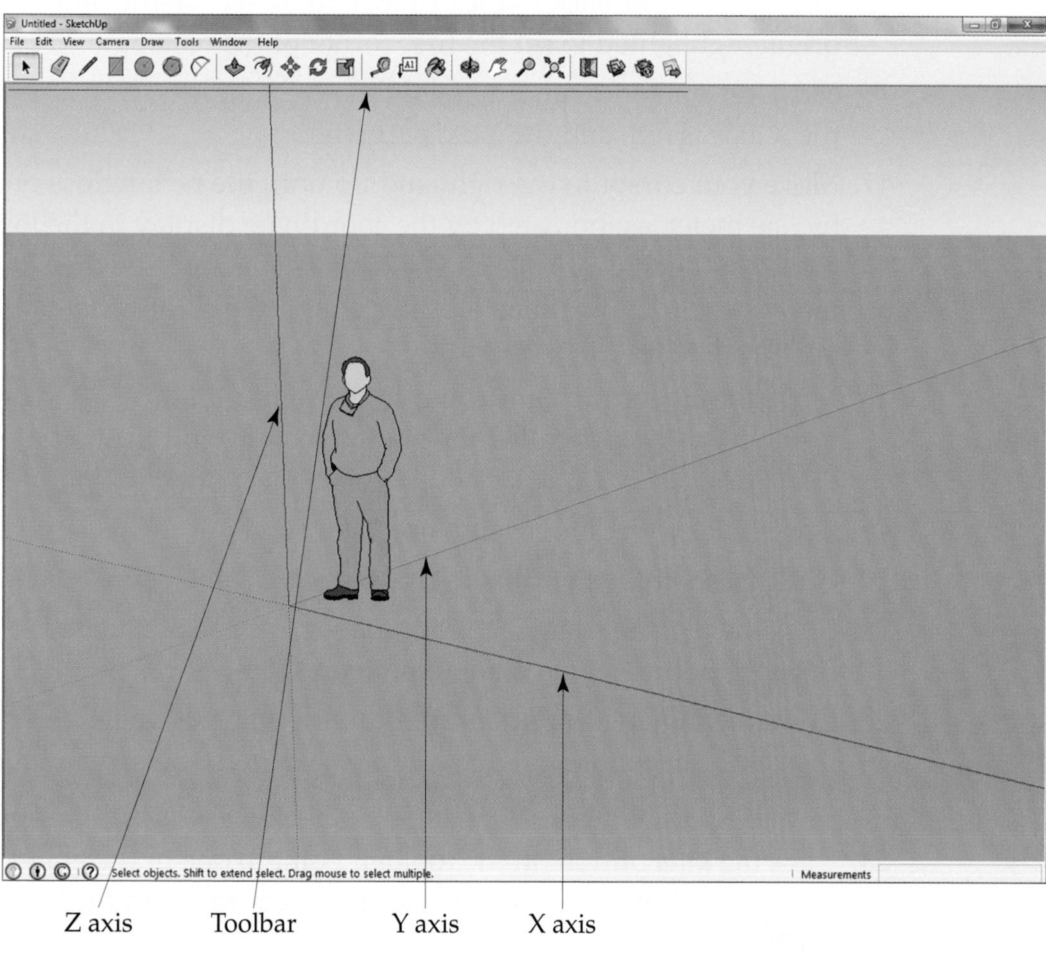

Goodheart-Willcox Publisher

Figure 22-5. The default appearance of SketchUp with a blank model file.

9. Place the cursor near the vertical middle of the screen, and then click and drag the mouse up. The view is zoomed in, and the origin of the screen comes closer. Dragging the cursor down zooms out on the view, and origin of the screen moves further away.

Eraser

10. Click the **Eraser** button on the toolbar.
11. Click on the person and drag until a blue selection box appears around the model, and then release the mouse button. The model of the person is erased.

Using SketchUp to Visualize Geometry

Rectangle

12. Click the **Rectangle** button on the toolbar.
13. Move the cursor until the dot is at the origin of the coordinate system. The dot changes to yellow, and the help text Origin appears.
14. Move the cursor over one of the axis lines. A dot appears on the axis to indicate the cursor has snapped onto the axis.
15. Move the cursor back to the origin, and then click the mouse with the origin highlighted to set the first corner of the rectangle.
16. Move the cursor up and to the right. A rectangle is drawn on XY plane—the X axis is red, and the Y axis is green.
17. Move your cursor to the right and up until the rectangle is one meter by one meter, as indicated by the coordinate display in the lower-right corner of the screen. You may need to use the mouse wheel to zoom in or out as you draw. When all sides of a rectangle are equal, it is a square, and the help text indicates this.
18. Move the cursor further up and to the right until the rectangle is 1 × 1.6 meters. This ratio is called the golden section, and the help text indicates this.
19. Single-click to set the second, opposite corner of the rectangle.

Push/Pull

20. Click the **Push/Pull** button on the toolbar.
21. Click the rectangle, and drag the cursor up. The rectangle is extruded upward, becoming a rectangular box.
22. Continue moving the cursor up until the shape is one meter tall, and then click the mouse again to set the height, as shown in **Figure 22-6.**
23. Use the **Orbit** tool to look at the model from different angles.

Line

24. Click the **Line** button on the toolbar. Point to one of the edges on the rectangular box until a small red square appears and the help text reads On Edge.
25. Move the cursor to the end of one of the edges. A green dot is displayed, and the help text reads Endpoint.

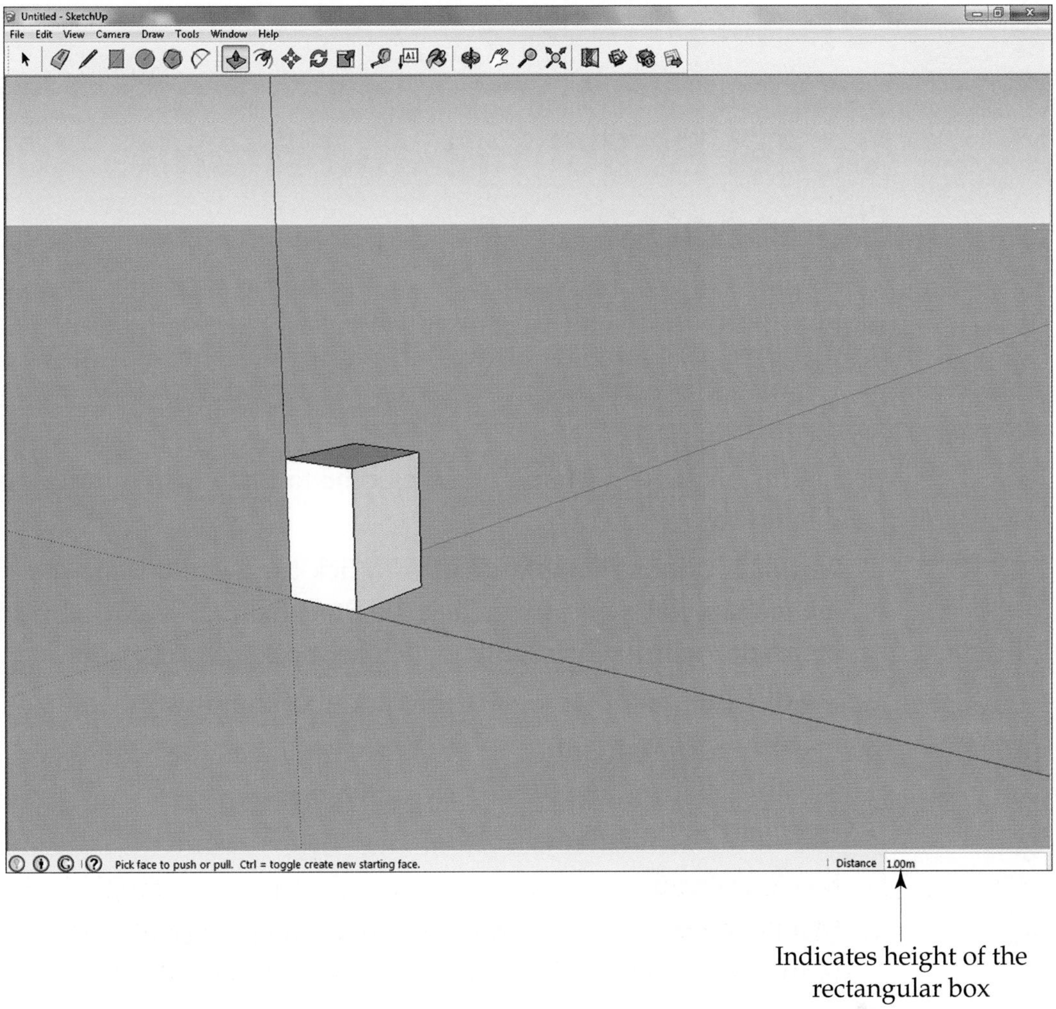

Indicates height of the rectangular box

Goodheart-Willcox Publisher

Figure 22-6. Drawing a basic rectangular shape and extruding it into a 3D object.

26. Move the cursor to the middle of one of the edges. A blue dot is displayed, and the help text reads a Midpoint.

The indications of midpoint and endpoint allow you to easily determine the beginning, middle, and ending of line segments and more accurately draw additional lines and shapes.

27. Draw a line from the midpoint on the top-front edge of the model to the top-back edge of the model.
28. Close SketchUp without saving.

Lesson 22-2

Model Buildings and Architectural Concepts

Creating a spatial model of a building is one way to demonstrate architectural concepts. It allows others to see what you have in mind and make suggestions for changes—changes that can be made immediately.

1. Launch SketchUp Make. The **Welcome to SketchUp** window is displayed.
2. Click the **Choose Template** button, click the **Simple Template – Feet and Inches** template, and then click the **Start using SketchUp** button. If the **Instructor** window is displayed, close it.

Eraser

3. Use the **Eraser** tool to delete the model of the person.

Rectangle

Push/Pull

Zoom Extents

4. Create a rectangular box of any size as long as the base is a golden section. The height may be of your choice.
5. Click the **Zoom Extents** button. The view is zoomed so the entire model fills the screen.
6. Use the **Orbit**, **Pan**, and **Zoom** tools to adjust to see a 3D view of the view of the top of model. This is the base spatial model for a building.
7. Use the **Line** tool to draw a line from the midpoint of one short side of the top face to the midpoint of the other short side of the top face. This line bisects the top face.

8. Click the **Move** button on the toolbar.
9. Click the bisecting line to select it, and move the cursor straight up. A dashed blue line will appear if the cursor is being moved straight up, and the help text will state On Blue Axis, which is the Z axis.
10. Move the line straight up a distance equal to about one-third of the height of the box, and click to set the new position. As the line is moved, the faces are adjusted and a sloped roof is created, as shown in **Figure 22-7.**
11. Use the **Zoom** and **Pan** tools to rotate the image so the triangular roof line is visible.

Tip A quick way to display flat, or orthographic, views is to click **Standard Views** in the **Camera** pull-down menu, and then select the side you want to view.

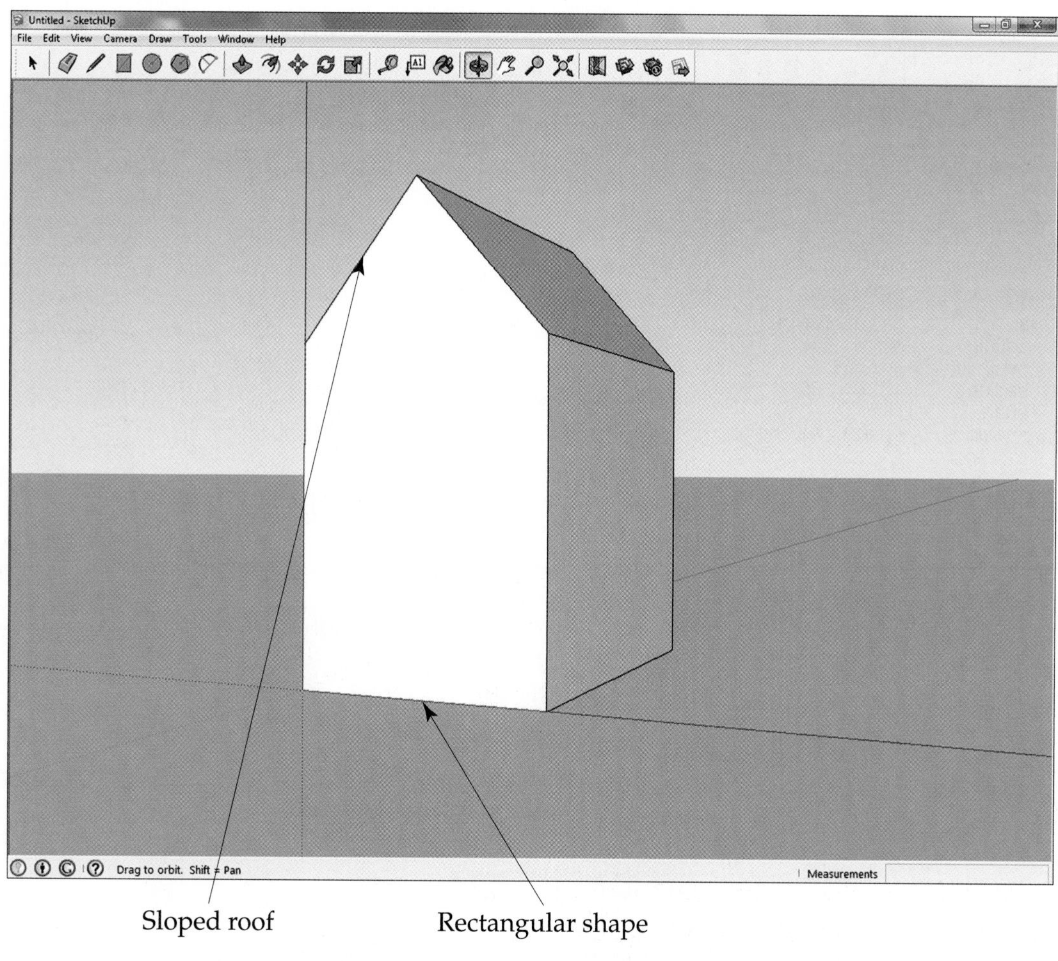

Goodheart-Willcox Publisher

Figure 22-7. A bisecting line has been added to the top face, and the line moved upward to create a roof peak.

12. Use the **Line**, **Rectangle**, **Circle**, and **Push/Pull** tools to create windows and doors on all sides of the building. See **Figure 22-8.** The spatial model is complete.

Tip When using the **Move** tool, holding the [Ctrl] key creates a copy instead of moving the object. This can be used to quickly create additional windows on the side of the building. Use the **Select** tool and the [Ctrl] key to select multiple objects.

13. Click **Save As...** in the **File** pull-down menu. A standard Windows save dialog box is displayed.
14. Navigate to your working folder, enter My First Building in the **Name:** text box, and click the **Save** button. SketchUp files are automatically saved with the .skp file extension.
15. Close SketchUp.

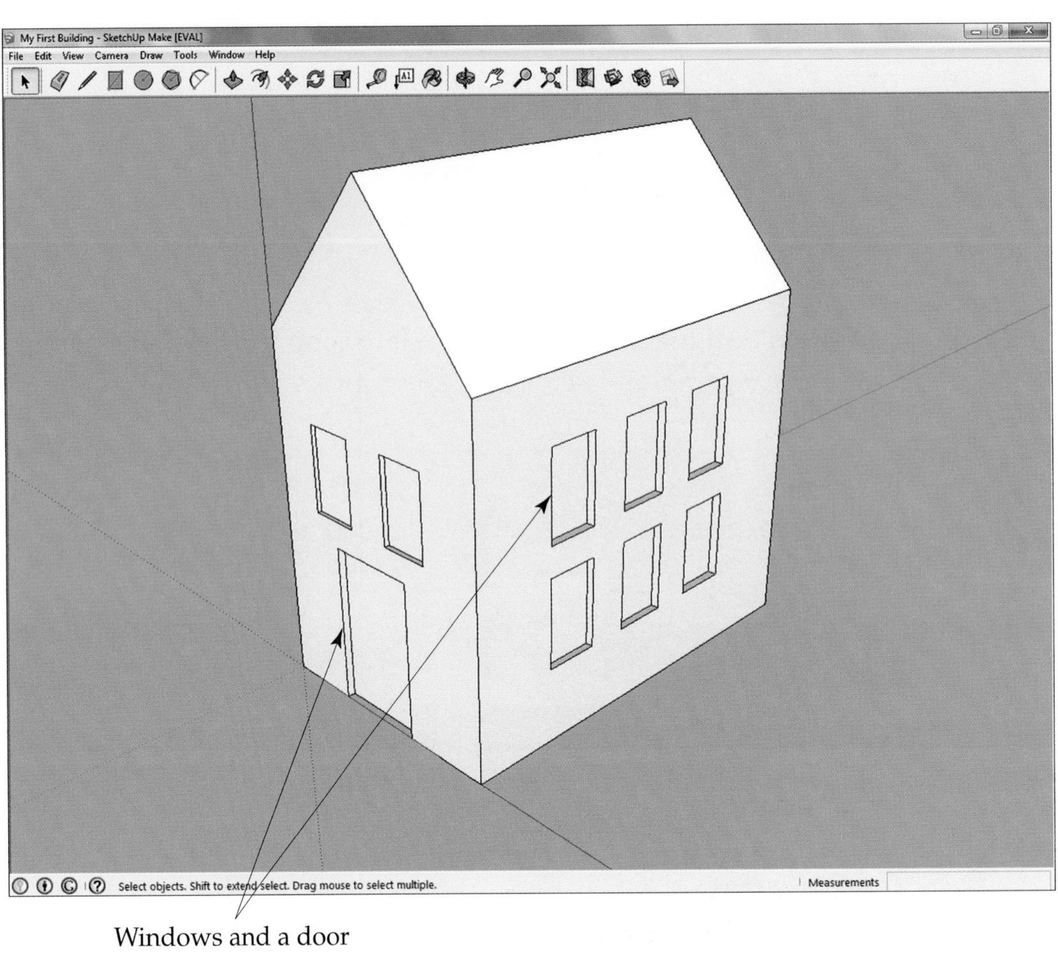

Goodheart-Willcox Publisher

Figure 22-8. Shapes have been added to the faces of the model, and then extruded inward to represent windows and doors.

Lesson 22-3

Full-Scale 3D Buildings and Environments

When designing a full-scale model, using precise dimensions are extremely important. SketchUp allows for keyboard entry of exact values.

Designing Full-Scale 3D Buildings

1. Launch SketchUp Make. The **Welcome to SketchUp** window is displayed.
2. Click the **Choose Template** button, click the **Architectural Design – Feet and Inches** template, and then click the **Start using SketchUp** button. If the **Instructor** window is displayed, close it.

Eraser

3. Use the **Eraser** tool to delete the model of the person.

Rectangle

4. Click the **Rectangle** button, and click at the origin (0,0) to set the first corner.
5. Using the keyboard, enter 20′,40′. These are the X and Y dimensions of the rectangle, and are reflected in the coordinate display as entered. Press the [Enter] key to set the dimensions.

Push/Pull

6. Click the **Push/Pull** button, and click inside the rectangle.
7. Using the keyboard, enter 10′. This is the Z dimension of the extrusion, and is reflected in the coordinate display as entered. Press the [Enter] key to set the dimension.

Line

8. Add a bisecting line to the top face of the building. The line should be between the short sides.

9. Click the **Move** button, and click the bisecting line to select it.
10. Move the mouse upward, and using the keyboard enter 4′. This is the offset value on the Z axis, as reflected in the coordinate display, to form the peak of the building. Press the [Enter] key to set the offset.
11. Add windows and doors to the building, paying attention to the size and placement of each. Consult an online source for standard sizes.
12. Save the model in your working folder as My Full-Scale Building.

Designing Environments

Paint Bucket

13. Click the **Paint Bucket** button on the toolbar. The **Materials** palette appears, as shown in **Figure 22-9.**

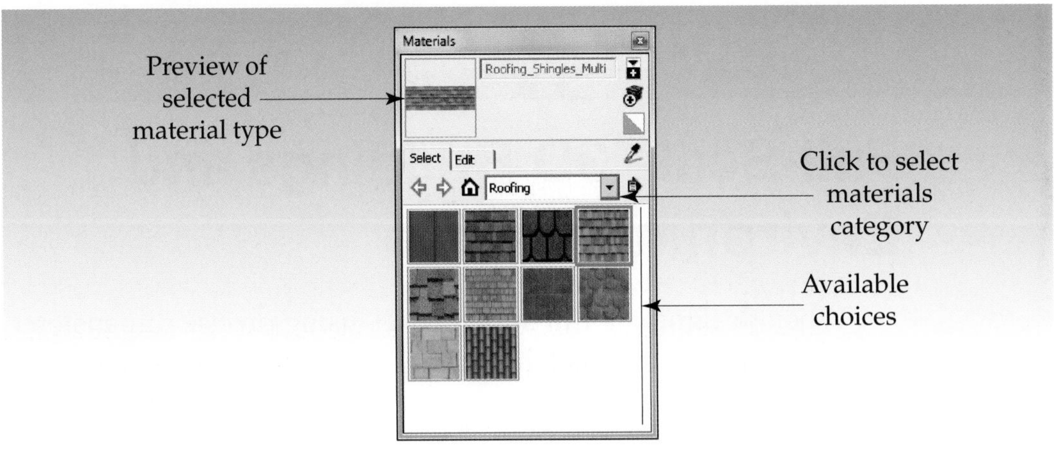

Goodheart-Willcox Publisher

Figure 22-9. The **Materials** palette is the control center for creating and applying materials to the model.

14. Click the **Materials** drop-down arrow in the **Materials** palette, and click **Roofing** in the list. The material samples in the palette change to only roofing materials, and the name changes to **Roofing**.
15. Click the Roofing_Shingles_Multi material sample (or the sample of your choice).
16. Click both roof faces. The material is applied to each face.

Tip Use the view-navigation tools as needed to view both faces on the roof.

17. Click the **Materials** drop-down arrow, now labeled **Roofing**, and click **Brick and Cladding** in the list.
18. Select a siding material for the model, and apply it to each outside wall. Notice that the windows and doors are separate spaces and the material is not applied to them.
19. Click the **Materials** drop-down arrow, now labeled **Brick and Cladding**, and click **Translucent** in the list.
20. Select a translucent material, and apply it to each window.
21. Click the **Materials** drop-down arrow, now labeled **Translucent**, and click **Wood** in the list.
22. Select a wood material, and apply it to each door.
23. Using what you know, create a thin rectangular object to be a patio for the house, and apply a stone paver material to it.

Get Models

24. Click the **Get Models...** button on the toolbar. The **3D Warehouse** window appears.

Tip While you can create your own models of trees and shrubbery in order to create a realistic environment for your building, it is far easier to download an existing model.

25. Click in the **Search** text box, enter tree, and click the **Search** button.
26. Scroll through the search results for a tree you would like to use.
27. Click the **Download Model** link for the tree you want to use. A message appears asking if you would like to load it into your model. Click the **Yes** button. The tree model is placed in the open SketchUp window.
28. Use the **Move** tool to place the tree near the house.
29. Continue adding models of trees, shrubs, and flowers to give your house nice landscaping. See **Figure 22-10.**
30. Using what you know, add a lawn, driveway, and model of a car.
31. Click **Save** in the **File** pull-down menu to save the model.
32. Close SketchUp.

Move

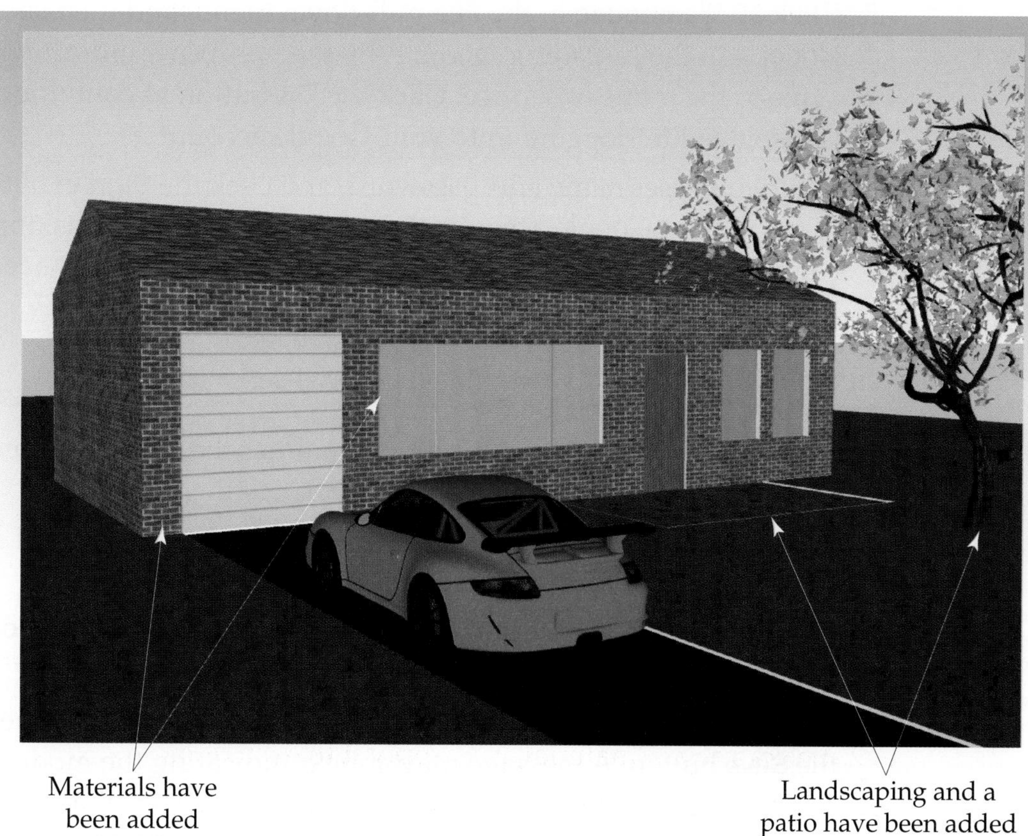

Goodheart-Willcox Publisher

Figure 22-10. Adding landscaping and other elements completes the scene.

Lesson 22-4

Collaborating with Others

Specific SketchUp users can be invited to view or edit a 3D model you have created. A user can also make his or her files available to all SketchUp users.

1. Launch SketchUp Make. The **Welcome to SketchUp** window is displayed.
2. Click the **Choose Template** button, click any template, and then click the **Start using SketchUp** button. If the **Instructor** window is displayed, close it.
3. Click **Open...** in the **File** pull-down menu. A standard Windows open dialog box is displayed.
4. Navigate to your working folder, select the My Full-Scale Building model created in Lesson 22-3, and click the **Open** button.
5. Click **3D Warehouse** in the **File** pull-down menu, and then click **Share Model...** in the cascading menu. A message appears indicating you must agree to the terms of service. Click the **OK** button to continue. A window is displayed for logging in to your Google account.
6. Enter your user name and password, and click the **Sign In** button to log in to your Google account. A new page is displayed asking you to confirm allowing access to your account. Click the **Allow Access** button.

Tip You can sign in to or out of your Google account at any time by clicking the **Sign In/Sign Out** button in the lower-left corner of the SketchUp screen.

7. A message may appear indicating you must choose a name and agree to the terms of service before continuing. Click the **OK** button to continue.
8. You may be asked to sign in to your Google account again. If so, sign in to continue. The terms of service are displayed.
9. Click the button to accept the terms of service. The **3D Warehouse Preferences** window is displayed, as shown in **Figure 22-11.**
10. Make the preference settings of your choice, enter a nickname, and click the **Save** button. A message may appear indicating the model contains unused items. Click the **Yes** button to continue. The 3D Warehouse upload window is displayed, as shown in **Figure 22-12.**
11. Click in the **Insert model title** text box, and enter a name for the model. The more descriptive the name, the easier the model will be to identify later.
12. Click in the **Insert model description** text box, and enter a brief explanation of what is shown in the model.

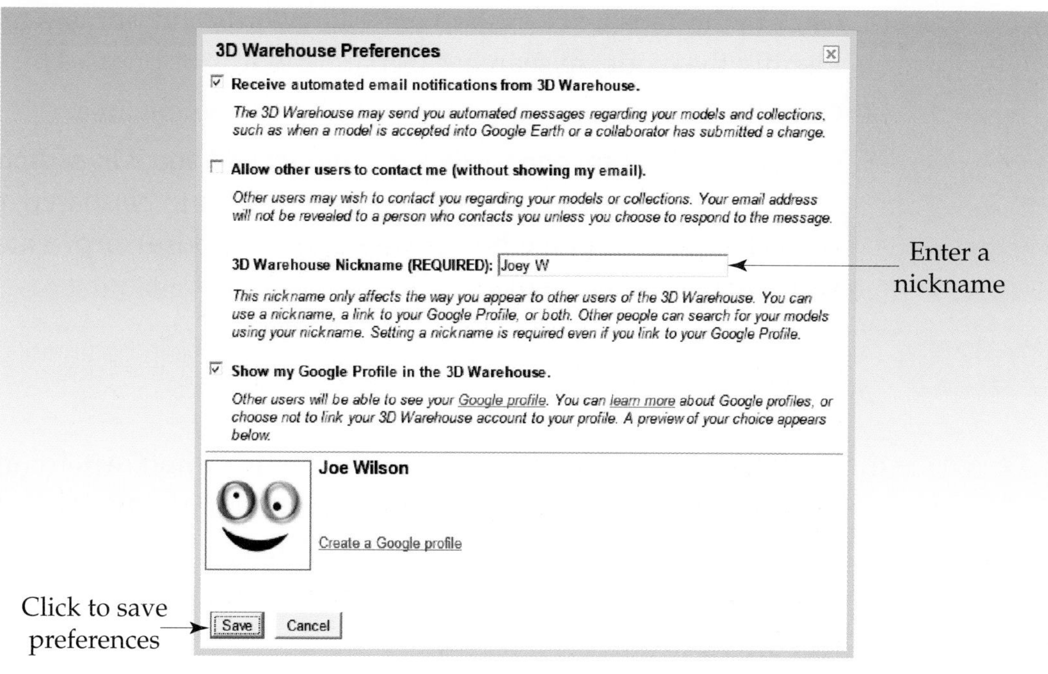

Goodheart-Willcox Publisher

Figure 22-11. Setting preferences for the 3D Warehouse.

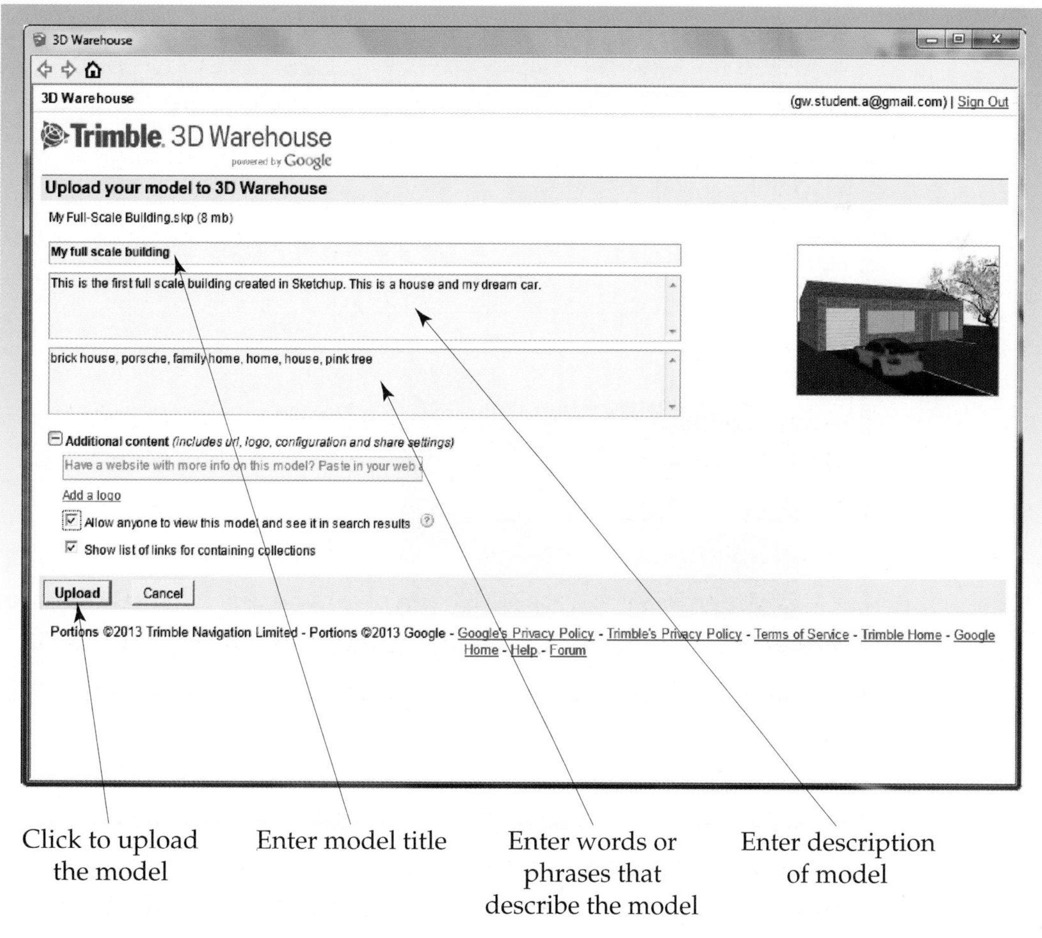

Goodheart-Willcox Publisher

Figure 22-12. Uploading a model to the 3D Warehouse.

13. Click in the **Tags** text box, and enter keywords and phrases that will help identify the model in searches. Separate words or phrases by commas.
14. Click the plus sign to expand the **Additional content** area.
15. Check the **Allow anyone to view this model and see it in search results** check box. This must be checked if the model is to be shared, either publicly (with anyone who accesses 3D Warehouse) or privately (just with people you choose).

A website URL and a logo, such as for your business, can be specified in the **Additional content** area.

16. Click the **Upload** button. A progress meter is shown. After your model is uploaded, a page is displayed containing information about the uploaded model, as shown in **Figure 22-13.**

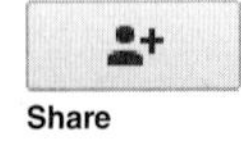

17. Click the **Share** button to display a drop-down menu, as shown in **Figure 22-14.**
18. Click **Invite others...** in the drop-down menu. A new page is displayed with choices to share the model, as shown in **Figure 22-15.**

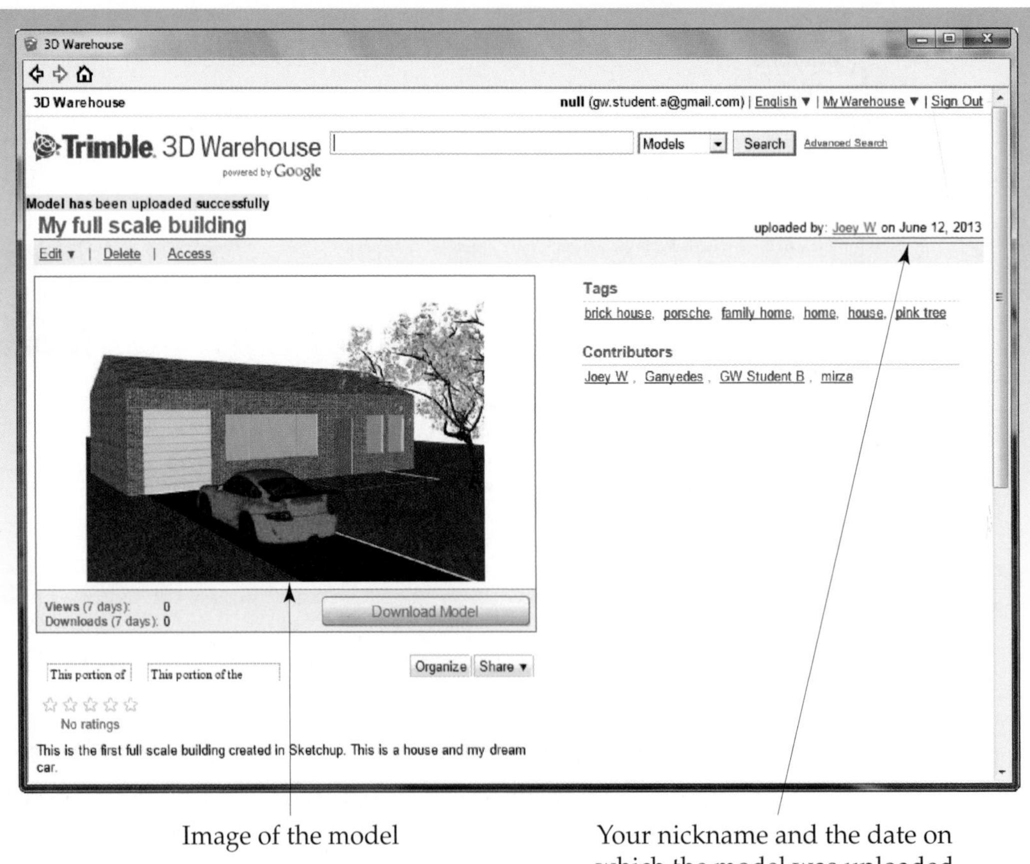

Goodheart-Willcox Publisher

Figure 22-13. The model has been uploaded to the 3D Warehouse.

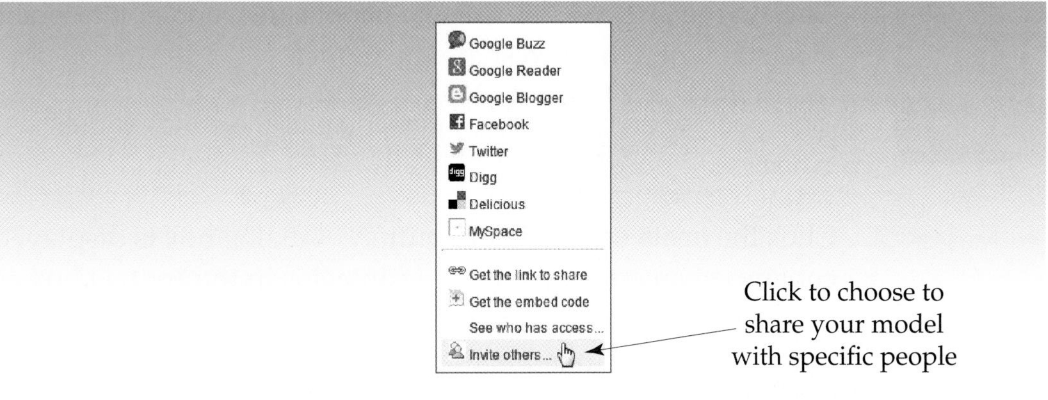

Goodheart-Willcox Publisher

Figure 22-14. The options for sharing a model in the 3D Warehouse.

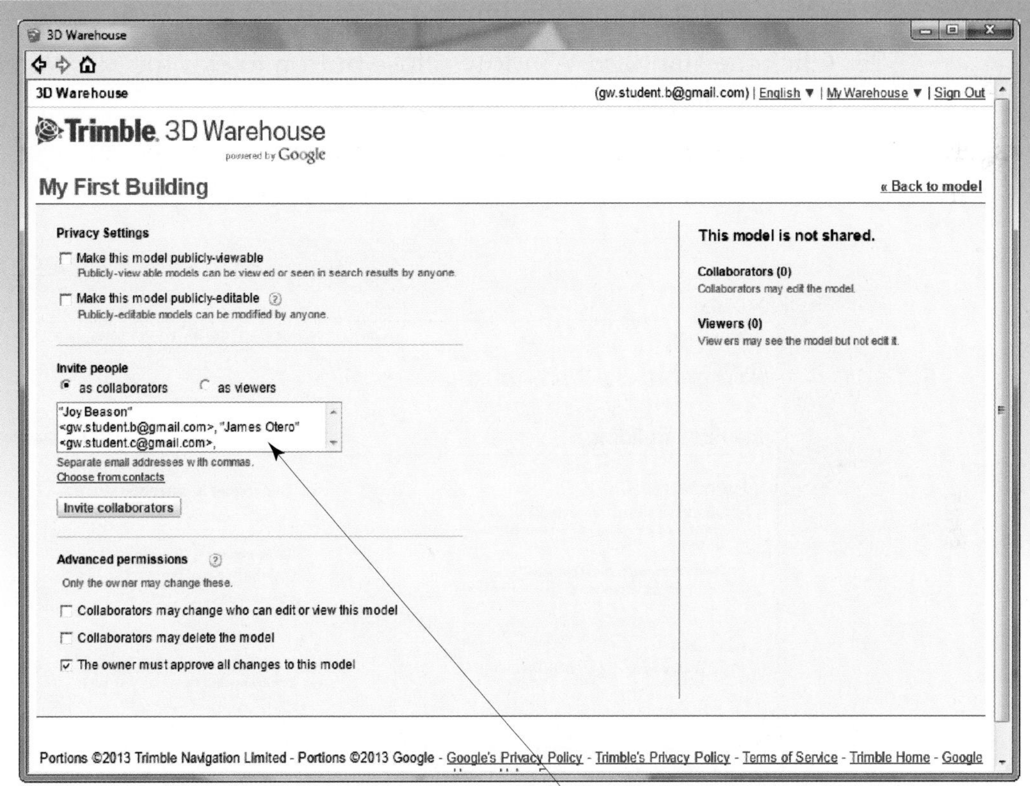

Goodheart-Willcox Publisher

Figure 22-15. Specifying settings for sharing a model in the 3D Warehouse.

19. In the **Privacy Settings** area of the page, uncheck both the **Make this model publically viewable** and **Make this model publically-editable** check boxes. This makes the model only visible to people you select.
20. In the **Invite people** area of the page, click the **As collaborators** radio button so it is on. This specifies the people you invite will be able to view and edit the model.

21. Click in the text box in the **Invite people** area, and enter e-mail address of a person with whom to share the model.

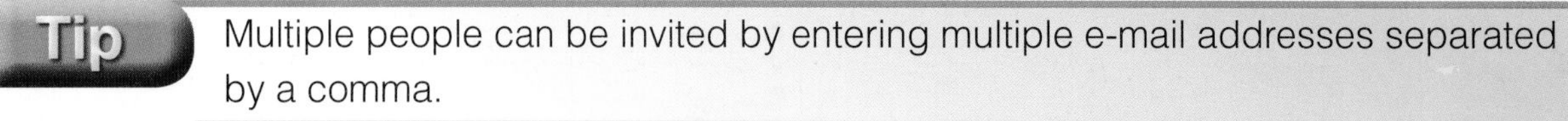

Multiple people can be invited by entering multiple e-mail addresses separated by a comma.

22. Click the **Invite collaborators** button. A dialog box is displayed containing an e-mail form. The contact is in the **To:** text box and the model name is in the **Subject:** text box. A link to the model will be automatically included in the e-mail.
23. Click in the **Message:** text box, and enter a brief message, for example, explaining what to do with the model.
24. Click the **Send** button. The sharing page is updated to show who is a collaborator on this model, as shown in **Figure 22-16.**
25. Click the standard Windows close button to exit the 3D Warehouse window to return to the model in SketchUp.
26. Save the model and close SketchUp.

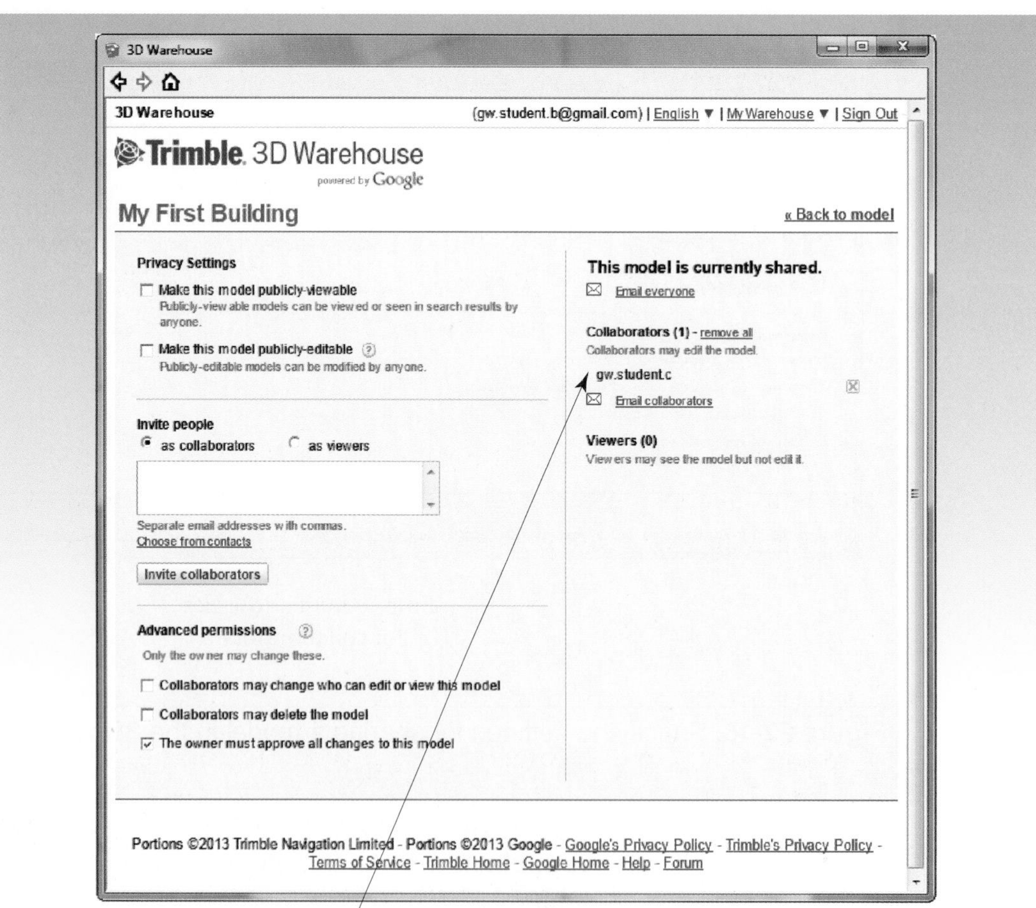

Goodheart-Willcox Publisher

Figure 22-16. When a model is shared, the collaborators are listed.

Check Your Google Apps IQ

Now that you have finished this chapter, see what you know about Google Apps by taking the chapter posttest.
www.m.g-wlearning.com
www.g-wlearning.com/informationtechnology/

Skill Review

Answer the following questions on a separate sheet of paper.

1. What is three-dimensional modeling?
2. Briefly describe the coordinate system used in 3D modeling.
3. What are the coordinates of the origin in SketchUp?
4. In terms of coordinates, what is the difference between a two-dimensional shape and a three-dimensional object?
5. How does a rectangle differ from a square?
6. What are the four basic geometric shapes that can be drawn in SketchUp?
7. Describe the purpose of a spatial model.
8. In general, what is the golden section used for?
9. What is the 3D Warehouse?
10. Briefly describe how to collaborate on a SketchUp model.

Lesson Application

These exercises are designed to apply the skills learned in this and previous chapters. General directions are provided, but you will need to draw on your knowledge to determine how to complete each exercise.

Exercise 22-1
Designing a Home

Use SketchUp to create a model of your own home, a home that you like, or a home that you design on your own. Be sure to consider relative size of features such as door heights, window dimensions, roof lines, and so on. Consult reference materials, either printed books or online resources, for correct dimensions of windows and doors. Upload the model to the 3D Warehouse, and share it with your instructor. Include a message when sharing the model indicating the model is ready for grading.

Exercise 22-2
Designing a Commercial or Public Building

Working with a team, design a model of a commercial or public building. This may be a retail space, office, town hall, post office, or any other public space you would like to create. Consult reference materials, either printed books or online resources, for correct dimensions of windows and doors. Assign tasks to each team member, such as one member creates the basic walls and another team member creates doors and windows. Share the model with the team, and have each team member complete his or her assigned task. Each team member should send an e-mail to the team when his or her task is done and the model is ready for the next task. When the model is complete, share it with your instructor, indicating it is ready for grading.

Exercise 22-3
Creating an Environment

Choose the building designed in Exercise 22-1 or Exercise 22-2. Add environmental features around the building to create a landscaped scene. Download models of trees, shrubs, roads, and so on to place around the building. Create your own models as needed. When complete, upload the model under a different name, and share it with your instructor, indicating it is ready for grading.

Chapter 23

Blogger

Objectives

After completing this chapter, you will be able to:

- **Create** a blog that is a reflective learning journal.
- **Post** messages, photos, and videos to a blog.
- **Share** schoolwork via a blog.

alexmillos/Shutterstock.com

Check Your Google Apps IQ

Before you begin this chapter, see what you already know about Google Apps by taking the chapter pretest.

www.m.g-wlearning.com
www.g-wlearning.com/informationtechnology/

Blogging

Google Blogger is an application that allows a user to create and publish blogs. ***Blog*** is short for web log, and it is an online location containing a series of entries, or ***posts,*** provided by the blog creator to share with others. Blog posts can include text, images, videos, or links. Through blogs, people can read and view each other's work and make comments about posts. Blogs are public spaces, accessible to anyone with an Internet connection, so avoid including information that would allow someone to personally identify you. For example, a user should not include his or her home address or social security number in a blog.

Initially, blogs were just textual. A person would post his or her thoughts and feelings on a particular topic and then others would respond. The blog creator might write something else in response to the comment. It was, essentially, a dialogue that might play out over weeks, months, or even years. A blog can still be textual, but it can also include photos and videos that enhance the blog. Some blogs are entirely video blogs.

Blogs are created for a variety of reasons. A blog can be created and maintained by an individual to share his or her experiences, such as a vacation log. An individual can also use Google Blogger to create and maintain a reflective learning journal. A ***reflective learning journal*** is a document where a user can add thoughts and reflections on what he or she is learning. Blogs can be created and maintained by a group or a company to promote its activities or products as well. For example a blog could be used by a student organization to keep supporters aware of the developments and events of that group.

Using Google Blogger

Google Blogger is one of the most popular blog services available. Two of the reasons it is well-liked are because of its ease of use and the ability to include images and videos. With Blogger, a user can create multiple blogs and follow the blogs of others. The main page of Blogger, as seen in **Figure 23-1,** is the Blogger ***dashboard*** and is topped by a list of blogs the user has created and maintains. Then blogs the user follows are displayed.

Creating a Blog

A user can compose a new post for blogs he or she has created from the dashboard using the **Compose New Post** button. A new composition page is displayed. The composition page is similar to a word processor window. A formatting toolbar is displayed along the top of the composition area.

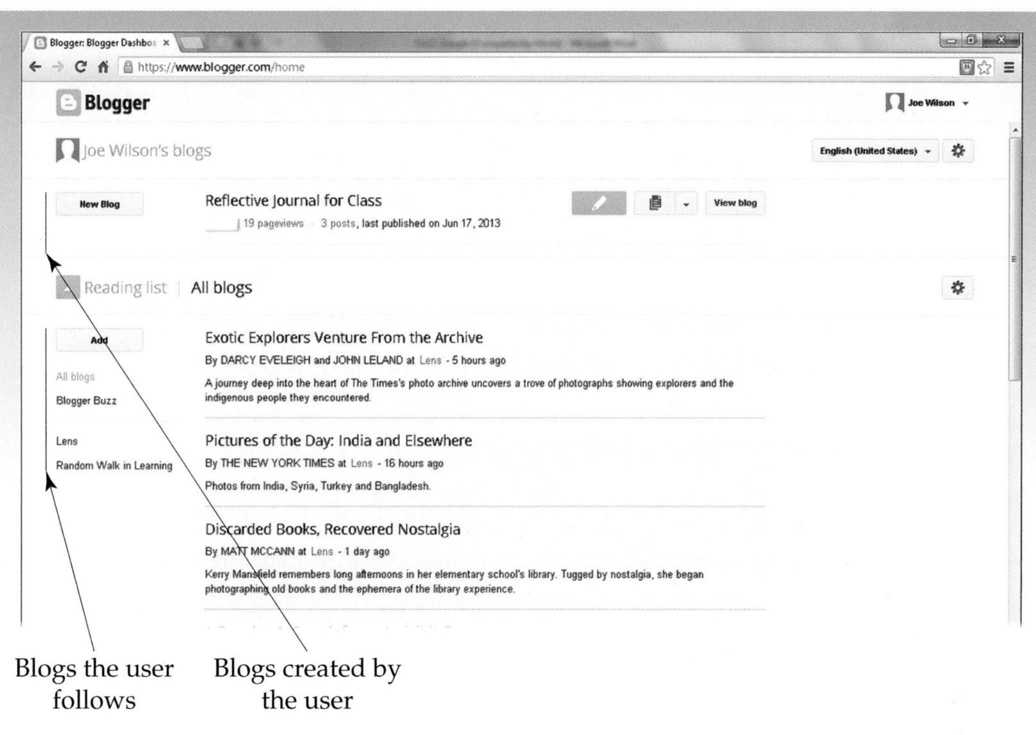

Goodheart-Willcox Publisher

Figure 23-1. Blogger can be used to quickly create a blog.

The toolbar includes options to format text with various font types and font size options along with the ability to bold, italicize, and underline text. A user can also insert images, videos, and links using the buttons on the toolbar.

When a new post is complete, it can be previewed before making it available online. Alongside the **Save** and **Close** buttons at the top of the new post page, the **Preview** button will display the new post in a separate tab. This version displays the post as it will look when it is published and available online. Once the new post is complete, the user clicks the **Publish** button to make it available online. Visitors to a blog will see new posts at the top of the blog page.

Following a Blog

A user can follow several blogs and view the latest posts from those blogs directly from the Blogger dashboard. In the **Reading list** section of the dashboard, a user can add blogs to follow by clicking the **Add** button. New content from these blogs will be displayed in the reading list when it is posted. A user can click the post title to have the post page displayed in a new tab of the browser. On the post page, a user can add comment to the blog.

Lesson 23-1

Creating a Reflective Learning Journal

A blog can be a good way to share information with others. Writing and formatting a blog post is similar to writing a document in Google Docs.

Launching Blogger for the First Time

1. Using your Internet browser, navigate to www.blogger.com.
2. Log in to your Google account. A page appears asking you to select between a Google+ profile and a Blogger profile, as shown in **Figure 23-2.**

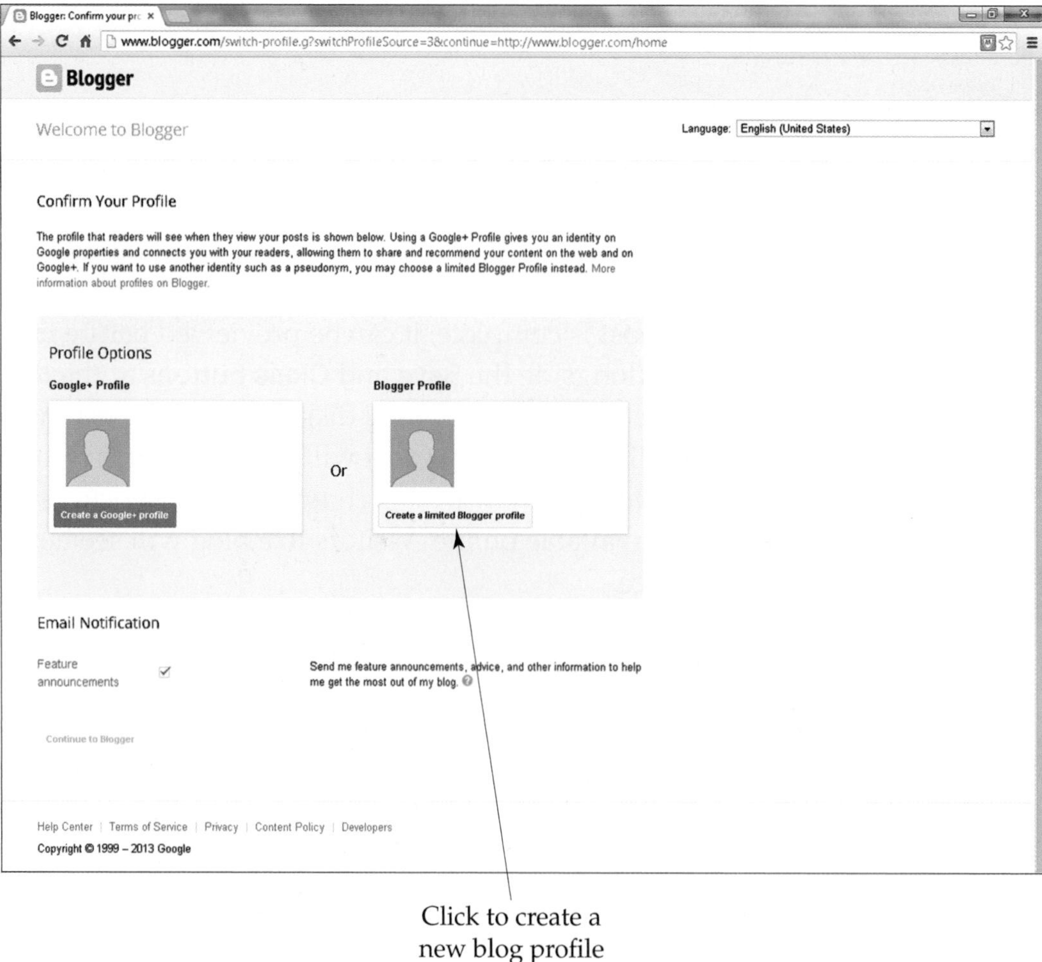

Goodheart-Willcox Publisher

Figure 23-2. The first time you log on to Blogger, you need to select a profile.

If your account is a Google+ account, a page is displayed asking to confirm your profile.

3. Click the **Create a Limited Blogger Profile** button. A new page is displayed on which you can enter a display name.

4. Click in the **Display Name** text box, enter the name you want others to see you as, and click the **Continue to Blogger** button. The Blogger home page—called the dashboard—is displayed, as shown in **Figure 23-3.** By default, the All blogs option is selected in the Reading list section of the page.

Creating a Blog

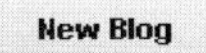

5. Click the **New Blog** button. The **Create a New Blog Window** dialog box is displayed, as shown in **Figure 23-4.**
6. Click in the **Title** text box, and enter Reflective Journal for Class.
7. Click in the **Address** text box, and enter ReflectiveJournal*YourLastName*. There can be no spaces, and .blogspot.com will be automatically added to the name.

A message will appear indicating if the address is valid and available. A valid and available address must be entered.

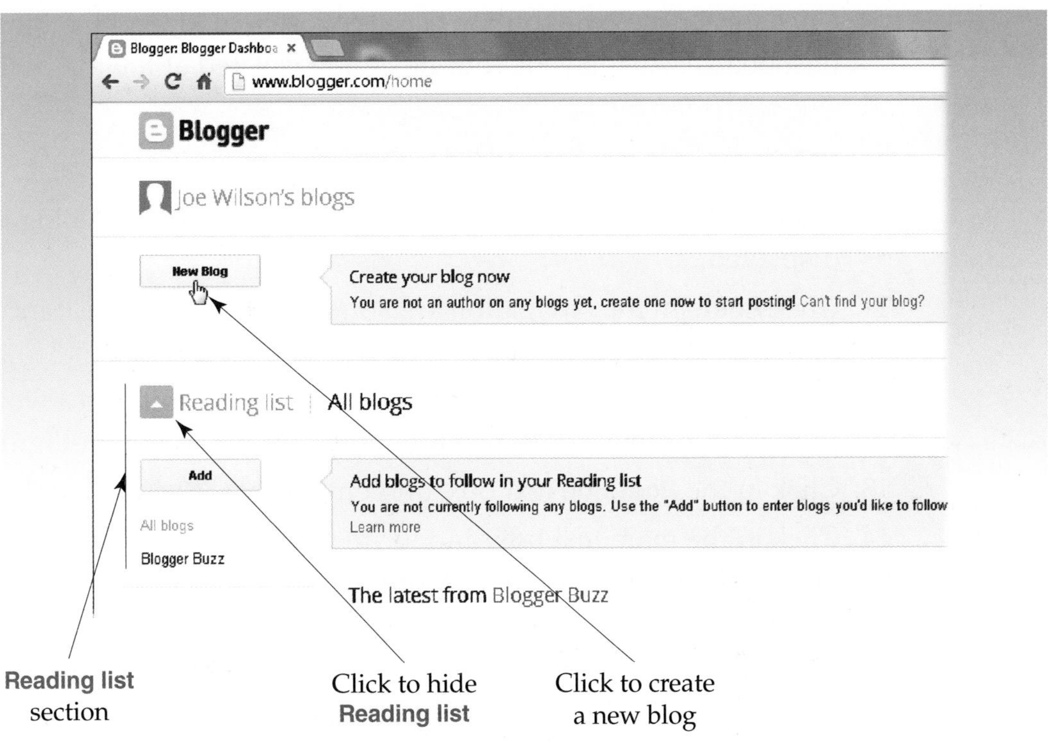

Goodheart-Willcox Publisher

Figure 23-3. The dashboard is a central control location for all of a user's blogs.

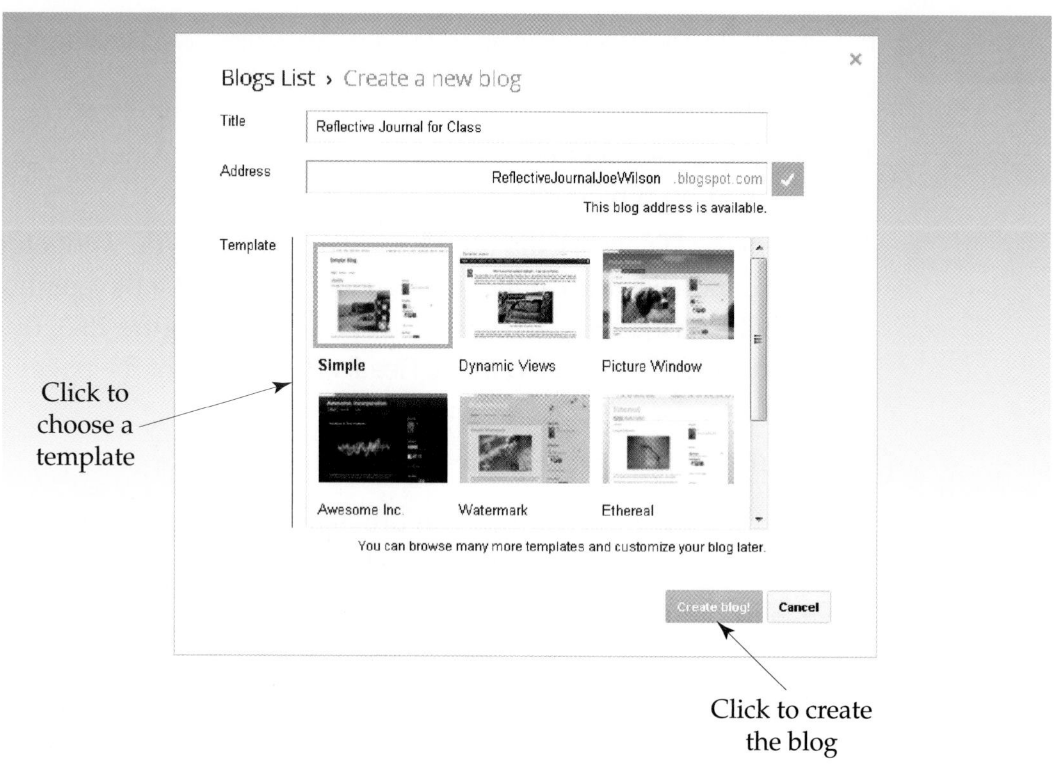

Goodheart-Willcox Publisher

Figure 23-4. Creating a new blog starts with selecting a template.

8. In the template area, click the **Simple** template.

Create blog!

9. Click the **Create blog!** button. The blog is created, and the Blogger dashboard is displayed. Your new blog is listed at the top of the page.

Using a Blog for Journaling

10. Click the name of your blog. An overview page for that blog is displayed.
11. Click **Posts** in the navigation area on the left of the page. Since there are no posts, the displayed page is blank.

Create New Post

12. Click the **Create New Post** button. A new page similar to a word processor is displayed for creating the post, as shown in **Figure 23-5.**
13. Click in the **Post title** text box, and enter What I Know About Blogging.
14. Click in the main text box, and write what you know about blogging. First, write what you knew before reading this chapter. Then, write what you have learned so far.

Publish

15. Click the **Publish** button. The post is published to the blog, and the Posts page is displayed, as seen in **Figure 23-6.**
16. Close the tab or window to exit Blogger.

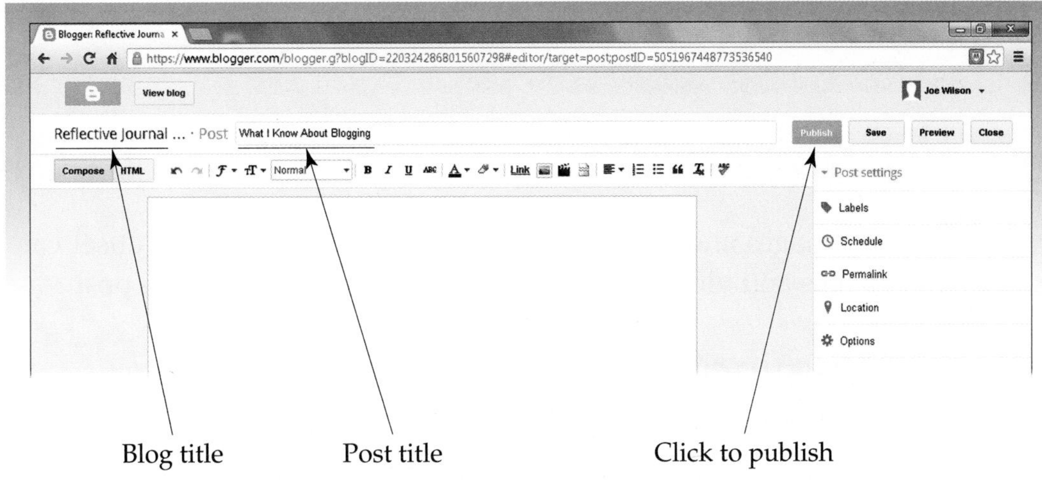

Goodheart-Willcox Publisher

Figure 23-5. Posts are created in Blogger using an interface similar to that of a word processor.

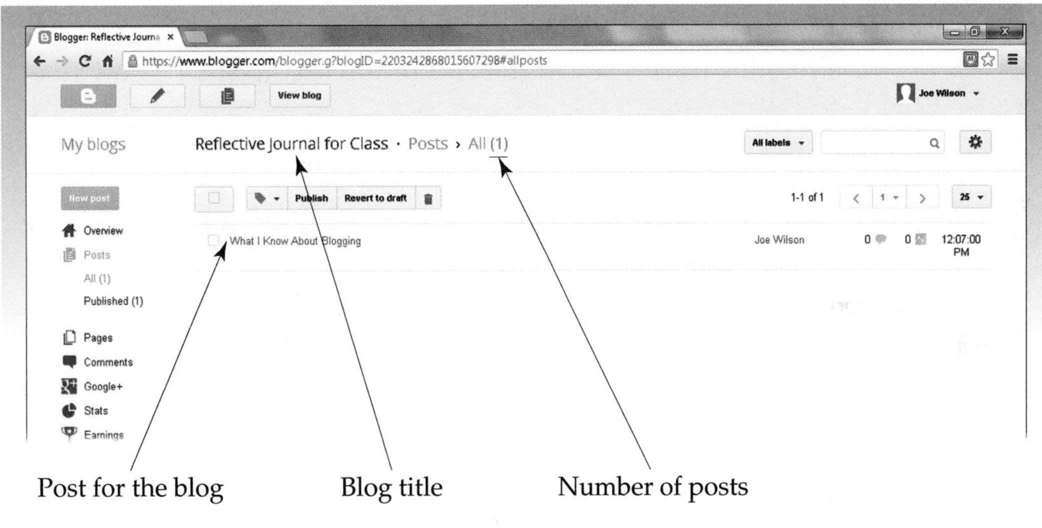

Goodheart-Willcox Publisher

Figure 23-6. A post has been added to the blog.

Lesson 23-2

Posting Photos and Videos in Blogger

Images and videos can be added to blog postings. A user can search for images and videos directly from Blogger to include in a post.

Creating Posts in Blogger

1. Using your Internet browser, navigate to www.blogger.com.
2. Log in to your Google account. The Blogger dashboard is displayed.
3. Click the Reflective Journal for Class name to display the overview of that blog.
4. Click the **New post** button. The page for creating a post is displayed.
5. Click in the **Post title** box, and enter Inserting Photos and Videos.
6. Click in the main text box, and key what you know about posting a photo in a word processing document.
7. Press the [Enter] key at the end of the text to start a new line.

New post

Posting Photos in Blogger

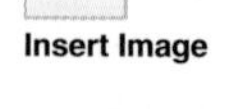

Insert Image

8. Click the **Insert image** button on the toolbar. The **Select a file** dialog box is displayed, as shown in **Figure 23-7.**

Tip Images can be selected from a local hard drive, those that already exist in the blog, a Picasa Web Album, a smartphone or webcam, or a specific URL.

9. Click the **From Picasa Web Albums** link. The Picasa albums created in Chapter 16 are displayed.
10. Click the Lincoln album or the album in which the Lincoln Photograph image file was stored in Chapter 17.
11. Click the Lincoln Photograph image. A blue box appears around the image to indicate it is selected.
12. Click the **Add Selected** button. The image is added to the draft of the blog post at the current location of the cursor.
13. Click the image in the draft of the blog post. A pop-up window containing options for placement of the image appears, as shown in **Figure 23-8.**
14. Click the **Small** link to set the size of the image. You may choose a different size, if needed.
15. Click the **Left** link to align the image to the left-hand margin.

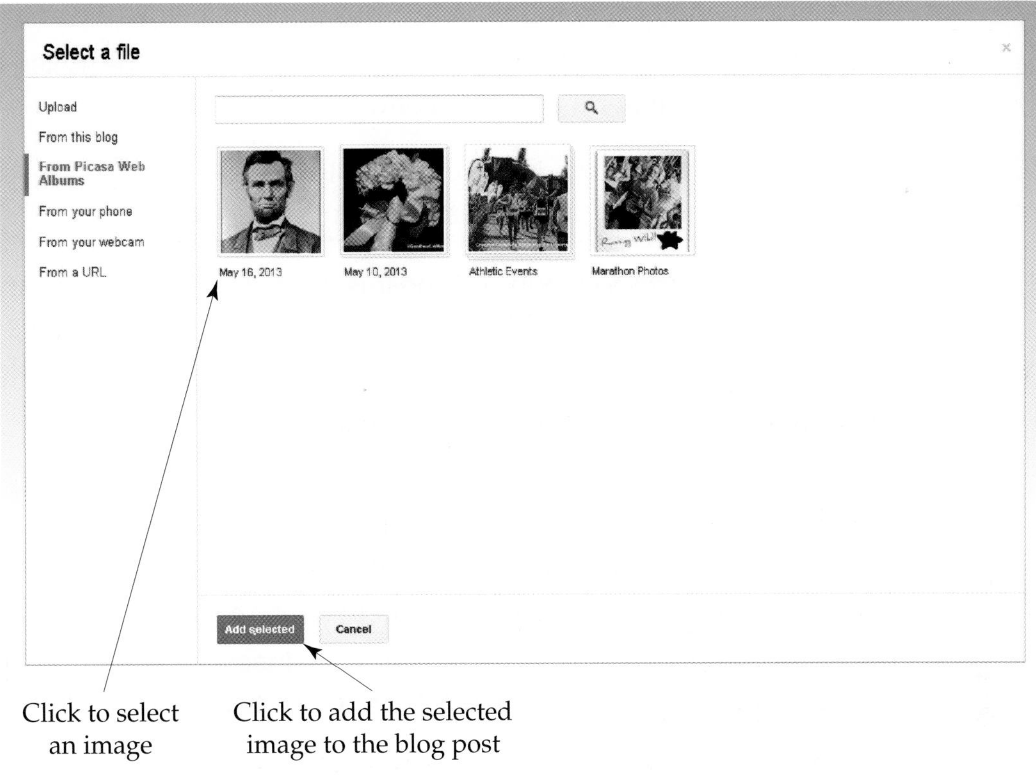

Goodheart-Willcox Publisher

Figure 23-7. There are several sources from which an image can be added to a blog.

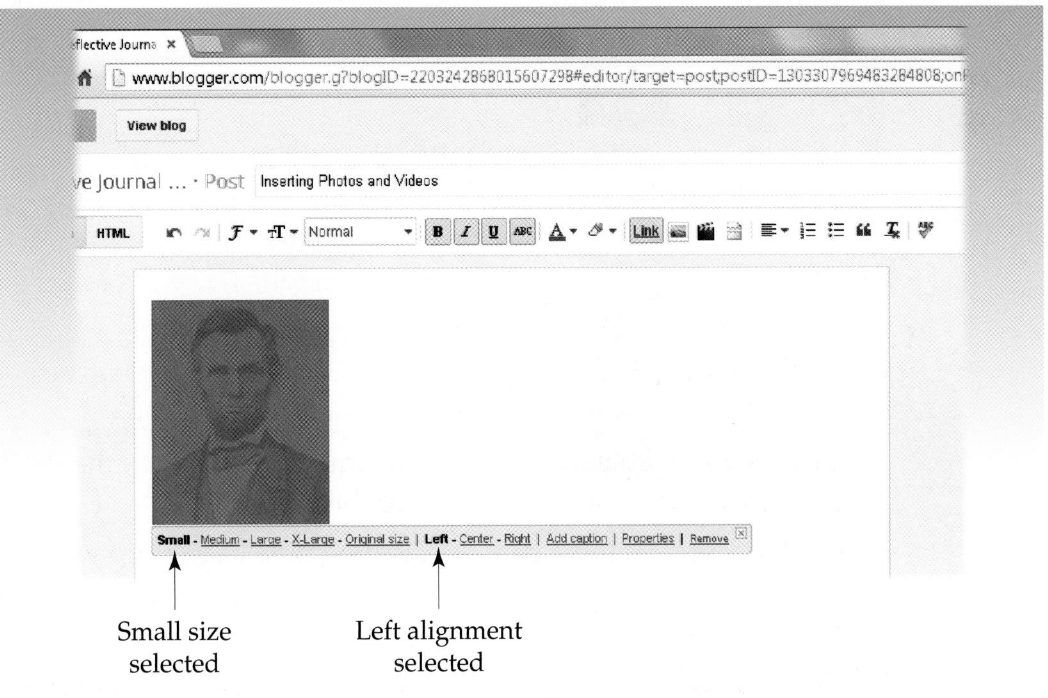

Goodheart-Willcox Publisher

Figure 23-8. Selecting an image in the draft of a post displays options for placement and size.

16. Click the **Add caption** link. A text box appears below the image.
17. Enter Abraham Lincoln in the text box. Do not press the [Enter] key unless you want to enter text on a second line.

An image can be removed by clicking the **Remove** link in the pop-up window or simply by pressing the [Delete] key with the image selected.

18. Click the **Publish** button. The post is published to the blog, and the overview page for the blog posts is displayed. The title of the new post appears on the page. As posts are added to the blog, their titles appear on this page as a list.

Posting Videos in Blogger

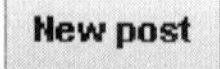

19. Click the **New post** button. The page for creating a post is displayed.
20. Click in the **Post title** box, and enter Historic Videos.

21. Click in the main text box, and click the **Insert video** button on the toolbar. The **Select a file** dialog box is displayed, as shown in **Figure 23-9.**

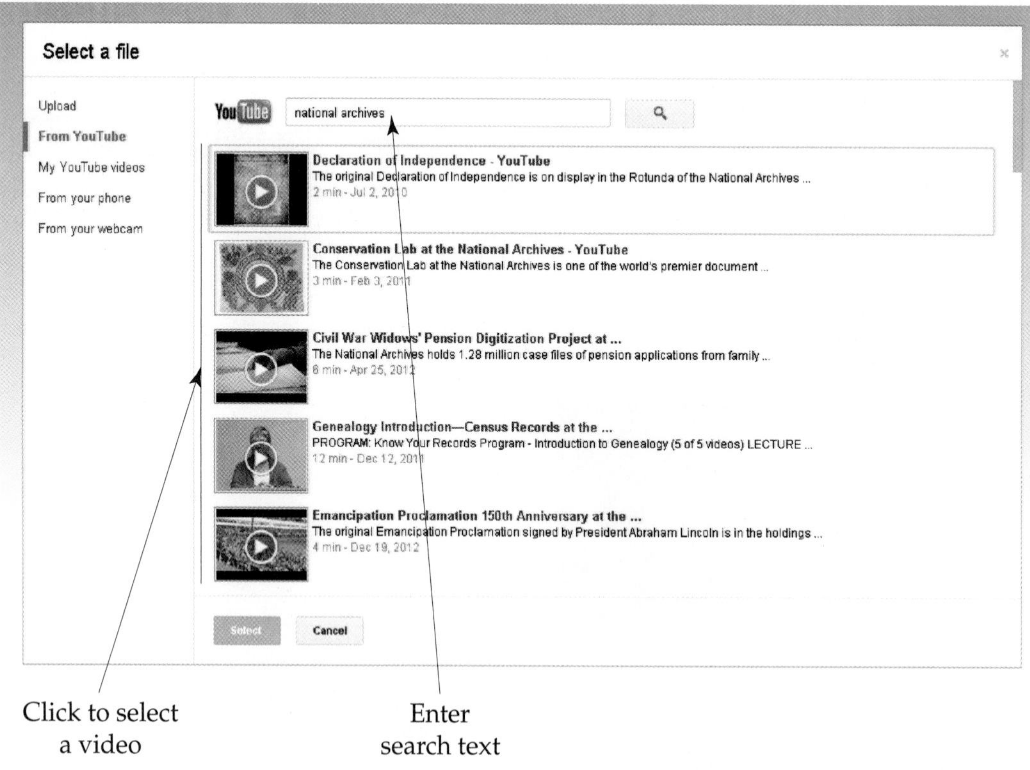

Goodheart-Willcox Publisher

Figure 23-9. A video can be inserted into a blog post, either from a file on your computer or from YouTube.

22. Click the **From YouTube** link. A search box appears.
23. Click in the search text box, enter national archives, and click the **Search** button. A list of YouTube videos from the National Archives is displayed.
24. Scroll through the list, and click the description of a video you would like to insert.

Tip A YouTube video can be previewed in the **Select a file** dialog box by clicking the thumbnail of the video.

25. Click the **Select** button. The video is inserted into the draft of the blog at the cursor's location. It is automatically in a player window so that those reading the blog can play the video.
26. Below the video, write a brief description of the video.
27. Click the **Publish** button. You now see three postings in your Reflective Journal for Class blog.
28. The post is published to the blog, and the overview page for the blog posts is displayed. The title of the new post appears on the page along with the previous post, as shown in **Figure 23-10.** Posts appear in chronological order, with the newest post at the top of the list.
29. Close the tab or window to exit Blogger.

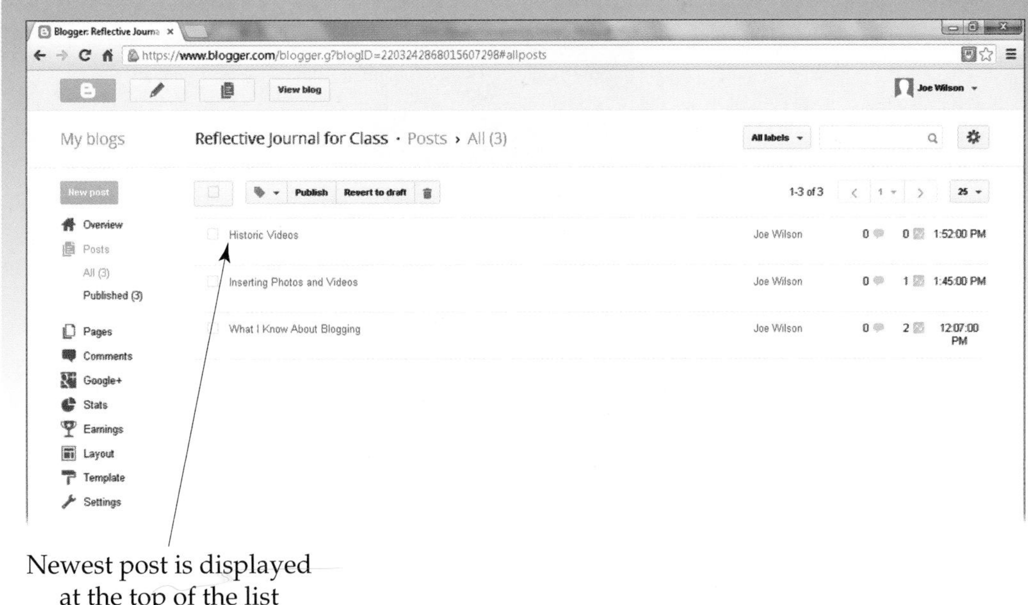

Goodheart-Willcox Publisher

Figure 23-10. A third post has been added to the blog.

Lesson 23-3

Sharing Schoolwork

Journaling, whether for a school assignment, a vacation, or just a personal record, is a popular use of Blogger. Blogger is also often used by teachers and students to communicate and further study beyond the classroom.

1. Working with a partner as assigned by your instructor, e-mail your partner a link to your blog. Remember, the blog address will end with .blogspot.com. At the same time, your partner will e-mail you a link to his or her blog.
2. Navigate to your partner's blog, which will appear similar to **Figure 23-11.**

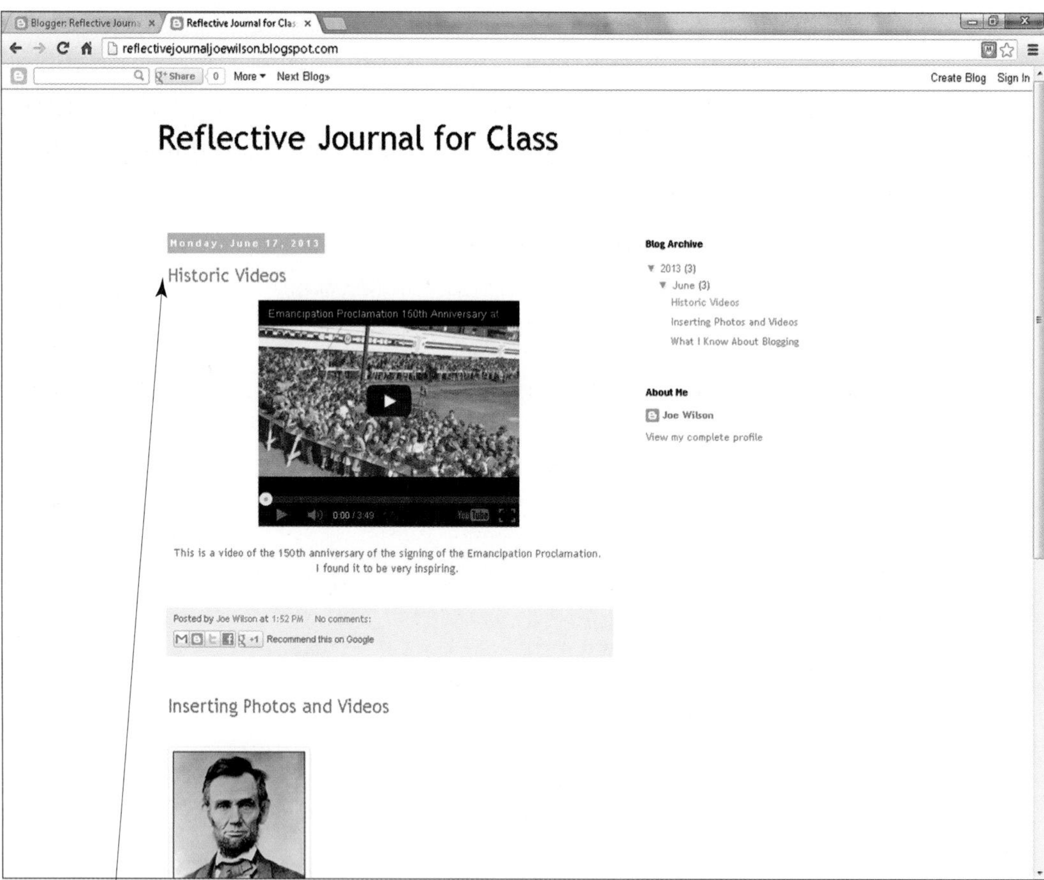

Goodheart-Willcox Publisher

Figure 23-11. A blog typically appears similar to the one shown here, depending on which template was used and how much customization the blog owner has done.

3. Click the title of the first post. The post is displayed with a comments text box at the bottom of the page.
4. Read the post. If the post contains a video, click the **Play** button on the video to watch it.
5. Click in the **Post a Comment** text box.
6. Write a comment that in some way addresses what your partner said in his or her blog post.
7. Click the **Comment as:** drop-down list, and click **Google Account** in the list.

Publish

8. Click the **Publish** button. If you are not logged in, you will be asked to do so. The comment is added below the blog post. Comments appear in chronological order, with the most recent comment at the top just below the blog post.
9. Click the **Home** link at the bottom of the page. The blog's home page is displayed.

Tip The archive can be used to navigate through posts without returning to the blog's home page.

10. Locate your partner's other post, and click on the title to display the post.
11. Read the post. If the post contains a video, click the **Play** button on the video to watch it.
12. Click in the **Post a Comment** text box.
13. Write a comment that in some way addresses what your partner said in his or her blog post.
14. Click the **Comment as:** drop-down list, and click **Google Account** in the list.

Publish

15. Click the **Publish** button. The comment is added below the blog post, after you log in, if needed.
16. Navigate to your own blog.
17. Review the comments your partner added to your blog posts.
18. Close the tab or window to exit Blogger.

Check Your Google Apps IQ

Now that you have finished this chapter, see what you know about Google Apps by taking the chapter posttest.
www.m.g-wlearning.com
www.g-wlearning.com/informationtechnology/

Skill Review

Answer the following questions on a separate sheet of paper.

1. Blog is short for ______.
2. What is a post in terms of a blog?
3. Why should a blog not share any personally identifying information?
4. List three types of information that can be included in a post on a Blogger blog.
5. A(n) ______ is a document to which you continually add thoughts and reflections on your learning.
6. What is one reason a student organization may maintain a blog?
7. What is the main page of Blogger called?
8. What type of software is the page for composing a blog post most like?
9. In Blogger, a post is not publicly available until the ______ button is clicked.
10. Where do blogs the user is following appear within Blogger?

Lesson Application

These exercises are designed to apply the skills learned in this and previous chapters. General directions are provided, but you will need to draw on your knowledge to determine how to complete each exercise.

Exercise 23-1 Reflective Journaling

Create a new blog based on a template of your choosing. The blog will be a reflective journal for one of your classes. The first post should describe the class and why you took it. After that, add a post each day reflecting on what was presented in class that day and what you learned. Be sure to use proper grammar and spelling, and follow common rules of etiquette. Use of texting language is not permitted. Compose an e-mail to your instructor describing the blog, and include a link to the blog.

Exercise 23-2 Photographic Journaling

Create a new blog based on a template of your choosing. The blog will be a photographic journal of a school trip or a personal outing, such as a vacation or an outing with friends. Create a post for each photograph, and include text to explain what is shown in the image. Be sure to use proper grammar and spelling, and follow common rules of etiquette. Use of texting language is not permitted. Compose an e-mail to your instructor describing the blog, and include a link to the blog.

Exercise 23-3 Sharing Blogs with Classmates

Working in a team as assigned by your instructor, brainstorm ideas for a blog related to your school. Decide on a template to use for the blog, and create the blog. Add posts related to the theme of the blog your team decided to use. Be sure to use proper grammar and spelling, and follow common rules of etiquette. Use of texting language is not permitted. Compose an e-mail to all members of your class describing the blog, and include a link to the blog. Working with your team, review the blog from every other team. Add comments to each post to make suggestions for improvements or that no changes are needed. Positive feedback and constructive criticism are to be provided. It is not acceptable to be insulting or otherwise inappropriate toward other teams and classmates.

Scenario

M&M Event Planning is organizing an educational-technology conference in Philadelphia. You are tasked with gathering information for the conference. Use the information learned in this unit to complete the activities. As much as possible, these activities should be completed without referring to the chapters for information.

Activities

1. To obtain as much information as you can on classroom technology, create three alerts. Possible topics include technology and teachers, technology and students, and schools and technology. Receive e-mail daily for two of the alerts and as-it-happens for the other alert. Forward one of the e-mails to your instructor.
2. Create two sections in Google News about education and technology. Search for the preset custom section titled Educational Technology, and add the section. Create your own custom section titled Educational Technology Conferences. Use search terms such as education conferences or technology in the classroom. Add the source Technology to your Google News, and make the necessary setting to receive information from it often.
3. The conference's keynote speaker will discuss technology in the classroom. Use Google Search to locate blogs on this topic, and e-mail yourself links to three blogs you would like to review. The keynote speaker would like to have pictures of technology being used in classrooms. Search for five photographs on the topic. Be sure the images are labeled for reuse or in the public domain. Save the image files to your working folder. In a Google Docs file, insert each image and include the website URL for each image.
4. The keynote speaker wants to use the images you located in Activity 3 as a slideshow. Upload the images to a Picasa Web Album. Title the album Technology in the Classroom, and include an appropriate description. Use the image-editing tools to add text to each image to briefly describe what is shown. Select an appropriate image for use as the album cover. Share the album with your instructor.
5. The conference is at the Pennsylvania Convention Center, and attendees need to be provided directions. Using Google Maps, create driving directions from the 30th Street train station to the convention center. Create a custom map of four places of interest attendees may wish to visit while in Philadelphia. For each place, include a description and an image or link in the details window. Share the map with your instructor.

Index